SOCIAL
PSYCHOLOGY

Second Edition

SOCIAL PSYCHOLOGY

Second Edition

Kenneth S. Bordens

Indiana University-Purdue University Fort Wayne

Irwin A. Horowitz

Oregon State University

http://bordens2e.com

LEA

2002

Lawrence Erlbaum Associates, Publishers

Mahwah, New Jersey   London

President/CEO:	Lawrence Erlbaum
Executive Vice-President, Marketing:	Joseph Petrowski
Senior Vice-President, Book Production:	Art Lizza
Director, Editorial:	Lane Akers
Director, Sales and Marketing:	Robert Sidor
Director, Customer Relations:	Nancy Seitz
Senior Editor:	Debra Riegert
Textbook Marketing Manager:	Marisol Kozlovski
Editorial Assistant:	Jason Planer
Cover Design:	Kathryn Houghtaling Lacey
Interior Design:	Cheryl Asherman
Textbook Production Manager:	Paul Smolenski
Full-Service & Composition:	Progressive Publishing Alternatives
Text and Cover Printer:	Hamilton Printing Company

This book was typeset in 10.5/12 pt. Minion.
The heads were typeset in 14/18 Gill Sans Extrabold and 10.5/12 Gill Sans Bold.

Lawrence Erlbaum Associates, Inc., Publishers
10 Industrial Avenue
Mahwah, New Jersey 07430

Library of Congress Cataloging-in-Publication Data

Horowitz, Irwin A.
  Social psychology / Irwin A. Horowitz, Kenneth S. Bordens. — 2nd ed.
    p. cm.
  Includes bibliographical references and index.
  ISBN 0-8058-3520-2
  1. Social psychology. I. Bordens, Kenneth S. II. Title.

HM1033 .H67 2001
302 – dc21

2001033635

Books published by Lawrence Erlbaum Associates are printed on acid-free paper,
and their bindings are chosen for strength and durability.

Printed in the United States of America

10 9 8 7 6 5 4 3 2 1

CONTENTS

CHAPTER 7

CONFORMITY, COMPLIANCE, AND OBEDIENCE   235

CHAPTER 11

ALTRUISM   405

PREFACE TO THE SECOND EDITION

When we set out to write the first edition of *Social Psychology,* our goal was to provide teachers and students with a book that covered the important research and theoretical areas in social psychology in a concise fashion. Although we strayed a bit from that original goal, we believe that we succeeded in writing a solid, research-based text for the introductory social psychology course. In the second edition, we decided to return to our original goal and have streamlined the book, while maintaining its scientific integrity.

Social psychology has become a diverse field and any attempt to present a totally comprehensive overview of all of its content area would be difficult to execute in a single volume or course. Instead, we have chosen to take the approach that we would like to present students with information concerning three questions:

1. What is social psychology?
2. What do we know about social psychological phenomena?
3. How do we know what we know about social psychological phenomena?

We believe that social psychology is important, interesting, relevant to the current world, and exciting. We think that this is truly the golden age of social psychology. We are impressed with the many bright, energetic people who have done so much interesting work. We hope to communicate to this generation of social psychology students the excitement that we felt as budding social psychologists when we first learned about Milgram's obedience research or Darley and Latané's bystander intervention research. Intrigued by the results of such studies, we began to wonder how they could be applied to real-life situations that confront each of us every day. In this edition, we believe that we have communicated the excitement of the field so that students new to the area will be as intrigued with social psychological research and theory as we were.

Most social psychology texts approach the field from the perspective of research and theory, using examples from everyday life as illustrations of social psychological phenomena. This approach often leaves students without a full appreciation of the applications of social psychology. By applications, we mean not only the usual applied social psychology topics that are interesting in their own right. By application, we also mean that the theory and research of social psychology can be used to understand the complexities of cultural, historical, and current events. Also, that social psychology can help us understand how we, as individuals, fit in with the wider social environment. Students will come away from this text with a sense that they are truly social creatures subject to the influence of the social and physical environment.

CHANGES TO THE SECOND EDITION

There have been substantive changes throughout the second edition that make it much different from the first edition. The first thing that you may notice is that we have dropped the use of four colors. In an era of rising textbook prices, we felt that students would appreciate a low-cost textbook that did not skimp on content. Consequently, this book is a "one color" book which keeps production costs down, and ultimately keeps the cost to the students down as well. Although we may have sacrificed color, we did not sacrifice content.

We have also rearranged and rewritten many of the chapters. The book now comprises 11 chapters representing the core of the field of social psychology. We have eliminated the "applied" chapters and placed relevant material from those chapters into the 11 core chapters. We felt that most instructors do not have the time to cover the core topics (e.g., social cognition, attribution, aggression, altruism, and attitudes) as well as separate applied chapters. As a consequence, we decided to eliminate the stand-alone applied chapters. This 11 chapter edition can legitimately be covered in a single semester or quarter.

We have made some major changes to the existing chapters. Here are some of the changes you will find:

Chapter 3: In this edition, we have combined elements of Chapters 3 (social cognition) and 4 (attribution processes) from the first edition into one chapter covering both social cognition and attribution processes. The chapter focuses on the basic processes involved in both of these important areas without overburdening students with esoteric research and theory.

Chapter 4: The core content of Chapter 4 (Prejudice) has been retained. However, a major new section has been added. This new section presents information on the consequences of being a target of prejudice and how people cope with prejudice.

Chapter 7: In the first edition, conformity and compliance (Chapter 8) and obedience (Chapter 9) were presented in separate chapters. We have combined these topics into a single chapter in this edition. Of course, there is less material on each of these topics. However, the core issues for each topic were covered in detail.

In addition to the reorganization of the chapters, we have updated existing research and have added material on newer issues (e.g., implicit attitudes and stereotypes). We have also eliminated the "Featured Discussions" that were part of the first edition. We have taken relevant material from those discussions and folded it into the chapters themselves. We feel that if something is important enough to be in the book, it should be in the chapter itself and not in a box rarely read by the student.

INTERNET SUPPORT

Each chapter now ends with an "Internet Activity." In this age of computers and the Internet, we felt it was important to introduce students to social psychology on the Internet. Each activity encourages the student to use an Internet resource to explore or investigate a social psychological phenomenon or issue. The Internet activities are:

Chapter 1: Taking Part in a Social Psychological Study

Chapter 2: Finding Out about Yourself

Chapter 3: What Is Your Locus of Control?

Chapter 4: Racism and the Internet

Chapter 5: How Did They Vote?

Additionally, there is a Web site, located at http://bordens2e.com, that accompanies the text. On the Web site, students will find links to interesting social psychology sites. They will also find the study guide that accompanies the text (more follows). The Web site can be used by instructors to integrate the Internet into their courses.

ANCILLARIES

The second edition comes with a similar ancillary package as did the first edition. There is an instructor's manual to help instructors organize and teach their course in social psychology. There is also an extensive computerized test bank of examination questions. The questions in the test bank have been written by the authors and not by someone paid a small amount of money per question. We hope that these author-prepared questions will be an asset to the instructor.

The first edition included a hardcopy student study guide. This time around we decided that this important resource should be available to all students at no cost. Consequently, the study guide can be found on our Web site. Each chapter is in both html and PDF format. Students can download materials for each chapter, print them out, and use them as they wish. The online study guide will include chapter outlines, key questions, practice questions, and suggested activities.

ACKNOWLEDGMENTS

A project of this scope requires much hard work and the support of many people. First and foremost we would like to thank our wives Ricky Karen Bordens and Kay F. Schaffer who provided much needed love and support while we toiled on this book. We would also like to thank the editorial staff at Lawrence Erlbaum and the production editors at Progressive Publishing Alternatives for the hard work they put in to make the second edition a reality. We would especially like to thank Debra Riegert, our sponsoring editor, for having faith that there was enough good in the first edition to justify going ahead with a second edition. We appreciate her devotion and the guidance she provided at every step of the process of producing this edition. A special note of thanks to Donna King our production manager at Progressive Publishing Alternatives and the many editors and staff members who made publication of this text possible.

REVIEWERS OF SOCIAL PSYCHOLOGY

This book owes its final shape to the academic reviewers who took the time to read drafts of chapters and provide helpful feedback. Their efforts contributed greatly to the quality and integrity of this book. These reviewers were Virgil H. Adams, *The University of Kansas;* Reuben M. Baron, *University of Connecticut;* Martin Bolt, *Calvin College;* Meredith Bombar, *Elmira College;* Paul C. Cozby, *California State University, Fullerton;* Robert T. Croyle, *University of Utah;* Lynda Dodgen, *North Harris College;* William J. Froming, *Pacific Graduate School of Psychology;* Jayne T. Gackenbach, *Athabasca University;* Ranald D. Hansen, *Oakland University;* Craig A. Hill, *Indiana University-Purdue University at Fort Wayne;* Marita R. Inglehart, *University of Michigan;* Donn L. Kaiser, *Southwest Missouri State University;* Martin F. Kaplan, *Northern Illinois University;* Mary E. Kite, *Ball State University;* Hilary M. Lips, *Radford University;* Angela Lipsitz, *Northern Kentucky University;* Dan P. McAdams, *Northwestern University;* Richard E. Petty, *Ohio State University;* Adrian Rapp, *North Harris College;* Cheryl A. Rickabaugh, *University of Redlands;* Tony Riley, *University of Massachusetts at Amherst;* Jerry I. Shaw, *California State University, Northridge;* Vaida D. Thompson, *University of North Carolina at Chapel Hill;* Teddy D. Warner, *Iowa State University;* Bernard Weiner, *University of California, Los Angeles;* Bernard E. Whitley, Jr., *Ball State University.*

A project of this magnitude is never the work of one or two people. We had the support of a talented team of editors and production experts.

CHAPTER 1

UNDERSTANDING SOCIAL BEHAVIOR

The scene inside Columbine High in Littleton, Colorado, must have been something right out of Dante's *Inferno*. Two students dressed in long black trench coats swept through the halls of Columbine High like avenging angels from hell. Eric Harris and Dylan Klebold carried with them a small arsenal, including several pipe bombs. After shooting several students outside the school, the pair entered the cafeteria and began throwing pipe bombs around the room. While their fellow students dove for cover wherever they could, Harris and Klebold left the cafeteria and headed for the library on the second floor.

On their way, they encountered a teacher, William "Dave" Sanders, outside the cafeteria, trying to get a group of students to the second floor to safety. On the second floor, Harris and Klebold opened fire, wounding Sanders twice in the back. Despite his wounds and the continuing danger, he got his students to a room on the second floor. There his students tried desperately to keep Sanders alive until help arrived. They were successful for about 2 hours. However, help did not come in time, and Sanders died from his wounds. His greatest concern was not for himself but for the safety and lives of his students.

Once in the library, according to surviving witnesses, Harris and Klebold began singling out students to be killed. First, they wanted all the "jocks" to stand up. Those who did were killed, including Isaiah Shoels, who was black. Although the killing rampage was not motivated by racism, Harris and Klebold made several racist statements before they shot Shoels in the head. Another student was singled out because she believed in God. Others were seemingly chosen at random.

As police arrived, it became apparent to Harris and Klebold that they were not going to be able to escape, so in the library, among their victims, Harris and Klebold took their own lives. They left behind the largest death toll of any such crime in the United States. They also left behind 30 pipe bombs and a large propane bomb in the school's kitchen. It was apparently their plan to destroy the entire school.

In the aftermath of the killings, several things came to light about Harris and Klebold. They were affiliated with a group of apparent outcasts, known as the Trench Coat Mafia, who other students considered weird and perhaps dangerous. Apparently, Harris and Klebold had been taunted by some "mainstream" students and, searching for a sense of belonging, had turned to this group of outcasts and misfits. Harris and Klebold were fascinated by movies glorifying killing, such as Oliver Stone's *Natural Born Killers*. They also played violent, bloody video games obsessively, and Harris had a Web site devoted to violence and hatred. They became enamored of Nazi culture and staged their murders on Adolph Hitler's birthday.

When we read or hear about incidents such as the one at Columbine High, many questions come to mind. We wonder, for example, how the dissatisfaction of two apparently normal students could explode into such levels of violence. Would the outcome of this confrontation have been different had the police responded more quickly, as some have speculated? We wonder about the teacher who sacrificed his life to save the lives of his students. What forces operated to cause this ultimate display of altruism? And what of Harris and Klebold themselves? Were they "bad" people, or were they caught up in a culture that glorifies violence and allows ready access to guns? What role did affiliation with a group of other disenchanted students play? How did the ready access to guns and information about bomb making on the Internet relate to the crime? Is there something about the high school social environment that pushes some students to, and sometimes, over the edge? These are some of the questions addressed in this chapter.

KEY QUESTIONS

AS YOU READ THIS CHAPTER, FIND THE ANSWERS TO THE FOLLOWING QUESTIONS:

1. *What is social psychology?*
2. *How do social psychologists explain social behavior?*
3. *How does social psychology relate to other disciplines that study social behavior?*
4. *How do social psychologists approach the problem of explaining social behavior?*
5. *What is experimental research, and how is it used?*
6. *What is correlational research?*
7. *What is the correlation coefficient, and what does it tell you?*
8. *Where is social psychological research conducted?*
9. *What is the role of theory in social psychology?*
10. *What can we learn from social psychological research?*
11. *What ethical standards must social psychologists follow when conducting research?*

SOCIAL PSYCHOLOGY AND THE UNDERSTANDING OF SOCIAL BEHAVIOR

The events that occurred at Columbine High School and the questions concerning why they happened all can be better understood and answered through a knowledge of social psychology. **Social psychology** is the scientific study of how individuals think and feel about, interact with, and influence one another, individually and in groups. It is the branch of psychology that studies social behavior—the thinking and behavior of individuals as they relate to other human beings.

Social psychology provides tools for understanding the events that occur around you every day. In your personal life, it can help you make sense of your day-to-day interactions—your friendships, love relationships, interactions at work, and performance at school. It can give you insight, for example, into why your most recent romantic relationship did not succeed, and why you find yourself attracted to one person in your afternoon math class but not to another. It can also help you understand why you may behave aggressively when someone cuts ahead of you in a cafeteria line, or why you get annoyed when someone sits right next to you in a theater when there are plenty of other empty seats. Social psychology can also help you understand why *other* people act the way the do. For example, social psychology can help us understand the forces that led to the massacre at Columbine High.

Your life also is touched by events beyond your immediate, day-to-day affairs—events that occur in the community and the nation. Although these events are more distant, you may still feel strongly about them and find a link between them and your personal life. If your friend's father were very sick, for example, you might want to share with him knowledge about a man whose determination kept him alive for 6 years. Perhaps the story would encourage him to keep on with his life. If something like the Columbine High incident happened in your city or town, you would experience directly the impact of disenfranchised teenagers exploding in anger. You probably would hear many people decrying the violence and talking about ways to deal with violent television and movies and the ready access of guns.

In one form or another, all the events at Columbine High represent recurring themes in human history. No, people haven't always been exposed to violent movies or had such easy access to guns. But humans have always been both aggressive and altruistic toward one another. Human beings have always had to find ways to live with each other. We have always functioned together in groups; had love relationships; tried to persuade others of our point of view; followed or rebelled against authority; and sought ways to resolve conflicts, whether through negotiation or through coercion. We help each other, and we hurt each other. We display prejudice and discrimination; we even have tried to kill entire populations. History is a tapestry of the best and the worst that human beings can do. Social psychology can help us understand these human social events in their infinite variety.

It's important to note, however, that social psychologists do not simply wonder and speculate about social behavior. Instead, they use scientific methods involving carefully designed and executed research studies to help explain complex, uncertain social issues. Social psychology is first and foremost a science. Through theory, research, and thoughtful application of concepts and principles to real-life situations, social psychologists provide

social psychology
The scientific study of how individuals think about, interact with, and influence each other.

insights into everyday events, both past and present, as well as those monumental events that are the stuff of history.

More than any other branch of psychology, social psychology offers a broad perspective on human behavior. Rather than focusing on the personal histories of individuals, or on how individuals respond to their environment, it looks at how people interact with and relate to each other *in social contexts.* As we have seen, a wide range of behavior and events falls within its domain.

A Model for Understanding Social Behavior

Social psychologists are interested in the forces that operate on individuals and cause them to engage in specific examples of social behavior. But social behavior is typically complex and has many contributing causes. Consequently, explaining social behavior is a difficult task. To simplify this task, we can assign the multiple causes of social behavior to one of two broad categories: the situation and the individual. According to a formula first proposed by Kurt Lewin (1936), one of the important early figures in social psychology, social behavior is a function of the interaction of the situation and the individual's characteristics, or

$$\text{Behavior} = \int (\text{social situation} \times \text{individual characteristics}).$$

Lewin's model of social behavior was inspired by his observation that the individual's perception of a situation is influenced by the tasks he or she has to accomplish. Lewin was a soldier in the German Army during World War I. He noticed that as he came nearer the battlefield, his view of the world changed. Where he once might have seen beautiful flowers and beckoning forests, he now saw boulders to hide behind and gullies from which he could ambush the enemy. Lewin came to believe that a person's perception of the world is influenced by what he or she has to do in that situation. He termed

As noted by Lewin, as soldiers march toward battle their perceptions of their environment change. Where they may have been aware of the birds and clouds far from the battleground, as they approach they become more aware of things that can help them survive in combat.

the combination of individual needs and situational factors the *psychological field* in which the individual lives (Pratkanis & Aronson, 1992).

According to this view, individuals with different needs and tasks would come to see the same event in dissimilar ways (Pratkanis & Aronson, 1992). Although Lewin looked at the individual's needs and tasks, he emphasized the importance of social context in producing the forces that control the individual's actions. Lewin was aware that we often fail to take situational factors into account when we try to explain why people behave as they do (Ross & Nisbett, 1991). For example, there were undoubtedly other students at Columbine High who were taunted by other students. However, their differing needs and interpretations of the social situation did not manifest itself in an overt act of mass killing.

Thus far we have seen that the situation and individual characteristics are central to the understanding of social behavior. How do social psychologists define *situation* and *individual characteristics*? Let's take a closer look.

THE SOCIAL SITUATION The *social situation* comprises all influences on behavior that are external to the individual. A situational factor might be any aspect of the physical and/or social environment (the presence of other people, real or imagined) that influences behavior. Different individuals will react differently to the social situation.

Sometimes the situation works on us in more subtle ways. We may modify our behavior even if there is no pressure on us to do so. We may imagine or believe that we are expected to act a certain way in a certain situation, and those beliefs can be as powerful as the situation itself. For example, let's say that you are in a restaurant with a group of friends. You are trying to decide what to order. You are leaning toward the sauteed buffalo, but the stewed rabbit sounds good too. When the waiter comes to the table, you order last, intending to try the buffalo. However, each of your friends orders the rabbit. When your turn comes, you also order the rabbit. You modified your behavior based on your friends' actions, because you didn't want to appear different. You felt and responded to social pressure of your own making!

Situational or social determinants of behavior exist on several levels simultaneously. Sometimes the social environment leads to temporary changes in behavior, as was the case in the restaurant. Ordering the rabbit may be specific to that one situation; you may never order rabbit again. In other cases, the social environment is a more pervasive influence and may lead to relatively permanent, enduring patterns of behaviors. The culture within which a person lives exerts a long-lasting influence over a wide range of behaviors. Culture influences the foods we like, how we relate to members of the other sex, the amount of personal space we require (the area immediately surrounding us that we claim and defend), what we plan and expect to accomplish in life, and a host of other behaviors.

INDIVIDUAL CHARACTERISTICS Individual characteristics include sex, age, race or ethnicity, personality characteristics, attitudes, self-concept, ways of thinking, and so on. In short, individual characteristics consist of anything internal to the person that might influence behavior. Physical traits are individual characteristics that are relatively enduring and for the most part known to others. Personality characteristics also tend to be enduring, but they are not necessarily obvious to others. Personality is an area of growing interest in social psychology today (Larsen & Ketelaar, 1991). Other internal characteristics, like attitudes, opinions, self-concept, and so on, can change over time. People often have some choice about how much of these areas of themselves they reveal to others.

Let's consider Columbine High again. What of the other students at the bottom of the social ladder? These individuals were subjected to very similar situational pressures as those who committed the violent acts. However, they were able to withstand the social pressure and not act violently. Did some combination of personal traits and attitudes mix with the situation to produce this different behavior? Since the situation was similar for other students, we look to individual characteristics such as personality traits to understand why some acted in violent ways and others did not.

Another important individual characteristic that is somewhat different from personality characteristics is the particular way each individual perceives and thinks about his or her social world. **Social cognition** refers to a general process we use to make sense out of social events, which may or may not include other people. For example, after reading about the Columbine High tragedy, you may begin to interpret those events, attempting to determine a cause. Eventually, you probably begin to make inferences about the motives of the individuals involved and to form impressions of them. Social psychologists call this process **social perception.** For example, thinking about the teacher who gave his life for his students may lead you to an inference that he was a highly empathic, caring person and was not simply doing his job as a teacher. Once you infer these characteristics and form an impression that he was a caring, compassionate person, you then settle on these internal characteristics as the primary motivation for his behavior.

Social cognition and social perception are central to our interpretation of situations. When we are exposed to a particular situation, how we respond depends on how we interpret that situation. Social cognition gives direction to our interpretation. The decisions we make based on our perception and cognition will influence our response. Every individual has a slightly different view of the world, because everyone has unique personal traits and a unique history of life experiences. This is because each of us actively constructs our own view of our social world, based on interpretations of social information.

Expanding Lewin's Model

Lewin's model tells us that both the social situation (physical setting, the presence of other people, real or imagined) and individual characteristics (physical traits, personality traits, attitudes and habitual ways of thinking, perceptual and cognitive processes, needs and tasks) influence social behavior. Lewin's model, however, does not specify how situational factors and individual characteristics fit together into a broad, general model of social behavior. We need to expand on Lewin's original model to gain a better understanding of the forces that shape social behavior. An expansion of Lewin's original model is shown in Figure 1.1.

As shown in this model, input from the social situation and individual characteristics do not directly influence social behavior. Instead, they both contribute to how we process information via mechanisms of social cognition and social perception. How that information is processed yields a particular evaluation of the situation. For example, after the Columbine High School shootings, a memorial was constructed on a hill above the school. The memorial comprised 15 crosses: 13 for the victims and 2 for the killers. As

---

social cognition
The general process we use to make sense out of social events, which may or may not include other people.

---

social perception
The social processes by which we come to comprehend the behavior, the words and actions, of other people.

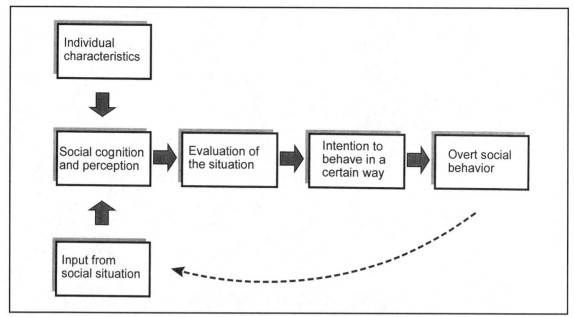

Figure 1.1 *An expanded model of social behavior. How we act in a given situation depends on input from the situation and individual characteristics that are mediated by the processes of social cognition and perception and the formation of an intention to behave in a certain way.*

you might expect, opinion was divided about including crosses for Harris and Klebold. A person (individual characteristics) who opposed including Harris and Klebold in the memorial may interpret the situation (social cognition) in a way that suggests that Harris and Klebold were cold-blooded killers because of the way they went about their crime, allegedly taking glee in killing others (input from the situation). Another person might focus on the social conditions that led to Harris and Klebold's murderous spree, pointing to the culture of violence, the social pressures in the school, and the availability of guns when explaining the incident. Such a person might likely favor inclusion of Harris and Klebold among the fold of victims of the Columbine massacre.

According to Figure 1.1, our evaluation of the social situation does not translate immediately into overt social behavior. Instead, based on our evaluation of the situation, we form a behavioral intention. For example, one parent of a victim might form an intention to sue the school district and the parents of Harris and Klebold. Another parent might form an intention to direct his or her energies into programs and laws to prevent such a tragedy from happening again.

It is important to realize that just because we form a behavioral intention does not mean we will act on that intention. For example, a person can form the intention of filing a law suit but never follow through, thinking perhaps that more harm than good would be done.

This view of social behavior implies that it is a dynamic process. Our monitoring of the social situation does not end with an evaluation of the situation, or the formation of an intention, or social behavior. Instead, we are constantly monitoring the social situation (our own behavior and that of others) and may modify our assessment of it on a moment-to-moment basis. Thus, we fine-tune our behavioral intentions up to the point that we engage in social behavior. So, even though the various processes underlying social behavior are presented in Figure 1.1 in a sequence of discrete boxes, they are really quite fluid and involve constant updating of our evaluation of the situation.

One final aspect of this model needs to be addressed. Notice that there is a dotted arrow going from social behavior to the social situation. In any social situation in which we are directly involved, our own behavior influences the social environment and probably will cause changes in the behavior of others. For example, imagine that you are talking to someone you have just met. Based on the first thing she says, you determine that she is not very friendly. Consequently, you become defensive (you fold your arms, lean away from her) and respond to her in a cold way. She picks up on your behavior and becomes colder herself. This cycle continues until one of you breaks off the conversation. How might this situation have played out if you had interpreted her initial behaviors as nervousness and responded to her in a positive way? You may have made a new friend. Thus, your own interpretations and behaviors had a profound effect on the situation.

SOCIAL PSYCHOLOGY AND RELATED FIELDS

We have seen that social psychology is a field of study that seeks to understand and explain social behavior — how individuals think and act in relation to other people. Yet many other disciplines are also concerned with the thoughts and actions of human beings, both individually and in groups. In what ways does social psychology differ from its two parent disciplines, sociology and psychology? And how is it similar to and different from other fields of study, such as biology, anthropology, and history?

To see how these fields differ in their approaches, let's consider a single question: Why do groups of people, including nations, display hostility toward one another? Although social psychologists are interested in this social problem, they have no unique claim to it (nor to others). Biologists, psychologists, anthropologists, sociologists, historians, and others all have explanations for the never-ending cycle of human violence. Let's consider first those fields that look for the causes of violent behavior within the individual and then move on to fields that focus increasingly on factors in the environment.

Many biologists say the answer to the puzzle of human violence resides not in our social situations, organizations, or personalities but rather in our genetic structure. Recently, for example, scientists have identified a tiny genetic defect that appears to predispose some men toward violence. Scientists studied a large Dutch family with a history of violent and erratic behavior among many, although not all, of the males. They found that those males who were prone to violence had an enzyme deficiency due to a mutation of a gene carried by the X chromosome (Brunner, Nelon, Breakefield, Ropers, & van Oost, 1993). Because men have only one X chromosome, they were the only ones who manifested the defect. Women may be carriers of the deficiency, but they are protected from expressing it by their second X chromosome with its backup copy of the gene. Geneticists do not argue that genetic defects are the sole cause of violence, but they do say that these factors play a definite role in determining who is violent.

Another biologically oriented view of this question comes from developmental psychologists (who study the development of human beings across

Different fields that concern themselves with behavior would look at a Klan member's behavior from different perspectives. A biologist would focus on genetic factors, a sociologist on the role of society, a historian on the events that gave rise to the clan, and a social psychologist on the immediate social environment.

the lifespan). They suggest that human beings may have an innate fear of strangers. They point out that at about 4 or 5 months, infants begin to react with fear to novel or unusual stimuli, such as the faces of strangers (Hegg & Thompson, 1968). Between 6 and 18 months, infants may experience intense *stranger anxiety*. These psychologists, as well as some biologists, argue that fear of strangers may be part of our genetic heritage. Early humans who possessed this trait may have been more likely to survive than those who didn't, and they passed the trait down to us. On a group or societal level, this innate mistrust of strangers might be elaborated into hostility, aggression, or even warfare. Other psychologists, however, are not convinced that fear of the novel is inborn (Hebb & Thompson, 1968).

Along similar lines, anthropologists (who study the physical and cultural development of the human species) have documented that some tribal societies view strangers with suspicion and may even attempt to kill them. Some anthropologists argue that hostility to strangers may have benefitted early human groups by helping them unite against threats from the outside.

Other scientists emphasize the psychological makeup of individuals as a way of explaining behavior. Personality psychologists suggest that aggressiveness (or any other behavioral trait) is a characteristic of the individual. The person carries the trait from situation to situation, expressing it in any number of different circumstances (Derlega, Winstead, & Jones, 1991). Personality psychologists would argue that some internal characteristic drove William "Dave" Sanders to behave altruistically in the Columbine shooting, just as some other personality traits affected the behavior of Dylan Klebold.

One researcher studied the aggressive behavior of adolescent boys in Sweden over 3 years (Olweus, 1984). He found that boys who were aggressive (started fights, were bullies) in the sixth grade were also physically aggressive in the ninth grade. Personality researchers take this as evidence that individual factors are an important determinant of aggression. Over the course of the 3 years, the boys had different teachers, were in different buildings, and had a variety of classmates. Yet their behavior remained consistently aggressive despite the change in their social situation (Derlega et al., 1991).

Social psychologists study the individual in the social situation. They are concerned with determining what characteristics of a situation increase or decrease the potential for violence. In looking at the question of hostility between groups, social psychologists focus on the forces both in individuals and in situations that lead to this outcome.

Whereas psychology (including social psychology) focuses on the role of the individual, other fields look for causes of behavior in more impersonal and general causes outside the individual. For example, sociologists are concerned primarily, although not exclusively, with larger groups and systems in society. A sociologist interested in violence might study the development of gangs. Interviews with gang members, observation of gang activity, or even participation in a gang as a participant–observer, if possible, would be potential methods of study.

Although sociology and social psychology are related, there are important differences between them. The sociologist asks what it is about the structure of society that promotes violence; the social psychologist, in contrast, looks at the individual's particular social situation as the potential cause of violence. The social psychologist is interested primarily in the behavior of individuals or of small groups, such as a jury. Sociology may be empirical in the sense that it attempts to gather quantitative information. A sociologist might compare rates of violent behavior in two societies and then try to determine how those societies differ. Social psychology is much more an experimental, laboratory-based science.

Historians take an even broader view of intergroup hostility than sociologists. They are primarily concerned with the interplay of large forces such as economic, political, and technological trends. Historians have shown, for example, that one nation can express power against other nations only if it has sufficient economic resources to sustain armed forces and if it has developed an adequate technological base to support them (Kennedy, 1987; O'Connell, 1989). One historian documented the importance of a single technological advance—the invention of stirrups—in accelerating violence between groups in the early Middle Ages (McNeill, 1982). Before stirrups were invented, knights on horseback were not very effective fighters. But once they were able to steady themselves in the saddle, they became capable of delivering a powerful blow with a lance at full gallop. The use of stirrups quickly spread throughout Europe and led to the rise of cavalry as an instrument of military power.

History and sociology focus on how social forces and social organization influence human behavior. These fields tend to take a top-down perspective; the major unit of analysis is the group or the institution, whether a nation, a corporation, or a neighborhood organization. Psychology, with its emphasis on individual behavior and the individual's point of view, offers a bottom-up approach. Social psychology offers a distinct perspective on social behavior.

Social psychologists look at how social forces affect the individual's thinking and behavior. Although the field takes a bottom-up perspective, focusing on the individual as the unit of analysis, behavior is always examined in social situations. Social psychology, therefore, tries to take into account individual factors, such as personality, as well as social and historical forces that have shaped human behavior.

As indicated earlier, social psychology is a science. The use of scientific methods is the primary contribution of social psychology to the understanding of complex, uncertain social behaviors such as intergroup hostility.

RESEARCH IN SOCIAL PSYCHOLOGY

In January 1992, a celebrity basketball game was held in New York City. There was open seating at a college basketball arena that held slightly more than 4,000 people. Therefore, the first people in the arena would get the best seats. As the crowd outside the arena grew into the thousands, anticipation built. People began pushing and shoving to get closer to the doors. As the crowd pressed forward toward the arena, the situation got out of control, and in the crush that followed, nine people were killed.

Even if you only read about this in the newspaper, you probably would wonder how it could happen and try to come up with an explanation. You might ask yourself, Could it be that there were thousands of highly aggressive, mean-spirited individuals waiting to see the game? That would be hard to believe. Well then, could the fact that the event occurred in New York City explain it? This also seems unlikely, because similar things have happened in smaller cities with more benign reputations, such as Cincinnati, Ohio. Or could it be that the presence of celebrities, the limited number of good seats, and the excitement of the event somehow influenced the crowd's behavior, causing them to act in ways they wouldn't act as individuals? This seems more likely, but is it true?

When we devise explanations for events like these, based on our prior knowledge and experiences, our attitudes and biases, and the limited information the newspaper provides, we don't know if they are accurate or not. Such common-sense explanations—simplistic explanations for social behavior that are based on what we believe to be true of the world (Bordens & Abbott, 1999)—serve us well in our day-to-day lives, providing easy ways to explain complex events. People would be hopelessly bogged down in trying to understand events if they didn't devise these explanations and move on to the next concern in their lives. Unfortunately, common-sense explanations are usually inadequate; that is, there is no evidence or proof that they pinpoint the real causes of events.

The aim of social psychology is to provide valid, reliable explanations for events such as the one in New York City. Rather than relying on conjecture, rumor, and simplistic reasoning, social psychologists approach the problem of explaining complex social behavior in a systematic, scientific way. They develop explanations for phenomena by applying the **scientific method,** which typically involves the four steps shown in Figure 1.2. First, you identify a phenomenon to study. This can come from observation of everyday behavior, reading research literature, or your own previous research. Next, a testable research **hypothesis** must be formed. A hypothesis is a tentative statement about the relationship between variables. The third step is to design a research study to test your hypothesis. Finally, the study is

scientific method
A method of developing scientific explanations involving four steps: identifying a phenomenon to study, developing a testable research hypothesis, designing a research study, and carrying out the research study.

hypothesis
A tentative statement about the relationship between variables.

Figure 1.2

The scientific method used in social psychology begins with the identification of a problem to study and then moves to the formation of testable hypotheses. Next, a research study is designed and carried out.

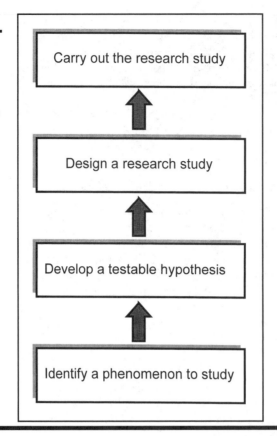

Carry out the research study

↑

Design a research study

↑

Develop a testable hypothesis

↑

Identify a phenomenon to study

actually carried out and the data analyzed. Only after applying this method to a problem and conducting careful research will a social psychologist be satisfied with an explanation.

Throughout this book, we refer to and describe research that social psychologists have conducted to test their ideas, to gain information about events, and to discover the causes of social behavior. We turn now to some of the basic principles of research, including the major research methods, the role of theory in research, the settings for social psychological research, and the importance of ethical conduct in research involving human participants.

The principal aim of the science of social psychology is to uncover scientific explanations for social behavior. A scientific explanation is an interpretation of the causes of social behavior that is based on objective observation and logic and is subject to empirical test (Bordens & Abbott, 1999). To this end, social psychologists use a wide variety of techniques to study social behavior. Generally, they favor two research strategies in their quest for scientific knowledge: **experimental research** and **correlational research.** Let's consider the characteristics of each of these methods, along with their advantages and disadvantages.

experimental research
Resarch involving manipulating a variable suspected of influencing behavior to see how that change affects behavior; results show causal relationships among variables.

correlational research
Research that measures two or more dependent variables and looks for a relationship between them; causal relationships among variables cannot be established.

Experimental Research

The goal of research in social psychology is to understand the causes of social behavior. The researcher usually has an idea he or she wants to test about how a particular factor affects an event or a behavior, that is, whether a particular factor *causes* a particular behavior. To establish a causal relationship between factors, researchers have to use the research method known as the experiment. Because experimental research is the only kind of study that can establish causality, it is the method most social psychologists prefer. An experiment has three essential features: the manipulation of a variable, ensuring that groups comprising the experiment are equivalent at the beginning of the experiment, and exercising control over extraneous variables.

MANIPULATING VARIABLES   In an experiment, a researcher manipulates, or changes the value or nature of, a variable. For example, in an experiment conducted by Henri Tajfel (1981, 1982), participants were shown an array of dots on a screen and were asked to estimate the number of dots that were present in the array. After each participant made a guess about the number of dots, Tajfel told some participants that they were "overestimators" (overestimated the number of dots) and others that they were "underestimators" (underestimated the number of dots). In reality, Tajfel assigned participants to one group or another randomly. Later, the participants were placed into a competitive game in which they could assign points to other participants. Tajfel found that overestimators gave more points to other overestimators and underestimators gave more points to other underestimators.

In this experiment, Tajfel manipulated the type of information given to participants (over- or underestimator). This variable that the researcher manipulates is called the **independent variable.** The researcher wants to determine whether changes in the value of the independent variable cause changes in the participant's behavior. To this end, the researcher obtains some measure of behavior. For example, Tajfel measured the number of points his participants awarded to other participants. This second variable is called the **dependent variable:** It is the measure the researcher assesses to determine the influence of the independent variable on the participant's behavior. The essence of experimental research is to manipulate an independent variable (or two or even more independent variables) and look for related changes in the value of the dependent variable.

independent variable
The variable that the researcher manipulates in an experiment, which must have at least two levels.

dependent variable
The measure the researcher assesses to determine the influence of the independent variable on the participant's behavior.

THE EQUIVALENCE OF GROUPS   The second essential characteristic of an experiment is that there are at least two groups involved who are comparable at the outset of the experiment. In the simplest type of experiment, one group of participants receives a treatment (for example, they are told there is open seating). The participants who receive the experimental treatment comprise the **experimental group.** To know for sure that an experimental treatment (the independent variable) is causing a particular effect, you have to compare the behavior of participants in the experimental group with the behavior of participants who do not receive the treatment (they are told nothing about seating arrangements). The participants who do *not* receive the experimental treatment comprise the **control group.** The researcher then compares the behavior of the participants in the experimental and control groups. In essence, the control group provides a baseline of behavior in the absence of the treatment against which the behavior of the treated participants is compared.

experimental group
A group comprising participants who receive the experimental treatment in an experiment.

control group
A group in an experiment comprising participants who do *not* receive the experimental treatment.

In the real world of research, experiments are usually more complex than the simple experimental group – control group design. Real-world experiments often have more than two levels of an independent variable. For example, if you were interested in the effects of norepinephrine on aggression, participants could receive either a 5-mg, 10-mg, or 15-mg dose of

factorial experiment
An experimental design in which two or more independent variables are manipulated.

norepinephrine. Additionally, most experiments have more than one independent variable. These are called **factorial experiments.** You could add an independent variable to the experiment on the effects of norepinephrine on aggression to make it a factorial experiment. For example, you could anger half of your participants and not anger the other half.

In order to establish a clear cause-and-effect relationship between the independent and dependent variables in an experiment, the participants in the groups must have the same characteristics at the outset of the experiment. For example, in the experiment on norepinephrine and aggression, you would not want to assign individuals with bad tempers to the 15-mg group. If you did this and found that 15-mg produces the highest levels of aggression, one could argue that the heightened aggression was due to the fact that all the participants in that group were hotheads.

random assignment
A method of assigning participants to groups in an experiment that involves each participant's having an equal chance of being in the experimental or control group.

The best way to ensure that two or more groups will be comparable at the outset of an experiment is **random assignment** of individuals to groups, which means that each participant has an equal chance of being assigned to the experimental or control group. Researchers can then be fairly certain that participants with similar characteristics or backgrounds are distributed among the groups. If the two or more groups in an experiment are comparable at the outset, the experiment is said to have *internal validity*, and it can legitimately demonstrate a causal relationship.

Researchers are also concerned about another kind of validity, known as *external validity*, or generality. When researchers study how experimental treatments affect groups of participants, they want to be able to generalize their results to larger populations. To do so, they have to be reasonably sure that the participants in their experiments are representative (typical) of the population to which they wish to generalize their results. For example, if the participants of a study were all male science majors at a small religious college, the researchers could not legitimately generalize the results to females or mixed populations, to younger or older people, or to music majors. If the researchers have gotten a representative sample of their population of interest, then they can legitimately generalize the results to that population, and the study is said to have external validity.

CONTROLLING EXTRANEOUS VARIABLES   The goal of any experiment is to show a clear, unambiguous causal relationship between the independent and dependent variables. In order to show such a relationship, the researcher must ensure that no other variables influence the value of the dependent variable. The researcher must tightly control any **extraneous variable** that might influence the value of the dependent variable. An extraneous variable is any variable not controlled by the researcher that could affect the results. For example, if the temperature in the room where an experiment is run fluctuates widely, it could influence participants' behavior. When it is hot, participants may get irritable and impatient. When it is cold, participants may become sluggish and uninterested in the task at hand.

extraneous variable
Any variable not controlled by the researcher that could affect the results of a study.

confounding variable
An extraneous variable in an experiment that varies systematically with the independent variable, making it difficult or impossible to establish a causal connection between the independent and dependent variables.

As just described, extraneous variables affect the outcome of an experiment by adding a random influence on behavior. In short, extraneous variables make it more difficult to establish a causal connection between your independent and dependent variable. In some cases, an extraneous variable can exert a systematic effect on the outcome of an experiment. This happens when the extraneous variable varies systematically with the independent variable. The result is that a **confounding variable** exists in the experiment.

For example, let's say you are running an experiment on the relationship between frustration and aggression. Participants in the experimental group perform a puzzle for which there is no solution (frustration group), whereas participants in the control group do a puzzle the is solvable (no frustration group). As it happens, on the days when you run the experimental group, the room you are using is hot and humid, whereas on the days when you run the control group the temperature and humidity are normal. Let's say you find that participants in the experimental group show higher levels of aggression than those in the control group. You want to attribute the difference in aggression between your two groups to the frustration levels. However, it may be that the higher levels of aggression recorded in the experimental group are due to the high temperature and humidity and not the frustrating task.

In the real world of research, confounding is seldom as obvious and blatant as in our example. More often, confounding results because a researcher is careless when designing an experiment. Confounding variables often creep into experiments because independent variables are not clearly defined or executed. The presence of confounding variables in an experiment render the results useless. The confounding variable provides an *alternative explanation* for any results that emerge. Because of this, a clear causal connection between the independent and dependent variables cannot be established. Consequently, it is essential that a researcher identify potential sources of confounding and take steps to avoid them. The time to do this is during the design phase of an experiment. Careful attention to detail when designing an experiment can go a long way toward achieving an experiment that is free from confounding variables.

EVALUATING EXPERIMENTS Most of the research studies described in this book are experimental studies. When evaluating these experiments, ask yourself these questions:

- What was the independent variable, and how was it manipulated?
- What were the experimental and control groups?
- What was the dependent variable?
- What methods were employed to test the hypothesis, and were the methods sound?
- Were there any confounding variables that could provide an alternative explanation for the results?
- What was found? That is, what changes in the dependent variable were observed as a function of manipulation of the independent variable?
- What was the nature of the sample used? Was the sample representative of the general population, or was it limited with respect to demographics such as age, gender, culture, or some other set of characteristics?
- Based on the methods and sample used, does the experiment have internal and external validity?

Correlational Research

Although most research in social psychology is experimental, some research is *correlational*. In correlational research, researchers do not manipulate an independent variable. Instead, they measure two or more dependent variables and look for a relationship between them. If changes in one variable are associated with changes in another, the two variables are said to be correlated. When the values of two variables change in the same direction, increasing or decreasing in value, there is a positive correlation between them. For example, if you find that crime increases along with increases in temperature, a positive correlation exists. When the values change in opposite directions, one increasing and the other decreasing, there is a negative correlation between the variables. For example, if you find that less help is given as the number of bystanders to an emergency increases, a negative correlation exists. When one variable does not change systematically with the other, they are uncorrelated.

Even if correlations are found, however, a causal relationship cannot be inferred. For example, height and weight are correlated with each other—the greater one is, the greater the other tends to be—but increases in one do not cause increases in the other. Changes in both are caused by other factors, such as growth hormone and diet. Similarly, aggressive behavior in children is correlated with violent TV viewing, but it isn't known which factor causes the other or if a third factor causes both. Correlational research indicates whether changes in one variable are related to changes in another, but it does not indicate *why* the changes are related. Cause and effect can be demonstrated only by experiments.

In correlational studies, researchers are interested in both the direction of the relationship between the variables (whether it is positive or negative) and the degree, or strength, of the relationship. They measure these two factors with a special statistical test known as the **correlation coefficient** (symbolized as r). The size of the correlation coefficient, which can range from -1 through 0 to $+1$, shows the degree of the relationship. A value of r that approaches -1 or $+1$ indicates a stronger relationship than a value closer to 0.

In Figure 1.3, the five graphs illustrate correlations of varying strengths and directions. Figure 1.3a shows a 0 correlation: Points are scattered at random within the graph. Figures 1.3b and 1.3c show positive correlations of different strengths. As the correlation gets stronger, the points start to line up with each other (Figure 1.3b). A **positive correlation** exists when the values of two variables increase or decrease in the same direction. In a perfect positive correlation ($r = +1$), all the points line up along a straight line (Figure 1.3c). Notice that in a positive correlation, the points line up along a line that slopes in an upward direction, beginning at the lower left of the graph and ending at the upper right.

In a negative correlation (shown in Figures 1.3d and 1.3e), the same rules concerning strength apply that held for the positive correlation. However, in a **negative correlation,** as the value of one variable *increases* the value of a second *decreases*. Figure 1.3e shows a perfect negative correlation (-1).

An excellent example of a correlational study is one conducted by Nancy Eisenberg and her colleagues (1989). This study addressed the relationship between an individual's feelings of sympathy and personal distress and their likelihood of helping. Each participant was shown a film depicting a mother talking about an accident in which her children were severely injured and describing their problems adjusting to their injuries. The participants were led to believe that they were watching the film as part of a study for a public television station interested in reactions to actual unaired programs. As part of the study, participants were told that their physiological responses to the film

correlation coefficient (r)

A measure of association between two variables that provides two important pieces of information: the degree of relationship between variables (indicated by the size of the coefficient) and the direction of the relationship (indicated by the sign of the coefficient).

positive correlation

The direction of a correlation in which the values of two variables increase or decrease in the same direction.

negative correlation

The direction of a correlation in which the value of one variable increases whereas the value of a second decreases.

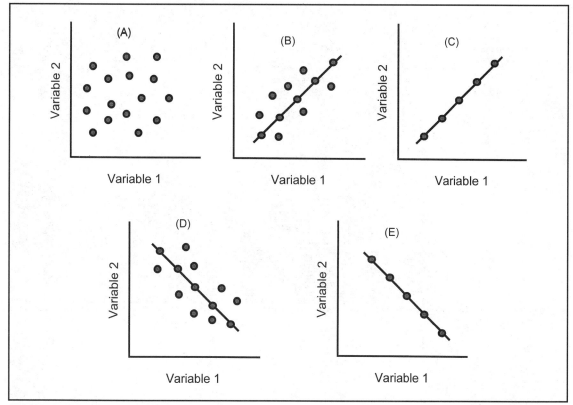

Figure 1.3 Scatterplots showing correlations of different directions and strength: (A) correlation of 0 indicated by dots randomly arrayed; (B) strong positive correlation; (C) perfect positive correlation (+1) indicated by the dots lined up perfectly, sloping from bottom left to upper right; (D) strong negative correlation; (e) perfect negative correlation indicated by the dots lined up perfectly, sloping from upper left to lower right.

would be measured. Consequently, they were hooked up to a heart rate monitor. The participants' facial expressions were also videotaped and later evaluated for the expression of several emotions (sympathy, sadness, personal distress, happiness). Independent raters evaluated each of the emotional expressions on scales ranging from 0 (no sign of the given emotion) to 5 (exceptionally strong display).

After viewing this film, each participant was asked to fill out a questionnaire dealing with how he or she felt about the film and the individuals portrayed in the film. The experimenter told the participant that a page of the questionnaire was missing and then left to look for it. The experimenter returned carrying an envelope from the principal investigator of the study. The envelope was addressed to "the student scheduled to watch tape 24" (each participant had been led to believe that he or she would be the only one to view that particular film). Inside the envelope was a request for the participant to help the person portrayed in the film. Participants indicated their willingness to help by checking off the number of hours they would be willing to donate to the family described in the film. They then completed the remainder of the questionnaire.

Based on this brief summary, you can see that four variables were measured: heart rate, facial expressions, participants' self-reports of how they felt about the film, and participants' willingness to help the victims

Social psychologists have discovered that when there are many bystanders present, individuals are less likely to help than if one is alone when a helping situation arises. This shows a negative correlation. As the number of bystanders increases, the number of individuals helping decreases.

depicted in the film. However, notice that Eisenberg and her colleagues did not manipulate any of the variables. Therefore, there were no independent variables.

Eisenberg found that the correlation between willingness to help and verbal self-reports of sympathy was .25; the correlation between willingness to help and self-reports of personal distress was .23. In other words, the more sympathetic the subjects reported feeling, the more likely they were to help. The correlations between willingness to help and happy facial expressions during the film and while reading the request for help were negative ($-.06$ and $-.15$). In other words, the happier the participants appeared while watching the film and while reading the request for help, the less likely they were to help. This pattern of results suggests that feelings and expressions of sympathy and sadness for a victim are positively correlated with offers of help. That is, the greater the sympathy expressed by the participant, the more likely the participant was to offer help. These findings suggest that we give money to the homeless because we feel sympathy for their predicament, not just because we are afraid it might ruin our day if we don't.

Although correlational research does not demonstrate causal relationships, it does play an important role in science. Correlational research is used in situations where it is not possible to manipulate variables. Any study of individual characteristics (age, sex, race, and so on) is correlational. After all, you cannot manipulate someone's age or sex. Correlational research is also used when it would be unethical to manipulate variables. For example, if you were interested in how alcohol consumption affects the human fetus, it would not be ethical to expose pregnant women to various dosages of alcohol and see what happens. Instead, you could *measure* alcohol consumption and the rate of birth defects and look for a correlation between those two variables. Finally, correlational research is useful when you want to study variables as they occur naturally in the real world.

Settings for Social Psychological Research

Social psychological research is done in one of two settings: the laboratory or the field. Laboratory research is conducted in a controlled environment the researcher creates; participants come into this artificial environment to participate in the research. Field research is conducted in the participant's natural environment; the researcher goes to the participant, in effect taking the study on the road. Observations are made in the participant's natural environment; sometimes independent variables are even manipulated in this environment.

LABORATORY RESEARCH Most research in social psychology is conducted in the laboratory. This allows the researcher to exercise tight control over extraneous (unwanted) variables that might affect results. For example, the researcher can maintain constant lighting, temperature, humidity, and noise level within a laboratory environment. This tight control over the environment and over extraneous variables allows the researcher to be reasonably confident that the experiment has internal validity—that is, that any variation observed in the dependent variable was caused by manipulation of the independent variable. However, that tight control also has a cost: The researcher loses some ability to apply the results beyond the tightly controlled laboratory setting (external validity). Research conducted in highly controlled laboratories may not generalize very well to real-life social behavior, or even to other laboratory studies.

FIELD RESEARCH Field research comes in three varieties: the field study, the field survey, and the field experiment. In a **field study,** the researcher makes unobtrusive observations of the participants without making direct contact or interfering in any way. The researcher simply watches from afar. In its pure form, the participants should be unaware that they are being observed, because the very act of being observed tends to change the participants' behavior. The researcher avoids contaminating the research situation by introducing any changes in the participants' natural environment.

Jane Goodall's original research on chimpanzee behavior was a field study. Goodall investigated social behavior among chimpanzees by observing groups of chimps from a distance, initially not interacting with them. However, as Goodall became more accepted by the chimps, she began to interact with them, even to the point of feeding them. Can we be sure that Goodall's later observations are characteristic of chimp behavior in the wild? Probably not, because she altered the chimps' environment by interacting with them.

In the **field survey,** the researcher directly approaches participants and asks them questions. For example, he or she might stop people in a shopping mall and collect information on which make of car they plan to buy next. The ubiquitous political polls we see during election years are examples of field surveys.

Field studies and surveys allow us to describe and catalogue behavior. Political polls, for example, may help us discover which candidate is in the lead, whether a proposition is likely to pass, or how voters feel about important campaign issues. However, they cannot tell us what causes the differences observed among voters, because we would need to conduct an experiment to study causes. Fortunately, we can conduct experiments in the field.

The field experiment is probably the most noteworthy and useful field technique for social psychologists. In a **field experiment,** the researcher

field study
A descriptive research strategy in which the researcher makes unobtrusive observations of the participants without making direct contact or interfering in any way.

field survey
A descriptive research strategy in which the researcher directly approaches the participants and asks them questions.

field experiment
A research setting in which the researcher manipulates one or more independent variables and measures behavior in the participant's natural environment.

manipulates independent variables and collects measures of the dependent variables (the participant's behavior). In this sense, a field experiment is like a laboratory experiment. The main difference is that in the field experiment, the researcher manipulates independent variables under naturally occurring conditions. The principal advantage of the field experiment is that it has greater external validity—that is, the results can be generalized beyond the study more legitimately than can the results of a laboratory experiment.

As an example, let's say you are interested in seeing whether the race of a person needing help influences potential helpers. You might consider a field experiment in which you had someone, a confederate of yours (a *confederate* is someone working for the experimenter), pretend to faint on a subway train. In the experiment, you use two different confederates, one a black male, the other a white male. The two are as alike as they can be (in age, dress, and so on) except, of course, for skin color. You then observe how many people help each man and how quickly they do so. Such an experiment would be very realistic and would have a high degree of external validity. Consequently, the results would have broad generality.

A disadvantage of the field experiment is that the researcher cannot control extraneous variables as effectively as in the laboratory. Thus, internal validity may be compromised. In the subway experiment, for example, you have no control over who the participants are or which experimental condition (white or black confederate) they will walk into. Consequently, the internal validity of your experiment—the legitimacy of the causal relationship you discover—may suffer. The experiment also poses some ethical problems, one of which is that the people who purchased a ride on the subway did not voluntarily agree to participate in an experiment. We discuss the ethics of research in a later section of this chapter.

THE ROLE OF THEORY IN SOCIAL PSYCHOLOGICAL RESEARCH

theory
A set of interrelated statements (propositions) concerning the causes for a social behavior that help social psychologists organize research results, make predictions about the influence of certain variables, and give direction to future social behavior research.

On many occasions throughout this book, we refer to social psychological theories. A **theory** is a set of interrelated statements of propositions about the causes of a particular phenomenon. Theories help social psychologists organize research results, make predictions about how certain variables influence social behavior, and give direction to future research. In these ways, social psychological theories play an important role in helping us understand complex social behaviors.

There are a few important points to keep in mind as you read about these theories. First, a theory is not the final word on the causes of a social behavior. Theories are developed, revised, and sometimes abandoned according to how well they fit with research results. Rather than tell us how things are in an absolute sense, theories help us understand social behavior by providing a particular perspective. Consider attribution theories—theories about how people decide what caused others (and themselves) to act in certain ways in certain situations. Attribution theories do not tell us exactly how people assign or attribute causality. Instead, they suggest rules and make predictions about how people make such inferences in a variety of circumstances. These predictions are then tested with research.

The second important point about social psychological theories is that, often, more than one theory can apply to a particular social behavior. For example, social psychologists have devised several attribution theories to help us understand how we make decisions about the causes for behaviors. Each theory helps provide a piece of the puzzle of social behavior. However, no single theory may be able to account for all aspects of a social behavior. One theory helps us understand how we infer the internal motivations of another individual; a second theory examines how we make sense of the social situation in which that individual's behavior took place.

Theory and the Research Process

Theories in social psychology are usually tested by research, and much research is guided by theory. Research designed to test a particular theory or model is referred to as **basic research.** In contrast, research designed to address a real-world problem is called **applied research.** The distinction between these two categories is not rigid, however. The results of basic research can often be applied to real-world problems, and the results of applied research may affect the validity of a theory.

For example, research on how stress affects memory may be primarily basic research, but the findings of this research apply to a real-world problem: the ability of an eyewitness to recall a violent crime accurately. Similarly, research on how jurors process evidence in complex trials (e.g., Horowitz & Bordens, 1990) has implications for predictions made by various theories of how people think and make decisions in a variety of situations. Both types of research have their place in social psychology.

basic research
Research that has the principal aim of empirically testing a theory or a model.

applied research
Research that has a principal aim to address a real-world problem.

Theory and Application

Application of basic theoretical ideas may take many forms. Consider, for example, the idea that it is healthy for individuals to confront and deal directly with psychological traumas from the past. Although various clinical theories have made this assumption, evidence in support of it was sparse.

In one study, social psychologist Jamie Pennebaker (1989) measured the effects of disclosure on mind and body. The research showed that when the participants confronted past traumas, either by writing or talking about them, their immunological functioning improved and their skin conductance rates were lowered. This latter measure reflects a reduction in autonomic nervous system activity, indicating a lessening of psychological tension. In other words, people were "letting go" as they fully revealed their feelings about these past traumas. Those who had trouble revealing important thoughts about the event—who could not let go of the trauma—showed heightened skin conductance rates. Pennebaker's work shows that the act of confiding in someone protects the body from the internal stress caused by repressing these unvoiced traumas. Here is an example of basic research that had clear applications for real-life situations.

WHAT DO WE LEARN FROM RESEARCH IN SOCIAL PSYCHOLOGY?

Two criticisms are commonly made of social psychological research. One is that social psychologists study what we already know, the "intuitively obvious." The other is that because exceptions to research results can nearly always be found, many results must be wrong. Let's consider the merits of each of these points.

Do Social Psychologists Study the Obvious?

William McGuire, a prominent social psychologist, once suggested that social psychologists may appear to study "bubba psychology"—things we learned on our grandmother's knee. That is, social psychologists study what is already obvious and predictable based on common sense. Although it may seem this way, it is not the case. The results of research seem obvious only when you already know what they are. This is called **hindsight bias,** or the "I-knew-it-all-along" phenomenon (Slovic & Fischoff, 1977; Wood, 1978). With the benefit of hindsight, everything looks obvious. For example, after the Columbine High incident, it seemed obvious to all that the police should have responded more quickly. However, the police were concerned that a bold move into an uncertain situation in which explosives were known to be present might have increased the number killed. Similarly, after Klebold and Harris killed their victims, people began to point to "signs" that should have been interpreted as signals for antisocial behavior to come. Of course, in both situations we have the benefit of knowing how things turned out. After an event, it seems obvious what should have been done. However, before the event, it is not so easy to predict what will happen as it would seem in hindsight.

Although the results of some research may seem obvious, studies show that when individuals are given descriptions of research without results, they can predict the outcome of the research no better than chance (Slovic & Fischoff, 1977). In other words, the results were not so obvious when they were not already known!

Do Exceptions Mean Research Results Are Wrong?

When the findings of social psychological research are described, someone often points to a case that is an exception to the finding. Suppose a particular study shows that a person is less likely to get help when there are several bystanders present than when there is only one. You probably can think of a situation in which you were helped with many bystanders around. Does this mean that the research is wrong or that it doesn't apply to you?

To answer this question, you must remember that in a social psychological experiment, groups of participants are exposed to various levels of the independent variable. In an experiment on the relationship between the number of bystanders and the likelihood of receiving help, for example, one group of participants is given an opportunity to help a person in need with no other bystanders present. A second group of participants gets the same opportunity but with three bystanders present. Let's say that our results in this hypothetical experiment look like those shown in Table 1.1. Seven out of 10 participants in the no-bystander condition helped (70%), whereas only 2 out of 10 helped in the 3-bystander condition (20%). Thus, we would conclude that you are more likely to get help when there are no other bystanders present than if there are three bystanders.

Notice, however, that we do not say that you will never receive help when three bystanders are present. In fact, two participants helped in that condition. Nor do we say that you will always receive help when no other bystanders are present. Three of the 10 participants did not help in that condition.

Table 1.1

Results from a Hypothetical Study of Helping Behavior

Participant Number	No Bystanders	Three Bystanders
1	No help	No help
2	No help	No help
3	Help	No help
4	Help	Help
5	No help	Help
6	Help	No help
7	Help	No help
8	Help	No help
9	Help	No help
10	Help	No help

The moral to the story here is that the results of experiments in social psychology represent differences between groups of participants, not differences between specific individuals. Based on the results of social psychological research, we can say that *on the average,* groups differ. Within those groups, there are nearly always participants who do not behave as most of the participants behaved. We can acknowledge that exceptions to research findings usually exist, but this does not mean that the results reported are wrong.

ETHICS AND SOCIAL PSYCHOLOGICAL RESEARCH

Unlike research in chemistry and physics, which does not involve living organisms, research in social psychology uses living organisms, both animal and human. Because social psychology studies living organisms, researchers must consider research ethics. They have to concern themselves with the treatment of their research participants and with the potential long-range effects of the research on the participants' well-being. In every study conducted in social psychology, researchers must place the welfare of the research participants among their top priorities.

Questions about ethics have been raised about some of the most famous research ever done in social psychology. For example, you may be familiar with the experiments on obedience conducted by Stanley Milgram (1963; described in detail in chapter 8). In these experiments, participants were asked to administer painful electric shocks to an individual who was doing poorly on a learning task. Although no shocks were actually delivered, participants believed they were inflicting intense pain on an increasingly unwilling victim. Following the experiment, participants reported experiencing guilt and lowered self-esteem as well as anger toward the researchers. The question raised by this and other experiments with human participants is how far researchers can and should go to gain knowledge.

Research conducted by social psychologists is governed by an ethical code of conduct developed by the American Psychological Association

Table 1.2

Ethical Principles of Psychologists and Code of Conduct for Research with Human Participants

1. When collecting, storing, or destroying any data collected from research participants, confidentiality must be preserved. No confidential information may be disclosed without the prior consent of the participant.

2. Psychologists must plan research so that the results will not be misleading, carry out the research according to accepted ethical principles, and protect the rights and welfare of the research participants and anyone else who might be affected by the research.

3. A psychologist must act with the dignity and welfare of the research participants in mind and is responsible for his or her conduct and the conduct of any subordinates. When special populations are used (e.g., children), special care must be taken to protect the participants' welfare and the welfare of anyone else affected by the research.

4. Research must comply with relevant federal and state laws and with professional standards governing research with human participants.

5. Approval from host institutions or organizations must be obtained before research is carried out. The psychologists must provide accurate information in any research proposals and conduct the research as approved.

6. Before conducting research (excepting anonymous surveys, naturalistic observation, or similar research), the nature of the research and what is expected from the researcher and participants must be clarified.

7. In appropriate instances, the psychologist is obligated to obtain informed consent from research participants, which should include statements describing the research, informing participants that they may withdraw without penalty, indicating any aspects of the study that might affect a participant's decision to participate, and explaining any aspects of the study about which participants ask.

8. When research participants are students or subordinates, special care must be taken to protect them from any consequences of declining participation or withdrawing. If research participation is a course requirement or an opportunity for extra course credit, an equitable alternative must be offered to fulfill the requirement or obtain the credit. If a person is legally incapable of giving informed consent, the psychologists must still provide an appropriate explanation of the research, obtain the participant's consent, and obtain permission from a legally authorized individual (if the latter is allowed by law).

9. Deception is not permitted in research unless it is justified by the scientific, educational, or applied value of the research and that alternatives to deception are not feasible. Deception is never allowed when it involves information that might affect a participant's willingness to participate (e.g., potential risks, adverse effects, discomfort, physical or emotional harm). Any deception used must be explained to the participant as early as possible, preferably at the end of participation but no later than the end of the research.

10. The psychologist must not interfere with the participant or the research environment from which data are collected unless it is warranted by appropriate research design and is consistent with the psychologist's role as a researcher.

11. The psychologist has an obligation to provide participants with a prompt opportunity to receive information about the nature, results, and conclusions of research in which they have participated. The psychologist also has an obligation to correct any misconceptions participants may have about the research. The psychologist must take reasonable measures to honor all commitments made to research participants.

Source: Adapted from "Ethical Principles of Psychologists and Code of Conduct," Sections 5 and 6. *American Psychologist, 47,* 1597–1611.

(APA). The main principles of the APA (1992) code are summarized in Table 1.2. Notice that the code mandates that participation in psychological research be voluntary. This means that participants cannot be compelled to participate in research. Researchers must also obtain **informed consent** from the participants, which means that they must inform them of the nature of the study, the requirements for participation, and any risks or benefits associated with participating in the study. Subjects must also be told they have the right to decline or withdraw from participation with no penalty.

Additionally, the APA code restricts the use of deception in research. Deception occurs when researchers tell their participants they are studying one thing but actually are studying another. Deception can be used only if no other viable alternative exists. When researchers use deception, they must tell participants about the deception (and the reasons for it) as soon as possible after participation.

Following ethical codes of conduct protects subjects from harm. In this sense, ethical codes help the research process. However, sometimes ethical research practice conflicts with the requirements of science. For example, in a field experiment on helping, it may not be possible (or desirable) to obtain consent from participants before they participate in the study. When such conflicts occur, the researcher must weigh the potential risks to the participants against the benefits to be gained.

informed consent
An ethical research requirement meaning that participants must be informed of the nature of the study, the requirements for participation, any risk or benefits associated with participating in the study, and the right to decline or withdraw from participation with no penalty.

COLUMBINE HIGH SCHOOL REVISITED

How can we explain the behavior of Eric Harris and Dylan Klebold? Social psychologists would begin by pointing to the two factors that contribute to social behavior: individual characteristics and the social situation. Was there something about Harris and Klebold's personalities, attitudes, or other characteristics that predisposed them toward violence. Or, was it the social environment that was more important. Social psychologists focus on the latter, and apparently the social situation played a major role in their behavior. They were outcasts in the social environment at Columbine High School which led them to associate with other outcasts. They enjoyed playing violent video games and were fans of Adolph Hitler. Evidently, the social forces came together in such a way that violence was seen as the best course of behavior. Of course, there were others who were outcasts who did not behave as did Harris and Klebold. Their unique way of viewing the social situation led them down the path they took.

Social psychology is not the only discipline that would be interested in explaining Harris and Klebold's behavior. Sociologists would look at the incident from the perspective of problems in the wider culture and society that contribute to an atmosphere that accepts such violent acts. Biologists might be interested in how such behavior fits within an evolutionary model of the species. Each discipline has its own way of collecting information about issues of interest. Social psychology would fact the daunting task of explaining Harris and Klebold's behavior by conducting carefully designed research. Through the scientific method, one could isolate the variables that contribute to aggressive acts such as those that occurred at Columbine High School.

1. **What is social psychology?**

   Social psychology is the scientific study of how we think and feel about, interact with, and influence each other. It is the branch of psychology that focuses on social behavior, specifically how we relate to other people in our social world. Social psychology can help us to understand everyday things that happen to us, as well as past and present cultural and historical events.

2. **How do social psychologists explain social behavior?**

   An early model of social behavior proposed by Kurt Lewin suggested that social behavior is caused by two factors: individual characteristics and the social situation. This simple model has since been expanded to better explain the forces that shape social behavior. According to modern views of social behavior, input from the social situation works in conjunction with individual characteristics to influence social behavior through the operation of **social cognition** (the general process of thinking about social events) and **social perception** (how we perceive other people). Based on our processing of social information, we evaluate the social situation and form an intention to behave in a certain way. This behavioral intention may or may not be translated into social behavior. We engage in social behavior based on our constantly changing evaluation of the situation. Once we behave in a certain way, it may have an effect on the social situation, which in turn will affect future social behavior.

3. **How does social psychology relate to other disciplines that study social behavior?**

   There are many scientific disciplines that study social behavior. Biologists, developmental psychologists, anthropologists, personality psychologists, historians, and sociologists all have an interest in social behavior. Although social psychology has common interests with these disciplines, unlike biology and personality psychology, social psychology focuses on the social situation as the principal cause of social behavior. Whereas sociology and history focus on the situation, social psychology takes a narrower view, looking at the individual in the social situation rather than the larger group or society. In other words, history and sociology take a top-down approach to explaining social behavior, making a group or institution the focus of analysis. Social psychology takes a bottom-up approach, focusing on how individual behavior is influenced by the situation.

4. **How do social psychologists approach the problem of explaining social behavior?**

   Unlike the layperson who forms commonsense explanations for social behavior based on limited information, social psychologists rely on the **scientific method** to formulate scientific explanations—tentative explanations based on observation and logic that are open to empirical testing. The scientific method involves identifying a phenomenon to study, developing a testable research **hypothesis,** designing a research study, and carrying out the research study. Only after applying this method to a problem and conducting careful research will a social psychologist be satisfied with an explanation.

5. **What is experimental research, and how is it used?**

   Experimental research is used to uncover causal relationships between variables. Its main features are (1) the manipulation of an **independent variable** and the observation of the effects of this manipulation on a **dependent variable,** (2) the use of two or more initially comparable groups, and (3) exercising control over **extraneous** and **confounding variables.** Every experiment includes at least one independent variable with at least two levels. In the simplest experiment, one group of participants (the **experimental group**) is exposed to an experimental treatment and a second group (the **control group**) is not. Researchers then compare the behavior of participants in the experimental group with the behavior of participants in the control group. Independent variables can be manipulated by varying their quantity or quality. Researchers use **random assignment** to ensure that the groups in an experiment are comparable before applying any treatment to them.

The basic experiment can be expanded by adding additional levels of an independent variable or by adding a second or third independent variable. Experiments that include more than one independent variable are known as **factorial experiments.**

6. What is correlational research?

In **correlational research,** researchers measure two or more variables and look for a relationship between them. When two variables both change in the same direction, increasing or decreasing in value, they are **positively correlated.** When they change in opposite directions, one increasing and the other decreasing, they are **negatively correlated.** When one variable does not change systematically with the other, they are uncorrelated. Even if a correlation is found, a causal relationship cannot be inferred.

7. What is the correlation coefficient, and what does it tell you?

Researchers evaluate correlational relationships between variables with a statistic called the **correlation coefficient** (symbolized as r). The sign of r (positive or negative) indicates the direction of the relationship between variables; the size of r (ranging from -1 through 0 to $+1$) indicates the strength of the relationship between variables.

8. Where is social psychological research conducted?

Social psychologists conduct research either in the laboratory or in the field. In laboratory research, researchers create an artificial environment in which they can control extraneous variables. This tight control allows the researchers to be reasonably confident that any variation observed in the dependent variable was caused by manipulation of the independent variable. However, results obtained this way sometimes cannot be legitimately generalized beyond the laboratory setting.

There are several kinds of field research. In the **field study,** the researcher observes participants but does not interact with them. In the **field survey,** the researcher has direct contact with participants and interacts with them. Both of these techniques allow the researcher to describe behavior, but causes cannot be uncovered. In the **field experiment,** the researcher manipulates an independent variable in the participant's natural environment. The field experiment increases the generality of the research findings. However, extraneous variables may cloud the causal relationship between the independent and dependent variables.

9. What is the role of theory in social psychology?

A **theory** is a set of interrelated statements of propositions about the causes of a phenomenon that help organize research results, make predictions about how certain variables influence social behavior, and give direction to future research. A theory is not the final word on the causes of a social behavior. Theories are developed, revised, and sometimes abandoned according to how well they fit with research results. Theories do not tell us how things are in an absolute sense. Instead, they help us understand social behavior by providing a particular perspective. Often, more than one theory can apply to a particular social behavior.

Sometimes one theory provides a better explanation of one aspect of a particular social behavior and another theory provides a better explanation of another aspect of that same behavior. Some research, called **basic research** is designed to test predictions made by theories. **Applied research** is conducted to study a real-wold phenomenon (e.g., jury decisions). Basic and applied research are not necessarily mutually exclusive. Some basic research has applied implications, and some applied research has theoretical implications.

10. *What can we learn from social psychological research?*

Two common criticisms of social psychological research are that social psychologists study things that are intuitively obvious and that because exceptions to research results can nearly always be found, many results must be wrong. However, these two criticisms are not valid. The findings of social psychological research may *appear* to be intuitively obvious in hindsight (the **hindsight bias**), but individuals cannot predict how an experiment will come out if they don't already know the results. Furthermore, exceptions to a research finding do not invalidate that finding. Social psychologists study groups of individuals. Within a group, variation in behavior will occur. Social psychologists look at average differences between groups.

11. *What ethical standards must social psychologists follow when conducting research?*

Social psychologists are concerned with the ethics of research—how participants are treated within a study and how they are affected in the long term by participating. Social psychologists adhere to the code of research ethics established by the American Psychological Association. Ethical treatment of participants involves several key aspects, including **informed consent** (informing participants about the nature of a study and requirements for participation prior to participation), protecting participants from short-term and long-term harm, and ensuring anonymity.

INTERNET ACTIVITY

TAKING PART IN A SOCIAL PSYCHOLOGICAL STUDY

In days past, the only way one could participate in a social psychological experiment was to go physically to a certain place and take part in the experiment. The Internet has changed all that. Now, anyone with access to a computer can be a participant in a social psychological study. You can find a wide range of experimental and correlational research studies on the Internet. One rich source for these studies is the Web site for the American Psychological Society. Or, you can type in the search term "social psychology experiments" and hunt arount for a study to take part in.

For this exercise, you are to find and participate in an on-line social psychological study. You may choose either an experimental or a correlational study. After you have completed the study, answer the following questions:

1. What was the main goal of the study?

2. Was an informed consent form used? If so, how did you complete it?

3. If the study was an experiment, what were the independent and dependent variables? How were the independent variables manipulated? How was the dependent variable collected?

4. If the study was correlational (e.g., a questionnaire), which variables do you think were going to be used to predict the values of others?

5. Was there any debriefing done? If so, what was it?

6. What, if any, opportunity were you given to ask questions and/or obtain a copy of the results of the study?

Agnew, N., & Pike, S. (1994). *The science game* (6th ed.). Englewood Cliffs, NJ: Prentice-Hall.

This book is an innovative, even humorous look at the research methods and concepts used in the social sciences.

American Psychological Association. (1992). Ethical principles of psychologists. *American Psychologist, 47,* 1597–1611.

This book details the ethical concerns that researchers should attend to when doing research with human participants.

Koocher, G. P., & Keith-Spiegel, P. (1998). *Ethics in psychology: Professional standards and cases* (2nd ed.). New York: Oxford University Press.

This book is a comprehensive treatment of ethics in psychology. It includes chapters on ethics in psychotherapy, psychological assessment, research, and publication as well as a host of other areas in which psychologists must be concerned with ethics.

Nickerson, R. (1992). *Looking ahead: Human factors and challenges in a changing world.* Hillsdale, NJ: Erlbaum.

A book that examines, in part, what social psychology and psychology in general can contribute to solving the challenges of the 21st century. An interesting view for anyone contemplating a career in psychology.

CHAPTER 2

THE SOCIAL SELF

James Carroll is a best-selling author, novelist, and journalist. He comes from a remarkable family whose members played important, sometimes decisive roles in the events of the late 20th century. Carroll's life illustrates how the interlocking influences of birth, family life, education, and historical forces all influence the development of one's sense of self.

Carroll's father was the most important influence in his life. His father's dream was to be a priest, and James lived that dream for his father. He was the altar boy who became the priest and the college chaplain. Carroll loved his life as a priest. Events transpired, however, to change Carroll's life in ways that were unexpected and traumatic. These events forged a breach between son and father, a breach only partially closed before the father died.

It is easy to see why Carroll's father so strongly influenced him as a young man. He was a figure of mythic proportions; he led a life almost impossible to be real, surely a figment of Hollywood imagination. As a young lawyer, Carroll's father caught the eye of the FBI Director, J. Edgar Hoover, and became a top agent. When the Vietnam War began, the air force recruited the FBI agent and made him director of the agency that selected the bombing targets in Vietnam. Improbably, the now General Carroll—James's father— was the individual in charge of the U.S. Air Force's war against North Vietnam.

The Vietnam War forced the young Carroll to confront exactly who he was. On the one hand, his father was helping to run the war in Vietnam, and James's brother, who was an FBI agent, was tracking down draft evaders and keeping tabs on antiwar protesters. James's superiors in the Catholic church also strongly supported the war. But Carroll, as a young seminarian, was turning against the war that his father was directing. In a moving account of his crisis of conscience and self-identity, Carroll in his memoir *An American Requiem* (1996) chronicles his conflict with church hierarchy, his government, his father, and most of all himself. The son, who still admired and loved his father the general, began to align himself with antiwar protestors, draft resisters, and Catholic antiwar radicals.

In *Memorial Bridge,* Carroll's stirring novel of the Vietnam War period, the author artfully and seamlessly painted a barely fictionalized picture of the conflict between his father and himself, a conflict that forever changed his sense of who he was. Carroll recalls being a participant in the famous antiwar demonstration at the Pentagon and looking up at the sixth floor of the building, knowing that his father was looking down on his son, the protestor, the radical, who had just left the priesthood. But perhaps the most defining moment of Carroll's life was an earlier event, the moment that he publicly and irrevocably created a self-identity separate and distinct from his father, much of his family, and the experiences of his life. When as a newly ordained priest Carroll conducted his first mass at an air force base in front of his family and his father's colleagues, the generals who were directing the Vietnam War, he expressed his moral outrage at their conduct, taking that moment to express clearly—a clarity he may have regretted later—his personal identity as distinct from his family's image of him.

In Carroll's life, we can see the interplay of the various parts of the self: the personal self—his own beliefs, knowledge, and principles—and that part of the self influenced by his relationships with family, friends, and church. Finally, we see the impact of the great social events of the time. It is no wonder that Carroll the novelist can write movingly and fervently about the effects on the self of family, church, and country. Carroll notes that he was much like his father, that he tried to live his father's dream, but events conspired to break both their hearts (Carroll, 1996).

KEY QUESTIONS

AS YOU READ THIS CHAPTER, FIND THE ANSWERS TO THE FOLLOWING QUESTIONS:

1. *What is the self?*
2. *How do we know the self?*
3. *What is distinctiveness theory?*
4. *How is the self organized?*
5. *What is authobiographical memory?*
6. *What is self-esteem?*
7. *How do we evaluate the self?*
8. *What is self-evaluation maintenance (SEM) theory?*
9. *What is self-consistency?*
10. *How do we present the self to others?*
11. *What is self-monitoring?*
12. *What is self-handicapping?*
13. *How accurate are we in assessing the impression we convey?*
14. *What is the spotlight effect?*
15. *What is the illusion of transparency?*

SELF-CONCEPT

How do we develop a coherent sense of who we are? The vignette describing James Carroll suggests that our personal experiences, interaction with others, and cultural forces all play some role in our definition of self. Who am I? The answer to this question is the driving force in our lives. If you were asked to define yourself, you most likely would use sentences containing the words *I, me, mine,* and *myself* (Cooley, 1902; Schweder, Much, Mahapatra, & Park, 1997).

The self may be thought of as a structure that contains the organized and stable contents of one's personal experiences (Schlenker, 1987). In this sense, the self is an object, something inside us that we may evaluate and contemplate. The self is "me," the sum of what I am. A significant part of what we call the *self* is knowledge. All the ideas, thoughts, and information that we have about ourselves—about who we are, what characteristics we have, what our personal histories have made us, and what we may yet become—make up our **self-concept.**

self-concept
All the knowledge and thoughts related to whom you believe you are, comprising the cognitive component of the self.

Self-Knowledge: How We Know the Self

There are several sources of social information that we use to forge our self-concept. One comes from our view of how other people react to us. These **reflected appraisals** shape our self-concept (Cooley, 1902; Jones & Gerard, 1967). A second social source is the comparisons we make with other people (Festinger, 1950). Self-knowledge comes from the **social comparison process** by which we compare our own reactions, abilities, and attributes to others (Festinger, 1950). We do this because we need accurate information so that we may succeed. We need to know if we are good athletes or students or race car drivers so that we may make rational choices. Social comparison is a control device, because it makes our world more predictable.

A third source of information comes from the self-knowledge gained by observing our own behavior. Daryl Bem (1967) suggested that people really do not know why they do things, so they simply observe their behavior and

reflected appraisal
A source of social information involving our view of how other people react to us.

social comparison process
A source of social knowledge involving how we compare our reactions, abilities, and attributes to others'.

Various characteristics enter into our self-concept. Often, we express our self-concept, as this biker is doing, by displaying aspects of it to others.

assume that their motives were consistent with their behavior. Someone who rebels against authority may simply observe her behavior and conclude, "Well, I must be a rebel." Therefore, we may obtain knowledge of our self simply by observing ourselves behave and then infer that our private beliefs must coincide with our public actions. Another method of knowing the self is through **introspection,** the act of examining our own thoughts and feelings. Introspection is a method we all use to understand ourselves, but there is evidence to suggest that we may get a somewhat biased picture of our own internal state. Thinking about our attitudes and the reasons we hold them can sometimes be disruptive and confusing (Wilson, Dunn, Kraft, & Lisle, 1989). More generally, the process of introspecting—of looking into our own mind, rather than just behaving—can have this effect. For example, if you are forced to think about why you like your romantic partner, you might find it disconcerting if you are not able to think of any good reasons why you are in this relationship. This doesn't mean that you don't have reasons, but they may not be accessible, easy to retrieve. Much depends on the strength of the relationship. If the relationship is not strong, thinking about the relationship could be disruptive because we might not think up many positive reasons in support of the relationship. If it is pretty strong, then reasoning might further strengthen it. The stronger our attitude or belief, the more likely that thinking about it will increase the consistency between the belief and our behavior (Fazio, 1986).

PERSONAL ATTRIBUTES AND SELF-CONCEPT Now that we have noted some of the methods we may use to form and gain access to our self-concept, let's see what is inside. What kind of information and feelings are contained in the self? First of all, the self-concept contains ideas and beliefs about **personal attributes.** A person may think of herself as female, American, young, smart, compassionate, the daughter of a single mother, a good basketball player, reasonably attractive, hot-tempered, artistic, patient, and a movie fan. All of these attributes, and many more, go into her self-concept.

Researchers investigated the self-concepts of American school children by asking them the following kinds of questions (McGuire & McGuire, 1988, p. 99):

- Tell us about yourself.
- Tell us what you are not.
- Tell us about school.
- Tell us about your family.

These open-ended probes revealed that children and adolescents often defined themselves by characteristics that were unique or distinctive. Participants who possessed a distinctive characteristic were much more likely to mention that attribute than were those who were less distinctive on that dimension (McGuire & McGuire, 1988).

According to **distinctiveness theory,** people think of themselves in terms of those attributes or dimensions that make them different, that are distinctive, rather than in terms of attributes they have in common with others. People, for example, who are taller or shorter than others, or wear glasses, or are left-handed are likely to incorporate that characteristic into their self-concept.

People usually are aware of the attributes they have in common with other individuals. A male going to an all-male high school is aware that he is male. But being male may not be a defining part of his self-concept because everybody around him has that same characteristic. He will define himself by

---

introspection
The act of examining our own thoughts and feelings to understand ourselves, which may yield a somewhat biased picture of our own internal state.

---

personal attributes
An aspect of the self-concept involving the attributes we believe we have.

---

distinctiveness theory
A theory suggesting that individuals think of themselves in terms of those attributes or dimensions that make them different rather than in terms of attributes they have in common with others.

attributes that make him different from other males, such as being a debater or a football player. At least, being male will not be a defining attribute in that high school. It may certainly be important in another social context, such as when taking part in a debate about changing gender roles.

People who belong to nondominant or minority groups are more likely to include their gender, ethnicity, or other identity in their self-concept than are those in dominant, majority groups (e.g., white male). Among the school children in the study (McGuire & McGuire, 1988), boys who lived in households that were predominately female mentioned their gender more often as did girls who lived in households that were predominately male.

Of course, not all knowledge about the self is conscious simultaneously. At any given time, we tend to be aware of only parts of our overall self-concept. This *working self-concept* varies depending on the nature of the social situation and how we feel at the moment (Markus & Gnawers, 1986). So when we are depressed, our working self-concept would be likely to include all those thoughts about ourselves that have to do with failure or negative traits.

Although the self-concept is relatively stable, the notion of a working self-concept suggests that the self can vary from one situation to another (Kunda, 1999). For example, as Ziva Kunda (1999) pointed out, if you are shy but are asked to give examples of when you were very outgoing, at least momentarily you might feel less shy than usual. However, the ease with which the self may change may depend on how self-knowledge is organized and how important the behavior is.

THE SELF AND MEMORY In addition to personal attributes, the self-concept contains memories, the basis for knowledge about oneself. The self is concerned with maintaining positive self-feelings, thoughts, and evaluations. One way it does this is by influencing memory. Anthony Greenwald (1980) suggested that the self acts as a kind of unconscious monitor that enables people to avoid disquieting or distressing information. The self demands that we preserve what we have, especially that which makes us feel good about ourselves.

According to Greenwald, the self employs biases that work somewhat like the mind-control techniques used in totalitarian countries. In such countries, the government controls information and interpretations of events so that the leadership is never threatened. Similarly, we try to control the thoughts and memories we have about ourselves. The self is totalitarian in the sense that it records our good behaviors and ignores our unsavory ones, or at least rationalizes them away. The self is a personal historian, observing and recording information about the self—especially the information that makes us look good. Like a totalitarian government, Greenwald claims, the self tends to see itself as the origin of all positive things and to deny that it has ever done anything bad.

Is it true, as Greenwald predicted, that the self is a kind of filter that makes us feel good by gathering self-serving information and discarding information that discomfits us? The study of **autobiographical memory**—memory for information relating to self—shows that the self does indeed play a powerful role in the recall of events (Woike, Gerskovich, Piorkowski, & Polo, 1999). The self is an especially powerful memory system, because events and attributes stored in the self have many associations (Greenwald & Banaji, 1989). Let's say, for example, that you are asked to recall whether you have done anything in your life that exemplifies a trait such as honesty or creativ-

autobiographical memory
Memory for information relating to the self that plays a powerful role in recall of events.

ity. A search of your self memory system perhaps would conjure up a recent event in which you devised a creative solution to a problem. The memory of that event might trigger similar memories from earlier periods in your history. You probably would be able to generate a flood of such memories.

Most people take only about 2 seconds to answer questions about their traits (Klein, Loftus, & Plog, 1992). This is because we have a kind of summary knowledge of our self traits, especially the most obvious ones. Such a handy summary makes it harder to access memories that conflict with our positive self-concept, however. As noted earlier, memories that match a person's self-concept are recalled more easily than those that clash with that concept (Neimeyer & Rareshide, 1991). If you perceive yourself as an honest person, you will have trouble digging up memories in which you may have behaved dishonestly.

A research study of social memory of everyday life among college students bore out these findings (Skowronski, Betz, Thompson, & Shannon, 1991). Participants were asked to keep two diaries: In one, they recorded events that occurred in their own lives, and in the other, they recorded events that occurred in the life of a close relative or friend, someone they saw on a daily basis. The students had to ask the consent of the other person, and they recorded the events discreetly. Participants made entries in the diaries for self and other for roughly 10 weeks, the length of the academic quarter. At the end of the quarter, the participants took a memory test on the events recorded in the two diaries. The were presented with the recorded events from the diaries in a random order and were asked to indicate how well they remembered the event, the date it occurred, and whether it was a unique episode.

The researchers found that participants recalled recent events more quickly than earlier ones, with faster retrieval of the oldest episodes than of those in the middle. They also found that pleasant events were recalled better than unpleasant ones, and extreme events, pleasant and unpleasant, were recalled better than neutral episodes. Pleasant events that especially fit the person's self-concept were most easily recalled. The self, then, monitors our experiences, processing information in ways that make us look good to ourselves. We interpret, organize, and remember interactions and events in self-serving ways, recalling primarily pleasant, self-relevant events that fit our self-concept. Obviously, this built-in bias influences the manner in which we understand our social world and how we interact with other people. Without realizing it, we are continually constructing a view of the world that is skewed in our favor.

MOODS AND AUTOBIOGRAPHICAL MEMORIES Some of you may be thinking as you read this, "These findings don't square with what happens to me sometimes when I think about my past." It is true that we don't always retrieve memories that are positive, pleasant, or bolster good feelings. Indeed, sometimes the precise opposite is true. Cathy McFarland and Roger Buehler (1998) examined how negative moods affect autobiographical memory. Generally, the kind of memories you may recall seem to fit the mood that you are in. The explanation for this mood-congruence recall is that our mood makes it more likely that we will find memories of events that fit that mood: positive mood, positive recall; negative mood, negative recall. People who experience lots of negative moods can enter into a self-defeating cycle wherein their negative moods prime or key negative memories that in turn make the individual even more sad or depressed.

Why do some people in negative moods perpetuate that mood and others make themselves feel better? It appears that the approach to how we retrieve these memories is the key (Lyubomirsky, Caldwell, & Nolen-Hoeksema, 1998). If you adopt a focused *reflective* attitude, which means that you may admit that you failed at this task, you explore the nature of why you feel bad and work to regulate that mood. This is in contrast to people who *ruminate* over their moods. That is, they focus neurotically and passively on negative events and feelings (Mcfarland & Buehler, 1998).

SOCIAL INFLUENCES Peers, school experiences, and involvement in religious activities and institutions may have profound effects on self-knowledge. The self-concept is not an unchanging vault of personal information but is powerfully influenced by social and situational as well as cultural forces. We saw the influence of the church on the life of James Carroll, the priest. In novelist Carroll's books after he left the priesthood, we can see that the church still has an enormous influence on his thinking and his view of himself and the world.

Bruce E. Blaine and his coworkers investigated the impact of religious belief on the self-concept (Blaine, Trivedi, & Eshleman, 1998). Blaine pointed out that religion ought to be a powerful influence on the self-concepts of believers. Religious beliefs typically set standards for character and behavior, emphasizing positive behaviors and exhorting believers to refrain from negative ones. Blaine found that individuals who indicated that they maintained religious beliefs (Protestant, Catholic, or Jewish) provided more positive and certain self-descriptions. These positive self-descriptions were not limited in Blaine's study to religious spheres solely but were also related to positive self-descriptions in the individuals' work and social lives.

Blaine and his colleagues (1998) suggested several reasons for these findings. The first is that religious teachings may have clear relevance to the business world to the extent that people who hold religious beliefs actually apply them to other life activities. As one example, Blaine notes the Jewish Torah warns that interest ought not be charged on goods sold to needy countrymen. Religion also may be an organizing principle for the self-concept and thereby embrace all facets of life

The Influence of Groups and Culture on the Self

Thus far we have focused on the **individual self,** that part of the self that refers to our self-knowledge, our private thoughts and evaluations of who and what we are. But as we saw in James Carroll's life, the groups to which we belong and the culture in which we live play crucial roles in sculpting our self-concept.

The **collective self** is that part of our self-concept that comes from our membership in groups. This collective self is reflected in thoughts such as, "In my family I am considered the responsible, studious one." It reflects the evaluation of the self by important and specific groups to which the person belongs (Greenwald & Pratkanis, 1984). Basic research on groups shows that the groups we belong to have a strong influence on the self-concept (Gaertner, Sedikides, & Graetz, 1999). Our behavior is often changed by what other group members demand of us.

These two representations, the individual and the collective selves, do not occupy equal space and influence in the self-concept. The relative

individual self
The part of the self that refers our self-knowledge, including our private thoughts and evaluations of who and what we are.

collective self
The part of our self-concept that comes from our membership in groups.

Group affiliation, such as being a member of a team, makes up our collective self and provides an important part of our self-concept.

importance of each component of the self for an individual is determined in large part by the culture in which the person lives. In some cultures, the individual self is dominant. Cultures that emphasize individual striving and achievement—societies that are concerned with people "finding themselves"—produce individuals in which the private self is highly complex, containing many traits and beliefs. Other cultures may emphasize specific groups, such as family or religious community, and therefore the collective self is primary. Collectivist societies show a pattern of close links among individuals who define themselves as interdependent members of groups such as family, co-workers, and social groups (Vandello & Cohen, 1999). However, even within societies, the degree of collectivism may vary. Joseph Vandello and Dov Cohen (1999) argued that collectivist tendencies in the United States would be highest in the Deep South, because that region still maintains a strong regional identity. Vandello and Cohen also thought that the greatest individualistic tendencies would be found in the West and mountain states. Figure 2.1 shows a map that identifies regional differences in collectivism. You can see that Vandello and Cohen's predictions were confirmed. Note that the states with the highest collectivism scores contain either many different cultures (i.e., Hawaii) or a strong and dominant religion (Utah).

One way to determine whether the individual or collective self is the dominant representation of who we are is to observe what occurs when one or another of these images of the self is threatened. Is a threat to the individual self more or less menacing than a threat to our collective self? If the status of the important groups to which we belong is threatened, is this more upsetting to us than if our individual, personal self is under attack?

In as series of experiments, Lowell Gaertner, Constantine Sedikides, and Kenneth Graetz (1999) tried to answer these questions by comparing individuals' responses to threats to collective or individual self. For example, in one study, women at a university were given a psychological test and were told either that they personally had not done very well on the test or that an important group to which they belong (women at the university) had not done well. Similar procedures were used in other experiments. Gaertner and his colleagues found that compared to a threat to the collective self, a threat to the individual self resulted in: the perception that the threat was more severe, a more negative mood, more anger, and the participants' denial of the accuracy or validity of the test or source of the threat.

The results suggest that the individual self is primary, and the collective self is less so. Of course, this does not mean that the collective self is not crucial. It and our group memberships provide protection and financial and social rewards. But all things being equal, it appears that, in this country, our individual self is more important to us than our collective self.

WHO AM I? THE INFLUENCE OF CULTURE ON SELF-CONCEPT Nothing, it seems, could be more personal and individual than how we answer the question, Who am I? But as it turns out, our answer is powerfully shaped by the culture in which we grew up and developed our self-concept. As we have suggested, some cultures place more emphasis on the uniqueness of the individual—the private self—whereas others focus on how the individual is connected to important others—the collective self.

In a culture that emphasizes the collective self, such as Japan, individuals are more likely to define themselves in terms of meeting the expectations of others rather than of fulfilling their own private needs. In fact, if you asked Japanese participants to answer the question, Who am I? (a common technique for investigating self-concept), you would find that they give many more social responses ("I am an employee at X") than do Americans (Cousins, 1989). In contrast, Americans are more likely to emphasize the content of the individual (private) self, defining themselves with such statements as "I am strong willed." The Japanese view themselves as part of a social context, whereas Americans tend to assume they have a self that is less dependent on any set of social relations (Cousins, 1989; Ross & Nisbett, 1991).

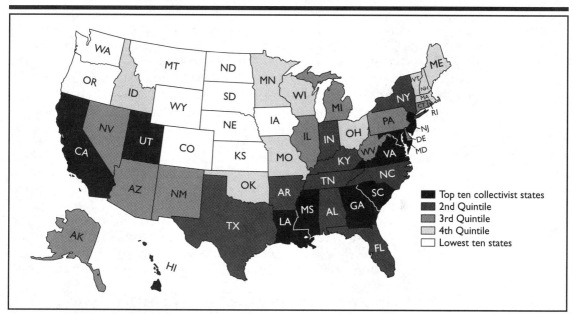

Figure 2.1 *Map of the United States showing regional patterns of collectivism. From Vandello and Cohen (1999). Reprinted with permission.*

Individuals in cultures that emphasize the collective self are also less likely to view themselves as the focus of attention in social interactions (Markus & Kitayama, 1991; Ross & Nisbett, 1991). Japanese appear to view their peers, rather than themselves, as the focus of attention. Consequently, social interactions in Japan are quite different from those in a society such as the United States.

Individual-self societies emphasize self-fulfillment at the expense of communal relationships; collective-self societies are more concerned with meeting shared obligations and helping others. In Haiti, for example, where the culture emphasizes the collective self, people are willing to share houses and food with relatives and friends for long periods of time.

Of course, no matter the dominant sense of self in each culture, sometimes situational factors will determine which self is dominant. Wendi Gardner, Shira Gabriel, and Angela Lee (1999) showed that the individual self may be temporarily more dominant in a collectivist culture when people are focused on personal issues, say, one's intelligence or one's goals in life. Similarly, people who live in an individualistic culture may temporarily focus on collectivist factors when confronted by issues involving group belongingness ("I am a member of Kappa Kappa Gamma").

However, whatever the effects of temporary situational factors, obviously, the thoughts and traits that make up the core of the self of a Japanese or Haitian person are likely to differ from the content of the self of an American. We would expect many more individual attributes to be part of an American self-concept. Japanese or Haitian individuals would probably emphasize attributes that reflect their similarities with others, whereas Americans are more likely to emphasize attributes that make them different from other people.

This tendency to emphasize attributes that make an individual stand out in American society and to blend in and not be conspicuous in Japanese society may very well be due to historical and cultural processes that affect how individuals behave. For example, in the United States, our sense of well-being, of being happy or pleased with ourselves, depends to a great extent on whether we are seen as better—more accomplished, perhaps richer—than other people. But, Shinobu Kitayama, a Japanese social psychologist familiar with the United States suggests that a sense of well-being in Japan depends less on attributes that make individuals different from others and more on correcting shortcomings and deficits (Kitayama, Markus, Matsumoto, & Norasakkunkit, 1997). Research shows that the psychological *and* physical well-being of Japanese persons can be predicted quite accurately from the lack of negative characteristics and not from the presence of positive attributes (Kitayama et al., 1997). In the United States, in contrast, how positive we feel about ourselves is directly related to our sense of personal well-being (Diener & Diener, 1995). So these social psychological aspects of self-representations—the individual and the collective selves—are caused by historical forces that emphasized individuality in the United States and group harmony in Japan.

We see in this example both the pervasive role of the self-concept in directing behavior and the widespread role of culture in determining ideas about the self. The self-concept is not just a private, personal construct; culture plays a part in shaping the individual's deepest levels of personal knowledge.

ORGANIZING KNOWLEDGE: SELF-SCHEMAS Whatever the culture one lives in, people don't think of themselves as just chaotic masses of attributes and memories. Instead, they arrange knowledge and information about themselves and their attributes into **self-schemas** (Markus, 1977; Markus & Zajonc, 1985). A *schema* is an organized set of related cognitions—bits of knowledge and information—about a particular person, event, or experience. A self-schema is an arrangement of information, thoughts, and feelings about ourselves, including information about our gender, age, race or ethnicity, occupation, social roles, physical attractiveness, intelligence, talents, and so on. People have many different self-schemas for the different areas of life activities.

Self-schemas serve a very important function: They organize our self-related experiences so that we can respond quickly and effectively in social situations. They help us interpret situations, and they guide our behavior. Schemas also help us understand new events (Scheier & Carver, 1988). You may have a self-schema about how you act in an emergency, for example. From past experience and from your ideals and expectations about yourself, you may believe that you are a person who stays calm, acts responsibly, and takes care of others, or one who panics and has to be taken care of by others. These beliefs about yourself influence your behavior when an emergency arises in the future. Or perhaps you have a self-schema about being a runner. When you hear people talking about keeping fit or eating the right foods you know what they are talking about and how it relates to you. In these ways, self-schemas contribute to our sense of control over our social world.

Self-schemas lend order to our past experiences as well. They guide what we encode (place) into memory and influence how we organize and store that memory. Memories that match our self-schemas are recalled more easily than are those that do not (Neimeyer & Rareshide, 1991). Self-schemas also influence how we think we will behave in the future. A person who thinks of himself as socially awkward, for example, may behave inappropriately in social situations. And based on his behavior in the past, he expects to behave inappropriately in future social situations.

People tend to have elaborate schemas about areas of life that are important to their self-concepts. Hazel Markus (1977) observed that people may be either schematic or aschematic with respect to various attributes that are in the self-concept. The term *schematic* means that the individual has an organized self-schema in an activity that the individual rates as important. In other areas of life, those that are not important to us or that may not even exist for us, people are said to be *aschematic*. That is, they do not have an organized self-schema in that domain.

SEXUALITY AND SELF-SCHEMAS Sexuality is clearly a fundamental behavior, and therefore, we expect people to have sexual self-schemas of varying degrees of organization. A **sexual self-schema** refers to how we think about the sexual aspects of the self. Sexual schemas are derived from past sexual knowledge and experience and, as all schemas do, they guide our future (sexual) activity. Cyranowski and Andersen (1998) studied the sexual self-schemas of university women and found that four different schemas emerged. Women who were schematic, that is, had well-developed schemas, displayed either positive or negative schemas. These positive and negative schemas reflected their individual past sexual history as well as their current sexual activity. As the sexual schema graph shows, positive-schema women had more previous sexual relationships (Figure 2.2) and scored higher measures of passionate attachment to their partners (Figure 2.3). These women were more likely to be in a current sexual relationship. Negative sexual

self-schemas
Self-conceptions that guide us in ordering and directing our behavior involving how we represent our thoughts and feelings about our experiences in a particular area of life.

sexual self-schema
How we think about the sexual aspects of the self, derived from past sexual knowledge and experience; guide future sexual activity.

Figure 2.2

The relationship between an individual's sexual schema and the number of his or her past relationships.

Based on data from Cyranowski and Anderson (1998).

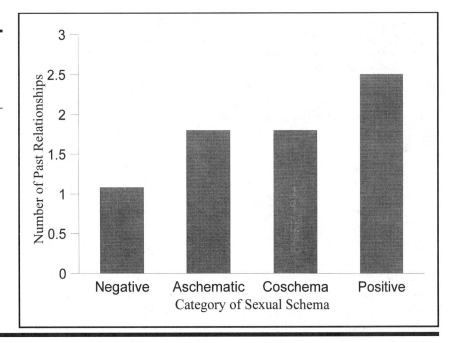

schema women displayed an avoidance of intimacy and passion and were much more anxious about sexual activity.

Some women had both negative and positive aspects to their self-schemas, and they were labeled *co-schematic*. Whereas co-schematic women see themselves as open, passionate, and romantic (as do the positive schema women), they differ from the positive-schema women in that they hold negative self-views, and this lead to anxieties about being rejected or abandoned by their partners.

Figure 2.3

The relationship between an individual's sexual schema and his or her passionate love score.

Based on data from Cyranowski and Anderson (1998).

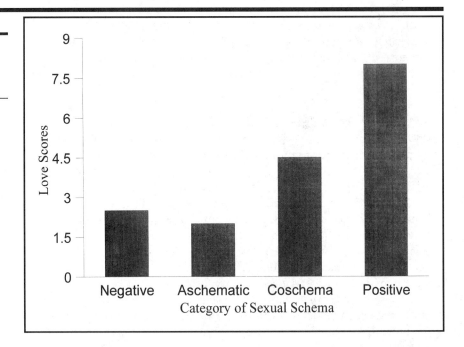

Table 2.1

Sexual Schemas and Sexual Behaviors

	Sexual Schemas			
	Schematic			
Sexual Behaviors	**Positive**	**Negative**	**Co-Schematic**	**Aschematic**
Previous sex experiences	Many	Few	Moderate	Few
Passionate	High	Low	High	Low
Intimacy	High	Low	Low	Low
Anxiety	Low	High	High	High
Self-views	Positive	Negative	Negative	Moderate

Derived from data from Cyranowski and Anderson (1998). No permission required.

Aschematic women, like negative-schema women, have fewer romantic attachments, less passionate emotions about love, and avoid emotional intimacy. Aschematic women tend to avoid sexual situations and display anxiety about sex. A major difference between aschematic women and negative-schema women is that aschematic women do not have negative self-views. They are just less interested in sexual activity. Table 2.1 summarizes these findings.

Whereas women express sexual self-schemas that fit roughly into categories, men's sexual self-schemas appear to flow along a continuum, ranging from highly schematic to aschematic (Andersen, Cyranowski, & Espindle, 1999). Men who are schematic have sexual schemas that reflect strong emotions of passion and love, attributes shared with positive-schematic women. However, these men see themselves as strong and aggressive, with liberal sexual attitudes (Andersen et al., 1999). Schematic men lead varied sexual lives, may engage in quite casual sex, but are also capable of strong attachments. On the other end of the scale, we find aschematic men, who lead quite narrow sexual lives and have few if any sexual partners.

The more varied and complex our self is, the more self-schemas we will have. We can see that men and women have sexual self-schemas of varying degrees of organization, and these schemas reflect their sexual past and guide their current (and future) sexual behavior. These cognitive representations or self-schemas reflect both the importance of the behavior represented and the emotional tone of that behavior.

People differ in the number of attributes, memories, and self-schemas that are part of their self-concept. Some people have highly complex selves, others much less complex. Self-complexity is important in influencing how people react to the good and bad events in life. Someone who is, say, an engineer, an opera lover, a mother, and an artist can absorb a blow to one of her selves without much damage to her overall self-concept (Linville, 1985, 1987). If her latest artistic endeavors meet unfavorable reviews, this woman's sense of self is buffered by the fact that there is much more to her than being an artist. She is still a mother, an engineer, an opera lover, and much more. People who are low in self-complexity may be devastated by negative events, because there is little else to act as a buffer.

SELF-ESTEEM: EVALUATING THE SELF

The self is more than a knowledge structure. The self also has a larger sense of our overall worth, a component that consists of both positive and negative self-evaluations. This is known as **self-esteem.** We evaluate, judge, and have feelings about ourselves. Some people possess high self-esteem; they regard themselves highly and are generally pleased with who they are. Others have low self-esteem, feel less worthy and good, and may even feel that they are failures and incompetent.

Self-esteem is affected both by our ideas about how we are measuring up to our own standards and by our ability to control our sense of self in interactions with others. Both these processes—one primarily internal, the other primarily external—have important repercussions on our feelings about ourselves.

Internal Influences on Self-Esteem

Our feelings about ourselves come from many sources. Some, perhaps most, we carry forward from childhood, when our basic self-concepts were formed from interactions with our parents and other adults. Research in child development indicates that people develop basic feelings of trust, security, and self-worth or mistrust, insecurity, and worthlessness from these early relationships and experiences.

SELF-ESTEEM AND STIGMA We have seen that people often define themselves in terms of attributes that distinguish themselves from others. Sometimes these attributes are positive ("I was always the best athlete"), and sometimes they are negative ("I was always overweight"). Some individuals have characteristics that are stigmatized—marked by society—and, therefore, they risk rejection whenever those aspects of themselves are recognized. One would expect that culturally defined stigmas would affect a person's self-esteem.

Frable, Platt, and Hoey (1998) wondered what effect stigmas that were either visible or concealable had on self-esteem. These researchers had Harvard University undergraduates rate their momentary self-esteem and feelings during everyday situations in their lives. Some of these students had concealable stigmas; that is, these culturally defined faults were hidden from the observer. The individuals were gay, bulimic, or came from poor families. Others had more visible socially defined stigmas; they were African American, or stutterers, or 30 pounds overweight.

Frable and her coworkers thought that those people with concealable stigmas would be most prone to low self-esteem, because they rarely would be in the company of people who had similar stigmas. Other people who belong to the "marked" group can provide social support and more positive perceptions of the membership of the stigmatized group than can nonmembers. For example, cancer patients who belong to support groups and have other strong social support generally have more favorable prognoses than do those patients who remain isolated (Frable et al., 1998). In fact, these researchers found that those who were gay, poor, bulimic, or had other concealable stigmas had lower self-esteem and more negative feelings about themselves than both those with visible stigmas or people without any social stigmas at all. This suggests that group membership that can offer support and positive feelings raises our self-esteem and buffers us against negative social evaluations.

Although the Frable study indicates that visible stigmas have a less negative influence on self-esteem than do the concealable ones, conspicuous stigmas, such as being overweight, have definite negative effects on self-esteem as well. Early in life we get a sense of our physical self. Western culture pays particular attention to physical attractiveness, or lack of the same, and it should not be surprising that our sense of our physical appearance affects our self-esteem. An aspect of appearance, body weight, plays a role in self-esteem. One need only gaze at the diet books and magazines at supermarket checkout counters to confirm the importance of body types in our society.

Miller and Downey (1999) examined the relationship between self-esteem and body weight. They found that individuals who were classified as "heavyweights" (to distinguish these people from individuals who were obese because of glandular problems) reported lower self-esteem. This finding was particularly true for females, but heavyweight males also tended to have lower self-esteem. Interestingly, those individuals who were in fact in the heavyweight category but did not think that they were did not have lower self-esteem. This suggests that what is important is whether the individual is marked with disgrace—stigmatized—in his or her own eyes. It may be that those who are heavyweight but do not feel that they have to match some ideal body type do not carry the same psychological burden that other heavyweights do. This suggest that feelings about ourselves come from our evaluations of ourselves in terms of our internal standards, our self-guides. It is probable that heavyweights who had higher self-esteem had a better match between their ideal and actual selves than did other overweight individuals.

SELF-REGULATION AND SELF-ESTEEM It seems that people who are distinctly overweight but still maintain a pretty good match between who they are and who they would like to be do not suffer loss of self-esteem. Indeed, the opposite may be true. Obtaining a good sense of who we are helps us guide our behavior in ways that are rational and productive. A crucial task of the self is to guide and regulate our behavior so we can control our social world as much as possible. It does this principally through the development and use of various self-guides.

Social psychologist E. Tory Higgins (1989) proposed that people think of themselves from two different standpoints: their own perspective and that of a significant other, such as a parent or a close friend. He also suggested that people have three selves that guide their behavior. The first is the **actual self,** the person's current self-concept. The second is the **ideal self,** the mental representation of what the person would like to be or what a significant other would like him or her to be. The third is the **ought self,** the mental representation of what the person believes he or she should be.

Higgins (1989) assumed that people are motivated to reach a state in which the actual self matches the ideal and the ought selves. The latter two selves thus serve as guides to behavior. When there is a discrepancy between the actual self and the self-guides, we are motivated to try to close the gap. That is, when our actual self doesn't match our internal expectations and standards, or when someone else evaluates us in ways that fail to match our standards, we try to narrow the gap. We try to adjust our behavior to bring it into line with our self-guides. The process we use to make such adjustments is known as **self-regulation,** which is our attempt to match our behavior or our self-guides to the expectations of others and is a critical control mechanism.

actual self
A person's current self-concept.

ideal self
The mental representation of what a person would like to be or what a significant other would like him or her to be.

ought self
The mental representation of what a person believes he or she should be.

self-regulation
A critical control mechanism used by individuals to match behavior to internal standards of the self or to the expectations of others.

Not only will individuals differ on the need to self-regulate, so will people who live in different cultures. Steven Heine and Darrin Lehman (1999) observed that whereas residents of the United States and Canada showed a strong bias towards adapting to others' expectations, Japanese citizens are less likely to try to self-regulate. Heine and Lehman found that their Japanese participants were much more self-critical than were North Americans and had greater discrepancies between their actual self and the ideal or ought selves, but these differences were less distressful for the Japanese and did not motivate them to change.

The closer the match among our various self-concepts, the better we feel about ourselves. Additionally, the more information we have about ourselves and the more certain we are of it, the better we feel about ourselves. This is especially true if the self-attributes we are most certain of are those that are most important to us (Pelham, 1991). Our ability to self-regulate, to match our performance to our expectations and standards, also affects our self-esteem. In sum, then, we tend to have high self-esteem if we have a close match among our selves; strong and certain knowledge about ourselves, especially if it includes attributes that we value; and the ability to self-regulate.

We know that the inability to regulate our self leads to negative emotions. Higgins (1998) investigated the emotional consequences of good matches versus discrepancies among the selves. When there is a good match between our actual self and our ideal self, we experience feelings of satisfaction and high self-esteem. When there is a good match between our actual self and our ought self, we experience feelings of security. (Recall that the actual self is what you or another currently think you are; the ideal self is the mental representation of the attributes that either you or another would like you to be or wishes you could be; and the ought self is the person that you or others believe you should be.) Good matches may also allow people to focus their attention outside themselves, on other people and activities.

But what happens when we can't close the discrepancy gap? Sometimes, of course, we simply are not capable of behaving in accord with our expectations. We might not have the ability, talent, or fortitude. In this case, we may have to adjust our expectations to match our behavior. And sometimes it seems to be in our best interests not to focus on the self at all; to do so may be too painful, or it may get in the way of what we're doing.

In general, however, these discrepancies, if sizable, lead to negative emotions and low self-esteem. As with good matches, the exact nature of the negative emotional response depends on which self-guide we believe we are not matching (Higgins & Tykocinsky, 1992). Higgins, Shah, and Friedman (1997) reported that the larger the differences between the actual and ideal selves, the more dejected and disappointed the individuals felt, but only if they were aware of that difference. In a similar vein, the larger the discrepancy between the actual self and the ought self, the more people felt agitated and tense, just as the theory predicts. Again, this was true only for those people who were aware of the discrepancy. These findings mean that when self-guides are uppermost in people's minds, when people focus on these guides, then the emotional consequences of not meeting the expectations of those guides have their strongest effects. People who indicated, for instance, that they were punished or criticized by their parents for not being the person they ought to be reported that they frequently felt anxious or uneasy (Higgins, 1998).

Having positive self-esteem does not mean that people have only positive self-evaluations. They do not. When normal people with positive self-esteem think about themselves, roughly 62% of their thoughts are positive and 38% are negative (Showers, 1992). What is important is how those thoughts are arranged. People with high self-esteem blend the positive and negative aspects of their self-concept. A negative thought tends to trigger a counterbalancing positive thought. A person who learns she is "socially awkward," for example, may think, "But I am a loyal friend." This integration of positive and negative self-thoughts helps to control feelings about the self and maintain positive self-esteem.

But some people group positive and negative thoughts separately. The thought "I am socially awkward" triggers another negative thought, such as "I am insecure." This is what happens in people who are chronically depressed: A negative thought sets off a chain reaction of other negative thoughts. There are no positive thoughts available to act as a buffer.

MAINTAINING SELF-ESTEEM IN INTERACTIONS WITH OTHERS

In order to feel good about ourselves, it is not enough to self-regulate. We also need to maintain and enhance our self-esteem in our interactions with others as well as to defend it against the inevitable threats that life throws in our path. When interacting with others, human beings have two primary self-related motives: to enhance self-esteem and to maintain self-consistency (Berkowitz, 1988). Obviously, people have a powerful need to feel good about themselves. They prefer positive responses from the social world. They become anxious when their self-esteem is under threat. What steps do they take to maintain and enhance self-esteem?

Enhancing the Self According to Abraham Tesser's **self-evaluation maintenance (SEM) theory** (1988), the behavior of other people, both friends and strangers, affects how we feel about ourselves, especially when the behavior is in an area that is important to our own self-concept. The self carefully manages emotional responses to events in the social world, depending on how threatening it perceives those events to be. Tesser gave this example to illustrate his theory: Suppose, for example, that Jill thinks of herself as a math whiz. Jill and Joan are close friends; Joan receives a 99 and Jill a 90 on a math test. Because math is relevant to Jill, the comparison is important. Therefore, Joan's better performance is a threat, particularly since Joan is a close other. There are a variety of things that Jill can do about this threat. She can reduce the relevance of Joan's performance. If math were not important to Jill's own self-definition she could bask in the reflection of Joan's performance. Jill could also reduce her closeness to Joan, then Joan's performance would be less consequential. Finally, Jill could try to affect their relative performance by working harder or doing something to handicap Joan (Tesser & Collins, 1988).

This story neatly captures the basic elements of SEM theory. The essential question that Jill asks about Joan's performance is, What effect does Joan's behavior have on my evaluation of myself. Notice that Jill compares herself to Joan on a behavior that is important to her own self-concept. If Joan excelled at bowling, and Jill cared not a fig about knocking down pins with a large ball, she would not be threatened by Joan's rolling a 300 game or winning a bowling championship. In fact, she would *bask in the reflected glory* (BIRG) of her friend's performance; Jill's self-esteem would be enhanced because her friend did so well.

The comparison process is activated when you are dealing with someone who is close to you. If you found out that 10% of high school students who

self-evaluation maintenance (SEM) theory
A theory explaining how the behavior of other people affects how you feel about yourself, especially when they perform some behavior that is important to your self-conception.

took the math SAT did better than you, it would have less emotional impact on your self-esteem than if you learned that your best friend scored a perfect 800, putting her at the top of all people who took the exam (provided, that is, that math ability was important to your self-concept).

SEM theory is concerned with the self's response to threat, the kinds of social threats encountered in everyday life. Tesser formulated SEM theory by investigating people's responses to social threats in terms of the two dimensions just described—relevance of the behavior to the participant's self-concept and closeness of the participant to the other person (Tesser & Collins, 1988). Participants were asked to remember and describe social situations in which a close or distant other performed better or worse than they did. Half the time the task was important to the participant's self-concept, and half the time the task was unimportant. The participants also reported the emotions they felt during those episodes.

Results indicate that when the behavior was judged relevant to the self, emotions were heightened. When participants did better than the other, distant or close, they felt happier, and when they did worse, they felt more personal disgust, anger, and frustration. When the behavior was not particularly relevant to the self, emotions varied, depending on the closeness of the relationship. When a close friend performed better than the participant, the participant felt pride in that performance. As you would expect, participants felt less pride in the performance of a distant person, and, of course, they felt less pride in the friend's performance when the behavior was self-relevant.

One conclusion we can draw from this research and from SEM theory is that people are willing to make *some* sacrifices to accuracy if it means a gain in self-esteem. People undoubtedly want and need accurate information about themselves and how they compare to significant others, but they also display an equally powerful need to feel positive about themselves. This need for self-enhancement suggests that in appraising our own performances and in presenting ourselves to others, we tend to exaggerate our positive attributes.

In sum, then, one way the self maintains esteem is to adjust its responses to social threats. If a friend does better than we do at something on which we pride ourselves, we experience a threat to that part of our self-concept. Our friend's achievement suggests that we may not be as good in an important area as we thought we were. To preserve the integrity and consistency of the self-concept and to maintain high self-esteem we can try to downplay the other's achievement and put more distance between ourselves and the other, because we feel less threatened by the performance or try to handicap our friend. In each case, the self subtly adjusts our perceptions, emotions, and behaviors in the service of enhancing self-esteem.

Self-Serving Cognitions   In Garrison Keillor's mythical Minnesota town of Lake Wobegon, all the women are strong, all the men are good-looking, and all the children are above average. In thinking so well of themselves, the residents of Lake Woebegon are demonstrating the **self-serving bias,** which leads people to attribute positive outcomes to our own efforts and negative results to situational forces beyond our control. A person typically thinks, I do well on examinations because I'm smart; I failed because it was an unfair examination. We take credit for success and deny responsibility for failure (Mullen & Riordan, 1988; Weiner, 1986).

There is a long-standing controversy about why the self-serving bias occurs in the attribution process (Tetlock & Levi, 1982). One proposal, the

self-serving bias
Our tendency to attribute positive outcomes of our own behavior to internal, dispositional factors and negative outcomes to external, situational forces.

motivational strategy, assumes that people need to protect self-esteem and therefore take credit for successes (Fiske & Taylor, 1984). We know that protecting and enhancing self-esteem is a natural function of the self, which filters and shapes information in self-serving ways.

Another way of looking at self-serving biases emphasizes *information-processing strategies.* When people expect to do well, success fits their expectations; when success occurs, it makes sense, and they take credit for it. This bias, however, does not always occur and is not always "self-serving." Constantine Sedikides and his colleagues noted that people in close relationships did not demonstrate the self-serving bias. The bias, according to these researchers takes a gracious turn for people who are close and is reflected in the following quote: "If more than one person is responsible for a miscalculation and the persons are close, both will be at fault" (Sedikides, Campbell, Reeder, & Eliot, 1998). What this means is that neither you or your partner is likely to take more credit for success, nor will you or your partner give more blame to the other for failure. Less close pairs, however, do show the self-serving bias (taking credit for success or giving blame for failure). The closeness of a relationship puts a barrier in place against the individual's need to self-enhance as revealed by the self-serving bias.

Maintaining Self-Consistency   Another driving motive of the self in social interactions is to maintain high self-consistency—agreement between our self-concept and the views others have of us. We all have a great investment in our self-concepts, and we make a strong effort to support and confirm them. Motivated by a need for **self-verification**—confirmation of our self-concept from others—we tend to behave in ways that lead others to see us as we see ourselves (Swann, Hixon, & De La Ronde, 1992). The need for self-verification is more than just a simple preference for consistency over inconsistency. Self-verification lends orderliness and predictability to the social world and allows us to feel that we have control (Swann, Stein-Seroussi, & Giesler, 1992).

self-verification
A method of supporting and confirming your self-identity involving behavior that encourages others to see you as you see yourself, providing orderliness to and control over your social world.

People seek to confirm their self-concepts regardless of whether others' ideas are positive or negative. One study showed that people with unfavorable self-concepts tended not to pick roommates who had positive impressions of them (Swann, Pelham, & Krull, 1989). In other words, people with negative self-concepts preferred to be with people who had formed negative impressions of them that were consistent with their own views of themselves.

Another study tested the idea that people search for partners who will help them self-verify (Swann, Hixon, & De La Ronde, 1992). Half the participants in this experiment had positive self-concepts and half had negative self-concepts. All participants were told that they would soon have the chance to converse with one of two people (an "evaluator") and could choose one of the two. Every participant saw comments that these two people had made about the participant. One set of comments was positive; the other set was negative (all comments were fictitious).

People with negative self-concepts preferred to interact with an evaluator who had made negative comments, whereas people with positive self-concepts preferred someone who had made positive comments. Why would someone prefer a negative evaluator? Here is one participant's explanation: "I like the (favorable) evaluation, but I am not sure that is, ah, correct, maybe. It *sounds* good, but the (unfavorable evaluator) . . . seems to know more about me. So I'll choose the (unfavorable evaluator)" (Swann, Hixon, & De La Ronde, 1992, p. 16).

In another study, spouses with positive self-concepts were found to be more committed to their marriage when their mates thought well of them. No surprise there. But in keeping with self-verification theory, spouses with negative self-concepts were more committed to their partners if their mates thought poorly of them (Swann, Hixon, & De La Ronde, 1992).

People with low self-esteem do appreciate positive evaluations, but in the end, they prefer to interact with people who see them as they see themselves (Jones, 1990). It is easier and less complicated to be yourself than to live up to someone's impression of you that, although flattering, is inaccurate.

Individuals tend to seek self-verification in fairly narrow areas of the self-concept (Jones, 1990). You don't seek out information to confirm that you are a good or bad person but that your voice is not very good or that you really are not a top-notch speaker. If your self-concept is complex, such negative feedback gives you accurate information about yourself but doesn't seriously damage your self-esteem.

People not only choose to interact with others who will verify their self-concepts but also search for situations that will serve that purpose. If, for example, you think of yourself as a storehouse of general knowledge, you may be the first to jump into a game of Trivial Pursuit. You have control over that kind of situation. But if you are the kind of person who can't remember a lot of trivial information or who doesn't care that FDR had a dog named Fala, then being forced to play Trivial Pursuit represents a loss of control.

Finally, keep in mind that most people have a positive self-concept. Therefore, when they self-verify, they are in essence enhancing their self-image, because they generally get positive feedback. So for most of us, self-verification does not contradict the need for self-enhancement. But as Swann's research shows, people also need to live in predictable and stable worlds. This last requirement is met by our need for self-verification.

SELF-AWARENESS

Self-verification suggests that at least some of the time, we are quite aware of how we are behaving and how other people are evaluating us. In fact, in some situations we are acutely aware of ourselves, monitoring, evaluating, and perhaps adjusting what we say and do. Although sometimes our behavior is mindless and unreflective, we probably spend a surprising amount of time monitoring our own thoughts and actions. Of course, there are some situations that force us to become more self-aware than others. When we are in a minority position in a group, for example, we become focused on how we respond (Mullen, 1986). Other situations that increase **self-focus** include looking in a mirror, being in front of an audience, and seeing a camera (Scheier & Carver, 1988; Wicklund, 1975).

When people become more aware of themselves, they are more likely to try to match their behavior to their beliefs and internal standards. In one study, two groups of participants—one in favor of the death penalty, the other opposed—had to punish another participant, a confederate of the experimenter (Carver, 1975). Some participants held a small mirror up to

self-focus

The extent to which one has a heightened awareness of oneself in certain situations (e.g., when a minority within a group).

When individuals become more self-focused, or more aware of themselves, they are more likely to attempt to match their internal standards and attitudes. This often happens when we find ourselves a minority, such as this black student in a class with a large majority of white classmates.

their faces as they administered an electric shock (no shock was actually transmitted).

When participants self-focused (looked into the mirror), they were truer to their beliefs: Their attitudes and their actions were more in harmony. Highly punitive individuals (those who favored capital punishment) gave much more shock when the confederate made errors than did the less punitive, anti-death penalty individuals. No such differences existed when participants did not self-focus.

Self-focus means that the individual tends to be more careful in assessing his or her own behavior and is more concerned with the self than with others (Gibbons, 1990). Self-focused individuals are concerned with what is proper and appropriate given their self-guides. Self-focused individuals probably have an increased need for accuracy and try to match their behavior to their self-guides. That is, they try to be more honest or moral.

Self-focusing may lead to positive or negative outcomes, depending on how difficult it is to match performance with the self's standards and with the expectations of others. Sometimes, for example, sports teams perform better on the road, especially in important games, than they do on their home field or arena. There is a definite home field advantage, that is, teams generally win more games at home than on the road. However, baseball teams win fewer final games of the World Series than expected when they play on their home fields (Baumeister, 1984). Their performance declines due to the pressure of the home fans' expectations ("choking").

Does audience pressure always lead to choking? It depends on whether the performer is more concerned with controlling the audience's perceptions or with living up to internal standards. If concern centers on pleasing the audience, the pressure may have a negative effect on performance. If concern centers on meeting personal standards, then audience pressure will have less impact (Heaton & Sigall, 1991).

Self-Knowledge and Self-Awareness

Accurate information about ourselves as we actually are is essential to effective self-regulation (Pelham & Swann, 1989). Such knowledge may lead us to adjust our self-guides, to lower our expectations or standards, for instance, in order to close the gap between what we are and what we want to be or think we ought to be. Although it is effortful to adjust our standards, it is important to minimize discrepancies between the actual and the other selves. Small discrepancies—that is, good matches between the actual self and self-guides—promote a strong sense of who we really are (Baumgardner, 1990). This knowledge is satisfying, because it helps us predict accurately how we will react to other people and situations. It increases our sense of control over our behavior and our social world. In other words, the stronger our sense of personal identity, the better we feel about ourselves and the more confident we are. It is therefore in or best interest to obtain accurate information about ourselves (Pelham & Swann, 1989).

Research confirms that people want to have accurate information about themselves, even if that information is negative (Baumgardner, 1990). It helps them know which situations to avoid and which to seek out. If you know that you are lazy, for example, you probably will avoid a course that promises to fill your days and nights with library research. There is evidence, however, that people prefer some sugar with the medicine of negative evaluations; they want others to evaluate their negative attributes a little more positively than they themselves do (Pelham, 1991).

People who are not certain about their attributes can make serious social blunders. If you are unaware that your singing voice has the same effect on people as someone scratching a fingernail on a chalkboard, then you might one day find yourself trying out for the choir, thereby making a fool of yourself. Greater knowledge of your vocal limitations would have saved you considerable humiliation and loss of face.

The Cost and Ironic Effects of Self-Control

We have seen the self has the capacity to engage in effortful behavior to deal with the external world. Now, it is very likely that most of the time, the part of the self that carries out this executive function does it in an automatic, nonconscious fashion, dealing with the world in neutral gear (Bargh & Chartrand, 1999). But when the self has to actively control and guide behavior, much effort is required. Roy Baumeister and his coworkers wondered whether the self had a limited amount of energy to do its tasks. If this is so, what were the implications of self-energy as a limited resource (Baumeister, Bratslavsky, Muraven, & Tice, 1998)?

In order to explore the possibility that expending energy on one self-related task would diminish the individual's ability (energy) to do another self task, Baumeister and his coworkers did a series of experiments in which people were required to exercise self-control or required to make an important personal choice or suppress a emotion. For example, in one study, some people forced themselves to eat radishes rather then some very tempting chocolates. This, as you might imagine, was an exercise in self-control. Others were allowed to have the chocolates without trying to suppress their desires and without having to eat the radishes. All were then asked to work on unsolvable puzzles. As shown in Figure 2.4, those who suppressed their desire for the chocolate and ate the radishes quit sooner

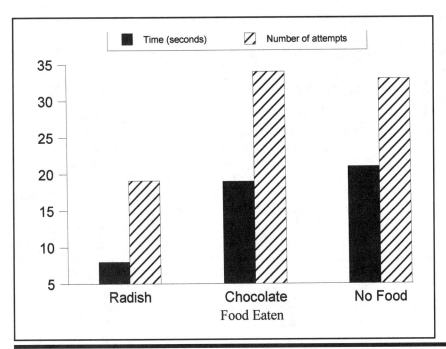

Figure 2.4

Persistence on an unsolvable puzzle as a function of the type of food eaten.

Based on data from Baumeister and colleagues (1998).

on the puzzle than those who did not have to suppress their desire to eat the chocolate. Baumeister argued that the "radish people" depleted self-energy. Baumeister calls this **ego-depletion,** using the Freudian term (ego) for the executive of the self.

We all have had the experience of seeing a particularly distressing movie and walked out of the theater exhausted. Research reveals that if people see a very emotional movie, they show a decrease in physical stamina (Muraven, Tice, & Baumeister, 1998). In a related study, participants were given a difficult cognitive task to perform and were asked to suppress any thought of a white bear. Research shows that trying to suppress thoughts takes much effort (Wegner, 1993). Try not thinking of a white bear for the next 5 minutes, and you will see what we mean. After doing this task, the individuals were shown a funny movie but were told not to show amusement. People who had expended energy earlier on suppressing thoughts were unable to hide expressions of amusement compared to others who did not have to suppress thoughts before seeing the movie (Muraven et al., 1998). All this suggests that active control of behavior is costly. The irony of efforts to control is that the end result may be exactly what we are trying so desperately to avoid. We have to expend a lot of energy to regulate the self. The research shows that there are finite limits to our ability to actively regulate our behavior.

ego depletion
The loss of self-energy that occurs when a person has to contend with a difficult cognitive or emotional situation.

MANAGING SELF-PRESENTATIONS

Eventually, we all try to manage, to some degree, the impressions others have of us. Some of us are very concerned about putting on a good front, others less so. Several factors, both situational and personal, influence how and when people try to manage the impressions they make on others. Situational factors include such variables as the social context, the "stakes" in the situation, and the supportiveness of the audience. Personal factors include such variables as whether the person has high or low self-esteem and whether the person has a greater or lesser tendency to self-monitor, to be very aware of how he or she appears to other people.

Self-Esteem and Impression Management

One research study looked at how people with high and low self-esteem differed in their approaches to making a good impression (Schlenker, Weigold, & Hallam, 1990). People with low self-esteem were found to be very cautious in trying to create a positive impression. In general, they simply are not confident of their ability to pull it off. When presenting themselves, they focus on minimizing their bad points. On the other hand, people with high self-esteem tend to focus on their good points when presenting themselves.

As might be expected, people with low self-esteem present themselves in a less egotistical manner than those with high self-esteem. When describing a success, they tend to share the credit with others. People with high self-esteem take credit for success even when other people may have given them help (Schlenker, Soraci, & McCarthy, 1976). Interestingly, all people seem to have an **egotistical bias;** that is, they present themselves as responsible for success whether they are or are not.

Social context makes a difference in how people present themselves but in different ways for people with high and low self-esteem. When participants were told to try to make a good impression in front of an audience, people with high self-esteem presented themselves in a very egotistical and boastful way, pointing out their sterling qualities (Schlenker et al., 1990). People with low self-esteem toned down egotistical tendencies in this high-pressure situation, becoming more timid. It seems that when the social stakes increase, people with high self-esteem become more interested in enhancing their self-presentation, whereas their low self-esteem counterparts are more concerned with protecting themselves from further blows to the self (Schlenker, 1987).

Self-Monitoring and Impression Management

Another factor that influences impression management is the degree to which a person engages in **self-monitoring**—that is, focuses on how he or she appears to other people in different situations. Some people are constantly gathering data on their own actions. These high self-monitors are very sensitive to the social demands of any situation and tend to fit their behavior to those demands. They are always aware of the impressions they are making on others; low self-monitors are much less concerned with impression management.

High self-monitors are concerned with how things look to others. For example, they tend to choose romantic partners who are physically attractive (Snyder, Berscheid, & Glick, 1985). Low self-monitors are more concerned with meeting people with similar personality traits and interests. Most high self-monitors are aware that they fit their behavior to the expectations of others. If they were to take a self-assessment like the one presented in Table 2.2, they would agree with the "high self-monitor" statements (Snyder, 1987).

It may be that low self-monitors have less need to manage other people's impressions of them. They may have high self-esteem or strong, consistent self-concepts. Remember, people who know themselves well like themselves

egotistical bias
The tendency to present oneself as responsible for success, whether you are or not, and the tendency to believe these positive presentations.

self-monitoring
The degree, ranging from low to high, to which a person focuses on his or her behavior when in a given social situation.

Table 2.2

Self-Monitoring Scale

1. I would probably make a good actor. (H)
2. My behavior is usually an expression of my true inner feelings. (L)
3. I have never been good at games like charades of improvisations. (L)
4. I'm not always the person I appear to be. (H)
5. I can deceive people by being friendly when I really dislike them. (H)
6. I can argue only for ideas that I already believe in. (L)
7. I find it hard to imitate the behavior of other people. (L)
8. In order to get along and be liked, I tend to be what people expect me to be rather then anything else. (H)

Adapted from Snyder and Gangestad (1986).

more than those who don't have a lot of self-knowledge (Baumgardner, 1990). All these factors may influence people's need to manage and control the impressions they make on others.

Self-Presentation and Manipulative Strategies

When people engage in impression management, their goal is to make a favorable impression on others. We have seen that people work hard to create favorable impressions on others. Yet we all know people who seem determined to make a poor impression and to behave in ways that are ultimately harmful to themselves. Why might these kinds of behavior occur?

Self-Handicapping

Have you ever goofed off before an important exam, knowing that you should study? Or have you ever slacked off at a sport even though you have a big match coming up? If you have—and most of us have at one time or another—you have engaged in what social psychologists call self-handicapping (Berglas & Jones, 1978). People self-handicap when they are unsure of future success and, by putting an obstacle in their way, protect their self-esteem if they should perform badly.

The purpose of **self-handicapping** is to mask the relationship between performance and ability should you fail. If you do not do well on an examination because you did not study, the evaluator doesn't know whether your bad grade was due to a lack of preparation (the handicap) or a lack of ability. Of course, if you succeed despite the handicap, then others evaluate you much more positively. This is a way of controlling the impression people have of you, no matter what the outcome.

Although the aim of self-handicapping is to protect the person's self-esteem, it does have some dangers. After all, what are we to make of someone who goes to a movie rather than studying for a final exam? In one research study, college students negatively evaluated the character of a person who did not study for an important exam (Luginbuhl & Palmer, 1991). The self-handicappers succeeded in their self-presentations in the sense that

self-handicapping
Self-defeating behavior engaged in when you are uncertain about your success or failure at a task to protect your self-esteem in the face of failure.

the student evaluators were not sure whether the self-handicappers' bad grades were due to lack of ability or lack of preparation. But the students did not think very much of someone who would not study for an exam. Therefore, self-handicapping has mixed results for impression management.

Still, people are willing to make this trade-off. They are probably aware that their self-handicapping will be seen unfavorably, but they would rather have people think they are lazy or irresponsible than dumb or incompetent. A study found that people who self-handicapped and failed at a task had higher self-esteem and were in a better mood than people who did not handicap and failed (Rhodewalt, Morf, Hazlett, & Fairfield, 1991).

Self-handicapping can take two forms (Baumeister & Scher, 1988). The first occurs when the person really wants to succeed but has doubts about the outcome. This person will put some excuse in place. An athlete who says that she has had a nagging injury while knowing that she is capable of winning is using this kind of impression-management strategy. People will really be impressed if she wins despite her injury; if she loses, they will chalk it up to that Achilles tendon problem.

The second form also involves the creation of obstacles to success but is more self-destructive. In this case, the individual fears that some success is a fluke or a mistake and finds ways to subvert it, usually by handicapping himself in a destructive and internal manner. For example, a person who is suddenly propelled to fame as a movie star may find himself showing up late for rehearsals, or blowing his lines, or getting into fights with the director. It may be because he doesn't really believe he is that good an actor, or he may fear he won't be able to live up to his new status. Perhaps being rich and famous doesn't match his self-concept. Consequently, he handicaps himself in some way.

The abuse of alcohol and drugs may be an example of self-handicapping (Beglas & Jones, 1978). Abusers may be motivated by a need to have an excuse for possible failure. They would rather that others blame substance abuse for their (anticipated) failure than lack of ability. Like the athlete with the injured leg, they want ability to be discounted as the reason for failure but credited as the basis for success. Because the self-handicapper will be embarrassed if the excuse that clouds the link between performance and outcome is absurd, it is important that the excuse be reasonable and believable. Self-handicapping is thus another way people attempt to maintain control over the impression others have of them.

Although self-handicapping may have short-term benefits (if you fail at something, it is not really your fault, because you have an excuse in place), the behavior has some long-term drawbacks. Zuckerman, Kieffer, and Knee (1998) did a long-term study of individuals who used self-handicapping strategies and found that self-handicappers performed less well academically because of bad study habits and had poorer adjustment scores. They tended to have more negative feelings, and withdrew more from other people than did others who did not self-handicap. As you might have predicted, all of this negativity started a vicious cycle that led to even more self-handicapping.

THE IMPRESSION WE MAKE ON OTHERS

How accurate are we in assessing the impression we convey? In general, most people seem to have a good sense of the impression they make on others. In one study designed to look at this question, participants interacted with partners who they had not previously met (DePaulo, Kenny, Hoover, Webb, & Oliver, 1987). After each interaction with their partners, participants had to report on the impressions they had conveyed to the partner. The researchers found that the participants were generally accurate in reporting the kind of impression their behavior communicated. They also were aware of how their behavior changed over time during the interaction and how it changed over time with different partners.

Another study also found that people are fairly accurate in identifying how they come across to others (Kenny & Albright, 1987); they also consistently communicate the same impression over time (Colvin & Funder, 1991). People tend to overestimate how favorably they are viewed by other people, however. When they err, it is on the side of believing that they have made a better impression than they actually have.

However, sometimes we can assume that other people recognize how we are really feeling, especially when we wish they could not. It appears, according to research by Thomas Gilovich and his coworkers, that we believe our internal feelings show more than they actually do (Gilovich, Savitsky, & Medvec, 1998). In general, we seem to overestimate the ability of others to "read" our overt behavior, how we act and dress. Gilovich and his colleagues called this the **spotlight effect,** suggesting that we as actors think others have us under a spotlight and notice and pay attention to what we do. This increased self-consciousness seems to be the basis of adult shyness: Shy people are so aware of their actions and infirmities that they believe others are focused (the spotlight) on them and little else. The reality of social life is quite different and most of us would be relieved to know that few in the crowd care what we do or think. For example, in one study, college students wore a T-shirt with the ever-popular Barry Manilow on the front, and the wearers much overestimated the probability that others would notice the T-shirt. The spotlight does not shine as brightly as we think.

Gilovich and colleagues (1998) believe that we have the same preoccupation (that others notice and pay attention to our external actions and appearance) with respect to our hidden, internal feelings. They called this the **illusion of transparency,** the belief that observers can read our private thoughts and feelings because they somehow "leak out." In one of the studies designed to test the illusion of transparency, Gilovich and colleagues hypothesized that participants asked to tell lies in the experiment would think that the lies were more obvious than they really were. Indeed, that was the result. In a second experiment, participants had to taste something unpleasant but keep a neutral expression. If, say, your host at a dinner party presented a dish you thoroughly disliked, you might try to eat around the edges for politeness' sake and not express disgust. How successful might you be at disguising your true feelings? The tasters in the Gilovich studies thought that they would not be very successful at all. Instead, observers were not likely to discern that the tasters were disgusted with the food or drink. Again, people overestimated the ability of others to determine their true, internal feelings.

Although most people seem to have a good sense of the impression they make on other people, some do not. In fact, some people never figure out that they are creating a bad impression. In a study designed to look at why some people do not seem to pick up on the cues that they are making a bad impression, individuals were observed interacting with people who had continually made either good or bad impressions (Swann, Stein-Seroussi, & McNulty, 1992). Swann and his co-workers found that participants said basically the

spotlight effect
A phenomenon occurring when we overestimate the ability of others to read our overt behavior, how we act and dress, suggesting that we think others notice and pay attention to whatever we do.

illusion of transparency
The belief that observers can read our private thoughts and feelings because they somehow leak out.

same generally positive things to both types of individuals. However, they acted differently toward the two types of individuals. They directed less approving nonverbal cues (such as turning away while saying nice things) at negative-impression individuals than at those who made positive impressions.

The researchers concluded that there are two reasons why people who continually make bad impressions do not learn to change. First, we live in a "white-lie" society in which people are generally polite even to someone who acts like a fool. Second, the cues that people use to indicate displeasure may be too subtle for some people to pick up (Swann et al., 1992).

THE LIFE OF JAMES CARROLL REVISITED

In our brief examination of the life and work of the best-selling author James Carroll, we had the opportunity to see how the author's personal life, his family, his teachers, and his religion, as well the momentous social events that occurred during his formative years, shaped and influenced both his personal and social selves. Certainly, these events provided Mr. Carroll with rich materials for his writings, which include ten fiction and nonfiction books.

CHAPTER REVIEW

1. What is the self?

The self is, in part, a cognitive structure, containing ideas about who and what we are. It also has an evaluative and emotional component, because we judge ourselves and find ourselves worthy or unworthy. The self guides our behavior as we attempt to make our actions consistent with our ideas about ourselves. Finally, the self guides us as we attempt to manage the impression we make on others.

2. How do we know the self?

Several sources of social information help us forge our **self-concept.** The first is our view of how other people react to us. From earliest childhood and through-out life, these **reflected appraisals** shape our self-concept. We also get knowledge about ourselves from comparisons with other people. We engage in a **social comparison process**—comparing our reactions, abilities, and **personal attributes** to those of others—because we need accurate information in order to succeed. The third source of information about ourselves is observation of our own behavior. Sometimes we simply observe our behavior and assume that our motives are consistent with our behavior. Finally, one may know the self through introspection, the act of examining our own thoughts and feelings.

3. What is distinctiveness theory?

Distinctiveness theory suggests that people think of themselves in terms of the characteristics or dimensions that make them different from others, rather than in terms of characteristics they have in common with others. An individual is likely to incorporate the perceived distinctive characteristic into his or her self-concept. Thus, distinctive characteristics help define our self-concept.

4. How is the self organized?

People arrange knowledge and information about themselves into self-schemas. A **self-schema** contains information about gender, age, race or ethnicity, occupation, social roles, physical attractiveness, intelligence, talents, and so on. Self-schemas help us interpret situations and guide our behavior. For example, a sexual self-schema refers to how we think about the sexual aspects of the self.

5. What is autobiographical memory?

The study of **autobiographical memory**—memory of information relating to the self—shows that the self plays a powerful role in the recall of events. Researchers have found that participants recalled recent events more quickly than older ones, pleasant events more quickly than unpleasant ones, and extreme events, pleasant and unpleasant, more quickly than neutral episodes. Pleasant events that especially fit the person's self-concept were most easily recalled.

6. What is self-esteem?

Self-esteem is an evaluation of our overall worth that consists of both positive and negative self-evaluations. We evaluate, judge, and have feelings about ourselves. Some people possess high self-esteem, regard themselves highly, and are generally pleased with who they are. Others have low self-esteem, feel less worthy and good, and may even feel that they are failures and incompetent.

7. How do we evaluate the self?

By continually adjusting perceptions, interpretations, and memories, the self works tirelessly behind the scenes to maintain positive self-evaluations, or high self-esteem. Self-esteem is affected both by our ideas about how we are measuring up to our own standards and by our ability to control our sense of self in interactions with others. Positive evaluations of the self are enhanced when there is a good match between who we are—the actual self—and what we think we'd like to be (the ideal self) or what others believe we ought to be (the ought self). When there are differences between our actual self and either what we would like to be or what we ought to be, we engage in self-regulation, our attempts to match our behavior to what is required by the ideal or the ought self.

8. What is self-evaluation maintenance (SEM) theory?

According to Abraham Tesser's **self-evaluation maintenance (SEM) theory,** the high achievement of a close other in a self-relevant area is perceived as a threat. In response we can downplay the other's achievement, put more distance between ourselves and the other, work hard to improve our own performance, or try to handicap the other.

9. What is self-consistency?

An important driving motive of the self in social interactions is to maintain high self-consistency—agreement between our self-concept and the views others have of us. Motivated by a need for **self-verification**—confirmation of our self-concept—we tend to behave in ways that lead others to see us as we see ourselves. Self-verification suggests that at least some of the time we are quite aware of how we are behaving and how other people are evaluating us. In fact, when people become more aware of themselves, when they self-focus, they are more likely to try to match their behavior to their beliefs and internal standards.

10. How do we present the self to others?

We engage in impression management, the process of presenting ourselves in certain ways in order to control the impressions that others form of us. People with low self-esteem are cautious in trying to create a positive impression and focus on minimizing their bad points. People with high self-esteem focus on maximizing their good points. Everyone, however, demonstrates an **egotistical bias,** the tendency to take credit for successes, whether appropriate or not.

11. What is self-monitoring?

Another factor that influences impression management is the degree to which a person engages in **self-monitoring,** that is, focuses on his or her own behavior in a given social situation. High self-monitors are very sensitive to the social demands of any situation and tend to fit their behavior to those demands; low self-monitors are much less concerned with impression management.

12. What is self-handicapping?

Self-handicapping involves actions that are harmful but that the person believes may produce some positive outcomes. An excuse is put in place that masks the relationship between performance and ability. It is an attempt to manage the impressions others have of the individual, but in the end it is self-defeating.

13. How accurate are we in assessing the impression we convey?

In general, most people seem to have a good sense of the impression they make on others People tend to overestimate how favorably they are viewed by other people, however. When they err, it is on the side of believing that they have made a better impression than they actually have.

14. What is the spotlight effect?

We sometimes assume that other people can recognize how we are really feeling, especially when we wish they could not. This the **spotlight effect,** suggesting that we think others have us under a spotlight and notice and pay attention to what we do. This increased self-consciousness seems to be the basis of adult shyness.

15. What is the illusion of transparency?

Some individuals harbor the belief that others can read their hidden, internal feelings. This is the **illusion of transparency,** or the belief that observers can read our private thoughts and feelings because they somehow leak out. Despite this illusion, people usually overestimate the ability of others to determine their true, internal feelings.

INTERNET ACTIVITY

FINDING OUT ABOUT YOURSELF

Each of us has a sense about what we are like. We know if we are friendly or shy, driven by external rewards or internal satisfaction, dependent on external information or internal motives, and so on. The Internet has several sites where you can self-test for a variety of personality characteristics. One such site, "Tests, Tests, Tests . . ." at http://www.queendom.com/personty.html has tests you can take on such things as driving personality, Type A behavior patterns, and an optimism–pessimism test. You can find other sites by using a search engine and typing in the search term: "personality tests." For this exercise, take one of these on-line personality tests and do the following:

1. Evaluate the personality test itself.
   a. Do you think the test was long enough to give an accurate picture of one's personality?
   b. Were the items on the test appropriate for testing the aspect of personality on which the test focused?
   c. Was any information provided on the source of the test or its reliability and validity?
   d. What would you do to improve the test?
2. How well did the results of the test match how you perceive yourself to actually be? In what areas was the test accurate or inaccurate?

SUGGESTIONS FOR FURTHER READING

Caspi, A. (2000). The child is the father of the man: Personality continuities from childhood to adulthood. *Journal of Personality and Social Psychology, 78,* 158–172.
This very insightful study shows how the self remains relatively stable throughout life.

Carroll, J. (1996). *An American requiem.* Boston: Houghton Mifflin.
This book is an engrossing memoir of an important American author and his conflict with his father and his religion during the Vietnam War period.

Vandello, J. A., & Cohen, D. (1999). Patterns of individualism and collectivism across the United States. *Journal of Personality and Social Psychology, 77,* 279–292.
These authors present another in the series of studies by Dov Cohen and his colleagues that show how regional differences affect the self and behavior.

Kunda, Z. (1999). *Social cognition.* Cambridge, MA: MIT Press.
This book's chapter on the self is probably the best general summary of research currently available.

CHAPTER 3

SOCIAL PERCEPTION: UNDERSTANDING OTHER PEOPLE

In July 1988, the U.S. guided missile frigate Vincennes was on patrol in the Persian Gulf. A state-of-the-art ship carrying the most sophisticated radar and guidance systems, the Vincennes became embroiled in a skirmish with some small Iranian naval patrol boats. During the skirmish, Captain Will Rogers III received word from the radar room that an unidentified aircraft was heading toward the ship. The intruder was on a descending path, the radar operators reported, and appeared to be hostile. It did not respond to the ship's IFF (identify friend or foe) transmissions, nor were further attempts to raise it on the radio successful. Captain Rogers, after requesting permission from his superior, ordered the firing of surface-to-air missiles; the missiles hit and destroyed the plane. The plane was not an Iranian fighter. It was an Iranian Airbus, a commercial plane on a twice-weekly run to Dubai, a city across the Strait of Hormuz. The airbus was completely destroyed, and all 290 passengers were killed.

Following the tragedy, Captain Rogers defended his actions. But Commander David Carlson of the nearby frigate Sides, 20 miles away, reported that his crew accurately identified the airbus as a passenger plane. His crew saw on their radar screen that the aircraft was climbing from 12,000 to 14,000 feet (as tapes later verified) and that its flight pattern resembled that of a civilian aircraft (*Time*, August 15, 1988). The crew of the Sides did not interpret the plane's actions as threatening, nor did they think an attack was imminent. When Commander Carlson learned that the Vincennes had fired on what was certainly a commercial plane, he was so shocked he almost vomited (*Newsweek*, July 13, 1992). Carlson's view was backed up by the fact that the "intruder" was correctly identified as a commercial aircraft by radar operators on the U.S.S. Forrestal, the aircraft carrier and flagship of the mission (*Newsweek*, July 13, 1992).

What happened during the Vincennes incident? How could the crew of the Vincennes have "seen" a commercial plane as an attacking enemy plane on their radar screen? How could the captain have so readily ordered the firing of the missiles. And how could others—the crews of the Sides and the Forrestal, for instance—have seen things so differently?

The answers to these questions reside in the nature of human cognition. The captain and crew of the Vincennes constructed their own view of reality based on their previous experiences, their expectations of what was likely to occur, and their interpretations of what was happening at the moment—as well as their fears and anxieties. All these factors were in turn influenced by the context of current international events, which included a bitter enmity between the United States and what was perceived by Americans as an extremist Iranian government.

The captain and crew of the Vincennes remembered a deadly attack on an American warship the previous year in the same area. They strongly believed that they were likely to be attacked by an enemy aircraft, probably one carrying advanced missiles that would be very fast and very accurate. If this occurred, the captain knew he would need to act quickly and decisively. The radar crew saw an unidentified plane on their screen. Suddenly they called out that the aircraft was descending, getting in position to attack. The plane didn't respond to their radio transmissions. Weighing the available evidence, Captain Rogers opted to fire on the intruder.

The commander and crew of the Sides had a different view of the incident. They saw the incident through the filter of their belief that the Vincennes was itching for a fight. From their point of view, a passenger plane was shot down and 290 lives were lost as a result of the hair-trigger reaction of an overly aggressive crew.

These different views and understandings highlight a crucial aspect of human behavior: Each of us constructs a version of social reality that fits with our perception and interpretation of events (Jussim, 1991). We come to understand our world through the processes of social perception, the strategies and methods we use to understand the motives and behavior of other people.

This chapter looks at the tools and strategies people use to construct social reality. We ask, What cognitive processes are involved when individuals are attempting to make sense of the world? What mechanisms come into play when we form impressions of others and make judgments about their behavior and motives? How accurate are these impressions and judgments? And what accounts for the errors in perception and judgment that seem to inevitably occur in social interactions? How do we put all of the social information together to get a whole picture of our social world? These are some of the questions addressed in this chapter.

KEY QUESTIONS

AS YOU READ THIS CHAPTER, FIND THE ANSWERS TO THE FOLLOWING QUESTIONS:

1. *What is impression formation?*
2. *What are automatic and controlled processing?*
3. *What is meant by a cognitive miser?*
4. *Why is automatic processing so important in social perception, behavior, and emotion?*
5. *Are our impressions of others accurate?*
6. *What factors affect the confidence we have in our impressions?*
7. *What is the attribution process?*

8. *What are internal and external attributions?*
9. *What is correspondent inference theory, and what factors enter into forming a correspondent inference?*
10. *What are covariation theory and the covariation principle?*
11. *How do consensus, consistency, and distinctiveness information lead to an internal or external attribution?*
12. *What is the dual process model of attribution, and what does it tell us about the attribution process?*
13. *What is meant by attribution biases?*
14. *What is the fundamental attribution error?*
15. *What is the sinister attribution error, and when is it made?*
16. *What is the actor–observer bias?*
17. *What are the false consensus and the self-serving biases?*
18. *What is the importance of first impressions?*
19. *What are schemas, and what role do they play in social cognition?*
20. *What is the self-fulfilling prophecy, and how does it relate to behavior?*
21. *What roles do stories play in social cognition?*
22. *What are the various types of heuristics that often guide social cognition?*
23. *What is meant by metacognition?*
24. *How do optimism and pessimism relate to social cognition and behavior?*
25. *How do distressing events affect happiness?*

IMPRESSION FORMATION: AUTOMATICITY AND SOCIAL PERCEPTION

impression formation
The process by which we make judgments about others.

The process by which we make judgments about others is called **impression formation**. We are primed by our culture to form impressions of people, and Western culture emphasizes the individual, the importance of "what is inside the person" as the cause of behavior (Jones, 1990). We also may be programmed biologically to form impressions of those who might help or hurt us. It is conceivable that early humans, who were better at making accurate inferences about others, had superior survival chances—and those abilities are part of our genetic heritage (Flohr, 1987). It makes sense that they were able to form relatively accurate and slow (effortful) impressions of others rather effortlessly. Because grossly accurate impressions—is this person dangerous or not, trustworthy or not, friend or foe—could be life threatening, humans learned to make those judgments efficiently. Those who could not were less likely to survive. So, efficiency and effortlessness in perception are critical goals of human cognition.

automatic processing
The idea that because of limited information processing capacity we construct social impressions without much thought or effort, especially when we lack the motivation for careful assessment or when our initial impressions are confirmed.

Social psychologists interested in cognition are primarily concerned with how the individual tries to make sense out of what is occurring in his or her world under the uncertain conditions that are a part of normal life (Mischel, 1999). Much of our social perception involves **automatic processing**—forming impressions without much thought or attention (Logan, 1989). Thinking that is conscious and requires effort is referred to as **controlled processing**.

controlled processing
An effortful and careful processing of information that occurs when we are motivated to accurately assess information or if our initial impressions or expectations are disconfirmed.

Automatic Processing

Automatic processing is thinking that occurs primarily outside consciousness. It is effortless in the sense that it does not require us to use any of our conscious cognitive capacity. We automatically interpret an upturned mouth as a smile, and we automatically infer that the smiling person is pleased or happy (Fiske & Taylor, 1991). Such interpretations and inferences, which may be built into our genetic makeup, are beyond our conscious control.

Running through all our social inference processes—the methods we use to judge other people—is a thread that seems to be part of our human makeup: our tendency to prefer the least effortful means of processing social information (Taylor, 1981). This is not to say we are lazy or sloppy; we simply have a limited capacity to understand information and can deal with only relatively small amounts at any one time (Fiske, 1993). We tend to be **cognitive misers in** the construction of social reality: Unless motivated to do otherwise, we use just enough effort to get the job done. In this business of constructing our social world, we are pragmatists (Fiske, 1992). Essentially we ask ourselves, What is my goal in this situation, and what do I need to know to reach that goal?

cognitive miser
A label suggesting that because humans have a limited capacity to understand information, we deal only with small amounts of social information and prefer the least effortful means of processing it.

Although automatic processing is the preferred method of the cognitive miser, there is no clear line between automatic and controlled processing. Rather, they exist on a continuum, ranging from totally automatic (unconscious) to totally controlled (conscious), with degrees of more and less automatic thinking in between.

Much of our processing of social information is done automatically, with little or no thought. For example, we automatically interpret this woman's smile as indicating happiness.

The Importance of Automaticity in Social Perception

Recall the work of Roy Baumeister discussed in chapter 2. His work concluded that even small acts of self-control such as forgoing a tempting bite of chocolate uses up our self-control resources for subsequent tasks. However, Baumeister and Kristin Sommer (1997) suggested that although the conscious self is important, it plays a causal and active role in only about 5% of our actions. This suggests that despite our belief in free will and self-determination, it appears that much if not most of our behavior is determined by processes that are nonconscious, automatic (Bargh & Chartrand, 1999). Daniel Wegner and his coworkers showed that people mistakenly believe they have intentionally caused a behavior when in fact they were forced to act by stimuli of which they were not aware (Wegner, Ansfield, & Pilloff, 1998). Wegner and Whealey (1999) suggested that the factors that actually cause us to act are rarely, if ever, present in our consciousness.

John Bargh (1997) wrote that automatic responses are learned initially from experience and then are used passively, effortlessly, and nonconsciously each time we encounter the same object or situation. For example, Chartrand and Bargh showed that when individuals have no clear-cut goals to form impressions of other people, those goals can be brought about nonconsciously. It is possible to present words or images so quickly that the individual has no awareness that anything has been presented, and furthermore the person does not report that he or she has seen anything (Kunda, 1999). But the stimuli can still have an effect on subsequent behavior. Employing this technique of presenting stimuli subliminally in a series of experiments, Chartrand and Bargh (1996) primed participants to form an impression of particular (target) individuals by presenting some subjects with words such as *judge* and *evaluate* and other impression-formation stimuli. Other experimental participants were not primed to form impressions subliminally. Soon thereafter, the participants in the experiment were given a description of behaviors that were carried out by a particular (target) individual but told only that they would be questioned about it later. Chartrand and Bargh reported that those participants who were primed by impression-formation words (judge, evaluate, etc.) below the level of conscious awareness (subliminally) were found to have a fully formed impression of the target. Subjects not primed and given the same description did not form an impression of the target. Therefore, the participants were induced nonconsciously to form an impression, and this nonconsciously primed goal guided subsequent cognitive behavior (forming the impression of the target person presented by the experimenter).

Automaticity and Behavior

A couple, married for a quarter of a century, sit at the dinner table vigorously discussing the day's events. The dinner guest cannot help but notice how husband and wife mimic, clearly unconsciously, each other's gestures. When he makes a strong point, the husband emphasizes his comments by hitting the table with his open hand. His wife, although not quite so vigorously, tends to do the same. Neither is aware of the gestures.

Indeed, there is evidence that such mimicry is common in social interaction (Macrae, Bodenhausen et al., 1998). Chartrand and Bargh (1999) termed this nonconscious mimicry the *chameleon effect,* indicating that like the chameleon changing its color to match its surroundings, we may change our behavior to match that of people with whom we are interacting.

Chartrand and Bargh (1999) suggested that there exists an automatic, unintended, and entirely passive effect of perception on behavior. In other words, perception automatically, without our awareness, may trigger behaviors. Recall the Chartrand and Bargh (1996) studies just discussed: When individuals are primed subliminally to form impressions of a target, that is precisely what they do. If nonconscious forces can affect social perception, can it also affect our behavior? Research on the chameleon effect indicates that the answer is yes.

Why does the chameleon effect exists? What social purpose does it serve? Chartrand and Bargh (1999) suggested that mimicry and behavioral coordination lead to smoother social interaction and interpersonal bonding. Research suggests that interacting individuals tend to match facial expression, bodily postures (behavioral coordination), and other mannerisms and that this is an entirely nonconscious phenomenon. It is, in Chartrand and Bargh's felicitous phrase, a kind of "social glue" that increases liking and understanding between individuals without any conscious intent to do these things.

What is the research evidence for these ideas? In one study, Chartrand and Bargh (1999) had people interact with each other. One of the two people was a confederate of the experimenter. Confederates either rubbed their face or shook their foot. Facial expressions were varied as well, primarily by smiling or not. The participant and the confederate sat in chairs half-facing each other, and the entire session was videotaped and analyzed. Figure 3.1 shows the results of this experiment. Experimental subjects tended to rub their faces when the confederate did so, and the subjects tended to shake their foot when the confederate did. Frank Bernieri, John Gillis, and their

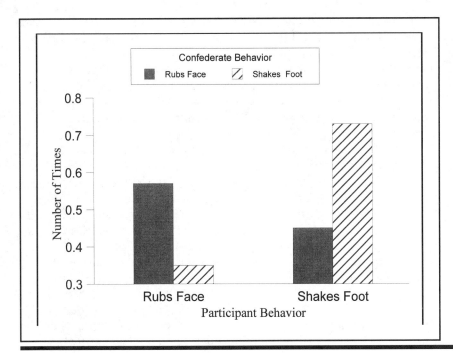

Figure 3.1

Behavior of research participants as it relates to the behavior of a confederate of the experimenter.

From Chartrand and Bargh (1999). Reprinted with permission.

co-workers also showed that when observers see two people in synchrony, that is, when their physical movements and postures seem to mimic or follow each other, the observers assume that the individuals have high compatibility or rapport (Bernieri, Gillis, Davis, & Grahe, 1996; Gillis, Bernieri, & Wooten, 1995).

In another experiment, Chartrand and Bargh showed the social value of such mimicry. For individuals whose partner mimicked their behavior, the interaction was rated as smoother, and they professed greater liking for that partner than did individuals whose partner did not mimic their expression or behavior. These experiments and others demonstrate the adaptive function of nonconscious behavior. Not only does it smooth social interactions, but it does away with the necessity of actively choosing goal-related behavior at every social encounter. Because our cognitive resources are limited and can be depleted, it is best that these resources are saved for situations in which we need to process social information in a conscious and controlled manner.

Automaticity and Emotions

If cognitive activity occurs primarily below the level of conscious awareness, what about emotions? We all know that our emotional responses to events often are beyond our conscious control. We may not be aware of why we reacted so vigorously to what was really a small insult or why we went into a "blue funk" over a trivial matter. Where we need conscious control is to get out of that bad mood or to overcome that reaction. It appears that our emotional responses are not controlled by a conscious will (LeDoux, 1996). As Wegner and Bargh (1998) indicated, the research on cognition and emotion focuses primarily on what we do after we express an emotion, not on how we decide what emotion to express.

Sometimes we can be aware of what we are thinking and how those thoughts are affecting us but still not know how the process started or how we may end it. For example, have you ever gotten a jingle stuck in your mind? You can't say why the jingle started, nor can you get it out of your mind, no matter how hard you try. You think of other things, and each of these distractors works for a while. But soon the jingle pops up again, more insistent than ever. Suppressing an unwanted thought seems only to make it stronger.

This phenomenon was vividly demonstrated in an experiment in which subjects were told not to think of a white bear for 5 minutes (Wegner, 1989). Whenever the thought of a white bear popped into mind, subjects were to ring a bell. During the 5-minute period, subjects rang the bell often. More interesting, however, was the discovery that once the 5 minutes were up, the white bears really took over, in a kind of *rebound effect*. Subjects who had tried to suppress thoughts of white bears could think of little else after the 5 minutes expired. The study demonstrates that even if we successfully fend off an unwanted thought for a while, it may soon return to our minds with a vengeance.

Because of this strong rebound effect, suppressed thoughts may pop up when we least want them. A bigot who tries very hard to hide his prejudice when he is with members of a particular ethnic group will, much to his surprise, say something stupidly bigoted and wonder why he could not suppress the thought (Wegner, 1993). This is especially likely to happen when people are under pressure. Automatic processing takes over, reducing the ability to control thinking.

Of course, we do control some of our emotions but apparently only after they have surfaced. If our boss makes us angry, we may try to control the expression of that anger. We often try to appear less emotional than we actually feel. We may moderate our voice when we are really angry, because it would do us no good to express that emotion. However, as Richards and Gross (1999) showed, suppressing emotion comes at a cost. These researchers demonstrated that suppressing emotions impairs memory for information during the period of suppression and increases cardiovascular responses. This suggests, as does Wegner's work, that suppressing emotions depletes one's cognitive resources.

Controlled Processing

As mentioned earlier, controlled processing involves conscious awareness, attention to the thinking process, and effort. It is defined by several factors: First, we know we are thinking about something; second, we are aware of the goals of the thought process; and third, we know what choices we are making. For example, if you meet someone, you may be aware of thinking that you need to really pay attention to what this person is saying. Therefore, you are aware of your thinking process. You will also know that you are doing this because you expect to be dealing with this person in the future. You may want to make a good impression on the person, or you may need to make an accurate assessment. In addition, you may be aware that by focusing on this one person, you are giving up the opportunity to meet other people.

People are motivated to use controlled processing, that is, to allocate more cognitive energy to perceiving and interpreting. They may have goals they want

When the impressions we form and social judgments we make are important, we tend to use controlled processing. A judge listening to evidence will be motivated to be correct in his judgments, so he will use controlled processing.

to achieve in the interaction, for example, or they may be disturbed by information that doesn't fit their expectancies. Processing becomes more controlled when thoughts and behavior are intended (Wegner & Pennebaker, 1993).

THE IMPRESSION OTHERS MAKE ON US: HOW DO WE "READ" PEOPLE?

It is clear then that we process most social information in an automatic way, without a great deal of effort. As we said earlier, perhaps only 5% of the time do we process it in a controlled and systematic way. What does this mean for accurate impression formation?

How Accurate Are Our Impressions?

How many times have you heard, "I know just how you feel?" Well, do we really know how someone else feels? Laura A. King (1998) noted that the ability to recognize the emotions of others is crucial to social interaction and an important marker of interpersonal competence. King found that our ability to accurately read other individuals' emotions depends on our own emotional socialization. That is, some individuals have learned, because of their early experiences and feedback from other people, that it is safe to clearly express their emotions. Others are more conflicted, unsure, and ambivalent about expressing emotions. Perhaps they were punished somehow for emotional expression and learned to adopt a poker face. This personal experience with emotional expressivity, King reasoned, should have an effect on our ability to determine the emotional state of other people.

King (1998) examined the ability of people who were unsure, ambivalent, about emotional expressivity to accurately read others' emotions. She found that compared to individuals who had no conflict about expressing emotions, those who were ambivalent about their own emotional expression tended to be confused about other people's expression of emotion. The ambivalent individuals, when trying to read people in an emotional situation or to read their facial expressions, quite often inferred the opposite emotion than the one the individuals actually felt and reported. Ambivalent individuals who spend much energy in being inexpressive or suppressing emotional reactions quite easily inferred that others also were hiding their emotions, and what they saw was not what was meant. This simply may mean that people who are comfortable with their own emotional expressiveness are more accurate in reading other people's emotional expressions.

King's work, then, suggests that in our ability to accurately read other people, much depends on our own emotional life. Take another example of this: Gifford Weary and John A. Edwards (1994) suggested that mild or moderately depressed people are much more anxious than others to understand social information. This is because depressives often feel that they have little control over their social world and their efforts to effect changes meet with little success.

Research by John A. Edwards and his co-workers shows that depressives are much more tuned to social information and put more effort into trying to determine why people react to them as they do. Depressives are highly vigilant processors of social information (Edwards, Weary, von Hippel, & Jacobson, 1999). One would think that depressives' vigilance would make them more accurate in reading people. Depressed people often have problems with social interactions, and this vigilance is aimed at trying to figure out why and perhaps alter these interactions for the better. But here again, we can see the importance of nonconscious behavior. Edwards and colleagues pointed out that depressed people behave in ways that "turn others off." These turnoffs are difficult to alter precisely because they are nonconscious. For example, depressives have trouble with eye contact, voice pitch, and other gestures that arouse negative reactions in others. In fact, Edwards and colleagues suggested that all this effortful processing detracts depressed individuals from concentrating on enjoyable interactions.

Confidence and Impression Formation

Our ability to read other people may depend on the quality of our own emotional life, but the confidence we have in our impressions of others appears to depend, not surprisingly, on how much we think we know about the other person. Confidence in our impressions of other people is important because, as with other beliefs held with great conviction, we are more likely to act on them. If, for example, we are sure that our friend would not lie to us, we then make decisions based on that certainty. The commander of the Vincennes certainly was confident in his interpretation of the deadly intent of the aircraft on his radar screen.

However, confidence in our judgment may not necessarily mean that it is accurate. Wells (1995) showed that the correlation between accuracy and confidence in eyewitness identification is very modest, and sometimes there is no relationship at all. Similarly, Swann and Gill (1997) reported that confidence and accuracy of perception among dating partners and among roommates were not very good.

Gill and his colleagues found that when individuals are required to form a careful impression of an individual, including important aspects of the target's life—intellectual ability, social skills, physical attractiveness, and so forth—and they had access to information derived from a videotaped interview with the target person, they had high confidence in their judgments of the target. This is not surprising, of course. But, what might be surprising is that confidence had no impact on the accuracy of the participants' judgment (experiment 1; Gill, Swann, & Silvera, 1998). In another series of studies, these researchers amply demonstrated that having much information about a target makes people even more confident of their judgments, because they can recall and apply information about these people easily and fluently. But, the judgments are no more accurate than when we have much less information about someone. What is most disturbing about these findings is that it is precisely those situations in which we have much information and much confidence that are most important to us. These situations involve close relationships of various kinds with people who are very significant in our lives. But the research says we make errors nevertheless, even though we are confident and possess much information.

Our modest ability to read other people accurately may be due to the fact that our attention focuses primarily on obvious, expressive cues at the expense of more subtle but perhaps more reliable cues. Bernieri, Gillis, and their co-workers showed in a series of experiments that observers pay much attention to overt cues such as when people are extraverted and smile a great deal. Bernieri and Gillis suggested that expressivity (talking, smiling, gesturing) drives social judgment, but people may not recognize that expressivity determines their judgments (Bernieri et al., 1996).

It Is Hard to Catch a Liar: Detecting Deception

If, as the research shows, we are not very good at reading people, even those with whom we have close relationships, then you might suspect that we are not very good at detecting lies and liars. In general, you are right. But some people can learn to be quite accurate in detecting lies. Paul Ekman and his co-workers asked 20 males (ages 18 to 28) to indicate how strongly they felt about a number of controversial issues. Choosing the social issue about which the individuals felt most strongly, these males were then asked to speak to an interrogator about it. Some were asked to tell the truth; others were asked to lie about how they felt (Ekman, O'Sullivan, & Frank, 1999). If the truth tellers were believed, they were rewarded with $10.00; liars who were believed were given $50.00. Liars who were caught and truth tellers who were disbelieved received no reward. So, the 20 males were motivated to do a good job. Ekman and his colleagues filmed the faces of the 20 participants and found that there were significant differences in facial movements between liars and truth tellers.

The researchers were interested in whether people in professions in which detection of lies is important were better than the average person in identifying liars and truth tellers. Ekman tested several professional groups, including federal officers (CIA agents and others), federal judges, clinical psychologists, and academic psychologists. In previous research, the findings suggested that only a small number of U.S. Secret Service agents were better at detecting lies than the average person, who is not very effective at recognizing deception. Figure 3.2 shows that federal officers were most accurate at detecting whether a person was telling the truth. Interestingly, these officers

Figure 3.2

Accuracy of individuals in various professions in detecting who is deceptive.

Based on data from Ekman, O'Sullivan, and Frank (1999).

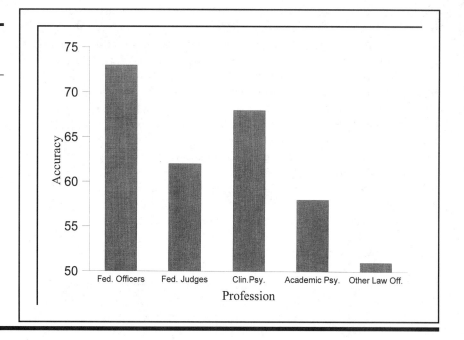

were more accurate in detecting lies than truth. Clinical psychologists interested in deception were next in accuracy, and again, they were better at discerning lies than truth telling.

The best detectors focused not on one clue but rather on a battery of clues or symptoms. Ekman notes that no one clue is a reliable giveaway. Perhaps the most difficult obstacle in detecting liars is that any one cue or series of cues may not be applicable across the board. Each liar is different; each detector is different as well. Ekman found a wide range of accuracy within each group, with many detectors being at or below chance levels.

In fact, there is some evidence that training people to detect lies does not help at all. Saul Kassin and Christina Fong (1999) provided some individuals with training typically used to prepare police interrogators. The trained individuals were provided with lessons in detecting verbal cues (liars are thought to be guarded and unhelpful in their answers) and nonverbal cues (deceivers are thought to slouch backwards, sit rigidly, avoid eye contact). Kassin and Fong reported that their subjects were unable to distinguish between truth tellers and deceivers, and trained individuals were less accurate than were untrained individuals. We can conclude that some professionals may be able to detect lies with some degree of accuracy, but the rest of us ought to be quite skeptical about our own ability to do so (Ekman et al., 1999).

However, skeptical we are not. If people are not very good at detecting lies, then they ought not to have much confidence in their ability to do so. But as Bella DePaulo and her colleagues have shown, people's confidence in their judgments as to whether someone else is telling the truth is not reliably related to the accuracy of their judgments (DePaulo, Charlton, Cooper, Lindsay, & Muhlenbruck, 1997). People are more confident in their judgments when they think that the other person is telling the truth, whether that person is or not, and men are more confident, but not more accurate, than are women. The bottom line is that we cannot rely on our feelings of confidence to reliably inform us if someone is lying or not. As suggested by the work of Gill and colleagues (1998) discussed earlier, being in a close relationship and knowing the other person well is no great help in detecting lies (Anderson, Ansfield, & DePaulo, 1998). However, we can take some comfort in the results of research that shows that people tell fewer lies to the individuals to whom they felt closer and were more uncomfortable if they did lie. When people lied to close others, the lies were other-oriented, aimed at protecting the other person or making things more pleasant or easier (DePaulo & Kashy, 1999).

In a book by neurologist Oliver Sacks, *The Man Who Mistook His Hat for His Wife,* there is a scene in which brain-damaged patients, all of whom had suffered a stroke, accident, or tumor to the left side of the brain (aphasics) and therefore had language disorders, were seen laughing uproariously while watching a TV speech by President Ronald Reagan. Dr. Sacks speculated that the patients were picking up lies that others were not able to catch.

There is now some evidence that Sacks's interpretation may have been right. Etcoff, Ekman, & Frank (2000) suggested that language may hide the cues that would enable us to detect lying, and therefore, those with damage to the brain's language centers may be better at detecting lies. The indications are that when people lie, their true intent is reflected by upper facial expressions, whereas the part of the face around the mouth conveys the false emotional state the liar is trying to project. It may be that aphasics use different brain circuitry to detect liars. For the rest of us, it's pretty much pure chance.

THE ATTRIBUTION PROCESS: DECIDING WHY PEOPLE ACT AS THEY DO

We make inferences about a person's behavior because we are interested in the cause of that behavior. When a person is late for a meeting, we want to know if the individual simply didn't care or if something external, beyond his or her control, caused the late appearance. Although there is a widespread tendency to overlook external fact as causes of behavior, if you conclude that the person was late because of, say, illness at home, your inferences about that behavior will be more moderate than if you determined he or she didn't care (Vonk, 1999).

Each of the theories developed to explain the process of attribution provides an important piece of the puzzle in how we assign causes and understand behavior. The aim of these theories is to illuminate how people decide what caused a particular behavior. The theories are not concerned with finding the true causes of someone's behavior. They are concerned with determining how we, in our everyday lives, think and make judgments about the perceived causes of behaviors and events.

In this section, two basic influential attribution theories or models are introduced, as well as additions to those models:

- Correspondent inference theory.
- Covariation theory.
- Dual process models.

The first two, correspondent inference theory and covariation theory, are the oldest and most general attempts to describe the attribution process. Others represent more recent, less formal approaches to analyzing attribution.

Heider's Early Work on Attribution

The first social psychologist to systematically study causal attribution was Fritz Heider. He assumed that individuals trying to make sense out of the social world follow simple rules of causality. The individual, or perceiver, operates as a kind of "naive scientist," applying a set of rudimentary scientific rules (Heider, 1958). **Attribution** theories are an attempt to discover exactly what those rules are.

Heider made a distinction between **internal attribution,** assigning causality to something about the person, and **external attribution,** assigning causality to something about the situation. He believed that decisions about whether an observed behavior has an internal (personal) or external (situational) source emerge from our attempt to analyze why others act as they do (causal analysis). Internal sources involve things about the individual—character, personality, motives, dispositions, beliefs, and so on. External sources involve things about the situation—other people, various environmental stimuli, social pressure, coercion, and so on. Heider (1944, 1958) examined questions about the role of internal and external sources as perceived causes of behavior. His work defined the basic questions that future attribution theorists would confront. Heider (1958) observed that perceivers are less sensitive to situational (external) factors than to the behavior of the individual they are observing or with whom they are interacting (the actor). We turn now to the two theories that built directly on Heider's work.

Correspondent Inference Theory

Assigning causes for behavior also means assigning responsibility. Of course, it is possible to believe that someone caused something to happen yet not consider the individual responsible for that action. A 5-year-old who is left in an automobile with the engine running, gets behind the wheel, and steers the car through the frozen food section of Joe's convenience store caused the event but certainly is not responsible for it, psychologically or legally.

Nevertheless, social perceivers have a strong tendency to assign responsibility to the individual who has done the deed—the actor. Let's say your brakes fail, you are unable to stop at a red light, and you plow into the side of another car. Are you responsible for those impersonal brakes failing to stop your car? Well, it depends, doesn't it? Under what circumstances would you be held responsible, and when would you not?

How do observers make such inferences? What sources of information do people use when they decide someone is responsible for an action? In 1965, Edward Jones and Keith Davis proposed what they called *correspondent inference theory* to explain the processes used in making internal attributions about others, particularly when the observed behavior is ambiguous, that is, when the perceiver is not sure how to interpret the actor's behavior. We make a **correspondent inference** when we conclude that a person's overt behavior is caused by or corresponds to the person's internal characteristics or beliefs. We might believe, for example, that a person who is asked by others to write an essay in favor of a tax increase really believes that taxes should be raised (Jones & Harris, 1967). There is a tendency not to take into account the fact that the essay was determined by someone else, not the essayist. What factors influence us to make correspondent inferences?

attribution
The process of assigning causes of behavior, both your own and that of others.

internal attribution
The process of assigning the cause of behavior to some internal characteristic rather than to outside forces.

external attribution
The process of assigning the cause of behavior to some situation or event outside a person's control rather than to some internal characteristic.

correspondent inference
An inference that occurs when we conclude that a person's overt behavior is caused by or corresponds to the person's internal characteristics or beliefs.

According to correspondent inference theory, two major factors lead us to make a correspondent inference:

1. We perceive that the person *freely chose* the behavior.
2. We perceive that the person *intended to do* what he or she did.

Early in the Persian Gulf War of 1991, several U.S.-coalition aircraft were shot down over Iraq. A few days later, some captured pilots appeared in front of cameras and denounced the war against Iraq. From the images, we could see that it was likely the pilots had been beaten. Consequently, it was obvious that they did not freely choose to say what they did. Under these conditions, we do not make a correspondent inference. We assume that the behavior tells us little or nothing about the true feelings of the person. Statements from prisoners or hostages always are regarded with skepticism for this reason. The perception that someone has been coerced to do or say something makes an internal attribution less likely. The second factor contributing to an internal attribution is intent. If we conclude that a person's behavior was intentional rather than accidental, we are likely to make an internal attribution for that behavior. To say that a person intended to do something suggests that the individual wanted the behavior in question to occur. To say that someone did not intend an action, or did not realize what the consequences would be, is to suggest that the actor is less responsible for the outcome.

Covariation Theory

Whereas correspondent inference theory focuses on the process of making internal attributions, *covariation theory,* proposed by Harold Kelley (1967, 1971), looks at external attributions—how we make sense of a situation, the factors beyond the person that may be causing the behavior in question (Jones, 1990). The attribution possibilities that covariation theory lays out are similar to those that correspondent inference theory proposes. What is referred to as an *internal attribution* in correspondent inference theory is referred to as a *person attribution* in covariation theory. What is called an *external attribution* in correspondent inference theory is called a *situational attribution* in covariation theory.

Like Heider, Kelley (1967, 1971) viewed the attribution process as an attempt to apply some rudimentary scientific principles to causal analysis. In correspondent inference theory, in contrast, the perceiver is seen as a moral or legal judge of the actor. Perceivers look at intent and choice, the same factors that judges and jurors look at when assigning responsibility. Kelley's perceiver is more a scientist: just the facts, ma'am.

According to Kelley, the basic rule applied to causal analysis is the **covariation principle,** which states that if a response is present when a situation (person, object, event) is present and absent when that same situation is absent, then that situation is the cause of the response (Kelley, 1971). In other words, people decide that the most likely cause of any behavior is the factor that covaries—occurs at the same time—most often with the appearance of that behavior.

As an example, let's say your friend Keisha saw the hit movie *Titanic* and raved about it. You are trying to decide whether you would like it too and whether you should go see it. The questions you have to answer are, What is the cause of Keisha's reaction? Why did she like this movie? Is it something about the movie? Or is it something about Keisha?

covariation principle
The rule that if a response is present when a situation (person, object, or event) is present and absent when that same situation is absent, the situation is presumed to be the cause of the response.

In order to make an attribution in this case, you need information, and there are three sources or kinds of relevant information available to us:

1. Consensus information.
2. Distinctiveness information.
3. Consistency information.

Consensus information tells us about how other people reacted to the same event or situation. You might ask, How did my other friends like *Titanic?* How are the reviews? How did other people in general react to this stimulus or situation? If you find high consensus—everybody liked it—well, then, it is probably a good movie. In causal attribution terms, it is the movie that caused Keisha's behavior. High consensus leads to a situational attribution.

Now, what if Keisha liked the movie but nobody else did? Then it must be Keisha and not the movie: Keisha always has strange tastes in movies. Low consensus leads to a person attribution (nobody but Keisha liked it, so it must be Keisha).

The second source or kind of data we use to make attributions is *distinctiveness information.* Whereas consensus information deals with what other people think, distinctiveness information concerns the situation in which the behavior occurred: We ask if there is something unique or distinctive about the situation that could have caused the behavior. If the behavior occurs when there is nothing distinctive or unusual about the situation (low distinctiveness), then we make a person attribution: If Keisha likes all movies, then we have low distinctiveness: There's nothing special about *Titanic.* It must be Keisha. If there is something distinctive about the situation, then we make a situational attribution. If this is the only movie Keisha has ever liked, we have high distinctiveness and there must be something special about the movie. Low distinctiveness leads us to a person attribution; high distinctiveness leads us to a situational attribution. If the situation is unique—very high distinctiveness—then the behavior probably was caused by the situation and not by something about the person. The combination of high consensus and high distinctiveness always leads to a situational attribution. The combination of low consensus and low distinctiveness always leads to a person attribution.

The third source or kind of input is *consistency information,* which confirms whether the action occurs over time and situations (Chen, Yates, & McGinnies, 1988). We ask, Is this a one-time behavior (low consistency), or is it repeated over time (high consistency)? In other words, is this behavior stable or unstable? Consistency is a factor that correspondent inference theory fails to take into account.

What do we learn from knowing how people act over time? If, for example, the next time we see Keisha, she again raves about *Titanic,* we would have evidence of consistency over time (Jones, 1990). We would have less confidence in her original evaluation of the movie if she told us she now thought the movie wasn't very good (low consistency). We might think that perhaps Keisha was just in a good mood that night and that her mood affected her evaluation of the movie. Consistency has to do with whether the behavior is a reliable indicator of its cause.

The three sources of information used in making attributions are shown in Figures 3.3 and 3.4. Figure 3.3 shows the combination of information— high consensus, high consistency, and high distinctiveness—that leads us to

Figure 3.3

Information mix leading to a situational attribution.

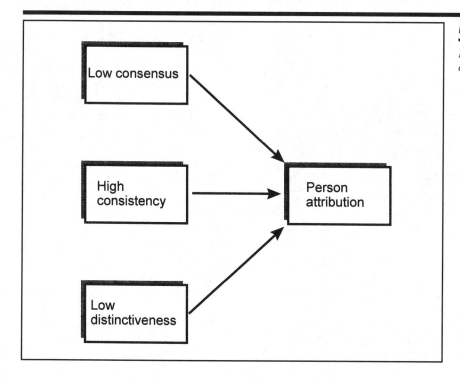

make a situational attribution. Go see the movie: Everybody likes it (high consensus); Keisha who likes few, if any, movies likes it as well (high distinctiveness of this movie); and Keisha has always liked it (high consistency of behavior).

Figure 3.4 shows the combination of information—low consensus, high consistency, and low distinctiveness—that leads us to a person attribution.

Figure 3.4

Information mix leading to a person attribution.

None of our friends likes the movie (low consensus); Keisha likes the movie, but she likes all movies, even *The Thing That Ate Newark* (low distinctiveness); and Keisha has always liked this movie (high consistency). Maybe we ought to watch TV tonight.

Not surprisingly, research on covariation theory shows that people prefer to make personal rather than situational attributions (McArthur, 1972). This conforms with the (correspondence) bias we found in correspondence inference theory and highlights again the tendency toward overemphasizing the person in causal analysis. It also fits with our tendency to be cognitive misers and take the easy route to making causal attributions.

Dual Process Models

We have emphasized that people are cognitive misers, using the least effortful strategy available. But they are not cognitive fools. We know that although impression formation is mainly automatic, sometimes it is not. People tend to make attributions in an automatic way, but there are times when they need to make careful and reasoned attributions (Chaiken & Trope, 1999).

Yaacov Trope (1986) proposed a theory of attribution that specifically considers when people make effortful and reasoned analyses of the causes of behavior. Trope assumed, as have other theorists, that the first step in our attributional appraisal is an automatic categorization of the observed behavior followed by more careful and deliberate inferences about the person (Trope, Cohen, & Alfieri, 1991).

The first step, in which the behavior is identified, often happens quickly, automatically, and with little thought. The attribution made at this first step, however, may be adjusted in the second step. During this second step, you may check the situation to see the target was controlled by something external to him. If so, if something "made him do it," then you might hold him less (internally) responsible for the behavior. In such instances, an inferential adjustment is made (Trope et al., 1991).

What information does the perceiver use to make these attributions? Trope plausibly argued that perceivers look at the behavior, the situation in which the behavior occurs, and prior information about the actor. Our knowledge about situations helps us understand behavior even when we know nothing about the person. When someone cries at a wedding, we make a different inference about the cause of that behavior than we would if the person cried at a wake. Our prior knowledge about the person may lead us to adjust our initial impression of the person's behavior.

A somewhat different model was developed by Daniel Gilbert (1989, 1991) and his colleagues. Influenced by Trope's two-step model, they proposed a model with three distinct stages. The first stage is the familiar automatic categorization of the behavior (that action was aggressive); the second is characterization of the behavior (George is an aggressive guy); and the third, correction, consists of adjusting that attribution based on situational factors (George was provoked needlessly). Gilbert essentially divided Trope's first step, the identification process, into two parts, categorization and characterization. The third step is the same as Trope's inferential-adjustment second step.

For example, if you say "Good to see you" to your boss, the statement may be categorized as friendly and the speaker may be characterized as someone who likes the other person; finally, this last inference may be corrected because the statement is directed at someone with power over the speaker (Gilbert, McNulty, Guiliano, & Benson, 1992). The correction is based on the inference that you had better be friendly to your boss. Gilbert suggests that *categorization* is an automatic process; *characterization* is not quite automatic but is relatively effortless, requiring little attention; but *correction* is a more cognitively demanding (controlled and effortful) process (Gilbert & Krull, 1988). Of course, we need to have the cognitive resources available to make these corrections. If we become overloaded or distracted, then we are not able to make these effortful corrections, and our default response is to make internal and dispositional attributions and to disregard situational information (Trope, & Alfieri, 1997; Gilbert & Hixon, 1991).

ATTRIBUTION BIASES

We know that individuals are not always accurate in determining what other people are really like. Although these attribution models assume people generally can make full use of social information, much of the time we take shortcuts, and we make a number of predictable errors. These errors or biases are examples of the cognitive miser as social perceiver. We deviate from the rules that a "pure scientist" would apply as outlined in the correspondent inference and especially the covariation models. Note, however, that some theorists argue that these biases are a consequence of the fact that people use a somewhat different attribution model than earlier theorists had assumed. In other words, there are no biases in the sense that people do something wrong in the way they make attributions; people just use the models in a different way than the earlier theorists thought they did.

Misattributions

A famous example of how our attributions may be misdirected is illustrated by a now classic experiment by Schachter and Singer (1962). Stanley Schachter and Jerome E. Singer demonstrated that two conditions are required for the production of an emotional response: physiological arousal and cognitions that label the arousal and, therefore, identify the emotion for the person experiencing it. Schachter and Singer injected participants with epinephrine, a hormone that produces all the symptoms of physiological arousal; rapid breathing, increased heart rate, palpitations, and so on. Half these people were accurately informed that the injection would create a state of arousal, and the other half were told the injection was only a vitamin, and would not have any effect. In addition, subjects in a control group were not given any drug.

Participants were then placed in a room to await another part of the experiment. Some subjects were in a room with a confederate of the experimenters who acted in a happy, excited, even euphoric manner, laughing, rolling up paper into balls, and shooting the balls into the wastebasket. Others encountered a confederate who was angry and threw things around the room. All subjects thought that the confederate was just another subject.

Schachter and Singer (1962) argued that the physiological arousal caused by the injection was open to different interpretations. The subjects who had been misinformed about the true effects of the injection had no reasonable explanation for the increase in their arousal. The most obvious stimulus was the behavior of the confederate. Results showed that aroused subjects who were in a room with an angry person behaved in an angry way; those in a room with a happy confederate behaved in a euphoric way. What about the subjects in the group who got the injection and were told what it was? These informed subjects had a full explanation for their arousal, so they simply thought that the confederate was strange and waited quietly.

The research shows that our emotional state can be manipulated. When we do not have readily available explanations for a state of arousal, we search the environment to find a probable cause. If the cues we find point us toward anger or aggression, than perhaps that is how we will behave. If the cues suggest joy or happiness, then our behavior may conform to those signals. It is true, of course, that this experiment involved a temporary and not very involving situation for the subjects. It is probable that people are less likely to make misattributions about their emotions when they are more motivated to understand the causes of their feelings and when they have a more familiar context for them.

The Fundamental Attribution Error

fundamental attribution error
The tendency to automatically attribute the causes for another person's behavior to internal rather than situational forces.

One pervasive bias found in the attributional process is the the tendency to attribute causes to people more readily than to situations. This bias is referred to as the **fundamental attribution error**.

If you have ever watched the television game show *Jeopardy*, you probably have seen the following scenario played out in various guises: A nervous contestant selects "Russian history" for $500. The answer is, "He was known as the 'Mad Monk.'" A contestant rings in and says, "Who was Molotov?" Alex Trebek, the host, replies, "Ah, noooo, the correct question is 'Who was Rasputin?'" As the show continues, certain things become evident. The

The fundamental attribution error involves automatically making an internal attribution for another person's behavior rather than an external attribution. For example, you would be making the fundamental attribution error if you automatically attributed this homeless person's plight to internal factors such as lack of motivation to find a job.

contestants, despite knowing a lot of trivial and not so trivial information, do not appear to be as intelligent or well informed as Trebek.

Sometimes we make attributions about people without paying enough attention to the roles they are playing. Of course Trebek looks smart—he may be smart; but he also has all the answers in front of him. Unfortunately, this last fact is sometimes lost on us. This so-called quiz show phenomenon was vividly shown in an experiment in which researchers simulated a TV game show for college students (Ross, Amabile, & Steinmetz, 1977). A few subjects were picked to be the questioners, not because they had any special skill or information but by pure chance, and had to devise a few fairly difficult but common-knowledge questions. A control group of questioners asked questions formulated by others. Members of both groups played out a simulation quiz game. After the quiz session, all subjects rated their own knowledge levels as well as the knowledge levels of their partners.

Now, all of us can think of some questions that might be hard for others to answer. Who was the Dodgers' third baseman in the 1947 World Series? Where is Boca Grande? When did Emma Bovary live? Clearly, the questioners had a distinct advantage: They could rummage around in their storehouse of knowledge, trivial and profound, and find some nuggets that others would not know.

When asked to rate the knowledge levels of the questioners as opposed to the contestants, both the questioners and the contestants rated the questioners as more knowledgeable, especially in the experimental group in which the questioners devised their own questions. Only a single contestant rated herself superior in knowledge to the questioner.

The fundamental attribution error can be seen clearly in this experiment: People attribute behavior to internal factors even when they have information indicating situational factors are at work. Because the questioners appeared to know more than the contestants, subjects thought the questioners were smarter. Everyone failed to account for the situation.

The quiz show phenomenon occurs in many social situations. The relationship between doctor and patient or teacher and student can be understood via this effect. When we deal with people in positions of high status or authority who appear to have all the answers, we attribute their behavior to positive internal characteristics such as knowledge and intelligence. Such an attribution enhances their power over us.

The Sinister Attribution Error: Paranoid Social Cognition

Steven Fein (1996) noted that suspicion is a unique aspect of social perception and that we are all aware that the people with whom we interact may behave in ways that are designed to deceive us. If love means not having to say you are sorry, then suspicion means not having to say that you will take what others do or say at face value. This suggests that suspicion can counter the fundamental attribution error.

Roderick Kramer (1998a) developed the notion of suspicion in social cognition and suggested that there is a variant of the fundamental attribution error that he calls the **sinister attribution error,** the tendency for certain people to overattribute lack of trustworthiness to others (p. 262). That is, the sinister attribution error refers to an assumption that other people are generally untrustworthy. This sinister attribution bias is part of what Kramer calls

sinister attribution error
The tendency for certain people to overattribute lack of trustworthiness to others.

paranoid social cognition. This is not so much a personality trait as is clinical paranoia but rather is derived from social situations. Three groups of social factors that make people distrusting of others and suspicious of their motives are listed here.

1. BEING DIFFERENT AND DISTINCTIVE   Factors in this category include age, race, and gender. They also may be based on social categories such as religion and social class. A woman in an all-male group is more salient, "looms larger," and may suspect, often quite rightly, that gender is a focal issue in the way the group responds to her (Kramer, 1998a, p. 257). Kramer suggested that although the "tokens" (e.g., the woman) no doubt had a "kernel of truth" in their perceptions that they were being treated differently, nevertheless, their attributions of others' motives were still cognitive distortions of the real situation.

Jennifer Crocker and her colleagues provided strong evidence that racial categorization can lead to the sinister attribution bias. Crocker, Luhtanen, Broadnax, & Blaine (1999) found that African Americans are more likely than Caucasian Americans to believe in theories about conspiracies by the United States Government against blacks. For example, 77% of blacks compared to 34% of whites thought it might be true that "The government deliberately singles out and investigates black elected officials to discredit them in a way it doesn't do with white officials" (p. 941). Nineteen percent of blacks believe that it might be true that AIDS was deliberately created to infect blacks. Crocker and colleagues presented evidence that suggests that these beliefs serve to blame an unresponsive system and that conspiracy beliefs were associated with higher self-esteem for blacks but not for whites who endorsed the same conspiracy theories. It appears in this instance that conspiracy beliefs serve to self-enhance blacks who hold them.

2. DEPENDENCE AND PARANOID COGNITION   It appears that when a person feels that he or she is under intense scrutiny, extreme self-consciousness results. Self-consciousness is a factor that may lead to the sinister attribution error. For example, in a well-known MBA program he studied, Kramer noted that students are motivated to pay greater attention to the faculty than vice versa, because faculty evaluate the students. Therefore, one would expect, given students' greater dependency and vulnerability, anything a faculty member might do or say with reference to the student would undergo lots of pondering. A missed phone call, a cool hello, a tart word might take on meaning for the student that did not reflect reality.

3. UNCERTAINTY ABOUT SOCIAL STANDING   Another factor that would heighten an anxious self-consciousness and thereby contribute to paranoid cognition and the sinister attribution error is uncertainty of social status. First-year students in MBA programs or in law school, new hires in business, untenured teachers and faculty members, all show heightened concerns about what others think and say about them. Heightened causal uncertainty about what people are saying about you and why they are saying it leads to confusion and anxiety according to John A. Edwards and Gifford Weary (1998). Such vigilance may lead to a cognitive bias such that people overestimate the importance of personal motives ("He's out to get me" — and there *is* the chance that he just may be) and to underestimate the importance of situational factors ("She just forgot to return my phone call"). Of course, as Kramer (1998) noted, distrust is not always irrational or even exaggerated.

Why We Make the Fundamental Attribution Error

Why do we err in favor of internal attributions? Several explanations have been offered for the fundamental attribution error, but two seem to be most useful: a focus on personal responsibility and the salience of behavior. Western culture emphasizes the importance of individual personal responsibility (Gilbert & Malone, 1995); we expect individuals to take responsibility for their behavior. We expect to be in control of our fates—our behavior—and we expect others to have control as well. We tend to look down on those who make excuses for their behavior. It is not surprising, therefore, that we perceive internal rather than external causes to be primary in explaining behavior (Forgas, Furnham, & Frey, 1990).

The second reason for the prevalence of the fundamental attribution error is the salience of behavior. In social situations as in all perception situations, our senses and attention are directed outward. The "actor" becomes the focus of our attention. His or her behavior is more prominent than the less commanding background or environment. The actor becomes the "figure" (focus in the foreground) and the situation, the "ground" (the total background) in a complex figure–ground relationship. A well-established maxim of perceptual psychology is that the figure stands out against the ground and thus commands our attention.

The perceiver tends to be "engulfed by the behavior," not the surrounding circumstances (Heider, 1958). If a person is behaving maliciously, we conclude he is a nasty person. Factors that might have brought on this nastiness are not easily available or accessible to us, so it is easy, even natural, to disregard or slight them. Thus, we readily fall into the fundamental attribution error.

Correcting the Fundamental Attribution Error

So, are we helpless to resist this common misattribution of causality? Not necessarily. As you probably already know from your own experience, the fundamental attribution error does not always occur. There are circumstances that increase or decrease the chances of making this mistake. For example, you are less likely to make the error if you become more aware of information external to another person that is relevant to explaining the causes for his or her behavior. However, even under these circumstances, the error does not disappear; it simply becomes weaker. Although the error is strong and occurs in many situations, it can be lessened when you have full information about a person's reason for doing something and are motivated to make a careful analysis.

The Actor–Observer Bias

Actors prefer external attributions for their own behavior, especially if the outcomes are bad, whereas observers tend to make internal attributions for the same behavior. The **actor–observer bias** is especially strong when we are trying to explain negative behaviors, whether our own or others'. This bias alerts us to the importance of perspective when considering attributional errors, because differing perspectives affect the varied constructions of reality that people produce.

actor–observer bias
An attribution bias showing that we prefer external attributions for our own behavior, especially if outcomes are negative, whereas observers tend to make internal attributions for the same behavior performed by others.

Figure 3.5

Self-test demonstrating the actor–observer bias.

From Fiske and Taylor (1984). Reprinted with permission.

First, rate a friend on the following characteristics using the scale that follows. Then go back and do the same for yourself.

Rating Scale

−2 Definitely does not describe
−1 Usually does not describe
 0 Sometimes describes, sometimes not
+1 Usually describes
+2 Definitely describes

	Friend	Self
Aggressive	_____	_____
Introverted	_____	_____
Thoughtful	_____	_____
Warm	_____	_____
Outgoing	_____	_____
Hard driving	_____	_____
Ambitious	_____	_____
Friendly	_____	_____
Total	_____	_____

Now, go back, ignore the pluses and minuses, and find the total of each column.

A simple experiment you can do yourself demonstrates the prevalence of the actor–observer bias (Fiske & Taylor, 1984). Using Figure 3.5, rate a friend on the adjectives listed and then rate yourself. Ignoring the plus and minus signs, go back and add up all the numbers in both columns. If you are like most people, you will have given your friend higher ratings than you gave yourself.

Why these results? It is likely that you see your friend's behavior as relatively consistent across situations, whereas you see your own behavior as more variable. You probably were more likely to choose the 0 category for yourself, showing that sometimes you see yourself as aggressive, thoughtful, or warm and other times not. It depends on the situation. We see other people's behavior as more stable and less dependent on situational factors.

The crucial role of perspective in social perception situations can be seen in a creative experiment in which the perspectives of both observer and actor were altered (Storms, 1973). Using videotape equipment, the researcher had the actor view his own behavior from the perspective of an observer. That is, he showed the actor a videotape of himself as seen by somebody else. He also had the observer take the actor's perspective by showing the observer a videotape of how the world looked from the point of view of the actor. That is, the observer saw a videotape of herself as seen by the actor, the person she was watching.

When both observers and actors took these new perspectives, their attributional analyses changed. Observers who took the visual perspective of the actor made fewer person attributions and more situational ones. They began to see the world as the actor saw it. When the actor took the perspective of the observer, he began to make fewer situational attributions and more personal ones. Both observers and actors got to see themselves as others see them—always an instructive, if precarious, exercise. In this case, it provided insight into the process of causal analysis.

The False Consensus Bias

When we analyze the behavior of others, we often find ourselves asking, What would I have done? This is our search for consensus information (What do other people do?) when we lack such information. In doing this, we often overestimate the frequency and popularity of our own views of the world (Ross, Greene, & House, 1977). The **false consensus bias** is simply the tendency to believe that everyone else shares our own feelings and behavior (Harvey & Weary, 1981). We tend to believe that others hold similar political opinions, find the same movies amusing, and think that baseball is the distinctive American game.

The false consensus bias may be an attempt to protect our self-esteem by assuming that our opinions are correct and are shared by most others (Zuckerman, Mann, & Bernieri, 1982). That is, the attribution that other people share our opinions serves as an affirmation and a confirmation of the correctness of our views. However, this overestimation of the trustworthiness of our own ideas can be a significant hindrance to rational thinking, and if people operate under the false assumption that their beliefs are widely held, the false consensus bias can serve as a justification for imposing one's beliefs on others (Fiske & Taylor, 1991).

false consensus bias
The tendency to believe that our own feelings and behavior are shared by everyone else.

CONSTRUCTING AN IMPRESSION OF OTHERS

After attributions are made, accurate or not, about the causes of other people's behavior we are still left with determining what processes perceivers use to get a whole picture of other individuals. We know that automatic processing of social information is widely used. We also know how people make attributions and what their biases are in making those attributions. Let's see how they might put all this social information together in a coherent picture.

The Significance of First Impressions

How many times have you met someone about whom you formed an immediate negative or positive impression? How did that first impression influence your subsequent interactions with that person? First impressions can be powerful influences on our perceptions of others. Researchers have consistently demonstrated **a primacy effect** in the impression-formation process, which is the tendency of early information to play a powerful role in our eventual impression of an individual.

Furthermore, first impressions can, in turn, bias the interpretation of later information. This was shown in a study in which individuals watched a person take an examination (Jones, Rock, Shaver, Goethals, & Ward, 1968). Some of the observers saw the test-taker do very well at the start and then get worse as the test continued. Other observers saw the test-taker do poorly at the beginning and then improve. Although both test-takers wound up with the same score, the test-taker who did well in the beginning was rated as more intelligent than the test-taker who did well at the end. In other words, the initial impression persisted even when later information began to contradict it.

This **belief perseverance,** the tendency for initial impressions to persist despite later conflicting information, accounts for much of the power of first impressions. A second reason that initial impressions wear well and long is

primacy effect
The observation that information encountered early in the impression formation process plays a powerful role in our eventual impression of an individual.

belief perseverance
The tendency for initial impressions to persist despite later conflicting information, accounting for much of the power of first impressions.

that people often reinterpret incoming information in light of the initial impression. We try to organize information about other people into a coherent picture, and later information that is inconsistent with the first impression is often reinterpreted to fit the initial belief about that person. If your first impression of a person is that he is friendly, you may dismiss a later encounter in which he is curt and abrupt, as an aberration—"He's just having a bad day." We can see that our person *schemas* are influenced by the primacy effect of the social information together.

Schemas

The aim of social perception is to gain enough information to make relatively accurate judgments about people and social situations. Next, we need ways of organizing the information we do have. Perceivers have strategies that help them know what to expect from others and how to respond. For example, when a father hears his infant daughter crying, he does not have to make elaborate inferences about what is wrong. He has in place an organized set of cognitions—related bits of information—about why babies cry and what to do about it. Psychologists call these sets of organized cognitions **schemas.** A schema concerning crying babies might include cognitions about dirty diapers, empty stomachs, pain, or anger.

schema
A set of organized cognitions that help us interpret, evaluate, and remember a wide range of social stimuli including events, persons, and ourselves.

ORIGINS OF SCHEMAS   Where do schemas come from? They develop from information about or experience with some social category or event. You can gain knowledge about sororities, for example, by hearing other people talk about them, by interacting with people who are in them, by reading about them, or by joining one. The more experience you have with sororities, the richer and more involved your schema will be. When we are initially organizing a schema, we place the most obvious features of an event or a category in memory first. If it is a schema about a person or a group of people, we begin with physical characteristics that we can see: gender, age, physical attractiveness, race or ethnicity, and so on.

We have different types of schemas for various social situations (Gilovich, 1991). We have self-schemas, which help us organize our knowledge about our own traits and personal qualities. Person schemes help us organize people's characteristics and store them in our memory. People often have a theory—known as an **implicit personality theory**—about what kinds of personality traits go together. *Intellectual,* for example, is often linked to *cold,* and *strong* and *adventurous* are often thought to go together (Higgins & Stangor, 1988). An implicit personality theory may help us make a quick impression of someone, but, of course, there is no guarantee that our initial impression will be correct.

implicit personality theory
A common person-schema belief that certain personality traits are linked together and may help us make a quick impression of someone, but there is no guarantee that initial impression will be correct.

THE RELATIONSHIP BETWEEN SCHEMAS AND BEHAVIOR
As happened with the crew of the Vincennes, schemas sometimes lead us to act in ways that serve to confirm them. In one study, for example, researchers convinced subjects that they were going to interact with someone who was hostile (Snyder & Swann, 1978). When the subjects did interact with that "hostile" person (who really had no hostile intentions) they behaved so aggressively that the other person was provoked to respond in a hostile way. Thus, the expectations of the subjects were confirmed, an outcome referred to as a **self-fulfilling prophecy** (Jussim, 1986; Rosenthal & Jacobson, 1968). The notion of self-fulfilling prophecies suggests that we often create our own

self-fulfilling prophecy
A tendency to expect ourselves to behave in ways that lead to confirmation of our original expectation.

realities through our expectations. If we are interacting with members of a group we believe to be hostile and dangerous, for example, our actions may provoke the very behavior we are trying to avoid.

This does not mean that we inhabit a make-believe world in which there is no reality to what we think and believe. It does mean, however, that our expectations can alter the nature of social reality. Consider the effect of a teacher's expectations on students. How important are these expectations in affecting how students perform? In one study, involving nearly 100 sixth-grade math teachers and 1,800 students, researchers found that about 20% of the results on the math tests were due to the teachers' expectations (Jussim & Eccles, 1992). Twenty percent is not inconsiderable: It can certainly make the difference between an A and a B or a passing and a failing grade. The researchers also found that teachers showed definite gender biases. They rated boys as having better math skills and girls as trying harder. Neither of these findings appeared to have been correct in this study, but it showed why girls got better grades in math. The teachers incorrectly thought that girls tried harder and, therefore, rewarded them with higher grades because of the girls presumed greater effort.

The other side of the self-fulfilling prophecy is **behavioral confirmation** (Snyder, 1992). This phenomenon occurs when perceivers behave as if their expectations are correct, and the targets then respond in ways that confirm the perceivers' beliefs. Although behavioral confirmation is similar to the self-fulfilling prophecy, there is a subtle distinction. When we talk about a self-fulfilling prophecy, we are focusing on the behavior of the perceiver in eliciting expected behavior from the target. When we talk about behavioral confirmation, we are looking at the role of the target's behavior in confirming the perceiver's beliefs. In behavioral confirmation, the social perceiver uses the target's behavior (which is partly shaped by the perceiver's expectations) as evidence that the expectations are correct. The notion of behavioral confirmation emphasizes that both perceivers and targets have goals in social interactions. Whether a target confirms a perceiver's expectations depends on what they both want from the interaction.

As an example, imagine that you start talking to a stranger at a party. Unbeknown to you, she has already sized you up and decided you are likely to be uninteresting. She keeps looking around the room as she talks to you, asks you few questions about yourself, and doesn't seem to hear some of the things you say. Soon you start to withdraw from the interaction, growing more and more aloof. As the conversation dies, she slips away, thinking, "What a bore!"

You turn and find another stranger smiling at you. She has decided you look very interesting. You strike up a conversation and find you have a lot in common. She is interested in what you say, looks at you when you're speaking, and laughs at your humorous comments. Soon you are talking in a relaxed, poised way, feeling and acting both confident and interesting. In each case, your behavior tends to confirm the perceiver's expectancies. Because someone shows interest in you, you become interesting. When someone thinks you are unattractive or uninteresting, you respond in kind, confirming the perceiver's expectations (Snyder, Tanke, & Berscheid, 1977).

As can be seen, whether the perceiver gets to confirm her preconceptions depends on what the target makes of the situation. To predict the likelihood of behavioral confirmation, we have to look at social interaction from the target's point of view. If the goal of the interaction from the target's

behavioral confirmation
A tendency for perceivers to behave as if their expectations are correct and the targets then to respond in ways that confirm the perceivers' beliefs.

viewpoint is simply to socialize with the other person, behavioral confirmation is likely. If the goal is more important—if the target needs to get to know the perceiver or if the perceiver's expectations threaten the target's self-concept—then behavioral disconfirmation is likely (Snyder, 1993). Note that the decision to confirm or disconfirm someone's expectations is by no means always a conscious one.

ASSIMILATING NEW INFORMATION INTO A SCHEMA
Schemas have some disadvantages, because people tend to accept information that fits their schemas and reject information that doesn't fit. This reduces uncertainty and ambiguity, but it also increases errors. Early in the formation of a schema of persons, groups, or events, we are more likely to pay attention to information that is inconsistent with our initial conceptions because we do not have much information (Bargh & Thein, 1985). Anything that doesn't fit the schema surprises us and makes us take notice. However, once the schema is well formed, we tend to remember information that is consistent with that schema. Remembering schema-consistent evidence is another example of the cognitive miser at work. Humans prefer the least effortful method of processing and assimilating information; it helps make a complex world simpler (Fiske, 1993).

If new information continually and strongly suggests that a schema is wrong, the perceiver will change it. Much of the time we are uncomfortable with schema-inconsistent information. Often we reinterpret the information to fit with our schema, but sometimes we change the schema because we see that it is wrong.

Stories

People often organize information in a form with which they feel most comfortable. There is evidence that people tend to integrate information by packaging their reasons for believing something in a form that is most persuasive and reasonable to both themselves and others. According to the *story model approach* to constructing social reality (Pennington & Hastie, 1986, 1988, 1992), we impose a structure on complex information by creating a coherent story and using it to connect facts and feelings about events.

A *story* is a schema that organizes information according to certain rules. That is, a story has a beginning, a middle, and an end. There are characters—good guys and bad guys—and, there are motives and reasons for behavior. All these aspects of the story motives, characters, and themes are woven together into a narrative. A story is an elaborate schema constructed to make sense of various, disjointed, or confusing pieces of information.

For example, imagine that you are a juror on a complex murder trial. Over the course of a week, many witnesses testify. Each witness provides evidence concerning various aspects of the crime. Some evidence makes you think that the defendant is guilty; other evidence makes you think he is innocent. How do you make sense out of such diverse information?

Studies show that in a complex murder case, jurors spontaneously devise a story narrative that helps them explain the evidence (Pennington & Hastie, 1986, 1988, 1992). They start to form a story fairly early and place this story in memory. It then guides the subsequent interpretation of the evidence. In other words, the juror actively searches for evidence that fits the preferred story. Evidence that fits the story is remembered and incorporated, and evidence that does not fit the story is forgotten (ForsterLee, Horowitz, &

Bourgeois, 1993). Where the story has gaps, the jurors fill them with their own interpretations and beliefs to make it more plausible.

People can, of course, consider more than one story that might fit the facts of any situation. We do more than simply identify and accept the most plausible story. Decision makers also, according to Keith Niedermeier and his colleagues, evaluate the relative plausibility of alternative stories. For example, in the O. J. Simpson trial, evidence was presented to the effect that the blood at the scene of the murders matched Mr. Simpsons' and the odds were that only one person in 170 million had the same genetic blueprint (Niedermeier, Kerr, & Messe, 1999). Despite the strength of that evidence, the jury did not convict. It appears that an alternative story or explanation, that the blood may have been planted by the police, was entertained by the jurors and found to be plausible. The jury was reluctant to convict because, apparently, they could easily picture a scenario in which police misconduct occurred. We see here a tendency for people to confirm the story or the bias that they favor. Indeed, this confirmation bias is one of the ways our construction of social information may go off track.

The Confirmation Bias

When we try to determine the cause or causes of an event, we usually have some hypothesis in mind. Say your college football team has not lived up to expectations, or you are asked to explain why American students lag behind others in standardized tests. When faced with these problems, we may begin by putting forth a tentative explanation. We may hypothesize that our football team has done poorly because the coach is incompetent. Or we may hypothesize that the cause of American students' poor performance is that they watch too much TV. How do we go about testing these hypotheses in everyday life?

When we make attributions about the causes of events, we routinely overestimate the strength of our hypothesis (Sanbonmatsu, Akimoto, & Biggs, 1993). We do this by the way we search for information concerning our hypothesis, typically tending to engage in a search strategy that confirms rather than disconfirms our hypothesis. This is known as the **confirmation bias**.

confirmation bias
A tendency to engage in a search strategy that confirms rather than disconfirms our hypothesis.

One researcher asked subjects to try to discover the rule used to present a series of three numbers, such as 2, 4, 6. The question was, What rule is the experimenter using? What is your hypothesis? Let's say the hypothesis is consecutive even numbers. Subjects could test their hypothesis about the rule by presenting a set of three numbers to see if it fit the rule. The experimenter would tell them if their set fit the rule, and then they would tell the experimenter what they hypothesized the rule was.

How would you test your hypothesis? Most individuals would present a set such as 8, 10, 12. Notice the set is aimed at confirming the hypothesis, not disconfirming it. The experimenter would say, yes, 8, 10, 12 fits the rule. What is the rule? You say, any three ascending even numbers. The experimenter says that is not the rule. What happened? You were certain you were right.

The rule could have been any three ascending numbers. If you had tried to disconfirm your hypothesis, you would have gained much more diagnostic information than simply trying to confirm it. If you said 1, 3, 4 and were told it fit the rule, you could throw out your hypothesis about even numbers.

We tend to generate narrow hypotheses that do not take into account a variety of alternative explanations.

In everyday life we tend to make attributions for causes that have importance for us. If you hate the football coach, you are more likely to find evidence for his incompetence than to note that injuries to various players affected the team's performance. Similarly, we may attribute the cause of American students' poor performance to be their TV-watching habits rather than search for evidence that parents do not motivate their children, or that academic performance is not valued among the students' peers. Of course, we should note there may be times that confirmation of your hypothesis is the perfectly rational thing to do. But, to do nothing but test confirmatory hypotheses leaves out evidence that you might very well need to determine the correct answer.

Shortcuts to Reality: Heuristics

heuristics
Handy rules of thumb that serve as shortcuts to organizing and perceiving social reality.

As cognitive misers, we have a grab bag of tools that help us organize our perceptions effortlessly. These shortcuts, handy rules of thumb that are part of our cognitive arsenal, are called **heuristics**. Like illusions, heuristics help us make sense of the social world, but also like illusions, they can lead us astray.

availability heuristic
A shortcut used to estimate the frequency or likelihood of an event based on how quickly examples of it come to mind.

THE AVAILABILITY HEURISTIC   If you are asked how many of your friends know people with AIDS, or have AIDS themselves, you quickly will think of those who do. The **availability heuristic** is defined as a shortcut used to estimate the frequency or likelihood of an event based on how quickly examples of it come to mind (Tversky & Kahneman, 1973). If AIDS is uncommon in your community, you will underestimate the overall incidence of AIDS; if you live in a community with many cases, you will overestimate its incidence.

As cognitive misers, we often default to rules of thumb known as heuristics. For example, many people are more afraid to fly than to drive a car. This is because when an airplane crashes, it is big news and such events can be more easily called to mind than a publicized car crash. This illustrates the availability heuristic.

Figure 3.6

Using the representativeness heuristic we will conclude that Steve is a lawyer if we are told that he is ambitious, argumentative, and very smart.

The availability heuristic tends to bias our interpretations, because the ease with which we can imagine an event affects our estimate of how frequently that event occurs. Television and newspapers, for example, tend to cover only the most visible, violent events. People, therefore, tend to overestimate incidents of violence and crime as well as the number of deaths from accidents and murder, because these events are most memorable (Kahneman, Slovic, & Tversky, 1982). As with all cognitive shortcuts, a biased judgment occurs, because the sample of people and events that we remember is unlikely to be fair and full. The crew and captain of the Vincennes undoubtedly had the recent example of the Stark in mind when they had to make a quick decision about the Iranian airbus.

THE REPRESENTATIVENESS HEURISTIC Sometimes we make judgments about the probability of an event or a person falling into a category based on how representative it or the person is of the category (Kahneman & Tversky, 1982). When we make such judgments, we are using the **representativeness heuristic**. This heuristic gives us something very much like a prototype (an image of the most typical member of a category).

To understand how this heuristic works, consider Steve, a person described to you as ambitious, argumentative, and very smart. Now, if you are told that Steve is either a lawyer or a dairy farmer, what would you guess his occupation to be (Figure 3.6)? Chances are, you would guess that he is a lawyer. Steve seems more representative of the lawyer category than of the dairy farmer category. Are there no ambitious and argumentative dairy farmers? Indeed there are, but a heuristic is a shortcut to a decision, a best guess.

Let's look at Steve again. Imagine now that Steve, still ambitious and argumentative, is 1 of 100 men; 70 of these men are dairy farmers, and 30 are lawyers. What would you guess his occupation to be under these conditions? The study that set up these problems and posed these questions found that most people still guess that Steve is a lawyer (Kahneman &

representativeness heuristic

A rule used to judge the probability of an event or a person falling into a category based on how representative it or the person is of the category.

Tversky, 1982). Despite the odds, they are misled by the powerful representativeness heuristic.

The subjects who made this mistake failed to use *base-rate data,* information about the population as opposed to information about just the individual. They knew that 70 of the 100 men in the group were farmers; therefore, there was a 7 out of 10 chance that Steve was a farmer, no matter what his personal characteristics. This tendency to underuse base-rate data and to rely on the special characteristics of the person or situation is known as the *base-rate fallacy.*

COUNTERFACTUAL THINKING   The tendency to run scenarios in our head—to create positive alternatives to what actually happened—is most likely to occur when we easily can imagine a different and more positive outcome. For example, let's say you leave your house a bit later than you had planned on your way to the airport and miss your plane. Does it make a difference whether you miss it by 5 minutes or 30 minutes? Yes, the 5-minute miss causes you more distress, because you can easily imagine how you could have made up those 5 minutes and now been on your way to Acapulco. Any event that has a negative outcome but allows for a different and easily imagined outcome is vulnerable to **counterfactual thinking,** an imagined scenario that runs opposite to what really happened.

counterfactual thinking

The tendency to create positive alternatives to a negative outcome that actually occurred, especially when we can easily imagine a more positive outcome.

As another example, imagine that you took a new route home from school one day because you were tired of the same old drive. As you drive this unfamiliar route, you are involved in an accident. It is likely that you will think, "If only I had stuck to my usual route, none of this would have happened!" You play out a positive alternative scenario (no accident) that contrasts with what occurred. The inclination of people to do these counterfactual mental simulations is widespread, particularly when dramatic events occur (Wells & Gavanski, 1989).

Generally, we are most likely to use and counterfactual thinking if we perceive events to be changeable (Miller, Turnbull, & McFarland, 1989; Roese & Olson, 1997). As a rule, we perceive dramatic or exceptional events (taking a new route home) as more mutable than unexceptional ones (taking your normal route). Various studies have found that it is the mutability of the event—the event that didn't have to be—that affects the perception of causality (Gavanski & Wells, 1989; Kahneman & Tversky, 1982). People's reactions to their own misfortunes and those of others may be determined, in great part, by the counterfactual alternatives evoked by those misfortunes (Roese & Olson, 1997).

Consider how tragic people perceived the fate of school teacher Christa McAuliffe to be. As a volunteer on the 1986 Challenger space shuttle flight, she was the only nonprofessional astronaut on board when the shuttle exploded and all seven crew members were killed. The public perceived her death in that context as more abnormal, more dramatic, and more mutable than the deaths of the six professional astronauts. We couldn't help but think she need not have been on that flight. We could easily imagine her in her normal routine, back in the classroom or at home. If only she hadn't been interested in going into space, if only she hadn't been selected from among the teachers who had applied, she would be alive today. It was less easy to imagine alternatives for the six others, because they were doing their appointed jobs. Just as we imagined alternative scenarios for McAuliffe, we can be sure that the crew of the Vincennes imagined endless what-if scenarios after the shooting of the Airbus.

HOW WE VIEW OUR SOCIAL WORLD: THINKING ABOUT THINKING

We seem to maintain an optimistic and confident view of our abilities to navigate our social world even though we seem to make a lot of errors. Perhaps this is because our **metacognition,** the way we think about thinking, is primarily optimistic. We know that in a wide variety of tasks, people believe they are above average, a logical impossibility because, except in Lake Wobegon, Garrison Keillor's mythical hometown, not everyone can be above average. So let's examine the possibility that the pursuit of happiness, or at least optimism and confidence, is a fundamental factor in the way we construct our social world.

metacognition
The way we think about thinking, which is primarily optimistic.

Janet Metcalfe (1998) examined the case for cognitive optimism and determined from her own research and that of others' that in most cognitive activities individuals express a consistent pattern of overconfidence. Metcalfe finds, among other results, that individuals think they can solve problems that they cannot; that they are very confident they can produce an answer when they are in fact about to make an error; that they think they know the answer to a question when in fact they do not; and they think the answer is on the "tip of their tongue" when there is no right or wrong answer.

In one of Metcalfe's studies, she gave subjects several different types of problems to solve. Some were easy, others required "insight," while a third group were anagrams. At certain points, a beep would sound and the problem-solvers would have to indicate how close they were to solving the problem on a "warmth" scale that ranged from "very cold" to "very warm." If you checked "very warm," it meant that you thought that you were very close to a solution. For example, here's one problem used in the research: "Suppose you are a museum curator, and a man comes in and offers you an ancient-looking bronze coin that is stamped 544 B.C. You have accepted objects from suspicious-looking people before but in this case you immediately call the police. Why?" (Metcalfe, 1998, p. 101). The answer, of course, is that the B.C. stamp is fraudulent. Interestingly, Metcalfe reports that in general the "warmth" ratings were low just before problem-solvers were about to give the right answer but high before they were about to give the wrong answer.

We know that optimism is sometimes extraordinarily helpful in human affairs. Laughter and a good mood appear to help hospitalized patients cope with their illnesses (Taylor & Gollwitzer, 1995). An optimistic coping style also appears to help individuals recover more rapidly and more effectively from coronary bypass surgery. Research demonstrates that optimistic bypass patients had fewer problems after surgery than pessimistic patients (Scheir et al., 1986). Following their surgery, the optimists reported more positive family, sexual, recreational, and health-related activities than pessimistic patients.

Many individuals react to threatening events by developing **positive illusions,** beliefs that include unrealistically optimistic notions about their ability to handle the threat and create a positive outcome (Taylor, 1989). These positive illusions are adaptive in the sense that ill people who are optimistic will be persistent and creative in their attempts to cope with the psychological and physical threat of disease. The tendency to display positive illusions has been shown in individuals who have tested positive for the HIV virus but have not yet displayed any symptoms (Taylor, Kemeny, Aspinwall, & Schneider, 1992). These individuals often expressed the belief that they had

positive illusions
Beliefs that include unrealistically optimistic notions about individuals' ability to handle a threat and create a positive outcome.

developed an immunity to the virus and that they could "flush" the virus from their systems. They acted on this belief by paying close attention to nutrition and physical fitness.

However, the cognitive optimism discussed by Metcalfe is different from that of AIDS or cancer patients. In these instances, optimism is both a coping strategy (I can get better, and to do so I must follow the medical advice given to me) and a self-protective or even self-deceptive shield. Metcalfe argued that the cognitive optimism seen in everyday life, however, is not self-deceptive but simply a faulty, over-optimistic methodology. The result of this optimistic bias in cognition is that people often quit on a problem because they think they will get the right answer or they convince themselves they have really learned new material when in fact they have not. Optimism may simply be the way we do our cognitive daily business.

Cognitive Optimism and Happiness

Diener and Diener (1996) found that about 85% of Americans rate their lives as above average in satisfaction. More than that, 86% of the population place themselves in the upper 35% of contentment with their lives (Lykken & Tellegren, 1996; Klar & Gilardi, 1999). It is clearly quite crowded in that upper 35%. Although 86% obviously cannot all be in the top 35%, Klar and Gilardi (1999) suggest that people feel this way because they have unequal access to other people's states of happiness compared to their own. Therefore, when a person says that he or she is really happy, it is difficult for him or her to anticipate that others may be quite so happy, and therefore, most (although certainly not all) people may conclude that they are well above average.

The pursuit of happiness, enshrined no less in the Declaration of Independence, is a powerful if occasionally elusive motive and goal. But what factors account for happiness? Can it be the usual suspects: money, sex, baseball? Edward Diener's long-time research concerning happiness suggests that subjective factors (feeling in control, feeling positive about oneself) are more important than objective factors such as wealth (Diener, Suh, Lucas, & Smith, 1999). Yes, wealth counts, but not as much as one would think. For example, one of Diener's studies showed that Americans earning millions of dollars are only slightly happier than those who are less fortunate. Perhaps part of the reason those with more are not significantly happier than those with less is that bigger and better "toys" simply satiate, they gratify no more, and so one needs more and more and better and better to achieve a positive experience (Lyubomirsky & Ross, 1999). One's first automobile, as an example, may bring greater gratification than the one we buy if and when money is no object.

Sonja Lyubormirsky and Lee Ross (1999) examined how happy and unhappy individuals dealt with situations in which they either obtained goals they wanted or were rejected or precluded from reaching those goals, such as admission to a particular college. In one study, these researchers examined how individuals dealt with either being accepted or rejected from colleges. Figure 3.7 shows what happened. Notice that happy participants (self-rated) show a significant increase in the desirability of their chosen college (the one that accepted them, and they in turn accepted) whereas unhappy (self-rated) participants show no difference after being accepted and, in fact, show a slight decrease in the desirability ratings of their chosen college. Furthermore, happy seniors sharply decreased the desirability of colleges that rejected them, whereas their unhappy counterparts did not.

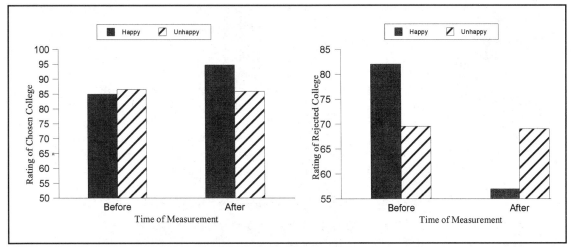

Figure 3.7   *Student ratings of their chosen school to which they were rejected and from which they were rejected before and after acceptance or rejection.*

Adapted from Lyubormirsky and Ross (1999). Reprinted with permission.

These results, according to Lyubomirsky and Ross (1999), illustrate the way happy and unhappy individuals respond to the consequences of choices that they made and were made for them (being accepted or rejected). Happy seniors seemed to make the best of the world: If they were accepted to a college, well then, that was the best place for them. If they were rejected, then maybe it wasn't such a good choice after all. Unhappy people seem to live in a world of unappealing choices, and perhaps it seems to them that it matters not which alternative they pick or is chosen for them. It also appears that if unhappy people are distracted or stopped from ruminating—from focusing on the dark state of their world—they tend to respond like happy people: Obtained goals are given high ratings, unobtainable options are downgraded.

The Incompetent, the Inept: Are They Happy?

Justin Kruger and David Dunning (1999) found in a series of studies that incompetent people are at times supremely confident in their abilities, perhaps even more so that competent individuals. It seems that the skills you need to behave competently are the same skills you need to recognize competence. That is, the incompetent do not have the ability to recognize that they are incompetent. If they could recognize incompetence, they would be competent. Life is indeed unfair. For example, students who scored lowest in a test of logic were most likely to wildly overestimate how well they did. For example, those scoring in the lowest 12% of the test-takers estimated that they scored in the low 60s percentiles. In tests of grammar and humor, the less competent individuals again overestimated their performance.

The less competent test-takers, when given the opportunity to compare their performance with high performing individuals, did not recognize competence: That is, the inept thought that their own performance measured up. The competent subjects, in contrast, when confronted with better performances, revised estimates of their own work in light of what they accurately saw as really competent performances by others.

These results, although intriguing, may be limited by a couple of factors. It may be that the nature of the tasks (which involved logic, grammar, humor) was rather vague, so it may not have been intuitively clear to everyone what was being tested. Also, when you ask people to compare themselves to "average" others, they may have varying notions of what average is. In any event, we see an example of the false consensus effect here: Other people must be performing about as well as I am, so the 60% level (a bit better than average; remember Lake Woebegone) is okay. Alternately, if you go bowling and throw 20 straight gutter balls, the evidence is undeniable that you are inept.

The Effects of Distressing and Joyful Events on Future Happiness

Lou Gehrig, the great Yankee first baseman afflicted with Amyotropic Lateral Sclerosis (ALS; also known as Lou Gehrig's disease), told a full house at Yankee Stadium in July of 1939 that still and all, he considered himself the luckiest man on the face of the earth. Gehrig spoke bravely and movingly, but surely he must have thought his luck had turned bad.

Perhaps not, according to recent research by Daniel Gilbert and his associates. Gilbert suggested that there is a "psychological immune" system, much like its physiological counterpart, which protects us from the ravages of bacterial and viral invasions. The psychological immune system fights off doom and gloom, often under the most adverse circumstances (Gilbert, Pinel, Wilson, Blumberg, & Wheatley 1998).

Gilbert and his colleagues suggested that the psychological immune system works best when it is unattended, for when we become aware of its functioning, it may cease to work. Gilbert notes that we may convince ourselves that we never really cared for our ex-spouse, but that protective cover won't last long if someone reminds us of the 47 love sonnets that we forgot we wrote. In an initial series of studies, Gilbert and collegues asked their participants to predict their emotional reactions to both good and bad events. First, the subjects reported on their own happiness. All individuals were asked if they were involved in a romantic relationship and whether they had experienced a breakup of a relationship. Those in a relationship who had not experienced a breakup ("luckies") were asked to predict how happy they would be 2 months after a breakup. Those who had been in a romantic relationship but were no longer ("leftovers") were asked to report how happy they were. Others not in a relationship ("loners") were asked to predict how happy they would be 6 months after becoming involved romantically.

First, we find that being in a romantic relationship means greater happiness than not being in one. Loners thought that 6 months after being in a relationship they would be as happy as people in a romantic relationship. So loners were accurate in their predictions, because people in relationships report as much happiness as loners predicted they would experience if they were in a 6-month relationship. But, most interestingly, luckies were no happier than were leftovers. Luckies thought that if their relationship broke up they would be very unhappy. But, those who experienced a breakup, the archly named leftovers, were in fact pretty happy, so, the luckies were wrong.

The college students in the first study made grave predictions about the state of their happiness after the end of a romantic involvement. Gilbert and colleagues found that professors denied tenure and voters whose candidate lost an important election all overestimated the depth of their future unhappiness because of the negative outcome and, in fact, about 3 months later all were much at the same state of happiness that existed before the negative event. Indeed, Gilbert's research suggest that even more harmful events yield the same result. People overestimate how durable their negative reaction will be (the "durability bias") and don't take into account that the psychological immune system tends to regulate our emotional state. Rather, they may explain their ability to bounce back afterward by saying something like, "I can deal with things better than I thought," to explain why they mispredicted their long-range emotional reactions. It appears that most of us can rely on this immune system to maintain a degree of stability in the face of life's ups and downs. Much research remains to be done, but it may be that there are significant individual differences in the workings of the psychological immune system, and that may account for different perceptions of happiness among individuals.

Bottom Line

Much of what we discussed in this chapter suggests that we, as social perceivers, make predictable errors. Also, much of what we do is automatic, not under conscious control. The bottom line is that we are cognitive tacticians who expend energy to be accurate when it is necessary but otherwise accept a rough approximation. Accuracy in perception is the highest value, but it is not the only value; efficiency and conservation of cognitive energy also are important. And so, we are willing to make certain trade-offs when a situation does not demand total accuracy. The more efficient any system is, the more its activities are carried out automatically. But when we are motivated, when an event or interaction is really important, we tend to switch out of this automatic, nonconscious mode and try to make accurate judgments. Given the vast amount of social information we deal with, most of us are pretty good at navigating our way.

THE VINCENNES REVISITED

The events that resulted in the firing of a missile that destroyed a civilian aircraft by the U.S.S. Vincennes are clear in hindsight. The crew of the Vincennes constructed their own view of reality, based on their previous experiences, their expectations of what was likely to occur, and their interpretations of what was happening at the moment, as well as their fears and anxieties. All of these factors were in turn influenced by the context of current international events, which included a bitter enmity between the United States and what was perceived by Americans as an extremist Iranian government. The Vincennes had reason to expect an attack from some quarter and that is the way they interpreted the flight path of the aircraft. This is true despite that fact that later analysis showed that the aircraft had to be a civilian airliner. The event clearly shows the crucial influence of our expectations and previous experience on our perception of new events.

CHAPTER REVIEW

1. What is impression formation?

Impression formation is the process by which we form judgments about others. Biological and cultural forces prime us to form impressions, which may have adaptive significance for humans.

2. What are automatic and controlled processing?

Much of our social perception involves **automatic processing or** forming impressions without much thought or attention. Thinking that is conscious and requires effort is referred to as **controlled processing**. If, however, we have important goals that need to be obtained, then we will switch to more controlled processing and allocate more energy to understanding social information. Automatic and controlled processing are not separate categories but rather form a continuum, ranging from complete automaticity to full allocation of our psychic energy to understand and control the situation.

3. What is meant by a cognitive miser?

The notion of **cognitive miser** suggests that humans process social information by whatever method leads to the least expenditure of cognitive energy. Much of our time is spent in the cognitive miser mode. Unless motivated to do otherwise, we use just enough effort to get the job done.

4. Why is automatic processing so important in social perception, behavior, and emotion?

It makes sense both biologically and psychologically that most of our social perception is accomplished effortlessly, given the vast amount of information that we may have to confront. We tend to be cognitive misers in the construction of social reality: Not only is much of social perception carried out without conscious awareness but also research indicates that the same is true of behavior and of emotional states. We may act without knowing why we do so, because we have been primed by stimuli that have not been consciously perceived.

5. Are our impressions of others accurate?

There are significant differences among social perceivers in their ability to accurately evaluate other people. Those who are comfortable with their own emotions are best able to express those emotions and to read other people. Individuals who are unsure of their own emotions, who try to hide their feelings from others, are not very good at reading the emotions of other people.

6. What factors affect the confidence we have in our impressions?

Despite distinct differences in abilities to read others, most of us are apparently confident in out ability to accurately do so. This is especially true if we have a fair amount of information about that person. However, research shows that no matter the information at our disposal, our accuracy levels are less then we think. In part, this appears to be true because we pay attention to obvious cues but do not attend to more subtle nonverbal ones. We are especially incompetent at determining if someone is lying, even someone very close to us.

7. What is the attribution process?

The **attribution** process involves assigning causes for the behavior we observe, both our own and that of others. Several theories have been devised to uncover how perceivers decide the causes of other people's behaviors. The correspondent inference and the covariation models were the most general attempts to describe the attribution process.

8. **What are internal and external attribution?**

When we make an **internal attribution** about an individual, we assign the cause for behavior to an internal source. For example, one might attribute failure on an exam to a person's intelligence or level of motivation. **External attribution** explains the cause for behavior as an external factor. For example, failure on an exam may be attributed to the fact that a student's parents were killed in an automobile accident a few days before the exam.

9. **What is correspondent inference theory, and what factors enter into forming a correspondent inference?**

Correspondent inference theory helps explain the attribution process when perceivers are faced with unclear information. We make a **correspondent inference** if we determine that an individual entered into a behavior freely (vs. being coerced) and conclude that the person intended the behavior. In this case, we make an internal attribution. Research shows that the perceiver acting as a cognitive miser has a strong tendency to make a correspondent inference—to assign the cause of behavior to the actor and downplay the situation—when the evidence suggest otherwise.

10. **What are covariation theory and the covariation principle?**

The **covariation principle** states that people decide that the most likely cause of any behavior is the factor that covaries, or occurs at the same time, most often with the appearance of that behavior. Covariation theory suggests that people rely on consensus (What is everyone else doing?); consistency (Does this person behave this way all the time?); and distinctiveness (Does this person display the behavior in all situations or just one?) information.

11. **How do consensus, consistency, and distinctiveness information lead to an internal or external attribution?**

When consensus (Everyone acts this way.); consistency (The target person always acts this way.); and distinctiveness (The target person only acts this way in a particular situation.) are high, we make an external attribution. However, if consensus is low (Nobody else behaves this way.); consistency is high (The target person almost always behaves this way.); and distinctiveness is low (The target person behaves this way in many situations.), we make an internal attribution.

12. **What is the dual process model of attribution, and what does it tell us about the attribution process?**

Trope's two-stage model recognized that the initial stage of assigning causality is an automatic categorization of behavior; a second stage may lead to a readjustment of that initial categorization, especially when the behavior or the situation is ambiguous. Trope's model led theorists to think about how and when people readjust their initial inferences.

13. **What is meant by attribution biases?**

Both the correspondent inference and covariation models emphasized that people often depart from the (causal) analysis of the attribution models they present and make some predictable errors in their casual analyses.

14. **What is the fundamental attribution error?**

The **fundamental attribution error** highlights the fact that people prefer internal to external attributions of behavior. The fundamental attribution error may be part of a general tendency to confirm what we believe is true and to avoid information that disconfirms our hypotheses. This is known as the confirmation bias.

15. **What is the sinister attribution error, and when is it made?**

The **sinister attribution error** is the tendency for certain people to overattribute lack of trustworthiness to others. In other words, it is an assumption that other people are generally untrustworthy. This sinister attribution bias is part of paranoid social cognition.

16. What is the actor–observer bias?

The **actor–observer bias** occurs when observers emphasize internal attributions whereas actors favor external attributions. That is, when we observe someone else, we make the familiar internal attribution, but when we ourselves act, we most often believe that our behavior was caused by the situation in which we acted. This seems to occur because of a perspective difference. When we observe other people, what is most obvious is what they do. But when we try to decide why we did something, what is most obvious are extrinsic factors, the situation.

17. What is the false consensus?

The **false consensus bias** occurs when people tend to believe that others think and feel the same way they do.

18. What is the importance of first impressions?

First impressions can be powerful influences on our perceptions of others. Researchers have consistently demonstrated a **primary effect** in the impression-formation process, which is the tendency of early information to play a powerful role in our eventual impression of an individual. Furthermore, first impressions, in turn, can bias the interpretation of later information.

19. What are schemas, and what role do they play in social cognition?

The aim of social perception is to gain enough information to make relatively accurate judgments about people and social situations. One major way we organize this information is by developing **schemas,** sets of organized cognitions about individuals or events. One type of schema important for social perception is **implicit personality theories,** schemas about what kinds of personality traits go together. *Intellectual,* for example, is often linked to *cold,* and *strong* and *adventurous* are often thought to go together.

20. What is the self-fulfilling prophecy, and how does it relate to behavior?

Schemas also influence behavior, as is illustrated by the notion of **self-fulfilling prophecies**. This suggests that we often create our own realities through our expectations. If we are interacting with members of a group we believe to be hostile and dangerous, for example, our actions may provoke the very behavior we are trying to avoid, which is the process of behavioral confirmation. The other side of the self-fulfilling prophecy is behavioral confirmation. This occurs when perceivers behave as if their expectations are correct and the targets of those perceptions respond in ways that confirm the perceivers' beliefs.

When we make attributions about the causes of events, we routinely overestimate the strength of our hypothesis concerning why events happened the way they did. This bias in favor of our interpretations of the causes of behavior occurs because we tend to engage in a search strategy that confirms our hypothesis rather than disconfirms it. This is known as the confirmation bias.

21. What roles do stories play in social cognition?

Individuals tend to integrate information by "packaging" their reasons for believing something in a form that is most persuasive and reasonable both to themselves and others. According to the story model approach to constructing social reality, we impose a structure on complex information that takes the form of a coherent story and use it to connect facts and feelings about events.

22. What are the various types of heuristics that often guide social cognition?

A **heuristic** is a shortcut, or a rule of thumb that we use when constructing social reality. The **availability heuristic** is defined as a shortcut used to estimate the likelihood or frequency of an event based on how quickly examples of it come to mind.

The **representativeness heuristic** involves making judgments about the probability of an event or of a person's falling into a category based on how representative it or the person is of the category. The simulation heuristic is a tendency to play out alternative scenarios in our heads. **Counterfactual thinking** involves taking a negative event or outcome and running scenarios in our head to create positive alternatives to what actually happened.

23. What is meant by metacognition?

Metacognition is the way we think about thinking, which can be primarily optimistic or pessimistic.

24. How do optimism and pessimism relate to social cognition and behavior?

We tend to maintain an optimistic and confident view of our abilities to navigate our social world even though we seem to make a lot of errors. Many individuals react to threatening events by developing **positive illusions,** beliefs that include unrealistically optimistic notions about their ability to handle the threat and create a positive outcome. These positive illusions are adaptive in the sense that people who are optimistic will be persistent and creative in their attempt to handle threat or illness. Most people think they are very happy with their lives, certainly happier than others. Happy and unhappy individuals respond differently to both positive and negative events. For example, happy individuals accepted by a college believe that it is the best place for them. If they are rejected, they think maybe it wasn't such a good choice after all. Unhappy people seem to live in a world of unappealing choices, and perhaps it seems to them that it doesn't matter which alternative they pick or is chosen for them. It seems that incompetents maintain happiness and optimism in part because they are not able to recognize themselves as incompetent.

25. How do distressing events affect happiness?

Research also suggests that we may have a psychological immune system that regulates our reactions and emotions in response to negative life events. Social psychological experiments suggest that this psychological immune system—much like its physiological counterpart that protects us from the ravages of bacterial and vial invasions—fights off doom and gloom, often under the most adverse circumstances. So the effects of negative events wear after a time no matter how long people think the effects will last.

INTERNET ACTIVITY

WHAT IS YOUR LOCUS OF CONTROL?

In chapter 3, attribution theory was discussed. Recall that one can make an internal or external attribution about behavior (our own and others). Certain individuals are more predisposed than others to make either internal or external attributions. This is known as *locus of control.* An individual with an internal locus of control tends to attribute behavior internally, whereas an individual with an external locus of control tends to attribute behavior externally. You can determine where you are in this dimension by taking an on-line locus of control test. One test can be found at http://www.queendom.com/tests/lc.html. You can find this test or others by entering the search term "attribution style" into a search engine.

Once you have found a locus of control site, take the test and obtain your results. Then answer the following questions:

1. Where did you score on the main locus of control dimension?

2. Do you think that the test gave an accurate picture of your locus of control?

3. Where did you score on subscales (e.g., attributions about success or failure)?
4. Did the Web site give any advice about your attribution style? If so, what was it?
5. How useful do you think the advice given is?

SUGGESTIONS FOR FURTHER READING

Gilovich, T. (1991). *How we know what isn't so: The fallibility of human reason in everyday life.* New York: Free Press.

This is a well-written overview of the flaws all social perceivers exhibit. Interesting and insightful analysis by one of the leading thinkers in the area.

Rachlin, T. (1994). *Behavior and the mind.* Oxford University Press.

An expert in the field shows how mental mechanisms relate to human behavior.

Bargh, J. A., & Chartrand, T. L. (1999). The unbearable automaticity of being. *American Psychologist, 54,* 462–479.

This is a concise summary of well-constructed, interesting research on automaticity in everyday life.

Gilbert, D. T., Pinel, E. C., Wilson, T. D., Blumberg, S. J., & Wheatley, T. P. (1998). Immune neglect: A source of durability bias in affective forecasting. *Journal of Personality and Social Psychology, 75,* 617–638.

This is a well-written series of studies on how and why we overestimate the degree of unhappiness that would be produced by negative life events. An exploration of the psychological immune system. This interesting study, one in a series, shows how perverse our cognitive processes can be.

Kunda, Z. (1999). *Social cognition.* MIT Press: Cambridge, MA.

This book is an excellent up-to-date and accessible overview of the field of social cognition by a leading researcher.

CHAPTER 4

PREJUDICE AND DISCRIMINATION

The seeds for conflict and prejudice were planted somewhere in the hills of Palmyra, New York, in 1830. There a young man named Joseph Smith, Jr., received a vision from the angel Moroni. Centuries before, Moroni as a priest of the Nephites wrote the history of his religion on a set of golden plates and buried them in the hills of Palmyra. When Moroni appeared to Smith he revealed the location of the plates and gave him the ability to transcribe the ancient writings into English. This translated text became the *Book of Mormon*, the cornerstone of the Mormon religion. The *Book of Mormon* contained many discrepancies from the Bible. For example, it suggested that God and Jesus Christ were made of flesh and bone.

The conflicts between this newly emerging religion and established Christianity inevitably led to hostile feelings and attitudes between the two groups. Almost from the moment of Joseph Smith's revelations, the persecution of the Mormons began. Leaving Palmyra, the Mormons established a

settlement in Kirtland, Ohio, in 1831, but it was a disaster. The Mormons didn't fit in well with the existing community. For example, the Mormons supported the Democratic Party, whereas most of the Christian population in Kirtland supported the Whigs. Mormonism also was a threat to the colonial idea of a single religion in a community. At a time when heresy was a serious crime, the Mormons were seen as outcast heretics. As a result, the Mormons were the targets of scathing newspaper articles that grossly distorted their religion. Mormons were socially ostracized, denied jobs, the targets of economic boycotts, and under constant threat of attack.

Because of the hostile environment in Kirtland, the Mormons moved on, splitting into two groups. One group began a settlement in Nauvoo, Illinois, and the other in Independence, Missouri. In neither place did the Mormons find peace. Near Nauvoo, for example, a Mormon settlement was burned to the ground and its inhabitants forced to take cover in a rain-soaked woods until they could make it to Nauvoo. At the Independence settlement in 1833, Mormon Bishop Edward Partridge was tarred and feathered after refusing to close a store and print shop he supervised. The tensions in Missouri grew so bad that then Governor Lilburn W. Boggs issued the following order: "The Mormons must be treated as enemies and must be exterminated or driven from the State if necessary, for the public peace" (Arrington & Bitton, 1979).

As a result of the prejudice experienced by the Mormons, they became more clannish, trading among themselves and generally keeping to themselves. As you might imagine, this further enraged the Christian community that hoped to benefit economically from the Mormon presence. It was not uncommon for Mormons to become the targets of vicious physical attacks or even to be driven out of a territory. There was even talk of establishing an independent Mormon state, but eventually, the Mormons settled in Utah.

The fate of the Mormons during the 1800s eerily foreshadowed the treatment of other groups later in history (e.g., Armenians in Turkey, Jews in Europe, Ethnic Albanians in Yugoslavia). How could the Mormons have been treated so badly in a country with a constitution guaranteeing freedom of religion and founded on the premise of religious tolerance?

Attitudes provide us with a way of organizing information about attitude objects and a way to attach an affective response to that object (e.g., like or dislike). Under the right circumstances, attitudes predict one's behavior. In this chapter, we explore a special type of attitude directed at groups of people: prejudice. We look for the underlying causes of incidents such as the Mormon experience and the other acts of prejudice outlined. We ask, How do prejudiced individuals arrive at their views? Is it something about their personalities that leads them to prejudice-based acts? Or do the causes lie more in the social situations? What cognitive processes cause them to have negative attitudes toward those they perceive to be different from themselves? How pervasive and unalterable are those processes in human beings? What are the effects of being a target of prejudice and discrimination? What can we do to reduce prejudice and bring our society closer to its ideals?

First, we define just what social psychologists mean when they use the term *prejudice,* and the related concepts *stereotype* and *discrimination.*

KEY QUESTIONS

AS YOU READ THIS CHAPTER, FIND THE ANSWERS TO THE FOLLOWING QUESTIONS:

1. *How are prejudice, stereotypes, and discrimination defined?*
2. *What is the relationship among prejudice, stereotypes, and discrimination?*
3. *What evidence is there for the prevalence of these three concepts from a historical perspective?*
4. *What are the personality roots of prejudice?*
5. *How does gender relate to prejudice?*
6. *What are the social roots of prejudice?*
7. *What is modern racism, and what are the criticisms of it?*
8. *What are the cognitive roots of prejudice?*
9. *How do cognitive biases contribute to prejudice?*
10. *Are stereotypes ever accurate, and can they be overcome?*
11. *What are implicit and explicit stereotypes?*

12. How do prejudiced and nonprejudiced individuals differ?
13. What is the impact of prejudice on those who are its target?
14. How can a person who is the target of prejudice cope with being a target?
15. What can be done about prejudice?

THE DYNAMICS OF PREJUDICE, STEREOTYPES, AND DISCRIMINATION

When we consider prejudice we really must consider two other interrelated concepts: stereotyping and discrimination. Taken together these three make up a triad of processes that contribute to negative attitudes, emotions, and behaviors directed at members of certain social groups. First, we define just what social psychologists mean by the term prejudice and the related concepts, stereotype, and discrimination.

Prejudice and Stereotypes

prejudice
A biased attitude, positive or negative, based on insufficient information and directed at a group, which leads to prejudgment of members of that group.

The term **prejudice** refers to a biased, often negative, attitude toward a group of people. Prejudicial attitudes include belief structures, containing information about a group of people as well as a set of expectations concerning their behavior. When prejudice is directed toward a group, it leads to prejudgment of the individual members of that group.

Of course, prejudice can be either positive or negative. Fans of a particular sports team, for example, are typically prejudiced in favor of their team. They often believe calls made against their team are unfair, even when the referees are being impartial. Social psychologists, however, have been more interested in prejudice that involves a negative bias, that is, in cases in which one group assumes the worst about another group and may base negative behaviors on these assumptions. It is this latter form of prejudice that is the subject of this chapter.

Prejudice comes in a variety of forms, the most visible of which are racism and sexism. *Racism* is the negative evaluation of others primarily because of their skin color. It includes the belief that one racial group is inherently superior to another. *Sexism* is the negative evaluation of others because of their gender (Lips, 1993). Of course other forms of prejudice exist, such as religious and ethnic prejudice and heterosexism (negative attitudes toward

As these desecrated Jewish graves show, prejudice is often a negative or hostile attitude based on insufficient evidence that is directed at a particular person or group.

gay men and lesbians), but racism and sexism are the two most widespread prejudices within U.S. society.

An important note should be added here about the concept of race. Throughout U.S. history, racial categories have been used to distinguish groups of human beings from one another. However, biologically speaking, race is an elusive and problematic concept. A person's race is not something inherited as a package from his or her parents; nor are biological characteristics such as skin color, hair texture, eye shape, facial features, and so on valid indicators of one's ethnic or cultural background. Consider, for example, an individual whose mother is Japanese and father is African American, or a blond, blue-eyed person who is listed by the U.S. Census Bureau as Native American, because her maternal grandmother was Cherokee. To attempt to define these individuals by race is inaccurate and inappropriate. Although many scientists maintain that race does not exist as a biological concept, it does exist as a social construct.

People perceive and categorize others as members of racial groups and often act toward them according to cultural prejudices. In this social sense, race and racism are very real and important factors in human relations. When we refer to race in this book, such as when we discuss race-related violence, it is this socially constructed concept, with its historical, societal, and cultural significance, that we mean.

Stereotypes

Prejudicial attitudes do not stem from perceived physical differences among people, such as skin color or gender. Rather, prejudice relates more directly to the characteristics we assume members of a different racial, ethnic, or other group have. In other words, it relates to the way we think about others.

People have a strong tendency to categorize objects based on perceptual features or uses. We categorize chairs, tables, desks, and lamps as *furniture*. We categorize love, hate, fear, and jealousy as *emotions*. And we categorize people on the basis of their race, gender, nationality, and other obvious features. Of course, categorization is adaptive in the sense that it allows us to direct similar behaviors toward an entire class of objects or people. We do not have to choose a new response each time we encounter a categorized object.

Categorization is not necessarily the same as prejudice, although the first process powerfully influences the second. We sometimes take our predisposition to categorize too far, developing rigid and overgeneralized images of groups. This rigid categorization—this rigid set of positive or negative beliefs about the characteristics or attributes of a group—is a **stereotype** (Judd & Park, 1993; Stangor & Lange, 1994). For example, we may believe that all lawyers are smart, a positive stereotype, or we may believe that all lawyers are devious, a negative stereotype. Many years ago, the political journalist Walter Lippmann (1922) aptly called stereotypes "pictures in our heads." When we encounter someone new who has a clear membership in one or another group, we reach back into our memory banks of stereotypes, find the appropriate picture, and fit the person to it.

In general, stereotyping is simply part of the way we do business cognitively every day. It is part of our cognitive "toolbox" (Gilbert & Hixon, 1991). We all have made judgments about individuals (Boy Scout leader, police officer, college student, feminist) based solely on their group membership. Stereotyping is a time saver; we look in our toolbox, find the appropriate utensil,

stereotype
A rigid set of beliefs, positive or negative, about the characteristics or attributes of a group, resulting in rigid overgeneralized images of members of that group.

and characterize the *college student*. It certainly takes less time and energy than trying to get to know that person (individuation; Macrae, Milne, & Bodenhausen, 1994). Again, this is an example of the cognitive miser at work. Of course, this means we will make some very unfair, even destructive judgments of individuals. All of us recoil at the idea that we are being judged solely on the basis of some notion that the evaluator has of group membership.

Stereotypes, like prejudicial attitudes, exist on the explicit and implicit level. *Explicit stereotypes* are those of which we are consciously aware, and they are under the influence of controlled processing. *Implicit stereotypes* operate on an unconscious level and are activated automatically when a member of a minority group is encountered in the right situation. The operation of implicit stereotypes was demonstrated in an interesting experiment conducted by Banaji, Harden, and Rothman (1993). Participants first performed a "priming task," which involved unscrambling sentences indicating either a male stereotype (aggressiveness), a female stereotype (dependence), or unscrambled neutral sentences (neutral prime). Later, in a supposedly unrelated experiment, participants read a story depicting either a dependent (male or female) or an aggressive (male or female). Participants then rated the target person in the story for the stereotypic or nonstereotypic trait.

The results of this experiment are shown in Figure 4.1. Notice that for both the male and female stereotypic traits, the trait was rated the same when the prime was neutral, regardless of the gender of the target. However, when the prime activated an implicit gender stereotype, the female stereotypic trait (dependence) was rated higher for female targets than for male targets. The opposite was true for the male stereotypic trait (aggressiveness). Here, aggressiveness was rated higher for male targets than for female targets. An incidental encounter with a stereotype (in this experiment, the prime) can affect evaluations of an individual who is a member of a given social category

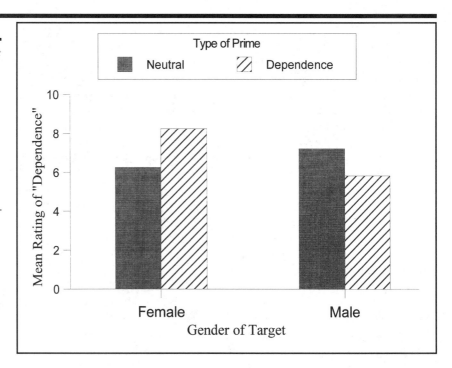

Figure 4.1

Results from an experiment on implicit stereotypes. When a prime activates an implicit female gender stereotype, a female stereotypic trait (dependence) was rated higher for female than for male targets. The opposite was true for the implicit male stereotypic trait (aggressiveness).

Based on data from Banaji, Harden, and Rothman (1993).

(e.g., male or female). Participants judged a stereotypic trait more extremely when the stereotype had been activated with a prime than when it had not. Thus, stereotyped information can influence how we judge members of a social group even if we are not consciously aware that it is happening (Banaji, et al., 1993).

Explicit and implicit stereotypes operate on two separate levels (controlled processing or automatic processing) and affect judgments differently depending on the type of judgment a person is required to make (Dovidio, Kawakami, Johnson, Johnson, & Howard, 1997). Dovidio and colleagues found that when a judgmental task required some cognitive effort (in this experiment, to determine whether a black defendant was guilty or not guilty of a crime), explicit racial attitudes correlated with judgments. However, implicit racial attitudes were not correlated with the outcome on the guilt–judgment task. Conversely, on a task requiring a more spontaneous, automatic response (in this experiment, a word completion task on which an ambiguous incomplete word could be completed in a couple of ways; e.g., b_d could be completed as *bad* or *bed*), implicit attitudes correlated highly with outcome judgments. Thus, explicit and implicit racial attitudes relate to different tasks. Explicit attitudes related more closely to the guilt–innocence task, which required controlled processing. Implicit attitudes related more closely to the word completion task which was mediated by automatic processing.

Another way that implicit stereotypes manifest themselves is by acting as *judgmental heuristics* (Bodenhausen & Wyer, 1985). For example, if a person commits a crime that is stereotype consistent (compared to one that is not stereotype consistent), observers assign a higher penalty, recall fewer facts about the case, and use stereotype-based information to make a judgment (Bodenhausen & Wyer, 1985). Generally, when a negative behavior is stereotype consistent, observers attribute the negative behavior to internal, stable characteristics. Consequently, the crime or behavior is seen as an enduring character flaw likely to lead to the behavior again.

This effect of using stereotype-consistent information to make judgments is especially likely to occur when we are faced with a difficult cognitive task. Recall from chapter 3 that many of us are cognitive misers, and we look for the path of least resistance when using information to make a decision. When faced with a situation in which we have both stereotype-consistent and stereotype-inconsistent information about a person, we are likely to recall stereotype-inconsistent information best under conditions of low cognitive load. Under conditions of high cognitive load, conversely, more stereotype-consistent than inconsistent information is likely to be recalled (Macrae, Hewstone, & Griffiths, 1993). As Macrae and colleagues suggested, "when the information-processing gets tough, stereotypes (as heuristic structures) get going" (p. 79).

There are also individual differences in the extent to which stereotypes are formed and used. Sheri Levy, Steven Stroessner, and Carol Dweck (1998) suggested that individuals use implicit theories to make judgments about others. That is, individuals use their past experience to form a theory about what members of other groups are like. According to Levy and colleagues, there are two types of implicit theories: *entity theories* and *incremental theories*. Entity theorists adhere to the idea that another person's traits are fixed and will not vary according to the situation. Incremental theorists do not see traits as fixed. Rather, they see them as having the ability to change over time and situations (Levy et al., 1998). A central question addressed by Levy and colleagues was whether entity and incremental theorists would differ in their predisposition to form and use stereotypes. Based on the results of five experiments, Levy and colleagues concluded that compared to incremental theorists, entity theorists:

- Were more likely to use stereotypes.
- Were more likely to agree strongly with stereotypes.
- Were more likely to see stereotypes as representing inborn, inherent group differences.
- Tended to make more extreme judgments based on little information about the characteristics of members of a stereotyped group.
- Perceived a stereotyped group as having less intramember diversity.
- Were more likely to form stereotypes.

In addition to the cognitive functions of stereotypes, there is also an emotional component (Jussim, Nelson, Manis, & Soffin, 1995). According to Jussim and colleagues, once you stereotype a person, you attach a label to that person that is used to evaluate and judge members of that person's group. Typically, a label attached to a stereotyped group is negative. This negative label generates negative affect and mediates judgments of members of the stereotyped group. Jussim and colleagues pointed out that this emotional component of a stereotype is more important in judging others than is the cognitive function (information storage and categorization) of the stereotype.

Discrimination

discrimination
Overt behavior—often negatively directed toward a particular group—tied to prejudicial attitudes, which involves behaving in different ways toward members of different groups.

More often than we would like to see, someone or some group is the victim of a prejudice-based criminal act, or a *hate crime*. The American Psychological Association (1998) defines hate crimes as "violent acts against people, property, or organizations because of the group to which they belong

Discrimination is the behavioral expression of a prejudicial attitude. At one time in the United States, discrimination against blacks was so bad that blacks were forced to drink from fountains separate from whites. Discrimination also forced blacks into inferior schools and jobs until laws were passed prohibiting such discrimination.

or identify with" (http://www.apa.org/pubinfo/hate/). The victim is targeted by an individual (or group) who is prejudiced against the group to which that person belongs. Perhaps the most infamous hate crime in recent years is the case of Charles Byrd, a black man who was hitchhiking along a road in Jasper County, Texas. Three white men in a pickup truck stopped and picked Byrd up. However, their motive was not altruistic. They drove Byrd to a remote area where they beat him, chained him by the ankles to the back of a pickup truck, and then dragged him two miles down a lonely country road.

Such hate crimes certainly do not make up a majority of crimes committed in the United States. However, they occur frequently enough that politicians have taken notice. According to a 1995 (the latest year for which statistics are available) FBI report, there were 7,497 hate crimes reported that year. These crimes were race based (4,831), religion based (1,277) and sexual orientation based (1,019). In the race category, most hate crimes were directed against blacks (2,988). In the religion category, most hate crimes were directed against Jews (1,058). In the sexual orientation category, most were directed against male homosexuals (735). Interestingly, a vast majority of hate crimes are not committed by members of hate groups. Indeed, only 5% of hate crimes are committed by members of such groups (American Psychological Association, 1998). The majority of hate crimes are committed by ordinary people, mostly young people who see little wrong with such actions (American Psychological Association, 1998). Oftentimes, other factors contribute to the commission of a hate crime, including alcohol and drug use. However, personal prejudice is the main driving force behind hate crimes (American Psychological Association, 1998).

You have probably noticed that hate crimes do not make up a majority of crimes committed in the United States. You are correct in your observation. Compared to other crime categories, hate crimes are relatively rare. However, they have a greater psychological impact on victims than other crimes. The American Psychological Association (1998) reports that some hate crime victims take as long as 5 years to get over the trauma of the crime, whereas victims of other similar crimes take about 2 years. There is also the impact of hate crimes on wider society. Highly publicized hate crimes inflame intergroup conflicts and instill fear in members of groups from which victims come.

Of course, hate crimes and the forces that drive them are not new. In fact, such incidents and attitudes have a rich tradition that includes slavery, lynching of blacks, the near extermination of Native Americans, and the persecution of Irish, Asian, Jewish, Moslem, Mormon, and other Americans. This long history of hate in the United States begs the question, Why do hate crimes occur? What could possibly have led to Charles Byrd being dragged horribly to his death? The answer lies in the dynamics that underlie such acts including prejudicial attitudes, stereotypes, and discrimination.

THE PERSISTENCE AND RECURRENCE OF PREJUDICE AND STEREOTYPES

Throughout history, members of *majority* groups (those in power) have held stereotypical images of members of *minority* groups (those not in power). These images supported prejudicial feelings, discriminatory behavior, and even wide-scale violence directed against minority-group members.

History teaches us that stereotypes and prejudicial attitudes are quite enduring. For example, some stereotypes of Jews and Africans are hundreds of years old. Prejudice appears to be an integral part of human existence. However, stereotypes and feelings may change, albeit slowly, as the context of our feelings toward other groups changes. For example, during and just after World War II, Americans had negative feelings toward the Japanese. For roughly the next 40 years, the two countries were at peace and had a harmonious relationship. This was rooted in the fact that the postwar American occupation of Japan (1945–1951) was benign. The Americans helped the Japanese rebuild their war-shattered factories, and the Japanese began to compete in world markets. But in the difficult economic times of the 1980s and early 1990s, many of the beliefs that characterized Japanese–American relations during World War II reemerged, although in somewhat modified form. Compared to how Japanese view Americans, Americans tend to see Japanese as more competitive, hard working, prejudiced, and crafty (see Figure 4.2). Japanese have a slight tendency to see Americans as undereducated, lazy, and not terribly hard working. Americans see Japanese as unfair, arrogant, and overdisciplined, as grinds who do nothing but work hard because of their conformity to group values (Weisman, 1991). Japanese, for their part, see Americans as arrogant and lacking

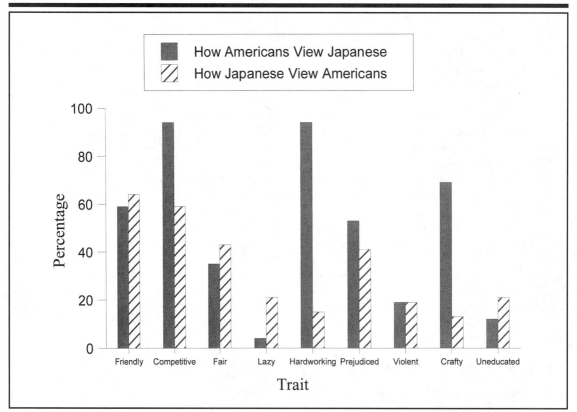

Figure 4.2 *How the Americans and Japanese view one another. Both Americans and Japanese hold stereotypical views of the other group.*

Based on data from a 1992 Times/CNN poll, cited in Holland (1992).

in racial purity, morality, and dedication (Weisman, 1991). The stereotypes on both sides have been altered and transformed by the passage of time, but like short skirts and wide ties, they tend to recycle. The periodicity of stereotypes suggests that they are based more on external factors such as economics and competition than on any stable characteristics of the group being categorized.

It is interesting to note that stereotypes and the cues used to categorize individuals change over time. For example, there was a time before skin color was a salient feature for prejudice. Some historians of the ancient Mediterranean suggest that there was a time before color prejudice. The initial encounter of black Africans and white Mediterraneans is the oldest chapter in the chronicle of black–white relations. Frank M. Snowden, Jr., (1983) traced the images of Africans as seen by Mediterraneans from Egyptian to Roman times. The first Africans encountered by Mediterraneans were soldiers or mercenaries. Mediterraneans knew that these black soldiers came from a powerful independent African state, Nubia, located in what today would be southern Egypt and northern Sudan. Nubians appear to have played an important role in the formation of Egyptian civilization (Wilford, 1992). Positive images of Africans appear in the artwork and writings of ancient Mediterranean peoples (Snowden, 1983).

These first encounters between blacks and whites were encounters between equals. The Africans were respected for their military skill and their political and cultural sophistication. Slavery existed in the ancient world but was not tied to skin color; anyone captured in war might be enslaved, whether white or black (Snowden, 1983). Prejudice, stereotyping, and discrimination existed too. Athenians may not have cared about skin color, but they cared deeply about national origin. Foreigners were excluded from citizenship. Women were also restricted and excluded. Only males above a certain age could be citizens and participate fully in society.

It is not clear when color prejudice came into existance. It may have been with the advent of the African–New World slave trade in the 16th century. Whenever it began, it is likely that race and prejudice were not linked until some real power or status differences arose between groups. Although slavery in the ancient world was not based exclusively on skin color, slaves were almost always of different ethnic group, national origin, religion, or political unit than their owners. In the next sections, we explore the causes of prejudice, focusing first on its roots in personality and social life and then on its roots in human cognitive functioning.

PERSONALITY AND PREJUDICE: AUTHORITARIANISM AND GENDER

What are the causes of prejudice? In addressing this question, social psychologists have looked not only at our mental apparatus, our inclination to categorize, but also at characteristics of the individual. Is there such a thing as a prejudiced personality? Are men or women more prone to prejudice? We explore the answers to these questions in this section.

Social psychologists and sociologists have long suspected a relationship between personality characteristics and prejudice. One important personality dimension relating to prejudice, stereotyping, and discrimination is

authoritarianism

A personality
characteristic that relates
to a person's
unquestioned acceptance
of and respect for
authority.

authoritarianism. Authoritarianism is a personality characteristic that relates to unquestioned acceptance of and respect for authority. Authoritarian individuals tend to identify closely with those in authority and also tend to be prejudiced.

The Authoritarian Personality

In the late 1940s, T. W. Adorno and other psychologists at the University of California at Berkeley studied people who might have been the prototypes of Archie Bunker—individuals who wanted different ethnic groups to be suppressed and degraded, preferably by an all-powerful government or state. Archie Bunker embodies many of the characteristics of the **authoritarian personality,** which is characterized by submissive feelings toward authority, rigid, unchangeable beliefs, and racism and sexism (Adorno, Frenkel-Brunswik, Levinson, & Sanford, 1950).

**authoritarian
personality**

A personality dimension
characterized by
submissive feelings
towards authority, rigid
and unchangeable beliefs,
and a tendency toward
prejudicial attitudes.

Motivated by the tragedy of the murder of millions of Jews and other Eastern Europeans by the Nazis, Adorno and his colleagues conducted a massive study of the relationship between the authoritarian personality and the Nazi policy of *genocide*, the killing of an entire race or group of people. They speculated that the individuals who carried out the policy of mass murder were of a personality type that predisposed them to do whatever an authority figure ordered, no matter how vicious or monstrous.

The massive study produced by the Berkeley researchers, known as *The Authoritarian Personality*, was driven by the notion that there was a relationship, an interconnectedness, between the way a person was reared and various prejudices he or she later came to hold. The study surmised that prejudiced people were highly ethnocentric; that is, they believed in the superiority of their own group or race (Dunbar, 1987). The Berkeley researchers argued that individuals who were ethnocentric were likely to be prejudiced against a whole range of ethnic, racial, and religious groups in their culture. They found this to be true, that such people were indeed prejudiced against many or all groups that were different from themselves. A person who was anticolored tended to be anti-Semitic as well. These people seemed to embody a prejudiced personality type, the authoritarian personality.

The Berkeley researchers discovered that authoritarians had had a particularly rigid and punishing upbringing. They were raised in homes in which children were not allowed to express any feelings or opinions except those considered correct by their parents and other authority figures. People in authority were not to be questioned and, in fact, were idolized. Children handled pent-up feelings of hostility toward these suppressive parents by becoming a kind of island, warding these feelings off by inventing very strict categories and standards. They became impatient with uncertainty and ambiguity and came to prefer clear-cut and simple answers. Authoritarians had very firm categories: This was good, that was bad. Any groups that violated their notions of right and wrong were rejected.

This rigid upbringing engendered frustration and a strong concealed rage, which could be expressed only against those less powerful. These children learned that those in authority had the power to do as they wished. If the authoritarian obtained power over someone, the suppressed rage came out in full fury. Authoritarians were at the feet of those in power and at the throats of those less powerful. The suppressed rage was usually expressed against a *scapegoat*, a relatively powerless person or group, and tended to occur most often during times of frustration, such as during an economic slump.

The authoritarian personality, the individual who is prejudiced against all groups perceived to be different, may gravitate toward hate groups. On July 2, 1999, Benjamin Smith went on a drive-by shooting rampage that killed two and injured several others. Smith took his own life while being chased by police. Smith had a history of prejudicial attitudes and acts. Before his deadly rampage, he was known to be affiliated with the World Church of the Creator which is allegedly a fast-growing hate group in America. Smith came under the influence of the philosophy of Matt Hale, who became the leader of the World Church in 1996. Hale's philosophy was that the white race was the elite race in the world and that members of any other races or ethnic groups (which he called "inferior mud races") were the enemy. Smith himself believed that whites should take up arms against those inferior races. The early research on prejudice, then, emphasized the role of irrational emotions and thoughts that were part and parcel of the prejudiced personality. These irrational emotions, simmered in a pot of suppressed rage, were the stuff of prejudice, discrimination, and eventually intergroup violence. The violence was usually set off by frustration, particularly when resources, like jobs, got scarce.

Social psychologists have also looked at whether there is a prejudiced personality (Dunbar, 1995; Gough, 1951). Gough, for example, developed a prejudiced personality scale (PR scale) using items from the Minnesota Multiphasic Personality Inventory. Gough (1951) reported that the PR scale correlated with anti-Semitic attitudes among midwestern high school students.

Dunbar (1995) administered the PR scale and two other measures of racism to white and Asian American students. He also administered a measure of anti-Semitism to see if the PR scale still correlated with prejudiced attitudes. Dunbar found that Asian Americans had higher scores on both the PR scale and the measure of anti-Semitism than did whites, indicating greater anti-Semitism among Asians than whites. However, the only significant relationships on the PR scale between anti-Semitic and racist attitudes were among the white participants.

Gender and Prejudice

Another characteristic relating to prejudice is gender. Research in this area has concentrated on male and female attitudes toward homosexuality. Generally, males tend to have more negative attitudes toward homosexuality than women (Kite & Whitley, 1998; Kite, 1984). Do men and women view gay men and lesbians differently? There is evidence that males have more negative attitudes toward gay men than toward lesbians (Kite & Whitley, 1998; Gentry, 1987; Kite, 1984). The findings for females is less clear. Kite and Whitley, for example, reported that women tend not to make distinctions between gay men and lesbians. Other research, however, shows that females show more negative attitudes toward lesbians than gay men (Gentry, 1987; Kite, 1984).

Janet Baker and Harold Fishbein (1998) investigated the development of gay and lesbian prejudice among a sample of 7th, 9th, and 11th graders. They found that males tended to be more prejudiced against gays and lesbians than females were, and male participants showed greater prejudice against gay males than toward lesbians. Prejudice against gays and lesbians increased between 7th and 9th grade for both males and females. However, between 9th and 11th grades, gay prejudice *decreased* for female participants, whereas it *increased* for male participants. Baker and Fishbein suggested the increase in male antigay prejudice may be rooted in the male's increased defensive reactions to intimate relationships.

A central question emerging from this research is whether there are gender differences in other forms of prejudice. One study, for example, confirmed that males show more ethnic prejudice than females on measures concerning friendship and allowing an ethnic minority to live in one's neighborhood. Males and females did not differ when interethnic intimate relations were considered (Hoxter & Lester, 1994). There is relatively little research in this area, and clearly, more is needed to investigate the relationship between gender and prejudice for a wide range of prejudices.

THE SOCIAL ROOTS OF PREJUDICE

The research on the authoritarian personality and gender provides an important piece of the puzzle of prejudice and discrimination. However, it is only one piece. Prejudice and discrimination are far too complex and prevalent to be explained by a single, personality-based cause. Prejudice occurs in a social context, and another piece of the puzzle can be found in the evolution of the feelings that form the basis of relations between dominant and other groups in a particular society.

To explore the social roots of prejudice, let's consider the situation of African Americans in the United States. During the years before the Civil War, black slaves were considered the property of white slave owners, and this arrangement was justified by the notion that blacks were in some way less human than whites. Their degraded condition was used as proof of their inferiority.

Social norms often play a role in defining stereotypes and prejudice. Before the Civil War blacks were assumed to be inferior to whites. Once the war broke out, Frederick Douglas lobbied President Abraham Lincoln to allow blacks to serve in the Union Army. Although blacks were eventually allowed to serve, prejudice was still evident. Black soldiers were initially assigned manual labor roles only, had white officers, and were paid less than their white counterparts.

In 1863, in the middle of the Civil War, President Lincoln issued the Emancipation Proclamation, setting slaves free. But abolition did little to end prejudice and negative attitudes toward blacks. The Massachusetts 54th Regiment, for example, was an all-black Union Army unit—led by an all-white officer corps. Blacks were said to lack the ability to lead, thus no black officers were allowed. Because of these stereotypes and prejudices, members of the 54th were also paid less than their white counterparts in other regiments. Initially also, they were not allowed in combat roles; they were used instead for manual labor, such as for building roads.

Despite prejudice, some blacks did rise to positions of prominence. Frederick Douglass, who escaped from slavery and became a leader and spokesperson for African Americans, was instrumental in convincing President Lincoln to issue the Emancipation Proclamation and to allow black troops to fight in the Civil War. Toward the end of the war, over 100,000 black troops were fighting for the North, and some historians maintain that without these troops, the result of the Civil War may have been different.

Over the course of the next hundred years, African Americans made strides in improving their economic and social status, but most changes met with intense resistance from the majority community. Then in 1954, the U.S. Supreme Court ruled in *Brown v. Board of Education* that segregated (separate but equal) schools violated the Constitution and mandated that schools and other public facilities be integrated. Since then, the feelings of white Americans toward African Americans have become more positive (Goleman, 1991). This change in attitude and behavior reflects the importance of social norms in influencing and regulating the expression of feelings and beliefs.

Yet there is a curious nature to these feelings. White Americans almost unanimously endorse such general principles as integration and equality, but they are generally opposed to steps designed to actualize these principles, such as mandatory busing or affirmative action (Katz, Wackenhut, & Hass, 1986). It may be that white Americans pay lip service to the principle of racial equality. They perceive African Americans as being *both* disadvantaged by the system *and* deviant. In other words, white Americans are aware that African Americans may have gotten a raw deal, but they also see them as responsible for their own plight (Katz et al., 1986). Remember, the human tendency to attribute behavior to internal rather than external causes makes it more likely that people will ascribe the reasons for achievement or lack of it to the character of an individual or group.

Although we may no longer have tarring and feathering of members of different groups, prejudice still exists in more subtle forms. If acquired early enough, prejudice seems to become part of one's deepest feelings:

> Many southerners have confessed to me, for instance, that even though in their minds they no longer feel prejudice towards African Americans, they still feel squeamish when they shake hands with an African American. These feelings are left over from what they learned in their families as children. (Pettigrew, 1986, p. 20)

Given the importance of things racial in U.S. history and given the way people process information in a categorical and automatic way, some observers assume that racist feelings are the rule for Americans (Gaertner & Dovidio, 1986).

Incidents from daily life seem to bear out this conclusion. In 1992, for example, the owner of the Cincinnati Reds baseball team, Marge Schott, drew fire for her use of offensive epithets about her black players (*Time*, December, 1992). Most pundits painted her as a racist, but her supporters claimed she wasn't a bigot or a hatemonger, just "from the old school."

In 1993, an AT&T company magazine published a drawing in which humans were shown talking on the telephone on several continents. But in Africa, a monkey was shown using the phone. AT&T issued an apology to its workers and to the NAACP, who called it truly offensive. An AT&T spokesperson said he couldn't imagine how the drawing had gotten past the magazine's editors and proofreaders (*Wall Street Journal*, September 17, 1993). In another incident, presidential candidate Ross Perot ran into trouble in 1992 when addressing the NAACP. He used the phrases like *you people* and *your people* when talking about who would suffer the most from economic problems and runaway crime. Critics said the phrase reflected how out of touch he was with his audience. He also offended many listeners with his description of his father's generosity toward African Americans in the South: "The only words I ever heard him say were, 'Son, these are people too, and they have to live.'" Joseph H. Duff, president of the Los Angeles chapter of the NAACP, commented, "When he tried to tell us we're people, he made a big mistake. We know we're people" (*New York Times*, July 12, 1992, p. 22). Perot himself was baffled by his listeners' response. He commented that if he had offended anyone, he was sorry.

Modern Racism

Although racist beliefs and prejudicial attitudes still exist, they have certainly become less prevalent than they had once been. For example, according to data from the General Social Survey (1999) attitudes toward blacks have improved between 1972 and 1996. Figure 4.3 shows some of the data from this survey. As shown in Figure 4.3, responses reflecting more positive racial attitudes can be seen in questions concerning whether whites have a right to keep blacks out of their neighborhood (blacks out), whether one would vote for a black presidential candidate (black president), whether whites would send their children to a school where more than 50% of the children were black (send children), whether they would vote to change a rule excluding blacks from a social club (change rule), and supporting a law preventing housing discrimination (housing law).

Despite these gains, prejudice still exists. Why this contradiction? Since the study of the authoritarian personality was published several decades ago, it has become more difficult (socially and legally) to overtly express prejudice against individuals from particular racial groups. It is not unusual, for example, for an individual to be removed from his or her job because of a racist statement. For example, in 1996 WABC (a New York) radio station fired Bob Grant, one of its most popular on-air personalities because of a history of racist statements. Even calling a racist a racist can get you fired. Alan Dershowitz, a prominent attorney, was fired from his talk show after calling Grant despicable and racist. Even if racism was not the intent, one can still be fired for using racial (or other ethnic) slurs. Even the appearance of prejudice from someone in an official position is unacceptable today.

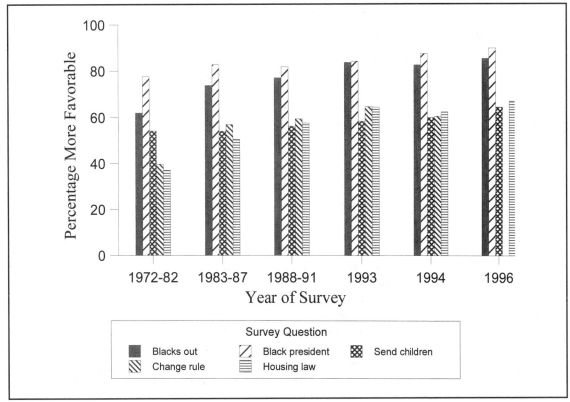

Figure 4.3 *The changing face of racial prejudice. Between the years 1972 and 1996, whites have shown more favorable attitudes toward blacks.*

Based on data from General Social Survey (1999).

Some social psychologists believe that many white Americans currently are *aversive racists*, people who truly believe they are unprejudiced, who want to do the right thing but, in fact, feel very uneasy and uncomfortable in the presence of someone from a different racial group (Gaertner & Dovidio, 1986). When they are with members of other groups, they smile too much, are overly friendly, and are sometimes very fearful. These feelings do not lead the aversive racist to behave in a negative way toward members of other groups; rather, they lead him or her to avoid them.

This more subtle prejudice is marked by an uncertainty in feeling and action toward people from different racial groups. J. C. McConahay (1986) referred to this configuration of feelings and beliefs as **modern racism,** also known as *symbolic racism.* Modern racists moderate their responses to individuals from different racial groups to avoid showing obvious prejudice; they express racism but in a less open manner than was formerly common. Modern racists would say that yes, racism is a bad thing and a thing of the past; still, it is a fact that African Americans "are pushing too hard, too fast, and into places where they are not wanted" (p. 93).

McConahay devised a scale to measure modern racism. In contrast to older scales, the modern racism scale presents items in a less racially charged manner. For example, an item from the modern racism scale might ask participants whether African Americans have received more economically

modern racism

Subtle racial prejudice, expressed in a less open manner than is traditional overt racial prejudice and characterized by an uncertainty in feeling and action toward minorities.

than they deserve. On an old-fashioned scale, an item might ask how much you would mind if an African-American family moved in next door to you. According to McConahay, modern racists would be more likely to be detected with the less racist items on the modern racism scale than the more racist items on an old-fashioned scale. McConahay found that the modern racism scale is sensitive enough to pick up more subtle differences in an individual's racial feelings and behaviors than the older scales. The modern racism scale tends to reveal a more elusive and indirect form of racism than the older scales.

In one of McConahay's experiments, participants (all of whom were white) were asked to play the role of a personnel director of a major company. All had taken a version of the modern racism scale. The "personnel director" received a resume of a graduating college senior who was a very ordinary job candidate. The race of the candidate was manipulated: For half of the participants, a photograph of an African American was attached, and for the other half a photograph of a white person was attached.

Another variable was added to the experiment in addition to the race of the applicant. Half of each group of participants were told that there were no other qualified candidates for the job. This was called the *no anchor* condition, because the personnel directors had no basis for judgment, no other candidate against which to evaluate the ordinary candidate. The other half of each group saw the resumes of two other candidates, both white, who were far superior to the ordinary candidate, white or African American. This was called the *anchor* condition, because the personnel directors now had a basis for comparison.

Personnel directors in all four groups were asked to make a decision about the candidate on a scale ranging from "definitely would hire" to "definitely would not hire." McConahay's findings are shown in Figure 4.4.

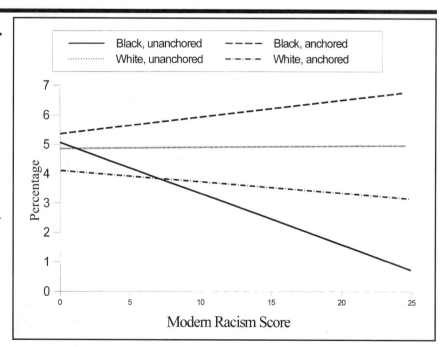

Figure 4.4

Hiring preferences as a function of modern racism scores, race of candidate, and decision context. Nonprejudiced individuals rated an African-American candidate the same regardless of the anchoring candidate. Prejudiced individuals rated African-American candidates highly as long as there were no other candidates.

From McConahay (1986). Reprinted with permission.

As shown on the graph, individuals who have high scores on the modern racism scale (indicating that they are prejudiced) do not treat white candidates any differently than their nonprejudiced counterparts. Whether they score 0 or 25 or somewhere in between on the scale, all participants rated the white candidates in both the anchor and the no-anchor condition in a similar way. Participants with low scores (near 0) rated white candidates about the same, whereas high scorers (closer to 25) rated the white no-anchor candidate a little higher than the white anchor candidate.

More interesting are the ratings of African American candidates. For nonprejudiced participants, African Americans, anchored or not, were rated precisely the same. But look at the very large differences between candidates for the prejudiced participants. An unanchored African American candidate was absolutely dismissed, whereas the anchored African American candidate, compared to more qualified whites, was given the highest rating.

Why these differences? Recall that modern racists are rather uncertain about how to feel or act in situations with members of different racial or ethnic groups. They particularly do not want to discriminate when others will find out about it and can label what they did as racist (Donnerstein & Donnerstein, 1973). To reject a very ordinary African American candidate when there were no other candidates probably would not be seen as prejudiced, because the candidate was not qualified. Note how much more favorably the modern racist judged the white candidate in the same anchor circumstances.

But when there is a chance that his or her behavior might be termed racist, the modern racist overvalues African Americans. This is seen when there were qualified white candidates (anchor condition). The modern racist goes out of his or her way to appear unprejudiced and therefore gives the ordinary African-American candidate the highest rating. Participants who scored low on the modern racism scale felt confident about how to feel and act in racial situations. People from different racial groups do not make them uncomfortable, they "call it like they see it" (Hass, Katz, Rizzo, Bailey, & Eisenstadt, 1991).

The concept of modern racism is not without its critics. Some suggest that it is illogical to equate opposition to an African American candidate or affirmative action programs with racism (Sykes, 1992). Other critics point out that modern racism researchers have not adequately defined and measured modern racism (Tetlock, 1986). They also point out that high correlations exist (ranging from about $r = .6$ to .7) between old-fashioned racism and modern racism. That is, if a person is a modern racist, he or she also is likely to be an old-fashioned racist. According to these critics, there simply may not be two forms of racism.

The fact is that race is a complex issue and contains many facets. In the past, according to public opinion surveys, whites were essentially either favorable or unfavorable to the cause of African Americans. But racial feelings are more subtle now. Someone might be against busing of school children but not opposed to having an African American neighbor (Sniderman & Piazza, 1994). Additionally, a person's racial attitudes are often affected by his or her politics. Individuals who have favorable attitudes toward African Americans but who perceive affirmative action policies to be unfair may come to dislike African Americans as a consequence (Sniderman & Piazza, 1994).

Changing Social Norms

What accounts for the changes we see in the expression of racist sentiments and for the appearance of modern racism? Our society, primarily through its laws, has made the obvious expression of racism undesirable. Over the past 30 years, social norms have increasingly dictated the acceptance of members of different racial and ethnic groups into mainstream society. Overt racism has become socially unacceptable. But for many individuals, deeply held racist sentiments remain unchanged. Their racism has been driven underground by society's expectations and standards.

Because of changed social norms, charges of prejudice and discrimination are taken seriously by those against whom they are made. In 1993, the Denny's restaurant chain was charged with discriminating against black customers. In one incident, a group of black high school students in San Jose, California, were allegedly told they had to pay in advance for their late-night meal. In another, six black Secret Service officers in Maryland complained that they waited for service whereas a nearby table of white officers ordered, were served, ate their meal, and left. As other similar incidents came to light, it began to seem that discrimination against African Americans was a company policy at Denny's (*Newsweek*, July 19, 1993, p. 36).

Denny's parent company, Flagstar Cos., launched a public relations campaign to defuse the charges. Television ads pledged that everyone who came to Denny's would be treated with respect and that any departures from that policy were unintentional. Nevertheless, business at Denny's declined, as did the price of Flagstar's stock. Consumer research indicated that the public was well aware of the incidents. The head of Flagstar expressed regret that he had not paid enough attention to running a corporation in an increasingly culturally diverse society. Only 1 of the 378 Denny's franchises, for example, was owned by an African American. The corporation had to suffer the consequences of his neglect: In 1994, Denny's was ordered to pay $46 million to customers who had been treated unfairly by the restaurant. The settlement was the largest ever awarded in a discrimination case involving public facilities (Herhold, 1994).

Despite such consequences, it appears that societal norms have been altered, allowing racial and ethnic animosities and prejudices to be expressed. One good example of these shifting norms is the proliferation of hate on the Internet. It is nearly impossible to get an accurate count of the number of hate sites on the Internet. However, according to the Antidefamation League (1999), hate groups such as Neo-Nazis, Skinheads, and the Ku Klux Klan are using the Internet to spread their message of hate. The Internet has allowed hate speech and the advocacy of violence against minorities to cross national boundaries. For example, on one Web site, one can peruse a variety of racist cartoons and purchase hate-related products. Hate-based "educational materials" are also easily obtained on the Internet. One program called *The Jew Rats* portrays Jews as rats who are indoctrinated to hate others and take over the world. Racist video games are also readily available. One game called *Bloodbath in Niggeria* involves shooting caricatures of Africans who pop up in huts. In addition, the Internet provides a medium that can help hate groups organize more easily. In addition to organizing on a local level, hate sites can now easily link hate groups across land and ocean, making the spread of hate and prejudice much easier.

On the other hand, there is evidence that attitudes, although not necessarily behavior, toward specific groups have become more positive. For example, gender stereotypes seem to have lessened recently at least among college students, if not among older individuals (Swim, 1994). In this case, social norms in favor of greater equality seem to be holding.

THE COGNITIVE ROOTS OF PREJUDICE: FROM CATEGORIES TO STEREOTYPES

What, then, has happened to the prejudiced personality? It appears that it remains with us. Only the form of expression seems to have changed. The irrational forces that drive prejudice have not been seriously affected by historical or social change. In fact, cognitive social psychologists have argued that although prejudice may have personality and social causes, it also exists because of the mental strategies people use to structure their social worlds.

Cognitive social psychologists believe that one of the best ways to understand how stereotypes form and persist is to look at how humans process information. As we saw in chapters 2 and 3, human beings tend to be cognitive misers, preferring the least effortful means of processing social information (Taylor, 1981). We have a limited capacity to deal with social information and therefore can deal with only relatively small amounts at any one time (Fiske & Taylor, 1991).

Given these limitations, people try to simplify problems by using shortcuts, primarily involving category-based processes (Bodenhausen & Wyer, 1985; Brewer, 1988). In other words, it is easier to pay attention to the group to which someone belongs than to the individual traits of the person. It takes less effort and less time for someone to use category-based (group-based) information than to try to deal with people on an individual basis (Macrae et al., 1994). For example, in June, 1998 when James Byrd was dragged to death in Texas, he was chosen as a victim purely because of his race. Byrd, a black man, was hitchhiking home from a party when three white men stopped to pick him up. The three men beat Byrd and then chained him to their truck and dragged him to death—all because he was black and in the wrong place at the wrong time. Research studies of the cognitive miser demonstrate that when people's ability or motivation to process information is diminished, they tend to fall back on available stereotypes. For example, in one study, when a juror's task was complex, he or she recalled more negative things about a defendant if the defendant was Hispanic than if the defendant did not belong to an identifiable group. When the jurors' task was simple, no differences in judgment were found between a Hispanic and a non-Hispanic defendant (Bodenhausen & Lichtenstein, 1987). When the situation gets more complicated, individuals tend to rely on these stereotypes.

Individuals are more likely to fall back on stereotypes when they are not at the peak of their cognitive abilities (Bodenhausen, 1990). Bodenhausen tested participants to determine if they were "night people"—individuals who function better in the evening and at night—or "day people"—individuals who function better in the morning. He then had participants make judgments about a student's misconduct. Sometimes the student was described in nonstereotypic terms (his name was "Robert Garner"), and in other situations he was portrayed as Hispanic ("Roberto Garcia"), as African American, or as an athlete.

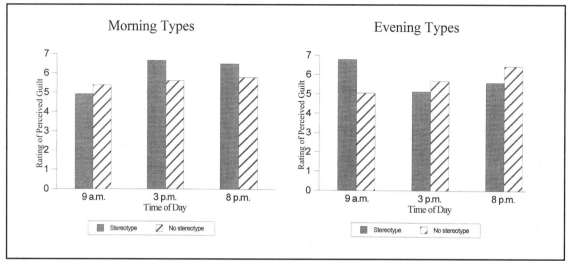

Figure 4.5 *Ratings of perceived guilt as a function of time of day, personality type, and stereotype activation. When individuals are not at their cognitive peak, they are more likely to rely on stereotypes when making judgments.*

Based on data from Bodenhausen, 1990.

The experiment showed that when people are not at their peak (morning people at night or night people in the morning), they tend to solve problems by using stereotypes. As shown in Figure 4.5, morning types relied on the stereotype to judge the student when presented with the case in the evening; evening types fell back on stereotypes in the morning. These findings suggest that category-based judgments take place when we do not have the capacity, the motivation, or the energy to pay attention to the target, and these lead human beings into a variety of cognitive misconceptions and errors.

Identify with the In-Group

in-group bias

The powerful tendency of humans to favor over other groups the group to which they belong.

One of the principal cognitive processes common to all human beings seems to be the tendency to identify with and prefer one's own group, the **in-group bias**, and at the same time to identify "different" others as belonging to a less favored out-group. Henri Tajfel, a social psychologist whose work we examined in chapter 1, studied the phenomenon of in-group favoritism as a way of exploring out-group hostility. He was preoccupied with the issue of genocide, the systematic killing of an entire national or ethnic group. As a survivor of Nazi genocide of European Jews from 1939 to 1945, Tajfel had a personal as well as a professional interest in this issue (Brown, 1986).

Unlike earlier researchers, who emphasized the irrational thoughts and emotions of the prejudiced personality as the source of intergroup violence, Tajfel believed that cognitive processes were involved. He believed that the process of categorizing people into different groups led to loyalty to the in-group, which includes those people one perceives to be similar to oneself in meaningful ways. Inevitably, as in-group solidarity forms, those who are perceived to be different are identified as members of the out-group (Allport, 1954; Billig, 1992).

Tajfel was searching for the minimal social conditions needed for prejudice to emerge. In his experiments with British school boys, he found that there was no situation so minimal that some form of in-group solidarity did not take shape. He concluded that the need to favor the in-group, known as the in-group bias, was a basic component of human nature. What are the reasons for this powerful bias?

As noted in chapter 2, we derive important aspects of our self-concepts from our membership in groups (Turner, 1987). These memberships help us establish a sense of positive social identity. Think of what appears to be a fairly inconsequential case of group membership, being a fan of a sports team. When your team wins a big game, you experience a boost, however temporary, to your sense of well-being. Recall from chapter 2 the concept of BIRGing—basking in reflected glory. You don't just root for the team, you become part of the team. You say, "We beat the heck out of them." Think for a moment about the celebrations that have taken place in Detroit, New York, Boston, and elsewhere after home teams won professional sports championships. It is almost as if it wasn't the Tigers or the Mets or the Celtics who won, but the fans themselves.

When your team loses the big game, on the other hand, you feel terrible. You're tempted to jump ship. It is hard to read the newspapers or listen to sportscasts the next day. When your team wins, you say, "We won." When your team loses, you say, "They lost." (Cialdini, 1988). It appears that both BIRGing and jumping ship serve to protect the individual fan's self-esteem. The team becomes part of the person's identity.

SOCIAL IDENTITY THEORY   Tajfel's (1982) social identity theory assumes that human beings are motivated to positively evaluate their own groups, and value them over other groups, in order to maintain and enhance self-esteem. The group confers on the individual a social identity, that part of a person's self-concept that comes from her membership in social groups and from her emotional connection with those groups (Tajfel, 1981).

Fundamental to **social identity theory (SIT)** is the notion of categorizing the other groups, pigeonholing them, by the use of stereotypes, those general beliefs that most people have about members of particular social groups (Turner, 1987). People are motivated to hold less than positive stereotypes of out-groups; by doing so they can maintain the superiority of their own group and thereby maintain their positive social (and self) identity.

Generally, any threat to the in-group, whether economic, military, or social tends to heighten in-group bias. Additionally, anything that makes a person's membership in a group more salient, more noticeable, will increase in-group favoritism. One series of experiments showed that when people were alone, they were likely to judge an out-group member on an individual basis, but when they were made aware of their in-group membership by the presence of other members of their group, they were likely to judge the out-group person solely on the basis of stereotypes of the out-group (Wilder & Shapiro, 1984, 1991). The increase of in-group feelings promoted judgments of other people on the basis of social stereotypes. When group membership gets switched on, as it does, for example when you are watching the Olympics or voting for a political candidate, then group values and social stereotypes play a larger role in how you react.

SELF-CATEGORIZATION THEORY   Increase in self-esteem as a result of group membership is central to SIT (Grieve & Hogg, 1999). To increase members' self-esteem, the in-group needs to show that it is distinct from other groups in positive ways (Mummenday & Wenzel, 1999). Central

social identity theory (SIT)
An assumption that we all need to have a positive self-concept, part of which is conferred on us through identification with certain groups.

self-categorization theory (SCT)

A theory suggesting that people need to reduce uncertainty about their perceptions of the world and seek affirmation of their beliefs from fellow group members.

to an extension of SIT, **self-categorization theory (SCT)** is the notion that self-categorization is also motivated by the need to reduce uncertainty (Hogg & Mullin, 1999). The basic idea is that people need to feel that their perceptions of the world are correct and this correctness is defined by people—fellow group members—who are similar to oneself in important ways. In a study by Haslam, Oakes, Reynolds, and Turner (1999), when the category *Australian* was made salient for a group of Australian students, it tended to reduce uncertainty about the characteristics that comprise one's social group. Consequently, it regulated and structured the members social cognition. This is consistent with SCT. When reminded of their common category or group membership, the Australian students were more likely to agree on what it meant to be Australian.

What are the consequences of uncertainty? Grieve and Hogg (1999) showed that when uncertainty is high (i.e., when group members did not know if their performance was adequate or would be successful in achieving group goals), groups were more likely to downgrade or discriminate against other groups. In other words, uncertainty is a threat. Uncertainty was also accompanied by increased group identification. So threat creates a kind of rally-round-the-flag mentality. Self-categorization theory suggests, then, that only when the world is uncertain does self-categorization lead to discrimination against other groups (Grieve & Hogg, 1999). Self-categorization theory adds a bit of optimism to its parent theory's (SIT) outlook by suggesting that categorization does not always lead to discrimination, and if threat can be managed or alleviated, little discrimination or intergroup antagonism need occur.

A BIOLOGICAL PERSPECTIVE ON IN-GROUP BIAS Tajfel's research has shown us that the formation of an in-group bias serves basic social and self needs primarily by maintaining personal self-esteem. Some scientists, specifically sociobiologists—scientists who take a biological approach to social behavior—believe that ethnocentrism (the increased valuation of the in-group and the devaluation of out-groups has a foundation in human biological evolution. They point out that for the longest part of their history, humans lived in small groups ranging from 40 to 100 members (Flohr, 1987). People had to rely on the in-group and gain acceptance by its members; it was the only way to survive. It would make sense, then, that a strong group orientation would be part of our human heritage: Those who lacked this orientation would not have survived to pass their traits on to us.

Sociobiologists also point out that people in all cultures seem to show a naturally occurring *xenophobia*, or fear of strangers. This fear may also be part of our genetic heritage. Because early populations were isolated from one another (Irwin, 1987), people may have used similar physical appearance as a marker of blood relationship (Tonnesmann, 1987). Clearly, there was always the possibility that people who looked different could be a threat to the food supply or other necessities of survival. Sociobiologists argue that it is reasonable to expect that people would be willing to cooperate only with humans of similar appearance and biological heritage and that they would distrust strangers (Barkow, 1980).

In modern times, as Tajfel showed, we still derive much of our identity from group membership; we fear being excluded from groups (Baumeister & Tice, 1990). High respect for our own groups often means a devaluing of other groups. This is not necessarily a big problem until groups have to compete for resources. Because the world does not appear to offer a surplus of resources, competition among groups is inevitable. Of particular interest to sociobiologists is a study by Tajfel (1982) and his co-workers in which it was demonstrated that children show a preference for their own national group long before they have a concept of country or nation. Children ranging in age from 6 to 12 years old were shown photographs of young men and were asked how much they liked those men. Two weeks later, the children were shown the same photographs again. They were also told that some of the men belonged to their nation and others did not. The children had to decide which young men were "theirs" (belonged to their country) and which were not. The researchers found that the children were more likely to assign the photographs they liked to their own nation. Therefore, liking and in-group feelings go together at an age when children cannot really comprehend fully the idea of a nation (Flohr, 1987).

In sum, those who offer a biological perspective on intergroup prejudice say that strong in-group identification can be understood as an evolutionary survival mechanism. We can find examples throughout human history of particular ethnic, racial, and religious groups that have strengthened in-group bonds in response to threats from the dominant group (Eitzen, 1973; Myrdal, 1962). Strengthening of these in-group bonds may help the group survive, but this is only one way of looking at the in-group bias. Acceptance of this notion does not require us to neglect our social psychological theories; it simply gives us some idea of the complexity of the issue (Flohr, 1987).

The Role of Language in Maintaining Bias

Categorization is, generally, an automatic process. It is the first step in the impression formation process. As mentioned earlier, it is not the same as stereotyping and prejudice, but it powerfully affects these other processes. One way in which categorizing can lead to prejudice is through language. The way we sculpt our world via the words and labels we use to describe people connects the category to prejudice. Social psychologist Charles Perdue and his colleagues tested the hypothesis that the use of words describing in-groups and out-groups unconsciously forms our biases and stereotypes (Perdue, Dovidio, Gurtman, & Tyler, 1990).

Perdue suggested that the use of collective pronouns—we, us, ours, they, their, theirs—is very influential in how we think about people and groups. We use these terms to assign people to in-groups and out-groups. In one study, Perdue and his colleagues showed participants a series of nonsense syllables (xeh, yof, laj) paired with pronouns designating in-group or out-group status (we, they). Participants were then asked to rate each of the nonsense syllables they had just seen in terms of the pleasantness or unpleasantness of the feelings they evoked. As shown in Figure 4.6, nonsense words paired with in-group pronouns were rated much more favorably than the same nonsense words paired with out-group pronouns or with control stimuli. Out-group pronouns gave negative meaning to previously unencountered and neutral nonsense syllables.

In a second experiment, these investigators demonstrated that in-group and out-group pronouns bias the processing of information about those groups. Participants saw a series of positive- and negative-trait words, such as helpful, clever, competent, irresponsible, sloppy, and irritable. Now, a positive trait ought to be positive under any circumstances, and the same should hold

Figure 4.6

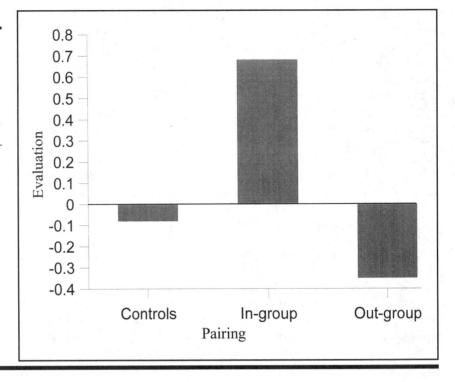

Standardized ratings of target syllables as a function of pronoun pairing. Syllables paired with in-group pronouns were judged more pleasant than those paired with out-group pronouns.

From Perdue, Dovidio, and Tyler (1990). Reprinted with permission.

true for negative traits, wouldn't you agree? *Skillful* is generally positive, *sloppy* is generally negative. But as Figure 4.7 shows, it took participants longer to describe a negative trait as negative when that trait had been associated with an in-group pronoun. Similarly, it took participants longer to

Figure 4.7

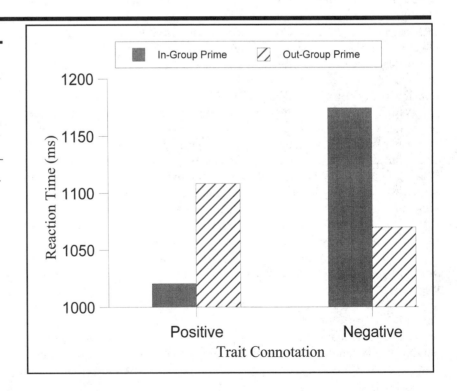

Reaction times to positive and negative trait descriptors as a function of pronoun type (in-group or out-group). Information processing is affected by in-group and out-group thinking.

From Perdue, Dovidio, and Tyler (1990). Reprinted with permission.

describe a positive trait as positive when it had been associated with an out-group pronoun. It took them little time to respond to a positive trait associated with an in-group pronoun and to a negative trait associated with an out-group pronoun.

These findings suggest that we have a nonconscious tendency (after all, the participants were not aware of the associations) to connect in-group labels with positive attributes rather than negative ones and out-group labels with negative attributes rather than positive ones. These associations are so strong that they shape the way we process subsequent information. They also seem to be deep and long lasting, a fact that may help explain why stereotypes remain so tenacious.

Illusory Correlations

The tendency to associate negative traits with out-groups is explained by one of the fundamental cognitive bases of stereotyping, the illusory correlation. An **illusory correlation** is an error in judgment about the relationship between two variables or, in other words, a belief that two unrelated events co-vary (are systematically related) (Hamilton & Sherman, 1989). For example, a person may notice that each time he wears his old high school bowling shirt when he goes bowling, he bowls very well. He may come to believe that there is a connection between the two events. Similarly, if you think that members of a minority group are more likely than members of a majority group to have a negative trait, then you perceive a correlation between group membership and behavior relating to that trait (Schaller, 1991).

Sometimes this cognitive bias crops up even among trained professionals. For example, a physician diagnosed a young, married African American woman with chronic pelvic inflammatory disease, an ailment related to a previous history of sexually transmitted disease. This diagnosis was made despite the fact that there was no indication in her medical history that she had ever had such a disease. As it turned out, she actually had endometriosis, a condition unrelated to sexually transmitted diseases (*Time*, June 1, 1992). The physician's beliefs about young black women, that they are sexually promiscuous, led to a diagnosis consistent with those beliefs. Research supports this anecdote. For example, participants have been found to ascribe different abilities to a girl depending on whether she is portrayed as having a lower or higher socioeconomic status background (Darley & Gross, 1983).

These examples illustrate the human tendency to overestimate the co-occurrence of pairs of distinctive stimuli (Sherman, Hamilton, & Roskos-Ewoldsen, 1989). In the case of the misdiagnosis, the presence of two distinctive stimuli—a young black woman and a particular symptom pattern—led the physician to conclude that the woman's disorder was related to her sexual history. The tendency to fall prey to this illusion has been verified in other experiments (Chapman & Chapman, 1967).

The illusory correlation helps explain how stereotypes form. The reasoning goes like this: Minority groups are distinctive because they are encountered relatively infrequently. Negative behavior is also distinctive because it is, in general, encountered less frequently than positive behavior. Because both are distinctive, there is a tendency for people to overestimate the frequency with which they occur together, that is, the frequency with which minority group members do undesirable things (Sherman et al., 1989).

illusory correlation
An error in judgment about the relationship between two variables in which two unrelated events are believed to covary.

Research shows that if people are presented with information about a majority group and a minority group and these groups are paired with either rare or common traits, people associate the smaller group with the rarer trait (Hamilton & Sherman, 1989). If both a minority and majority group have the same negative trait, say a tendency toward criminal behavior, the negative behavior will be more distinctive when paired with the minority as compared to the majority group. Our cognitive apparatus seems to lead us to make an automatic association between negative behavior and minority-group membership.

Distinctive characteristics are also likely to play a critical role in the formation of category-based responses. In any gathering of people, we pay more attention to those who appear to be different from others, such as a white in an otherwise all-black group, or a man in an all-woman group. Skin color, gender, and ethnicity are salient characteristics.

One function of automatic evaluation is to point to events that may endanger the perceiver (Pratto & John, 1991). Certainly, sociobiologists would agree with that notion. The human ability to recognize friend from foe, safety from danger, would have fundamental survival value (Ike, 1987). For example, people automatically responded to an angry (salient) face in a happy crowd (Hansen & Hansen, 1988). An angry person among friends is dangerous. Another study demonstrated that individuals automatically turn their attention from a task to words, pictures, or events that might be threatening (Pratte & John, 1991). Participants attended more rapidly to salient negative traits than to positive ones. This automatic vigilance may lead people to weigh undesirable attributes in those around them differently than positive attributes.

When we encounter other groups, then, it is not surprising that we pay more attention to the bad things about them than the good. Negative social information grabs our attention. This greater attention to negative information may protect us from immediate harm, but it also helps perpetuate stereotypes and may contribute to conflict between groups (Pratto & John, 1991).

From Illusory Correlations to Negative Stereotypes via the Fundamental Attribution Error

The fact that a negative bit of information about a different group has grabbed our attention does not necessarily lead to discrimination against that group. There must be a link between the salience of negative information and prejudiced behavior. The fundamental attribution error—the tendency to overestimate internal attributes and underestimate the effect of the situation—supplies this link and plays a role in the formation of discriminatory stereotypes. This is particularly true when perceivers do not take into account the roles assigned to people. Recall the quiz show study described in chapter 3 in which participants thought that the quiz show questioners were smarter than the contestants (Ross, Arnabile, & Steinmetz, 1977), even though roles had been randomly assigned.

This confusion between internal dispositions and external roles has led to punishing negative stereotypes of different groups. Let's consider just one example, the experience of the Jews in Europe over the past several hundred years (Ross & Nisbitt, 1991). Historically, Jews had many restrictions imposed on them in the countries where they resided. They were prevented from owning land; they often had to be in certain designated areas; they could not enter politics; and mainly professions were closed to them.

This exclusion from the greater society left the Jews with two options: either convert to Christianity or maintain their own distinctive culture. Most Jews opted for the latter, living within the walls of the ghetto assigned to them by the Christian majority and having little to do with non-Jews. Exclusion and persecution strengthened their in-group ties and also led the majority to perceive them as clannish. However, one segment of the Jewish population was highly visible to the mainstream society, the moneylenders. Money lending was a profession forbidden to Christians and open to Jews (Ross & Nisbett, 1991). Although it was held in contempt, it was an essential function in national and international business, especially as capitalism began to develop. Jewish moneylenders became important behind-the-scenes figures in the affairs of Europe. Thus, the most distinctive members of the group—distinctive for their visibility, their economic success, and their political importance—were invariably moneylenders.

The distinctive negative role of money lending, although restricted to only a few Jews, began to be correlated with Jews in general. Jews were also seen as distinctive because of their minority status, their way of life, their unique dress, and their in-group solidarity. All of these characteristics were a function of the situation and roles thrust on the Jews by the majority, but they came to be seen, via the fundamental attribution error, as inherent traits of Jewish people in general. These traits were then used as a justification for discrimination, based on the rationale that Jews were different, clannish, and money grubbing.

Jews have been depicted in negative ways throughout history. For example, in Shakespeare's *The Merchant of Venice*, the Jewish moneylender, Shylock, is depicted as a bloodthirsty person who will stop at nothing to extract his pound of flesh for repayment of a defaulted debt. However, do these stereotypes still crop up today in "enlightened" American communities? Movie director Steven Speilberg grew up in New Jersey and Arizona but never experienced anti-Semitism until his family moved to Saratoga, California,

Often stereotypes can be traced to some historical root. For example, the stereotypes of Jews as money grubbing, characteristic embodied in Shakespeare's character Shylock, came from the time in Europe when Christians were not permitted to be moneylenders because it was considered a sin. Jews stepped into this role and provided a valuable service. However, the Jewish moneylenders collected interest on the money they lent to Christians. Thus was born the Shylock image of the Jew as money grubbing.

during his senior year in high school. "He encountered kids who would cough the word Jew in their hands when they passed him, beat him up, and throw pennies at him in study hall. 'It was my six months of personal horror. And to this day I haven't gotten over it nor have I forgiven any of them' " (*Newsweek*, December 20, 1993, p. 115).

Historically, Jews were not the only group to suffer from majority exclusion and the fundamental attribution error (Ross & Nisbett, 1991). The Armenians in Turkey, the Indians in Uganda, and the Vietnamese boat people were all money middlemen who took on that role because no other positions were open to them. All of these groups suffered terrible fates.

The Confirmation Bias

People dealing with Jews in the 18th century in Europe or with Armenians in Turkey at the turn of the 20th century found it easy to confirm their expectancies about these groups; perceivers could recall the moneylenders, the strange dress, the different customs. Stereotypes are both self-confirming and resistant to change.

Numerous studies show that stereotypes can influence social interactions in ways that lead to their confirmation. In one study, some participants were told that a person with whom they would soon talk was in psychotherapy; other participants were told nothing about the person (Sibicky & Dovidio, 1986). In actuality, the individuals they talked to were randomly chosen students from basic psychology courses; none were in therapy. After the interviews, participants were asked to evaluate the person with whom they had interacted. Those individuals identified as therapy clients were rated less confident, less attractive, and less likable than the individuals not described as being in therapy.

We can see from this study that once people have a stereotype, they evaluate information within the context of that stereotype. After all, none of the people being interviewed in the experiment were in fact in therapy The differences between the ratings had to be due to the participants' stereotypical view of what somebody in therapy must be like. Describing a person as being in therapy seems to lead to a negative perception of that person. People who hold negative stereotypes about certain groups may behave so that group members act in a way that confirms the stereotype (Crocker & Major, 1989). The confirmation bias contributes in many instances to self-fulfilling prophecies. If you expect a person to be hostile, your very expectation and the manner in which you behave may bring on that hostility. In the study just described, participants who thought they were interacting with someone in therapy probably held a stereotypical view of all people with psychological problems. It is likely that they behaved in a way that made those individuals uneasy and caused them to act in a less confident manner.

The Out-Group Homogeneity Bias

An initial effect of categorization is that members of the category are thought to be more similar to each other than is the case when people are viewed as individuals. Because we have a fair amount of information about the members of our own group (the in-group), we are able to differentiate among them. But we tend to view members of other groups (out-groups) as being very similar to one another (Wilder, 1986). This phenomenon of perceiving members of the out-group as all alike is called the **out-group homogeneity bias** (Linville, Fischer, & Salovey, 1989).

The out-group homogeneity hypothesis was tested in one study involving students from Princeton and Rutgers universities (Quattrone & Jones, 1980). Participants, who were either Rutgers or Princeton students, saw a videotape of a student supposedly from the other school. The videotaped person had to decide whether he wanted to wait alone or with other people before being a participant in a psychological experiment. The actual participant then had to predict what the average student at the target university (Rutgers for Princeton students and Princeton for Rutgers students) would do in a similar situation.

Would the participants see students at the other university as similar to the student they had viewed? Would they predict that most Princeton students (or Rutgers students) would make the same choice as the Princeton student (or Rutgers student) in the film clip? These questions get at the issue of whether people see out-group members as more similar to one another than to the in-group members. In fact, this is pretty much what the study showed, although there was a greater tendency to stereotype Princeton students than Rutgers students. That seems logical, because it is probably easier to conjure up a stereotype of Princeton student. In general, however, results supported the notion that the out-group homogeneity bias leads us to think that members of out-groups are more similar to one another than to members of in-groups.

A second outcome of out-group homogeneity bias is the assumption that any behavior of an out-group member reflects the characteristics of all group members. If a member of an out-group does something bad, we tend to conclude, "That's the way those people are." In contrast, when an in-group member does something equally negative, we tend to make a dispositional attribution, blaming the person rather than our own in-group for the negative behavior. This has been referred to as the **ultimate attribution error:** We are more likely to give in-group members the benefit of the doubt than out-group members (Pettigrew, 1979).

Once we construct our categories, we tend to hold on to them tenaciously, which may be both innocent and destructive. It is innocent because the process is likely to be automatic and nonconscious. It is destructive because stereotypes are inaccurate and often damaging; individuals cannot be adequately described by reference to the groups to which they belong.

In general, social psychologists have not made a consistent attempt to determine the accuracy of stereotypes. Much of the early research on stereotypes assumed that stereotypes were inaccurate by definition. More recently, the issue of stereotype accuracy has been addressed by Charles Judd and Bernadette Park (1993). They suggested several technical standards against which the accuracy of a stereotype can be measured. For example, consider the notion that Germans are efficient. One standard that Judd and Park suggested to measure the accuracy of that stereotype is to find data that answers the questions: Are Germans in reality more or less efficient than the stereotype? Is the group attribute (efficiency) exaggerated?

Of course, to apply these standards we need some objective data about groups. We need to know how groups truly behave with respect to various characteristics. For some attributes, say, kindness or sensitivity, it is probably impossible to obtain such information. For others, there may be readily available data.

---

out-group homogeneity bias
The predisposition to see members of an out-group as having similar characteristics or being all alike.

---

ultimate attribution error
The tendency to give in-group—but not out-group—members the benefit of the doubt for negative behaviors.

In MaCauley and Stitt's 1978 study of the accuracy of stereotypes, white participants' estimates of certain attributes of the African-American population were compared with public records (as cited in Judd & Park, 1993). The attributes estimated were percentage of high school graduates, number of crime victims, and number of people on the welfare rolls. This study showed that whites underestimated the differences between African Americans and themselves with respect to these attributes. In other words, whites thought more African Americans graduated from high school than was true and they thought fewer African Americans were victims of crime than the data showed.

Is it important to know if a stereotype is accurate? Technically it is, because many of the earlier definitions of stereotypes assume that inaccuracy is part of the definition of the concept (Stangor & Lange, 1994). Most stereotypes are unjustified generalizations; that is, they are not accurate. But, even if they are accurate, stereotypes still have a damaging effect on our perception of others. None of us would wish to be judged as an individual by the worst examples of the group(s) to which we belong.

In previous chapters, we have seen how automatic and controlled processing enter into the social cognition process. Some people use controlled processing to readjust initial impressions of others in instances where new information conflicts with existing categorization (Fiske & Neuberg, 1990, Trope, 1986). Automatic and controlled processing again come into play when we consider how stereotypes are maintained and how prejudiced and nonprejudiced individuals differ.

The Difference Between Prejudiced and Nonprejudiced Individuals

Patricia Devine (1989) contends that stereotypes are automatically activated when we encounter a member of a particular social group. According to Devine, some people are able to consciously alter their prejudiced responses, whereas others are not. Devine found that those interested in being nonprejudiced think differently from those who are not. For example, prejudiced individuals are more willing to indulge in negative thoughts and behaviors toward members of different racial and ethnic groups than nonprejudiced individuals. Devine also found that both high- and low-prejudiced whites hold almost the same stereotypes of African Americans. However, nonprejudiced individuals think those stereotypes are wrong.

Devine also found that the main difference between prejudiced and nonprejudiced whites was that nonprejudiced whites are sensitive to and carefully monitor their stereotypes. The nonprejudiced person wants his or her behavior to be consistent with his or her true beliefs rather than his or her stereotypes. When given a chance to use controlled processing, nonprejudiced individuals show behavior that is more consistent with nonprejudiced true beliefs than stereotyped beliefs. In contrast, the behavior of prejudiced individuals is more likely to be guided by stereotypes. In another study, nonprejudiced individuals were more likely than prejudiced individuals to feel bad when they had thoughts about gay men and lesbians that ran counter to their beliefs (Monteith, Devine, & Zuwerink, 1993). When nonprejudiced individuals express prejudicial thoughts and feelings, they feel guilty about doing so (Devine, Montieth, Zuwerink, & Elliot, 1991).

What happens if automatic processing takes over? According to Devine, activating a stereotype puts a person into automatic mode when confronting a person from the stereotyped group. The automatically activated stereotype will be acted on by both prejudiced and nonprejudiced individuals unless there is an opportunity to use controlled processing (Devine, 1989). Devine found that when participants in an experiment were prevented from switching to controlled processing, both prejudiced and nonprejudiced individuals evaluated the behavior of an African American negatively.

We can draw several conclusions from Devine's research. First, prejudiced individuals are less inhibited about expressing their prejudice than nonprejudiced individuals. Second, no differences exist between prejudiced and nonprejudiced individuals when stereotype activation is beyond conscious control. Third, nonprejudiced people work hard to inhibit the expression of negative stereotypes when they have the opportunity to monitor behavior and bring stereotypes under conscious control. Fourth, nonprejudiced individuals realize that there is a gap between their stereotypes and their general beliefs about equality and they work continually to change their stereotyped thinking.

THE CONSEQUENCES OF BEING A TARGET OF PREJUDICE

Imagine being awakened several times each night by a telephone caller who inundates you with racial or religious slurs. Imagine being a second-generation Japanese-American soldier on December 8, 1941 (the day after the Pearl Harbor attack) and being told you are no longer trusted to carry a gun in defense of your country. Imagine being an acknowledged war hero who is denied the Medal of Honor because of race-related suspicions of your loyalty to the country for which you had just fought. In each of these instances, a person becomes the target of prejudicial attitudes, stereotypes, and discriminatory behavior directed at him or her. What effect does being the

Being the target of prejudice has several negative consequences for those who are targeted. After the Japanese attack on Pearl Harbor on December 7, 1941, Japanese Americans, many of whom were second and third generation citizens of the United States, were rounded up and sent to internment camps because their loyalty to the United States was questioned. In addition, their homes, businesses and property were also confiscated.

target of such prejudice have on an individual? To be sure, being a target of discrimination generates a great deal of negative affect and has serious emotional consequences for the target (Dion & Earn, 1975). Next, we explore some of the effects that prejudice has on those who are its targets.

Ways Prejudice Can Be Expressed

In his monumental work on prejudice called *The Nature of Prejudice*, Gordon Allport (1954) suggested that there are five ways that prejudice can be expressed. These are *antilocution*, talking in terms of prejudice or making jokes about an out-group; *avoidance*, avoiding contact with members of an out-group; *discrimination*, actively doing something to deny members of an out-group something they desire; *physical attack*, beatings, lynchings, and the like; and *extermination*, an attempt to eliminate an entire group. One issue we must address is the reaction shown by members of an out-group when they are targeted with prejudice. It is fairly obvious that those faced with overt discrimination, physical attack, and extermination will respond negatively. But, what about reactions to more subtle forms of prejudice? What toll do they take on a member of a minority group?

everyday prejudice
Prejudice that comprises recurrent and familiar events considered to be commonplace.

Janet Swim, Laurie Cohen, and Lauri Hyers (1998) characterized some forms of prejudice as **everyday prejudice,** "recurrent and familiar events that can be considered commonplace" (p. 37). These include short-term interaction such as remarks and stares, and incidents that can be directed at an individual or an entire group. According to Swim and colleagues, such incidents can be initiated either by strangers or by those with intimate relationships with the target and have a cumulative effect and contribute to the target's experience with and knowledge of prejudice.

PREJUDICE-BASED JOKES   How do encounters with everyday prejudice affect the target? Let's startby looking at one form of antilocution discussed by Allport that mostpeople see as harmless: prejudice-based jokes. Most of us have heard(and laughed at) jokes that make members of a group the butt of the joke. Many of us may have even told such jokes, assuming that they do no harm. But how do those on the receiving end feel? Women, for example, find sexist jokes less funny and less amusing than nonsexist jokes (LaFrance & Woodzicka, 1998). They also tend to report feeling more disgusted, angry, hostile, and surprised by sexist versus nonsexist jokes. They also tend to roll their eyes indicating disgust, and touch their faces, indicating embarassment, more in response to sexist than to nonsexist jokes (LaFrance & Woodzicka, 1998).

Kathryn Ryan and Jeanne Kanjorski (1998) directly compared the reactions of men and women to sexist jokes. They found that compared to men, women enjoyed sexist humor less and found it less acceptable and more offensive. Interestingly, men and women did not differ in terms of telling sexist jokes. A more ominous finding was that for men, there were significant positive correlations between enjoyment of sexist humor and rape myth acceptance, adversarial sexual beliefs, acceptance of interpersonal violence, likelihood of engaging in forced sex, and sexual aggression. This latter finding may lend some credence to Allport's (1954) idea that antilocution, once accepted, sets the stage for more serious expressions of prejudice.

STEREOTYPE-BASED THREAT As noted earlier, affiliation with groups often contributes to a positive social identity. What about membership in a group that does not confer a positive social identity? Not all social groups have the same social status and perceived value. What happens when an individual is faced with doing a task for which a negative stereotype exists for that person's group? For example, it is well-established that blacks tend to do more poorly academically than whites. What happens when a black individual is faced with a task that will indicate academic aptitude?

One intriguing hypothesis about why blacks might not score well on standard tests of IQ comes from an experiment conducted by Steele & Aronson (1995). According to Steele and Aronson, when a person is asked to perform a task for which there is a negative stereotype attached to their group, that person will perform poorly, because the task is threatening. They called this idea a **stereotype threat**. To test the hypothesis that members of a group perform more poorly on tasks that relate to prevailing negative stereotypes, Steele and Aronson conducted the following experiment. Black and white participants took a test comprising items from the verbal section of the Graduate Record Exam. One-third of the participants were told that the test was diagnostic of their intellectual ability (diagnostic condition). One-third were told that the test was a laboratory tool for studying problem solving (nondiagnostic condition). The final third were told that the test was of problem solving and would present a challenge to the participants (nondiagnostic–challenge condition). Steele and Aronson then determined the average number of items answered correctly within each group.

The results of this experiment showed that when the test was said to be diagnostic of one's intellectual abilities, black and white participants differed significantly, with black participants performing more poorly than white participants. However, when the *same* test was presented as nondiagnostic, black and white participants did equally well. There was no significant difference between blacks and whites in the nondiagnostic-challenge condition. Overall across the three conditions, blacks performed most poorly in the diagnostic condition. In a second experiment, Steele and Aronson (1995) produced results that were even more pronounced than in their first. They also found that black participants in the diagnostic condition finished fewer items and worked more slowly than black participants in the nondiagnostic condition. Steele and Aronson pointed out that this is a pattern consistent with impairments caused by test anxiety, evaluation apprehension, and competitive pressure.

In a final experiment, Steele and Aronson (1995) had participants perform word-completion tasks (e.g., __ __ ce; la __ __; __ __ ack; __ __ or) that could be completed in a racially stereotyped way (e.g., race: lazy) or a nonstereotyped way (e.g., pace; lace). This was done to test if stereotypes are activated when Participants were told that a test was either diagnostic or nondiagnostic. Steele and Aronson found that there was greater stereotype activation among blacks in the diagnostic condition compared to the nondiagnostic condition. They also found that in the diagnostic condition, blacks were more likely than whites to engage in self-handicapping strategies (i.e., developing behavior patterns that actually interfere with performance, such as losing sleep the night before a test). Blacks and whites did not differ on self-handicapping behaviors in the nondiagnostic condition.

stereotype threat
The condition that exists when a person is asked to perform a task for which there is a negative stereotype attached to their group and performs poorly because the task is threatening.

These findings help us understand why blacks consistently perform more poorly than whites on intelligence tests. Intelligence tests by their very nature and purpose are diagnostic of one's intellectual abilities. According to Steele and Aronson's (1995) analysis, when a black person is faced with the prospect of taking a test that is diagnostic of intellectual ability, it activates the common stereotype threat that blacks are not supposed to perform well on tests of intellectual ability. According to Steele and Aronson, the stereotype threat impairs performance by generating evaluative pressures. Recall that participants who were under stereotype threat in the diagnostic condition spent more time doing fewer items. As they became more frustrated, performance was impaired. It may also impair future performance, because more self-handicapping strategies are used by blacks facing diagnostic tests. In short, the stereotype threat creates an impairment in the ability to cognitively process information adequately, which in turn, inhibits performance. So, lower scores on IQ tests by blacks may relate more to the activation of the stereotype threat than to any genetic differences between blacks and whites.

Recently, Steele and his colleagues extended the notion of the stereotype threat to other groups. For example, Spencer, Steele, and Quinn (cited in Aronson, Quinn, & Spencer, 1998) found that men and women equated for math ability performed differently on a math test depending on whether they were told that there were past results showing no gender differences in performance on the test (alleviating the stereotype threat) or given no information about gender differences (allowing the stereotype threat to be activated). Specifically, when the "no gender differences" information was given, men and women performed equally well on the test. However, when the stereotype threat was allowed to be activated (i.e., that women perform more poorly on math tests than do men), men scored significantly higher than women. Aronson and Alainas reported similar effects for Latino versus white participants and white males versus Asian males (cited in Aronson et al., 1998).

In a more direct test of the relationship between gender, stereotype threat, and math performance, Brown and Josephs (1999) told male and female students that they would be taking a math test. One-half of the participants of each gender were told that the test would identify exceptionally strong math abilities, whereas the other half was told that the test would uncover especially weak math skills. Brown and Josephs reasoned that for males the test for strong math skills would be more threatening, because it plays into the stereotype that males are strong in math. On the other hand, the test for weakness would be more threatening to females, because females stereotypically are viewed as being weak in math. Their results were consistent with Steele and Aronson's stereotype threat notion. Males performed poorly on the test that supposedly measured exceptional math skills. Conversely, females performed poorly on the test that was said to identify weak math skills. In both cases, a stereotype was activated that was relevant to gender, which inhibited performance. According to Brown and Josephs, the stereotype threat for math performance is experienced differently for males and females. Males feel more threatened when faced with having to prove themselves worthy of the label of being strong in math skills, whereas females feel more threatened when they face a situation that may prove a stereotype to be true.

Stereotype threat also operates by reducing positive expectations a person has going into a situation. For example, based on a person's previous experience, he or she may feel confident about doing well on the SATs, having a positive expectation about his or her performance on the exam. Now, let's say that a stereotype of this person's group is activated prior to taking the exam. The resulting stereotype threat may lower that person's expectations about the test, and as a consequence, the person does not do well.

The fact that this scenario can happen was verified in an experiment by Charles Stangor, Christine Carr, and Lisa Kiang (1998). Female participants in this experiment all performed an initial task of identifying words. Afterward, some participants were told that their performance on the task provided clear evidence that they had an aptitude for college-level work. Other participants were told that the evidence concerning college performance was unclear. Next, participants were told that there was either strong evidence that men did better than women on the second test (stereotype threat) or that there were no sex differences (no stereotype threat). Before working on the second task, participants were asked to rate their ability to perform the second task successfully. The results of this experiment, shown in Figure 4.8 were clear. When a stereotype threat was not activated, performance was affected by the feedback given after the first task. Those participants who believed that there was clear, positive evidence of college aptitude had higher expectations of success than those given unclear feedback. In the stereotype threat condition, the two groups did not differ in their expectations concerning the second task.

Thus, in addition to arousing anxiety about testing situations, stereotype threats also lower one's expectations about one's performance. Once these negative expectations develop, a self-fulfilling prophecy is most likely developed that "Because I am a female, I am not expected to do well on this task." Poor performance then confirms that prophecy.

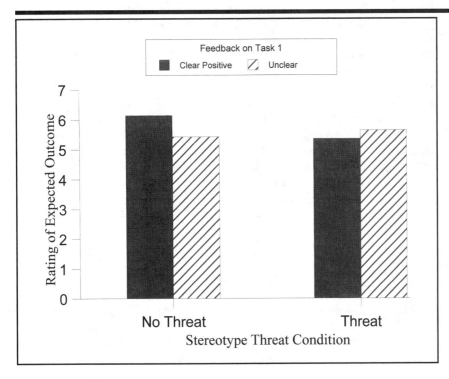

Figure 4.8

Task performance as a function of feedback about prior performance and activation of a stereotype threat. When no threat was activated, participants used performance on a prior task to form expectations about future performance. When a threat was activated, performance was affected by what was expected based on the stereotype.

From Charles Stangor, Christine Carr, and Lisa Kiang (1998). Reprinted with permission.

Coping with Prejudice

It should be obvious from our previous discussion that being a target of prejudice has a variety of negative consequences. Individuals facing instance after instance of everyday prejudice must find ways to deal with its effects. How, for example, can an overweight person who is constantly the target of prejudice effectively manage its consequences? In this section, we explore some strategies that individuals use to cope with being a target of prejudice.

One method of coping with prejudice when your group is stigmatized, oppressed, or less valued than other groups is to raise its value. This is done by first convincing group members of their own self-worth and then convincing the rest of society of the group's worth. The function of all consciousness-raising efforts and positive in-group slogans is to persuade the members of scorned or less-valued groups that they are beautiful or smart or worthy or competent. This first step, maintaining and increasing self-esteem, can be approached in at least two ways (Crocker & Major, 1989; Crocker, Voelkl, Testa, & Major, 1991): attributing negative events to prejudice of the majority and comparing oneself to members of one's own group.

First, for example, supposed that an African-American woman is denied a job or a promotion. She can better maintain her self-esteem if she attributes this outcome to the prejudice of the person evaluating her. Of course, people are usually uncertain about the true motives of other people in situations like this. Although a rejection by a majority group member can be attributed to the evaluator's prejudice, the effects on the self-esteem of the minority person are complex.

Some of these effects were investigated in a study in which African-American participants were evaluated by white evaluators (Crocker & Major, 1989). When participants thought that evaluators were uninfluenced by their race, positive evaluations increased their self-esteem. But when participants knew that evaluators were influenced by their race, positive evaluations decreased their self-esteem. Compared to whites, African Americans were more likely to attribute both positive and negative evaluations to prejudice. Any judgment, positive or negative, that the recipient thought was based on racism led to a decrease in self-esteem (Crocker et al., 1991).

Uncertainty about such evaluations thus has important consequences for self-esteem. In our society, African Americans are often evaluated primarily by whites, which suggests that they may always feel uncertain about their evaluators' motives (Crocker et al., 1991). This uncertainty may be exacerbated for African-American females who are evaluated by white males (Coleman, Jussim, & Isaac, 1991).

Second, members of less-favored groups can maintain self-esteem by comparing themselves with members of their own group rather than with members of the more favored or fortunate groups. In-group comparisons may be less painful and more rewarding for members of stigmatized groups. Research supports this hypothesis in a number of areas, including pay, abilities, and physical attractiveness (Crocker & Major, 1989). Once group members have raised their value in their own eyes, the group is better placed to assert itself in society.

As the feelings of cohesiveness and belonging of the in-group increase, there is often an escalation in hostility directed toward the out-group

(Allport, 1954). History teaches us that self-identifying with an in-group and identifying others with an out-group underlie many instances of prejudice and intergroup hostility.

Swim, Cohen, & Hyers (1998) suggested that another strategy for individuals from a stigmatized group is to try to anticipate situations in which prejudice will be encountered. By doing this, the individual can decide how to best react or to minimize the impact of prejudice. The individual may decide to alter their demeanor, manner of dress, or even where they go to school or live in an effort to minimize the likelihood of encountering prejudice (Swim et al., 1998).

Once a person has made an assessment of a situation for anticipated prejudice, that person must next decide what course of action to take. The individual could choose to confront the prejudice and move toward the original goal or choose to avoid the prejudiced situation and find some alternative (Swim et al., 1998). For example, a black family may anticipate prejudice if they move into an all-white neighborhood. The family could choose to move into the all-white neighborhood (original goal) and cope with the prejudice they may experience. An alternative course of action would be to move into a racially mixed neighborhood and avoid the threat of prejudice inherent in the original situation. Of course, it is not possible or even desirable to completely avoid situations in which prejudice can arise. In cases where it does, other coping strategies must be developed.

Members of a stigmatized group can also engage in *compensation* to cope with prejudice (Miller & Myers, 1998). According to Carol Miller and Anna Myers, there are two modes of compensation in which a person can engage. When **secondary compensation** is used, an individual attempts to change their mode of thinking about situations to psychologically protect themselves against the outcomes of prejudice. For example, a person who wants to obtain a college degree but faces prejudice that may prevent reaching the goal would be using secondary compensation if he or she devalued the goal (a college education is not all that important) or disidentified with the goal (members of my group usually don't go to college). On the other hand, **primary compensation** reduces the actual threats posed by prejudice. Coping strategies are developed that allow the targets of prejudice to achieve their goals. For example, the person in the example could increase his or her effort (study harder in school), use latent skills (become more persistent), or develop new skills to help achieve goals that are blocked by prejudice. When primary compensation is used, it reduces the need for secondary compensation (Miller & Myers, 1998).

Interestingly, coping with prejudice is different if you are talking about individual coping as opposed to group coping. Mummendey, Kessler, Klink, and Mielke (1999) tested coping strategies tied to two theories relating to being a target of prejudice: social identity theory and relative deprivation theory. As you read earlier, social identity theory proposes that individuals derive part of their self-concept from affiliation with a group. If the group with which you affiliate has negative stereotypes attached to it, the social identity will be negative. According to *relative deprivation theory*, members of a stereotyped group recognize that they are undervalued and reap fewer benefits from society than more preferred groups. In theory, negative social identity should lead to individually based coping strategies, whereas perceived relative deprivation should lead to group-based coping (Mummendey et al., 1999).

secondary compensation
A method of handling prejudice involving attempts to change one's mode of thinking about situations to psychologically protect oneself against the outcomes of prejudice.

primary compensation
A method of managing prejudice that reduces threats posed by prejudice and using coping strategies that allow targets of prejudice to achieve their goals.

To test this hypothesis, residents of former East Germany were administered a questionnaire concerning social identity and relative deprivation. The questionnaire also measured several identity management strategies. Mummendey and colleagues (1999) found that social identity issues were handled with management strategies (e.g., mobility and recategorization of the self to a higher level in the group) that stressed one's individual attachment with an in-group. Management techniques relating to relative deprivation were more group based, focusing on group-based strategies such as collective action to reduce relative deprivation. In addition, social identity issues were tied closely with cognitive aspects of group affiliation, whereas relative deprivation was mediated strongly by emotions such as anger.

REDUCING PREJUDICE

A rather gloomy conclusion that may be drawn from the research on the cognitive processing of social information is that normal cognitive functioning leads inevitably to the development and maintenance of social stereotypes (Mackie, Allison, Vorth, & Asuncion, 1992). Social psychologists have investigated the strategies that people can use to reduce prejudice and intergroup hostility. In the following sections, we explore some of these actions.

Contact Between Groups

contact hypothesis
A hypothesis that contact between groups will reduce hostility, which is most effective when members of different groups have equal status and a mutual goal.

In his classic book *The Nature of Prejudice* (1954), Gordon Allport proposed the **contact hypothesis**. According to this hypothesis, contact between groups will reduce hostility when the participants have equal status and a mutual goal. However, the contact hypothesis has not been strongly supported by research evidence (Miller & Brewer, 1984). Even if there is friendly contact, people still manage to defend their stereotypes. Friendly interaction between individual members of different racial groups may have little effect on their prejudices, because the person they are interacting with may be seen as exceptional and not representative of the out-group (Horwitz & Rabbie, 1989).

In one early study, two groups of boys at a summer camp were made to be competitive and then hostile toward each other (Sherif, Harvey, White, Hood, & Sherif, 1961). At the end of the camp experience, when the researchers tried to reduce the intergroup hostility, they found that contact between the groups and among the boys was not sufficient to reduce hostility. In fact, contact only made the situation worse. It was only when the groups had to work together in pulling a vehicle out of the mud so that they could continue on a long-awaited trip that hostility was reduced. This cooperation on a goal that was important to both groups is called a *superordinate goal*, which is essentially the same as Allport's notion of a mutual goal.

Further evidence that under certain circumstances contact does lead to a positive change in the image of an out-group member comes from other research. College students were asked to interact with another student described as a former patient at a mental hospital (Desforges et al., 1991). Students were led to expect that the former patient would behave in a manner similar to a typical mental patient. Some of the participants were initially prejudiced toward mental patients, and others were not. After working with the former mental patient in a 1-hour-long cooperative task, the initially prejudiced participants showed a positive change in their feelings about the former patient.

As shown in Figure 4.9, participants experienced a three-stage alteration. At first, they formed a category-based impression: "This is a former mental

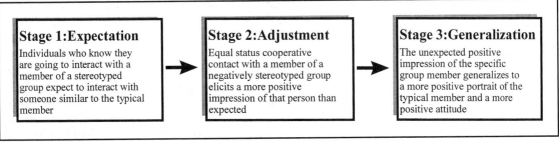

Stage 1: Expectation	Stage 2: Adjustment	Stage 3: Generalization
Individuals who know they are going to interact with a member of a stereotyped group expect to interact with someone similar to the typical member	Equal status cooperative contact with a member of a negatively stereotyped group elicits a more positive impression of that person than expected	The unexpected positive impression of the specific group member generalizes to a more positive portrait of the typical member and a more positive attitude

Figure 4.9   *Three stages in the alternation of characteristics attributed to the typical group member and general attitudes toward the group through structured contact with a group member.*

From Desforges (1991). Reprinted with permission.

patient, and this is the way mental patients behave." But equal status and the necessity for cooperation (Allport's two conditions) compelled the participants to make an adjustment in their initial automatically formed impression (Fiske & Neuberg, 1990). This is the second stage. Finally, once the adjustment was made, participants generalized the change in feelings to other mental patients (although they might have concluded, as tends to be more common, that this patient was different from other former mental patients). Note that the readjustment of the participants' feelings toward the former mental patient was driven by paying attention to the personal characteristics of that individual.

In another setting (a school room), Eliot Aronson found that the use of tasks that require each person to solve some part of the whole problem reduces prejudice among school children (Aronson, Blaney, Stephan, Sikes, & Snapp, 1978). This approach, called the *jigsaw classroom*, requires that each group member be assigned responsibility for a part of the problem. Group members then share their knowledge with everyone else. The concept works because the problem cannot be solved without the efforts of all members; thus, each person is valued. This technique also tends to increase the self-esteem of members of different ethnic groups, because their efforts are valued.

Does the contact hypothesis work? Yes, but with very definite limits. It seems that both parties have to have a goal they both want and cannot achieve without the other. This superordinate goal also has to compel both to attend to each other's individual characteristics. It also seems to be important that they be successful in obtaining that goal.

Even when all these conditions are met, individuals may revert to their prior beliefs when they leave the interaction. Palestinians and Israelis meeting in Egypt to resolve differences and conclude peace may find their stereotypes of the other side lessening as they engage in face-to-face, equal, and (perhaps) mutually rewarding contact. But when they go home, the pressure from other members of their groups may compel them to take up their prior beliefs again.

Personalizing Out-Group Members

According to Henri Tajfel (1982), the Nazis attempted to deny Jews and others their individuality, their identity, by defining them as outside the category of human beings, as *Untermenschen*, subhumans. This dehumanization made it easy for even humane individuals to brutalize and kill because they did not see the individual men, women, and children who were their victims (Horwitz & Rabbie, 1989).

If dehumanizing people makes it easier to be prejudiced, even to carry out the worst atrocities, then perhaps humanizing people, personalizing them, can reduce stereotyping and prejudice. People are less likely to use gender stereotypes, for example, when they have the time to process information that tells them about the distinctive traits of individual males and females (Pratto & Bargh, 1991). Humanizing members of a group does not necessarily mean that we must know or understand each individual in that group (Bodenhausen, 1993). It means we understand that we and they have a shared humanity and that we all feel the same joys and pains. Overall, although personalization is not always successful, especially if the individual is disliked, it does make it more difficult for people to act in a prejudiced manner (Fiske & Neuberg, 1990).

In the 1993 movie *Schindler's List*, an event occurs that illustrates the notion of humanizing the other group. Schindler has managed to save 1,200 Jews otherwise destined for the gas chambers by employing them in his factory. Schindler knows that the German guards have orders to kill all the Jews should the war end. When news comes that the war is over, the guards stand on a balcony overlooking the factory floor, their weapons pointed at the workers. But these Germans have had contact with the Jews; they have seen Schindler treat them humanely, and they have heard them praying and celebrating the Sabbath. Schindler, desperate to save his charges, challenges the Germans: "Do you want to go home as men or as murderers?" The guards hesitate and then slowly leave. Did the Germans put up their weapons out of a sense of shared humanity, or were they simply tired of killing people? In any event, the Jews survived.

Reducing the Expression of Prejudice Through Social Norms

In the spring of 1989, four African-American students at Smith College received anonymous notes containing racial slurs. The incident led to campuswide protests. It also inspired an experiment designed to determine the most effective way to deter such expressions of hatred (Blanchard, Lilly, & Vaughn, 1991). The answer? Attack the behaviors—the acts of hatred themselves—not people's feelings about racial issues.

In one experiment, students were asked how they felt the college should respond to these anonymous notes. Some participants then "overheard" a confederate of the experimenters express the opinion that the letter writer, if discovered, should be expelled. Other participants "overheard" the confederate justify the letters by saying the African-American students probably did something to deserve it. The study showed that clear antiracist statements (the person should be expelled) set a tone for other students that discouraged the expression of racial sentiment. Because, as we have seen, racial stereotypes are automatically activated and resistant to change, the best way to discourage racial behavior is through the strong expression of social norms—disapproval from students, campus leaders, and the whole college community (Cook, 1984).

Another kind of prejudice, *heterosexism*, has been deflected in recent years by appeal to social norms as well as by the threat of social sanctions.

The Gay and Lesbian Alliance Against Defamation (GLAAD), increasingly supported by public opinion, has targeted pop musicians who sing antigay lyrics and make antigay statements. Facing the cancellation of concerts and TV appearances, targeted musicians such as reggae star Shabba Ranks and rap singer Marky Mark have apologized and promised to refrain from spouting hate lyrics (Farber, 1993).

Is it realistically possible to reduce racist, sexist, heterosexist, and ethnic hate acts? Strengthening social norms may be our best hope in approaching this problem. We turn now to one success story, the U.S. Army. Granted, it is a special case, and not all the lessons learned are applicable to other situations. But even in this case, things seemed hopeless at one point. The army began to attack its problems only when it was about to disintegrate because of racial hatred.

A Success Story: The Disarming of Racism in the U.S. Army

During the Vietnam War, race relations in the U.S. Army were abysmal (Moskos, 1991). Fights between white and African American soldiers were commonplace in army life in the 1970s. By the early 1980s, the army was making an organized and determined effort to eliminate racial prejudice and animosities. It appears to have succeeded admirably. Many of the strategies the Army used are based on principles discussed in this chapter. Let's consider what they were.

One important strategy used by the army was the *level playing field*. (Moskos, 1990, 1991). This means that from basic training onward, everyone is treated the same—the same haircuts, the same uniforms, the same rules and regulations. This helps to reduce advantages and handicaps and to make everyone equal. The army also has a basic remedial education program that is beneficial for those with leadership qualities but deficits in schooling.

A second factor is a rigid no-discrimination policy. Any expression of racist sentiments results in an unfavorable rating and an end to a military career. This is not to say that officers are free of racist sentiments; it merely means that officers jeopardize their careers if they express or act on such sentiments. A racial insult can lead to a charge of incitement to riot and is punishable by time in the brig. The army uses social scientists to monitor the state of racial relations. It also runs training programs for equal-opportunity instructors, whose function is to see that the playing field remains level.

The army's ability to enforce a nonracist environment is supported enormously by the *hierarchy* that exists both within the officer corps and among the noncommissioned officers. The social barriers that exist in the army reflect rank rather than race. A sergeant must have a stronger identification with his or her peer sergeants than with members of the same race in lower ranks.

Finally, the army's nondiscriminatory environment is visible in its leadership. Many African Americans have leadership roles in the army, including General Colin Powell, the former chairman of the Joint Chiefs of Staff.

What lessons can we learn from the Army's experience? First, a fair implementation of the contact hypothesis is a good starting point for reducing prejudice. Equal-status interaction and clear mutual goals, even superordinate goals, are essential ingredients of effective contact. Clear and forceful support of the program by leadership is another ingredient. Anyone who violates the policy suffers. At the same time, positive action is taken to level prior inequalities. The army's special programs ensure that everyone has an equal chance.

Some of these lessons cannot be transferred from the army setting. Civilian society does not have the army's strict hierarchy, its control over its members, or its system of rewards and punishments. But the fundamental lesson may be that race relations can best be served by strengthening positive social norms. When social norms are very clear, and when there is a clear commitment to nondiscrimination by leadership—employers, politicians, and national leaders—individual members of society have the opportunity to transcend their prejudices and act on their shared humanity.

THE MORMON EXPERIENCE REVISITED

We opened this chapter with a discussion of the experience of the Mormons in the 1800s. The Mormons were the victims of stereotyping (branded as heretics), prejudice (negative attitudes directed at them by the population and the press), and discrimination (economic boycotts). They were viewed as the out-group by Christians (the in-group) to the extent that they began living in their own, homogeneous enclaves, and even became the target of an extermination order. Once the "us" versus "them" mentality set in, it was easy enough for the Christian majority to pigeonhole Mormons and act toward individual Mormons based on what was believed about them as a group. This is what we would expect based on social identity theory and self-categorization theory. By perceiving the Mormons as evil and themselves the protector of all that is sacred, the Christian majority undoubtedly was able to enhance the self-esteem of its members.

The reaction of the Mormons to the prejudice also fits nicely with what we know about how prejudice affects people. Under conditions of threat, we tend to ban more closely together as a protection mechanism. The Mormons became more clannish and isolated from mainstream society. This is an example of using primary compensation to cope with the prejudice. The Mormons decided to keep to themselves and tried not to antagonize the Christian majority. Unfortunately, this increased isolation was viewed as the majority as further evidence for the stereotypes about the Mormons. Ultimately, the cycle of prejudice continued until the Mormons were driven to settle in Utah.

CHAPTER REVIEW

1. **How are prejudice, stereotypes, and discrimination defined?**

   Prejudice is defined as a biased, often negative, attitude about a group of people. Prejudicial attitudes include belief structures housing information about a group and expectations concerning the behavior of members of that group. Prejudice can be positive or negative, with negative prejudice—dislike for a group—being the focus of research and theory. A **stereotype** is a rigid set of positive or negative beliefs about the characteristics of a group. A stereotype represents pictures we keep in our heads. When a prejudiced person encounters a member of a group, he or she will activate the stereotype and fit it to the individual. Stereotypes are not abnormal ways of thinking. Rather, they relate to the natural tendency for humans to categorize. Categorization becomes problematic when categories become rigid and overgeneralized. Stereotypes may also form the basis for judgmental heuristics about the behavior of members of a group. **Discrimination** is the behavioral component of a prejudicial attitude. Discrimination occurs when prejudicial feelings are turned into behavior. Like stereotyping, discrimination is an extension of a natural tendency to discriminate among stimuli. Discrimination becomes a problem when it is directed toward people simply because they are members of a group. It is important to note that discrimination can occur in the absence of prejudice, and prejudice can exist without discrimination.

2. **What is the relationship among prejudice, stereotypes, and discrimination?**

   Prejudice, stereotypes and discrimination, are related phenomena that help us understand why we treat members of certain groups with hostility. Prejudice comes in a variety of forms, with sexism (negative feelings based on gender category) and racism (negative feelings based on apparent racial category) being most common. Stereotyped beliefs about members of a group often give rise to prejudicial feelings, which may give rise to discriminatory behavior.

   Stereotypes also may serve as judgmental heuristics and affect the way we interpret the behavior of members of a group. Behavior that is seen as stereotype consistent is likely to be attributed internally and judged more harshly than behavior that is not stereotype consistent.

3. **What evidence is there for the prevalence of these three concepts from a historical perspective?**

   History tells us that stereotyping, prejudice, and discrimination have been with human beings for a long time. Once formed, stereotypes and prejudices endure over time. Stereotyped views of Japanese by Americans (and vice versa) endured from the World War II era through the present. Prejudicial feelings also led to religious persecution in the United States against groups such as the Mormons.

4. **What are the personality roots of prejudice?**

   One personality dimension identified with prejudice is **authoritarianism**. People with **authoritarian personalities** tend to feel submissive toward authority figures and hostile toward different ethnic groups. They have rigid beliefs and tend to be racist and sexist. Social psychologists have also explored how members of different groups, such as whites and blacks, perceive each other. The United States has a long history of racist feelings and behavior. White Americans today may acknowledge that African Americans have received a raw deal, but they may still blame them, at least partially, for their problems. Although few whites today admit to overt prejudice, they may be aversive racists, professing unprejudiced attitudes but still feeling uncomfortable around African Americans. Another demonstration of prejudice is modern racism, a less open form of racism in which racist sentiments come out only under certain circumstances.

5. How does gender relate to prejudice?

Research on male and female attitudes about homosexuality generally shows that males demonstrate a more prejudiced attitude toward homosexuals than do females. Males tend to have more negative feelings toward gay men than toward lesbians. Whether females show more prejudice against lesbians than against gay men is not clear. Some research shows that women don't make a distinction between gays and lesbians, whereas other research suggests greater prejudice against lesbians than against gay men. Other research shows that males tend to show more ethnic prejudices than females.

6. What are the social roots of prejudice?

Prejudice must be considered within the social context within which it exists. Historically, dominant groups have directed prejudice at less dominant groups. Although most Americans adhere to the notion of equity and justice toward minorities such as African Americans, they tend to oppose steps to reach those goals and only pay lip service to the notion of equity.

7. What is modern racism, and what are the criticisms of it?

In modern culture, it is no longer acceptable to express prejudices overtly, as they were in the past. However, prejudice is still expressed in a more subtle form: **modern racism**. Adherents of the notion of modern racism suggest that opposing civil rights legislation or voting for a candidate who opposes affirmative action are manifestations of modern racism.

Critics of modern racism point out that equating opposition to political ideas with racism is illogical and that the concept of modern racism has not been clearly defined or measured. Additionally, the correlation between modern racism and old-fashioned racism is high. Thus, modern and old-fashioned racism may be indistinguishable.

8. What are the cognitive roots of prejudice?

Cognitive social psychologists have focused on stereotypes and intergroup perceptions when attempting to understand prejudice. As humans, we have a strong predisposition to categorize people into groups. We do this even when we have only the most minimal basis on which to make categorizations. We classify ourselves and those we perceive to be like us in the in-group, and others whom we perceive to be different from us, we classify in the out-group. As a result of this categorization, we tend to display an in-group bias: favoring members of the in-group over members of the out-group.

Henri Tajfel proposed his **social identity theory** to help explain **in-group bias**. According to this theory, individuals are motivated to maintain a positive self-concept, part of which comes from membership in groups. Identification with the in-group confers us with a social identity. Categorizing dissimilar others as members of the out-group is another aspect of the social identity process. When we feel threatened, in-group bias increases, thereby enhancing our self-concept. **Self-categorization theory** suggests that self-esteem is most likely to be enhanced when members of the in-group distinguish themselves from other groups in positive ways.

The in-group bias may also have biological roots. We have a strong wariness of the unfamiliar, called xenophobia, which sociobiologists think is a natural part of our genetic heritage. It may have helped us survive as a species. It is biologically adaptive, for example, for a child to be wary of potentially dangerous strangers. The in-group bias may serve a similar purpose. Throughout history there are examples of various groups increasing solidarity in response to hostility from the dominant group to ensure group survival. Prejudice, then, may be seen as an unfortunate by-product of natural biologically based behavior patterns.

Because it is less taxing to deal with a person by relying on group-based stereotypes than to find out about that individual, categorizing people using stereotypes helps us economize our cognitive processing effort. Quick categorization of individuals via stereotypes contributes to prejudicial feelings and discrimination. Automatic language associations, by which we link positive words with the in-group and negative words with the out-group, contribute to these negative feelings.

9. How do cognitive biases contribute to prejudice?

Cognitive biases and errors that lead to prejudice include the illusory correlation, the fundamental attribution error, the confirmation bias, the out-group homogeneity bias, and the ultimate attribution error. An **illusory correlation** is the tendency to believe that two unrelated events are connected if they are systematically related. If you have a tendency to believe that members of a minority group have a negative characteristic, then you will perceive a relationship between group membership and a behavior related to that trait. Additionally, illusory correlations help form and maintain stereotypes. A prejudiced person will overestimate the degree of relationship between a negative trait and a negative behavior. The fundamental attribution error (the tendency to overestimate the role of internal characteristics in the behavior of others) also helps maintain stereotypes and prejudice. Because of this error, individuals tend to attribute negative behaviors of a minority group to internal predispositions rather than to situational factors. The confirmation bias maintains prejudice because individuals who hold negative stereotypes about a group look for evidence to confirm those stereotypes. If one expects a minority-group member to behave in a negative way, evidence will be sought to confirm that expectation. The **out-group homogeneity bias** is the tendency to see less diversity among members of an out-group than among members of an in-group. As a consequence, a negative behavior of one member of an out-group is likely to be seen as representative of the group as a whole. The **ultimate attribution error** occurs when we attribute a negative behavior of a minority group to the general characteristics of individuals who make up that group, whereas we attribute the same behavior of an in-group member to situational factors.

10. Are stereotypes ever accurate, and can they be overcome?

There are studies that show that some stereotypes sometimes are accurate. However, accurate or not, stereotypes are still harmful, because they give us a damaging perception of others. There is a tendency to judge individuals according to the worst example of a group represented by a stereotype. Stereotypes can be overcome if one uses controlled processing rather than automatic processing when thinking about others.

11. How do prejudiced and nonprejudiced individuals differ?

One important way in which more and less prejudiced individuals differ is that the latter are aware of their prejudices and carefully monitor them. Less prejudiced persons tend not to believe the stereotypes they hold and act accordingly. Prejudiced individuals are more likely to use automatic processing and energize stereotypes than are less prejudiced individuals who used controlled processing. However, even nonprejudiced persons will fall prey to stereotyping if stereotypes are activated beyond their conscious control.

12. What is the impact of prejudice on those who are its target?

There are many ways that prejudice can be expressed, some more serious than others. However, it is safe to say that even the lowest level of expression (antilocution) can have detectable emotional and cognitive consequences for targets of prejudice. **Everyday prejudice** has a cumulative effect on a person and contributes to the target's knowledge and experience with prejudice. Targets of prejudice-based jokes report feelings of disgust, anger, and hostility in response to those jokes.

Another way that targets of prejudice are affected is through the mechanism of the **stereotype threat**. Once a stereotype is activated about one's group, a member of that group may perform poorly on a task related to that threat, a fact confirmed by research.

13. How can a person who is the target of prejudice cope with being a target?

Usually, individuals faced with everyday prejudice must find ways of effectively managing it. If one's group is devalued, stigmatized, oppressed relative to other groups, prejudice can be countered by raising the value of the devalued group. This is done by first convincing group members of their own self-worth and then by convincing the rest of society of the worth of the group. Another strategy used by individuals from a stigmatized group is to try to anticipate situations in which prejudice will be encountered. Individuals can then decide how to best react to or minimize the impact of prejudice, for example by modifying their behavior, the way they dress, or the neighborhood in which they live. A third way to cope with stress is through the use of compensation. There are two modes of compensation in which a person can engage. When **secondary compensation** is used, an individual's attempt to change his or her mode of thinking about situations to psychologically protect him- or herself against the outcomes of prejudice. For example, a person who wants to obtain a college degree but faces prejudice that may prevent reaching the goal would be using secondary compensation if he or she devalued the goal (a college education is not all that important) or disidentified with the goal (members of my group usually don't go to college). On the other hand, **primary compensation** reduces the actual threats posed by prejudice. Coping strategies are developed that allow the target of prejudice to achieve his or her goals.

14. What can be done about prejudice?

Although prejudice has plagued humans throughout their history, there may be ways to reduce it. The **contact hypothesis** suggests that increased contact between groups should increase positive feelings. However, mere contact may not be enough. Positive feelings are enhanced when there is a superordinate goal toward which groups work cooperatively. Another strategy is to personalize out-group members; this prevents failing back on stereotypes. It is also beneficial to increase the frequency of antiracist statements that people hear, a form of strengthening social norms. A strong expression of social norms, disapproval of prejudice in all of its variations, is probably the best way to discourage and reduce prejudiced acts.

INTERNET ACTIVITY

RACISM AND THE INTERNET

The Internet provides a wealth of information, some good and some not so good. *U.S. News and World Report* (September 25, 2000) ran an article indicating how hate groups are using the Internet to disseminate racist, antisemitic, and misogynist ideas nationally and internationally. The article points out that the Internet has allowed for the globalization of hate. Gordon Allport in his classic work, *The Nature of Prejudice* (1951), identified several levels on which prejudice can be expressed. These are antilocution, avoidance, discrimination, physical attack, and extermination. The first, antilocution, involved talking in terms of prejudice and expressing prejudice in various verbal forms (e.g., racist jokes, racist propaganda, etc.). According to Allport, once antilocution is accepted, it can set the stage for more serious outlets for prejudice.

For this activity, you are going to explore the world of hatred on the Internet. Use your search engine to find a Web site related to a racist group (e.g., the Ku Klux Klan,

White Aryan Resistance, the American Nazi Party). Next, analyze what is on the site (the White Aryan site is a good one for this activity), and answer the following questions:

1. What positions does the site present on issues such as race, gender, religion, and immigration.
   a. How are women, Jews, blacks, and other minorities described?
   b. What, if any, stereotypical terms or images are associated with members of out-groups?
2. Are there any racist images portrayed on the site (e.g., cartoons)? If so, how are members of various nonwhite groups portrayed in these images?
3. Does the site present any specific types of persuasive argument (e.g., an emotional appeal, such as fear; or facts and figures)? If so, what types are presented?
4. How would you counter some of the statements made on the site?
5. What, if any, action is recommended on the site to address the issues raised on the site?

As an extension of this exercise, find a Web site dedicated to reducing prejudice and discrimination (e.g., the Antidefamation League), and determine what specific measures are recommended to combat prejudice.

SUGGESTIONS FOR FURTHER READING

Fiske, S. T. (1993). Controlling other people. *American Psychologist, 48,* 621–628.
   One of the leading social cognitivists examines the relationship between stereotyping and power. Fiske demonstrates that stereotyping is a way of maintaining the status quo for the powerful.

Levin, J., & McDevitt, J. (1993). *Hate crimes: The rising tide of bigotry and bloodshed.* New York: Plenum.
   This book presents a thoughtful and thorough examination of the distressing increase in prejudice-driven violence. The authors examine the origins of hate crimes and ask whether such crimes are part of our mainstream culture.

Sniderman, P. M., & Piazza, T. (1994). *The scar of race.* Cambridge, MA: Harvard University Press.
   This book examines current public attitudes on race, showing their complexities and subtleties.

Swim, J. K., & Stangor, C. (Eds.). (1998). *Prejudice: The target's perspective.* San Diego, CA: Academic Press.
   This edited book provides several insights into how it feels to be the target of prejudice and discrimination.

Sykes, C. J. (1992). *A nation of victims.* New York: St. Martin's Press.
   This is an examination of how fragmented American society has become. Sykes shows that almost every group in the United States claims that it has been victimized and therefore should be compensated in some form.

Wilford, J. N. (1992, February 11). Nubian treasures reflect black influence on Egypt. *The New York Times,* p. 29.
   This is an interesting report on a time before racial prejudice in the Mediterranean region.

CHAPTER 5

ATTITUDES

Ida Tarbell is not a name most of us recognize. A history of American women doesn't give her even a single line (Hymowitz & Weissman, 1984). Yet, she was at the center of American life for the first 3 decades of the 20th century. Teddy Roosevelt hurled the mocking epithet *muckraker* at her. It was a label she eventually wore proudly, for she, perhaps more than anyone else, told the American people about the corruption, conspiracies, strong-armed tactics, and enormous greed that went into "business as usual" at the turn of the century (Fleming, 1986).

Tarbell grew up in Titusville, Pennsylvania. In the last decades of the 19th century, it was the center of the booming oil industry. It was also the town that would make Standard Oil Company, and its founder, John D. Rockefeller, richer than anyone could imagine.

Tarbell grew up among derricks and oil drums, in oil-cloaked fields, under oil-flecked skies. In 1872, her father's business was threatened by a scheme devised by Rockefeller and his partners that

would allow them to ship their oil via the railroads at a much cheaper fare than any other producer, thus driving their competition out of business. Frank Tarbell and the others fought this scheme and forced the railroads to treat everyone fairly, at least temporarily. Ida was well informed about the conspiracy and, possessing her father's strong sense of justice, was outraged. She vowed that if she were given the chance, she would make people aware of the greed and dishonesty she had witnessed. At this time she was 15 years old (Weinberg & Weinberg, 1961).

Tarbell decided that she would have to understand the nature of oil. She was determined to go to college, become a scientist, and never marry. Now, in the 19th century, women simply did not go to college. Most people thought that too much education would endanger a woman's health and, worse, affect her chances of marriage. But Tarbell had made up her mind, and her parents were not deterred by prevailing attitudes. She enrolled in the science curriculum at Allegheny College in Pennsylvania.

In college, Tarbell was a free spirit. She became friends with whomever she wanted, ignored all the unwritten social rules, learned to be critical and disciplined in her work, and graduated with a degree in natural science. After working as a school teacher, she went off to Paris to become a writer. For years, she wrote articles and biographies, but in 1900, she started to write about oil. She began to form an idea about a series of articles on the Standard Oil Company, which supplied almost all the oil that was used to light American homes in the days before electricity. Although Standard Oil had been investigated on charges of bribery and other illegal tactics by authorities for almost the entire 30 years of its existence, very little evidence existed in the public domain. Tarbell got around that by getting to know one of the company's vice presidents, Henry Rogers, who let her have access to private records. Rogers was unapologetic about his role. He cheerfully admitted that Rockefeller lied, cheated, double-dealt, and used violence or the threat of it to build an enormously successful, powerful, and efficient company (Fleming, 1986).

Tarbell's book, *The History of the Standard Oil Company*, published in 1904, appeared in monthly installments in McClure's magazine. It was a sensation. It read like a suspense story, and readers couldn't wait until the next month's issue. The book had a ready made villain: John D. Rockefeller. He was portrayed as a money-hungry rogue without a shred of humanity, and that is the image of him that has come down to us 100 years later. After the book came out, he tried to restore his image by giving some $35 million to charity. At the time, he was estimated to be worth over $900 million, a sum equivalent to several billion dollars in today's currency.

Tarbell's work had a tremendous impact on the nation. It led not only to a number of lawsuits against the oil industry for their monopolistic practices, but also to federal antitrust laws that dismantled the original Standard Oil Company. Today, we have a number of independent Standard Oil companies (Ohio, New Jersey, etc.) as a result of Tarbell's work.

Tarbell completed the Standard Oil articles in 1904, but for the next 30 years she was an important voice in economic and international issues. She never married, continued to write, did what she wanted, supported herself and, in fact, became quite wealthy. She remained tough and inquisitive; above all, she maintained her exquisite sense of justice.

Even more remarkable than what Tarbell did was the way she did it. She was entirely skeptical of all the common beliefs of her time. She did not believe in the theory of the inferiority of women, prevalent in the early years of her life, nor did she believe in the turn-of-the-century theory that women were morally superior and evolutionarily more advanced. She joined no organizations or social reform movements. Yet she took on the most powerful men in the country and became a formidable adversary (Fleming, 1986).

What made Tarbell the way she was? To some degree, she was no doubt born a fighter. By temperament, she was determined, controlled, and unafraid, but her attitudes and behavior were also shaped and informed by her experience. She grew up in a family that supported her in her independent ways and encouraged her to do what she thought was right. She was powerfully influenced by her father, within whom she saw a strong sense of justice. Events that occurred during her formative years motivated and inspired her and forever altered the way she viewed the world.

The attitudes that Tarbell held played a fundamental role in the way she perceived the world around her. Like other mechanisms of social cognition, they organized her experiences, directed her behavior, and helped define who she was. In chapter 4, we looked at prejudiced attitudes; here, we look at attitudes more broadly. We begin by exploring what attitudes are and what role they play in the life of a person like Tarbell. What are the elements that go into attitudes? How do they flow from and express our deepest values? What are the processes by which we acquire or develop attitudes? And what is the relationship between attitudes and behavior in our day-to-day life? How do attitudes express the relationships among what we think, what we feel, what we intend to do, and what we actually do? These are some of the questions addressed in this chapter.

KEY QUESTIONS

AS YOU READ THIS CHAPTER, FIND THE ANSWERS TO THE FOLLOWING QUESTIONS:

1. *What is an attitude?*
2. *What components make up an attitude?*
3. *What is the relationship of attitudes to values?*
4. *What are terminal and instrumental values?*
5. *What function do attitudes serve in day-to-day life?*
6. *What is an attitude survey?*
7. *How are attitude surveys conducted?*
8. *What are the potential sources of bias in a survey?*
9. *What are behavioral measures of attitudes?*
10. *What processes are involved in attitude formation?*
11. *Can attitudes be inherited?*
12. *What is the relationship between attitudes and behavior?*
13. *Why aren't attitudes always good predictors of behavior?*
14. *What is the theory of reasoned action?*
15. *What is the theory of planned behavior?*
16. *How does conviction of an attitude affect the attitude–behavior relationship?*
17. *How does one's ideology relate to behavior?*
18. *What is the notion of the nonrational actor?*
19. *How has the controversy over the rational and nonrational actor been resolved?*

WHAT ARE ATTITUDES?

The study of attitudes has been of fundamental concern to social psychologists throughout the history of the field. Other issues may come and go, dictated by fashion in theory and research and influenced by current events, but interest in attitudes remains. This preoccupation with attitudes is easy to understand. The concept of attitudes is central to explaining our thoughts, feelings, and actions with regard to other people, situations, and ideas.

In this section, we explore the basic concept of attitudes. First we look at and elaborate on a classic definition of the term. Then we consider how attitudes relate to values, what functions attitudes serve, and how attitudes can be measured.

Allport's Definition of Attitudes

The word *attitude* crops up often in our everyday conversation. We speak of having an attitude about someone or something. In this usage, attitude usually implies feelings that are either positive or negative. We also speak of someone who has a "bad attitude." You may, for example, think that a co-worker has an "attitude problem." In this usage, attitude implies some personality characteristic or behavior pattern that offends us.

Social psychologists use the term *attitude* differently than this. In order to study and measure attitudes, they need a clear and careful definition of the term. Gordon Allport, an early attitude theorist, formulated the following definition: "An **attitude** is a mental and neural state of readiness, organized through experience, exerting a directive or dynamic influence upon the individual's response to all objects and situations with which it is related" (1935). This is a rich and comprehensive definition, and although there have been many redefinitions over the years, Allport's definition still captures much that is essential about attitudes (see Figure 5.1). Consequently, we adopt it here as our central definition. The definition can be broken into three parts, each with some important implications (Rajecki, 1990).

First, because attitudes are mental or neural states of readiness, they are necessarily private. Scientists who study attitudes cannot measure them directly in the way, for example, that medical doctors can measure blood pressure. Only

attitude

A mental and neural state of readiness, organized through experience, exerting a directive or dynamic influence on the individual's response to all objects and situations with which it is related.

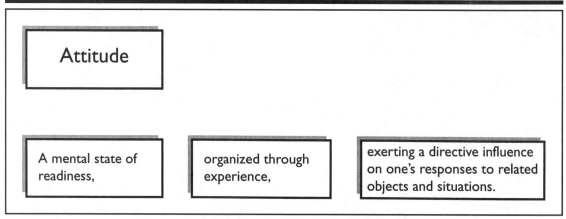

Figure 5.1 *A schematic diagram of Allport's definition of an attitude showing the important components of an attitude.*

the person who holds an attitude is capable of having direct access to it. The social psychological measures of an attitude must be indirect.

Second, if attitudes are organized through experience, they are presumably formed through learning from a variety of experiences and influences. Our attitudes about, say, appropriate roles for men and women are shaped by the attitudes passed on by our culture, especially by parents, friends, and other agents of socialization, such as schools and television. Recall that even though the wider society was not supportive of women in nontraditional roles in Ida Tarbell's time, her parents were very supportive. The notion that our attitudes arise only from experience is too limiting, however. There is also increasing evidence that some attitudes also have a genetic element (Tesser, 1993).

Finally, because attitudes exert a directive or dynamic influence on a person's response to objects, people, and situations, attitudes are directly related to our actions or behavior. The attitudes we hold predispose us to act in positive or negative ways toward the objects of those attitudes. Tarbell's early experience with Standard Oil clearly affected her later behavior.

Attitude Structures

An attitude is made up of four interconnected components: cognitions, affective responses, behavioral intentions, and behaviors. To understand this interconnectedness, let's consider the attitude of someone opposed to gun-control legislation. Her attitude can be stated as, "I am opposed to laws in any way controlling the ownership of guns."

This attitude would be supported by cognitions, or thoughts, about laws and gun ownership. For example, she might think that unrestricted gun ownership is a basic right guaranteed by the Second Amendment to the Constitution. The attitude would also be supported by affective responses, or feelings. She might feel strongly about her right to do what she wants to do without government interference, or she might feel strongly about protecting her family from intruders.

The attitude, and the cognitions and feelings that support it, can result in behavioral intentions and behaviors. Our hypothetical person might intend to send money to the National Rifle Association or to call her representative to argue against a gun-control bill. Finally, she might turn that intention into some real action and send the money or call her legislator.

An attitude is really a summary of an **attitude structure**, which consists of these interconnected components (Zimbardo & Leippe, 1992) Thus, the attitude "I oppose laws that restrict handgun ownership" comprises a series of interrelated thoughts, feelings, and intentions; this attitude structure is shown in Figure 5.2.

As can be seen from the figure, a change in one component of an attitude structure might very well lead to changes in the others (Zimbardo & Leippe, 1992), because an attitude structure is dynamic, with each component influencing the others. For example, if a close relative of yours lost his job because of a new gun-control law, a person who favors strong gun-control laws may change her mind. The neat structure displayed in Figure 5.2 would now be in turmoil. New feelings about guns might lead to new thoughts; intentions might change and, with them, behaviors.

Generally, the affective component dominates the attitude (Breckler & Wiggins, 1989). When we think of a particular object or person, our initial

attitude structure
The fact that attitudes comprise a cognitive, affective, and behavioral component in their basic structure.

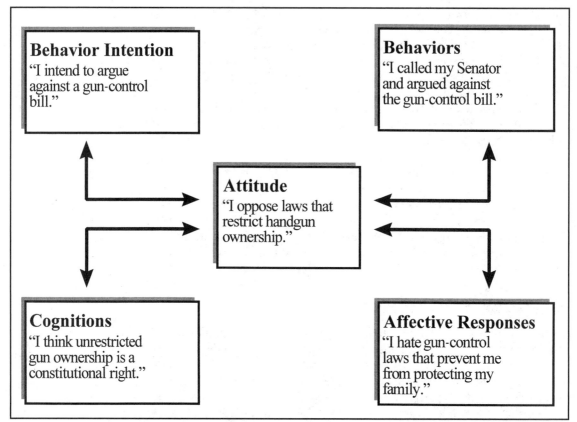

Figure 5.2 *An example of an attitude structure.*

Adapted from Zimbardo & Leippe, 1992. Reprinted with permission.

response is usually some expression of affect, as in, "I feel women will make good political candidates." We do not simply have attitudes about war, or the president, or baseball: We like these things, or we do not. When an attitude is evoked, it is always with positive or negative feeling, although, to be sure, the feeling varies in intensity. It is likely that our most intensely held attitudes in particular are primarily affective in nature (Ajzen, 1989). Thus, you might think of an attitude as primarily a response emphasizing how you *feel* about someone or something, as primarily an evaluation of the person or object. But keep in mind also that this evaluation is based on all the thoughts, intentions, and behaviors that go into the structure of the attitude (Zanna & Rempel, 1988).

Explicit and Implicit Attitudes

In many cases we freely express and are aware of our attitudes and how they influence our behavior. An attitude falling into this category is known as an **explicit attitude**. Explicit attitudes operate on a conscious level, so we are aware of them—aware of the cognitive underpinnings of them—and are conscious of how they relate to behavior. They operate via controlled processing and take some cognitive effort to activate. For example, you may know how you feel toward a given political candidate and match your behavior (e.g., voting for him or her) to that attitude. It is these explicit attitudes that we often find having a directive effect on behavior.

explicit attitude

An attitude operating via controlled processing about which we are aware of its existence, its cognitive underpinnings, and how it relates to behavior.

Although many of our attitudes operate on this conscious level, there are others that operate unconsciously. This form of an attitude is known as an **implicit attitude**. Specifically, an implicit attitude is defined as "actions or judgments that are under control of automatically activated evaluation without the performer's awareness of that causation (Greenwald, McGhee, & Schwartz, 1998, p. 1464). In other words, implicit attitudes affect behaviors automatically, without conscious thought, and below the level of awareness. For example, an individual may have a quick negative reaction toward a member of a minority group even though the individual professes positive and tolerant attitudes toward that group. The "gut level" reaction occurs without thought and is often distasteful to the individual (Wilson, Lindsey, & Schooler, 2000).

Timothy Wilson, Samuel Lindsey, and Tonya Schooler (2000) proposed a *model of dual attitudes* to explain the relationship between explicit and implicit attitudes. They suggested that when one develops a new attitude, the new attitude does not erase the old attitude. Instead, the two attitudes coexist. The new attitude serves as the explicit attitude; the old attitude remains in memory and takes on the role of the implicit attitude. This implicit attitude can override the explicit attitude when the situation is right. For example, a person who has changed from a racially prejudiced attitude to a nonprejudiced attitude may still have an automatic negative reaction to a member of a minority group despite the newly formed positive attitude. In this case, the underlying unconscious implicit attitude has overridden the explicit attitude.

According to the dual model of attitudes, implicit and explicit attitudes are separate and distinct attitude structures (Wilson et al., 2000). Dual attitudes are not merely different ways of categorizing an attitude object. Nor are they the same as ambivalent attitudes (that is, having mixed feelings about an attitude object). Finally, dual attitudes are not a product of a conflict between the various components of an attitude (as between thoughts and feelings). Several lines of research support the notion that attitudes can exist on unconscious and conscious levels simultaneously. For example, Banaji, Hardin, and Rothman (1993) found that stereotype-related information (e.g., about gender) can influence how we judge others outside our level of awareness. However, the implicit–explicit attitude distinction is not limited to stereotypes. Other attitudes can be activated directly from memory automatically when an attitude object is encountered, and this activation is both spontaneous and unavoidable (Fazio, Sanbonmastsu, Powell, & Kardes, 1986).

Attitudes as an Expression of Values

Our attitudes flow from and express our values (Ball-Rokeach, Rokeach, & Grube, 1984). A **value** is a conception of what is desirable; it is a guideline for a person's actions, a standard for behavior. Thus, for example, the attitude that more women and members of different ethnic groups should be elected to office might flow from the value of equality. The attitude that public officials who lie or cheat should be punished severely might flow from the value of honesty. Ida Tarbell placed a high value on fairness and justice and was outraged by the actions of Standard Oil Company.

Notice that whereas attitudes are directed toward objects, people, and situations, values are broad, abstract notions. Because values are more general than attitudes, there are few values but many attitudes. Just as an attitude can

implicit attitude
An attitude that affects behavior automatically, without conscious thought and below the level of awareness.

value
A concept closely related to an attitude that is a standard of what is desirable for one's actions.

be seen as a system of cognitive, affective, and behavioral components, so a value can be seen as containing many interrelated attitudes. The value of equality could give rise not only to the attitude that more women and members of different ethnic groups should hold office but also to countless other attitudes relating to the innumerable people, objects, issues, and ideas toward which one might direct thoughts, feelings, and behaviors.

Milton Rokeach, a social psychologist who spent most of his professional life studying how people organize their value systems, argued that there are two distinct categories of values (1973, 1979). He called one category *terminal values*. These are preferred end states, such as freedom, equality, and happiness. The other category he called *instrumental values*. These are preferred ways of doing things. Honesty and ambition are instrumental values.

According to Rokeach, two fundamental terminal values, equality and freedom, are especially predictive of a whole range of attitudes. Attitudes about the role of government, for example, often can be predicted by knowing how someone ranks these two values. A person who values equality more highly probably would want the government to take an active role in education, health, and other social welfare issues. A person who values freedom more highly probably would prefer that government stay out of the way and let everyone fend for him- or herself. Consider a person who rates equality higher than freedom. How might this affect her attitudes on specific issues? A high value placed on equality implies that the individual is more concerned with the common good than with individual freedoms (although freedom might still be ranked relatively highly by that person). This individual might be in favor of "sin taxes" (such as high tobacco and alcohol taxes) to raise money for national health care and also might be in favor of stronger gun-control laws. A person who considers freedom to be more desirable than equality probably would be against sin taxes ("It's none of the government's business if people want to kill themselves") and also against government regulation of gun ownership.

When asked, do people account for their attitudes by referring to specific values? And do people on opposing sides of an issue hold opposing values? In one study, researchers measured participants' attitudes toward two issues, abortion and nuclear weapons (Kristiansen & Zanna, 1988). Next, participants were asked to rank the (personal) importance of 18 values, such as freedom, equality, an exciting life, family security, and so on, and then relate each value to their attitudes on these two issues.

People with different attitudes consider different values important. People who oppose the right to abortion, for example, give a higher ranking to certain values (e.g., mature love, wisdom, true friendship, salvation, and a world of beauty) than do people who support the right to abortion. Those who support the right to abortion give a higher ranking to other values (e.g., happiness, family security, a comfortable life, pleasure, an exciting life, and a sense of accomplishment) than do those who oppose the right to abortion.

At the same time, both groups shared many values. Both ranked freedom, inner harmony, and equality as the values most important to their attitude. Differences in the rankings of other values were slight. The results also suggest that people on either side of volatile issues might be much closer in their values than they realize.

What Do Attitudes Do for Us? The Function of Attitudes

Attitudes serve several important functions. First, they define us. The person who opposes gun control is telling us something important about herself. Her attitude has a kind of **badge value**; that is, it is an up-front statement about who she is or would like others to think she is (Abelson & Prentice, 1989).

Second, attitudes direct our future feelings and thoughts about the objects of those feelings and thoughts. In other words, a negative attitude toward gun control would lead the person holding it to search out and remember information that confirms the attitude. Certainly, Ida Tarbell's attitudes about greedy oil men affected her later action in a very clear way. Like schemas and stories, discussed in chapters 2 and 3, attitudes are cognitive structures that guide perception and help us fill the gaps when information is lacking.

Finally, attitudes summarize our feelings, thoughts, intentions, and behavior for the cognitive miser. When a topic comes up, especially one with which you have some experience and familiarity, your attitude helps you respond. You don't have to diagram the whole attitude structure; the cognitive miser has neither the time nor the inclination to conjure up all the relevant feelings and thoughts. You simply express the attitude. "Oh, yes," you say, "I would vote for a woman for president," or "I support gun control," or "I think the government should increase funding of AIDS research." In essence, then, our attitudes help us operate efficiently in our social world.

Several specific functions of attitudes have been identified. Attitudes can serve a utilitarian, or adaptive, function when they lead us to value objects that help us reach our goals. Attitudes serve a knowledge function, helping us to make sense out of the world by categorizing objects and people. By

badge value
The aspect of a value that provides an up-front statement about who a person is or would like others to think he or she is.

One function of an attitude is badge value, which is the aspect of an attitude that provides an upfront statement about what one believes in. This woman is clearly making an upfront statement about her attitude toward abortion.

expressing our values, attitudes can serve a value-expressive function. Finally, attitudes serve an ego-defensive function when they protect us against our fears and anxieties (Katz, 1960; McGuire, 1989).

Let's consider how racially prejudiced attitudes might serve all four functions. Someone might be prejudiced because if another group is kept down, there are more jobs for his group (utilitarian function). Prejudice might also make life simpler for him, allowing him to categorize people simply by virtue of their membership in a group (knowledge function). If his life feels unsatisfactory and his job and place in the world seem insecure, his prejudice might enable him to shift his resulting feelings of hostility to others (ego-defensive function). Finally, his prejudice might be expressive of basic values, such as a sense that people of different races are inherently unequal (value-expressive function).

The implications of the functions of attitudes were shown in a study that looked at people's hostile attitudes toward co-workers with AIDS (Pryor, Reeder, & McManus, 1991). Could this hostility be reduced by supplying co-workers with accurate information? Workers viewed a film that showed that working with a person who had AIDS was not dangerous. Workers whose negative attitude had a utilitarian function—they were worried about the possibility of contagion—were influenced by the information in the film. Other workers, however, had strong feelings against gay men; people with AIDS symbolized values they rejected. This was true even when the co-workers had contracted AIDS through a blood transfusion, not through any sexual activity. The workers' negative attitude, in other words, had a value-expressive function. This group of workers was not influenced by the information in the film. In short, attitudes that serve an instrumental function may be influenced by information and reason; attitudes that serve a value-expressive function are more difficult to change.

HOW ARE ATTITUDES MEASURED?

What happens when investigators want to learn about people's attitudes on a particular issue, such as affirmative action, illegal aliens, or capital punishment? As pointed out earlier in this chapter, attitudes are private; we can't know what a person's attitudes are just by looking at her or him. For this reason, social psychologists use a variety of techniques to discover and measure people's attitudes. Some of these techniques rely on direct responses, whereas others are more indirect.

The Attitude Survey

attitude survey

A self-report method of measuring attitudes that involves a researcher's mailing a questionnaire to a potential respondent, conducting a face-to-face interview, or asking a series of questions on the telephone.

The most commonly used techniques for measuring attitudes are attitude surveys. In an **attitude survey**, the researcher mails a questionnaire to a potential respondent, conducts a face-to-face interview, or asks a series of questions on the telephone. Because respondents report on their own attitudes, an attitude survey is a self-report measure. A respondent indicates his or her attitude by answering a series of questions.

There may be several types of questions on an attitude survey. Open-ended questions allow respondents to provide an answer in their own words (Oskamp, 1991). For example, respondents might be asked, What qualifications do you think are necessary in a President of the United States? Although this type of question yields rich, in-depth information, the answers can be difficult to analyze. Consequently, most of the questions on an attitude survey are close ended, or restricted, questions such as, Are women qualified to be President of the United States? Notice that this type of question forces respondents into making one of a limited number of choices.

Another kind of attitude survey is the *rating scale*, in which respondents indicate the extent to which they agree or disagree with a statement by circling a number on a scale. One of the most popular of these methods is the Likert Scaling. Likert items ask the person to agree or disagree with such attitude statements as the following on a 5-point scale: I believe women are qualified to serve in national office. Likert's technique is a summated rating scale, so called because individuals are given an attitude score based on the sum of their responses.

In evaluating election preferences or other attitudes, social psychologists usually are interested in the attitudes of a large group. Because it is not possible to survey every member of the group, researchers conducting an attitude survey select a sample or small subgroup of individuals from the larger group, or population. Don't think that you need a huge sample to have a valid survey. In fact, most nationwide surveys use a sample of only about 1,500 individuals.

Although a sample need not be large, it must be representative. As you recall from chapter 1, a representative sample is one that resembles the population in all important respects. Thus, for any category that is relevant to the attitude being measured (e.g., race and ethnicity, socioeconomic class, gender, age), the sample would contain the same proportion of people from each group within the category (e.g., from each race and ethnic group) as does the population whose attitudes are being measured. A representative sample contrasts with a biased sample, which is skewed toward one or more characteristics and does not adequately represent the larger population.

Potential Biases in Attitude Surveys

Although attitude surveys, containing various types of questions, are very popular, they do have several problems that may make any responses made by research participants invalid. Norbert Schwarz (1999) suggested that the way a person responds to a survey question depends on a variety of factors, including question wording, the format of the question, and the context within which the question is placed.

For example, presidential candidate Ross Perot commissioned a survey in March 1993 that included the following question: Should laws be passed to eliminate all possibilities of special interests giving huge sums of money to candidates? Ninety-nine percent of the people who responded to the survey said yes. A second survey done by an independent polling firm, asked the same question in a different way: Do groups have the right to contribute to the candidate they support? In response to this question, only 40% favored limits on spending. This is a textbook example of how the wording of the question can influence polling data (Goleman, 1993).

Phrasing is important but so are the specific words used in a question. For example, in one survey commissioned some years ago by the American Stock Exchange, respondents were asked how much stock they owned. Much to everyone's surprise, the highest stock ownership was found in the Southwest. It seems that the respondents were thinking of stock of the four-legged kind, not the Wall Street type. The moral is that you must consider the meaning of the words from the point of view of the people answering the questions.

The format of a question is also important. If a respondent is given a question with several alternatives from which to choose, the response made may be different from that with a question asked in an open-ended format. For example, when asked to choose an alternative to the question, What is the most important thing to prepare children for for life? Sixty-one point five percent of respondents chose the alternative, to think for themselves. Yet, when an open-ended question was used, only 4.6% of respondents spontaneously produced that answer (Schwarz, 1999).

Schwarz also pointed out that the context within which a question is asked can affect its meaning to respondents. That is, the questions around a particular question set a context for the target question. The answer given to the target question depends on the nature of the questions that surround it.

Another potential bias is that individuals give opinions on subjects they know nothing about. In one classic study, for example, respondents were asked to rate how they felt about a number of national groups, including fictitious groups such as Danerins and Pirenians and Wallonians. Respondents liked the first two but were prejudiced against Wallonians (Hartley, 1946).

Finally, respondents may lie, or to put it somewhat differently, they may not remember what they actually did or thought. Kipling Williams (1994) and his students asked voters whether they had voted in a very recent election; almost all said they had. Williams was able to check the actual rolls of those who had voted (not how they voted) and found that only about 65% of his respondents had voted. Now, some may have forgotten, but many simply did not want to admit they had failed to do a socially desirable thing, to vote in an election (Paulhus & Reid, 1991).

Behavioral Measures

Because of the problems associated with self-report techniques, social psychologists have developed behavioral techniques of measuring attitudes. These techniques, in one way or another, avoid relying on responses to questions.

unobtrusive measure
A method of assessing attitudes such that the individuals whose attitudes you are measuring are not aware of your interest in them.

Unobtrusive measures assess attitudes by indirect means; the individuals whose attitudes are being measured simply are never aware of it. For example, in one early study, investigators measured voting preferences by tallying the number of bumper stickers for a particular candidate on cars in a parking lot (Wrightsman, 1969). Other researchers measured attitudes toward competing brands of cola by searching through garbage cans. Still others attempted to determine the most popular exhibit at a museum by measuring the amount of wear and tear on various parts of the carpet (Webb, Campbell, Schwartz, Sechrist, & Grove, 1981).

Another example of unobtrusive measurement of attitudes is the *lost-letter technique* (Milgram, Mann, & Hartner, 1965). If a researcher wants to measure a community's attitudes toward, say, its foreign residents, she might not get honest answers on a Likert-type questionnaire. But, if she has some stamps and envelopes, she can try the lost-letter technique. This is what the researcher does: She addresses an envelope to someone with a foreign-sounding name at a local address. She puts a stamp on the envelope and then drops it on a crowded street near the post office so that it can easily be found and mailed. As her baseline control, she drops a stamped envelope addressed to someone whose name doesn't sound foreign. She repeats the procedure as many times as necessary to get a large enough sample. Then all she has to do is count the envelopes that turn up in the mail and compare the number with names that sound foreign to the number with names that don't. This is her measure of that community's attitude toward foreigners.

Attitudes can also be studied by measuring participants' physiological responses when answering questions about their attitudes. Psychophysiological measurements of attitudes again involve questions about attitudes, as in surveys, but the focus is not so much on the verbal reply as on the accompanying physiological arousal. Can you, in truth, measure people's bodily responses to attitude issues and get an accurate reading of their real attitudes? John Cacioppo and Richard Petty (1983), who wrought a revolution in how we study and measure attitudes, made a strong case for it. They pointed out that any production of emotion by attitudes must be reflected in responses by the sympathetic nervous system, the part of the nervous system that is involved in arousing the body to respond to stress-related situations. For example, the facial muscles, particularly those around the eyes and mouth, appear to react quickly to emotional stimuli.

At the same time, Cacioppo and Petty were very careful about their claims for psychophysiological measurements of attitudes. This caution is especially in order because any physiological response may have several different causes. For example, a researcher trying to assess the degree of emotion some issue aroused in a person might measure the amount of electricity the skin conducts. An increase in skin conductance means greater emotional response. But the greater emotional response can be caused by such factors as stress or the novelty of the situation, not just by the attitude object (Cacioppo & Petty, 1983). The researcher would know there was a physiological response but could not be entirely sure of its cause.

As noted, facial muscle movements seem to be especially promising as physiological indicators of feelings about attitudes (Cacioppo, Petty, & Tassinary, 1989). Depending on the results of research along these and similar lines, the relatively undeveloped field of psychophysiological measurement could make an important contribution to our ability to measure attitudes objectively.

HOW ARE ATTITUDES FORMED?

Attitudes affect how we think, feel, and behave toward a wide range of people, objects, and ideas that we encounter. Where do our attitudes come from? Are they developed, as Allport suggested, through experience? If so, just how do our attitudes develop through experience? And are there other ways in which we acquire our attitudes?

The term *attitude formation* refers to the movement we make from having no attitude toward an object to having some positive or negative attitude toward that object (Oskamp, 1991). How you acquire an attitude plays a very important role in how you use it. In this section, we explore a range of mechanisms for attitude formation. Most of these mechanisms—mere exposure, direct personal experience, operant and classical conditioning, and observational learning—are based on experience and learning. However, the last mechanism we will look at is based on genetics.

Mere Exposure

Some attitudes may be formed and shaped by what Robert Zajonc (1968) called **mere exposure**, which means that simply being exposed to an object increases our feelings, usually positive, toward that object. The

mere exposure
The phenomenon that being exposed to a stimulus increases one's feelings, usually positive, toward that object; repeated exposure can lead to positive attitudes.

mere-exposure effect has been demonstrated with a wide range of stimuli, including foods, photographs, words, and advertising slogans (Bornstein, 1989).

In one early study, researchers placed ads containing nonsense words such as NANSOMA in college newspapers (Zajonc & Rajecki, 1969). Later, they gave students lists of words that included NANSOMA, to rate. Mere exposure to a nonsense word, such as NANSOMA was enough to give it a positive rating. In another study, participants were exposed to nonsense syllables and to Chinese characters (Zajonc, 1968). Repeated exposure increased the positive evaluations of both the nonsense syllables and the Chinese characters.

Generally, this means that familiarity, in fact, may not breed contempt. Familiar faces, ideas, and slogans become comfortable old friends. Think of the silly commercial jingle you sometimes find yourself humming almost against your will.

In fact, repeated exposures often work very well in advertising. The Marlboro man, invented to convince male smokers that taking a drag on a filtered cigarette would enhance their manhood, lasted through a generation of smokers. (The ad lasted, the original model didn't—he died of lung cancer.) When we walk down the aisle to buy a product, be it cigarettes or soap suds, the familiar name brand stands out and says, "Buy me." And we do.

Now, there are limits to the effect, at least in the experimental studies. A review of the mere-exposure research concluded that the effect is most powerful when it occurs randomly over time, and that too many exposures actually will decrease the effect (Bornstein, 1989). A constant bombardment does not work very well.

Repeated exposures increase liking when the stimuli are neutral or positive to begin with. What happens when the stimuli are negative? It seems that continual exposure to some object that was disliked initially increases that negative emotion (Bornstein, 1989; Perlman & Oskamp, 1971). Say, for example, a person grew up disliking a different ethnic group because of comments she heard her parents make. Then, on repeated encounters with members of that group, she might react with distaste and increasing negativity. Over time, these negative emotions are likely to produce hostile beliefs about the group (Krosnick, Betz, Jussim, & Lynn, 1992). Thus, negative feelings of which a person might hardly be aware can lead, with repeated exposure, to the object of those feelings, to increased negative emotions and, ultimately, to a system of beliefs that support those emotions. Stimuli, ideas, and values to which we are exposed shape us in ways that are not always obvious to us.

Direct Personal Experience

A second way we form attitudes is through *direct personal experience*. If we get mugged one Saturday night coming home from a movie, for example, we may change our attitudes toward criminals, the police, personal safety, and a range of other concerns. Or if we have a flat tire and someone stops to help, we may change our attitude about the value of going out of our way to assist others. If our father's business is put in peril because of the dirty tactics of a large corporation like that of Ida Tarbell's, we would resent such organizations for the rest of our lives. Direct personal experience has the power to create and change attitudes.

Attitudes acquired through direct experience are likely to be strongly held and to affect behavior. People are also more likely to search for information to support such attitudes. For example, people who had experience with flu shots gathered further information about the shots and were more likely to get vaccinated each flu season (Davison, Yantis, Norwood, & Montano, 1985). People are also less likely to be vulnerable to someone trying to persuade them to abandon the attitude. If, for example, your attitude that the environment needs preserving was formed because you lived near a river and observed directly the impact of pollution, you will be less likely to be persuaded even by powerful counterarguments (Wood, 1982).

Direct experience continues to form and shape our attitudes throughout life. One study examined the effects of direct experience with government agencies on younger and older individuals' attitudes toward government (Tyler & Schuller, 1991). The experiences involved, for example, getting a job, job training, unemployment compensation, and medical and hospital care. The older people changed their attitudes following a positive or negative experience as much as, if not more than, the younger people. This finding argues against the impressionable-years model, which assumes that young people are more open to forming new attitudes, and supports the lifelong-openness model, which emphasizes that people can form new attitudes throughout their life. We should note here that in later years, Ida Tarbell came to know John D. Rockefeller's successor, Judge Gary, who caused her to write a more favorable second edition to *The History of the Standard Oil Company*.

Operant and Classical Conditioning

Most social psychologists would agree that the bulk of our attitudes are learned. That is, attitudes result from our experiences not our genetic inheritance. Through socialization, individuals learn the attitudes, values, and behaviors of their culture. Important influences in the process include parents, peers, schools, and the mass media.

As an example, let's look at the formation of attitudes about politics. The formation of some of these attitudes begins early, perhaps at age 6 or 7. In one early study, grade-school students thought that the American system was the best and that "America is the best country in the world" (Hess & Torney, 1967). When children are young, parents exert a major influence on their political attitudes, but later, peers and the mass media have a greater impact. In fact, by the time young adults are seniors in high school, there is a fairly low correlation between the political attitudes of children and those of their parents (Oskamp, 1991). Parents and children may identify with the same political party, but their attitudes about politics are likely to differ.

During the course of socialization, a person's attitudes may be formed through operant and classical conditioning, two well-known learning processes. In **operant conditioning**, the individual's behavior is strengthened or weakened by means of reward or punishment. Parents may, for example, reward their daughter with praise when she expresses the attitude that doing math is fun. Each time the child is rewarded, the attitude becomes stronger. Or, parents may punish their son with a verbal rebuke when he expresses that same attitude. In these examples, operant conditioning serves to impart attitudes.

operant conditioning
A method by which attitudes are acquired by rewarding a person for a given attitude in the hopes it will be maintained or strengthened.

Simply rewarding people for expressing an attitude can affect what they believe. In one study, participants took part in a debate and were randomly assigned to one or the other side of an issue (Scott, 1957). Those debaters who were told, again randomly, that they won were more likely to change their attitudes in the direction of their side of the topic than those who were told that they lost.

In **classical conditioning**, a stimulus comes to evoke a response it previously did not call up. Classical conditioning occurs by repeatedly pairing this stimulus (the conditioned stimulus) with a stimulus that does have the power to evoke the response (the unconditioned stimulus).

How might attitudes be learned through classical conditioning? In one experiment, when an attitude object (a person) was paired with positive or negative stimuli, participants came to associate the person with the positive or negative emotions (Krosnick et al., 1992). Participants were shown nine different slides in which a target person was engaged in various activities, such as walking on a street or getting into a car. Immediately before each slide there were very short exposures (13 milliseconds) of positive slides (e.g., newlyweds, a pair of kittens) or negative slides (e.g., a face on fire, a bloody shark). The participants then reported their impressions of the person. Generally, participants who had seen the person paired with warm, positive stimuli rated the person as having a better personality and as more physically attractive than did those who had seen the person paired with violent negative stimuli.

Observational Learning

Although we often learn attitudes by getting rewarded, we can also learn simply by observing. One often hears parents, shocked by the aggressive attitudes and behavior of their child, ask, "Now, where could she have gotten that from?" Research shows that children may learn to act aggressively by watching violent movies or by seeing their friends fight (Bandura, 1977). **Observational learning** occurs when we watch what people do and then model, or imitate, that behavior. For example, a child who hears her mother say, "We should keep that kind of people out of our schools," will very likely express a version of that attitude.

Observational learning does not depend on rewards, but rewards can strengthen the learning. In the preceding example, when the child expresses the attitude she has imitated, the mother might reward her with an approving smile. Furthermore, people are more likely to imitate behavior that is rewarded. Thus, if aggressive behavior seems to be rewarded—if children observe that those who use violence seem to get what they want—it is more likely to be imitated.

When there are discrepancies between what people say and what they do, children tend to imitate the behavior. A parent may verbally instruct a child that violence is a bad way of solving conflicts with other children. However, if the child observes the parent intimidate the newspaper carrier into bringing the paper to the front door rather than dropping it on the driveway, the child has noticed the truth of the matter. The parent thinks she is imparting one attitude toward violence but in fact is conveying another.

The Effect of Television and Books

Mass media play an important role in our society. For example, media heroes tend to be a very important influence in the development of our attitudes toward all manner of things: race, gender, violence, crime, love, and sex. Issues given extensive coverage in the media become foremost in the public's consciousness. For example, the saturation coverage of the 2000 presidential election elevated politics to a level not often considered by the average person. Television is a particularly pervasive medium, with 99% of children between the ages of 2 and 10 living in homes with a television, and 89% living in homes with more than one television. (Kaiser Family Foundation, 1999). Research shows that children spend an average of 5.5 hours per day watching television, with children 8 to 18 years of age watching nearly 7 hours per day (Kaiser Family Foundation, 1999).

What do they see during those hours? Most get a constant fare of violence. This violence affects the attitudes of at least some children in their interactions with peers, and the more violence they see, the more aggressive their interaction style. This effect is strongest for children in neighborhoods where violence is commonplace; the TV violence evidently serves as reinforcement.

In addition to providing aggressive models, many TV programs emphasize situations that are linked to violence. People who watch a lot of TV are likely to overestimate by far the amount of violence and crime that occurs in the world (Jowett & O'Donnell, 1992). As a result, they are more likely to anticipate violence in their own lives. In other words, by emphasizing some events and ignoring others, television, along with other mass media, defines reality for us. It directly affects how many of us think and feel about the world.

Evidence for this can be found in research looking at the relationship between sexist portrayals in children's books and how children think about the world in terms of sex roles. Kortenhaus and Demarest (1993) analyzed award-winning children's books to find out how males and females were portrayed. They pointed out, that although portrayals got better from the 1970s to the early 1990s, there is still a 2:1 ratio of males to females in central characters, pictures, and characters in children's stories. They also found that males were more likely to be portrayed in independent, instrumental roles (i.e., carrying out some activity); whereas girls were more likely to be portrayed in nurturant and dependent roles. When male and female characters appeared together, boys were shown in roles of dominance and authority, whereas girls were portrayed in roles depicting helplessness, incompetence, and lack of ambition. Even if a female character were portrayed in an active, independent role, a male character was often portrayed in a more active, independent role.

In one study, Chinese and Canadian children were asked to imagine that they were an animal and then write a story including themselves as that animal. The results showed that male children selected animals that were dangerous, strong, and wild. On the other hand female children selected animals that were safe, weak, and tame (Harvey, Ollila, Baxter, & Guo, 1997). In another study, Trepanier and Romatowski (1985) analyzed stories written by male and female children for a "young author's" competition. Specifically, they analyzed the stories for portrayals of male and female characters. As one might expect, male authors included more male characters in their stories, and female authors included more female characters. However, overall, male characters outnumbered female characters. Positive attributes were more likely to be attributed to male characters (74%) than to female characters (26%). Both male and female authors assigned fewer occupational roles to female characters than male characters. Additionally, males tended to have a wider variety of interesting roles assigned to them than females. Thus, the themes in children's stories reflect the content of books to which they are exposed. The media has a definite role in shaping a child's world view of appropriate gender-based roles.

The Effect of Textbooks

Did you find your elementary and high school textbooks dull? Textbooks, especially for areas other than the sciences, can sometimes be bland, because it is in their interest to avoid controversy. They also have an interest in presenting accepted, conventional views held by most people in the society in order to socialize students to prevailing social norms.

In an unusual look at history textbooks written earlier in the 20th century, Frances Fitzgerald contended that American history books and courses in grade school and high school neither made students good citizens nor "[left] them with very much information about the American government" (1979). Fitzgerald made a strong argument that the fury of many American college students during the 1960s came in part from their feeling that officials, teachers, and textbooks had hidden the truth about American history and politics, such as how European settlers treated Native Americans, how involved the United States was in overthrowing other governments, and so on.

The way in which textbooks treat issues can have serious consequences for the formation of attitudes. Do you recall your history book's unit on the American Civil War? There was probably a section on Billy Yank and Johnny Reb. Here is a version of the common portrayal of Johnny Reb: Johnny Reb had always known slaves. They were as much a part of his life as eating and sleeping. Johnny liked the black slaves. He believed that he treated them well. They had rocked him to sleep when he was little. He had played with them as a boy. He probably had worked with them in the fields. But he still wanted to keep the blacks as slaves (Allen & Howland, 1974). This bit of "history" is historically inaccurate, because most Confederate soldiers did not own slaves. In fact, in 1862, the second year of the Civil War, the Confederate Congress passed a law exempting all slave owners who held more than 20 slaves from military service. The ordinary Southern soldier began to speak of "a rich man's war, a poor man's fight."

Accuracy aside, what does a passage like this convey? How might it influence attitudes about the Civil War and race? In the passage, Johnny Reb's owning slaves is presented as if it were just a quirk or a bad habit, nothing to get all excited about. Yet, the fundamental fact of the American Civil War was slavery. No other civilized country in the world in 1860 had slavery. This is what unleashed the furies of the war, a war whose effects are still felt. Frances Fitzgerald (1979) wondered how anyone could learn to deal with issues of slavery and race if attitudes formed in childhood were based on misinformation.

Textbooks also can affect our attitudes, albeit in a more generalized, less obvious way, through their selective coverage. For example, especially in older texts, the role of women, blacks, Asians, and other groups in shaping American history is minimized, because little is said about them. We noted earlier that Ida Tarbell seems to be virtually unknown even in books specifically about women in American history. Texts that present a one-sided picture of history contribute to one-sided attitudes.

Attitudes are formed, then, through a variety of socializing forces, including families, schools, the media, TV, and textbooks. But some attitudes may be rooted at least partially in our biology. We turn to this topic next.

The Heritability Factor

Most theories about the formation of attitudes are based on the idea that attitudes are formed primarily through experience. However, some research suggests that attitudes as well as other complex social behaviors may have a genetic component (Plomin, 1989).

When studying the origins of a trait or behavior, geneticists try to calculate what proportion of it may be determined by heredity rather than by learning or other environmental influences involved. **Heritability** refers to the extent to which genetics accounts for differences among people in a given characteristic or behavior. For example, eye color is entirely determined by genetics; there are no environmental or learning influences. If the heritability of a characteristic is less than 100%, then other influences are involved. Height, for example, is about 90% heritable; nutrition also plays a determining role.

heritability
An indicator of the degree to which genetics accounts for differences among people for any given behavior or characteristic.

Eye color and height are clearly based in one's heredity. But how can complex social structures such as attitudes have a genetic basis? The answer is that genetics may have an indirect effect on our attitudes. That is, characteristics that are biologically based might predispose us to certain behaviors and attitudes. For example, genetic differences in sensory structures, such as hearing and taste, could affect our preferences for certain kinds of music and foods (Tesser, 1993). As another example, consider aggressiveness, which, as research has shown, has a genetic component. Level of aggressiveness can affect a whole range of attitudes and behaviors, from watching violent TV shows and movies, to hostility toward women or members of other groups, to attitudes toward capital punishment (Oskamp, 1991). In this case, a biologically based characteristic affects how one thinks, feels, and acts.

Plomin, Corley, Defries, and Fulker (1990) were interested in children's attitudes and behaviors related to television viewing. Learning—particularly the influence of parents and friends—certainly plays a role in the formation of TV-viewing attitudes and behaviors. Is it possible that genetics could also play a role? If so, how could we know this? To answer these questions, Plomin studied the TV viewing of adopted children, comparing it to the TV-viewing habits of the children's biological parents and adoptive parents. The question he asked was, Would the child's behavior more closely resemble that of the biological parents or that of the adoptive parents? A close resemblance to the habits of the biological parents would argue for a biological interpretation, because the biological parents did not share the child's environment. A close resemblance to the habits of the adoptive parents, on the other hand, would argue for an environmental interpretation. Thus, the study of adoptive children made it possible to calculate the extent to which TV viewing is determined, indirectly, by genetics.

Plomin's findings were surprising. There was a very high resemblance between the TV viewing of the children and that of the biological parents. Although shared environment influenced the amount of viewing, the genetic component was much higher. This doesn't mean that children whose biological parents watch a lot of TV are doomed to be glued to the TV for the rest of their days. It simply suggests that there is something in our genetic makeup that may incline us to certain behaviors and attitudes.

Attitudes that have a high heritability factor might be expected to differ in certain ways from those that are primarily learned. Specifically, they might be expected to be more strongly held. Is this in fact the case? There are at least two indicators of attitude strength: A person responds quickly on encountering the object of that attitude, and the person is unlikely to give in to pressure to change the attitude. Evidence suggests that both these indicators are indeed present with attitudes that have a high heritability factor (Tesser, 1993).

ATTITUDES AND BEHAVIOR

Intuitively, it makes sense that if we know something about a person's attitudes we should be able to predict his or her behavior. In Allport's definition of attitude given at the beginning of this chapter, attitudes exert a directive influence on the individual's behavior. There is a rationality bias in all of this, a belief that people will act in a manner consistent with their innermost feelings and ideas. Do we, in fact, behave in accordance with our attitudes? Early researchers assumed that a close link did exist between attitudes and behavior. However, a review of attitude–behavior research revealed quite a different picture: Attitudes appeared to be, at best, only weak predictors of behavior (Wicker, 1969).

We begin this section by looking at one early study that appeared to show little correlation between attitudes and behavior. Social psychologists eventually concluded that a relationship exists but is more complex than they suspected. We look at their attempts to unravel the complexities and to thereby show that attitudes can predict behavior. More recently, other social psychologists have argued that our behavior often is nonrational and has nothing to do with our attitudes. We conclude the section by seeing how the rational and nonrational approaches can be reconciled.

An Early Study of Attitudes and Behavior

In one well-known study from the 1930s, a young sociologist traveled around the United States with a young Chinese couple (LaPiere, 1934). They traveled 10,000 miles and visited over 200 places (Oskamp, 1991). The 1930s were a time of relatively overt expression of prejudice against many groups, including Asians. What did LaPiere and the Chinese couple encounter? Interestingly, during their entire trip, they were refused service by only one business. Several months after the trip, LaPiere wrote to every establishment he and his friends had visited and asked the owners if they would object to serving a Chinese couple. About half the establishments answered; of these, only nine said they would offer service, and only under certain conditions.

The visits measured the behavior of the business owners. The follow-up question about offering service was a measure of attitudes. Clearly, the expressed attitudes (primarily negative) and the behavior (primarily positive) were not consistent. This kind of finding led to a great deal of pessimism among attitude researchers concerning the link between attitudes and behavior. But let's consider the inconsistency more closely. Our behavior is determined by many attitudes, not just one. LaPiere measured the owners' attitudes about Asians. He did not measure their attitudes about losing money or creating difficulties for themselves by turning away customers.

Although attitudes may not predict behavior all the time, there are instances where attitudes and behavior match well. For example, a specific attitude toward abortion (for or against) often matches well with a specific behavior (protesting). Attitudes and behaviors match well for those issues we feel strongly about.

Furthermore, it is easier to express a negative attitude when you are not face-to-face with the object of that attitude. Think how easy it is to tell the aluminum-siding salesperson over the phone that you never want to hear about aluminum siding again as long as you live. Yet when the person shows up at your door, you are probably less blunt and might even listen to the sales pitch. In the case of LaPiere's study, being prejudiced is easy by letter, harder in person.

To summarize, LaPiere's findings did not mean there is little relationship between attitudes and behavior. They just indicated that the presence of the attitude object (in this case, the Chinese couple) is not always enough to trigger the expression of the attitude. Other factors can come into play.

There are several reasons why attitudes aren't good predictors of behavior. First, research showed that it was when investigators tried to link general attitudes and specific behaviors that the link appeared weak. When researchers looked at a specific attitude, they often were able to find a good relationship between that attitude and behavior. However, when researchers asked people about a general attitude, such as their religious beliefs, and assessed a specific behavior related to that attitude, such as praying before meals, they found only a weak correlation (Eagly, 1992).

Another reason why attitudes and behaviors may not relate strongly is the fact that a behavior may relate to more than one attitude. For example, whether you vote for a particular candidate may depend on how she stands on a range of issues (e.g., abortion, health care, defense spending, civil rights). Measuring any single attitude may not predict very well how you vote. However, if the entire range of attitudes is measured, the relationship between attitudes and behavior improves. Similarly, if only one behavior is measured, your attitude may not relate to that behavior very well. It is much better if a behavioral trend (several behaviors measured over time) is measured. Attitudes tend to relate better to behavioral trends than a single behavior.

The Theory of Reasoned Action

theory of reasoned action
A theory of attitudes stating that people are relatively thoughtful creatures and are aware of their attitudes and behavior.

Years ago, Martin Fishbein and Icek Ajzen (1975), in their **theory of reasoned action**, stated that people were relatively thoughtful creatures and were aware of their attitudes and behavior. But they may demonstrate the link between their attitudes and behavior in ways that differ from those expected by social psychologists. A person with strong religious attitudes may go to church only occasionally. However, this does not mean that the person is not committed to his or her religious attitude system. It simply means that the social psychologist has to measure a number of behaviors that are reasonably related to the attitudes. Strong religious attitudes should be related not only to going to religious services but also to doing charitable work, sending children for religious instruction, and expressing interest in theology among other behaviors. Fishbein and Ajzen said that if we measure the aggregate — the entire mix of behaviors that are related to the attitude — we will find that attitudes and behavior in fact are related. In other words, to get at the true relationship between general attitudes and behavior, it is necessary to look at many different kinds of behavior, all plausibly related to the attitude.

Theory of Planned Behavior

theory of planned behavior
A theory that explains attitude–behavior relationships, focusing on the relationship between the strength of our behavioral intentions and our performance of them.

Continuing their work on attitudes and behavior, Ajzen and Fishbein (1980) proposed the **theory of planned behavior**. This theory sensibly assumes that the best predictor of how we will behave is the strength of our intentions (Ajzen, 1987). As shown in Figure 5.3, the theory is essentially a three-step process to the prediction of behavior. The likelihood that individuals will

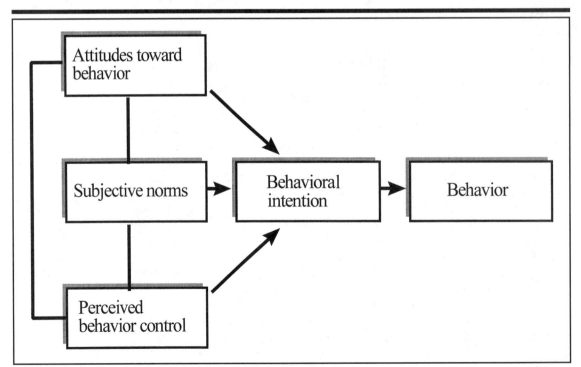

Figure 5.3 *A schematic diagram of the theory of planned behavior. An important component is the behavioral intention based on attitudes toward a behavior, subjective norms, and perceived behavioral control. The behavioral intention directly influences behavior.*

Based on Fishbein & Ajzen, 1980. Reprinted with permission.

carry out a behavior consistent with an attitude they hold depends on the strength of their intention, which is in turn influenced by three factors. By measuring these factors, we can determine the strength of intention, which enables us to predict the likelihood of the behavior.

The first factor that influences behavioral intention is *attitude toward the behavior*. Be careful here: We are talking about the attitude toward the behavior, not toward the object. For example, you might have a positive attitude about exercise, because you believe that it reduces tension. Exercise is the object of the attitude. But you might not like to sweat. In fact, you hate to sweat. Will you exercise? The theory says that the attitude toward the behavior, which includes sweating, is a better predictor of your actions than your attitude about exercise because it affects your intentions.

The second factor, *subjective norms*, refers to how you think your friends and family will evaluate your behavior. For example, you might think, "All my friends exercise, and they will think that it is appropriate that I do the same." In this case, you may exercise despite your distaste for it. Your friends' behavior defines exercise as normative, the standard. Wellness programs that attempt to change dietary and exercise habits rely heavily on normative forces. By getting people into groups, they encourage them to perceive healthy lifestyles as normative (everyone else is involved).

Perceived behavioral control, the third factor, refers to a person's belief that the behavior he or she is considering is easy or hard to accomplish. For example, a person will be more likely to engage in health-related preventive behaviors such as dental hygiene or breast self-examination if he or she believes that they can be easily done (Ronis & Kaiser, 1989).

In summary, the theory of planned behavior emphasizes that behavior follows from attitudes in a reasoned way. If a person thinks that a particular behavior associated with an attitude will lead to positive outcomes, that other people would approve, and that the behavior can be done readily, then the person will engage in the behavior (Eagly, 1992). People essentially ask themselves if they can reasonably expect that the behavior will achieve their individual and social needs.

Let's use the theory of planned behavior to analyze voting behavior. Assume you have a positive attitude about voting (the object). Will you actually vote? Let's say you think that it is the duty of every citizen to vote. Furthermore, your friends are going to vote, and you believe they will think badly of you if you don't (subjective norms). Finally, you feel that you will be able to easily rearrange your schedule on election day (perceived behavioral control). If we know all this about you, we can conclude you have a strong intention to vote and can make a pretty confident prediction that in keeping with your attitude, you are likely to vote.

The accuracy of behavioral intentions in predicting behavior is evident in the Gallup Poll. The Gallup organization has been conducting voting surveys since 1936, the year Franklin Delano Roosevelt ran against Alf Landon, governor of Kansas. Figure 5.4 shows the record of the Gallup Poll in national elections from 1968 to 2001. In general, the polls are quite accurate. Yes, there have been a few exceptions over the past 57 years. They certainly got it wrong in 1948: The data indicated that Harry Truman did not have much of a chance to win. But rarely in history books do we hear mention of Dewey, the governor of New York who ran against Truman and who was projected as the winner. In this case, the pollsters were wrong primarily because they stopped polling a little too early. They had not yet learned that people

Figure 5.4

Gallup Poll data showing predicted and actual outcomes for presidential elections from 1968 to 2000. Gallup Polls are remarkably accurate in predicting not only the winner but also the margin of victory.

Note: Average error = −1.93.

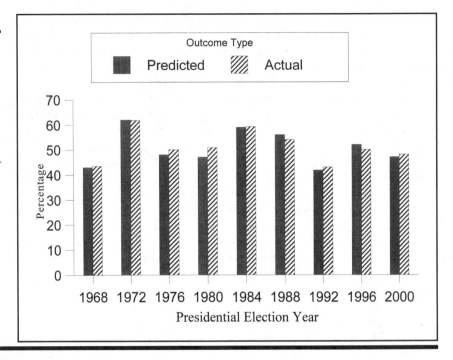

have other things on their minds than elections and may not start to pay serious attention to the campaign until a week or so before the actual vote. Pollsters will not make that error again.

Although the question, For whom will you vote, candidate X or candidate Y? might appear to be a measure of attitude, it is really a measure of behavioral intention. Voting is a single act and can be measured by a single direct question. These are the circumstances in which consistency between attitude and behavior is likely to be the highest. Pollsters often try to determine the strength of these intentions by asking such questions as: How strongly do you feel about your preferred candidate? How intense are your feelings? Although refinements like these may add to the accuracy of voting surveys in the future, what is needed is a concrete way of measuring behavioral intentions.

The Importance of Conviction

Some of our attitudes are important to us; others are much less important. One reason researchers underestimated the attitude–behavior link is because they did not focus on attitudes that are important to people (Abelson, 1988). Attitudes held with conviction are central to the person holding them. Examples include attitudes of racial and gender equality, racism and sexism, patriotism, religious fundamentalism, and occultism. Attitudes held with conviction are like possessions (Abelson, 1988). Recall that one function of an attitude is that it defines us; it tells people who we are. The person owns his or her attitudes, proudly displaying them to those who would appreciate them and defending them against those who would try to take them away. For example, someone deeply committed to one side or the other of the abortion issue will likely defend his view against the other side and show his solidarity with those on the same side. Such attitudes will be hard to change, as a change would mean a major alteration in the way the person sees the world.

Because attitudes to which people are strongly committed are hard to manipulate in a laboratory experiment, researchers tended to stay away from them. As a result, social psychologists overestimated the ease with which attitudes might be changed and underestimated the relationship between attitudes and behavior. If an attitude is important to people, they expect that behavior in agreement with that attitude will help them get what they want. Thus, important attitudes and behavior tend to be closely linked.

An attitude held with conviction is easily accessible. This means that if you discuss with someone a subject about which they feel strongly, they respond quickly and have a lot of ideas about it. Moreover, attitude accessibility—the ease with which one can bring a particular attitude to mind—is increased by constant use and application of that attitude (Doll & Ajzen, 1992). In a study several years ago, researchers measured latencies (speed of response) with respect to questions about women's rights, abortion, and racial integration (Krosnick, 1989). Whatever the issue, people who considered an attitude important responded more quickly than those who considered it unimportant. Important attitudes are more available in memory and are more likely to correspond to behavior. If your stand on abortion, women's rights, gun ownership, or the Dallas Cowboys is important, you are more likely to act in a manner consistent with that attitude.

You can get a sense of how accessible an attitude is by noting how long it takes you to recall it. For example, notice how long it takes you to recall your attitude toward the following: living wills, parent–teacher associations, the death penalty, aisle seats, snakes, water filters, political action committees, the clergy, daylight-saving time, baseball. Some of these notions brought feelings and thoughts to mind quickly; others may not have.

If attitude accessibility indicates strength of conviction, we might expect attitudes high in accessibility to be better predictors of behavior than attitudes lower in accessibility. Russell Fazio, who has extensively studied attitude accessibility, investigated this issue in connection with the 1984 presidential election (Fazio & Williams, 1986). The summer before the election, potential voters were asked whether they agreed with each of the following two statements: "A good president for the next 4 years would be Walter Mondale," and "A good president for the next 4 years would be Ronald Reagan." The respondents had to indicate how strongly they agreed or disagreed by pressing one of five buttons: strongly agree, agree, don't care, disagree, strongly disagree.

The researchers measured the time that passed before respondents pressed the button. The delay interval between the moment you are confronted with an object and the moment you realize your attitude is called the *latency* (Rajecki, 1990). The longer respondents took to hit the button, the longer the latency and the less accessible the attitude. Not only were the researchers able to get a reading of the attitude toward the candidates but also they were able to get a measure of accessibility.

On the day after the election, respondents were asked whether they had voted and, if so, for whom they had voted. Was there a relationship between latency times and voting behavior? That is, did attitude accessibility predict behavior? The answer is, yes it did. Attitude accessibility measured in June and July 1984 accurately predicted voting behavior in November. Those who had responded quickly for Reagan were more likely to vote for him than those who had taken longer to respond. The same relationship held, although not quite as strongly, for Mondale supporters.

Ideology

ideology
A person's doctrines, opinions, or ways of thinking that characterize an overarching view of the world.

One's **ideology** refers to the doctrines, opinions, or ways of thinking that are characteristic of a person. Ideologies form an overarching way of viewing the world. For example, a Supreme Court justice may hold a conservative ideology that, at its core, would oppose abortion, seek to put limits on affirmative action laws, and generally favor laws that keep the government out of the lives of individual citizens. Is there a strong connection between one's ideology and behavior? Apparently there is. In a study of the voting of Supreme Court justices, Baum (1985) analyzed the voting records of Supreme Court justices during the 1982 session to see if the ideology of the justices (liberalism or conservatism) matched their voting record on freedom issues. Baum, as shown in Figure 5.5, found remarkable consistency between a justice's ideology and how the justices voted. For example, the late Justice Thurgood Marshall, a very liberal justice, voted almost exclusively in the liberal direction. Coversely, Justice William Rehnquist, a very conservative justice, voted almost exclusively in the conservative direction.

This general finding is supported by a study of the relationship between religious ideology and sexual behavior (Brody et al., 1996). Brody and colleagues had German college students complete a questionnaire measuring their sexual behaviors and experience. Participants also indicated their political (left wing or right wing) and religious ideology on rating scales.

Although there is sometimes a weak relationship between one's general attitudes and specific behaviors, there is a stronger relationship between one's ideology and behavior. Liberal justices tend to vote in a liberal direction, whereas conservative justices tend to vote in a conservative direction.

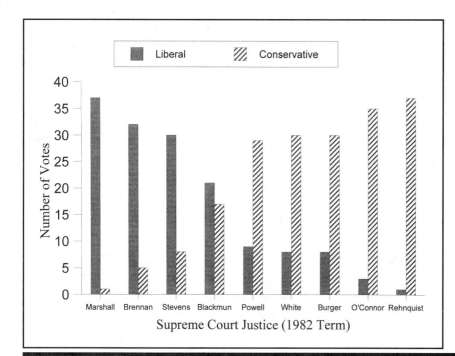

Figure 5.5

Voting records of Supreme Court Justices for cases relating to social issues. A justice's ideology is a strong predictor of how that justice voted on these types of cases.

Based on data from Baum, 1985.

Brody and colleagues found that participants with strong religious beliefs tended to have few or no sex partners and little other sexual experience. Participants with a left-wing political ideology tended to have more sexual experience. Specifically, left-wing men had more experience with oral sex; whereas left-wing women tended to have more sexual partners than right-wing women. Left-wing political leanings also were associated with a greater willingness to consider having homosexual relationships, higher rates of masturbation, and for women having one's first sexual experience at an early age.

The Nonrational Actor

The theories and ideas about attitudes and behavior discussed so far tend to assume a rational, almost calculated approach to behavior. In the theory of planned behavior, if you can get measures of people's attitude toward a behavior, their perception of how important others might approve or disapprove of what they do, and their sense of control over that behavior, then you can predict their intentions and, therefore, their likely behavior. If there is a significant criticism of the theory of planned behavior, it is that when you ask people to tell you about the components of their intentions, they know that their answers should be logical. If you reported that you voted but you had no interest in the candidates and you thought all candidates were crooks, this hardly makes you look like a logical individual.

Some theorists have taken the opposite approach: They assume that human beings are **nonrational actors** (Ronis & Kaiser, 1989), and our attitudes may often be totally irrelevant to our behavior. Cigarette smoking, for example is so habitual as to be automatic, totally divorced from any attitude or behavioral intention the smoker may have. Most of our behaviors are like

nonrational actor

A view that humans are not always rational in their behavior and their behavior can be inconsistent with their attitudes.

that (Ronis & Kaiser, 1989). We do them over and over without thought (Gilbert, 1991). You floss your teeth, but your attitude and intentions about dental hygiene are activated only when you run out of floss. Even though you believe flossing is important, and even though you remember that sign in your dentist's office that reads, "No, you don't have to floss all you teeth — only the ones you want to keep," you now have to act on your attitude. Are you willing to get in the car at 11 P.M. and drive to the store to buy more dental floss? Similarly, if your regular aerobics class becomes inconvenient, is your attitude about the importance of exercise strong enough that you will rearrange your whole schedule?

In sum, people usually behave habitually, unthinkingly, even mindlessly. They make active decisions only when they face new situations. Thus, there is a good chance of inconsistencies between our attitudes and our behavior.

Mindless Behavior in Everyday Life

Have you ever arrived home after work or school and not been able to recall a single thing about how you got there? In everyday life, we often run on a kind of automatic pilot. Our behavior becomes so routine and automatic that we are hardly aware of what we are doing. We are in a state of mind that Ellen Langer (1989) termed *mindlessness*, one that involves reduced attention and a loss of active control in everyday activities. Mindlessness occurs when we're engaging in behaviors that have been overlearned and routinized. In this state, we carry out the behaviors rigidly, according to a preconceived pattern and without thought or appraisal. Mindlessness is fairly common in our everyday interactions. The cashier at a restaurant asks you, "How was everything?" You say that your steak was overcooked, your potato was cold, and the service was terrible. The cashier replies, "Here's your change, have a nice day." In this example, the cashier's question and response were automatic; she really didn't care how you enjoyed your meal.

Langer was interested in studying this state of mind (Langer, Blank, & Chanowitz, 1978). She had a researcher approach people waiting to use a copy machine in a library and ask to use it first. The request was phrased in one of several ways: "Excuse me, I have five pages to copy. May I use the machine because I am in a rush?" "Excuse me, I have five pages to copy. May I use the machine?" "Excuse me, I have five pages to copy. May I use the machine because I have to make copies?" The researcher also asked to make 20 copies in these three different ways. Request 2 offers no reason for using the copier first, and request 3 offers a mindless reason ("because I have to make copies"); only request 1 provides a minimally acceptable reason ("because I am in a rush"). If the participants in this situation were dealing with the request in a mindless fashion, they would fail to distinguish between legitimate and illegitimate (or ridiculous) reasons. As it turns out, any kind of excuse works as long as the request is small. When the request was to make five copies, people apparently did not appraise the quality of the excuse as long as one was offered: Having to make copies was just as good as being in a rush. People snapped out of their mindless state, however, when the request was to make 20 copies. It is clear that when the behavior (the request) had a significant impact, people paid more attention to the difference between bad and good excuses. Although we usually pay close attention to good and bad reasons for people's behavior, it may be that the request to copy five pages isn't worth the effort. When the ante is raised to 20 pages, then we are more mindful.

The fact that we hold a number of attitudes without really thinking about them means there can be some interesting consequences once we are forced to think about them. Thinking about our attitudes and the reasons we hold them can sometimes be disruptive and confusing (Wilson, Dunn, Kraft, & Lisle, 1989). More generally, the process of introspecting—of looking into our own mind, rather than just behaving—can have this effect.

Timothy Wilson's work showed that thinking about the reasons for our attitudes can often lead us to behave in ways that seem inconsistent with those attitudes (Wilson et al., 1989). For example, if you are forced to think about why you like your romantic partner, you might wind up ending the relationship in the near future. Much depends on the strength of the relationship. If the relationship is not strong, thinking about reasons might weaken it. If it is pretty strong, then reasoning might further strengthen it. The stronger our attitude or belief, the more likely that thinking about it will increase the consistency between it and our behavior (Fazio, 1986).

Why should thinking about reasons for our attitudes sometimes lead to inconsistency between our attitudes and behavior? The basic answer is that if we have never really thought about an attitude before, then thinking about it may cause us to change it (Wilson et al., 1989). If you are forced to count the ways you love your current partner, and it takes you a lot of time to use all the fingers on one hand, you have gotten some insight into how you really think about the relationship.

This explanation was supported by a study in which people were asked their attitudes about social issues, such as the death penalty, abortion, and national health insurance, in two separate telephone surveys conducted a month apart (Wilson & Kraft, 1988). In the first survey, some people were asked to give their reasons for their opinions whereas others were just asked their opinions. A month later, those people who had been asked to give reasons proved more likely to have changed their opinion. So thinking about reasons seems to lead to change. Why? The full explanation might lie in the biased sample hypothesis, proposed by Wilson and colleagues (1989). It goes like this: If you ask people why they believe something, they are not likely to say, "I don't know." Instead, they will conjure up reasons that seem plausible but may be wrong or incomplete. That is, because people often do not know their true reasons, they sample only part of those reasons. Thus, they present a biased sample of their reasons. People then assume the reasons in the biased sample are their true reasons for holding the belief. If these reasons don't seem compelling, thinking about them may persuade people to change their belief.

The Rational and Nonrational Actors: A Resolution

Sometimes we are rational actors, sometimes we are nonrational actors. Sometimes our behavior is "coupled" to our attitudes, sometimes it is "uncoupled" from them. Isn't this where we began? Let's see if we can now resolve the apparent conflict. It makes sense to see attitudes and behavior as ordinarily linked, with uncoupling occurring primarily under two kinds of circumstances.

The first circumstance is when an attitude is not particularly important to you. You may not have thought about the attitude object much or have expressed the attitude very often. So in this case, you don't really know what you think. True, capital punishment and national health care are important issues. But many of us may not have thought them through. When you are forced to consider these issues, you may be surprised by what you say. This may make you reconsider your attitude.

The second circumstance is slightly more complicated. Essentially, it is when you don't have a clear sense of your goals and needs. Let's go back to the theory of planned action for a moment. The theory says if you expect that a behavior can help you achieve your goals and social needs, you will do it. But people are often not clear about their goals and needs (Hixon & Swann, 1993). When you are not clear about what you want to accomplish, then your behavior will be relatively unpredictable and might well be uncoupled from your attitudes.

For example, we exercise, but only sporadically, because we are mainly concerned about looking good in front of our health-obsessed friends. Our reasons are weak, not clear to us, and therefore our exercising behavior is infrequent and unpredictable. But if we or a friend the same age has a heart attack, we develop a much stronger attitude toward exercise. We now know that our reasons for exercising are to improve cardiovascular function, to enhance our sense of well-being, and, in short, to save our lives. Now we change our schedule around to exercise every day, subscribe to *Runner's World* magazine, invest in better exercise shoes, and so on.

In sum, then, our behavior is more likely to be consistent with our attitudes when the attitudes concern an area that is important to us and when the behavior helps us achieve clear and strong social needs. Attitudes we hold with conviction are not vulnerable to uncoupling because we have expressed those attitudes in a variety of situations and have thought deeply about them.

IDA TARBELL REVISITED

Today, Ida Tarbell is not a well-known historical figure, but she held her attitudes with conviction and expressed them courageously. Although she didn't like being called a muckraker at first, she realized that there was a lot of "muck" in American life that needed to be raked. President Roosevelt and the American public came to agree.

Tarbell followed her beliefs with a powerful sense of purpose. Her early experiences, her family's support, and her own strong education and temperament combined to produce a woman whose attitudes and behavior were consistently in accord. No doubt this is an unusual situation. Ida was a rational actor; the coupling of her attitudes and her life's work was fierce and unshakable.

CHAPTER REVIEW

1. **What is an attitude?**
   Gordon Allport, an early attitude theorist, formulated the following definition: "An **attitude** is a mental and neural state of readiness, organized through experience, exerting a directive or dynamic influence upon the individual's response to all objects and situations with which it is related."

2. **What components make up an attitude?**
   Attitudes are constructed of thoughts about the object of the attitude (cognitions), feelings (affect), behavioral intentions, and behaviors related to the object of the attitude. An attitude is really a summary of an **attitude structure**, which consists of these interconnected components. An **explicit attitude** operates via controlled processing and we are aware of it, its cognitive underpinnings, and how it relates to behavior. An **implicit attitude** is under automatic control and we are not aware of its operation.

3. **What is the relationship of attitudes to values?**
   Our attitudes flow from and express our values. A **value** is a conception of what is desirable; it is a guideline for a person's actions, a standard for behavior.

4. **What are terminal and instrumental values?**
   A terminal value is a preferred end state. Examples of terminal values are freedom, equity, and happiness. Instrumental values are preferred ways of doing things and include values such as honesty and ambition. Two terminal values, equality and freedom, are especially predictive of a wide range of attitudes.

5. **What function do attitudes serve in day-to-day life?**
   First, attitudes define us. The person who opposes gun control is telling us something important about herself. Her attitude has a kind of **badge value**. Second, attitudes direct our future feelings and thoughts about the objects of those feelings and thoughts. Attitudes summarize our feelings, thoughts, intentions, and behavior for the cognitive miser. When a topic comes up, especially one with which we have some experience and familiarity, our attitude helps us respond.

6. **What is an attitude survey?**
   An **attitude survey** is a self-report measure of attitudes. On an attitude survey, a respondent indicates his or her attitude by answering a series of questions. Attitude surveys may include open-ended questions which simply ask respondents to write down an answer to a question. Attitude surveys may also include rating scales on which respondents indicate the extent to which they agree or disagree with a statement by circling a number on a scale. One of the most popular of these methods is Likert scaling on which the respondent agrees or disagrees with attitude statements on a 5-point scale.

7. **How are attitude surveys conducted?**
   Social psychologists are interested in the attitudes of large groups of individuals. However, it is not possible to survey everyone in the population. Consequently, a small sample of individuals is chosen for a survey. A survey sample need not be large, it must be representative. Ideally, the sample would contain the same proportion of individuals from different demographic categories (e.g., gender, race, age).

8. **What are the potential sources of bias in a survey?**
   Although we would like to believe that attitude surveys produce truthful data, some sources of bias exist in survey results. For example, the way a person answers a question depends on factors such as how a question is worded, the format of the question, and where the question appears on the questionnaire. Also, survey respondents may give opinions on issues or subjects about which they know very little or flat out lie.

9. What are behavioral measures of attitudes?

Because of the problems inherent in attitude surveys, social psychologists have developed other measures of attitudes that measure behavior directly. **Unobtrusive measures** assess attitudes indirectly. One could, for example, count the number of bumper stickers on cars that favor one or another political candidate. In the lost-letter technique, letters are dropped on a street, some addressed to ethnic minorities and others to nonminority people. The rate of return of each group of letters is used as an index of attitudes. Psychophysiological measures assess attitudes through the recording of physiological arousal.

10. What processes are involved in attitude formation?

The processes most frequently involved in attitude formation are **mere exposure**, direct personal experience, **operant conditioning, classical conditioning**, and **observational learning**. Additionally, the mass media (television, popular books, and text books) plays a role in the shaping of attitudes. Media heroes play an important role in attitude formation, such as gender role attitudes.

11. Can attitudes be inherited?

The content of attitudes is certainly learned. However, researchers are now pointing to the possibility that some characteristics that are biologically based may predispose us to certain behaviors and attitudes. **Heritability** refers to the extent to which genetics accounts for differences among people in a given characteristic or behavior. For example, genetic differences in sensory structures such as hearing and taste could affect our preferences for certain kinds of music and foods.

12. What is the relationship between attitudes and behavior?

The strength of the relationship depends on whether the attitude is strongly held, with conviction, or is weakly held. Research shows that strongly held attitudes tend to be firmly tied to behavior and are accessible. However, attitudes may be uncoupled from behavior, usually if the attitude object is not important to the person and if the person is unclear about his or her social goals and needs.

13. Why aren't attitudes good predictors of behaviors?

When attitude researchers measure general attitudes and try to predict specific behaviors, the attitude–behavior relationship is weak. The relationship is stronger when specific attitudes and specific behaviors are measured. Additionally, behaviors often relate to more than one attitude and attitudes tend to predict behavioral trends better than any single behavior.

14. What is the theory of reasoned action?

The **theory of reasoned action** states that people were relatively thoughtful creatures and were aware of their attitudes and behavior. But they may demonstrate the link between their attitudes and behavior in ways that differ from those expected by social psychologists. A person with strong religious attitudes may go to church only occasionally. However, this does not mean that the person is not committed to her religious attitude system. It simply means that the social psychologist has to measure a number of behaviors that are reasonably related to the attitudes.

15. What is the theory of planned behavior?

The **theory of planned behavior** assumes that the best predictor of how we behave is not our attitudes but the strength of our intentions. Three factors influence the strength of a behavioral intention: our attitudes toward the behavior (e.g., How do we feel about voting?), perceived behavior control (e.g., How easy or hard is voting and will it make a difference?), and subjective norms (e.g., Are my friends all voting?).

16. How does conviction of an attitude affect the attitude–behavior relationship?

If an attitude is important to us (e.g., attitudes about race and gender equality), then the relationship between that attitude and behavior will be stronger than if an attitude is unimportant to us.

17. **How does one's ideology relate to behavior?**
    Ideology refers to the doctrines, opinions, and ways of thinking that are characteristic of a person and represent overarching ways of viewing the world. Political conservatism and liberalism are examples of ideologies. There is a strong connection between one's ideology and behavior. For example, conservative judges most often vote in a conservative direction on issues relating to freedom. Conversely, liberals vote in a liberal direction on the same issues.

18. **What is the notion of the nonrational actor?**
    Some attitude theorists have criticized the theory of planned behavior, because it assumed that individuals are always rational when attitudes are concerned. Other theorists maintain that humans are **nonrational actors** and that sometimes attitudes are totally irrelevant to our behavior. In many cases, according to this view, people behave habitually, unthinkingly, and even mindlessly in everyday life.

19. **How has the controversy over the rational and nonrational actor been resolved?**
    The short answer is that sometimes we are rational actors and our attitudes are coupled with our behavior. Other times we are nonrational actors and our behaviors and attitudes are uncoupled. Uncoupling is likely to occur when an attitude is not particularly important to us or if we don't have a clear sense of our goals and needs.

INTERNET ACTIVITY

HOW DID THEY VOTE?

You can conduct your own miniature study of how Supreme Court justices voted on issues relating to social issues. Listed in the table below are seven social issues cases decided by the Supreme Court in the year 2000. For this exercise, you are going to use the Internet to find the cases listed below and determine whether a justice voted in a liberal or conservative direction. You can find the Court's opinions easily by using either the Legal Information Institute Web site http://supct.law.cornell.edu/supct/00highlts.html or FindLaw Court Decisions http://www.findlaw.com/casecode/supreme.html. Or, you can enter the search term: "supreme court decisions" into a search engine to find these or other sites that house Supreme Court opinions.

For the purposes of this exercise, define a conservative or liberal vote in the following way:

	CONSERVATIVE VOTE	LIBERAL VOTE
School prayer	Dissent	Opinion of Court
Gay scoutmaster	Opinion of Court	Dissent
Nude dancing	Opinion of Court	Dissent
Death penalty	Opinion of Court	Dissent
Miranda warnings	Dissent	Opinion of Court
Gender violence law	Opinion of Court	Dissent
Partial-birth abortions	Dissent	Opinion of Court

You can find out how each justice voted by reading the abstract of each case. At the end of each abstract you will find which justices voted with the opinion of the court and which justices dissented. You will find a listing that looks like this:

Breyer, J., delivered the opinion of the Court, in which Stevens, O'Connor, Souter, and Ginsburg, J., joined. Stevens, J., filed a concurring opinion, in which Ginsburg, J., joined. O'Connor, J., filed a concurring opinion. Ginsburg, J., filed a concurring opinion, in which Stevens, J., joined. Rehnquist, C. J., and Scalia, J., filed dissenting opinions. Kennedy, J., filed a dissenting opinion, in which Rehnquist, C. J., joined. Thomas, J., filed a dissenting opinion, in which Rehnquist, C. J., and Scalia, J., joined.

In this instance, Justices Breyer, Stevens, O'Connor, Souter, and Ginsburg, voted with the opinion of the Court and Justices Rehnquist, Scalia, Kennedy, and Thomas dissented.

In the chart that follows, place a "C" in the box to indicate a conservative vote and an "L" to indicate a liberal vote. When you have done this, tally the conservative and liberal votes for each justice and determine:

1. Which justices are the most conservative (consistently vote in the conservative direction).
2. Which justices are the most liberal (consistently vote in the liberal direction).
3. Which, if any, justices can be classified as *swing voters* (equally as likely to vote in the conservative or liberal direction).

	REHNQUIST	O'CONNOR	STEVENS	THOMAS	SOUTER	SCALIA	GINSBURG	KENNEDY	BREYER
Partial birth abortion *(Sternberg v. Carhart)*									
Boy Scouts and gay scoutmaster *(Boy Scouts of America v. Dale)*									
Nude dancing *(Erie v. Pap's A.M.)*									
Death penalty *(Weeks v. Aneelone, Director, Virginia)*									
Miranda warnings *(Dickerson v. United States)*									
Gender violence *(United States v. Morrison)*									
School prayer *(Santa Fe School Distric v. Doe)*									

SUGGESTIONS FOR FURTHER READING

Dalleck, R. (1991). *Lone star rising: Lyndon Johnson and his times, 1908–1960.* New York: Oxford University Press.

This is a fascinating portrait of a larger-than-life man, a study of attitudes in the making.

Goleman, D. (1993, September 7). Pollsters enlist psychologists in quest for unbiased results. *The New York Times,* p. 28.

This article shows how social psychologists can make public opinion polling more reliable.

Kamiiner, W. (1992). Crashing the locker room. *Atlantic, 270,* 58–71.

This is an engaging examination of sexism in journalism and elsewhere.

CHAPTER 6

PERSUASION AND ATTITUDE CHANGE

Chicago, 1924: Jacob Franks, a wealthy businessman, answered the telephone and listened as a young but cultivated voice told him that his 14-year-old son, Bobby, had been kidnaped and could be ransomed for $10,000. The next morning, while Mr. Franks arranged for the ransom, he was notified that the nude and bloody body of his son had been found in a culvert on Chicago's South Side. Franks was sure that the boy in the morgue was not Bobby, because the kidnappers had assured him that this was simply a business proposition. He sent his brother to the morgue to clear up the misidentification. Unfortunately, the body was that of his son; his head had been split open by a blow from a blunt instrument.

The case was solved quickly. The police found a pair of eyeglasses near the body and traced them to Nathan Leopold, Jr., the 20-year-old son of a prominent local entrepreneur. Leopold denied any connection to the murder, claiming he had spent the day with his friend, Richard Loeb, the son of a

vice president of Sears, Roebuck, and Company. However, both men soon confessed. Loeb, it seemed, had always dreamed of committing the "perfect crime." He had enlisted Leopold, and together they had gone to their old school playground and followed several different boys around. They finally settled on Bobby Franks and pushed him into their car. Loeb hit Bobby over the head with a chisel, and then he and Leopold drove in a leisurely fashion to the culvert, stopping along the way for a bite to eat.

The trial was a media circus. The Leopold and Loeb families hired the most famous trial lawyer of that time, Clarence Darrow, to plead for their sons. The men had already confessed, so the issue was not whether they were guilty. It was whether they would spend the rest of their lives in prison—or hang. The prosecution argued for hanging the murderers. Darrow pleaded for mercy.

Darrow had a tough fight: He needed all his persuasive skills to convince Judge Caverly of his point of view (a jury was not required). He spoke for 12 hours, trying to provide the judge with a rationale for sentencing the men to life imprisonment. He argued that life sentences would serve a better, more humane purpose than bowing to public opinion and hanging those two "mentally diseased boys." Darrow also claimed disinterest in the fates of his clients, an interesting ploy for a lawyer who spoke from morning to night on their behalf. In fact, he suggested that life in prison would be a worse fate than death. At the end of Darrow's oration, the judge was in tears, as were many spectators.

Darrow's arguments hit the mark. Judge Caverly sentenced Leopold and Loeb to life imprisonment for murder and 99 years for kidnaping. Darrow's impassioned, eloquent arguments persuaded the judge to spare his clients' lives (Weinberg, 1957).

Clarence Darrow's task was to convince the judge that his clients' lives should be spared. He knew that the judge favored the death penalty, as did almost all the American public. If Darrow couldn't change the judge's attitude, he had to convince him that his attitude should not be applied in this case, that is, that he should behave contrary to his beliefs.

KEY QUESTIONS

AS YOU READ THIS CHAPTER, FIND THE ANSWERS TO THE FOLLOWING QUESTIONS:

1. *What is persuasion?*
2. *What is the Yale communication model?*
3. *What factors about the communicator affect persuasion?*
4. *What message factors mediate persuasion?*
5. *What is the elaboration likelihood model of persuasion?*
6. *What is the impact of vividness on persuasion?*
7. *What is the need for cognition?*
8. *What is the heuristic and systematic information model of persuasion?*
9. *What is cognitive dissonance theory, and what are its main ideas?*
10. *What is self-perception theory?*
11. *What is self-affirmation theory?*
12. *What is psychological reactance?*
13. *How are the tactics of persuasion used on a mass scale?*

Darrow used all his powers of persuasion to influence the judge. **Persuasion** is the application of rational and/or emotional arguments to convince others to change their attitudes or behavior. It is a form of social influence used not only in the courtroom but also in every part of daily social life. The persuasion process goes on in the classroom, church, political arena, and the media. Persuasive messages are so much a part of our lives that we often are oblivious of the bombardment from billboards, TV, radio, newspapers, parents, peers, and public figures.

Persuasion, then, is a pervasive form of social influence. We are all agents of social influence when we try to convince others to change their attitudes or behavior. We are also targets of social influence when others try to persuade or coerce us to do what they want us to do.

In this chapter, we explore the process of persuasion, looking at the strategies communicators use to change people's attitudes or behavior. We consider the techniques of persuasion used by a brilliant trial lawyer such as Clarence Darrow. How was Darrow able to be so effective? He was a famous trial lawyer, highly regarded and highly credible. Was his persuasiveness a function of something about him? Or was it something about the argument he made? What role did his audience—Judge Caverly—play in the persuasiveness of the argument? In what ways might the judge have taken an active role in persuading himself of the validity of Darrow's case? And how does persuasion, both interpersonal and mass persuasion, affect us all every day as we go about our lives? These are some of the questions addressed in this chapter.

persuasion
A form of social influence that involves changing others' thoughts, attitudes, or behaviors by applying rational and emotional arguments to convince them to adopt your position.

THE YALE COMMUNICATION MODEL

What is the best way to communicate your ideas to others and persuade them to accept your point of view? An early view suggested that the most effective approach to persuasion was to present logical arguments that showed people how they would benefit from changing their attitudes. This view was formulated by Carl Hovland, who worked for the U.S. government in its propaganda efforts during World War II. After the war, he returned to Yale University, where he gathered a team of 30 co-workers and began to systematically study the process of persuasion. Out of their efforts came the **Yale communication model** (Hovland, Janis, & Kelley, 1953).

According to the Yale model, the most important factors comprising the communication process are expressed by the question, Who says what to whom by what means? This question suggests that there are four factors involved in persuasion. The "who" refers to the communicator, the person making the persuasive argument. The "what" refers to the *organization* and *content* of the persuasive message. The "whom" is the target of the persuasive message, the audience. Finally, the "means" points to the importance of the channel or medium through which the message is conveyed, such as television, radio, or interpersonal face-to-face communication. For each factor, there are several variables that can potentially influence the persuasion process.

The four factors are not independent of one another; they interact to create a persuasive effect. In practice, the content and presentation of the message depend on the communicator, the audience, and the channel. Darrow carefully chose his messages according to what arguments best suited the judge, the public, the trial setting, and his own preferences. We turn

Yale communication model
A model of the persuasion process that stressed the role of the communicator (source of a message), the nature of the message, the audience, and the channel of communication.

now to a discussion of the four factors, considering selected variables within each component. We also look at how the factors interact with one another.

The Communicator

Have you ever seen a late-night infomercial on TV? These half-hour commercials usually push a "miracle" product, such as the car wax that supposedly can withstand a direct hit from a hydrogen bomb. The car is vaporized but the wax survives. There is an "expert" (usually the inventor) who touts the product's virtues. Do you believe what this person tells you? Many people must, given the large amounts of money made from infomercials. However, many people clearly are not convinced. If you are not persuaded, one thing you may focus on is the communicator. You may find yourself questioning this fellow's integrity (because he will profit by persuading you to buy the atomic car wax) and, consequently, disbelieving his claims. In other words, you question his credibility.

CREDIBILITY: EXPERTISE AND TRUSTWORTHINESS

credibility
The believability (expertise and trustworthiness) of the communicator of a persuasive message.

Clarence Darrow knew the importance of **credibility**, the power to inspire belief. During his final arguments in the Leopold and Loeb case, Darrow continually tried to undermine the prosecution's credibility and increase his own in the eyes of the judge. For example, Darrow said of his opponent:

> I have heard in the last six weeks nothing but the cry for blood. I have heard from the office of the state's attorney only ugly hate. I have seen a court urged . . . to hang two boys, in the face of science, in the face of philosophy, in the face of the better and more humane thought. (Weinberg, 1957, p. 134)

Although other variables are important, including a communicator's perceived attractiveness and power, credibility is the most critical variable

A communicator's credibility is crucial to that person's ability to persuade. Credibility is made up of expertise and trustworthiness. Secretary of State Colin Powell is a persuasive communicator because he is perceived to have high levels of both expertise and trustworthiness.

affecting the ability to persuade. Credibility has two components: expertise and trustworthiness. **Expertise** refers to a communicator's credentials and stems from the person's training and knowledge. For example, your doctor has the ability to persuade you on health matters because she has the education and experience that give her words power. **Trustworthiness** refers to the audience's assessment of the communicator's character as well as his or her motives for delivering the message. We ask, "Why is this person trying to convince us?" Trustworthiness may be diminished when we perceive that the communicator has something to gain from persuading us. For example, you might trust a review of a product published in *Consumer Reports* (which accepts no advertising and runs independent tests) more than a similar review based on research conducted by the manufacturer of the product.

Expertise and trustworthiness do not always go together. A communicator may be high in one but low in the other. A research physician speaking about a new drug to treat AIDS may have expertise and derive credibility from that expert knowledge. But if we discover that the physician stands to gain something from the sale of this drug, we probably will question her trustworthiness. We wonder about her character and motives and may no longer consider her a credible source.

A political figure with the unfortunate mix of high expertise–low trustworthiness was President Richard Nixon. He was highly knowledgeable on matters of state but was not perceived as very trustworthy. During his period of political prominence, a poster appeared that depicted him looking particularly shifty and asked, "Would you buy a used car from this man?" Even before that—in fact, from the beginning of his political career—he was known as "tricky Dick." In contrast, a source can be highly trustworthy but low in expertise. This was the case with President Ronald Reagan. During speeches he often used unsubstantiated statistics, sending his aides scrambling for sources. However, the public generally saw him as trustworthy. People wanted to believe him. Public opinion surveys showed again and again that a majority of the public viewed President Reagan as personally attractive and likable, and these qualities prime us to accept a persuader's message (Roskos-Ewoldsen & Fazio, 1992).

Trustworthiness is, in part, a judgment about the motives of the communicator. If someone is trying very hard to persuade us, we are likely to question his or her motives (Eagly, Wood, & Chaiken, 1978). We may be more convinced by the communicator's arguments if we don't think he or she is trying to persuade us (Walster [Hatfield], & Festinger, 1962). This is the theory behind the hidden-camera technique used by television advertisers. Presumably, a person touting the virtues of a fabric softener on hidden camera must be telling the truth. The communicator is not trying to convince us; he or she is giving an unbiased testimonial.

A communicator who appears to argue against his or her own best interest is more persuasive than a communicator who takes an expected stance (Eagly et al., 1978). This was the case when newly appointed U.S. Attorney General Janet Reno took responsibility for the 1993 attack by federal agents on David Koresh's Branch Davidian headquarters in Waco, Texas. The attack, subsequently acknowledged by the government as ill planned, led to a fiery holocaust in which most of the cult members, including many children, died. At a time when everyone connected with the attack was denying responsibility for it, Reno publicly assumed the responsibility for ordering the assault. Although her statement was not in her own best interest, it enhanced the public's sense of her character and credibility. Clarence Darrow

expertise

A component of communicator credibility that refers to the communicator's credentials and stems from the individual's training and knowledge.

trustworthiness

A component of communicator credibility that involves our assessment of the communicator's motives for delivering the message.

also seemed to be arguing against his own best interest when he suggested to the judge that he did not care about the fate of his clients. Instead, he maintained, he was strongly interested in what the verdict meant for the future of humanity: "I am pleading for the future; I am pleading for a time when hatred and cruelty will not control the hearts of men, when . . . all life is worth saving, and that mercy is the highest attribute of man" (Weinberg, 1957, p. 134)

Darrow tried to increase his credibility by saying he was not acting out of self-interest or concern for the fate of Leopold and Loeb; he was fighting for a moral cause. Of course, Darrow did not mention that his fee was one of the highest ever paid to an attorney.

LIMITS ON CREDIBILITY: THE SLEEPER EFFECT Does a credible communicator have an advantage over a noncredible one in the long run? Apparently not. Research has shown that there are limits to a credible communicator's influence. The Yale group found that although the credibility of the communicator has a strong effect on attitude change, over time people forget who said what, so the effects of credibility wear off. Initially, people believe the credible source. But 6 weeks later, they are about as likely to show attitude change from a noncredible source as from a credible source. So, if you read an article in the *National Enquirer*, it probably would have little effect on you right away. But after a few weeks, you might show some change despite the source's low credibility. The phenomenon of a message having more impact on attitude change after a long delay than when it is first heard is known as the **sleeper effect**.

sleeper effect

A phenomenon of persuasion that occurs when a communication has more impact on attitude change after a long delay than when it is first heard.

One possible cause of the sleeper effect may be that the communicator's credibility does not increase the listener's understanding of the message (Kelman & Hovland, 1953). In other words, people understand messages from credible and noncredible communicators equally well. As the effects of credibility wear off over time, listeners are left with two equally understood (or misunderstood) messages (Gruder et al., 1979).

Three factors make it more likely that the sleeper effect will occur (Rajecki, 1990):

1. There is a strong persuasive argument.
2. There is a discounting cue, something that makes the receiver doubt the accuracy of the message, such as lack of communicator credibility or new information that contradicts the original message.
3. Enough time passes that the discounting cue and the message become disassociated, and people forget which source said what.

Studies show that the sleeper effect occurs most reliably when the receivers get the discounting cue after they hear the message rather than before (Pratkanis, Greenwald, Leippe, & Baumgardner, 1988). If the discounting cue comes before the message, the receiver doubts the message before it is even conveyed. But if the discounting cue comes after the message, and if the argument is strong, the receiver probably has already been persuaded. Over time, the memory of the discounting cue "decays" faster than the memory of the persuasive message (Pratkanis et al., 1988). Because the message is stored before the discounting cue is received, the message is less likely to be weakened. After a long period has elapsed, all the receiver remembers is the original persuasive message (Figure 6.1).

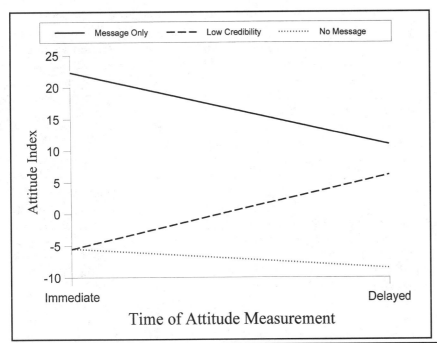

Figure 6.1

The sleeper effect in persuasion. When attitudes are measured immediately, a message from a low-credibility communicator is not persuasive. However, after a delay, the low-credibility communicator becomes more persuasive.

From data provided by Gruder and colleagues et al. (1979).

What can we say happens to a persuasive message after several weeks? When the discounting cue occurs before the message, the effect of the message diminishes. When the discounting cue occurs after the message, the power of the message is reinforced. The lesson for persuaders, then, is that they should attack their adversary before he or she makes a case or conveys a rebuttal.

The Message and the Audience

Thus far, we have seen that the characteristics of the communicator can influence the degree to which we modify our attitudes in response to a persuasive message. But what about the message itself? What characteristics of messages make them more or less persuasive, and how do these elements interact with the characteristics of the audience? We address these questions next.

WHAT KIND OF MESSAGE IS MOST EFFECTIVE? THE POWER OF FEAR

An important quality of the message is whether it is based on rational or emotional appeals. Early research showed that appeal to one emotion in particular—fear—can make a message more effective than can appeal to reason or logic. Psychologists found at first that an appeal containing a mild threat and evoking a low level of fear was more effective than an appeal eliciting very high levels of fear (Hovland et al., 1953). Then research suggested that moderate levels of fear may be most effective (Leventhal, 1970). That is, you need enough fear to grab people's attention but not so much you send them running for their lives. If the message is boring, people do not pay attention. If it is too ferocious, they are repelled.

However, persuaders need to do more than make the audience fearful; they also need to provide a possible solution. If the message is that smoking cigarettes results in major health risks, and if the communicator does not offer a method for smokers to quit, then little attitude or behavior change will occur. The smoker will be motivated to change behavior if effective ways of dealing with the threat are offered. This principle is in keeping with the Yale group's notion that people will accept arguments that benefit them.

Of course, individuals often avoid messages that make them uncomfortable. This simple fact must be taken into account when determining a persuasion strategy. For example, a strong fear appeal on the television is not very effective. The message is there only by our consent; we can always change the channel. This is why the American Cancer Society's most effective antismoking commercial involved a cartoon character named "Johnny Smoke," a long, tall cowboy cigarette. He was repeatedly asked, as he blew smoke away from his gun: "Johnny Smoke, how many men did you shoot today?" That was it: no direct threat, no explicit conclusion about the harm of smoking. It was low-key, and the audience was allowed to draw their own conclusions.

Despite evidence that high fear messages tend to repulse people, fear appeals are certainly used heavily in health education, politics, and advertising. The assumption is that making people afraid persuades them to stop smoking or to vote for a certain candidate or to buy a particular product (Gleicher & Petty, 1992). Does fear work? Sometimes it does.

In one study of the effect of low versus high fear, Faith Gleicher and Richard Petty (1992) had students at Ohio State University listen to one of four different simulated radio news stories about crime on campus. The broadcasts were either moderate in fear (crime was presented as a serious problem) or only mildly fearful (crime was not presented as a serious problem). Besides manipulating fear, the researchers varied whether the appeals had a clear assurance that something could be done about crime (a crime-watch program) or that little could be done (i.e., the crime-watch

Fear appeals are effective if they arouse significant fear, make a person believe that the dire consequences can happen, and provide a way to avoid the dire consequences. Wrecked cars brought to college campuses to deter drunk driving are an example of a fear appeal against drunk driving.

STAY ALIVE
DONT DRINK
AND DRIVE

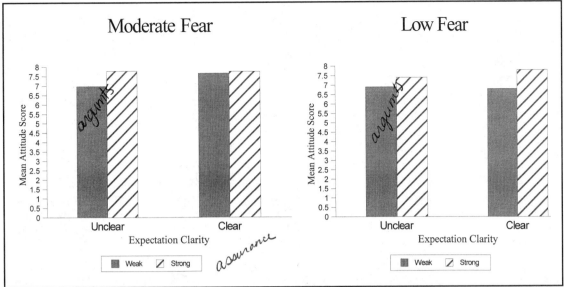

Figure 6.2 *Attitude toward a crime-watch program as a function of fear, expectation of effectiveness, and argument quality. Under low fear, attitudes depend on the strength of the arguments made. Under moderate fear, attitudes differ only when the expectation for success is unclear. This indicates that the arousal of moderate fear enhances effortful processing of the message content.*

From Gleicher and Petty (1992). Reprinted with permission.

programs do not work). The researchers also varied the strength of the arguments; some participants heard strong arguments, and others heard weak ones. In other words, some participants heard powerful arguments in favor of the crime-watch program whereas others heard powerful arguments that showed crime watch did not work. In the weak argument condition, some participants heard not very good arguments in favor of crime watch whereas others heard equally weak arguments against the effectiveness of crime watch. In all these variations of the persuasive message, the speaker was the same person with the same highly credible background.

The researchers found that under low fear conditions, strong persuasive arguments produced more attitude change than weak arguments, regardless of whether the programs were expected to be effective (Figure 6.2). In other words, if crime did not appear to be a crisis situation, students were not overly upset about the message or the possible outcome (effectiveness of the crime-watch program) and were simply persuaded by the strength of the arguments.

However, people who heard moderately fearful broadcasts focused on solutions to the crime problem. When there was a clear expectation that something could be done about crime on campus, weak and strong arguments were equally persuasive. If students were confident of a favorable outcome, they worried no further and did not thoroughly analyze the messages. But when the effectiveness of crime-fighting programs was in question, students did discriminate between strong and weak arguments. In other words, when there was no clear assurance that something effective could be done, fear motivated the participants to carefully examine the messages, so they tended to be persuaded by strong arguments. Again, concern for the outcome made them evaluate the messages carefully.

What we know from the Petty and Gleicher (1992) study is that fear initially motivates us to find some easily available, reassuring remedy. We will accept an answer uncritically if it promises us that everything will be okay. But if no such promise is there, then we have to start to think for ourselves. So, fear in combination with the lack of a clear and effective solution (a program to fight crime, in this case) leads us to analyze possible solutions carefully. Note that Petty and Gleicher were not dealing with really high fear. Ethical considerations prevent researchers from creating such a situation in the laboratory. It may be that very high fear shuts off all critical thinking for most of us.

What do we know, then, about the effectiveness of using fear to persuade? The first point is that if we do scare people, it is a good idea to give them some reassurance that they can protect themselves from the threat we have presented. The *protection–motivation* explanation of how fear appeals work argues that intimidation motivates us to think about ways to protect ourselves (Rogers, 1983). We are willing to make the effort to evaluate arguments carefully. But, in keeping with the cognitive miser strategy, if we don't need to analyze the arguments, we won't.

THE IMPORTANCE OF TIMING: PRIMACY VERSUS RECENCY

The effectiveness of any persuasive attempt hinges on the use of an effective strategy, including the timing of the message's delivery. When is it best to deliver your message? If you were given the option of presenting your message before or after your opponent in a debate, which should you choose? Generally, persuasive situations like these are governed by a law of primacy (Lawson, 1969). That is, the message presented first has more impact than the message presented second. However, the law of primacy does not always hold true. It depends on the structure of the situation. A primacy effect occurs when the two messages follow one another closely, and there is a delay between the second message and the audience response or assessment. In this situation, the first message has the greater impact. But when there is a delay between the two messages, and a response or assessment is made soon after the second message, we see a *recency effect*—the second message has a greater impact (Figure 6.3).

The primacy and recency effects apply most clearly under certain conditions—when both sides have equally strong arguments and when listeners are reasonably motivated to understand them. If one side has a much stronger argument than the other side, listeners are likely to be persuaded by the strong argument regardless of whether it is presented first or last (Haugtvedt & Wegener, 1993). When listeners are very motivated, very interested in the issue, they are more likely to be influenced by the first argument (the primacy effect) than by those they hear later on (Haugtvedt & Wegener, 1993).

FITTING THE MESSAGE TO THE AUDIENCE The Yale group also was interested in the construction and presentation of persuasive messages. One of their findings was that messages have to be presented differently to different audiences. For example, an educated or highly involved audience requires a different type of persuasive message than an uneducated or uninvolved audience. Rational arguments are effective with educated or analytical audiences (Cacioppo, Petty, & Morris, 1983). Emotional appeals work better with less educated or less analytical groups.

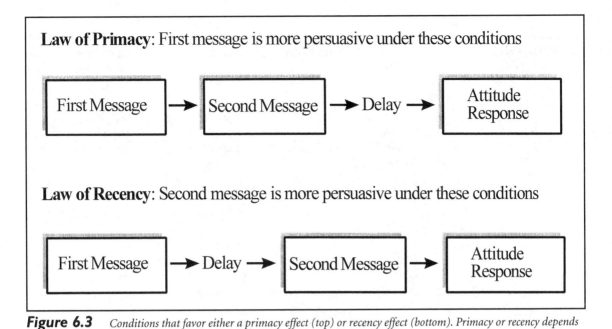

Law of Primacy: First message is more persuasive under these conditions

First Message → Second Message → Delay → Attitude Response

Law of Recency: Second message is more persuasive under these conditions

First Message → Delay → Second Message → Attitude Response

Figure 6.3   *Conditions that favor either a primacy effect (top) or recency effect (bottom). Primacy or recency depends on when a delay is introduced.*

ONE-SIDED VERSUS TWO-SIDED MESSAGES   The nature of the audience also influences how a message is structured. For less educated, uninformed audiences, a *one-sided message* works best. In a one-sided message you present only your side of the issue and draw conclusions for the audience. For a well-educated, well-informed audience, a *two-sided message* works best. The more educated audience probably is already aware of the other side of the argument. If you attempt to persuade them with a one-sided argument, they may question your motives. Also, well-educated audience members can draw their own conclusions. They probably would resent your drawing conclusions for them. Thus, a more educated audience will be more persuaded by a two-sided argument (Hovland, Janis, & Kelley, 1953).

One-sided and two-sided appeals also have different effects depending on the initial attitudes of the audience. Generally, a one-sided message is effective when the audience already agrees with your position. If the audience is against your position, a two-sided message works best. You need to consider both the initial position of audience members and their education level when deciding on an approach. A two-sided appeal is best when your audience is educated, regardless of their initial position. A one-sided appeal works best on an uneducated audience that already agrees with you.

INOCULATING THE AUDIENCE   When presenting a two-sided message, you don't want to accidentally persuade the audience of the other side. Therefore, the best approach is to present that side in a weakened form to "inoculate" the audience against it (McGuire, 1985). When you present a weakened message, listeners will devise their own counterarguments: "Well,

inoculation theory
The theory that if a communicator exposes an audience to a weakened version of an opposing argument, the audience will devise counterarguments to that weakened version and avoid persuasion by stronger arguments later.

that's obviously not true! Any fool can see through that argument! Who do they think they're kidding?" The listeners convince themselves that the argument is wrong. **Inoculation theory** is based on the medical model of inoculation. People are given a weakened version of a bacterium or a virus so that they can develop the antibodies to fight the disease on their own. Similarly, in attempting to persuade people of your side, you give them a weakened version of the opposing argument and let them develop their own defenses against it.

In a study of the inoculation effect, McGuire and Papageorgis (1961) exposed participants to an attack on their belief that brushing their teeth prevented tooth decay. Obviously, everybody believes that brushing your teeth is beneficial. This is a cultural truism, something we all accept without thinking or questioning. Therefore, we may not have any defenses in place if someone challenges those truisms.

Participants in one group heard an attack on the tooth-brushing truism. A second group received a supportive defense that reinforced the concept that brushing your teeth is good for you. A third group was inoculated, first hearing a mild attack on the truism and then hearing a defense of tooth brushing. A fourth group, the control group, received no messages. Of the three groups who heard a message, the "inoculated" group was most likely to believe tooth brushing was beneficial (Figure 6.4). In fact, people in the inoculated group, who were given a mild rebuttal of the truism, were *more likely* to believe in the benefits of tooth brushing than were the people who heard only a supportive defense of the truism.

This study highlights the fact that the inoculation defense is the best protection against an attack. It motivates people to generate their own counterarguments and makes them more likely to believe the persuader's side of the issue. In this case, forewarned is truly forearmed.

Figure 6.4

The inoculation effect. A persuasive attack on a truism caused a decrease in the belief of the validity of the truism unless participants were first "inoculated" with a weakened form of the persuasive message before receiving the attack message.

Based on data from McGuire and Papageorgis (1961).

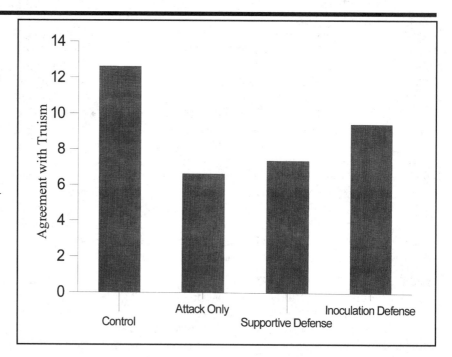

THE ROLE OF DISCREPANCY   Another aspect of the audience a persuader has to consider is their preexisting attitudes in relation to the message he or she wants to convey. For instance, imagine you are going to deliver a prochoice message to a room full of people with strong attitudes against abortion. Obviously, your message will be very different from the preexisting attitudes of your audience. This is a *high-discrepancy* situation. On the other hand, if you are trying to convince a room full of prochoice individuals, your message will not be very different from preexisting attitudes. This is an example of *low discrepancy*. In either of these cases, you would not expect much persuasion. In the first case, your message is too discrepant from the one your audience already holds; they will reject your message without giving it much thought. In the second case, you are basically saying what your audience already believes, so there won't be much persuasive effect or attitude change. Generally, a moderate amount of discrepancy produces the greatest amount of change.

Discrepancy interacts with the characteristics of the communicator. A highly credible communicator can induce change even when a highly discrepant message, one we ordinarily would reject or that contradicts a stereotype, is delivered. In one study, researchers found that Scottish participants had definite stereotypes of male hairdressers and of "skinheads" (Macrae, Shepherd, & Milne, 1992). Male hairdressers were perceived as meek, and skinheads were perceived as aggressive. However, a report from a psychiatrist that stated the contrary—that a particular hairdresser was aggressive or a skinhead was meek—altered the participants' opinions of those two groups. Of course, a credible communicator cannot say just anything and expect people to believe it. An effective communicator must be aware of the audience's likely perception of the message. Clarence Darrow carefully staked out a position he knew the judge would not reject. He didn't argue that the death penalty should be abolished, because he knew that the judge would not accept that position. Rather, he argued that the penalty was not appropriate in this specific case because of the defendants' ages and their mental state:

> And, I submit, Your Honor, that by every law of humanity, by every law of justice. . . . Your Honor should say that because of the condition of these boys' minds, it would be monstrous to visit upon them the vengeance that is asked by the State. (Weinberg, 1957, p. 163)

In other words, even highly credible communicators have to keep in mind how discrepant their message is from the audience's views. For communicators with lower credibility, a moderate amount of discrepancy works best.

Social Judgment Theory

How does discrepancy work? Muzafer Sherif suggested that the audience makes social judgments about the difference between the communicator's position and their own attitude on an issue (Sherif & Hovland, 1961; Sherif, Sherif, & Nebergall, 1965). This **social judgment theory** argues that the degree of personal involvement in an issue determines how the target will evaluate an attempt at persuasion.

Sherif suggested that an individual's perception of a message falls into one of three judgment categories, or latitudes. The **latitude of acceptance**

social judgment theory
An attitude theory suggesting that the degree of personal involvement with an issue determines how a target of persuasion will judge an attempt at persuasion.

latitude of acceptance
In social judgment theory, the region of an attitude into which messages that one will accept fall.

Figure 6.5

The effect of involvement with an issue on the size of the latitudes of rejection and acceptance in social judgment theory. Higher involvement leads to an increased latitude of rejection and a related decreased latitude of acceptance.

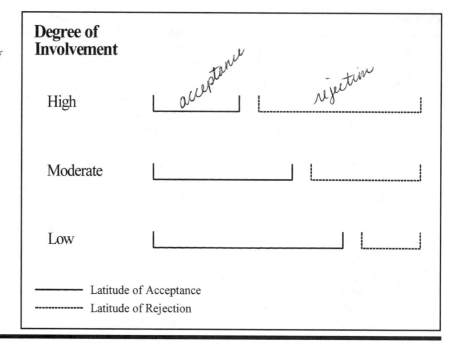

Degree of Involvement

High

Moderate

Low

————— Latitude of Acceptance

------------ Latitude of Rejection

---

latitude of rejection

In social judgment theory, the region of an attitude into which messages that one will reject fall.

latitude of noncommitment

In social judgment theory, the region of an attitude into which messages that one will neither accept nor reject fall.

is the set of positions the audience would find acceptable. The **latitude of rejection** is the set of arguments the individual would not accept. The **latitude of noncommitment** is a neutral zone falling between the other two and including positions the person does not accept or reject but will consider.

The breadth of the latitudes is affected by how strongly the person feels about the issue, how ego-involved he or she is. As Figure 6.5 shows, as involvement increases, the latitudes of acceptance and noncommitment narrow, but the latitude of rejection increases (Eagly & Telaak, 1972). In other words, the more important an issue is, the less likely you are to accept a persuasive message unless it is similar to your position. Only messages that fall within your latitude of acceptance, or perhaps within your latitude of noncommitment, will have a chance of persuading you. As importance of an issue increases, the number of acceptable arguments decreases. Sherif measured the attitudes of Republicans and Democrats in a presidential election and found that very committed Republicans and very committed Democrats rejected almost all the other side's arguments (Sherif, Sherif, & Nebergall, 1965). However, voters who were less extreme in their commitment were open to persuasion. Moderates of both parties usually accepted as many arguments from the opposition as they rejected. Therefore, as Darrow knew, a persuasive message must fall at least within the audience's latitude of noncommitment to be accepted.

The Problem of Multiple Audiences

In many circumstances, a communicator must persuade multiple audiences with diverse attitudes, education levels, levels of involvement, latitudes of acceptance, and so forth. Clarence Darrow's primary audience was the judge, but he also had to keep the public in mind. Similarly, a prisoner of war forced to make statements contrary to his beliefs has to convince his captors he is sincere but let his comrades know he is lying. And politicians often wish to appeal to one group without offending another. The same message must mean different things to different audiences. This is the **multiple audience problem**—how to send different meanings in the same message to diverse audiences (Fleming, Darley, Hilton, & Kojetin, 1990).

How do people manage these difficult situations? Researchers interested in this question had communicators send messages to audiences composed of friends and strangers (Fleming et al., 1990). The communicators were motivated to send a message that would convey the truth to their friends but deceive the stranger. Participants in this experiment were quite accurate at figuring out when their friends were lying. Strangers were not so accurate. Recall the fundamental attribution error and the correspondence bias from chapter 3: We tend to believe that people mean what they say. In general, we are not very good at detecting lies (Ekman, 1985).

Friends also were able to pick up on the communicator's hidden message, because they shared some common knowledge. For example, one communicator said she was going to go to Wales, a country her friends knew she loved, and was going to do her shopping for the trip in a department store her friends knew she hated. The message was clear to those in the know: She is lying. The department store reference was a private code or key that close friends understood. This is the way communicators can convey different meanings in the same message. They use special, private keys that only one audience understands. We often see private keys used in political ads, especially those ads aimed at evoking stereotypes and emotional responses. Consider the 1991 gubernatorial race in Mississippi. Incumbent Governor Ray Mabus, a Democrat campaigning on a plan to improve the state's education system, was in a tight race with Republican Kirk Fordice, a businessman. Fordice's campaign emphasized the bad economic times. It also became clear that Fordice was aiming exclusively at the white vote. His campaign ran several ads against welfare, including one that showed a photo of an African-American woman holding a baby. It also showed a middle-class African-American woman pushing a shopping cart (Jamieson, 1992). The presence of two African Americans, one "good" (middle class) and one "not so good" (lower class) protected Fordice from a direct attack that the ad was racist. However, the ad's intended audience (whites) knew the private keys: "Blacks are the welfare problem in Mississippi, and Fordice will take care of it. Fordice won the race by getting almost none of the African-American vote but a large majority of the white vote.

THE COGNITIVE APPROACH TO PERSUASION

You may have noted that in the Yale model of persuasion the audience seems to be nothing more than a target for messages. People just sit there and take it, either accepting the message or not. Cognitive response approaches, on the other hand, emphasize the active participation of the audience (Greenwald, 1968). The cognitive approach looks at *why* people react to a message the way they do, why they say that a message is interesting or that a communicator is biased.

Cognitively oriented social psychologists emphasize that a persuasive communication may trigger a number of related experiences, memories, feelings, and thoughts that individuals use to process the message. Therefore, both what a person thinks about when she hears the persuasive message and how the person applies those thoughts, feelings, and memories to analyzing the message are critical. We now turn to the individual's cognitive response to the persuasive message.

The Elaboration Likelihood Model

elaboration likelihood model (ELM)

A cognitive model of persuasion suggesting that a target's attention, involvement, distraction, motivation, self-esteem, education, and intelligence all influence central and/or peripheral reception to a persuasive attempt.

One well-known cognitive response model is the **elaboration likelihood model (ELM)**. This model, first proposed by Richard Petty and John Cacioppo (1986), makes clear that audiences are not just passive receptacles but are actively involved in the persuasion process. Their attention, involvement, distraction, motivation, self-esteem, education, and intelligence determine the success of persuasive appeals. The elaboration likelihood model owes a lot to the Yale model, incorporating much of the Yale research on the important roles of communicator and message. But its primary emphasis is on the role of the audience, especially their emotions and motivations. According to ELM, two routes to persuasion exist: a central processing route and a peripheral processing route. Persuasion may be achieved via either of these routes.

central route processing

In the ELM, information may be processed by effortful, controlled mechanisms involving attention to and understanding and careful processing of the content of a persuasive message.

CENTRAL ROUTE PROCESSING Central route processing involves elaboration of the message by the listener. This type of processing usually occurs when the person finds the message personally relevant and has preexisting ideas and beliefs about the topic. The individual uses these ideas and beliefs to create a context for the message, expanding and elaborating on the new information. Because the message is relevant, the person is motivated to listen to it carefully and process it in an effortful manner (Figure 6.6).

A juror listening to evidence that she understands and finds interesting, for example, will generate a number of ideas and responses. As she assimilates the message, she will compare it to what she already knows and believes. In the Leopold and Loeb trial, Judge Caverly may have elaborated on Darrow's argument for life imprisonment by recalling that in the Chicago courts, no one had been sentenced to death after voluntarily entering a guilty plea, and no one as young as the defendants had ever been hanged.

Elaboration of a message does not always lead to acceptance, however. If the message does not make sense or does not fit the person's knowledge and beliefs, elaboration may lead to rejection. For example, Judge Caverly might have focused on the brutal and indifferent attitude that Leopold and Loeb displayed toward Bobby Franks. If Darrow had not put together a coherent argument that fit the evidence, the judge probably would have rejected his argument. But the story Darrow told was coherent. By emphasizing the "diseased minds" of his clients, enhanced by the suggestion that they probably were born "twisted," he explained the unexplainable: why they killed Bobby Franks. At the same time, he made Leopold and Loeb seem less responsible. Thus, Darrow presented the judge with credible explanations on which he could expand to reach a verdict.

Central route processors elaborate on the message by filling in the gaps with their own knowledge and beliefs. Messages processed this way are more

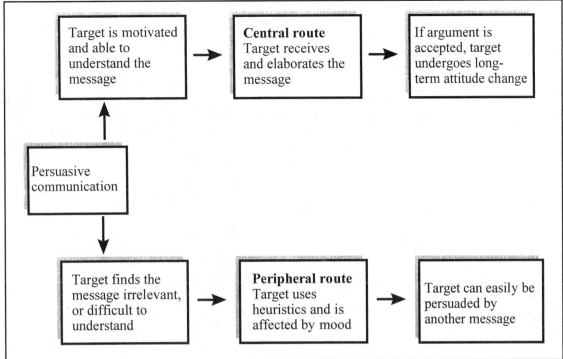

Figure 6.6 *The two routes to persuasion proposed in the elaboration likelihood model. Whether a person carefully processes a message (central route) depends on the person's motivation and ability to understand the message. If the person is motivated and can understand the message then central route processing is likely. If not, peripheral route processing is likely.*

From Petty and Cacioppo (1986). Reprinted with permission.

firmly tied to other attitudes and are, therefore, more resistant to change. Attitude change that results from central route processing is stable, long-lasting, and difficult to reverse.

PERIPHERAL ROUTE PROCESSING What if the listener is not motivated, is not able to understand the message, or simply does not like to deal with new or complex information? In these incidences, the listener takes another route to persuasion, a peripheral route. In **peripheral route processing**, listeners rely on something other than the message to make their decisions; they are persuaded by cues peripheral or marginal to the message. A juror may be favorably influenced by the appearance of the defendant, for example. Or perhaps he or she remembers when his or her uncle was in a similar predicament and thinks, "He wasn't guilty either."

Emotional cues are very effective in persuading peripheral route processors (Petty & Cacioppo, 1986). Recall the experiment on the effects of fear appeals in campus crime newscasts: A strong emotional appeal offering a reassuring solution was accepted regardless of whether the argument itself was strong or weak. Participants were not processing centrally; they paid no attention to the quality of the argument. They simply wanted reassurance, and the existence of a possible solution acted as a peripheral cue, convincing them that the argument must be valid. High or moderate fear makes us accept whatever reassuring solution is presented to us.

peripheral route processing
In the ELM, information may be processed using cues peripheral or marginal to the content message.

Familiar phrases or cliches included in persuasive messages can serve as peripheral cues to persuasion (Howard, 1997). Daniel Howard compared familiar (don't put all of your eggs in one basket) and literal (don't risk everything on a single venture) phrases for their ability to persuade via the peripheral route. Howard found that familiar phrases produced more persuasion under conditions of low attitude involvement (peripheral route) than under high involvement (central route). The familiar phrases were also more effective than the literal phrases when the individual is distracted from the message and when the target of the persuasive communication is low in the need for cognition.

Peripheral route processing often leads to attitude change, but because the listener has not elaborated on the message, the change is not very stable and is vulnerable to counterpressures (Kassin, Reddy, & Tulloch, 1990). A juror who processes centrally will be firm in his or her conclusions about the evidence, but a peripheral route juror will be an easy target for the next persuader in the courtroom (ForsterLee, Horowitz, & Bourgeois, 1993).

Although we have distinguished between the central and peripheral routes, message processing is not an either/or proposition. In fact, you may process some parts of a message centrally, others peripherally For example, a juror may be interested in and understand the scientific evidence presented at trial and process that information centrally. However, when an economist takes the stand, the juror may be bored or may think that people in bow ties are untrustworthy, and then process that testimony peripherally.

The Effect of Mood on Processing

Many speakers try to put their audience in a good mood before making their case. They tell a joke or an amusing story, or they say something designed to make listeners feel positive. Is this a good strategy? Does it make an argument more persuasive? It depends. When people are in a good mood, they tend to be distracted. Good moods bring out many related pleasant feelings and memories. Everything seems rosy. People in good moods cannot concentrate very well on messages; they cannot process information centrally. In one study on the influence of mood, people were put in either a good or a neutral mood and were given either an unlimited or very limited amount of time to listen to a message (Mackie & Worth, 1989). The strength of the persuasive messages also varied: One message contained strong arguments; the other, only weak arguments. The researchers reasoned that for the participants in good moods, strong and weak arguments would be equally effective. As shown in Figure 6.7, this was found to be the case, but only when there was a limited amount of time to study the messages. People in good moods did not distinguish between strong and weak arguments because they were not processing centrally.

Good feelings do not, however, always prevent central processing. If people in good moods are motivated to carefully evaluate and elaborate on a message, and if they have enough time, they will process centrally. A good mood will not have a direct effect on their attitudes, but it may make them think more positive thoughts about the message, if it is a strong one and they have time to consider it (Petty, Schumann, Richman, & Strathman, 1993). The good thoughts then lead to positive attitude change. For those using peripheral route processing, good moods don't lead to more positive thoughts

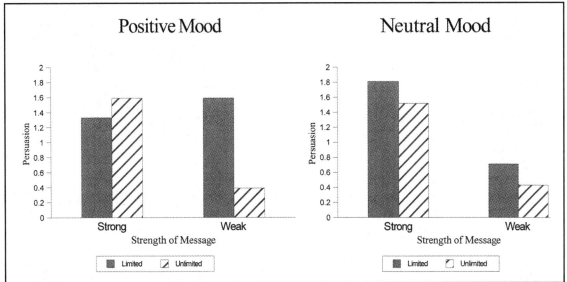

Figure 6.7 *The effect of mood and processing time on the impact of a persuasive message. When people are in a good mood and have limited time to process the message, there is no effect of argument strength. Given unlimited time, participants are more persuaded by the strong argument. In a neutral mood, participants are more persuaded by strong arguments than weak arguments, regardless of time limitation.*

Adapted from Mackie and Worth (1989).

and then to positive attitude change. These people aren't thinking about the message at all and are not elaborating on it. Instead, for them, good mood leads directly to attitude change. Figure 6.8 shows how good mood affects central and peripheral processors differently.

Thus, the relationship between potentially biasing factors in persuasion, such as mood or likeability of the communicator, is a complex one. Variables

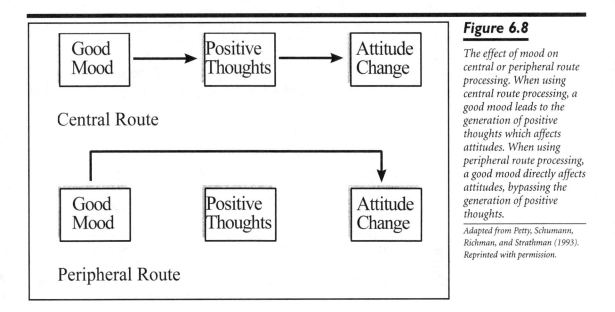

Figure 6.8

The effect of mood on central or peripheral route processing. When using central route processing, a good mood leads to the generation of positive thoughts which affects attitudes. When using peripheral route processing, a good mood directly affects attitudes, bypassing the generation of positive thoughts.

Adapted from Petty, Schumann, Richman, and Strathman (1993). Reprinted with permission.

that bias the persuasion process still operate when an individual is motivated to process a message centrally (Petty, Wegener, & White, 1998). Petty and Wegener (1993) proposed the **flexible correction model (FCM)** to help us understand how biasing variables influence the persuasion process. According to the FCM, individuals using central route processing (highly motivated) are influenced by biasing variables because they are not aware of the potential impact of the biasing variable (e.g., mood) during a persuasion situation (Petty, Wegener, & White, 1998). Furthermore, correction for biasing conditions, according to the FCM, should take place under the following conditions (p. 95):

When an individual is motivated to search for biasing variables.

When an individual finds sources of potential bias after a search.

When an individual generates ideas or theories about the nature of the bias.

When an individual is motivated and has the ability to make a correction for the biasing variable.

In two experiments, Petty, Wegener, and White (1998) tested the assumptions made by the FCM. In their first experiment, Petty and colleagues varied the likeability of the source of a message (likable and unlikable) along with whether participants received an instruction to correct for the likeability information. Petty and colleagues found that when no correction instruction was given, the likable source led to attitude change in the direction of the position advocated in a persuasive message (positive attitude change), whereas the unlikable source led to attitude change in the opposite direction (negative attitude change). This is the usual finding when such variables are manipulated. However, when participants were given an instruction to correct for the likeability of the source, the results were just the opposite. The unlikable source produced positive attitude change, whereas the likable source produced negative attitude change. Additionally, there was greater correction for the unlikable source than the likable source.

In their second experiment, Petty and colleagues added a third variable: whether participants used high- or low-elaboration strategies. When participants used low-elaboration and no correction instruction was given, the likable source yielded more persuasion than the unlikable source. However, when a correction instruction was given, the likable and unlikable sources were equally persuasive. The opposite occurred under high-elaboration strategies. Here, in the no-correction condition, the likable and unlikable sources produced the same levels of persuasion, whereas when the correction instruction was given, the unlikable source produced more attitude change than the likable source.

The results of both studies suggest that when individuals become aware of a biasing factor (likeability or mood), they will be motivated to correct for the biasing factor under high- or low-elaboration conditions. Thus, when individuals become aware of such biasing factors, they may not influence persuasion more when peripheral route processing is used. Additionally, such factors may not bias the processing of information relevant to the issue contained in a persuasive message when central route processing is used (Petty, Wegener, & White, 1998). It appears as though the mechanisms for correction for biasing factors operate independently from the mechanisms for processing the content of the message (Petty, Wegener, & White, 1998).

The Effect of Personal Relevance on Processing

Another factor affecting central versus peripheral route processing is personal relevance. If an issue is important to us and affects our well-being, we are more likely to pay attention to the quality of the message. In one study, college students were told that the university chancellor wanted to have all seniors pass a comprehensive examination before they could graduate (Petty, Cacioppo, & Goldman, 1981). Participants hearing the *high-relevance version* of this message were told the policy would go into effect the following year and, consequently, would affect them. Participants hearing the *low-relevance version* were informed that the policy wouldn't be implemented for several years and, therefore, would not affect them.

The researchers also varied the quality of the arguments and the expertise of the communicator. Half the participants heard persuasive arguments, and the other half heard weaker arguments. Half were told that the plan was based on a report by a local high school class (low communicator expertise), and the other half were told the source was the Carnegie Commission on Higher Education (high expertise).

Results indicated that relevance did influence the type of processing participants used (Figure 6.9). Students who thought the change would affect them were persuaded by the strong argument and not by the weak one. In other words, they carefully examined the arguments, using central processing. Students who thought the change wouldn't affect them simply relied on the expertise of the communicator. They were persuaded when they thought the plan was based on the Carnegie Commission report, regardless

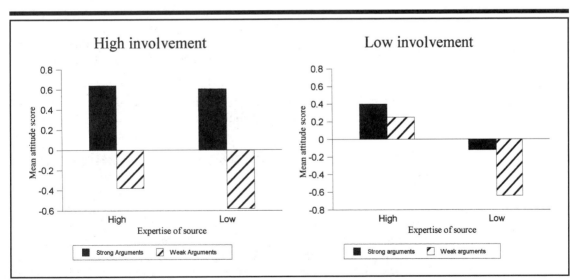

Figure 6.9   *The effects of audience involvement, expertise of source, and strength of arguments.*

From Cacioppo and Goldman (1981).

of whether the arguments were strong or weak. Low relevance, in other words, enhances the influence of communicator credibility and increases the likelihood that listeners will use peripheral processing.

Does high relevance mean that you always will be persuaded by strong and rational arguments? Not at all. An issue may be highly relevant to you because it involves an important personal value. In this case, even a very persuasive argument probably won't change your opinion. In the current abortion debate, for example, an extreme position on either side is based on fundamental values relating to privacy, coercion, and the nature of life. The issue is certainly relevant to individuals with extreme views, but they are unlikely to be persuaded to change their opinions by any argument.

If, however, an issue is highly relevant because of a particular outcome, rather than a value, then a strong, persuasive argument might work (Johnson & Eagly, 1989). If you are strongly opposed to taking a senior comprehensive exam, a persuasive message about outcome, such as the possibility that passing the exam would increase your chances of getting into graduate school, might well convince you to take it.

Personal relevance has been an issue for many people concerned about funding for AIDS research. Because this disease was originally associated with certain groups—gay men and injecting drug users—public officials were inclined to give it less attention and allocate less research money to it than to diseases that more commonly struck the majority of the population. Activists struggled with the issue of how to make people realize that AIDS is a problem for the entire society. One person, Mary Fisher, spoke persuasively about AIDS before the Republican National Convention in 1992. She attempted to establish a connection between people with AIDS and members of the audience by invoking their common humanity:

> Though I am white, and a mother, I am one with a black infant struggling with tubes in a Philadelphia hospital. Though I am female, and contracted this disease in marriage . . . I am one with the lonely gay man sheltering a flickering candle from the cold wind of his family's rejection. . . . We may take refuge in our stereotypes, but we cannot hide there long. Because HIV asks only one thing of those it attacks: Are you human? And this is the right question: Are you human? (cited in Osborne & Osborne, 1994, p. B20)

Those who hear this question—Are you human?—must admit that, in this sense at least, AIDS is personally relevant for them.

The Impact of Attitude Accessibility on Elaboration

In addition to the relevance of a persuasive message to an individual, processing of a persuasive message is also influenced by *attitude accessibility*. Attitude accessibility refers to the ease with which an attitude can be automatically activated when the correspondent attitude object is encountered (Fabrigar, Priester, Petty, & Wegener, 1998). Attitude accessibility is one dimension along which the strength of an attitude can be measured. Highly accessible attitudes tend to be stronger than less accessible attitudes. Fabrigar and colleagues reasoned that highly accessible attitudes may enhance message elaboration because attitude-relevant information is more readily available than with less accessible attitudes.

Fabrigar and colleagues (1998) conducted two experiments to investigate the role of attitude accessibility in persuasion. In the first experiment, attitude accessibility was measured, and participants' attitudes were classified as low, moderate, or high in accessibility. The researchers manipulated the quality of the arguments made within a persuasive message on nuclear power (high or low quality). The results of experiment 1 confirmed that individuals with high-accessibility attitudes were more likely to elaborate the persuasive message than those with low accessibility attitudes. Specifically, argument quality enhanced attitudes among moderately and highly accessible attitudes but not for low-accessibility attitudes. This effect was strongest for the individuals with highly accessible attitudes. Data from the second experiment confirmed the first.

The bottom line is that attitude accessibility mediates the amount of elaboration that an individual will display when exposed to a persuasive message. High accessibility (high attitude strength) is associated with increased examination of the content of the message (central route processing). When attitude accessibility is low (a weak attitude), an individual is less likely to scrutinize the content of the persuasive message carefully.

Do Vivid Messages Persuade Better Than Nonvivid Messages?

What about the effect of vividness on persuasion? Does it make a difference in our attitudes or behavior? Advertisers and other persuaders certainly believe that vivid messages, presented in eye- or ear-catching terms, are persuasive. Social psychologists interested in this issue stated, "Everybody knows that vividly presented information is impactful and persuasive" (Taylor & Thompson, 1982, p. 155). However, when these researchers surveyed the literature on vividness, they found very weak support for the persuasive power of vivid materials.

In one study of the *vividness effect*, people were given vivid and nonvivid versions of crime stories in the news (Collins, Taylor, Wood, & Thompson, 1988). The vivid versions used colorful language and provided bizarre details. People listened to a vivid or nonvivid story and then rated its quality in terms of emotion, imagery, interest, and so forth as well as its persuasiveness. In a second study, people also had to predict how others would respond to the stories.

The studies found no evidence of a vividness effect; vivid messages had about the same persuasive effect as nonvivid messages. However, people believed that vivid messages affected other people. What influenced the participants if vividness did not? Interest: If the message involved a topic that interested them, people felt the message was more effective. Remember the effects of personal relevance in the elaboration likelihood model of persuasion.

On the other hand, some messages, such as political ads, appear to benefit from vividness. Perhaps they work because they interest people and force them to pay more attention than they normally might. One study examined the effects of vivid language in a trial concerning a dispute between a contractor and a subcontractor on a building project (Wilson, Northcraft, & Neale, 1989). People playing the role of jurors watched different videotapes of the trial. One version had vivid phrasing; the other, nonvivid language (p. 135):

1. There was a *spiderweb* of cracks through the slab. (vivid)

   There was a *network* of cracks through the slab. (nonvivid)
2. The slab was *jagged* and had to be sanded. (vivid)

   The slab was *rough* and had to be sanded. (nonvivid)

The jurors tended to award the plaintiff more money when they heard vivid phrases. So, is there a vividness effect or not? Based on the evidence, it seems that vivid messages have an initial effect, especially if there is little else to compete with them. In the trial situation, vivid information had a strong impact when the jurors were presented with a lot of evidence that was not directly important for their decision, such as a history of the building project and pictures of the construction site. Then the jurors heard the vivid language ("a spiderweb of cracks through the slab"). Given the background of irrelevant information, they were influenced by the one or two vivid messages they heard.

How can we reconcile the seemingly conflicting results concerning the impact of vividness? One approach suggests that the impact of vividness depends on the number of cognitive resources that are devoted to processing a persuasive message (Meyers-Levy & Peracchio, 1995). According to Joan Meyers-Levy and Laura Peracchio, the impact of vivid information depends on the degree of correspondence between the resources a person has available to process a message and the resources required to adequately process information. Vivid language or illustrations, according to Myers-Levy and Peracchio, should have the greatest impact when a persuasive message requires relatively few resources, and a person is highly motivated to process the message. Conversely, for a highly motivated individual and a persuasive message that requires high levels of resources, vivid content should not have a strong impact. If an individual is not highly motivated to process a message, then vividness will serve as a peripheral cue and have a significant impact on persuasion.

Myers-Levy and Peracchio (1995) conducted two experiments to confirm these predicted relationships. In their first experiment, they found that for highly motivated individuals, a demanding persuasive message (an advertisement of a bicycle) was most effective when vividness was low (a black-and-white photo of the bicycle and model was used). For a less demanding message, a vivid message (a color advertisement) was more effective. In the second experiment, low-motivation and highly motivated individuals were included. They found that for low-motivation individuals, a vivid message was more effective than a less vivid message. For highly motivated individuals, the impact of vividness (color) depended on the level of resources needed to process the message (as described earlier). These results were supported by three experiments by Anand Keller Punam and Lauren Block (1997).

Thus, in a situation in which much information already has been made available (low demand), or when the audience is particularly interested in the issue, one vivid message may not have a significant impact. However, when people are not particularly interested, a vivid message may have significant impact. In other words, vividness is a peripheral cue. When individuals find the message interesting and personally relevant, they process centrally, and vividness has little effect. But when the cognitive miser is at work, a vivid message may have a definite influence on attitudes.

Need for Cognition: Some Like to Do It the Hard Way

Some people prefer central route processing no matter what the situation or how complex the evidence. These people have a high **need for cognition (NC)**. According to Cacioppo, Petty, and Morris (1983), high-NC people like to deal with difficult and effortful problems. On a scale assessing this cognitive characteristic, they agree with such statements as, "I really enjoy a task that invokes coming up with new solutions to problems," and they disagree with such statements as, "I only think as hard as I have to."

High-NC people are concerned with the validity of the messages they receive, which suggests that they rely mainly on central route processing (Cacioppo et al., 1983). High-NC individuals also organize information in a way that allows them to remember messages and use them later (Lassiter, Briggs, & Bowman, 1991). Those low in need for cognition tend to pay more attention to the physical characteristics of the speaker, indicating peripheral processing (Petty & Cacioppo, 1986).

Elaboration likelihood model research shows that people who have a need to process information centrally—high-NC people—accept and resist persuasive arguments in a different way than those low in need for cognition. Because they are processing centrally, they elaborate on the messages they hear. They are influenced by the qualities of the argument or the product advertised rather than by peripheral cues (Haugtvedt, Petty, & Cacioppo, 1992), and they tend to hold newly formed attitudes longer and be more resistant to counterpersuasion (Haugtvedt & Petty, 1992).

need for cognition (NC)
An individual difference dimension in persuasion concerning the degree to which individuals prefer effortful processing of information.

The Heuristic Model of Persuasion

A second cognitive model of persuasion is the **heuristic and systematic information-processing model (HSM)**. Proposed by Shelley Chaiken (1987), HSM has much in common with ELM. As in ELM, there are two routes for information processing: the systematic and the heuristic. Systematic processing in HSM is essentially the same as central processing in ELM, and heuristic processing is the same as peripheral processing. Heuristics, as you recall from chapter 3, are simple guides or shortcuts that people use to make decisions when something gets too complicated or when they are just too lazy to process systematically.

The main difference between the two theories lies in the claim of HSM that reliance on heuristics is more common than is usually thought (Chaiken, Liberman, & Eagly, 1989). If motivation and ability to comprehend are not high, individuals rely on heuristics most of the time. Some of these heuristics might be: "Experts can be trusted." "The majority must be right." "She's from the Midwest; she must be trustworthy." "If it was on the evening news, it must be true."

Heuristic processing can be compared to scanning newspaper headlines. The information you receive is minimal, and the truth or relevance of the headline will be determined by those simple rules. "Congress Cannot Agree on a Budget," reads the headline. Your response would be to quickly check the

heuristic and systematic information-processing model (HSM)
A cognitive model of persuasion suggesting that of the two routes to persuasion, systematic and heuristic, people choose to use heuristics or peripheral cues more often.

available heuristics that might explain the headline. Here it is: "Politicians are incompetent." Next headline, please. The HSM model suggests that people are more likely to agree with communicators who are expert and with messages with which most people agree. Again we see the cognitive miser at work.

COGNITIVE DISSONANCE THEORY: A MODEL OF SELF-PERSUASION

Direct persuasion by a communicator is not the only route to attitude or behavior change. Attitude change may also occur if we find our existing attitudes in conflict with new information, or if our behavior is inconsistent with our beliefs. Leon Festinger observed that people try to appear consistent. When we act counter to what we believe or think, we must justify the inconsistency. In other words, if we say one thing and do something else, we need a good reason. Usually, we persuade ourselves that we have a good reason, even if it means changing our previous attitudes. Inconsistency is thus one of the principal motivations for attitude change.

Cognitive Dissonance Theory

Festinger's cognitive dissonance theory proposed that if inconsistency exists among our attitudes, or between our attitudes and our behavior, we experience an unpleasant state of arousal called *cognitive dissonance* (Festinger, 1957). The arousal of dissonance motivates us to change something, our attitudes or our behavior, to reduce or eliminate the unpleasant arousal. Reducing the tension helps us achieve *consonance*, a state of psychological balance.

Cognitive dissonance theory is like *homeostatic theory* in biology. Consider what happens when you are hungry: Your brain detects an imbalance in your blood sugar levels, causing a physiological state of hunger. You are motivated to reduce this unpleasant state of arousal by finding and consuming food. Similarly, when cognitive consonance is disrupted, you feel tension and are motivated to reduce it.

The five key assumptions of **cognitive dissonance theory** can be summarized as follows:

cognitive dissonance theory
A theory of attitude change proposing that if inconsistency exists among our attitudes, or between our attitudes and our behavior, we experience an unpleasant state of arousal called cognitive dissonance, which we will be motivated to reduce or eliminate.

1. Attitudes and behavior can stand in a consonant (consistent) or a dissonant (inconsistent) relationship with one another.
2. Inconsistency between attitudes and behavior gives rise to a negative motivational state known as cognitive dissonance.
3. Because cognitive dissonance is an uncomfortable state, people are motivated to reduce the dissonance.
4. The greater the amount of dissonance, the stronger the motivation to reduce it.
5. Dissonance may be reduced by rationalizing away the inconsistency or by changing an attitude or a behavior.

HOW DOES COGNITIVE DISSONANCE LEAD TO ATTITUDE CHANGE? Exactly how does cognitive dissonance change attitudes? To find out, imagine that you have volunteered to be a participant in a social psychological experiment. You are instructed to sit in front of a tray of objects and repeatedly empty and refill the tray for the next hour. Then, to add more excitement to your day, you are asked to turn pegs in holes a little at a time. When your tasks are over, you are asked to tell the next participant how interesting and delightful they were. For doing this, you are paid the grand sum of $1. Unbeknown to you, other participants go through the same experience and also are asked to tell an incoming participant how interesting the tasks are, but each is paid $20.

When this classic experiment was done in 1959, almost all the participants agreed to misrepresent how much fun the experiment was (Festinger & Carlsmith, 1959). Several weeks later, the participants were contacted by a third party and asked whether they had enjoyed the study. Their responses turned out to depend on how much money they had been paid. You might predict that the participants who got $20 said that they enjoyed their experience more than those who got only $1. Well, that's not what happened. Participants paid $20 said the tasks were boring, and those paid $1 said they had enjoyed the tasks. A third group, the control participants, were given no reward and were not told that anyone else had received one. Like the $20 group, they said the tasks were boring.

Cognitive dissonance theory argues that change occurs when people experience dissonance. Where is the dissonance in this experiment? Being paid $1, a trifling sum even in 1959, was surely insufficient justification for lying. If a $1 participant analyzed the situation logically, it would look like this: "I lied to someone because the experimenter asked me to, and I got paid only a buck." Conclusion: "Either I am a liar or I am stupid." Neither conclusion fits with what we generally think of ourselves. The dissonance is between what we want to think of ourselves and how we have behaved. So, how does the participant resolve the dissonance? The behavior can't be undone, so the participant engages in self-persuasion: "I'm not a liar or stupid, so I must have meant what I said. I enjoyed the experiment. The $20-participant has an easily available, if not very flattering, justification for the lie: "I needed the money."

THE REVERSE INCENTIVE EFFECT   The implications of this study and many more that have replicated the effect over the years are intriguing. One concept that came from the original study is the *reverse-incentive effect*: When people are given a large payment for doing something, they infer that the activity must be difficult or tedious or risky (Freedman, Cunningham, & Krismer, 1992). Thus, professional athletes who once played the game just for fun may now moan about playing the game for $5 million a year. People seem to get suspicious when they are paid large sums for doing something they enjoyed doing in the first place. They feel a little apprehensive and develop a less positive view of the activity (Crano & Sivacek, 1984).

Dissonance theory argues, then, that the less the reward or the less the threatened punishment used to make people behave counter to their attitudes, the more people have to provide their own justifications for their behavior. The more they have to persuade themselves of the rightness of the behavior, the more their attitude is likely to change.

THE IMPORTANCE OF FREE CHOICE   We have seen that an important condition in the arousal of dissonance is whether behavior is freely chosen or coerced. In another study of cognitive dissonance, participants were asked to write an essay arguing a position that ran counter to their real beliefs (Elkin & Leippe, 1986). Furthermore, they did this attitude-inconsistent act when they felt they had freely chosen it. Dissonance theorists call this situation *induced compliance*. The researchers found that when participants wrote an essay counter to their beliefs, they showed greater physiological arousal than if they had written an essay consistent with their beliefs. This finding is compatible with predictions from cognitive dissonance theory, specifically that dissonance increases feelings of tension (physiological arousal).

This study reinforced the finding that people do not experience dissonance if they do not choose the inconsistent behavior (Brehm & Cohen, 1962). If they are forced to do something, the coercion is a sufficient external justification for the attitude-discrepant actions. If they don't have to justify their behavior to themselves, there is no self-persuasion. This suggests that attribution processes may play a role in mediating dissonance arousal and reduction. We explore this possibility later in this chapter.

POSTDECISION DISSONANCE   Free choice relates to dissonance in another way when you have to choose between two mutually exclusive, equally attractive alternatives (e.g., between two cars or two jobs). After a choice is made, dissonance is experienced. Here is how it works: Let's say you have enough money to buy a car. There are two cars you are considering that are equally attractive to you. For each car, there is a set of positive cognitions. Once you have made your choice (let's say you picked car 1), all the cognitions associated with your chosen alternative are consistent with your choice. However, all the positive cognitions associated with the unchosen alternative are now inconsistent with your choice. Dissonance theory predicts that you will take steps to reduce the dissonance associated with the unchosen alternative. One way to reduce dissonance would be to change your decision (that is, choose car 2). Of course, this won't work, because now all of the cognitions associated with car 1 are inconsistent with your new decision, and the dissonance remains. More likely, you will begin to think of negative things about the unchosen car to reduce dissonance. For example, you may reason that the insurance costs would be higher, the color isn't exactly what you wanted, and the warranty is not as good. At the same time, you may also think of more positive things about the chosen car. For example, you may point out how comfortable the seats are, how good the stereo sounds, and how the color fits you perfectly.

postdecision dissonance

Cognitive dissonance that is aroused after you have chosen between two equally attractive, mutually exclusive alternatives.

The arousal of **postdecision dissonance** and its subsequent reduction was demonstrated in a classic experiment by Brehm (1956). In this experiment, female participants first rated the desirability of several household products (e.g., a toaster). Brehm then offered the women one of the two products they had rated very closely or they had rated very differently. After the women made their choices, they again rated the products. Brehm found that when the two choice alternatives were close in desirability (a difficult decision), ratings of the chosen alternative became more positive, compared to the original ratings. At the same time, the ratings of the unchosen product became more negative. This effect was less pronounced when the choice was between two products that varied more widely in desirability (easy decision).

Generally, the greater the separation between alternatives the less dissonance will be produced after a decision. After all, a choice between a highly desirable product and an undesirable product is an easy one. On the other hand, the closer the alternatives are to one another (assuming they are not identical), the more difficult the decision and the more postdecision dissonance will be aroused. Thus, the greatest postdecision dissonance will be realized when you have to choose between two mutually exclusive (you can only have one), equally attractive, but different alternatives.

How do we explain these free-choice dissonance situations? Shultz and Lepper (1999) suggested that an analogy can be made between dissonance phenomena and the operation of artificial intelligence neural networks. Networks of cognitions underlie states of consonance and dissonance and are activated by a set of constraints imposed by a problem. For example, in a choice between two cars, you may be constrained by finances, model preference, and color desirability. According to Shultz and Lepper, the decision we make attempts to satisfy as many of the constraints as possible. In short, "the motivation to increase cognitive consonance, and thus to reduce dissonance, results from the various constraints on the beliefs and attitudes that a person holds at a given point in time" (p. 238). Consonance results when similar cognitions are activated and inconsistent cognitions are inhibited. Thus, in the free-choice situation, linkages among positive cognitions associated with an alternative produce consonance. However, for the unchosen alternative, the linkages between inconsistent elements (the unchosen alternative and the positive cognitions associated with it) produce dissonance.

Shultz and Lepper (1996) performed computer simulations of Brehm's (1956) original experiment and produced results that matched quite well with Brehm's results. That is, ratings of the unchosen alternative became more negative, and ratings of the chosen alternative became only slightly more positive. However, Shultz and Lepper pointed out that in Brehm's experiment, participants always made a decision that was both difficult (two products that were rated very similarly) and between two highly desirable products. Schultz and Lepper found that when participants had to choose between two similarly rated but undesirable products, the ratings of the chosen product became much more positive, but the ratings of the unchosen product became only slightly more negative.

An experiment by Thomas Shultz, Elene Leveille, and Mark Lepper (1999) sought to test the results from computer simulations of free-choice experiments against actual behavior of individuals. Participants in this experiment were given the choice between two posters after indicating on a rating scale how much they liked each poster. The choice parameters varied in difficulty. An easy choice was one between two posters, one with a high initial rating, and one with a low initial rating. In the "high-difficult" condition, a choice was to be made between two posters that had been rated very positively by participants. Finally, in the "low-difficult" condition, participants had to choose between two posters that had been poorly rated. Following the choice procedure, participants again rated the posters. The results paralleled the computer simulations. In the high-difficult condition, ratings of the unchosen alternative became substantially more negative, whereas ratings of the chosen alternative became only slightly more positive. In the low-difficult condition, the opposite was true; ratings of the chosen alternative became much more positive. However, ratings of the unchosen alternative became only slightly more negative. These results are consistent with Shultz and Lepper's (1996) *consonance constraint satisfaction model*.

**RESPONSIBILITY: ANOTHER VIEW OF CONGITIVE DISSO-
NANCE** Another view suggests that cognitive dissonance occurs only
when our actions produce negative consequences (Cooper & Scher, 1992).
According to this view, it is not the inconsistency that causes dissonance so
much as our feelings of personal responsibility when bad things happen
(Cooper & Fazio, 1984).

Let's say, for example, that you wrote a very good essay in favor of something you believed in, such as not raising tuition at your school. You knew
that the essay could be presented to the school's board of trustees, the body
that determines tuition rates. You then learned that your essay was actually
used to convince the board to raise tuition. Or perhaps you were asked to
write an essay taking a position you did not believe in—raising tuition. You
then learned that the essay convinced the board to raise tuition. How would
you feel?

According to this responsibility view, simply doing something counter
to your beliefs will not produce dissonance unless there are negative results. If you are opposed to tuition hikes and write an essay in favor of
them, but there are no hikes as a result, you do not experience dissonance.
In several similar studies, people were asked to write essays advocating a
position—raising tuition—that conflicted with their beliefs. When rates
were increased and essayists felt responsible for the outcome, they resolved
the dissonance by changing their attitude in the direction of the outcome.
That is, they began to say they were now more in favor of a fee increase
than before they wrote the essay. When students wrote essays in favor of a
fee increase, and fees were not increased, they did not experience dissonance and did not change their attitudes. When there is no tension, there is
no attitude change.

So, what creates dissonance, inconsistency or a sense of responsibility?
There have been hundreds, perhaps thousands, of experiments that support
the basic ideas of cognitive dissonance theory, namely, that inconsistency
leads to attitude change. That there are valid alternatives simply means the
theory may have to incorporate those ideas and continue to be revised.

ATTRIBUTION PROCESSES AND DISSONANCE We noted
earlier that dissonance is unlikely to be aroused when a person has a sufficient external justification (attribution) for their attitude-discrepant behavior. An experiment by Joel Cooper (1998) highlighted the role of attribution
processes in mediating dissonance reactions. Cooper had participants write a
counterattitudinal essay advocating the institution of 7:00 A.M. classes on
campus (something students opposed). They wrote the essays under
either a high-choice (participants were asked to write the essay "if you are
willing") or a low-choice condition (the "if you are willing" phrase was left
out). Participants were also randomly assigned to a misattribution condition
(an instruction that inconsistent lighting makes many feel tense and aroused)
or a no misattribution condition (the instruction about the lighting effects
was deleted). The main measure was the participants' ratings (positive or
negative) about instituting 7:00 A.M. classes.

Cooper found that greater attitude change occurred under the high-
choice condition. This confirms our earlier statement that under conditions
of free choice, dissonance is more likely to be aroused and attitude change
more likely to occur. Additionally, there was less attitude change in the
direction of the essay under the misattribution condition than the no

misattribution condition. Participants in the misattribution condition had an external explanation for their arousal (dissonance), and were consequently less likely to change their attitude. The greatest amount of attitude change in the direction of the essay was realized in the high-choice (participants chose to write the essay)—no misattribution condition. In a follow-up experiment using a different task, Cooper found that participants who had previously misattributed their arousal to the lighting did not show dissonance-consistent attitude change.

Attribution style also relates to the arousal of dissonance. Daniel Stalder and Robert Baron (1998) investigated the relationship between *attributional complexity (AC)* and dissonance-produced attitude change in a series of experiments. Specifically, attributional complexity refers to how complex a person's attributions are for explaining behavior and events. High-AC individuals are those who normally engage in thorough attributional searches for information. Thus, a high-AC person will search long and hard for the source of arousal in a given situation (e.g., a situation that arouses dissonance). A low-AC person is less likely to engage in such a search.

The results from their first experiment confirmed the idea that high-AC individuals show little dissonance-related attitude change, most likely because they are able to generate a wide variety of possible causes for the arousal associated with dissonance (Stalder & Baron, 1998). Having attributed the arousal to something other than the dissonance-arousing situation, the high-AC individual would not be expected to show much attitude change. In their second experiment, Stalder and Baron found that low-AC individuals showed the typical dissonance-related attitude change after dissonance arousal.

The two experiments just discussed suggest strongly that dissonance-related attitude change is mediated by the attributions made about the dissonance situation. If an alternative to dissonance is provided for an explanation for dissonance-related arousal, the typical dissonance result does not occur. Stalder and Baron's study shows us that there are individual differences in attributional style, which correlates with dissonance-related attitude change. Those individuals who are highly motivated to find causes for their arousal are less likely to show dissonance-related attitude change because they settle on an alternative attribution for their arousal, more so than a person who is not so motivated.

LESSONS OF COGNITIVE DISSONANCE THEORY What can we learn about persuasive techniques from cognitive dissonance theory? The first lesson is that cognitive inconsistency often leads to chance. Therefore, one persuasive technique is to point out to people how their behavior runs counter to their beliefs. Presumably, if people are aware of their inconsistencies, they will change. Persuasion may also occur if individuals are made aware that their behavior may produce a negative outcome (Cooper & Scher, 1992).

A second lesson is that any time you can induce someone to become publicly committed to a behavior that is counter to their beliefs, attitude change is a likely outcome. One reason for the change is that people use their public behavior as a kind of heuristic, a rule that says people stand by their public acts and bear personal responsibility for them (Baumeister & Tice, 1984; Zimbardo & Leippe, 1992). In other words, the rule is, "If I did it, I meant it."

COGNITIVE DISSONANCE AND CULT MEMBERSHIP Cognitive dissonance plays an important role in the formation and maintenance of cults. Once people make a public commitment to a leader and a movement, it is hard for them to acknowledge their misgivings. Instead, they have to throw more and more resources into maintaining their commitment, even when it becomes obvious to others that the loyalty is misplaced. This phenomenon has occurred many times in human history. It happened in 1978 in Guyana, in Jonestown, the "utopian" community of the Reverend Jim Jones. On his orders, his followers committed mass suicide by drinking Kool Aid laced with cyanide. It happened again more recently in Waco, Texas.

In March, 1993, a religious cult known as the Branch Davidians came to national attention at the beginning of its stand-off with the Bureau of Alcohol, Tobacco and Firearms (ATF). The cult was led by David Koresh, who claimed to receive orders from God. Koresh created the group's social reality. He separated cult members from the rest of the world, both physically and psychologically. He told them that he was Jesus and that "others" would deny the fact and try to destroy the cult. The Davidians stocked arms, food, and ammunition to prepare for apocalypse and confrontation with the outside world. Koresh's predictions seemed to come true when ATF agents came to seize the cult's automatic weapons. Guns blazed on both sides, leaving several agents dead and wounded.

A siege of the compound began that lasted nearly 2 months. Federal authorities grew increasingly concerned about the welfare of the many children inside and the lack of progress in the negotiations with Koresh. Finally, assured by experts that the Davidians would not commit mass suicide if threatened, agents pumped tear gas into the compound to force them outside. However, fires erupted inside the buildings, apparently started by the cult. Eighty-six cult members, including 23 children, were incinerated. Apparently, the Davidians chose self-destruction rather than destruction of their reality. Why were members so persuaded by Koresh's outrageous claims? How did they become so committed to the cult?

All cults have many characteristics in common. The primary feature is a charismatic leader. He or she takes on a supernatural aura and persuades group members to devote their lives and fortunes to the cult. Koresh was such a charismatic individual, able to convince large groups of people through clever arguments and persuasive appeals. For example, he refuted doubters by claiming to possess sole understanding of the Scriptures and changed interpretations often to keep cult members constantly uncertain and reliant on him. Koresh used charm and authority to gain control of followers' lives. However, charisma alone is not enough to account for the behavior of the Davidians. We must also look at the cognitive dynamics of the individual members to see how they became so committed to Koresh and his ideals.

Joining the cult was no easy feat. At first, few demands were made, but after a while, members had to give more. In fact, members routinely turned over all of their possessions, including houses, insurance policies, and money. Once in the group, life was quite harsh. Koresh enforced strict (and changeable) rules on every aspect of members' lives, including personally rationing all their food, imposing celibacy on the men while taking women as his wives and concubines, and inflicting physical abuse. In short, residents of the compound had to expend quite a bit of effort to be members.

All the requirements for membership relate directly to what we know about attitudes and behavior from dissonance theory. For example, dissonance research shows that the harder people have to work to get into a group, the more they value that group (Aronson & Mills, 1959). By turning over all of their possessions, members were making an irreversible commitment to the cult. Once such a commitment is made, people are unlikely to abandon positive attitudes toward the group (Festinger, Riecken, & Schachter, 1982). After expending so much effort, questioning commitment would create cognitive dissonance (Osherow, 1988). It is inconsistent to prove devotion to a belief by donating all of your possessions and then to abandon those beliefs. In other words, to a large extent, cult members persuade themselves. Dissonance theory predicts that the Davidians would come to value the group highly and be disinclined to question Koresh. This is, in fact, what happened.

Interestingly, cult members do not lose faith when the situation begins to sour. In fact, there is sometimes an increase in the strength of their commitment. One study investigated a "doomsday" society, a group that predicts the end of the world (Festinger et al., 1982). The study found that when a prophecy failed, members became more committed to the group. There are five conditions that must be met before this effect will occur.

1. The belief must be held with deep conviction and must be reflected in the believer's overt behavior.

2. The believer must have taken a step toward commitment that is difficult to reverse, for example, giving all of his or her money to the group.

3. The belief must be specific and well enough related to real-world events that it can be disconfirmed, or proven false, for example, the prediction that the world will end on a specified day.

4. There must be undeniable evidence that the belief is false (the world doesn't end).

5. The individual believer must have social support for the belief after disconfirmation.

Most, perhaps all, five conditions were present in the Waco tragedy. Members were committed to their beliefs and gave everything they had to Koresh. There was evidence that the situation was unstable; several members had left the cult, and some were even talking to federal officials. And when it started to become obvious that Koresh was not invincible, members had each other to turn to for social support. As negotiations deteriorated, Koresh altered his rhetoric to emphasize apocalyptic visions, rationalizing the cult's destruction and self-sacrifice. Cult members probably came to believe it was their destiny to die, if necessary. The power of persuasion can be seen in the tragic results.

ALTERNATIVES TO COGNITIVE DISSONANCE THEORY

Not all social psychologists believe cognitive dissonance theory is the best way to explain what happens when cognitive inconsistencies occur. Other theories have been proposed to explain how people deal with these discrepancies. In the sections that follow, we explore some alternatives to traditional cognitive dissonance theory.

Self-Perception Theory

Daryl Bem, a student of the great behaviorist psychologist, B. F. Skinner, challenged cognitive dissonance theory, because he asserted, he could explain people's behavior without looking at their inner motives. Bem (1972) proposed **self-perception theory**, which explains discrepant behavior by simply assuming that people are not self-conscious processors of information. People observe their own behavior and assume that their attitudes must be consistent with that behavior. If you eat a big dinner, you assume that you must have been hungry. If you take a public stand on an issue, the rule of self-perception theory is, "I said it, so I must have meant it." We don't look at our motives; we just process the information and conclude that there is no inconsistency.

self-perception theory
A theory suggesting that we learn about our motivations by evaluating our own behavior, useful especially in the area of attitude change.

Bem supported his theory with some interesting experiments. In one, he trained people to tell the truth whenever a "truth" (green) light was lit and to lie whenever a "lie" (red) light was lit. When the green light was on, people had to say something about themselves that was true. When the red light was on, people had to lie about themselves. Bem then asked the participants to make further statements that were either true or false under both truth and lie lights. Participants who told lies when the truth light was on came to believe that those false statements were true. Likewise, subjects who made true statements when the lie light was on reported that they lied.

The point of self-perception theory is that we make inferences about our behavior in much the same way an outside observer might. If you were observing the experiment, you would infer, quite reasonably, that whatever anyone said when the light was red was a lie and anything said under the green light was true. The participants assumed the same thing. According to self-perception theory, something does not have to happen "inside" the person for inconsistencies to be resolved—no tension, no motivation to reconcile attitudes and behavior, just information processing.

RATIONALIZATION AND SELF-AFFIRMATION THEORY

The fact that millions of people smoke is proof that dissonance does not always lead to behavior change. Everyone knows that smoking leads to lung cancer, heart disease, and other problems, including the strong and occasionally aggressive disapproval of nonsmokers. People have to reduce the dissonance between smoking and the knowledge that smoking causes such serious harm. The solution is to rationalize: "Nothing will happen to me," "I'll stop when I'm 40," or "My grandfather lived until 80, and he smoked like a chimney." Rationalizations are important in maintaining a coherent self-concept.

Dissonance may threaten a person's self-concept with negative implications, making the person appear stupid, unethical, or lazy (Steele, 1988). Nonsmokers probably view smokers as being all three. Then why don't people in dissonant situations alter their behavior? In the case of cigarette smoking, a large part of the answer is the highly addictive nature of nicotine. Many people try to quit and fail, or they can't face the prospect of never having another cigarette. So they are stuck with the dissonance. **Self-affirmation theory** suggests that people may not try to reduce dissonance if they can maintain (affirm) their self-concept by proving that they are adequate in other ways: "Yes, I may be a smoker, but I'm also a good mother, a respected professional, and an active citizen in my community." These self-affirmations remove the sting inherent in a dissonance situation (Zimbardo & Leippe,

self-affirmation theory
A theory that individuals may not try to reduce dissonance if they can maintain (affirm) their self-concept by showing they are morally adequate in other ways.

1992). People cope with a threat to one aspect of the self by affirming an unrelated part of the self (Steele, 1988).

PSYCHOLOGICAL REACTANCE   Psychological tension can be reduced in several ways. Sometimes, when people realize they have been coerced into doing or buying something against their wishes, they try to regain or reassert their freedom. This response is called **psychological reactance** (Brehm & Brehm, 1981). The theory of psychological reactance, an offshoot of cognitive dissonance theory, suggests that when some part of our freedom is threatened, we become aroused and motivated to restore that freedom.

The Coca-Cola Company found this out in 1985 when they tried to replace the traditional Coke formula with "New Coke." They conducted an in-depth marketing study of the new product that included 200,000 taste tests. The tests showed that people really liked New Coke. The company went ahead with plans to retire the old formula and to put New Coke in its place. However, the issue was not taste; it was perceived choice. People resented having a choice taken away and reacted by buying the traditional Coke as if it were manna from heaven, never to be seen again. Some people even formed Old Coke clubs. The company got over 1,500 angry calls and letters every day. Coca-Cola had to change its marketing plans, and "Classic Coke" still holds an honored place on the grocery shelves (Oskamp, 1991). Whether consumers liked New Coke did not matter. Their emotional ties to old Coke did matter, as did their freedom to buy it. New Coke just wasn't it for these folks.

PERSUADING THE MASSES

Throughout the chapter, the social psychology of persuasion was discussed primarily in interpersonal terms. That is, much of what we discussed deals with individuals constructing strategies and arguments to persuade people one-on-one or speak directly to an audience. However, in today's society, persuasion often takes place on a larger scale, through mass media or in situations in which the audience cannot interact with the persuader. Examples of mass persuasion abound: political candidates trying to obtain our vote, magazines telling us what the latest fads are, and endless advertisers vying for our money. In this section, we explore a sample of persuasion situations and techniques that occur on a mass level.

Public Health Campaigns: Educating People about AIDS

Although there is no cure for AIDS, a tremendous amount of information about it is available. This includes information about how the virus is transmitted and about the horrors of the disease itself. The focus of government and public health campaigns is on prevention through education. Messages about AIDS are aimed at persuading people to alter their sexual behaviors in order to minimize risk (Weisse, Nesselhof-Kendall, Fleck-Kandath, & Baum, 1990).

CHANGING SEXUAL ATTITUDES AND BEHAVIOR   Although educational efforts have been effective among some populations at risk for HIV infection, they have been far from successful among others. For

Persuasive attemps are not only directed at people on an individual level. There are also persuasive messages intended to reach a mass audience. This billboard is an example of a mass persuasive appeal concerning AIDS.

illusion of unique invulnerability

A tendency to underestimate the likelihood of bad things happening to oneself.

example, between 1997 and 1999 the number of males who have sex with other males with AIDS has dropped (Center for Disease Control and Prevention [CDC], 2001). In 1997, there were 20,369 cases of AIDS among this population, compared to 17,508 and 17,162 cases for the years 1998 and 1999, respectively. However, it is also clear that homosexual men continue to engage in risky sexual behavior. According to statistics from the CDC, homosexual males still have the highest number of cases of AIDS (348,657 in 1999) within the male population with AIDS. The rate of infection has been increasing most rapidly among adult and adolescent women (especially non-white women). For example, between 1985 and 1999, the rate of infection of adolescent and adult women has tripled from 7% to 23% (CDC, 2000a). Clearly, just getting information out is not enough to persuade people to stop engaging in risky behavior that could kill them (Gerrard, Gibbons, Warner, & Smith, 1993).

One reason people are not persuaded by information about AIDS or other threats is that they simply believe bad things will not happen to them. This phenomenon has been called the **illusion of unique invulnerability** (Perloff, 1987). We know that bad things happen — cars are stolen, unwanted pregnancies occur, people get lung cancer — but we think they happen only to others, not to us. Therefore, despite the evidence, we act as if we are invulnerable and resist precautions.

A survey of the sexual risk-taking behaviors and attitudes of college students and of an older, noncollege group — members of a health club — showed that almost everyone (96%) had extensive and tolerably accurate knowledge about the importance of using condoms to prevent HIV transmission and the dangers of having unprotected anal intercourse (Cronin & Rosa, 1990). However, knowledge and behavior were unrelated; people knew the dangers and still engaged in risky behavior. Moreover, amount of education did not affect sexual behavior: People who had attended graduate school did not behave differently than college students or high school graduates.

The survey revealed that less than 23% of the respondents always used condoms, even though over 50% of the health club members had over 10 sexual partners in their lifetime. Most of the participants simply did not think they were at risk: Only about 10% thought HIV infection could be a possibility for them. Besides, many of the respondents, nearly 90%, rationalized that a cure would be found for AIDS.

REACHING THE ADOLESCENT POPULATION Given the resistance of individuals to changing their sexual behavior, how can public health officials get people to stop killing themselves? If the facts about AIDS aren't persuasive enough, how can people be convinced to stop putting themselves at risk?

Let's look at one group that is particularly vulnerable to HIV infection — adolescents. Although young people (aged 13–19) do not have a high rate of AIDS (which is declining), they are showing a trend toward higher HIV infection rates (CDC, 2000b). This may be translated into a higher rate of AIDS among adolescents in the future. One important factor in targeting young people is that the image of "impressionable years" has some truth. It doesn't mean that older people do not change; they do. But susceptibility to attitude and behavior change is strongest during adolescence and early adulthood (Krosnick & Alwin, 1989). If adolescents can be motivated to pay attention to safe-sex messages, they may listen to the evidence and analyze it in order to make an informed decision. As you recall from the elaboration likelihood model, when individuals use central processing, they create a personally relevant context for the message and, as a result, experience long-term attitude change. In other words, if individuals form strong attitudes about safe-sex practices during adolescence, those attitudes are likely to stick.

How can health officials reach adolescents with persuasive messages about protecting themselves from AIDS? First of all, credible communicators are particularly important for this audience (Krosnick & Alwin, 1989). We have seen that the more credible the communicator, the more effective the persuasive message is. This is especially true with people whose attitudes are not well formed yet, specifically adolescents. Second, the message must be credible, in both form and content. The message that all teenagers should abstain from sex, for example, is unrealistic and, therefore, unconvincing. The message should contain enough interest and fear to get the audience's attention but not so much that they will reject the message as noncredible. Messages about AIDS that focus on safer sex practices, especially the use of condoms, are likely to have the most effect.

How often should a persuasive message be shown to an audience? What is the effect of frequent exposures? One study showed that repetition of a message was effective up to a point, and then listeners became weary of it (Cacioppo & Petty, 1979). In this study, the magic number was three exposures. Televised messages usually run longer than this, of course, and it may take a long time before a message loses its power to influence. Other studies have looked at the strength of the message as a variable in effectiveness. Results indicate that frequently repeated weak messages get negative reactions but that frequently repeated strong messages get positive reactions (Petty & Cacioppo, 1986).

Finally, the channel for the message must be accessible and appealing. Television, video, and rock music are all channels that are familiar and credible for an adolescent audience. Madonna's "Like a Prayer" is a good example of an effective format for persuading adolescents. It included advice and information about AIDS and risk reduction. The communicator was credible, particularly because she had nothing tangible to gain from conveying this message.

The message was strong without being threatening, and the channel (tape, CD) was familiar and accessible. What about self-persuasion? Jeff Stone and his colleagues (Stone, Aronson, Crain, Wenslow, & Fried, 1994) applied a new twist on cognitive dissonance theory to the prevention of HIV transmission among sexually active young adults. Stone asked participants to develop a speech about using condoms for the prevention of HIV transmission and to deliver it in front of a TV camera. These individuals were then systematically reminded of the fact that they had admitted to not using condoms in the past. Cognitive dissonance theory predicts that a conflict like this, between public statements and private behavior, leads to a change in behavior. Results showed that participants who were made aware of this inconsistency, this "hypocrisy," were more likely than other participants to purchase condoms in the future.

The Limits of Persuasion

However, we should not overstate the odds that persuasion efforts will work. There is limited empirical evidence that educating or informing people about the risk of HIV transmission increases precautionary behavior (Gerrard et al., 1993). This is not true for other health risks. You can persuade people to use seat belts or to stop smoking or to change their eating habits. What is different about AIDS? Sex. Sexual relationships are central to our personal identities (Gerrard et al., 1993). We are resistant to making changes recommended by others in something we perceive as so basic and so private. We would rather take risks than surrender our values or intimate "freedoms," or delude ourselves into thinking we are not really at risk.

THE LEOPOLD AND LOEB CASE REVISITED

Clarence Darrow used all his powers of persuasion to save his clients, Leopold and Loeb, from execution. As a skilled communicator, he knew how important it was to establish and maintain his credibility. Many of his arguments aimed, sometimes subtly, sometimes not, at destroying his opponent's credibility and enhancing his own.

Darrow also understood that a communicator who seems disinterested in persuading his audience is usually more successful than one who is clearly trying to persuade. He took the high moral ground, arguing that it would be inhumane to execute two young men who weren't entirely responsible for their actions.

Darrow did not neglect his audiences, the trial judge and the public. He carefully structured and presented his arguments in order to have the greatest effect on them. Darrow knew that arguments too far from the judge's "latitude of acceptance" would not succeed. He didn't argue against capital punishment (although he personally opposed it), just capital punishment in this particular case. He knew Judge Caverly was listening carefully to his arguments, elaborating on them and placing them in the context of American criminal justice. He knew the world was listening, too. The Leopold and

Loeb "thrill murder" case became one of the most infamous incidents in U.S. history, for Americans were shocked at the spectacle of two wealthy young men who killed just to see what it would feel like.

Judge Caverly handed down his decision on September 10, 1924. Leopold and Loeb were sentenced to life imprisonment for murder and 99 years for kidnaping. Loeb died in 1936 in a prison fight; a model prisoner, Leopold was released at the age of 70 and spent the rest of his life in Puerto Rico helping the poor.

CHAPTER REVIEW

1. What is persuasion?

Persuasion is a form of social influence whereby a communicator uses rational and/or emotional arguments to convince others to change their attitudes or behavior.

2. What is the Yale communication model?

The **Yale communication model** is a theoretical model that guides persuasion tactics. It is based on the assumption that persuasion will occur if a persuader presents a logical argument that clarifies how attitude change is beneficial.

3. What factors about the communicator affect persuasion?

The Yale model focuses on the **credibility** of the communicator, an important determinant of the likelihood that persuasion will occur. The components of credibility are **expertise** and **trustworthiness**. Although an important factor in the persuasiveness of a message, communicator credibility may not have long-lasting effects. Over time, a message from a noncredible source may be as persuasive as one from a credible source, a phenomenon known as the **sleeper effect**. This is more likely to occur if there is a strong persuasive argument, if a discounting cue is given, and if sufficient time passes that people forget who said what. Other communicator factors that increase persuasion are physical attractiveness, similarity to the target, and a rapid, fluent speech style.

4. What message factors mediate persuasion?

Messages that include a mild to moderate appeal to fear seem to be more persuasive than others, provided they offer a solution to the fear-producing situation. The timing of the message is another factor in its persuasiveness, as is the structure of the message and the extent to which the communicator attempts to fit the message to the audience. Research supports **inoculation theory**, which holds that giving people a weakened version of an opposing argument is an effective approach to persuasion. Good communicators also know their audience well enough not to deliver a highly discrepant message. When this cannot be avoided, as when there is a **multiple audience problem**, communicators use hidden messages and private keys and codes to get their point across.

Additionally, the amount of discrepancy between the content of a message and the audience members' existing attitudes makes a difference. According to **social judgment theory**, persuasion relates to the amount of personal involvement an individual has with an issue. A message can fall into a person's **latitude of acceptance** (positions found to be acceptable), **latitude of rejection** (positions found to be unacceptable), or **latitude of noncommitment** (positions neither accepted nor rejected, but to be considered).

5. What is the elaboration likelihood model of persuasion?

Cognitive response models focus on the active role of the audience. They assert that people respond to persuasive messages by connecting them with their own knowledge, feelings, and thoughts related to the topic of the message. The **elaboration likelihood model (ELM)**, which examines how individuals respond to the persuasive message, proposes two routes to persuasion. The first, **central route processing**, is used when people have the capacity and motivation to understand the message and analyze it in a critical and effortful manner. Central route processors elaborate on the message by connecting it to their knowledge and feelings. Sometimes this elaboration will persuade the recipient, depending on the strength of the message. Central route processors tend to experience more durable attitude changes.

The second avenue to persuasion is **peripheral route processing**. This occurs when individuals do not have the motivation or interest to process effortfully. Instead, they rely on cues other than the merits of the message, such as the attractiveness of the communicator. Whether a person uses central or peripheral route processing depends on a number of factors, including mood, personal relevance, and use of language. The **flexible correction model** augments the elaboration likelihood model. It suggests that individuals using central route processing are influenced by biasing factors when they are not aware of the potential impact of those factors, for example when they are in a good mood. Under these conditions, correction for biasing factors takes place.

6. What is the impact of vividness on persuasion?

Overall, the effect of vividness of a message on persuasion is not very strong. Studies show, however, that individuals exposed to vivid messages on an issue that was important to them felt the vivid message was effective. Vividness may be beneficial in political ads or in jury trials. For example, jurors awarded more money to a plaintiff when the evidence they heard was vivid as opposed to nonvivid. Vivid information has its greatest impact when a persuasive message requires few resources and a person is highly motivated to process the message. For a message with a highly motivated target that requires many resources, vividness does not have an effect on persuasion.

7. What is the need for cognition?

Need for cognition (NC) is an individual difference variable mediating persuasion. Individuals who are high in the need for cognition will process persuasive information along the central route, regardless of the situation or the complexity of the message. Conversely, individuals low in the need for cognition pay more attention to peripheral cues (e.g., physical characteristics of the speaker) and are more likely to use peripheral route processing of a persuasive message.

8. What is the heuristic and systematic information model of persuasion?

The **heuristic and systematic information processing model (HSM)** focuses more heavily on the importance of heuristics or peripheral cues than does the elaboration likelihood model. This model notes that often issues are too complex or too numerous for effortful, systematic processing to be practical.

9. What is cognitive dissonance theory, and what are its main ideas?

Cognitive dissonance theory proposes that people feel an uncomfortable tension when their attitudes, or attitude and behavior, are inconsistent. This psychological discomfort is known as cognitive dissonance. According to the theory, people are motivated to reduce this tension, and attitude change is a likely outcome. Dissonance theory suggests that the less reward people receive for a behavior, the more compelled they feel to provide their own justification for it, especially if they believe they have freely chosen it. Similarly, the more they are rewarded, the more they infer that the behavior is suspect. The latter is known as the reverse-incentive effect.

Additionally, cognitive dissonance theory states that an individual will experience dissonance after making a decision between two mutually exclusive, equally attractive alternatives. This is known as **postdecision dissonance**.

Another, more recent view suggests that cognitive dissonance results not so much from inconsistency as from the feeling of personal responsibility that occurs when inconsistent actions produce negative consequences.

10. What is self-perception theory?

One alternative to cognitive dissonance theory is **self-perception theory**, which argues that behavior and attitude change can be explained without assuming that people are motivated to reduce the tension supposedly produced by inconsistency.

Instead, self-perception assumes that people are not self-conscious processors of information. They simply observe their own behavior and assume that their attitudes must be consistent with that behavior.

11. What is self-affirmation theory?

Another alternative to cognitive dissonance, **self-affirmation theory** explains how people deal with the tension that dissonant thoughts or behaviors provoke. **Self-affirmation theory** suggests that people may not try to reduce dissonance if they can maintain their self-concept by proving that they are adequate in other ways, that is, by affirming an unrelated and positive part of the self.

12. What is psychological reactance?

Individuals may reduce psychological tension in another way as well. When people realize they have been coerced into doing or buying something against their will, they sometimes try to regain or reassert their freedom. This response is called **psychological reactance**.

13. How are the tactics of persuasion used on a mass scale?

The same persuasive tactics that operate in interpersonal settings can be and are used in mass communication. One example is the public health campaign to persuade people to change their sexual practices in order to protect themselves from HIV infection. Although these efforts have been effective among some populations, they have been far from successful among others. One reason people are not persuaded by information about AIDS or other serious threats is that they simply believe bad things will not happen to them. This phenomenon has been called the **illusion of unique invulnerability**.

Efforts to change people's sexual behaviors must be very persuasive, using credible communicators, familiar channels, and a moderate appeal to fear that includes a solution to the problem (e.g., the use of condoms).

INTERNET ACTIVITY

IDENTIFYING PERSUASIVE MESSAGES

Each day we are bombarded by hundreds of persuasive messages advertising everything from products to political candidates. Persuasion plays a key role during times of war. Entire populations can be motivated to get behind the war effort or, as was the case of Vietnam, protest against the war. Propaganda, a systematic attempt to persuade large groups of individuals, has been used for centuries to shape the minds and behavior of the populations of entire nations. On the Internet, you can find examples of propaganda posters used at various times during history. At one site, *Powers of Persuasion*, http://www.nara.gov/exhall/powers/powers.html, for example, there are several examples of propaganda posters used during World War II. You can find Web sites that have propaganda posters by typing in the keywords: "propaganda posters" in a search engine.

For this exercise, select two or three propaganda posters, and analyze them according to the Yale communication model:

1. Identify the source of the communication (e.g., government or private industry), and indicate whether you feel it was a credible source (and why).

2. Was the poster a fear appeal, a rational appeal, or both? If the poster was a fear appeal, what images were used to generate fear? Do you think this was an effective tool to generate fear (why or why not)?

3. What content did the message portray? That is, what was the poster showing, and what did it want people to do?

4. What do you think the major aim of the poster was?

SUGGESTIONS FOR FURTHER READING

Jamieson, K. H. (1992). *Dirty politics: Distraction, deception, and democracy.* New York: Oxford University Press.

The dean of the Annenberg School of Communication has given us an insightful and lively examination of not only the most recent elections but also the use of persuasion tactics in politics throughout American history.

Pratkams, A. R., & Ironstone, E. (1992). *The age of propaganda.* New York: Freeman.

This book is a well-written nontechnical examination of the application of the social psychology of persuasion to everyday events by two of the leading researchers in the area of persuasion and social influence.

Spence, G. (1990). *With justice for none.* New York: Penguin Books.

This is a personal examination of the legal system by a successful trial lawyer who knows all the tricks of persuasion.

CHAPTER 7

CONFORMITY, COMPLIANCE, AND OBEDIENCE

The jury had been empaneled to hear the case *State v. Leroy Reed*. Reed, a paroled felon, had been arrested for possessing a gun. Frank, a firefighter, sat in the jury box, carefully listening and watching. The prosecuting attorney argued that the defendant should be found guilty of violating his parole despite any sympathy jurors might feel for him. The defense attorney argued that even though Reed had bought a gun, he should not be found guilty. According to the defense, Reed bought the gun because he believed that it was required for a mail-order detective course in which he had enrolled. Reed wanted to better his life, and he thought that becoming a private detective was just the ticket. He admired real-life detectives very much. He had told a police detective at the county courthouse that he was learning to be a detective and had bought a gun. The detective was incredulous and told Reed to go home and get it. Reed did so and was promptly arrested, because possessing a gun is a criminal offense for felons. Evidence also showed that Reed was able to read at only a fifth-grade level

and probably did not understand that he was violating his parole by purchasing a weapon.

The judge told the jury that according to the law, they must find Reed guilty if he possessed a gun and knew that he possessed a gun. As he went into the jury room, Frank was convinced that Reed was guilty. After all, the prosecutor had presented sufficient evidence concerning the points of law that according to the judge must be fulfilled for conviction. Reed had bought a gun and certainly knew that he possessed that gun. As the deliberations began, however, it became obvious that not all jurors agreed with Frank.

The results of a first-ballot vote taken by the foreperson showed that nine jurors favored acquittal and only three, including Frank, favored conviction. After further discussion, two of the jurors favoring conviction changed their votes. Frank alone held firm to his belief in the defendant's guilt. As the deliberations progressed, the other jurors tried to convince Frank that a not-guilty verdict was the fairer verdict. This pressure made Frank very anxious and upset. He continually put his face in both hands and closed his eyes. Continued efforts to persuade Frank to change his verdict failed.

After a while, however, Frank, still unconvinced, decided to change his verdict. He told the other jury members that he would change his verdict to not guilty but that he "would just never feel right about it."

Why did Frank change his verdict, even though he did not agree with his fellow jurors? This case, vividly brought to life in the PBS film *Inside the Jury Room,* forces us not just to look at Frank's behavior but also to speculate about our own. Would each of us be as willing to compromise our beliefs in the face of a unanimous majority who think differently? Under what conditions can our behavior be modified by others? These questions are at the very core of what distinguishes social psychology from other areas of psychology: the influence of others on our behavior.

In chapter 6, we saw how persuasive arguments from others can influence our behavior. Frank was certainly exposed to such arguments. However, he did not accept them as a basis for changing his verdict. Rather, Frank modified his verdict in response to the knowledge that all of his fellow jurors believed that Leroy Reed should be found not guilty. Thus, as Frank's case illustrates, sometimes we modify behavior based on perceived pressure from others rather than through a process of accepting what they say.

Like Frank, we are often influenced by what those around us do. For example, when you are seated in a classroom, you will note that most people are behaving similarly: They are taking notes and listening to the professor. In social situations, such as the classroom, the behavior of others often defines the range of appropriate behavior. This is especially true when the situation is new or ambiguous. What if, for example, the fire alarm rang while you were sitting in class? Would you immediately get up and leave, or would you look around to see what others do? Most people insist that they would get up and leave. However, experience teaches us otherwise. If your classmates were just sitting in their seats calmly, you probably would do the same. The social influence processes that operate on you in the classroom situation can also be applied to understanding situations like Frank's changing his verdict.

In this chapter, we explore three types of social influence: conformity, compliance, and obedience. We ask: How does social influence sometimes cause us to do or say things that we don't necessarily believe in, as was the case with Frank? Why was Frank able to hold out when there were others on his side but finally gave in when he was the only one for conviction? What other factors and types of situations make us more or less likely to conform? When we conform, do we always conform with the majority, or can a minority sometimes lead us to conform to their point of view? Under what conditions do we comply with or agree to a direct request? And, finally, what factors lead us to obey the orders of a person in a position of authority? These are some of the questions addressed in this chapter.

KEY QUESTIONS

AS YOU READ THIS CHAPTER, FIND THE ANSWERS TO THE FOLLOWING QUESTIONS:

1. *What is conformity?*
2. *What is the source of the pressures that lead to conformity?*
3. *What research evidence is there for conformity?*
4. *What factors influence conformity?*
5. *Do women conform more than men?*

6. Can the minority ever influence the majority?
7. How does minority influence work?
8. Why do we sometimes end up doing things we would rather not do?
9. What are compliance techniques, and why do they work?
10. What do social psychologists mean by the term "obedience"?
11. Are evil deeds done by evil persons?
12. What research has been done to study obedience?
13. What factors influence obedience?
14. Are there gender differences in obedience?
15. Do Milgram's results apply to other cultures?
16. What criticisms of Milgram's experiments have been offered?
17. How does disobedience occur?

CONFORMITY: GOING ALONG WITH THE CROWD

As a juror, Frank was placed in an uncertain position because he was receiving conflicting input about the situation. From the judge and the prosecution, he received a message about the law that convinced him Reed was guilty and that his responsibility as a juror was to convict him of violating his parole. From his fellow jurors, on the other hand, he received a different message, a message that made him doubt this conclusion. The other jurors told him that in their opinion, Reed should be found not-guilty despite the evidence. They believed that extenuating circumstances, including Reed's lack of intent to commit a crime, made a not-guilty verdict appropriate. Additionally, Frank was well aware that he was the only juror holding out for conviction. The force brought to bear by the social situation eventually caused Frank to change his verdict, although privately he did not agree with most of his fellow jurors. Frank was the victim of social influence.

If Frank had had to decide Reed's fate on his own, he would have convicted him. But once he was in a social context, he had to reconsider his personal views in light of the views of others. He yielded to group pressure even though he felt the group was wrong. Frank's behavior is illustrative of what social psychologists call conformity. **Conformity** occurs when we modify our behavior in response to real or imagined pressure from others. Notice that nobody directly asked or ordered Frank to change his verdict. Instead, he responded to the subtle and not-so-subtle pressures applied by his fellow jurors.

conformity

A social influence process that involves modifying behavior in response to real or imagined pressure from others rather than in response to a direct request or order from another.

Informational and Normative Social Influence

What is it about the social situation that can cause us to change our opinion, even if we privately feel such an opinion shift is wrong? To adequately address this question, we need to make a distinction between two kinds of social influence: informational and normative (Deutsch & Gerrard, 1955).

Sometimes we modify our behavior in response to information that we receive from others. This is known as **informational social influence.** In many social situations, other people provide important information through their actions and words. Imagine yourself in the place of one of Frank's fellow jurors, say, the jury foreperson. You think the defendant is guilty, but nine of your fellow jurors think the opposite. They try to convince you of the defendant's innocence by sharing their perceptions of the evidence with you. One juror may remind you of an important piece of information that you had forgotten; another may share an interpretation of the defendant's behavior that had not occurred to you. If you modify your opinion based on such new or reinterpreted information, you are responding to informational social influence. The persuasion process discussed in chapter 6 illustrates informational social influence.

informational social influence

Social influence that results from a person's responding to information provided by others.

This is, in fact, what happened to the foreperson in the Reed case. Initially, he was among the three jurors who were voting to convict. But after hearing the group discuss the issues and the evidence, he came to see the crime and the surrounding circumstances in a different way. Based on his reinterpretation of the evidence, he decided to change his verdict. He did so in direct response to what was said and how other jurors said it.

In certain social situations it is expected that a person behave in a given way. We conform to social norms when we adhere to the norms that have been established. These individuals, who are all dressed alike, are conforming to a norm concerning how to dress for a situation. How would one of them feel if he were dressed differently?

Generally, we are subject to informational social influence because we want to be accurate in our judgments. We use other people's opinions as a source of information by which to test the validity of our own judgments. We conform because we perceive that others have correct information (Campbell & Fairey, 1989). Shifts in opinion based on informational social influence result from the sharing of arguments and factual information (Kaplan & Miller, 1987). Essentially, opinion and behavior change come about via the kind of persuasion processes discussed in chapter 6.

Conformity also comes about as a result of **normative social influence.** In this type of social influence situation, we modify our behavior in response to a **norm,** an unwritten social rule that suggests what constitutes appropriate behavior in a particular situation. Our behavior is guided not only by rational consideration of the issue at hand but also by the discomfort we experience when we are in disagreement with others. We are motivated to conform to norms and to the implicit expectations of others in order to gain social acceptance and to avoid appearing different or being rejected (Campbell & Fairey, 1989).

During deliberations, Frank was not influenced directly by the informational content of the jury deliberations. Instead, the fact that others disagreed with him became crucial. The arguments and opinions expressed by the other jurors suggested to him that the operational norm was that the law didn't apply in this case; Reed ought to be acquitted despite evidence pointing to his guilt. Frank changed his verdict in order to conform to this norm.

In a normative social influence situation, at least two factors are relevant. First, the input we obtain from others serves as a clue to the nature of the norm in effect at any given time (Kaplan & Miller, 1987). Frank was surprised to discover what the norm was in the jury room. Second, the size and unanimity of the majority convey information about the strength of the norm in effect. As we see later in the chapter, these two variables are important in determining the likelihood and amount of behavior change in a social influence situation.

normative social influence
Social influence in which a person changes behavior in response to pressure to conform to a norm.

norm
An unwritten social rule existing either on a wide cultural level or on a smaller, situation-specific level that suggests what is appropriate behavior in a situation.

Although both informational and normative social influence can exert powerful control over our behavior, their effects are different. The changes caused by informational social influence tend to be stronger and more enduring than those caused by normative social influence (Burnstein & Sentis, 1981). This is because changes caused by new information or a new interpretation of existing information may be persuasive and convincing. As we saw in chapter 6, the opinion changes that result from persuasion are usually based on our accepting information, elaborating on it, and altering our attitudes and behavior accordingly. This type of information processing tends to produce rather stable, long-lasting change.

For normative social influence to occur, we need not be convinced that our opinion is incorrect. We respond to our perception of what we believe others want us to do. Consequently, a change in opinion, attitude, or behavior brought about by normative pressure is often fragile. Once normative pressure eases up, we are likely to go back to our previous opinions. Frank went along with the other members of the jury, but he did not really believe they were right.

Because norms play such an important role in our behavior, and because normative social influence is so critical an element in conformity and other forms of social influence, we turn now to a more detailed discussion of these important forces.

Social Norms: The Key to Conformity

Norms play an important role in our everyday lives. These unwritten rules guide much of our social behavior. Humans seem to be predisposed to form norms—and conform to them—even in the most minimal situations. Norms exist on many levels, ranging from broad cultural norms to smaller-scale, situation-specific norms. We have cultural norms for how close we stand to another person when talking, for how men and women interact in business settings, and for the clothing we wear. We have situation-specific norms for how to behave in class or in the courtroom.

Violating norms makes us uncomfortable. We are embarrassed if we show up at a wedding reception in casual dress and find everyone else dressed formally, or if we go to tennis camp in tennis whites only to discover everyone else wearing the camp T-shirt. In general, standing out from the crowd, being the only different one, is something human beings don't like.

To get a better idea of how norms develop and how normative social influence works, imagine that you are taking part in an experiment. You are sitting in a totally dark room waiting for a point of light to appear on the wall across from where you are sitting. After the light is shone, you are asked to judge how far the light moved (in inches). In fact, unknown to you, the light is stationary and only appears to move, a phenomenon called the *autokinetic effect*. If asked to make successive judgments of the amount of movement that you perceive, what will occur? Will your judgments vary widely, or will they show some consistency? If you have to do the same task with two others, will your judgments remain independent or blend with those of the others?

These questions were asked by Muzafer Sherif (1936, 1972) in his classic studies on norm formation. When participants did the task alone, Sherif found that their judgments eventually reflected some internalized standard

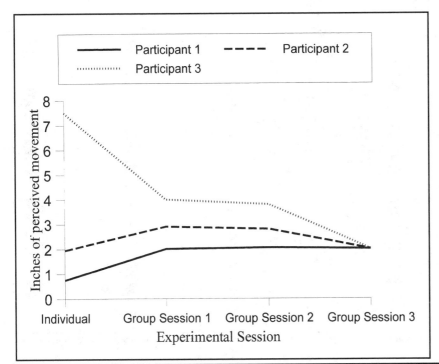

Figure 7.1

The formation of a group norm. When individuals judged the apparent movement of a stationary light, there was a considerable difference among their estimates. After three group sessions, estimates converged indicating that a group norm had formed.

Adapted from Sherif (1936). Reprinted with permission.

that put a limit on their estimates of how far the light moved. That is, rather than being haphazard, individual participants showed evidence of establishing a range and norm to guide their judgments. When these participants were then placed within a group context, the individualized ranges and norms blended into a single group norm. Some of Sherif's results are shown in Figure 7.1.

The left side of the figure shows the results from three individual participants who first did the task alone. Notice that individual judgments covered quite a range (from about 1 inch to 7.5 inches). But after three sessions in which the individuals judged the distance in groups, their judgments converged, producing a funnel-shaped graph. According to Sherif, this convergence shows that the group, without specific instructions to do so, developed a group norm. Interestingly, this group norm was found to persist even when the participants were brought back to do the task again a year later!

Classic Studies in Conformity

The convergence of judgments shown in Sherif's study should not be surprising. The autokinetic effect is misleading, so the task was ambiguous, depending on subjective estimates of the distance traveled by a light. Individual judgments eventually converged on a group norm, demonstrating conformity. But what happens if the task is less ambiguous? Do participants still conform to a group norm? Or do they maintain their independence? These are some of the questions Solomon Asch addressed in a now-classic series of experiments (1951, 1955, 1956).

Figure 7.2

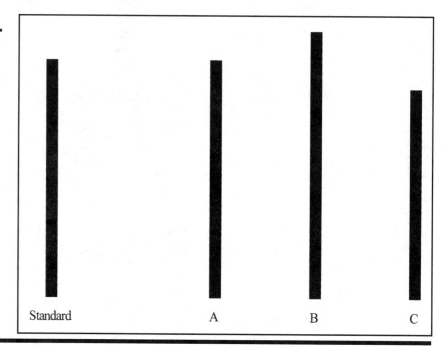

Standard   A   B   C

THE ASCH PARADIGM   Imagine that you have signed up for an experiment investigating perceptual judgments. When you arrive at the lab, you find that several other participants are already present. You take the only remaining seat. You are told that the experiment involves judging the length of lines presented on a card at the front of the room. You are to look at each of three lines and decide which one matches a standard presented to the left (Figure 7.2). The experimenter tells you that each of you will give your judgment orally one after another. Because you are in the last chair you will give your judgment last.

The experiment begins uneventfully. Each member of the group gives what you consider the correct response, and then you give your response. But soon the others begin to give answers you believe to be incorrect, and you must decide what to do. Should you give the correct answer (which is obvious) or go along with the majority, who are wrong?

Before we see what happened, let's take a closer look at the Asch paradigm. The "other participants" were not really participants at all. They were confederates of the experimenter who were instructed to give incorrect answers on several "critical trials." Misinformation provided by the incorrect majority places the real participant in a dilemma. On the one hand, he has the evidence of his own senses that tells him what the correct answer is. On the other hand, he has information from the majority concerning what is correct. The participant is placed in a situation in which he must decide between these two competing sources of information. From these competing sources of information, pressure on the participant arises.

Now, when you are faced with a situation like the one created in the Asch experiments, there are two ways you can test reality to determine which line really matches the standard. You can jump up, whip out your pocket measuring tape, rush to the front of the room, and measure the lines. This is directly testing your perceptions against reality. However, you probably won't do this, because it will violate your sense of the operative social norm—how you should act in this situation. The other way is to test the accuracy of your perceptions against those of others through a *social comparison* process (Festinger, 1954). Asch's paradigm strongly favors doing the latter. Given that participants in these experiments probably will not measure the lines, what do they do about the conflict between information from their own senses and information from the majority?

CONFORMITY IN THE ASCH EXPERIMENTS   Asch's experimental paradigm placed the participant's own perceptions into conflict with the opinions of a unanimous majority advocating a clearly incorrect judgment. When confronted with the incorrect majority, Asch's participants made errors in the direction of the incorrect majority on over 33% of the critical trials. Therefore, Asch showed a conformity rate of 33% on his line-judgment task. Almost all participants knew the correct answer. When they did the same task alone, the error rate (mismatching the line with the standard) was 7.4%, one fourth the error rate when other participants were present. Yet many changed their opinions to be in conformity with the group judgment. So, even with a simple perceptual task, an individual may abandon his or her own judgement and go with the majority. Why would we do this? As we see next, there are different reasons why people conform or remain independent.

PATHS TO CONFORMITY AND INDEPENDENCE   Based on his results and interviews with participants, Asch classified them as either yielding (conforming) or independent (nonconforming) (Asch, 1951). Of the yielding participants, some (but relatively few) gave in completely to the majority. These participants suffered from *distortion of perception* and saw the majority judgments as correct. They appeared to believe that the incorrect line was actually the correct one. The largest group of yielding participants displayed *distortion of judgment*. These participants yielded because they lacked confidence in their own judgments—"I'm not sure anymore." Without such confidence, they were not able to stick with their own perceptions and remain independent. Finally, some yielding participants experienced *distortion of action*. Here, participants knew that the majority was wrong but conformed so that they did not appear different to the other participants—"I'll go along" (Figure 7.3 on p. 244). This is what happened to Frank. Interestingly, there was a remarkable consistency among yielding participants. Once bound to the majority, they stayed on the path of conformity.

Of the independent participants, about 25% remained totally independent, never agreeing with the incorrect majority (Asch, 1955). These participants had a great deal of confidence in their own judgments and withstood the pressure from the majority completely. Other independent participants remained so because they felt a great need to remain self-reliant; still others remained independent because they wanted to do well on the task.

Asch's interviews tell us that there are many paths to conformity or independence. Some participants remain independent because they trust their own senses, whereas others remain independent because they feel a great need to do so. These latter participants appear to remain independent because of *psychological reactance* (Brehm, 1966). As described in chapter 6, psychological reactance occurs when individuals feel that their freedom of choice or action is threatened because other people are forcing them to do or

Figure 7.3

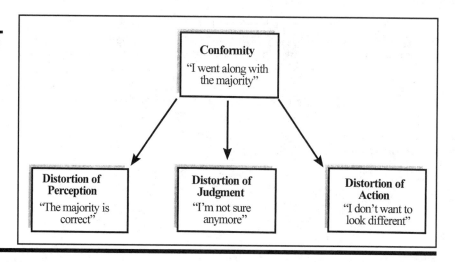

say things (Brehm & Brehm, 1981). To reestablish independence, they reject the majority's pressure and go their own way. Even when individuals choose to remain independent, however, they still feel the pressure the incorrect majority exerts. Resisting the pressure of the majority is not easy. Independent participants can withstand that pressure and stick with their own perceptions.

How Does Social Influence Bring about Conformity?

What is it about social influence situations that causes conformity? When your opinion is different from that of a unanimous majority, you are faced with a dilemma. On the one hand, your senses (or belief system) suggest one thing; on the other, the social situation (the majority) suggests something quite different. Placed in such a situation you experience conflict, which is psychologically uncomfortable (Moscovici, 1985). When you grapple with this conflict, your tendency is to pay attention to the views of the majority. Once the majority influence is removed, however, attention is focused back on the stimulus (e.g., the judgment of lines in the Asch studies). Once majority influence is removed, you will return to your previous judgments (Moscovici, 1985).

The effects of dividing attention between the majority and the stimulus were demonstrated in a study in which participants were asked to judge how similar two noises were in volume (Tesser, Campbell, & Mickler, 1983). Participants performed this task under conditions of high social pressure, when three members of a majority disagreed with the participant's evaluation of the noise, or under conditions of low social pressure, when only one person disagreed. Under high social pressure, participants responded by either attending very little or attending a great deal to the stimulus to be judged. Under low social pressure, participants paid a moderate amount of attention to the stimulus.

Researchers speculated that high social pressure would lead to high levels of arousal. This arousal is due to the competing tendencies to pay attention both to the stimulus and to the source of social influence, other people. The net result is that a person will default to his or her dominant way of behaving. Those who have a strong tendency to conform may resolve the conflict by adopting the view of the majority. Others less prone to the effects of social influence may increase their attention to the stimulus as a way to resolve the conflict. By focusing on the stimulus, they take their minds off the social pressure. Like Frank in the jury room, some participants in the Asch studies actually put their hands over their ears or eyes so that they did not hear or see what other people said. This was the only way they could resist conforming.

Factors That Affect Conformity

We have established that the opinions of others can alter our behavior. However, we have not yet explored how variables such as the nature of the task, the size of the majority, and the effect of one other person in agreement work to affect conformity. Next, we explore several variables relating to the amount of conformity observed in social influence situations.

NATURE OF THE TASK The first variable that can affect the amount of conformity observed relates to the task itself. One variable affecting conformity rates is the ambiguity of the task. As the task facing the individual becomes more ambiguous (i.e., less obvious), the amount of conformity increases (Crutchfield, 1955). Asch's task was a simple one, involving the judgment of the length of lines, and produced a conformity rate of about 33%. Conformity research conducted with more ambiguous stimuli shows even higher levels of conformity. For example, Sherif's (1936) experiment on norm formation using the autokinetic effect (an extremely ambiguous task) found conformity rates of about 70%.

Other research involving attitudinal issues with no clear right or wrong answer produced conformity rates similar to Sherif's. In one study, highly independent professionals such as army officers and expert engineers were led to believe that other professionals had answered an opinion item differently than they had (Crutchfield, 1955). For example, colonels in the army were told that other colonels had agreed with the item "I often doubt that I would make a good leader." Now, this is blasphemy for army officers, who are trained to lead. Yet when faced with a false majority, 70% of the officers said they agreed with that item. Privately, they disagreed strongly.

The type of task faced by a group may also determine the type of social influence (informational or normative) that comes into play. For example, informational social influence should be strongest when participants face an *intellective issue*, in which they can use factual information to arrive at a clearly correct answer (Kaplan & Miller, 1987). Normative social influence should be more crucial on a *judgmental issue*. A judgmental issue is based on moral or ethical principles, where there are no clear-cut right or wrong answers. Therefore, resolution of the issue depends on opinion, not fact. In a jury simulation study investigating the use of informational and normative social influence, Martin Kaplan and Charles Miller (1987) empaneled six-person juries to judge a civil lawsuit. The juries were required to award the plaintiff compensatory damages and punitive damages. Compensatory damages are awarded to reimburse the plaintiff for suffering and losses due to the defendant's behavior. Generally, awarding compensatory damages is a fact-based intellective task. If, for example, your lawn mower blows up because the No Pain, No Gain Lawn Mower Company put the gas tank in the wrong place, it is easy for the jury to add up the cost of the mower plus whatever medical costs were incurred. Punitive damages, on the other hand, are awarded to deter the defendant from repeating such actions in the future. The issue of awarding punitive damages is a judgmental task. How much should you punish the manufacturer so that they cease making mowers that blow up?

The results of the study indicated that juries doing an intellective task (awarding compensatory damages) were more likely to use informational social influence than normative social influence. When the task has a clear standard, then it is the information that majority members can bring forth that convinces other jurors. Juries doing a judgmental task, on the other hand, were more likely to use normative influence. Where there is no clear-cut answer, the jurors in the majority try to convince the minority to agree by pressuring them to conform to the group (majority) decision.

THE SIZE OF THE MAJORITY The size of the majority also affects conformity rates. As the size of the majority increases, so does conformity, up to a point (Asch, 1951, 1956; Milgram, Bickman, & Berkowitz, 1969). Generally, as shown in Figure 7.4, there is a nonlinear relationship between the size of the majority and conformity. That is, majority influence significantly increases until some critical majority size is reached. After that, the addition of more majority members does not significantly increase conformity. For example, Milgram and colleagues (1969) found that increasing the number of individuals (confederates of the experimenter) on a sidewalk who looked upward toward the sky increased conformity (the percentage of passersby looking upward) up to a majority size of five and then leveled off (see Figure 7.4).

Figure 7.4

The effect of majority size on conformity. Conformity initially increases but eventually levels off.

Adapted from Milgram, Bickman, and Berkowitz (1969). Reprinted with permission.

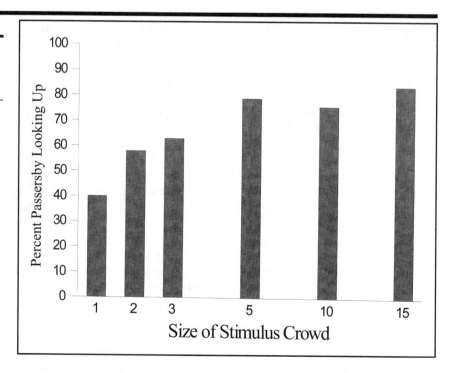

There is no absolute critical size of a majority after which addition of majority members does not significantly increase conformity. Milgram and colleagues found that conformity leveled off after a majority size of five. Asch (1951), using his line-judgment task, found that conformity leveled off after a majority size of three. Regardless of the critical size of the majority, the general nonlinear relationship between majority size and conformity is firmly established.

Why does conformity level off after some critical majority size? Two explanations have been suggested (Baron, Kerr, & Miller, 1992). First, as majority members are added beyond the critical point, the individual in the conformity situation might suspect that the additional majority members are going along to avoid making trouble in the group. If the individual conformer perceives this to be the motive for joining the majority, the power of the additional majority members is reduced. Second, as the size of the majority grows, each new majority member is probably noticed less. That is, the individual is more likely to notice a third person added to a majority of two than to notice a tenth person added to a majority of nine.

Increases in the size of a majority are most likely to produce increased conformity in normative social influence situations, when the situation causes us to question our perceptions and judgments (Campbell & Fairey, 1989). When a majority is arrayed against us, and we cannot obtain adequate information about the stimuli that we are to judge, we conform. This is exactly what happened in Asch's experiment.

Normative social influence also produces conformity when a judgment is easy and the individual is sure the group is wrong but cannot resist the pressure of the majority. This is what happened to Frank in the jury room. Informational influence was nil. The other jurors could not offer any information that Frank did not have already. They did not dispute the evidence. They made the judgment that the law, not the evidence, was wrong. The jurors wanted Frank to conform to this norm. Eventually, as we know, he did.

When you know you are right and the rest of the group is wrong, more conformity results when the majority comprises three members than if it comprises only one (Campbell & Fairey, 1989). This makes sense because it is normative influence that is operating in this situation. But what if you are not certain whether the majority is right or wrong? In this case, you search for information that could inform your decision, information that will help you make the right choice. It is informational influence that counts here. Just a few people, perhaps even one person can convince you through informational social influence if their information is persuasive (Campbell & Fairey, 1989).

HAVING A TRUE PARTNER   Often the changes caused by the forces producing conformity are fragile and easily disrupted. This is the case when we find that there is another person who supports our perceptions and actions in a given social situation. Imagine, for example, that you have been invited to a black-tie wedding reception at a posh country club on a Saturday night. When an invitation specifies black-tie, the norm is for men to wear tuxedos and women to wear formal dresses. Now, suppose that you don't want to dress so formally but feel you should because everyone else will (normative social influence). But then suppose that you speak to a friend who is also attending and who also doesn't want to wear a tuxedo or a formal dress. The two of you agree to wear less formal attire, and you feel comfortable with your decision. The next weekend, you are invited to another black-tie party, but this time your friend is not attending. What will you do this time? You decide to dress formally.

This example illustrates an important social psychological phenomenon. The **true partner effect** occurs when we perceive that there is someone who supports our position; we are then less likely to conform than if we are alone facing a unanimous majority. This effect was first demonstrated empirically by Asch (1951). In one variation of his experiment, Asch had a true partner emerge at some point during his conformity experiment. On a given trial, the true partner would break with the incorrect majority and support the real participant's judgments. The results of this manipulation were striking: Conformity was cut by nearly 80%! As in the example of the black-tie parties, when we have a true partner, we are better able to withstand the strong forces of normative social influence.

Why does this occur? There are many possible explanations. For example, when we violate a norm by ourselves, we draw attention to ourselves as deviant. Recall that some of Asch's participants conformed because they did not want to appear different. Apparently, it makes us very uncomfortable to be perceived by others as different. When we have a true partner, we can diffuse the pressure by convincing ourselves that we are not the only ones breaking a norm.

Another explanation for the true partner effect draws on the social comparison process (Festinger, 1954; Kruglanski & Mayseless, 1990). As discussed in chapter 2, social comparison theory proposes that we compare our thoughts, beliefs, and actions with those of others to find out if we are in agreement. When we find that we agree, we feel validated; it is rewarding when we receive such confirmation. Our confidence in our beliefs increases because they are shared with others.

Think back to the second black-tie party. Without a true partner, you bring your behavior into line with the norm in effect: wearing formal attire. Asch (1951) found the very same thing when he had the true partner withdraw his support of the participant. When the participant was abandoned, his conformity went back up to its previous level.

The true partner effect applies in jury deliberations; we saw that Frank experienced great distress when he was the only one holding out for conviction. Earlier in the deliberations, Frank had other jurors (true partners) who supported his view. When those jurors changed their votes, their support for Frank disappeared. Now, Frank faced not only a unanimous majority but also one that included two former true partners. Would things have turned out differently if one other juror had stuck with Frank? Perhaps. The courts have acknowledged that conformity pressures are greater when a person is the single advocate of a particular point of view.

GENDER AND CONFORMITY Besides investigating situational forces that affect conformity, social psychologists have investigated how individual characteristics affect conformity. Early research suggested that women were more likely to conform than men (Eagly & Carli, 1981). For example, 43% of the studies published before 1970 reported this phenomenon, in contrast to only 21% published after 1970. Did changes in the cultural climate make women less likely to conform? Or did early conformity studies have a

---

true partner effect
The phenomenon whereby an individual's tendency to conform with a majority position is reduced if there is one other person who supports the nonconforming individual's position.

male bias, as expressed in male-oriented tasks and a predominantly male environment? Research indicates that the nature of the task was not important in producing the observed gender differences, but the gender of the experimenter was. Generally, larger gender differences are found when a man runs the conformity experiment. No gender differences are found when a woman runs the experiment (Eagly & Carli, 1981).

An analysis of the research also shows that there are conditions under which women are more likely to conform than men and others under which men are more likely to conform than women (Eagly & Chrvala, 1986). For example, women are more likely to conform than men in group pressure situations—that is, under conditions of normative social influence—than in persuasion situations, where informational social influence is being applied (Eagly, 1978; Eagly & Carli, 1981).

Two explanations have been proposed for gender differences in conformity (Eagly, 1987). First, gender may serve as a status variable in newly formed groups. Traditionally, the female gender role is seen as weaker than the male role. In everyday life, males are more likely to hold positions of high status and power than women. Men are more likely to be in the position of "influencer" and women in the position of "influencee." The lower status of the female role may contribute to a greater predisposition to conform on the part of women, especially in group pressure situations. Second, women tend to be more sensitive than men to conformity pressures when their behavior is under surveillance—that is, when they have to state their opinions publicly (Eagly, Wood, & Fishbaugh, 1981). When women must make their opinions public, they are more likely than men to conform. In the Asch paradigm, participants were required to state their opinions publicly; this favors women conforming more than men.

HISTORICAL AND CULTURAL DIFFERENCES IN CONFORMITY
Asch conducted his classic experiment on conformity during the 1950s in the United States. The sociocultural climate that existed at the time favored conformity. The country was still under the stifling influence of "McCarthy-ism," which vilified those who failed to conform to "normal" American ideals. This climate may have contributed in significant ways to the levels of conformity Asch observed (Larsen, 1982; Perrin & Spencer, 1981). Researchers working in England failed to obtain conformity effects as strong as those Asch had obtained (Perrin & Spencer, 1981). This raised a question: Were the Asch findings limited to a particular time and culture?

Unfortunately, this question has no simple answer. Evidence suggests that within the United States, rates of conformity vary with the sociopolitical climate (Larsen, 1974, 1982). The conformity rate in the early 1970s was 62.5% (that is, 62.5% of participants conformed at least once in an Asch-type experiment) compared to a rate of 78.9% during the early 1980s (Larsen, 1982). Compare this to Asch's (1956) rate of 76.5%. Results like these suggest that conformity rates may be tied to the cultural climate in force at the time of a study.

The evidence for cross-cultural influences is less clear. A host of studies suggest that conformity is a fairly general phenomenon across cultures. Conformity has been demonstrated in European countries such as Belgium, Holland, and Norway (Doms & Van Avermaet, 1980; Milgram, 1961; Vlaander & van Rooijen, 1985) as well as in non-Western countries such as Japan, China, and some South American countries (Huang & Harris, 1973; Matsuda, 1985;

Sistrunk & Clement, 1970). Additionally, some research suggests that there may be cross-cultural differences in conformity when North Americans are compared to non-North Americans (see Furnham, 1984, for a review) and across other non-North American cultures (Milgram, 1961).

What is the bottom line? It is safe to say that the Asch conformity effect is fairly general across cultures. However, some cultural groups may conform at different levels than others. Conformity also appears to fluctuate in size across time within a culture.

MINORITY INFLUENCE

In the classic film *Twelve Angry Men*, Henry Fonda portrayed a juror who was firmly convinced that a criminal defendant was not guilty. The only problem was that the other 11 jurors believed the defendant was guilty. As the jurors began to deliberate, Fonda held fast to his belief in the defendant's innocence. As the film progressed, Fonda convinced each of the other 11 jurors that the defendant was innocent. The jury finally returned a verdict of not guilty.

In this fictional portrayal of a group at work, a single unwavering individual not only was able to resist conformity pressure but also convinced the majority that they were wrong. Such an occurrence would be extremely rare in a real trial (Kalven & Zeisel, 1966). With an 11 to 1 split, the jury would almost always go in the direction of the majority (Isenberg, 1986; Kalven & Zeisel, 1966). The film, however, does raise an interesting question: Can a steadfast minority bring about change in the majority? For almost 35 years after Sherif's original experiments on norm formation, this question went unanswered. It was not until 1969 that social psychologists began to investigate the influence of the minority on the majority. This line of investigation has been pursued more by European social psychologists than American social psychologists.

Can a Minority Influence the Majority?

In the first published experiment on minority influence, researchers devised an Asch-like conformity situation. Participants were led to believe that they were taking part in a study on color perception (Moscovici, Lage, & Naffrechoux, 1969). Participants were shown a series of slides and asked to say the color of the slide aloud. Unbeknown to the real participants (four, making up the majority), two confederates (comprising the minority) had been instructed to make an error on certain trials—by calling a blue slide green, for example. Researchers found that 8.42% of the judgments made by the real participants were in the direction of the minority, compared to only .025% of the judgments in a control condition in which there was no incorrect minority. In fact, 32% of the participants conformed to the incorrect minority. Thus, a minority can have a surprisingly powerful effect on the majority.

In this experiment, the minority participants were consistent in their judgments. Researchers theorized that consistency of behavior is a strong determinant of the social influence a minority can exert on a majority (Moscovici et al., 1969). An individual in a minority who expresses a deviant opinion consistently may be seen as having a high degree of confidence in his or her judgments. In the color perception experiment, majority participants rated minority members as more confident in their judgments than themselves. The consistent minority caused the majority to call into question the validity of their own judgments.

What is it about consistency that contributes to the power of a minority to influence a majority? Differing perceptions and attributions made about consistent and inconsistent minorities are important factors. A consistent minority is usually perceived as being more confident and less willing to compromise than an inconsistent minority (Wolf, 1979). A consistent minority may also be perceived as having high levels of competence, especially if it is a relatively large minority (Nemeth, 1986). Generally, we assume that if a number of people share a point of view, it must be correct. As the size of the minority increases, so does perceived competence (Nemeth, 1986).

Although research shows that consistency increases the power of a minority to influence a majority, consistency must be carefully defined. Will a minority that adopts a particular view and remains intransigent be as persuasive as one that is more flexible? Two styles of consistency have been distinguished: rigid and negotiating (Mugny, 1975). In the rigid style, the minority advocates a position that is counter to the norm adopted by the majority but is unwilling to show flexibility. In the negotiating style, the minority, although remaining consistent, shows a willingness to be flexible. Each of these styles contributes to the minority's image in the eyes of the majority (Mugny, 1975). The rigid minority is perceived in a less positive way than a negotiating minority, perhaps leading to perceptions that the rigid minority's goal is to block the majority. Conversely, the negotiating minority may be perceived as having compromise as its goal.

Generally, research suggests that a more flexible minority has more power to influence the majority than a rigid one, as long as the perception of minority consistency remains (Mugny, 1975; Nemeth, Swedlund, & Kanki, 1974). The perception of the minority is also partially dependent on the degree to which it is willing to modify its position in response to new information. A minority that adapts to new information is more influential than a minority that holds a position irrespective of any additional information (Nemeth et al., 1974).

Majority and Minority Influence: Two Processes or One?

Social influence, as we have seen, operates in two directions: from majority to minority and from minority to majority. The discovery of minority influence raised an issue concerning the underlying social psychological processes controlling majority and minority influence. Do two different processes control majority and minority influence, or is there a single process controlling both?

THE TWO-PROCESS MODEL Judgments expressed by a minority may be more likely to make people think about the arguments raised (Moscovici, 1980). This suggests that two different processes operate: majority influence, which occurs almost exclusively on a public level, and minority influence, which seems to operate on a private level. Majority influence, according to the two-process approach, operates through the application of pressure. People agree with a majority because of public pressure, but often they really don't accept the majority's view on a private level. The fact that the majority exerts great psychological pressure is reflected in the finding that people feel very anxious when they find themselves in disagreement with the majority (Asch, 1956; Nemeth, 1986). However, as soon as majority pressure is removed, people return to their original beliefs. Majority influence, in this model, is like normative influence—it does not necessarily have a lasting effect. For example, Frank, in the Leroy Reed case, changed his verdict in response to group pressure. However, he probably went home still believing, deep down, that Reed should have been convicted.

Minority influence, according to the two-process approach, operates by making people think more deeply about the minority's position (Nemeth, 1986). In doing so, they evaluate all the aspects of the minority view. The majority decides to agree with the minority because they are converted to its position (Nemeth, 1992). Minority influence is like informational influence. The character played by Henry Fonda in *Twelve Angry Men* convinced the majority members to change their votes through informational social influence. Thus, unlike the majority influencing Frank in the Reed case through normative pressure, Fonda changed the minds of the other jurors by applying persuasive informational arguments.

A SINGLE-PROCESS MODEL: SOCIAL IMPACT THEORY

The dual process model suggests that there are different psychological processes underlying majority and minority influence. A competing view, the single-process approach to social influence, suggests that one psychological process accounts for both majority and minority influence. The first theory designed to explain majority and minority influence with a single underlying process was proposed by Bibb Latané (Latané, 1981; Latané & Wolf, 1981). Latané's **social impact theory** suggests that social influence processes can be summed up by the formula:

$$Influence = f(SIN)$$

where S represents the strength of the source of the influence, I represents the immediacy (or closeness) of the source of influence, and N represents the number of influence sources.

Latané (1981) suggested an analogy between the effect of social influence and the effect of light bulbs. If, for example, you have a bulb of a certain strength (e.g., 50 watts) and place it 10 feet from a wall, it will cast light of a given intensity against the wall. If you move the bulb closer to the wall (immediacy), the intensity of the light on the wall increases. Moving it farther from the wall decreases the intensity. Increasing or decreasing the wattage of the bulb (the strength of the source) also changes the intensity of the light cast on the wall. Finally, if you add a second bulb (number), the intensity of light will increase. Similarly, the amount of social influence increases if the strength of a source of influence is increased (e.g., if the source's credibility is enhanced), if the source's immediacy is increased, or if the number of influence sources is increased.

Latané also suggested that there is a nonlinear relationship between the number of sources and the amount of influence. According to Latane, adding a second influence source to a solitary source will have greater impact than adding the 101st source to 100 sources. Social impact theory predicts that influence increases rapidly between zero and three sources and then diminishes beyond that point, which is consistent with the research on the effects of majority size.

Social impact theory can be used to account for both minority and majority influence processes. In a minority influence situation, social influence forces operate on both the minority and majority, pulling each other toward

social impact theory
A theory stating that social influence is a function of the combination of the strength, immediacy, and number of influence sources.

the other's position (Latané, 1981). Latané suggested that minority influence will depend on the strength, immediacy, and number of influence sources in the minority, just as in majority influence. Thus, a minority of two should have greater influence on the majority than a minority of one, a prediction that has received empirical support (Arbuthnot & Wayner, 1982; Moscovici & Lage, 1976).

Although there is evidence supporting the two-process and single-process models alike, the weight of the evidence favors the single-process model.

COMPLIANCE: RESPONDING TO A DIRECT REQUEST

Compliance occurs when you modify your behavior in response to a direct request from another person. In compliance situations, the person making the request has no power to force you to do as he or she asks. For example, your neighbor can ask that you move your car so that she can back a truck into her driveway. However, assuming your car is legally parked, she has no legal power to force you to move your car. If you go out and move your car, you have (voluntarily) complied with her request. In this section, we explore three compliance strategies: the foot-in-the-door technique, the door-in-the-face technique, and low-balling. We start by looking at the foot-in-the-door technique.

compliance
Social influence process which involves modifying behavior after accepting a direct request.

Foot-in-the-Door Technique

Imagine that you are doing some shopping in a mall and a person approaches you. The solicitor asks you to sign a petition condemning drunk driving. Now most people would be happy to sign such a petition. After all, it is for a cause that most people support, and it takes a minimal amount of effort to sign a petition. Imagine further that you agree to this initial request and sign the petition. After you sign the petition, the solicitor then asks you for a $5 donation to PADD (People Against Drunk Driving). You find yourself digging into your wallet for a $5 bill to contribute.

Consider another scenario. You are again in the mall doing some shopping, when a person from PADD approaches you and asks you for a $5 donation to help fight drunk driving. This time, instead of digging out your wallet, you tell the solicitor to hit the road, and you go back to your shopping.

These two scenarios illustrate a common compliance effect: the **foot-in-the-door technique (FITD)**. In the first scenario, you were first asked to do something small and effortless, to sign a petition. Next, you were asked for a donation, a request that was a bit more costly than simply signing a petition. Once you agreed to the first, smaller, request, you were more inclined to agree to the second, larger, request. This is the essence of the FITD technique. When people agree to a small request before a larger one is made, they are more likely to agree to the larger request than if the larger request was made alone.

foot-in-the-door technique (FITD)
A social influence process in which a small request is made before a larger request resulting in more compliance to the larger request than if the larger request were made alone.

In the experiment that first demonstrated the FITD technique (Freedman & Fraser, 1966), participants were contacted in their homes by a representative of a fictitious marketing research company under four separate conditions: (1) Some participants were asked if they would be willing to answer a few simple questions about the soap products used in their households (a request to which most participants agreed). The questions were asked only if the participant agreed. This was called the "performance" condition. (2) Other participants were also asked if they would be willing to answer a few simple questions, but when they agreed, they were told that the company was simply lining up participants for a survey and that they would be contacted later. This was called the "agree-only" condition. (3) Still other participants were contacted, told of the questionnaire, and told that the call was merely to familiarize people with the marketing company. This was the "familiarization" condition. (4) A final group of participants was contacted only once. This was the single-contact (control) condition.

Participants in the first three conditions were called again a few days later. This time a larger request was made. The participants were asked if they would allow a team of five or six people to come into their homes for 2 hours and do an inventory of soap products. In the single-contact condition, participants received only this request. The results of the experiment, shown in Figure 7.5, were striking. Notice that over 50% of the subjects in the performance condition (which is the FITD technique) agreed to the second, larger request, compared to only about 22% of the subjects in the single-contact group. Notice also that simply agreeing to the smaller request or being familiarized with the company was not sufficient to significantly increase compliance with the larger request. The FITD effect occurs only if the smaller task is actually performed.

Since this seminal experiment, conducted in 1966, many other studies have verified the FITD effect. Researchers quickly turned their attention to investigating the underlying causes for the effect.

Figure 7.5

Compliance to a large request as a function of the nature of an initial, smaller request. The highest level of compliance for a large request was realized after participants performed a smaller request first, illustrating the foot-in-the-door technique.

Based on data from Freedman and Fraser (1966).

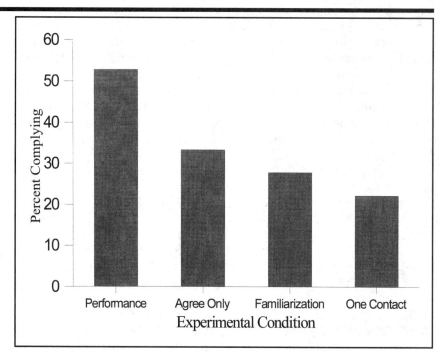

WHY IT WORKS: THREE HYPOTHESES One explanation for the FITD effect is provided by self-perception theory (Bem, 1972). Recall from chapter 6 that we sometimes learn about ourselves from observing our own behavior and making inferences about the causes for that behavior. According to the self-perception hypothesis, the FITD works because agreeing to the first request causes changes in our perceptions of ourselves. Once we agree to the smaller, original request, we perceive ourselves as the type of person who gives help in that particular situation, and thus we are more likely to give similar help in the future. Generally, research has supported this idea (Dejong, 1979; Goldman, Seever, & Seever, 1982; Snyder & Cunningham, 1975).

Originally it was believed that merely agreeing to any initial request was sufficient to produce the FITD effect. However, we now know differently. FITD works when the initial request is sufficiently large to elicit a commitment from an individual and the individual attributes the commitment to internal, dispositional factors. That is, the person reasons, "I am the type of person who cooperates with people doing a market survey" (or contributes to PADD, or helps in particular types of situations).

Although self-perception theory has been widely accepted as an explanation for FITD, another explanation has also been proposed. This is the *perceptual contrast hypothesis*, which suggests that the FITD effect occurs because the smaller, initial request acts as an "anchor" (a standard of reference) against which other requests are judged (Cantrill & Seibold, 1986). The later request can be either assimilated to or contrasted with the anchor. Theoretically, in the FITD situation, the second, larger request is assimilated to the anchor (the smaller, first request) and is seen as less burdensome than if it were presented alone. That is, the second and larger request is seen as more reasonable because of the first request with which the person has already agreed. Although this hypothesis has generated some interest, there is not as much support for it as there is for the self-perception explanation.

Another explanation for the effectiveness of the FITD effect focuses on the thought processes of its recipients. It was suggested that information about the solicitor's and recipient's behavior affects compliance in the FITD effect (Tybout, Sternthal, & Calder, 1983). According to this view, targets of the FITD technique undergo changes in attitudes and cognitions about the requested behavior. Compliance on a second request depends, in part, on the information available in the participant's memory that relates to the issue (Homik, 1988).

This hypothesis was put to test in a field experiment involving requests for contributions to the Israeli Cancer Society (ICA; Hornik, 1988). Participants were first asked to fulfill a small request: to distribute ICA pamphlets. Participants agreeing to this request were given a sticker to display on their doors. One version of the sticker touted the participant's continuing involvement in the ICA campaign. A second version suggested that participants had fulfilled their obligation completely. Ten days later participants were contacted again and asked to donate money to the ICA. Additionally, the control group of participants were contacted for the first time.

The results of this study confirmed the power of the FITD technique to produce compliance (compared to the control group). Those participants who received the sticker implying continued commitment to the ICA showed greater compliance with the later request than did either those who had received the sticker shoving that an obligation was fulfilled or those in the control group. Participants in the continued-commitment group most likely held attitudes about themselves, had information available, and had self-perceptions suggesting continued commitment. This translated into greater compliance.

LIMITS OF THE TECHNIQUE   As you can see, the FITD technique is a very powerful tool for gaining compliance. Although the effect has been replicated over and over, it has its limits. One important limitation of the FITD technique is that the requests being made must be socially acceptable (Dillard, Hunter, & Burgoon, 1984). People do not comply with requests they find objectionable. Another limitation to the FITD technique is the cost of the behavior called for. When a high-cost behavior is called for (e.g., donating blood), the FITD technique does not work very well (Cialdini & Ascani, 1976; Foss & Dempsey, 1979). Does this mean that the FITD technique cannot be used to increase socially desirable but high-cost behaviors like blood donation? Not necessarily. A small modification in the technique may prove effective: adding a moderately strong request between the initial small and final large requests. Adding such an intermediate request increases the power of the FITD technique (Goldman, Creason, & McCall, 1981). A gradually increasing, graded series of requests may alter the potential donor's self-perceptions, which are strongly associated with increased compliance in the FITD paradigm.

Interestingly, although the FITD technique does not increase blood donations significantly, it can be used to induce people to become organ donors (Carducci & Deuser, 1984). Why the difference between these two donation behaviors? It may be that the two behaviors involve differing levels of commitment. Blood donation takes time and involves some pain and discomfort. Organ donation, which takes place after death, does not. Blood donation requires action; organ donation requires only agreement. It appears that blood donation is seen as a higher cost behavior than organ donation. Under such high-cost conditions the FITD technique, in its original form, does not work very well.

Door-in-the-Face Technique

Imagine that you are sitting at home reading a book when the telephone rings. The caller turns out to be a solicitor for a charity that provides food baskets for needy families at Thanksgiving. The caller describes the charity program and asks if you would be willing to donate $250 to feed a family of 10. To this request you react as many people do: "*What!* I can't possibly give that much!" In response, the caller offers you several other alternatives, each requiring a smaller and smaller donation (e.g., $100, $50, $25, and $10). Each time the caller asks about an alternative you feel more and more like Ebenezer Scrooge, and finally you agree to provide a $25 food basket.

Notice the tactic used by the solicitor. You were first hit with a large request, which you found unreasonable, and then a smaller one, which you agreed to. The technique the solicitor used was just the opposite of what would take place in the FITD technique (a small request followed by a larger

Figure 7.6

The door-in-the-face technique may activate a norm of reciprocity. When we think a solicitor has made a concession, we may feel compelled to make one ourselves. This technique also works because we don't want to appear to be callous or cheap.

one). In this example you have fallen prey to the **door-in-the-face technique** (**DITF**; Figure 7.6).

After being induced into buying a candy bar from a Boy Scout who used the DITF technique, one researcher decided to investigate the power of this technique to induce compliance (Cialdini, 1993). Participants were approached and asked if they would be willing to escort a group of "juvenile delinquents" to a local zoo (Cialdini et al., 1975). Not surprisingly, most participants refused this request. But in the DITF condition, this request was preceded by an even larger one, to spend 2 hours per week as a counselor for juvenile delinquents for at least 2 years! It is even less surprising that this request was turned down. However, when the request to escort delinquents to the zoo followed the larger request, commitments for the zoo trip increased dramatically (Figure 7.7). Subsequent studies verified the power of the DITF technique to induce compliance (e.g., Cialdini & Ascani, 1976; Williams & Williams, 1989).

Some researchers have suggested that the DITF technique works because the target of the influence attempt feels compelled to match the concession (from the first, larger request to the smaller, second request) made by the solicitor (Cialdini et al., 1975). The social psychological mechanism operating here is the norm of reciprocity (Gouldner, 1960). The **norm of reciprocity** states that we should help those who help us. Remember Aesop's fable about the mouse who came across a lion with a thorn in its foot? Despite the obvious danger to itself, the mouse helped the lion by removing the thorn. Later, when the lion came on the mouse in need of help, the lion reciprocated by helping the mouse. This is an illustration of the norm of reciprocity. The norm of reciprocity is apparently a very powerful force in our social lives (Cialdini, 1988).

Implied in this original statement of the norm is the idea that we may feel compelled to reciprocate when we perceive that another person is making a concession to us. This norm helps explain the DITF effect. It goes something like this: When a solicitor first makes a large request and then immediately backs off when we refuse and comes back with a smaller request, we perceive that the solicitor is making a concession. We feel pressure to reciprocate by also making a concession. Our concession is to agree to the

door-in-the-face technique (DITF)
A social influence process in which a large request is made before a smaller request resulting in more compliance to the smaller request than if the smaller request were made alone.

norm of reciprocity
A social norm stating that you should help those who help you and should not injure those who help you.

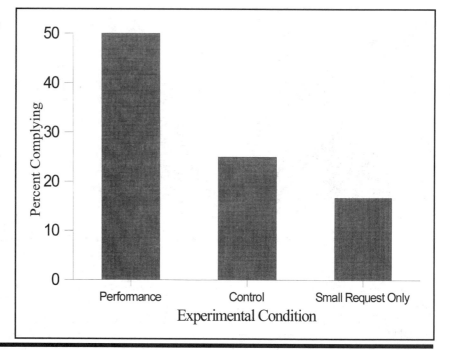

Figure 7.7

Compliance to a small request as a function of the nature of an initial request. Participants complied more with a second, smaller request if it followed a larger request, demonstrating the door-in-the-face technique.

Based on data from Cialdini and colleagues (1975).

smaller request, because refusing the smaller request would threaten our sense of well-being tied to the norm of reciprocity. In the DITF technique, then, our attention becomes focused on the behavior of the solicitor, who appears to have made a concession (Williams & Williams, 1989). If we don't reciprocate, we may later feel guilty or fear that we will appear unreasonable and cheap in the light of the concession the solicitor made.

The power of the norm of reciprocity has been shown in empirical research. For example, one study found that more participants agreed to buy raffle tickets from someone who had previously done them a favor (bought the participant a soft drink) than from someone who had not done them a favor (Regan, 1971). In this study, the norm of reciprocity exerted a greater influence than overall liking for the solicitor. Research has also shown that the norm of reciprocity is central to the DITF effect (Cialdini, 1993; Cialdini et al., 1975; Goldman & Creason, 1981). If a solicitor makes more than one concession (when a solicitor reads a list of smaller and smaller requests), compliance is higher than if the solicitor makes only one concession (Goldman & Creason, 1981). This is especially true if the intermediate request is moderate (Goldman, Creason, & McCall, 1981).

Although there is support for the role of reciprocity in the DITF effect, some researchers have questioned its validity and have suggested alternative explanations for these situations. One such alternative is the perceptual contrast hypothesis. As discussed earlier, this hypothesis focuses on the contrast in size between the first and second requests. Applied to the DITF effect, the perceptual contrast hypothesis suggests that individuals agree to the second (small) request because it appears more reasonable in the light of the first (large) request. The individual may perceive that the second request is less costly than the first. Although there is some evidence against this view

(Shanab & Isonio, 1982), there is also evidence to support it (Miller, Seligman, Clark, & Bush, 1976; Shanab & O'Neill, 1979).

A second possible explanation for the DITF effect is the *worthy person hypothesis* (Foehl & Goldman, 1983). In most DITF studies, the solicitation is made for a worthy cause (Foehl & Goldman, 1983). Refusing the second, smaller request in a DITF experiment may make individuals feel guilty because they have rejected a worthy request.

Finally, there is evidence that our fear of appearing cheap may be an important factor in falling prey to solicitations. The number of people contributing to the American Cancer Society was increased by simply tacking on the statement "even a penny would help" to a neutral solicitation pitch (Cialdini & Schroeder, 1976). Adding the even-a-penny statement makes even a paltry contribution legitimate and may make the individual feel cheap or guilty for not giving (Cialdini & Schroeder, 1976). The even-a-penny statement did not affect the amount of money contributed. Apparently, once we get over the hump of deciding to give, we give as much as we would have anyway.

Low-Ball Technique

Yet another technique for inducing compliance is the **low-ball technique** (also known as *low-balling*). In low-balling, a solicitor (usually a salesperson) makes you an offer that seems too good to be true. For example, a car salesperson may quote you an extremely low price for a car. The catch, of course, is that she must have it approved by the sales manager. She leaves for some time, leaving you to "stew." During this stewing period, you probably are convincing yourself that this is the car you want (Cialdini, 1988). When she returns, she informs you that the manager couldn't possibly sell the car for such a low price or that there was some error made in calculating the price (e.g., forgetting to add in the price of rustproofing). She makes a new offer that is higher than the original offer. If you find yourself buying the car for the higher price, you have fallen prey to low-balling.

Low-balling, much like the FITD and DITF techniques, is a two-step process. First, an initial commitment is obtained from the target. Car salespersons often try to get you to give them a check to "show good faith" and sign a form with your "offer" (the low price). The second step is to reveal the higher price, either through a hidden cost (e.g., dealer preparation,) or through management's refusal of the low offer.

Like the other compliance strategies, low-balling does induce compliance. For example, in one study, participants were asked to be in an experiment that began at 7:00 A.M. Under these conditions, only 31% of those asked said they would be willing to participate. However, if they were "low-balled"—told about the starting time only after they had agreed to participate—56% of those asked agreed (Cialdini, Cacioppo, Bassett, & Miller, 1978).

The two principal psychological mechanisms operating in the low-ball technique are commitment and consistency (Cialdini, 1993). Commitment occurs when you take significant steps toward a particular course of action. For example, once you decide to make an offer on a car and give a deposit, you are taking significant steps toward buying that car. Once you make this

low-ball technique (or low-balling)

A social influence process in which a solicitor makes you an offer that seems too good to be true but then backs off and proposes a less attractive alternative.

initial commitment to the salesperson, you are likely to follow through on it (Burger & Petty, 1981). There is evidence that commitment to a person (e.g., a salesperson) is more important than commitment to the behavior (e.g., buying a car) in compliance (Burger & Petty, 1981). So, you may not be so inclined to buy the car if you negotiate first with the salesperson and then with the sales manager than if you had continued negotiating with the original salesperson.

Commitment affects our behavior in two ways. First, we typically look for reasons to justify a commitment after making it (Cialdini, 1993). This is consistent with cognitive dissonance theory, as discussed in chapter 6. Typically, we devise justifications that support our decision to buy the car. Second, we also have a desire to maintain consistency between our thoughts and actions and among our actions (Cialdini, 1993; Festinger, 1957). When the salesperson returns with a higher offer, we may be inclined to accept the offer because refusal would be dissonant with all the cognitions and justifications we developed during the stewing period.

Compliance Techniques: Summing Up

We described and analyzed three different compliance techniques. Are they all equally effective, or are some more effective than others? Research indicates that the DITF technique elicits more compliance than the FITD technique (Brownstein & Katzev, 1985; Cialdini & Ascani, 1976). There is also evidence that a combined FITD–DITF strategy elicits greater compliance than either of the techniques alone (Goldman, 1986). However, low-balling may be more effective for gaining compliance than either the FITD or the DITF techniques (Brownstein & Katzev, 1985). In one experiment, participants were stopped and asked to donate money to a museum fund drive. The request was made under either FITD, DITF, low-ball, or a control condition. The average amount of money donated was highest under the low-ball conditions, compared to the FITD, DITF, and control conditions (which did not differ significantly from one another).

All of these compliance techniques have been and will be used to induce people to buy products (some of which they may want and some of which they may not want). The psychological mechanisms of reciprocity, commitment, consistency, and perceptual contrast operate to varying degrees to produce compliance. Because we all share these mechanisms, we all find ourselves on occasion doing something we don't really want to do. Sellers of all types use compliance techniques to sell their products (Cialdini, 1993). The best way to guard ourselves against these techniques is to recognize and understand them when they are used.

OBEDIENCE

obedience
A social influence process involving modification of behavior in response to a command from an authority figure.

When we modify our behavior in response to a direct order from someone in authority, **obedience** has occurred. Certainly no group, no society, could exist very long if it couldn't make its members obey laws, rules, and customs. Generally, obedience is not a bad thing. Traffic flows much easier when there are motor vehicle laws, for example. But when the rules and norms people are made to obey are negative, obedience is one of the blights of society. This kind of obedience is called *destructive obedience*. Destructive obedience occurs when a person obeys an authority figure and behaves in ways that are counter to accepted standards of moral behavior, ways that conflict with the demands of conscience.

Unfortunately, destructive obedience—the form of obedience we are most concerned with in this chapter—is a recurring theme in human history. Throughout human history, there are many instances when individuals carried out orders that resulted in harm or death to others. At the Nuremberg trials following World War II, many Nazi leaders responsible for murdering millions of people fell back on the explanation that they were following orders. More recently, in the ethnic violence between Serbs and Bosnians in the former Yugoslavia, Serbian soldiers allegedly received orders to rape Muslim women in captured towns or villages. Islamic tradition condemns women who have been raped or who become pregnant outside marriage; these orders were intended to destroy the fabric of Muslim family life. The Serbian soldiers had been ordered to engage in blatantly immoral and illegal behavior. More recently, mass murders took place in Kosovo at the behest of the Serbian leadership.

Destructive obedience doesn't only crop up in such large-scale situations. Destructive obedience can also manifest itself so that your everyday activities may be threatened. For example, Tarnow (2000) cites evidence that excessive obedience to the Captain's orders may be responsible for up to 25% of all airplane crashes. One form of obedience seems to be particularly problematic. When the nonflying crew member (copilot) does not correctly monitor and subsequently challenge an error made by the pilot. These types of errors are made in 80% of airline accidents (Tarnow, 2000). Tarnow suggests that the atmosphere in the cockpit is one of a Captain's absolute authority. The Captain is given these powers by law. However, more power flows from the Captain's greater flying experience than the copilot (to become a Captain, you need at least 1,500 hours of flight time vs. 200 hours for a first officer). The power stemming from the law and greater experience makes it difficult for junior officers to challenge the Captain, even in cases where the Captain's decision is clearly wrong (Tarnow, 2000). The consequences of this obedience dynamic may be tragic.

The Banality of Evil: Eichmann's Fallacy

It would be a relief to believe that those carrying out crimes of obedience are deviant individuals predisposed to antisocial behavior. Unfortunately, history tells us that those who perpetrate evil are often quite ordinary. William Calley, who was in command of the platoon that committed a massacre at the Vietnamese village of My Lai, was ordinary before and after My Lai. So was Adolph Eichmann, one of the architects of the Holocaust and the Nazi officer responsible for the delivery of European Jews to concentration camps in World War II.

Eichmann's job was to ensure that the death camps had a steady flow of victims. He secured the railroad cattle cars needed to transport the human cargo. His job was managerial, bureaucratic; often he had to fight with competing German interests to get enough boxcars. When the war was over, Eichmann, a most-wanted war criminal, escaped to Argentina. From 1945 to 1961, he worked as a laborer outside Buenos Aires. His uneventful existence ended in 1961 when he was captured by Israeli secret agents, who spirited him to Israel. There he stood trial for crimes against humanity. After a long trial, Eichmann was found guilty and was later hanged.

We often assume that evil deeds are done by evil individuals. Most often, however, evil deeds are done by quite ordinary individuals. This photo of the unassuming Adolph Eichmann, the architect of the Holocaust against the Jews, illustrates this point. What would you think of him if you bumped into him at the mall and did not know who he was?

The Israelis constructed a special clear, bulletproof witness box for Eichmann to appear in during the trial. They were afraid that someone in Israel might decide to mete out some personal justice. What did the man in the glass booth took like? Eichmann was a short, bald man whose glasses slipped down his nose now and then. You could walk past him a hundred times on the street and never notice him. During the trial, Eichmann portrayed himself as a man anxious to please his superiors, ambitious for advancement. Killing people was a distasteful but necessary part of his job. Personally, he had no real hatred of the Jews. He was just following orders.

Philosopher and social critic Hannah Arendt observed Eichmann in the dock. She was struck by the wide gap between the ordinariness of the man and the brutal deeds for which he was on trial. In her book, *Eichmann in Jerusalem: A Report on the Banality of Evil* (1963), Arendt essentially accepted Eichmann's defense. Her analysis of Eichmann suggested that evil is often very commonplace. Those who carry out acts of destructive obedience are often ordinary people, rather like you and me.

People were shocked by Eichmann and by Arendt's analysis. They had expected a Nazi war criminal to be the epitome of evil. There was a prevailing belief that evil deeds are done by evil people, a belief referred to as **Eichmann's fallacy** (Brown, 1986). This is really the question we would like to answer: Do evil deeds always lead us back to an evil person? Although it might make us feel better if the answer to this question were yes, we see in this chapter that things are not, unfortunately, so simple.

Eichmann's fallacy
The belief that evil deeds are done only by evil people.

Ultimately, Who Is Responsible for Evil Deeds?

After World War II, the Allies tried many of the high-ranking Nazis who, like Eichmann, claimed innocence. Their principal defense was to shift responsibility to their superiors: They were only following orders. More recently, a former East German border guard, Ingo Heinrich, was brought to trial for his role in preventing East German citizens from escaping to the west during the height of the cold war. Heinrich, along with his fellow border guards, had

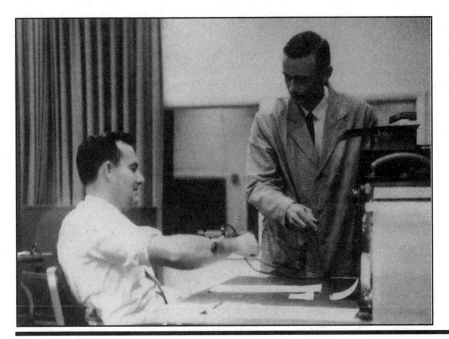

Stanley Milgram's "shock" machine used in his famous experiments on obedience. Participants used the switches shown to deliver an increasing level of electric shock to the learner. Of course, no shocks were delivered at all.

orders to shoot to kill anyone attempting to escape over the Berlin Wall. Heinrich did just that. But some of his comrades, under the same orders, shot over the heads of escapees. After the fall of the Berlin Wall and the reunification of Germany, Heinrich was arrested and charged with murder. He was eventually convicted and sentenced to 3.5 years in prison.

The cases of Eichmann and Heinrich raise some important issues about responsibility. Is "I was only following orders" a valid defense? Does it erase personal responsibility? Or should individuals be held accountable for their behavior, even if they were following orders? On the surface it would appear that Eichmann and Heinrich were personally responsible for their behavior. However, a deeper examination of authority and its effects on behavior suggests a more complex picture, a picture with many aspects. These issues and questions served as the catalyst for what are probably the most famous experiments in social psychology, the obedience experiments designed and conducted by Stanley Milgram.

Milgram's Experiments on Obedience

How does one test destructive obedience in a laboratory setting? The late Stanley Milgram devised a simple yet powerful situation. Before we look at it, let's consider the sociohistorical "climate" in the United States at the time. The year was 1962. Vietnam was but a blip on the back pages of the newspapers. The Kennedy assassinations had not yet occurred, nor had the murder of Martin Luther King, Jr., Watergate, or the riots in the streets of Newark, Detroit, and Watts. This was America before the real 1960s began, still holding on to some of the innocence, however illusory, of the 1950s. This context is important to consider because it may have influenced how people behaved in Milgram's experiments.

THE PARTICIPANT'S PERSPECTIVE   Let's begin by considering what these experiments looked like from a participant's perspective (Elms, 1972). Imagine you are living in New Haven, Connecticut. One day you notice an ad in the paper asking for volunteers for an experiment on learning and memory at nearby Yale University. The researchers are clearly seeking a good representation of the general population. The ad piques your curiosity, and you decide to sign up for the experiment.

When you arrive for the experiment, a young man, Mr. Williams, Dr. Milgram's associate, writes out a check to each of you for $4.50. Williams tells you that little is known about the impact of punishment on learning, and that is what this experiment is about. You become a bit concerned when Williams says that one of you will be a learner and the other will be a teacher. Your fears about getting punished soon evaporate when you draw lots to see who will be the learner and you draw the role of the teacher.

Preliminaries out of the way, Williams leads you both into a room past an ominous-looking piece of equipment labeled "Shock Generator, Thorpe ZLB . . . Output 15 volts–450 volts" (Milgram, 1974). The learner, Mr. Wallace, is told to sit in a straight-backed metal chair. Williams coolly tells you to help strap Wallace's arms down to prevent "excessive movement" during the experiment, which you do. Williams then applies a white paste to Wallace's arms, which he says is electrode paste, "to avoid blisters and burns." Wallace is now worried, and he asks if there is any danger. Williams says, "Although the shocks can be extremely painful, they cause no permanent tissue damage" (Elms, 1972, p. 114).

In front of the learner is a row of switches that he will use to respond to your questions. Williams tells you that a light panel in the other room will register the learner's responses. If his answers are correct, you, the teacher, tell him so. If incorrect, you deliver an electric shock from the shock generator.

It's time to start the experiment. You leave Wallace strapped to the shock generator and follow Williams into the next room. He places you before a control panel that has 30 levers, each with a little red light and a big purple light above. The lights have signs above them reading 15 volts, 30 volts, 45 volts, and so on, up to 450 volts. There are also printed descriptions of the shock levels above the labels, reading Slight Shock, Moderate Shock, Strong Shock, Intense Shock, Extreme Intense Shock, and finally, over the last few switches, in red, Danger: Severe Shock XXXXX. At this point, you hope that Wallace is brighter than he looks (Elms, 1972).

Before you begin the experiment, Williams gives you a sample shock of 45 volts, which gives you a little jolt. Next, you are told that your task is to teach Wallace several lists of word pairs, such as blue–box, nice–day, wild–duck. You read the entire list of word pairs and then test him, one pair at a time, by providing the first word from each pair.

At first the test is uneventful; Wallace makes no errors. Then he makes his first mistake, and you are required to give him a 15-volt shock. Williams tells you that for every error after that, you are to increase the shock by 15 volts. On subsequent trials Wallace makes frequent errors. When you get to 105 volts, you hear Wallace yell through the wall, "Hey, this really hurts!"

Williams, cool as ever, doesn't seem to notice. You certainly do. At 150 volts, the moaning Wallace yells, "Experimenter, get me out of here! I won't be in the experiment any more. I refuse to go on!" (Elms, 1972, p. 115). You look at Williams. He says softly but firmly, "Continue."

Williams brings you more word-pair lists. You begin to wonder what you and Wallace have gotten into for $4.50. You are now at 255 volts, Intense Shock. Wallace screams after every shock. Whenever you ask Williams if you can quit, he tells you to continue. At 300 volts, you wonder if Wallace is going to die. "But," you think, "they wouldn't let that happen at Yale . . . or would they?"

"Hey, Mr. Williams," you say, "whose responsibility is this? What if he dies or is seriously injured?" Williams does not bat an eye: "It's my responsibility, not yours, just continue with the experiment." He reminds you that, as he told you before, the labels apply to small animals, not humans.

Finally it is over. There are no more shock switches to throw. You are sweaty, uneasy. Wallace comes in from the other room. He is alive and seems okay. You apologize. He tells you to forget it, he would have done the same if he had been in your shoes. He smiles and rubs his sore wrists, everybody shakes hands, and you and Wallace walk out together.

Predicted Behavior and Results in the Milgram Experiment

How do you think you would behave in Milgram's experiment? Most people think they would refuse to obey the experimenter's orders. Milgram was interested in this question, so he asked a wide range of individuals, both expert (psychiatrists) and nonexpert (college students and noncollege adults), how they thought participants would behave in this situation. They all predicted that they would break off the experiment, defying the experimenter. The psychiatrists predicted that participants would break off when the learner began to protest, at the 150-volt level. So, if you believe that you would defy the experimenter and refuse to inflict pain on another person, you are not alone.

The underlying assumption of these predictions is that individual principles will be more powerful determinants of behavior than situational factors. The predictions reflect the notion that moral knowledge predicts moral behavior; in other words, if you know what is right, you will do it. However, the results of Milgram's first "baseline" experiment (in which there was no feedback from the victim) don't support these rosy predictions. A majority of participants (65%) went all the way to 450 volts. In fact, the average shock level delivered by the participants in this first experiment was 405 volts! We can infer from this result that under the right circumstances, most of us probably also would go all the way to 450 volts.

Of course, no electric shock was ever given to Wallace, who was, in fact, a professional actor, playing out a script. However, Milgram's participants did not know that the entire situation was contrived.

Situational Determinants of Obedience

Milgram himself was surprised at the levels of obedience observed in his first experiment. He and others conducted several additional experiments investigating the situational factors that influence levels of obedience. In the following sections, we explore some of these situational factors.

PROXIMITY OF THE VICTIM In his first series of experiments, Milgram tested the limits of obedience by varying the proximity, or closeness, between the teacher and the learner (victim). The conditions were:

1. *Remote victim.* The teacher and the learner were in separate rooms. There was no feedback from the victim to the teacher. That is, Wallace didn't speak, moan, or scream.

2. *Voice feedback.* The teacher and the learner were in separate rooms, but Wallace began to protest the shocks as they became more intense. This is the experiment just described. In one version of the voice-feedback condition, Wallace makes it clear that he has a heart condition. After receiving 330 volts he screams, "Let me out of here. Let me out of here. My heart is bothering me" (Milgram, 1974, p. 55).

3. *Proximity.* The teacher and the learner were in the same room, sitting only a few feet apart.

4. *Touch proximity.* The teacher and the learner were in the same room, but the learner received the shock only if his hand was placed on a shock plate. At one point the learner refused to keep his hand on the plate. The teacher was told to hold the learner's hand down while delivering the shock. The teacher often had to hand-wrestle the victim to be sure the hand was properly placed on the shock plate.

These four conditions decrease the physical distance between the teacher and the learner. Milgram found that reducing the distance between the teacher and the learner affected the level of obedience (Figure 7.8). In the remote-victim condition, 65% of the participants obeyed the experimenter and went all the way to 450 volts (the average shock intensity was 405 volts). As you can see from Figure 7.8, obedience was not substantially reduced in the voice-feedback condition. In this condition, obedience dropped only 2.5%, to 62.5%, with an average shock intensity of 368 volts.

Thus, verbal feedback from the learner, even when he indicates his heart is bothering him, is not terribly effective in reducing obedience. Significant

Figure 7.8

The effect of moving the learner closer to the teacher. In the remote condition, obedience was highest. Adding voice feedback did not reduce obedience significantly. It was only when the learner and teacher were in the same room that obedience dropped. The lowest level of obedience occurred when the teacher was required to touch the learner in order to administer the electric shock.

Based on data from Milgram (1974).

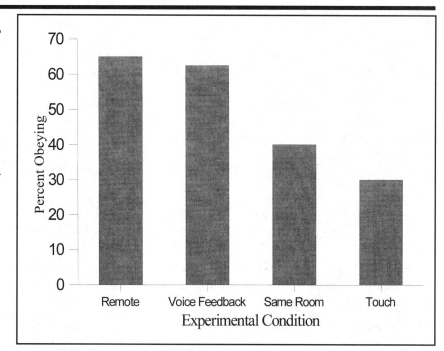

drops in the rates of obedience were observed when the distance between the teacher and the learner was decreased further. In the proximity condition, where the teacher and the learner were in the same room and only a few feet apart, 40% of the participants went to 450 volts (with an average shock intensity of 312 volts). Finally, when the teacher was required to hold the learner's hand on the shock plate in the touch-proximity condition, only 30% obeyed and went to 450 volts (the average shock intensity was 269 volts).

Why does decreasing the distance between the teacher and the learner affect obedience so dramatically? Milgram (1974) offered several explanations. First, decreasing the distance between the teacher and the learner increases empathic cues from the learner, cues about his suffering, such as screaming or hanging on the wall. In the remote-victim condition, the teacher receives no feedback from the learner. There is no way for the teacher to assess the level of suffering of the learner, making it easier on the teacher's conscience to inflict harm. In the feedback conditions, however, the suffering of the learner is undeniable. The teacher has a greater opportunity to observe the learner in voice-feedback, proximity, and touch conditions than in the remote-victim condition. It is interesting to note, however, that even in the touch-proximity condition, a sizable percentage of participants (39%) were willing to fully obey the experimenter. It is apparent that there are some among us who are willing to discount empathic cues and continue to do harm to others in a face-to-face, intimate-contact situation. For example, there was no shortage of Nazis willing to shoot Jews at close range during the early stages of the Holocaust.

Milgram also suggested that in the remote-victim condition a "narrowing of the cognitive field," or *cognitive narrowing*, occurs. That is, the teacher can put the learner out of mind and focus on the learning task instead. As the victim becomes more observable, such narrowing becomes more difficult, and obedience is reduced. These results suggest that it is more difficult to inflict harm on someone you can see, hear, or touch. This is why it is probably easier to drop bombs on a city of 500,000 from 30,000 feet than to strangle one person with your bare hands.

POWER OF THE SITUATION   A second variable Milgram investigated was the nature of the institution behind the authority. The original studies were conducted at Yale University. To test the possibility that participants were intimidated by the school's power and prestige, Milgram rented a loft in downtown Bridgeport, Connecticut, and conducted the experiment under the name "Research Associates of Bridgeport." He also had the experimenter represent himself as a high school biology teacher. Under these conditions, obedience fell to 47.5%, down from 65% in the original, baseline study. Although this difference of 17.5% does not meet conventional levels of statistical significance, it does suggest that removing some of the trappings of legitimacy from an authority source reduces obedience somewhat.

PRESENCE AND LEGITIMACY OF THE AUTHORITY FIGURE
What if the authority figure was physically removed from the obedience situation? In another variation on his original experiment, Milgram had the experimenter give orders by telephone, which varied the immediacy of the authority figure, as opposed to varying the immediacy of the victim. He

Figure 7.9

The trappings of authority. Individuals are more likely to obey someone in uniform than someone not in uniform. The uniform conveys authority to the individual.

found that when the experimenter is absent or tried to phone in his instructions to give shock, obedience levels dropped sharply, to as little as 20%. The closer the authority figure, the greater the obedience.

After Milgram's original research was publicized, other researchers became interested in the aspects of authority that might influence obedience levels. One line of research pursued the perceived legitimacy of the authority figure. Two different studies examined the effect of a uniform on obedience (Bickman, 1974; Geffner & Gross, 1984). In one (Geffner & Gross, 1984), experimenters approached participants who were about to cross a street and requested that they cross at another crosswalk. Half the time the experimenter was uniformed as a public works employee, and half the time the experimenter was not in uniform. The researchers found that participants were more likely to obey uniformed than nonuniformed individuals (Figure 7.9).

CONFLICTING MESSAGES ABOUT OBEDIENCE   Milgram also investigated the impact of receiving conflicting orders. In two variations, participants received such conflicting messages. In one, the conflicting messages came from the learner and the experimenter. The learner demanded that the teacher continue delivering shocks whereas the experimenter advocated stopping the experiment. In the second variation, two authority figures delivered the conflicting messages. One urged the teacher to continue whereas the other urged the teacher to stop.

When such a conflict arose, participants chose the path that lead to a positive outcome: termination of harm to the learner. When there was conflict between authority sources, or between the learner and the authority source, not one participant went all the way to 450 volts.

GROUP EFFECTS A fourth variation involved groups of teachers, rather than a single teacher. In this variation, a real participant was led to believe that two others would act as co-teachers. (These other two were confederates of the experimenter.) When the learner began to protest, at 150 volts, one confederate decided not to continue. Defying the experimenter's instructions, he walked away and sat in a chair across the room. At 210 volts the second confederate followed. Milgram's results showed that having the two confederates defy the experimenter reduced obedience markedly. Only 10% of the participants obeyed to 450 volts (mean shock intensity = 305 volts). Thirty-three percent of the participants broke off after the first confederate defied the experimenter but before the second confederate. An additional 33% broke off at the 210-volt level after the second confederate defied the experimenter. Thus, two-thirds of the participants who disobeyed the experimenter did so immediately after the confederates defied the experimenter.

Why does seeing two others disobey the experimenter significantly reduce the participant's obedience? One explanation centers on a phenomenon called *diffusion of responsibility*. Diffusion of responsibility occurs when an individual spreads responsibility for his or her action to other individuals present. In the obedience situation in which there were two other teachers delivering shocks, the participant could tell himself that he was not solely responsible for inflicting pain on the learner. However, when the two confederates broke off, he was left holding the bag; he was now solely responsible for delivering shocks. Generally, when people are in a position where they can diffuse responsibility for harming another person, obedience is higher than if they have to deliver the harm entirely on their own and cannot diffuse responsibility (Kilharn & Mann, 1974). In short, having two people defy the experimenter placed the participant in a position of conflict about who was responsible for harming the learner.

There is another explanation for the group effects Milgram observed. When the two confederates broke off from the experiment, a new norm began to form: disobedience. The old norm of obedience to the experimenter is placed into conflict with the new norm of disobedience. The norm of disobedience is more "positive" than the norm of obedience with respect to the harm to the learner. Remember that when participants were given the choice between a positive and a negative command, most chose the positive. The lone participants in the original studies, however, had no such opposing norms and so were more inclined to respond to the norm of obedience. Evidently, having role models who defy authority with impunity emboldens us against authority. Once new norms develop, disobedience to oppressive authority becomes a more viable possibility.

The Role of Gender in Obedience

In Milgram's original research, only male participants were used. In a later replication, Milgram also included female participants and found that males and females obeyed at the same levels. However, later research showed that there is a gender difference in obedience. In an experiment conducted in Australia, Wesley Kilham and Leon Mann (1974) found that males conformed more than females. In another study conducted in the United States, Robert Geffner and Madeleine Gross (1984) found that males obeyed a uniformed authority more than females did.

Figure 7.10

Obedience as a function of the gender of an authority figure and participant age. Younger participants were more likely to obey a male authority figure than older participants. Younger and older participants obeyed a female authority figure equally.

Based on data from Geffner and Gross (1984).

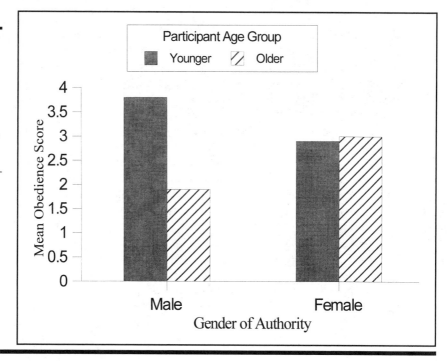

Another way to approach the issue of gender effects in obedience is to determine whether male or female authority figures are more effective in producing obedience. In Geffner and Gross's (1984) experiment, the effects of experimenter gender, participant gender, and participant age on obedience were investigated. The results showed no simple effect of experimenter gender on obedience. Instead, experimenter gender and participant age interacted, as shown in Figure 7.10. Notice that there was no difference between older and younger participants ("younger" participants being under age 30, and "older" participants being over age 50) when the experimenter was female. However, when the experimenter was male, younger participants obeyed the male experimenter more than older participants did.

Obedience or Aggression?

Milgram's experiment used an aggressive response as the index of obedience. Could it be that participants were displaying aggression toward the learner, which had little to do with obedience? Such an interpretation appears unlikely. In situations where participants were allowed to choose the level of shock to deliver to the learner, the average shock delivered was 82.5 volts, with 2.5% obeying completely. This is quite a drop from the 405 volts with 65% obeying completely in the baseline condition (Milgram, 1974).

These results were supported by a replication of Milgram's experiment by other researchers (Mantell, 1971). In one condition of this experiment, participants were allowed to set the level of shock delivered to the learner. Compared to 85% of participants who used the highest level of shock in a replication of Milgram's baseline experiment (no feedback from the learner), only 7% of the participants in the "self-decision" condition did so. These results and others (Kilham & Mann, 1974; Meeus & Raaijmakers, 1986; Shanab & Yahya, 1978) lead us to the conclusion that participants were displaying obedience to the experimenter rather than to their own aggressive impulses.

Obedience Across Culture, Situation, and Time

Milgram's original experiments were conducted in the United States, using a particular research technique. Would his results hold up across cultures and across experimental situations? Some critics of Milgram's study, Dutch researchers Meeus and Raaijmakers (1986), argued that the type of obedience required in Milgram's experiment—physically hurting another person—was not realistic. Such behavior is rare in everyday life. They argued that people are more often asked to hurt others in more subtle ways. For example, your employer might ask you to do something that makes another employee look bad. Would you obey?

Meeus and Raaijmakers (1986) studied a different form of obedience: *administrative obedience*. Dutch participants were told that the psychology department of a university was commissioned to screen applicants for various state and civic positions and that the department was using this opportunity to test the effects of stress on test achievement. According to instructions, participants made a series of disparaging statements about a person taking a test for a state job. Fifteen statements, each more disruptive than the previous, were used. The mildest statement was, "Your answer to question 9 was wrong"; a moderate statement was, "If you continue like this, you will fail the test"; and the strongest statement was, "According to the test, it would be better for you to apply for lower functions" (p. 323). Understandably, job applicants became increasingly upset with each comment.

Most of the Dutch participants obeyed; 90% read all 15 statements. This resembles the Milgram experiment in which participants had to increase shock in 15 stages as the victim became more upset. In Milgram's terms, they gave the full 450 volts. When questioned about it, they attributed responsibility for the harassment to the experimenter.

In another variation on Milgram's experiment, Australian participants assumed the role of either transmitter of the experimenter's instructions or executor (Kilham & Mann, 1974). In the transmitter condition, participants relayed orders to continue shocking a learner to a confederate of the experimenter who delivered the shocks. In the executor condition, participants received orders indirectly from the experimenter through a confederate of the experimenter. The hypothesis was that there would be greater obedience when the participant was the transmitter rather than the executor of orders, presumably because the participant is not directly responsible for inflicting harm on the victim. Results supported this hypothesis. Participants in the transmitter role showed higher levels of obedience than those in the executor role.

Milgram's obedience effect has been supported by other cross-cultural research. For example, obedience among Jordanian adults was found to be 62.5%—comparable to the 65% rate found by Milgram among Americans—and among Jordanian children, 73% (Shanab & Yahya, 1977). The highest rates of obedience were reported among participants in Germany. In a replication of Milgram's original baseline experiment, 85% of German men obeyed the experimenter (Mantell, 1971). Overall, it appears that obedience is an integral part of human social behavior.

Finally, Milgram's findings have withstood the test of time. Blass (2000) evaluated replications of Milgram's experiments conducted over a 22-year period (1963 to 1985) and found that obedience rates varied from a low of 28% to a high of 91%. However, there was no systematic relationship between the time that a study was conducted and the rate of obedience. According to Blass, it does not appear that an *enlightenment effect* has occurred. An enlightenment effect occurs when results of research are disseminated and behavior is altered. If this happened there should have been reliably less obedience in later studies of obedience than in earlier studies (Blass, 2000).

Reevaluating Milgram's Findings

Milgram sought to describe the dynamics of obedience by comparing obedience rates across different experimental conditions. A wholly different picture of Milgram's findings emerges when a careful analysis of the audiotapes made by Milgram of almost all sessions of his experiment was done (Rochat, Maggioni, & Modigliana, 2000). Such an analysis by Rochat, Maggioni, and Modigliana showed that obedience within an experimental session tended to develop slowly and incrementally through a series of steps. Rochat and colleagues classified participants' behavior as either acquiescence (going along with the experimenter's demands without comment), checks (the participant seeks clarification of a restricted part of the procedure), notifies (the participant provides information to the experimenter that could lead to breaking off of the experiment), questions (the participant overtly expresses doubt or requests additional information about the experimenter's demands), objects (the participant overtly disagrees with the experimenter and brings up some personal reason why he/she should not continue), or refuses (the participant overtly declines to continue the experiment, effectively disobeying the experimenter).

Rochat and colleagues found that the participants' acquiescence to the experimenter was relatively brief. At the 75-volt level (when the learner first indicates he is in pain), 10% of participants exhibited a low-level defiant response (at minimum checking). As the experiment progressed, opposition in the form of checking increased. By 150 volts, 49.7% of participants were checking, and by 270 volts all participants checked. Additionally, 30% of participants either questioned, objected to, or refused the experimenter's orders at or before 150 volts, with an additional 35% reaching this high level of opposition between 150 and 330 volts (Rochat et al., 2000). Interestingly, 57% of the participants who eventually refused to continue began to protest before 150 volts, whereas none of the fully obedient participants did so.

Regardless of the path chosen by a participant, he or she experienced a great deal of conflict as the experiment progressed. Participants dealt with the conflict aroused by the demands of the experimenter and the learner by becoming confused and uncertain, and by showing high levels of distress. (Rochat et al., 2000). Some participants dealt with the stress of the situation by rationalizing away the suffering of the learner, whereas others rushed through the remaining shock levels. According to Rochat and colleagues, participants resolved their conflict in one of two ways. Some participants completed the task to the 450-volt level in a "resigned or mechanical fashion" (p. 170). Others resolved the conflict by becoming oppositional toward the experimenter by first questioning and/or objecting to the experimenter and then later refusing, despite the pressure put on the participant by the experimenter to continue (Rochat et al., 2000).

Critiques of Milgram's Research

There were aspects of Milgram's experiments and others like them that were never precisely defined but probably influenced levels of obedience. Consider, for example, the gradual, stepwise demands made on the participant. Each 15-volt increment may have "hooked" the participants a little more. This is in keeping with the foot-in-the-door technique.

Obeying a small, harmless order (deliver 15 volts) made it likely that they would more easily obey the next small step, and the next, and so on (Gilbert, 1981). Each step made the next step seem not so bad. Imagine if the participant were asked to give 450 volts at the very start. It is likely that many more people would have defied the experimenter.

What about the protests made by many participants? Very few participants went from beginning to end without asking if they should continue or voicing some concern for the victim. But they were always told, "You must continue; you have no choice." Perhaps, as some observers suggest, the experiments are as much a study of ineffectual, and indecisive disobedience as of destructive obedience (Ross & Nisbett, 1991). When participants saw others disobey, they suddenly knew how to disobey too, and many of them did so.

There is another, even more subtle factor involved here. The experiments have a kind of unreal, "Alice-in-Wonderland" quality (Ross & Nisbett, 1991). Events do not add up. The participant's job is to give increasing levels of electric shock to a learner in order to study the effects of punishment on learning. The shocks increase as the learner makes errors. Then (in some variations), the learner stops answering. He can't be learning anything now. Why continue to give shocks? Furthermore, the experimenter clearly does not care that the victim is no longer learning.

Some observers suggest that because the situation does not really make sense from the participant's perspective, the participant becomes confused (Ross & Nisbett, 1991). The participant acts indecisively, unwilling or unable to challenge authority. Not knowing what to do, the participant continues, with great anxiety, to act out the role that the experimenter has prescribed.

This analysis suggests that Milgram's experiments were not so much about slavish obedience to authority as they were about the capacity of situational forces to overwhelm people's more positive tendencies. This may, however, be a futile distinction. Either way, the victim would have been hurt if the shock had been real.

Finally, Milgram's research came under fire for violating ethical research practices. Milgram explored the dimensions of obedience in 21 experiments over a 12-year period, and more than a thousand participants participated in these experimental variations. Because Milgram's participants were engaging in behavior that went against accepted moral standards, they were put through an "emotional wringer." Some participants had very unpleasant experiences. They would "sweat, tremble, stutter, bite their lips, groan, dig their fingernails into their flesh" (Milgram, 1963, p. 375). A few had "full-blown uncontrollable seizures" (p. 375). No one enjoyed it.

Milgram's research and its effects on the persons who participated raise an interesting question about the ethics of research. Should we put people through such experiences in the name of science? Was the participants' anguish worth it? Several observers, including Diana Baumrind (1964), criticized Milgram for continuing the research when he saw its effect on his participants. After all, the critics argued, the participants agreed to take part only in an experiment on memory and learning not on destructive obedience and the limits of people's willingness to hurt others.

But Milgram never doubted the value of his work. He believed it was important to find the conditions that foster destructive obedience. He further believed that his participants learned a great deal from their participation; he knew this because they told him so. Milgram went to great lengths to make sure the teachers knew that Wallace was not harmed and that he held no hard feelings. He also had a psychiatrist interview the participants a year or so after the experiment; the psychiatrist reported that no long-term harm had been done (Aron & Aron, 1989).

The current rules for using participants in psychological experiments would make it exceedingly difficult for anyone in the United States to carry out an experiment like Milgram's. All universities require that research proposals be evaluated by institutional review boards (IRB's), which decide if participants might be harmed by the research. A researcher must show the IRB that benefits of research to science or humankind outweigh any adverse effects on the participants. If a researcher were allowed to do an experiment like Milgram's, he or she would be required to ensure that the welfare of the participants was protected. In all likelihood, however, we will not see such research again.

DISOBEDIENCE

Although history shows us that obedience can and has become an important norm guiding human behavior, there are also times when disobedience occurs. In 1955, for example, a black seamstress named Rosa Parks refused to give up her seat on a Montgomery, Alabama, bus to a white passenger. Her action was in violation of a law that existed at the time. Parks was arrested, convicted, and fined $10 for her refusal.

Parks' disobedience served as a catalyst for events that shaped the civil rights movement. Within 2 days of her arrest, leaflets were distributed in the African-American community calling for a 1-day strike against the bus line. Her cause was taken up by Martin Luther King, Jr., and other African American leaders. The bus strike that was supposed to last only a day lasted for a year. Eventually, laws requiring African Americans to sit at the back of a bus, or to surrender a seat to a white passenger, were changed. From Rosa Parks's initial act of disobedience flowed a social movement, along with major social change.

agentic state

In the agentic state, an individual becomes focused on the source of authority, tuning in to the instructions issued.

Breaking with Authority

Milgram (1974) suggested that one factor contributing to the maintenance of obedience was that the individual in the obedience situation entered into an **agentic state,** which involves a person's giving up his or her normal moral and ethical standards in favor of those of the authority figure. In short, the

Humans have a strong predisposition to obey rules and laws. To disobey requires a person to buck existing norms and accept the consequences of disobedience. Rosa Parks defied discriminatory laws in Alabama which required blacks to ride at the back of a bus. She refused, setting off a boycott of busses by blacks in Montgomery, Alabama, and helping to spark the civil rights movement.

individual becomes an agent or instrument of the authority figure. Milgram suggested further that in this agentic state, a person could experience role strain (apprehension about the obedience behavior) that could weaken the agentic state. In an obedience situation, the limits of the role we play are defined for us by the authority source. As long as we are comfortable with, or at least can tolerate, that role, obedience continues. However, if we begin to seriously question the legitimacy of that role, we begin to experience what Milgram called **role strain.**

In this situation, the individual in the agentic state begins to feel tension, anxiety, and discomfort over his or her role in the obedience situation. In Milgram's (1974) experiment, participants showed considerable signs of role strain in response to the authority figure's behavior. As shown in Figure 7.11 on p. 276, very few participants were "not at all tense and nervous." Most showed moderate or extreme levels of tension and nervousness. Milgram suggested that this tension arose from several sources:

role strain
The discomfort one feels in an obedience situation that causes a person to question the legitimacy of the authority figure and weakens the agentic state.

- The cries of pain from the victim, which can lead the agent to question his or her behavior.
- The inflicting of harm on another person, which involves violating established moral and social values.
- Potential retaliation from the victim.
- Confusion that arises when the learner screams for the teacher to stop while the authority demands that he or she continue.
- Harmful behavior, when this behavior contradicts one's self-image.

How can the tension be reduced? Participants tried to deny the consequences of their actions by not paying attention to the victim's screams, by dealing only with the task of flipping switches. As mentioned earlier, Milgram (1974) called this method of coping *cognitive narrowing*. Teachers

Figure 7.11

Role strain in Milgram's
obedience experiment.
Most participants
experienced moderate to
extreme stress, regardless of
the fact that they knew they
were not ultimately
responsible for any harm to
the learner.

Adapted from Milgram (1974).
Reprinted with permission.

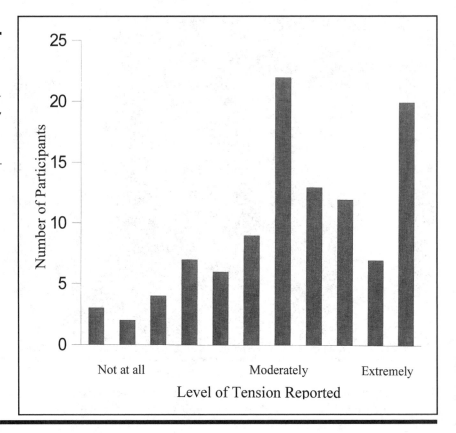

also tried to cheat by subtly helping the learner—that is, by reading the
correct answer in a louder voice. These techniques allowed teachers to tolerate doing harm that they wished they did not have to do. Other participants
resolved the role strain by breaking the role, by disobeying. This choice
was difficult; people felt they had ruined the experiment, which they considered legitimate.

Role strain can, of course, eventually lead to disobedience. However,
real-world obedience situations, such as those that occur within military
organizations, often involve significant pressures to continue obedience.
Nazi soldiers who made up the squads that carried out mass murders
(*Einsatzgruppen*) were socialized into obedience and closely allied themselves
with their authority sources. When role strain is felt by people in this type of
situation, disobedience is difficult, perhaps impossible.

However, this does not necessarily mean that the role strain is ignored.
Creative psychological mechanisms may develop to cope with it. A fair
number of members of the *Einsatzgruppen* experienced role strain. In his
study of Nazi doctors, Robert Lifton (1986) found that many soldiers who
murdered Jews firsthand experienced immediate psychological reactions, such
as physical symptoms and anxiety. For example, General Erich von dem Bach-
Zelewski (one of the Nazis' premier *Einsatzgruppen* generals) was hospitalized
for severe stomach problems, physical exhaustion, and hallucinations tied
to the shooting of Jews (Lifton, 1986). The conflict soldiers felt was severe:

They couldn't disobey, and they couldn't continue. As a result, they removed themselves from the obedience situation by developing psychological problems.

Reassessing the Legitimacy of the Authority

In their book *Crimes of Obedience,* Herbert Kelman and Lee Hamilton (1989) pointed out that authority is more often challenged when the individual considers the authority source illegitimate. Recall that when Milgram conducted his experiment in downtown Bridgeport instead of at Yale University, he found a decrease in obedience. When an authority source loses credibility, disobedience becomes possible.

Kelman and Hamilton suggested that two kinds of psychological factors precede disobedience. The first comprise cognitive factors—the way we think about obedience. In order to disobey, the individual involved in an obedience situation must be aware of alternatives to obedience. For example, Lt. Calley's men in Vietnam were not aware that a soldier may disobey what he has good reason to believe is an illegal order, one that violates the rules of war.

Disobedience is also preceded by motivational factors. An individual in the obedience situation must be willing to buck the existing social order (whether in the real world or in the laboratory) and accept the consequences. The importance of this motivation to disobey is supported by Milgram's finding that participants who saw another person disobey and suffer no consequences frequently disobeyed.

These same factors could explain the behavior of Lithuanians during the early part of 1990. The Lithuanians declared independence from the Soviet Union, disrupting the long-standing social order. They were willing to accept the consequences: sanctions imposed by the Soviets. Lithuanian disobedience came on the heels of the domino-like toppling of Communist governments in Eastern Europe. Having seen that those people suffered no negative consequences, Lithuanians realized that there was an alternative to being submissive to the Soviets. In this respect, the Lithuanians behaved similarly to Milgram's participants who saw the confederates disobey the experimenter.

According to Kelman and Hamilton (1989), these two psychological factors interact with material resources to produce disobedience. In response, the authority source undoubtedly will apply pressure to restore obedience. Those who have the funds or other material resources will be able to withstand that pressure best. Thus, successful disobedience requires a certain level of resources. As long as individuals perceive that the authority figure has the greater resources (monetary and military), disobedience is unlikely to occur.

Consider the events in Tiananmen Square in China during June 1989. Students occupied the square for several days, demanding more freedom. At first, it appeared that the students had gained the upper hand and had spurred an irreversible trend toward democracy! The government seemed unable to stem the tide of freedom. However, the government's inability to deal with the students was an illusion. Once the Chinese government decided to act, it used its vastly superior resources to quickly and efficiently end the democracy movement. Within hours, Tiananmen Square was cleared. At the cost of hundreds of lives, "social order" was restored.

Strength in Numbers

In Milgram's original experiment, the obedience situation consisted of a one-on-one relationship between the authority figure and the participant. What would happen if that single authority source tried to influence several participants?

In a study of this question, W. A. Gamson and his colleagues recruited participants and paid them $10 to take part in a group exercise supposedly sponsored by the Manufacturers' Human Resources Consultants (MHRC) (Gamson, Fireman, & Rytina, 1982). Participants arrived at a hotel and were ushered into a room with a U-shaped table that seated nine persons. In the room were microphones and television cameras. After some introductory remarks, the session coordinator (the experimenter) explained that MHRC was collecting information for use in settling lawsuits. The nine participants were told that the current group would be discussing a case involving the manager of a gas station (Mr. C). Mr. C had been fired by the parent company because he was alleged to be involved in an illicit sexual relationship. The experimenter explained that the courts needed information concerning "community standards" on such an issue to help reach a rational settlement in the case. Participants then signed a "participation agreement," which informed them that their discussions would be videotaped.

Next, they were given the particulars of the case and then were asked to consider the first question: "Would you be concerned if you learned that the manager of your local gas station had a lifestyle like Mr. C's?" (Gamson et al., 1982, p. 46). Before leaving the room, the experimenter conspicuously turned on a videotape recorder to record the group's discussions. A few minutes later, the experimenter came back into the room, turned off the video recorder, and gave the group a second question to consider: "Would you be reluctant to do business with a person like Mr. C because of his lifestyle?" (p. 46). Simultaneously, the experimenter designated certain members of the group to adopt a position against Mr. C, because people were only taking the side of the gas station manager.

He then turned the video recorder back on and left the room. This process was repeated for a third question. Finally, the experimenter came back into the room and asked each person to sign an affidavit stating that the tapes made could be used as evidence in court. The experimenter again left the room, apparently to get his notary public stamp so that the affidavits could be notarized. The measure of obedience was each person's willingness to sign the affidavit.

Let's consider what happened in this study up to this point. Imagine that you are a participant in this study. You are seen on videotape arguing a given position (against Mr. C) that you were told to take. However, because the experimenter turned off the video recorder each time he came into the room, his instructions to adopt your position are not shown. A naive observer — for example, a judge or a juror in a court in which these tapes would be used — would assume that what you say on the tape reflects your actual views. The question for you to evaluate is whether you would sign the affidavit.

Surprisingly, in 16 of the 33 nine-person groups all participants refused to sign. These groups staged what might be considered outright rebellion against the experimenter. Some members even schemed to smuggle the affidavit out of the room so that they would have evidence for future legal action against Mr. C. Disobedience was not a spur-of-the-moment decision, though. Some groups showed signs of reluctance even before the final request was made, such as during break periods between tapings. When the video recorder was off, members of these groups expressed concern about the behavior of the experimenter.

Furthermore, there were nine groups that the researchers termed factional successes. In these groups, most participants refused to sign, although some agreed to sign. Four other groups, called *fizzlers*, included a majority of members who showed signs of rebellion during the early stages of the experiment. However, when it came time to sign the affidavits, these majority members signed them anyway. Finally, four groups, called *tractables*, never showed signs of having a majority of rebellious members. Therefore, in all but four groups, there was a tendency to disobey the experimenter.

What differences are there between the Gamson and Milgram studies? The most important difference is that Gamson's participants were *groups* and Milgram's were *individuals*. The groups could talk, compare interpretations, and agree that this authority was illegitimate. Milgram's participants may have thought the same, but they had no way of confirming their opinions. One important lesson may be that rebellion is a group phenomenon. According to Gamson, people need to work together for disobedience to be effective.

The development of an organized front against authority may occur slowly. A core of committed individuals may mount the resistance, with others falling in later in a *bandwagon effect*. The Chinese student uprising in 1989 is an example. The protest began with a relatively small number of individuals. As events unfolded, more people joined in, until there were hundreds of thousands of protesters.

A second factor is the social climate. Disobedience—often in the form of social movements—occurs within social climates that allow such challenges to authority. Milgram's studies, for example, were conducted mainly between 1963 and 1968. By the time Gamson and his colleagues did theirs, in 1982, the social climate had changed dramatically. Trust in government had fallen sharply after Watergate and the Vietnam War. Furthermore, Gamson's situation involved a large oil company. By 1982, people's trust in the honesty of oil companies had reached a very low level.

Many nonlaboratory examples illustrate the role of social climate in rebellion. Communist governments in eastern Europe, for example, were overthrown only after major changes in the political system of the Soviet Union that had controlled eastern Europe since 1945, the end of World War II. Eventually, that climate caught up to the Soviet Union, which disintegrated completely in 1991.

Rebellion against authority may also occur within social climates that do not fully support such rebellion. The resistance movements in France during World War II, for example, helped undermine the German occupation forces, despite the fact that most of France was ruled with an iron fist by the Germans. Within Germany itself, there was some resistance to the Nazi regime (Peukert, 1987). Even the ill-fated student uprising in Tiananmen Square took place within a climate of liberalization that had evolved over several years before the uprising. Unfortunately, the climate reversed rapidly.

THE JURY ROOM REVISITED

Poor Frank! He never really had a chance did he? He was caught on the horns of a dilemma. On the one horn was the judge, a powerful authority figure, telling him that he must obey the law if the prosecutor proved his case. This was reinforced by the prosecutor in his closing statement when he reminded the jury of their duty to apply the law as provided by the judge. Certainly, in Frank's mind the prosecutor had met the burden of proof outlined by the judge. In comes the second horn which gored Frank when the deliberations began. He began to face normative and informational social influence from his fellow jurors. On the initial vote only two jurors sided with Frank. At this point he had his true partners and he might have been able to hold out and at least hang the jury if those true partners hadn't abandoned him. Eventually, Frank was left alone facing a majority who tried their best to get Frank to change his mind. They did this by directly applying pressure via persuasive arguments (informational social influence) and the more subtle channel of normative pressure.

As we know, Frank ultimately decided to disobey the judge's authority. He changed his vote to not guilty. However, consistent with what we now know about social influence, he was not convinced. His behavior change was brought about primarily through normative social influence. This is reflected in the sentiment he expressed just before he changed his vote: He changed his vote so as not to hold up the jury but he would "never feel right about it."

CHAPTER REVIEW

1. What is conformity?

Conformity is one type of social influence. It occurs when we modify our behavior in response to real or imagined pressure from others. Frank, the man cast into the role of juror in a criminal trial, entered the jury deliberations convinced that the defendant was guilty. Throughout the deliberations, Frank maintained his view based on the information he had heard during the trial. However, in the end, Frank changed his verdict. He did this because of the perceived pressure from the other 11 jurors, not because he was convinced by the evidence that the defendant was innocent. Frank's dilemma, pitting his own internal beliefs against the beliefs of others, is a common occurrence in our lives. We often find ourselves in situations where we must modify our behavior based on what others do or say.

2. What is the source of the pressures that lead to conformity?

The pressure can arise from two sources. We may modify our behavior because we are convinced by information provided by others, which is **informational social influence**. Or we may modify our behavior because we perceive that a **norm**, an unwritten social rule, must be followed. This is **normative social influence**. In the latter case, information provided by others defines the norm we then follow. Norms play a central role in our social lives. The classic research by Sherif making use of the autokinetic effect showed how a norm forms.

3. What research evidence is there for conformity?

Solomon Asch conducted a series of now-classic experiments that showed conformity effects with a relatively clear, simple perceptual line judgment task. He found that participants conformed to an incorrect majority on 33% of the critical trials where a majority (composed of confederates) made obviously incorrect judgments. In postexperimental interviews, Asch found that there were a variety of reasons why a person would conform (yield) or not conform (remain independent).

4. What factors influence conformity?

Research by Asch and others found several factors that influence conformity. Conformity is more likely to occur when the task is ambiguous than if the task is clear-cut. Additionally, conformity increases as the size of the majority increases up to a majority size of three. After a majority size of three, conformity does not increase significantly with the addition of more majority members. Finally, Asch found that conformity levels go down if you have another person who stands with you against the majority. This is the **true partner effect**.

5. Do women conform more than men?

Although early research suggested that women conformed more than men, later research revealed no such simple relationship. Research indicates that the nature of the task was not important in producing the observed sex differences. However, women are more likely to conform if the experimenter is a man. No gender differences are found when a woman runs the experiment. Also, women are more likely to conform than men under conditions of normative social influence than under informational social influence conditions. Two explanations have been offered for gender differences in conformity. First, gender may serve as a status variable in newly formed groups, with men cast in the higher status roles and women in the lower status roles. Second, women tend to be more sensitive than men to conformity pressures when they have to state their opinions publicly.

6. Can the minority ever influence the majority?
Generally, American social psychologists have focused their attention on the influence of a majority on the minority. However, in Europe, social psychologists have focused on how minorities can influence majorities. A firm, consistent minority has been found capable of causing change in majority opinion. Generally, a minority that is consistent but flexible and adheres to opinions that fit with the current spirit of the times has a good chance of changing majority opinion.

7. How does minority influence work?
Some theorists contend that majority and minority influence represent two distinct processes, with majority influence being primarily normative and minority influence primarily informational. However, other theorists argue that a single process can account for both majority and minority influence situations. According to Latané's **social impact theory**, social influence is related to the interaction between the strength of the influence source, the immediacy of the influence source, and the number of influence sources. To date, neither the two- nor the single-process approach can explain all aspects of minority, or majority, influence, but more evidence supports the single process model.

8. Why do we sometimes end up doing things we would rather not do?
Sometimes we modify our behavior in response to a direct request from someone else. This is known as **compliance**. Social psychologists have uncovered four main techniques that can induce compliance.

9. What are compliance techniques, and why do they work?
In the **foot-in-the-door technique (FITD)**, a small request is followed by a larger one. Agreeing to the second, larger request is more likely after agreeing to the first, smaller request. This technique appears to work for three reasons. First, according to the self-perception hypothesis, agreeing to the first request may result in shifts in one's self-perception. After agreeing to the smaller request, you come to see yourself as the type of person who helps. Second, the perceptual contrast hypothesis suggests that the second, larger request seems less involved following the smaller, first request. Third, our thought processes may undergo a change after agreeing to the first request. The likelihood of agreeing to the second request depends on the thoughts we developed based on information about the first request.

The **door-in-the-face technique (DITF)** reverses the foot-in-the-door strategy: A large (seemingly unreasonable) request is followed by a smaller one. Agreement to the second, smaller request is more likely if it follows the larger request than if it is presented alone. The door-in-the-face technique works because the **norm of reciprocity** is energized when the person making the request makes a "concession." The door-in-the-face technique may also work because we do not want to seem cheap, through perceptual contrast or to be perceived as someone who refuses a worthy cause. This latter explanation is the worthy person hypothesis.

The **low-ball technique** is another two-stage process. A product is offered at a very low price and then, after a commitment is made, the price is raised. Commitment and consistency are the principal forces that make low-balling work. The commitment occurs when you take significant steps toward buying the product. Once the commitment is made we then strive to maintain consistency between our thoughts and our actions. Refusal of the higher price would be inconsistent with all the positive thoughts we developed about the product.

10. What do social psychologists mean by the term "obedience"?
Obedience is the social influence process by which a person changes his or her behavior in response to a direct order from someone in authority. The authority figure has the power, which can stem from several sources, to enforce the orders. Generally,

obedience is not always bad. Obedience to laws and rules is necessary for the smooth functioning of society. However, sometimes obedience is taken to an extreme and causes harm to others. This is called destructive obedience.

11. Are evil deeds done by evil persons?
We might like to think that those who carry out orders to harm others are inhuman monsters. However, Hannah Arendt's analysis of Adolph Eichmann, a Nazi responsible for deporting millions of Jews to death camps, suggests that evil is often very commonplace. Those who carry out acts of destructive obedience are often very ordinary people. The false idea that evil deeds can be done only by evil people is referred to as **Eichmann's fallacy.**

12. What research has been done to study obedience?
Recurring questions about destructive obedience led Stanley Milgram to conduct a series of ingenious laboratory experiments on obedience. Participants believed that they were taking part in a learning experiment. They were to deliver increasingly strong electric shocks to a "learner" each time he made an error. When the participant protested that the shocks were getting too strong, the experimenter ordered the participant to continue the experiment. In the original experiment where there was no feedback from the learner to the participant, 65% of the participants obeyed the experimenter, going all the way to 450 volts.

13. What factors influence obedience?
In variations on his original experiment, Milgram uncovered several factors that influenced the level of obedience to the experimenter, such as moving the learner closer to the teacher. Explanations for the proximity effect include increasing empathic cues from the learner to the teacher and cognitive narrowing, which is focusing attention on the obedience task at hand, not on the suffering of the victim. Moving the experiment from prestigious Yale University to a downtown storefront resulted in a modest (but not statistically significant) decrease in obedience as well. Research after Milgram's suggests that the perceived legitimacy of authority is influential. We are more likely to respond to an order from someone in uniform than from someone who is not. Additionally, if the authority figure is physically removed from the laboratory and gives orders by phone, obedience drops.

Conflicting sources of authority also can disrupt obedience. Given the choice between obeying an authority figure who says to continue harming the learner and obeying one who says to stop, participants are more likely to side with the one who says to stop. Seeing a peer disobey the experimenter is highly effective in reducing obedience. Two explanations have been offered for this effect. The first explanation is diffusion of responsibility: When others are involved in the obedience situation, the participant may spread around the responsibility for doing harm to the learner. The second explanation centers on the development of a new antiobedience norm when one's peers refuse to go along with the experimenter. If an antiobedience norm develops among disobedient confederates, individuals are likely to disobey the authority figure.

14. Are there gender differences in obedience?
Although Milgram's original research suggested that there is no difference in levels of obedience between male and female participants, two later studies suggest that males obey more than females and that among younger individuals there is more obedience to male than female sources of authority.

15. Do Milgram's results apply to other cultures?
Milgram's basic findings hold up quite well across cultures and situations. Cross-cultural research done in Australia, Jordan, Holland, and Germany has reduced obedience levels that support Milgram's findings, even when the obedience tasks diverge from Milgram's original paradigm.

16. What criticisms of Milgram's experiments have been offered?

Milgram's research paradigm has come under close scrutiny. Some observers question the ethics of his situation. After all, participants were placed in a highly stressful situation and were deceived about the true nature of the research. However, Milgram was sensitive to these concerns and took steps to head off any ill effects of participating in his experiment. Other critiques of Milgram's research suggested that using the graded shock intensities made it easier for participants to obey. The foot-in-the-door effect may have been operating.

Another criticism of Milgram's research was that the whole situation had an unreal quality to it. That is, the situation confuses the participant, causing him to act indecisively. Thus, Milgram's experiments may be more about how a situation can overwhelm the normal positive aspects of behavior rather than about slavish obedience to authority.

Finally, Milgram's experiments have been criticized for violating ethical standards of research. Participants were placed into a highly stressful situation, one they reacted negatively to. However, Milgram was concerned about the welfare of his participants and took steps to protect them during and after the experiment.

17. How does disobedience occur?

Historically, acts of disobedience have had profound consequences for the direction society takes. When Rosa Parks refused to give up her bus seat, she set a social movement on course. Disobedience has played an important role in the development of social movements and social change.

Disobedience may occur when **role strain** builds to a point where a person will break the **agentic state**. If a person in an obedience situation begins to question his or her obedience, role strain (tension and anxiety about the obedience situation) may arise. If this is not dealt with by the individual, he or she may break the agentic state. One way people handle role strain is through cognitive narrowing. Disobedience is likely to occur if an individual is strong enough to break with authority, has the resources to do so, and is willing to accept the consequences. Finally, research on disobedience suggests that there is strength in numbers. When several people challenge authority, disobedience becomes likely.

INTERNET ACTIVITY

DO ONLY EVIL PEOPLE DO EVIL DEEDS?

Stanley Milgram's research stunned the world when it showed that ordinary people would willingly engage in behavior that harmed another person. It would be more comforting to believe that only evil people commit evil deeds. This belief is called "Eichmann's Fallacy" after the notorious Adolph Eichmann. Eichmann was an unassuming, meek looking man. If you were to meet him on the street you would not think he was responsible for the deaths of hundreds of thousands of Jews during World War II. For this exercise use the Internet to find a biography of one (or more) of the following Nazi leaders:

Klaus Barbie	Hermann Goering
Adolph Eichmann	Reinhard Heydrich
Joseph Goebbels	Heinrich Himmler

After exploring the life of the person you chose, consider Eichmann's Fallacy:

1. Was there anything serious in the person's background that would lead you to believe that he would willingly take part in the Holocaust?

2. If you saw a picture of this person, not knowing who he was, would you think that he could take part in the Holocaust?

3. Why do you think this person fell under the sway of the Nazis and Hitler?

4. How do you think you would have reacted if placed in the same situation? Would you have resisted the Nazis or would you have obeyed?

SUGGESTIONS FOR FURTHER READING

Blass, T. (1991). Understanding behavior in the Milgram obedience experiment: The role of personality, situations, and their interactions. *Journal of Personality and Social Psychology, 60,* 398–413.
This is an excellent article presenting the evidence for personality and situational variables in determining obedience. The article also presents an interactionist perspective on obedience.

Cialdini, R. B. (1993). *Influence: Science and practice* (3rd ed.). Glenview, IL: Scott Foresman.
This fascinating and easy-to-read book takes you inside the world of social influence. Cialdini, having had experience going undercover as a salesperson, gives a unique perspective on social influence. You will come away a bit wiser from this book!

Early, P. (1988). *Family of spies: Inside the John Walker spy ring.* New York: Bantam Books.
This book chronicles the Walker spy scandal. It gives some excellent insights into how compliance techniques operate when recruiting potential spies.

Gibson, J. T., & Haritos-Fatouros, M. (1986, November). The education of a torturer. *Psychology Today,* 50–58.
This article provides a highly readable overview of the research on the education of Greek recruits to be torturers. The article ties the methods used by the Greek secret police to elements of Milgram's model of obedience.

Heck, A. (1985). *A child of Hitler: Germany in the days when God wore a swastika.* Frederick, O.: Renaissance House.
Alphons Heck has written an autobiographical account of his experieces as a member of the Hitler Youth in Nazi Germany. He describes how he idolized Adolph Hitler, joined the Hitler Youth, and fought in World War II for the Nazis.

Kelman, H., & Hamilton, L. (1989). *Crimes of obedience: Toward a social psychology of authority and responsibility.* New Haven, CT: Yale University Press.
This book provides a readable excursion into the problem that obedience has caused historically. It also provides an overview of the conditions that favor disobedience.

Latane, B. (1981). The psychology of social impact. *American Psychologist, 36,* 343–356.
This article is an excellent introduction to Latane's social impact theory.

Maas, A., & Clark, R. D. (1984). Hidden impact of minorities: Fifteen years of minority influence research. *Psychological Bulletin, 95,* 428–450.

This article reviews the critical issues addressed in the research on minority influence. Discussions of minority style, normative context, and different types of minorities are included.

Milgram, S. (1974). *Obedience to authority.* New York: Harper & Row.

This offers an excellent overview of Milgram's research and writings on obedience. Milgram's ideas about the causes for obedience, as well as numerical data, are presented.

Sereny, G. (1974). *Into that darkness: An examination of conscience.* New York: Vintage Press.

Gitta Sereny, a journalist, conducted interviews with Franz Stangl, the commandant of the Treblinka death camp run by the Nazis. Stangl describes how he gradually was socialized into the role of a killer.

CHAPTER 8

GROUP PROCESSES

The mission was supposed to be the crown jewel of the American space program. The *Challenger* mission was supposed to show how safe space travel had become by sending along Christa McAuliffe, a teacher from Concord, New Hampshire, who would become the first civilian in space. She was supposed to teach a 15-minute class from space. The *Challenger* mission was supposed to be a success just like the 55 previous U.S. space flights. But, what wasn't supposed to happen actually did: Fifty-eight seconds into the flight the trouble started; a puff of smoke could be seen coming from one of the solid rocket boosters. About 73 seconds into the flight, *Challenger* exploded in a huge fireball that spread debris over several miles. The crew cockpit plummeted back to earth and hit the Atlantic Ocean, killing all seven astronauts. As millions of people watched, the two solid rocket boosters spiraled off in different directions making the image of the letter Y in smoke. The pattern formed would foreshadow the main question that was on everyone's mind in the days that followed the tragedy: Why?

The answer to this question proved to be complex indeed. The actual physical cause of the explosion was clear. Hot gasses burned through a rubber O-ring that was supposed to seal two segments of the solid rocket booster. Because of the exceptionally cold temperatures on the morning of the launch, the O-rings became brittle and did not seat properly. Hot gasses burned through and ignited the millions of gallons of liquid fuel on top of which *Challenger* sat. The underlying cause of the explosion, relating to the decision-making structure and process at NASA and Morton Thiokol (the maker of the solid rocket booster), took months to disentangle. What emerged was a picture of a flawed decision-making structure that did not foster open communication and free exchange of information. This flawed decision-making structure was the true cause for the *Challenger* explosion.

At the top of the decision-making ladder was Jesse Moore, Associate Administrator for Space Flight. It was Mr. Moore who made the final decision to launch or not to launch. Also in a top decision-making position was Arnold Aldrich, Space Shuttle Manager at the Johnson Space Center. At the bottom of the ladder were the scientists and engineers at Morton Thiokol. These individuals did not have direct access to Moore. Any information they wished to convey concerning the launch had to be passed along by executives at Morton Thiokol, who would then communicate with NASA officials at the Marshall Space Flight Center. These officials would, in turn, report to Aldrich, who was the only one in direct communication with Jesse Moore. Because of the cold weather, the Thiokol scientists and engineers had serious reservations about launching *Challenger*. In fact, one of the engineers later said that he "knew" that the shuttle would explode and felt sick when it happened. Unfortunately, the reservations about the O-ring never reached Moore, and he ordered the ill-fated launch.

In addition to the communication flaws, the group involved in making the decision suffered from other decision-making deficiencies, including a sense of invulnerability (after all, all other shuttle launches went off safely), negative attitudes toward one another (characterizing the scientists and engineers as overly cautious), and an atmosphere that stifled free expression of ideas (Thiokol engineer Alan McDonald testified before congressional hearings that he felt pressured to give the green light to the launch).

What went wrong? Here we had a group of highly intelligent, expert individuals who made a disastrous decision to launch *Challenger* in the cold weather that existed at launch time. In this chapter, we explore the effects of groups on individuals. We ask, What special characteristics distinguish a group like the *Challenger* decision-making group from a simple gathering of individuals? What forces arise within such groups that change individual behavior? Do groups offer significant advantages over individuals operating on their own? For example, would the launch director at NASA have been better off making a decision by himself rather than assembling and relying on an advisory group? And what are the group dynamics that can lead to such faulty, disastrous decisions? These are some of the questions addressed in this chapter.

KEY QUESTIONS

AS YOU READ THIS CHAPTER, FIND THE ANSWERS TO THE FOLLOWING QUESTIONS:

1. *What is a group?*
2. *Why do people join groups?*
3. *What effect does an audience have on performance?*
4. *How does being in a group affect performance and other behavior?*
5. *When it comes to decision making, are groups better than individuals, or are individuals better than groups?*
6. *How do groups reach decisions?*
7. *What factors affect the decision-making ability and effectiveness of a group?*
8. *How does group size affect group productivity?*
9. *What is group cohesiveness, and how does it affect group performance?*
10. *What role does leadership play in group process?*
11. *What is groupthink?*
12. *What conditions tend to favor the emergence of groupthink?*
13. *What steps can be taken to prevent groupthink?*
14. *What are the alternatives to groupthink?*

WHAT IS A GROUP?

Groups are critical to our everyday existence. We are born into a group, we play in groups, and we work and learn in groups. We have already learned that we gain much of our self-identity and self-esteem from our group memberships. But what is a *group*? Is it simply a collection of individuals who happen to be at the same place at the same time? If this were the case, the people standing on a street corner waiting for a bus would be a group. Your social psychology class has many people in it, some of whom may know one another. Some people interact, some do not. Is it a group? Well, it is certainly an *aggregate*, a gathering of people, but it probably does not feel to you like a group.

Groups have special social and psychological characteristics that set them apart from collections or aggregates of individuals. Two major features distinguish groups: In a group, members interact with each other, and group members influence each other through this social interaction. By this definition, the collection of people at the bus stop would not qualify as a group. Although they may influence one another on a basic level (if one person looked up to the sky, others probably would follow suit), they do not truly interact. A true **group** has two or more individuals who mutually influence one another through social interaction (Forsyth, 1990). That is, the influence arises out of the information (verbal and nonverbal) that members exchange. The *Challenger* decision-making group certainly fit this definition. The group members interacted during committee meetings, and they clearly influenced one another.

group
An aggregate of individuals who interact with and influence one another.

This definition of a group may seem broad and ambiguous, and in fact, it is often difficult to determine whether an aggregate of individuals qualifies as a group. To refine our definition and to get a closer look at groups, we turn now to a closer look at their characteristics.

Characteristics of Groups

Interaction and mutual influence among people in the group are only two of a number of attributes that characterize a group. What are the others?

First of all, a group typically has a purpose, a reason for existing. Groups serve many functions, but a general distinction can be made between *instrumental groups* and *affiliative groups*. Instrumental groups exist to perform some task or reach some specific goal. The *Challenger* group was an instrumental group, as are most decision-making groups. A jury is also an instrumental group. Its sole purpose is to find the truth of the claims presented in a courtroom and reach a verdict. Once this goal is reached, the jury disperses.

Affiliative groups exist for more general and, often, more social reasons. For example, you might join a fraternity or a sorority simply because you want to be a part of that group—to affiliate with people with whom you would like to be. You may identify closely with the values and ideals of such a group. You derive pleasure, self-esteem, and perhaps even prestige by affiliating with the group.

A second characteristic of a group is that group members share perceptions of how they are to behave. From these shared perceptions emerge **group norms,** or expectations about what is acceptable behavior. As pointed out in chapter 7, norms can greatly influence individual behavior. For example, the parents of the children on a soccer team might develop into a group on the sidelines of the playing fields. Over the course of the season or several seasons, they learn what kinds of comments they can make to the coach, how much

group norms
Expectations concerning the kinds of behaviors required of group members.

and what kind of interaction is expected among the parents, how to cheer and support the players, what they can call out during a game, what to wear, what to bring for snacks, and so on. A parent who argued with a referee or coach or who used abusive language would quickly be made to realize he or she was not conforming to group norms.

Third, within a true group, each member has a particular job or role to play in the accomplishment of the group's goals. Sometimes these roles are formally defined; for example, a chairperson of a committee has specific duties. However, roles may also be informal (DeLamater, 1974). Even when no one has been officially appointed leader, for example, one or two people usually emerge to take command or gently guide the group along. Among the soccer parents, one person might gradually take on additional responsibilities, such as organizing carpools or distributing information from the coach, and thus come to take on the role of leader.

Fourth, members of a group have affective (emotional) ties to others in the group. These ties are influenced by how well various members live up to group norms and how much other group members like them (DeLamater, 1974).

Finally, group members are interdependent. That is, they need each other to meet the group's needs and goals. For example, a fraternity or a sorority will fall apart if members do not follow the rules and adhere to the norms so that members can be comfortable with each other.

What Holds a Group Together?

cohesiveness

The strength of the relationships that link members of a group together and is essentially what keeps people in a group or causes them to stick together.

Once a group is formed, what forces hold it together? Group **cohesiveness**— the strength of the relationships that link the members of the group (Forsyth, 1990)—is essentially what keeps people in the group. Cohesiveness is influenced by several factors:

- *Group members' mutual attraction.* Groups may be cohesive because the members find one another attractive or friendly. Whatever causes people to like one another more increases group cohesiveness (Levine & Moreland, 1990).

- *Members' propinquity (physical closeness, as when they live or work near each other).* Sometimes simply being around people regularly is enough to make people feel that they belong to a group. The various departments in an insurance company—marketing, research, sales, and so on—may think of themselves as groups.

- *Their adherence to group norms.* When members live up to group norms without resistance, the group is more cohesive than when one or two members deviate a lot or when many members deviate a little.

- *The group's success at moving toward its goals.* Groups that succeed at reaching their goals are obviously more satisfying for their members and, therefore, more cohesive than those that fail. If groups do not achieve what the members wish for the group, they cease to exist or at the very least are reorganized.

HOW AND WHY DO GROUPS FORM?

We know that humans have existed in groups since before the dawn of history. Clearly, then, groups have survival value. Groups form because they meet needs that we cannot satisfy on our own. Let's take a closer look at what these needs are.

Meeting Basic Needs

Groups help us meet a variety of needs. In many cases, these needs, whether biological, psychological, or social, cannot be separated from one another. There are obvious advantages to group membership. Sociobiologists, who believe that there is a biological basis for all social behavior, suggest that early humans had a better chance of survival when they banded together in groups (Wilson, 1975). Psychology is developing an evolutionary perspective, and evolutionary social psychologists view groups as selecting individual characteristics that make it more probable that an individual can function and survive in groups (Caporael, 1997). Couched in terms of natural selection, evolution would favor those who preferred groups to those who preferred to live in isolation.

But groups meet more than biological needs. They also meet psychological needs. Our first experiences occur within the context of the family group. Some people believe that our adult reactions to groups stem from our feelings about our family. That is, we react toward group leaders with much the same feelings we have toward our fathers or mothers (Schultz, 1983). Many recruits to religious cults that demand extreme devotion are searching for a surrogate family (McCauley & Segal, 1987).

Groups also satisfy a variety of social needs, such as social support—the comfort and advice of others—and protection from loneliness. Groups make it easier for people to deal with anxiety and stress. Human beings are social beings; we don't do very well when we are isolated. In fact, research shows that social isolation, the absence of meaningful social contact, is as strongly associated with death as is cigarette smoking or lack of exercise (Brannon & Feist, 1992).

Groups also satisfy the human need for *social comparison*. We compare our feelings, opinions, and behaviors with those of other people, particularly when we are unsure about how to act or think (Festinger, 1954). We compare ourselves to others who are similar to us to get accurate information about what to do. Those in the groups with which we affiliate often suggest to us the books we read, the movies we see, and the clothes we wear.

Social comparison also helps us obtain comforting information (Taylor & Brown, 1988). Students, for example, may be better able to protect their self-esteem when they know that others in the class also did poorly on an exam. B students compare themselves favorably with C students, and D students compare themselves with those who failed. We are relieved to find out that some others did even worse than we did. This is *downward comparison*, the process of comparing our standing with that of those less fortunate.

As noted earlier, groups play a large role in influencing individual self-esteem. In fact, individuals craft their self-concept from all the groups with which they identify and in which they hold membership, whether the group is a softball team, a sorority, or a street gang.

Of course, groups are also a practical social invention. Group members can pool their resources, draw on the experience of others, and solve problems that they may not be able to solve on their own. Some groups, such as families, form an economic and social whole that functions as a unit in the larger society.

Roles in Groups

Not all members are expected to do the same things or obey precisely the same norms. The group often has different expectations for different group members. These shared expectations help to define individual roles, such as team captain, a formal role, or newcomer, an informal role (Levine & Moreland, 1990).

NEWCOMERS Group members can play different roles in accordance with their seniority. Newcomers are expected to obey the group's rules and standards of behavior (its norms) and show that they are committed to being good members (Moreland & Levine, 1989). More senior members have "idiosyncratic" credit and can occasionally stray from group norms (Hollander, 1985). They have proven their worth to the group and have "banked" that credit. Every now and then it is all right for them to depart from acceptable behavior and spend that credit. New members have no such credit. The best chance new members have of being accepted by a group is to behave in a passive and anxious way.

DEVIATES What happens when the new members find that the group does not meet their hopes or the senior members feel the recruit has not met the group's expectations? The group may try to take some corrective action by putting pressure on the member to conform. Groups will spend much time trying to convince someone who does not live up to group norms to change (Schachter, 1951). If the deviate does not come around, the group then disowns him or her. The deviate, however, usually bows to group pressure and conforms to group norms (Levine, 1989).

Deviates are rejected most when they interfere with the functioning of the group (Kruglanski & Webster, 1991). Imagine an advisor to the launch director at NASA objecting to the launch of *Challenger* after the decision had been made. No matter how persuasive the person's objection to the launch, it is very likely that the deviate would have been told to be silent; he or she would have been interfering with the group's ability to get the job done. Experimental research has verified that when a group member dissents from a group decision close to the group's deadline for solving a problem, the rejector is more likely to be condemned than if the objection is stated earlier (Kruglanski & Webster, 1991).

HOW DO GROUPS INFLUENCE THE BEHAVIOR OF INDIVIDUALS?

We have considered why people join groups and what roles individuals play in groups. Now let's consider another question: What effect does being in a group have on individual behavior and performance? Does group membership lead to self-enhancement, as people who join groups seem to believe? Does it have other effects? Some social psychologists have been particularly interested in investigating this question. They have looked not just at the effects of membership in true groups but also at the effects of being evaluated by an audience, of being in an audience, and of being in a crowd.

Recall that groups affect the way we think and act even when we only imagine how they are going to respond to us. If you practice a speech, just imagining that large audience in front of you is enough to make you nervous. The actual presence of an audience effects us even more. But how? Let's take a look.

The Effects of an Audience on Performance

Does an audience make you perform better? Or does it make you "choke"? The answer seems to depend, at least in part, on how good you are at what you are doing. The presence of others seems to help when the performer is doing something he or she does well: when the performance is a dominant, well-learned skill, a behavior that is easy or familiar (Zajonc, 1965). If you are a class A tennis player, for example, your serve may be better when people are watching you. The performance-enhancing effect of an audience on your behavior is known as **social facilitation**. If, however, you are performing a nondominant skill, one that is not very well learned, then the presence of an audience detracts from your performance. This effect is known as **social inhibition**.

The social facilitation effect, the strengthening of a dominant response due to the presence of other people, has been demonstrated in a wide range of species, including roaches, ants, chicks, and humans (Zajonc, Heingartner, & Herman, 1969). Humans doing a simple task perform better in the presence of others. On a more difficult task, the presence of others inhibits performance.

Why does this happen? How does an audience cause us to perform better or worse than we do when no one is watching? Psychologists have several alternative explanations.

INCREASED AROUSAL Robert Zajonc (1965) argued that a performer's effort always increases in the presence of others due to increased arousal. Increased arousal increases effort; the consequent increased effort improves performance when the behavior is dominant and impairs performance when the behavior is nondominant. If you are good at tennis, then increased arousal and, therefore, increased effort make you play better. If you are not a good tennis player, the increased arousal and increased effort probably will inhibit your performance (Figure 8.1 on p. 294).

EVALUATION APPREHENSION An alternative explanation for the effects of an audience on performance centers not so much on the increased effort that comes from arousal but on the judgments we perceive others to be making about our performance. A theater audience, for example, does not simply receive a play passively. Instead, audience members sit in judgment of the actors, even if they are only armchair critics. The kind of arousal this situation produces is known as **evaluation apprehension**. Some social scientists believe that evaluation apprehension is what causes differences in performance when an audience is present (Figure 8.2 on p. 295).

Those who favor evaluation apprehension as an explanation of social facilitation and social inhibition suggest that the presence of others will cause arousal only when they can reward or punish the performer (Geen, 1989). The mere presence of others does not seem to be sufficient to account for social facilitation and social inhibition (Cottrell, 1972). In one experiment, when the audience was made up of blindfolded or inattentive persons, social facilitation of performance did not occur. That is, if the audience could not see the performance, or did not care about it, then evaluation apprehension did not occur, nor did social facilitation or social inhibition (Cottrell, Wack, Sekerak, & Rittle, 1968).

social facilitation
The performance-enhancing effect of others on behavior; generally, simple, well-learned behavior is facilitated by the presence of others.

social inhibition
The performance-detracting effect of an audience or coactors on behavior; generally, complex, not-well-learned behaviors are inhibited by the presence of others.

evaluation apprehension
An explanation for social facilitation suggesting that the presence of others will cause arousal only when they can reward or punish the performer.

Figure 8.1

The arousal model of social facilitation. The presence of others is a source of arousal and increased effort. This increase in arousal and effort facilitates a simple, well-learned task but inhibits a complex, not well-learned task.

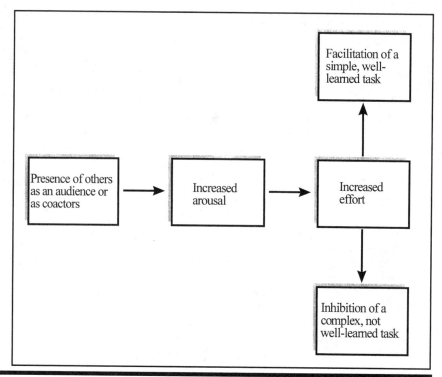

distraction–conflict theory

A theory of social facilitation suggesting that the presence of others is a source of distraction that leads to conflicts in attention between an audience and a task that affects performance.

THE DISTRACTION–CONFLICT EFFECT Another explanation of the presence-of-others effect is **distraction–conflict theory** (Baron, 1986). According to this theory, arousal results from a conflict between demands for attention from the task and demands for attention from the audience. There are three main points to the theory. First, the presence of other people distracts attention from the task. Our tennis player gets all kinds of attention-demanding cues—rewards and punishments—from those watching him play. He may be aware of his parents, his ex-girlfriend, his tennis coach, an attractive stranger, and his annoying little brother out there in the crowd. This plays havoc with a mediocre serve. Second, distraction leads to conflicts in his attention. Our tennis player has just so much attentional capacity. All of this capacity ought to be focused on throwing the ball in the air and hitting it across the net. But his attention is also focused on those he knows in the crowd. Third, the conflict between these two claims for his or her attention stresses the performer and raises the arousal level (Figure 8.3 on p. 296).

The Effects of Group Participation on Performance

We have seen that being watched affects how we perform. Let's take this a step further and examine how being a member of a group affects our performance.

We noted earlier that people who join groups do so largely for self-enhancement: They believe that group membership will improve them in

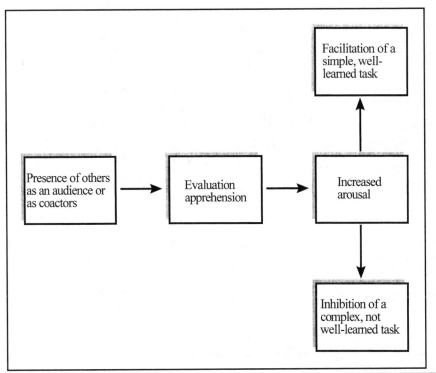

Figure 8.2

The evaluation apprehension model of social facilitation. According to this model, audience-related arousal is caused by apprehension about being evaluated.

some way. They will become better speakers, better citizens, better soccer players, better dancers or singers; they will meet people and expand their social circle; they will make a contribution to a cause, a political candidate, or society. Does group membership actually lead to improved performance? Or does it detract from individual effort and achievement, giving people the opportunity to goof off? Both effects have been documented, depending on a number of factors.

ENHANCED PERFORMANCE Imagine that you are a bicycling enthusiast. Three times a week you ride 20 miles, which takes you a little over an hour. One day you happen to come on a group of cyclists and decide to ride along with them. When you look at your time for the 20 miles, you find that your time is under 1 hour, a full 10 minutes under your best previous time. How can you account for your increased speed? Did the other riders simply act as a wind shield for you, allowing you to exert less effort and ride faster? Or is there more to this situation than aerodynamics? Could it be that the mere presence of others somehow affected your behavior?

This question was asked by Norman Triplett, one of the early figures in social psychology (1898). Triplett, a cycling enthusiast, decided to test a theory that the presence of other people was sufficient to increase performance. He used a laboratory in which alternative explanations for the improvement in cycling time (e.g., other riders being a wind shield) could be eliminated. He also conducted what is perhaps the first social psychological experiment. He had children engage in a simulated race on a miniature track. Ribbons were attached to fishing reels. By winding the reels the

Figure 8.3

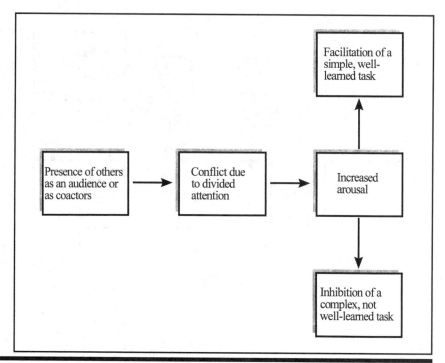

children could drag ribbons around a miniature racetrack. Triplett had the children perform the task either alone or in pairs. He found that the children who played the game in the presence of another child completed the task more quickly than children who played the game alone. The improved performance of the children and the cyclist when they participate in a group setting rather than alone gives us some evidence that groups do enhance individual performance.

SOCIAL LOAFING AND FREE RIDES Is it true that the presence of others is always arousing and that participating in a group always leads to enhanced individual performance? Perhaps not. In fact, the opposite may occur. Sometimes when we are in a group situation, we relax our efforts and rely on others to take up the slack. This effect is called **social loafing**.

social loafing
The performance-inhibiting effect of working in a group that involves relaxing individual effort based on the belief that others will take up the slack.

Sometimes people are not more effortful in the presence of others; they, in fact, may loaf when working with others in groups (Harkins & Szymanski, 1987; Latane, Williams, & Harkins, 1979; Williams & Karau, 1991). In one experiment, participants were informed that they had to shout as loudly as they could to test the effects of sensory feedback on the ability of groups to produce sound. The researchers compared the noise produced by individuals who thought they were shouting or clapping alone to the noise they made when they thought they were in a group. If groups did as well as individuals, then the group production would at least equal the sum of the individual production. But the research findings showed that groups did not produce as much noise as the combined amount of noise individuals made (Latane et al., 1979). Some group members did not do as much as they were capable of doing as individuals: They loafed. In some instances, then, participation of others in the task (e.g., in a tug-of-war game) lowers individual motivation

When individuals are acting as part of a group, there is a tendency to social loaf, or reduce individual output. This can be avoided if a person's work can be identified and evaluated. Factory workers whose work can be identified and evaluated show less tendency toward social loafing.

and reduces performance on the task. Simply put, people sometimes exert less effort when working on a task in a group context (Harkins & Petty, 1982).

Why should the group reduce individual performance in some cases and enhance it in others? The nature of the task may encourage social loafing. In a game of tug-of-war, if you do not pull the rope as hard as you can, who will know or care? If you don't shout as loud as you can, what difference does it make? You cannot accurately assess your own contribution, nor can other people evaluate how well you are performing. Also, fatigue increases social loafing. Claudia Hoeksema-van Orden and her coworkers had a group of people work for 20 hours continuously, individually or in a group. These researchers found that fatigue increased social loafing in groups, whereas individuals were less likely to loaf even when fatigued (Hoeksema-van Orden, Galillard, & Buunk, 1998).

Social loafing tends not to occur in very important tasks. However, many of our everyday tasks are repetitive and dull and are vulnerable to social loafing (Karau & Williams, 1993).

Regardless of the task, some individuals work harder than others in groups (Kerr, 1983). **Free riders** do not do their share of the work. Why not? They are cynical about the other members; they think others may be holding back, so they hold back also. People do not want to be suckers, doing more than their share while others take it easy. Even if they know that their coworkers are doing their share and are competent, individuals may look for a free ride (Williams & Karau, 1991).

The larger the group, the more common are social loafing and free riding. It is harder to determine individual efforts and contributions in big groups. People are likely to feel more responsible for the outcome in smaller groups (Kerr, 1989). Of course, not everyone loafs in groups, nor do people loaf in all group situations.

What decreases the likelihood of social loafing? It is less likely to occur if individuals feel that it is important to compensate for other, weaker group

free riders
Group members who do not do not do their share of the work in a group.

members (Williams & Karau, 1991). When the task is important and motivation to perform is high, then **social compensation**—working harder to make up for the weakness of others—seems to overcome the tendency toward social loafing and free riding.

Social loafing is also less likely when individual contributions can be clearly identified. Generally, when individuals can be identified and cannot simply blend in with the background of other workers, they are less likely to loaf (Williams, Harkins, & Latane, 1981). The members of an automobile manufacturing team, for example, are more careful about their tasks and less willing to pass on defective work if they have to sign for each piece they do. If responsibility for defects is clear, if positive effort and contribution are rewarded, and if management punishes free riders, then social loafing will be further diminished (Shepperd, 1993). Similarly, Shepperd and Taylor (1999) showed that if group members perceive a strong relationship between their effort and a favorable outcome for the group, social loafing does not happen, and there are no free riders.

Social loafing is a phenomenon that is very robust and occurs in a variety of situations and cultures (Karau & Williams, 1993). It has been found to be more common among men than women and among members of Eastern as opposed to Western cultures. These cultural and gender differences seem to be related to values. Many women and many individuals in Eastern cultures attach more importance to group harmony and group success and satisfaction. Many men, especially in Western cultures, attach more value to individual advancement and rewards and to other people's evaluations. Groups tend to mask individual differences. For this reason, Western men may have less inclination to perform well in group situations. The result is social loafing (Karau & Williams, 1993).

GROUPS, SELF-IDENTITY, AND INTERGROUP RELATIONSHIPS

Groups not only affect how we perform, but they also influence our individual sense of worth—our self-esteem—which, in turn, has an impact on how one group relates to other groups in a society. In 1971, Henri Tajfel and his colleagues showed that group categorizations along with an in-group identification are both necessary and sufficient conditions for groups to discriminate against other groups (Rubin & Hewstone, 1998). Recall that in chapter 4 Tajfel showed that even if people were randomly assigned to a group (minimal group categorization), they tended to favor members of that group when distributing very small rewards (the in-group bias; Tajfel, Billig, Bundy, & Flament, 1971). For example, boys in a minimal group experiment ("you overestimate the number of dots on a screen and, therefore, you are in the overestimator group") gave more money to members of their group (the in-group) than to members of the underestimator group (the out-group). So even the most minimal group situation appears to be sufficient for an in-group bias, favoring members of your group, to occur.

Tajfel's findings suggested to him that individuals obtain part of their self-concept, their social identity, from their group memberships and that they seek to nourish a positive social (group) identity to heighten their own self-esteem. Groups that are successful and are held in high esteem by society enhance the esteem of its members. The opposite is also true. All of this depends on the social comparison with relevant out-groups on issues that are important to both (Mummendey & Wenzel, 1999). Favorable comparisons enhance the group and its members. Social identity then is a definition of the self in terms of group membership (Caporael, 1997; Brewer, 1993). Changes in the fate of the group implies changes in the self-concept of the individual members.

Tajfels theory is called **self-identity theory (SIT)** and proposes that a number of factors predict one group's reaction to other competing groups in society. It pertains to what may arise from identification with a social category (membership in a social, political, racial, religious group, etc.). It does not say that once we identify with a group we inevitably will discriminate against other groups. However, SIT does lay out the conditions under which such discrimination may take place. Generally, SIT assumes that the potential that one group will tend to discriminate or downgrade another group will be affected by four factors:

1. How strongly the in-group members identify with their group.
2. The importance of the social category that the in-group represents.
3. The dimension on which the groups are competing (the more important the dimension, the greater the potential for conflict).
4. The group's relative status and the difference in status between the in-group and the out-group (Oakes, Haslam, & Turner, 1994).

Therefore, if members strongly identify with the group; the group represents a crucial identification category, say race, religion, or more affiliative groups such as a social organization; the competition occurs on a crucial dimension (jobs, college entrance possibilities, intense sports rivalries); and the result can be expected to affect the status of the group relative to its competitor, SIT predicts intergroup discrimination. Low or threatened self-esteem will increase intergroup discrimination because of the need to enhance one's social identity (Hogg & Abrams, 1990). Groups that are successful in intergroup discrimination will enhance social identity and self-esteem (Rubin & Hewstone, 1998).

When self-esteem is threatened by group failure, people tend to respond in ways that can maintain their positive identity and sense of reality. For example, Julie Duck and her colleagues examined the response of groups in a hotly contested political campaign. These researchers found that individuals who strongly identified with their political party were more likely to see the media coverage of the campaign as biased and favoring the other side (Duck, Terry, & Hogg, 1998). This was particularly strong for members of the weaker political party, as SIT would predict, because the weaker party was more threatened. However, when the weaker party won, they were less likely to think that the media was biased, whereas the losing, stronger party began to think the media was biased against them.

A member who threatens the success of a group also threatens the positive image of the group. This leads to the **black sheep effect**, the observation that whereas an attractive in-group member is rated more highly than an attractive member of an out-group, an unattractive in-group member is perceived more negatively than an unattractive out-group member (Marques & Paez, 1994). The SIT inference is that the an attractive in-group member is a serious threat to the in-group's image (Mummendey & Wenzel, 1999).

self-identity theory (SIT)
A theory proposing that a number of factors predict one group's reaction to competing groups and concerning what may arise from identification with a social category.

black sheep effect
The phenomenon in which an attractive in-group member is rated more highly than an attractive member of an out-group and an unattractive in-group member is perceived more negatively than an unattractive out-group member.

Why People Identify with a Social Category

Clearly some social categories are imposed on us, through accidents of birth and so forth. But identification with that category implies a psychological commitment to the category. Why make that commitment? Self-identity theory proposes that people apply social categorizations to themselves and others to reduce uncertainty in their world and to make their own place clear and predictable. Because social categories help to define one's self, people identify with those categories that have the potential of enhancing or at least maintaining their self-esteem (Grieve & Hogg, 1999).

Although SIT emphasizes the relationship between group membership and the maintenance of self-esteem, the theory also suggests that another function of group membership is to provide a social reality for its members. For example, in a study involving Australian college students, researchers found that the more the students were made to identify with membership in the social category known as *Australians*, the more they were likely to agree on a shared view of what traits categorized that group. Compared to Australian students who were not manipulated into increased identification with the social category Australians, those who were strongly identified were somewhat more likely to ascribe positive traits—happy-go-lucky, honest, witty—and much less likely to attribute negative traits—materialistic, loud, lazy, imitative—(Haslam, Oakes, Reynolds, & Turner, 1999). This is an example of a group consensus defining the reality of one's social world. Members of the social category Australians, when strongly identified with that category, agree on what constitutes being an Australian.

Self-Categorization Theory (SCT)

Increase in self-esteem as a result of group membership is central to the SIT (Grieve & Hogg, 1999). To increase members' self-esteem, the in-group needs to show that it is distinct from other groups in positive ways (Mummenday & Wenzel, 1999). Central to an extension of SIT, known as self-categorization theory (SCT), is the emphasis on the notion that self-categorization is also motivated by the need to reduce uncertainty (Hogg & Mullin, 1999). The basic idea is that people need to feel that their perceptions of the world are "correct" and this correctness is defined by people (fellow group members) who are similar to them in important ways. In the Haslam and colleagues (1999) study, when the Australian category was made salient and therefore uncertainty was reduced, it regulated and structured the members social cognition. This is consistent with SCT. When reminded of their common category or group membership, the Australian students were more likely to agree on what it meant to be Australian.

What are the consequences of uncertainty? Grieve and Hogg (1999) showed that when uncertainty is high (i.e., when group members did not know if their performance was adequate or would be successful in achieving group goals), groups were more likely to downgrade or discriminate against other groups. In other words, uncertainty is a threat. Uncertainty was also accompanied by increased group identification. So threat creates a kind of "rally 'round the flag" mentality. Self-categorization theory suggests that only when the world is uncertain does self-categorization lead to discrimination against other groups (Grieve & Hogg, 1999). Self-categorization theory, then, adds a bit of optimism to its parent theory's (SIT) outlook by suggesting that categorization does not always lead to discrimination, and if threat can be managed or alleviated then little discrimination or intergroup antagonism need occur.

The Power of Groups to Punish: Social Ostracism

Although groups may serve to increase our self-esteem by enhancing our social identity, groups have power to exact painful, even dreadful, punishment. Baumeister and Leary (1995) observed that there is little in life so frightful as being excluded from groups that are important to us. Most of us spend much of our time in the presence of other people. The presence of others provides us not only with opportunities for positive interactions but also for risks of being ignored, excluded, and rejected. Kipling Williams (1997; Williams & Zadro, in press) provided an innovative approach to the study of the effects of being ignored or rejected by the group. Such behavior is called social **ostracism** and is defined by Williams as the act of excluding or ignoring other individuals or groups. This behavior is widespread and universal. Williams noted that organizations, employers, co-workers, friends, and family all may ignore or disengage from people (the silent treatment) to punish, control, and vent anger. The pervasiveness of ostracism is reflected by a survey conducted by Williams and his co-workers that showed that 67% of the sample surveyed said they had used the silent treatment (deliberately not speaking to a person in their presence) on a loved one, and 75% indicated that they had been a target of the silent treatment by a loved one (Faulkner & Williams, 1995). As you might imagine, the silent treatment is a marker of a relationship that is disintegrating. From the point of view of the victim of this silent treatment, social ostracism is the perception of being ignored by others in the victim's presence (Williams, in press).

> **ostracism**
> The widespread and universal behavior of excluding or ignoring other individuals or groups.

Williams and his colleague Kristin Sommer identified several forms of ostracism (Williams & Sommer, 1997). First, they distinguish between social and physical ostracism. Physical ostracism includes solitary confinement, exile, or the time-out room in grade school. Social ostracism is summed up by phrases we all know: the cold shoulder, the silent treatment.

In the social psychological realm, *punitive ostracism* and *defensive ostracism* are among the various guises ostracism may take. Punitive ostracism refers to behaviors (ignoring, shunning) that are perceived by the victim as intended to be deliberate and harmful. Sometimes, Williams and Sommer pointed out, people also engage in defensive ostracism, a kind of preemptive strike when you think someone might feel negatively toward you.

The purpose of ostracism from the point of view of the ostracizer is clear: controlling the behavior of the victim. Ostracizers also report being rewarded when they see that their tactics are working. Certainly, defensive ostracism, ignoring someone before they can harm you or ignore you, seems to raise the self-esteem of the ostracizer (Sommer, Williams, Ciarocco, & Baumeister, 1999).

Williams developed a number of creative methods to induce the perception of being ostracized in laboratory experiments. Williams and Sommer (1997) used a ball-tossing game in which two individuals working as confederates of the experimenters either included or socially ostracized a participant during a 5-minute ball-tossing game. Participants who were waiting for a group activity to begin were placed in a waiting room that happened to have a number of objects, including a ball. Three people were involved, the two confederates and the unknowing research participant. All participants were thrown the ball during the first minute, but those in the ostracized condition were not thrown the ball during the remaining 4 minutes. The experimenter then returned to conduct the second part of the study.

After the ball-tossing ended in the Williams and Sommer (1997) experiment, participants were asked to think of as many uses for an object as possible within a specified time limit. They performed this task in the same room either collectively (in which they were told that only the group effort would be recorded) or coactively (in which their own individual performances would be compared to that of the other group members) with the two confederates. Williams and Sommer predicted that ostracized targets—those excluded from the ball tossing—would try to regain a sense of belonging by working comparatively harder on the collective task, thereby contributing to the group's success. Williams and Sommer found support for this hypothesis, but only for female participants. Whether they were ostracized in the ball-tossing task, males displayed social loafing by being less productive when working collectively than when working coactively. Females, however, behaved quite differently depending on whether they had been ostracized or included. When included, they tended to work about as hard collectively as coactively, but when ostracized, they were actually more productive when working collectively compared to when they worked coactively (Williams, in press).

Women also demonstrated that they were interested in regaining a sense of being a valued member of the group by displaying nonverbal commitment (i.e., leaning forward, smiling), whereas males tended to employ face-saving techniques such as combing their hair, looking through their wallets, and manipulating objects, all in the service of being "cool" and showing that they were unaffected by the ostracism. We can conclude that ostracism did threaten sense of belonging for both males and females, but ostracized females tried to regain a sense of belonging, whereas males acted to regain self-esteem (Williams & Sommer, 1997; Williams, in press).

Deindividuation and Anonymity: The Power of Groups to Do Violence

Although ostracism refers to essentially psychological methods of exclusion from the group, other more dangerous behaviors occur in group settings. We have seen that when certain individuals feel they can't be identified by their actions or achievements, they tend to loaf. This is a common group effect. A decline in individual identity seems to mean a decline in a person's sense of responsibility. Anonymity can alter people's ethical and moral behavior.

Observers of group behavior have long known that certain kinds of groups have the potential for great mischief. Groups at sporting events have engaged in murder and mayhem when their soccer teams have lost. One element present in such groups is that the individuals are not easily identifiable. People get lost in the mass and seem to lose their self-identity and self-awareness. Social psychologists have called this loss of inhibition while engulfed in a group **deindividuation** (Zimbardo, 1969).

People who are deindividuated seem to become less aware of their own moral standards and are much more likely to respond to violent or aggressive

deindividuation

A phenomenon that occurs in large-group (crowd) situations in which individual identity is lost within the anonymity of the large group, perhaps leading to a lowering of inhibitions against negative behaviors.

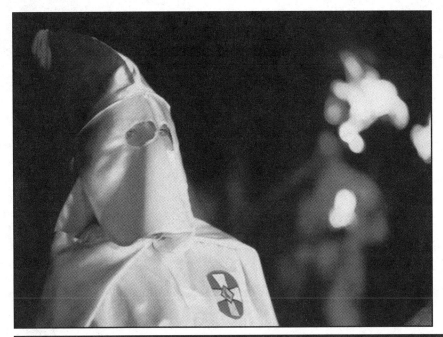

Deindividuation is an important social psychological process underlying violence by members of certain groups. Klansmen wear the hooded uniform so that they lose their sense of self-identity. Other groups, such as an army, also require uniforms to enhance the group experience and reduce self-identity.

cues (Prentice-Dunn & Rogers, 1989). In fact, deindividuated people are quick to respond to any cues. Research suggests that when people are submerged in a group, they become impulsive, aroused, and wrapped up in the cues of the moment (Spivey & Prentice-Dunn, 1990). Their action is determined by whatever the group does.

Groups and organizations whose primary purpose involves violence often attempt to deindividuate their members. Certainly, the white sheets covering the members of the Ku Klux Klan are a prime example of this. So, too, are the training methods of most military organizations. Uniforms serve to lower a sense of self-awareness and make it easier to respond to aggressive cues.

There is some evidence that the larger the group, the more likely it is that individual group members will deindividuate. Differences have been found in the behavior of larger and smaller crowds that gather when a troubled person is threatening to leap from a building or bridge (Mann, 1981). Out of 21 such cases examined, in 10, the crowds baited the victim to jump, whereas in the remaining 11, the victim was not taunted and was often rescued. What was the difference between these two sorts of cases?

The baiting crowds tended to be larger—over 300 people. The baiting episodes were more likely to take place after dark, and the victim was usually situated higher up, typically above the 12th floor. Additionally, the longer the episode continued, the more likely was the taunting. All these factors—the large size of the crowd, the distance between that crowd and the victim, the anonymity lent by darkness—contributed to the deindividuation of the members of the crowd. And the longer these deindividuated people waited, the more irritable they became.

Another study found that when a crowd is bent on violence, the larger the crowd, the more vicious the behavior (Mullen, 1986). Larger crowds and smaller numbers of victims can lead to atrocities such as hangings, torture, and rape.

GROUP DECISION MAKING AND GROUP PRODUCTIVITY

We turn to a final set of questions: How do groups operate to solve problems, make decisions, and reach group goals? Early in the chapter we distinguished between groups with an instrumental purpose and groups with an affiliative purpose. Many, if not most, groups are formed for the purpose of making decisions, a clearly instrumental purpose. This was the purpose of the *Challenger* group. We form decision-making groups because we believe that combining the talents of individuals will increase the effectiveness of decision making and thus the productivity of our endeavor. We extend the old saying "two heads are better than one" to groups of "heads." Let's see if the truisms are true.

Individual Decisions Versus Group Decisions

First of all, let's consider whether group decisions are in fact better than individual decisions. Is it better to have a team of medical personnel decide whether our CAT scan indicates we need surgery, or is that decision better left to a single surgeon? Did the launch director at NASA benefit from the workings of the group, or would he have been wiser to think through the situation on his own?

DOES A GROUP DO BETTER THAN THE AVERAGE PERSON?
In general, research shows that groups do outperform individuals—at least the average individual—on many jobs and tasks (Stasser, Kerr, & Davis, 1989). Three reasons have been proposed for the observed superiority of groups over the average person. First of all, groups do a better job than the average person because they recognize truth—accept the right answer—more quickly. Second, groups are better able to reject error—reject incorrect or implausible answers (Laughlin, 1980; Laughlin, VanderStoep, & Hollingshead, 1991; Lorge & Solomon, 1955). Third, groups have a better, more efficient memory system than do individuals. This permits them to process information more effectively.

transactive memory systems

Systems within groups that are sets of individual memories that allow group members to learn about each other's expertise and to assign memory tasks on that basis.

Groups may possess what has been called **transactive memory systems**, a shared system for placing events into memory (encoding), storing those memories, and retrieving that information (Wegner, 1986). Wegner (1996) used the example of a directory-sharing computer network to explain the three legs of a transactive memory system:

1. *Directory updating*, in which people find out what other group members know.
2. *Information allocation*, the place where new information is given to the person who knows how to store it.
3. *Retrieval coordination*, which refers to how information is recovered when needed to solve a particular problem.

Group members learn about each other's expertise and assign memory tasks on that basis. This not only leaves others to concentrate on the memory tasks they do best, it also provides the group with memory aids. Someone in the group may be good in math, for example, so that person is assigned the task of remembering math-related information. When the group wants to recall that information, they go to this expert and use him or her as an external memory aid. Memory thus becomes a transaction, a social event in the group. For some or all of these reasons, groups seem to outperform the average person on many decision-related tasks.

Andrea Hollingshead (1998) showed the effectiveness of transactive memory. She studied intimate couples as compared to strangers who worked on problems, some face to face, and others via a computer conferencing network. Intimate couples who were able to sit face-to-face and process their partner's verbal and nonverbal cues were able to solve problems better than couples comprised of strangers, because the intimate couples were able to retrieve more information. Intimate couples who worked via a computer conferencing system did not do as well, again suggesting that the nonverbal cues were important in pooling information.

DOES A GROUP DO BETTER THAN ITS BEST MEMBER?
We noted that research shows that groups outperform the average person. But what about the smartest person, the "best and brightest" member of the group?

To test the hypothesis that groups can find correct responses better than individuals, college students were asked to try to discover an arbitrary rule for separating a deck of cards into those that did and did not fit the rule (Laughlin, VanderStoep, & Hollingshead, 1991). If the rule was "hearts," for example, then all cards of the hearts suit would fit the rule, and all others would not. Subjects had to guess the rule, and then test it by playing a card. The feedback from the experimenter gave them information on which to base their next guess. The researchers also varied the amount of information that subjects had to process. They presented some subjects with only two arrays of cards, others with three, and others with four. The more arrays, the more difficult the task.

The performance of four-person groups was then compared to the performance of each of the four group members, who had to do a similar task individually. The best individual was able to generate more correct guesses than the group or any other individual member. The group's performance was equal to its second-best member. The third- and fourth-best members were inferior to the group. As the task became more difficult—the arrays increased to four, which made much more information available—the performance of both the best individual and the group fell. The researchers also compared the abilities of groups and their individual members in rejecting implausible hypotheses. The fewer implausible ideas subjects or groups raised, the better they did with respect to rejecting false leads. Groups and the best individual were better at rejecting false leads than were the second-, third-, and fourth-best individuals.

This research suggests that groups in general perform as well as their best or second-best individual member working independently. You might ask, Why not just have the best member do the task? But keep in mind that it is often not possible to identify the group's best member prior to completing the task. This finding tells us that groups tend to perform competently, particularly when the information load is not overwhelming.

THE HARDER THE PROBLEM, THE BETTER THE GROUP
However, recent work suggests that we may have underrated the ability of groups to reach solutions, especially more difficult problems. Crott, Giesel, and Hoffman (1998) argued that their research on group problem solving suggests

that difficult tasks provoke creativity in groups. When faced with a problem that required the group to come up with a number of hypotheses to discover the correct answers, groups more than individuals were able to generate a number of novel explanations. Groups were also shown to be less likely to be prone to the confirmation bias than were individuals (Crott et al., 1998).

Similarly Laughlin, Bonner, and Altermatt (1998) showed that groups were as good as the best individual in solving difficult inductive (proceeding from specific facts to general conclusions) problems and better than all the remaining group members. Groups are especially effective in dealing with information-rich problems because they have more resources (Tindale, Smith, Thomas, Filkins, & Sheffey, 1996).

We have seen how well groups perform with respect to the abilities of their members. Let's take a closer look at the workings, the dynamics, of how those decisions are made. How do groups gather and use the information possessed by individual members? How do they reach decisions?

THE GROUP'S USE OF INFORMATION One advantage groups have over individual decision makers is that a variety of individuals can usually bring to the discussion a great deal more information than can one person. This is usually seen as the great advantage of groups. But does the group make adequate use of that information?

Research shows that group members tend to discuss information that they share and avoid discussing information that only one person has. Individuals also avoid discussing or disclosing information that goes counter to the group's preferred decision (Stasser, Taylor, & Hanna, 1989).

In one experiment, each member of a committee received common information about three candidates for student government (Stasser & Titus, 1987). Each also received information about each candidate that none of the others received (unshared information). The committee members met in four-person groups to rank the candidates. The sheer number of facts available to the members varied from one group to the next. When the number of facts was high, the raters ignored information that was unshared. That is, they rated the candidates based solely on the information that they held in common. The information they chose to share tended to support the group decision; they did not share information that would have conflicted with the decision. Because the results of this study indicate that group members try to avoid conflict by selectively withholding information, the researchers concluded that face-to-face, unstructured discussion is not a good way to inform group members of unshared information (Stasser, 1992).

There appear to be at least two reasons for the failure of face-to-face groups to report and use unshared information. The first has to do with the way people think. Whatever is most salient (the shared information) tends to overwhelm that which recedes into the background (the unshared information). In other words, group members hear the shared information and simply neglect to bring up or take into account the unshared information. The second reason, as suggested earlier, is that individuals may be motivated to ignore or forget information (unshared) that they think may cause conflict.

The nature of a group's task may also affect how the group searches for information and uses shared and unshared facts. To investigate this possibility, experimenters hypothesized that groups would be more likely to share all information if they knew that the problem had a definitively correct answer than if the task called only for a judgment (Stasser & Stewart, 1992). Subjects in this study were given information about a crime. In some groups, all the information was given to all the members. In other groups, some information was given only to individual members. In other words, in the latter groups, some members had unshared information. In addition, half the groups were told that there was enough evidence to solve the crime, whereas others were informed that because the evidence was less than full, the group would have to make a judgment call.

The results showed that groups given the task with the correct answer were much more likely to search for the unshared information and get the right answer than groups given a judgment problem. What differed was the expectation that there was or was not a correct answer (Stasser & Stewart, 1992). When the group members think or know that the task has a definite answer, they are more forthright in bringing up anything (unshared) that could help the group. The group strategy changes. People want to search for any information that helps them to be successful.

THE IMPORTANCE OF UNSHARED INFORMATION The research of James R. Larson, Jr., showed that access to unshared information is crucial to good group decision making. For example, Larson, Christensen, Franz, and Abbot (1998) examined the decision making of medical teams. Three-person physician teams had to diagnose cases and were given shared information (to all three MDs), whereas the rest of the diagnostic data was divided among the three. Compared with unshared information, the medicos discussed shared information earlier in the discussion. However, the unshared information when discussed proved to lead to more accurate (correct diagnosis) outcomes.

In other research, Larsen's team reached similar conclusions. Winquist & Larsen (1998) gave three-person groups the task of nominating professors for teaching awards. Discussion focused more on shared information, but the quality of the decision was determined by the amount of unshared information that was pooled in the discussion.

The Effect of Leadership Style on Group Decision Making

How can we make sure groups gain access to unshared information? What is the best way of making sure that group members who have information that others do not are motivated to pool that information?

We know that leadership style is important in determining how groups function (Fiedler, 1967). In one study, researchers identified two common styles of leadership. The first, the **participative leader**, was someone who shares power with the other members of the group and includes them in the decision making. Another leadership style, the **directive leader**, gives less value to participation, emphasizes the need for agreement, and tends to prefer his or her own solution.

DIRECTIVE AND PARTICIPATIVE LEADERS Research using these leadership styles indicates that participative leaders provoked their groups to discuss more information, both shared and unshared, than did groups with a directive leader (Larson, Jr., Foster-Fishman, & Franz, 1998). However, directive leaders were more likely to repeat information that had been pooled, especially unshared information. In other words, directive leaders made unshared information more prominent.

participative leader
A leadership style characterized by a leader who shares power with the other members of the group and includes them in the decision making.

directive leader
A leadership style involving a leader who gives less value to participation, emphasizes the need for agreement, and tends to prefer his or her own solution.

It seems then that participative leaders worked to get the group to bring out more information but that directive leaders were more active in managing the information once it was put on the table. What about the quality of the decisions? Interestingly, groups under participative leadership made many more incorrect decisions. This was counter to the researchers' expectations (Larson, Jr. et al., 1998). If directive leaders have information that favors the best alternative, they use it and bring the group to a good quality decision. They do this much better than participative leaders. The downside to directive leaders is that they may not be able to get the group members to bring out all the necessary information for good decision making.

WHY GROUP MEMBERS OBEY LEADERS: THE PSYCHOLOGY OF LEGITIMACY Tom R. Tyler (1997) provided insight into when and why groups voluntarily follow their leaders. In order for groups to function, the members have to decide that the leader ought to be obeyed. Although leaders often have access to coercive methods to get members to follow their orders, voluntary compliance is necessary oftentimes for a group to successfully achieve its goals.

Tyler was interested in the judgment by group members that they should voluntarily comply with the rules laid down by authorities, regardless of the probability of punishment or reward. Tyler (1997) suggested the feeling of obligation to obey the leader is best termed **legitimacy**. Following earlier work by French and Raven (1959), a leader has legitimate power to influence, and the member has the obligation to obey when all have accepted (internalized) the central values of the group. Tyler's work suggests that the basis of a leader's legitimacy resides in its psychological foundations. That is, it is not enough for the leader to be successful in getting the group's work done, although clearly that is quite important.

Among the factors that are crucial for legitimacy is, first, how people are treated by authorities, regardless of how the leaders have evaluated them and, second, whether the members share group membership with the authorities. Finally, Tyler's work indicated that people value the leader's integrity more than they do the leader's competence. This description of legitimacy is called the *relational model*.

The relational model emphasizes that individuals are most likely to internalize group values when they are treated with procedural fairness (van den Bos, Wilke, & Lind, 1998). In fact, people make judgments about authorities when little information is available about them, based on whether the authorities give them dignified, fair treatment (van den Bos et al., 1998). Neidermeier, Horowitz, and Kerr (1999) reported that some groups (juries) may deliberately and willfully disobey the commands of authorities (judges) when they determine that following the authority's instructions would result in an unfair and unjust verdict. People will be more likely to accept a leader when that leader exhibits interpersonal respect, neutrality in judgment, and trustworthiness (Tyler, 1997).

Again, we should not overlook the importance of instrumental factors in leadership. Getting the group's work done is crucial. It is likely that under some circumstances, relational issues may not be important at all (Fiedler, 1967). If someone has the ability to lead a group out of a burning building, relational issues matter not. But, Tyler's earlier work indicated that in judging authorities with whom we have no contact (the U.S. Congress, the Supreme Court), concerns about fairness come into play (Tyler, 1994).

legitimacy
A group member's feeling of obligation to obey the group's leader.

Factors That Affect the Decision-Making Ability of a Group

What makes a good decision-making group? Is there a particular size that works best? A particular composition? What other factors have an impact on the abilities and effectiveness of a group? Consider President Kennedy's advisory group that decided to invade Cuba. It was fairly large, perhaps 12 or more people attended each session, and group members were similar in temperament, background, and education. Is that a good recipe for a decision-making group?

GROUP COMPOSITION   Several group investigators emphasize the composition of a group as its most fundamental attribute (Levine & Moreland, 1990). Questions often arise about how to best constitute groups, especially decision-making groups. For example, some people have asked whether random selection of citizens is the best way to put together a jury, especially for a complex trial (Horowitz, ForsterLee, & Brolly, 1996).

Some researchers have investigated whether groups with high-ability members perform better than groups composed of individuals of lesser abilities. In one study, the composition of three-person battle tank crews was varied (Tziner & Eden, 1985). Some crews had all high-ability members, some had mixtures of high- and low-ability members, and others had all low-ability members. Their results showed that tank groups composed of all high-ability individuals performed more effectively than expected from the sum of their individual talents. Groups composed of all low-ability members did worse than expected.

Psychologist Robert Sternberg believes that every group has its own intelligence level, or "group IQ" (Williams & Sternberg, 1988). The group's IQ is not simply the sum of each member's IQ. Rather, it is the blending of their intellectual abilities with their personalities and social competence.

In one study, Sternberg asked volunteers who had been tested on their intelligence and social skills to devise a marketing plan for a new product, an artificial sweetener (Williams & Sternberg, 1988). Other groups had similar tasks, all of which required creative solutions. The decision-making groups that produced the most creative solutions were those that contained at least one person with a high IQ and others who were socially skillful, or practical, or creative. In other words, the successful groups had a good mix of people with different talents who brought different points of view to the problem.

This research highlights the fact that everybody in the group must have the skills to make a contribution. If one member of the group is extremely persuasive or extremely good at the task, the other members may not be able to use their abilities to the best effect. According to one study, successful leaders should have IQ scores no more than 10 points higher than the average IQ score of the group (Simonton, 1985). This minimizes the possibility that the most talented person will dominate the group. If this person is more extraordinary, then the collective effort will be hurt by his or her presence (Simonton, 1985).

The gender of group members also influences problem-solving ability (Levine & Moreland, 1990). Research shows that although groups composed of all males are generally more effective than all-female groups, the success of the groups really depends on the kind of problem they have to solve. Male groups do better when they have to fulfill a specific task, whereas female groups do better at communal activities that involve friendship and social support (Wood, 1987).

GROUP SIZE Conventional wisdom tells us that two heads are better than one. If this is so, then why wouldn't three be better than two, four better than three, and so on? Does increasing a group's size also increase its ability to arrive at correct answers, make good decisions, and reach productivity goals?

Increasing the number of members of a group does increase the resources available to the group and therefore the group's potential productivity. On the other hand, increasing group size also leads to more **process loss** (Steiner, 1972). In other words, the increase in resources due to more group members is counterbalanced by the increased difficulty in arriving at a decision. Large groups generally take more time to reach a decision than small groups (Davis, 1969).

Another problem facing larger groups is unequal participation of members. This was clearly a problem for the Bay of Pigs advisors. Lower-status members and newcomers tend to say very little. In order for increased resources to increase productivity, those resources must be made available to the group. However, in larger groups, all members do not contribute equally to the discussion. In larger groups (of 6 to 10 members), two or three people dominate the discussion. Some members may be uncomfortable speaking up in this size group. The number of members actually contributing their resources falls short of the actual size of the group as the actual size increases (Bray, Kerr, & Atkin, 1978).

Yet, smaller is not always better. We often misperceive the effect of group size on performance. Researchers interested in testing the common belief that small groups are more effective than large groups gave a number of groups the task of solving social dilemmas, problems that require individuals to sacrifice some of their own gains so that the entire group benefits, such as conserving water during a drought (Kerr, 1989).

Those who participated in the study thought that the size of their group was an important determinant of their ability to satisfactorily resolve social dilemmas. People in larger groups felt there was very little they could do to influence the decisions of the group. They tended to be less active and less aware of what was going on than comparable members of smaller groups. They believed that smaller groups would more effectively solve social dilemmas than larger groups, mainly by cooperating.

In fact, there was no difference in effectiveness between the small and large groups in solving social dilemmas. People enjoyed small groups more than large ones, but the product and the quality of the decisions of both sizes of groups were much the same. Thus, small groups offer only an **illusion of efficacy**. That is, they think they are more effective than larger groups, but the evidence suggests they may not be, based on their actual productivity.

GROUP COHESIVENESS Does a cohesive group outperform a noncohesive group? When we consider decision-making or problem-solving groups, two types of cohesiveness become important: *task-based cohesiveness* and *interpersonal cohesiveness* (Zachary & Lowe, 1988). Groups may be cohesive because the members respect one another's abilities to help obtain the group's goals; this is task-based cohesiveness. Other groups are cohesive because the members find each other to be likable; this is interpersonal cohesiveness.

Each type of cohesiveness influences group performance in a somewhat different way, depending on the type of task facing the group. When a task does not require much interaction among members, task-based cohesiveness increases group productivity, but interpersonal cohesiveness does

process loss

The loss of group efficiency that results from increased group size and generally leads to a decrement in productivity.

illusion of efficacy

The illusion that members of small groups think they are more effective than larger groups, which may not be the case.

not (Zaccaro & McCoy, 1988). For example, if a group is working on writing a paper, and each member is responsible for different parts of that paper, then productivity is increased to the extent that the members are committed to doing a good job for the group. The group members do not have to like one another to do the job well.

Now, it is true that when members of the group like one another, their cohesiveness increases the amount of commitment to a task and increases group interaction as well (Zachary & Lowe, 1988). However, the time they spend interacting may take away from their individual time on the task, thus offsetting the productivity that results from task-based cohesiveness.

Some tasks require interaction, such as the *Challenger* decision-making group. On these tasks, groups that have high levels of both task-based and interactive cohesiveness perform better than groups that are high on one type but low on the other or that are low on both (Zaccaro & McCoy, 1988).

Cohesiveness can also detract from the successful completion of a task when group members become too concerned with protecting one another's feelings and do not allot enough attention to the actual task. Groups that are highly cohesive have members who are very concerned with one another. This may lead group members to stifle criticism of group decisions. This, in fact, is what happened in Kennedy's advisory group, according to the participants' memoirs and statements. People were afraid to say what they really thought of the plan to invade Cuba with a brigade of ill-trained exiles (Janis, 1972).

Members of strongly cohesive groups are less likely to disagree with one another than are members of less cohesive groups, especially if they are under time pressure to come up with a solution. Ultimately, then, very high cohesiveness may prevent a group from reaching a high-quality decision. Cohesiveness is a double-edged sword: It can help or hurt a group, depending on the demands of the task.

THE DYNAMICS OF GROUP DECISION MAKING: DECISION RULES, GROUP POLARIZATION, AND GROUPTHINK

Now that we have considered various aspects of group decision making, let's consider how the decision-making process works. Although we empower groups to make many important decisions for us, they do not always make good decisions. As we have seen, even a high-powered group of advisors to the President of the United States can make unfortunate decisions. We turn now to a consideration of three important and related aspects of group interaction and decision making.

How Groups Blend Individual Choices Into Group Decisions

A *decision rule* is a rule about how many members must agree before the group can reach a decision. Decision rules set the criteria for how individual choices will be blended into a group product or decision (Pritchard & Watson, 1992). Two common decision rules are *majority rule* (the winning alternative must receive more than half the votes) and *unanimity rule* (consensus, all members must agree).

Groups will find a decision rule that leads to good decisions and stick with that rule throughout the life cycle of the group (Miller, 1989). The majority rule is used in most groups (Davis, 1980). The majority dominates both through informational social influence—controlling the information the group uses (Stasser, Kerr, & Davis, 1989)—and through normative social influence—exerting the group's will through conformity pressure.

A unanimity rule, or consensus, forces the group to consider the views of the minority more carefully than a majority rule. Group members tend to be more satisfied by a unanimity rule, especially those in the minority, who feel that the majority paid attention and considered their point of view (Hastie, Penrod, & Pennington, 1983).

The decision rule used by a group may depend on what kind of task the group is working on. When the group deals with intellective tasks—problems for which there is a definitive correct answer, such as the solution to an equation—the decision rule is truth wins. In other words, when one member of the group solves the problem, all members (who have mathematical knowledge) recognize the truth of the answer. If the problem has a less definitively correct answer, such as, say, the solution to a word puzzle, then the decision rule is that truth supported wins. When one member comes up with an answer that the others support, that answer wins (Kerr, 1992).

When the group deals with judgmental tasks—tasks that do not have a demonstrably correct answer, such as a jury decision in a complex case— then the decision rule is majority wins (Laughlin & Ellis, 1986). That is, whether the formal decision rule (the one the judge gives to the jury) is unanimity, or a 9 out of 12 majority (a rule common in some states), a decision usually is made once the majority rule has been satisfied. Even if the formal rule is unanimity, unpersuaded jurors tend to go along with the majority once 9 or 10 of the 12 jurors agree.

Group Polarization

group polarization
The tendency for individual, prediscussion opinion to become more extreme following group discussion.

A commonplace event observed in group decision making is that groups tend to polarize. **Group polarization** (Moscovici & Zavalloni, 1969; Myers & Lamm, 1976) occurs when the initial-decision tendency of the group becomes more extreme following group discussion. For example, researchers asked French students about their attitudes toward Americans, which prior to group discussion had been negative (Moscovici & Zavalloni, 1969). After group discussion, researchers measured attitudes again and found that group discussion tended to polarize, or pull the attitude to a more extreme position. The initial negative attitudes became even more negative after discussion.

In another study, researchers found that if a jury initially was leaning in the direction of innocence, group discussion led to a shift to leniency. If, on the other hand, the jury was initially leaning in the direction of guilt, there was a shift to severity (Myers & Lamm, 1976). Group polarization can also be recognized in some of the uglier events in the real world. Groups of terrorists become more extreme, more violent, over time (McCauley & Segal, 1987). Extremity shifts, as we have seen, appear to be a normal aspect of group decision making (Blascovich & Ginsburg, 1974).

Why does group polarization occur? Researchers have focused on two processes in group discussion: *social comparison* and *persuasive arguments*. Group discussion, as we have seen, provides opportunities for social comparison. We can not compare how we think with how everyone else thinks. We might have thought that our private decision favored a daring choice, but then we find that other people took even riskier stands. This causes us to redefine our idea of riskiness and shift our opinion toward more extreme choices.

The second cause of the group polarization is persuasive arguments (Burnstein, 1982; Burnstein & Vinokur, 1977). We already have seen that people tend to share information they hold in common. This means that the arguments put forth and supported are those the majority of group members support. The majority can often persuade others to accept those arguments (Myers & Lamm, 1975). For example, most people in Kennedy's advisory group spoke in favor of a military response to Cuba and persuaded doubters of their wisdom.

Research supports the idea that discussion polarizes groups. In one early study on the risky shift, group meetings were set up under several conditions (Wallach & Kogan, 1965). In some groups, members merely exchanged information about their views by passing notes; there was no discussion, just information exchange. In others, individuals discussed their views face-to-face. In some of the discussion groups, members were required to reach consensus; in others, they were not. The researchers found that group discussion, with or without reaching consensus, was the only necessary and sufficient condition required to produce the risky shift. The mere exchange of information without discussion was not enough, and forcing consensus was not necessary (Wallach & Kogan, 1965).

Groupthink

The finding that group decisions tend to be more extreme than the decisions of individuals is an important one. It offers some insight into how it is that groups composed of competent, intelligent individuals can reach poor decisions, including the decision to launch the Bay of Pigs invasion. In fact, the disastrous outcome of that decision led to a new area of study called groupthink.

The late Irving Janis (1972, 1982) carried out several post hoc (after the fact) analyses of what he terms historical fiascos. Janis found common threads running through these decision failures. He called this phenomenon **groupthink**, "a mode of thinking that people engage in when they are deeply involved in a cohesive in-group, when the members' striving for unanimity overrides their motivation to realistically appraise alternative courses of actions" (Janis, 1982, p. 9). Groupthink is a breakdown in the rational decision-making abilities of members of a cohesive group. As we have seen, members of a highly cohesive group become motivated to reach unanimity and protect the feelings of other group members and are less concerned with reaching the best decision.

In examining poor decisions and fiascos, we have to acknowledge the benefits we gain from hindsight. From our privileged point of view here in the present, we can see what we believe to be the fatal flaws of many decisions of the past, especially those with disastrous outcomes. This is obviously dangerous from a scientific perspective (a danger that Janis recognized). It can lead us to overstate the power of groupthink processes. What would have happened, for example, if the invasion of Cuba had been a rousing success and a democratic government installed there? The decisions that we now view as disastrous would have been cheered, not jeered. How many historical decisions had all the markings of groupthink but led to good outcomes? It is important to keep a sense of perspective as we apply concepts such as groupthink to both historical and contemporary events.

groupthink
A group-process phenomenon that may lead to faulty decision making by highly cohesive group members more concerned with reaching consensus than with carefully considering alternative courses of action.

CONDITIONS THAT FAVOR GROUPTHINK The crux of Janis' groupthink concept involved pressures toward uniformity that hinder the complete evaluation of the available courses of action and dangers. Janis (1982) suggested that this tendency was directly related to three factors:

1. *The cohesiveness of the group.* Generally, the more cohesive the decision-making group, the greater the risk that it will fall victim to groupthink.

2. *Stress.* The more stress, the greater the group's susceptibility to groupthink. Indeed, groups under stress show a decrease in performance (Worchel & Shackelford, 1991).

3. *The persuasive strength of its leader.* A leader who is strong and highly directive (i.e., makes his or her views known and pushes the group in that direction) sets a tone that favors the emergence of groupthink.

Social psychologist Clark McCauley provided a slightly different analysis. McCauley (1989) identified three conditions that he believed are always involved when groupthink occurs:

1. *Group insulation.* The decision-making group does not seek analysis and information from sources outside the group.

2. *Promotional leadership.* The leader presents his or her preferred solution to the problem before the group can evaluate all the evidence.

3. *Group homogeneity.* Groups that are made up of people of similar background and opinions are prone to have similar views.

These three antecedents, according to McCauley, lead the group to a premature consensus.

SYMPTOMS OF GROUPTHINK Groups that suffer from groupthink show a fairly predictable set of symptoms. Unlike the antecedent conditions just discussed, which increase the likelihood of groupthink, the symptoms protect the group against negative feelings and anxieties during the decision process. Janis (1972) defined several major symptoms of groupthink.

1. The Illusion of Invulnerability Group members believe that nothing can hurt them. For example, officials at NASA suffered from this illusion. In the 25 space flights before *Challenger* exploded, not one astronaut was lost in a space-launch mission. Even when there was a near disaster aboard Apollo 13, NASA personnel were able to pull the flight out of the fire and bring the three astronauts home safely. This track record of extrodinary success contributed to a belief that NASA could do no wrong. Another example of this illusion can be seen in the decision on how to defend Pearl Harbor. Prior to the Japanese attack on Pearly Harbor in 1941, advisors to the U.S. commander believed that Pearl Harbor was invincible. Typically, this illusion leads to excessive optimism: The group believes that anything it does will turn out for the better.

2. Rationalization Group members tend not to realistically evaluate information presented to them. Instead, they engage in collective efforts to rationalize away damaging information. For example, when the space shuttle *Challenger* exploded in 1986, officials apparently rationalized away information

about the O-rings, whose failure caused the explosion. Negative information about the O-rings dating back as far as 1985 was available but ignored. Six months before the disaster, a NASA budget analyst warned that the O-rings were a serious problem. His warning was labeled an "overstatement."

3. An Unquestioned Belief in the Group's Morality   When a group believes that what they are doing is morally right, excessive risk taking is likely to occur. After all, God is on our side! The *Challenger* decision showed evidence of this belief. The space shuttle program was used for military as well as civilian missions. In 1986, the Soviet Union was still viewed as a major threat to U.S. interests. The military missions strengthened the U.S. military and made it easier to "keep the world free." Such a high moral goal justifies just about anything. This symptom was also seen in John F. Kennedy's group that decided to invade Cuba at the Bay of Pigs. Here were the "good guys" (a free democratic society) fighting the "bad guys" (the godless communists).

4. A Stereotyped View of the Enemy   If a group sees the enemy as too weak, evil, or stupid to do anything about the group's decision, they are displaying a stereotyped view of that enemy. An enemy need not be a military or other such foe. The enemy is any person or group that poses a threat to a group's emerging decision. The enemy in the *Challenger* decision was the group of Thiokol scientists and engineers who recommended against the launch. These individuals were characterized as being too concerned with the scientific end of things. In fact, one engineer was told to take off his engineer's hat and put on his management hat. The implication here is that engineers are too limited in their scope.

5. Conformity Pressures   We have seen that majority influences can operate within a group to change the opinions of dissenting members.

Strong conformity pressures are at work when groupthink emerges. That is, group members who raise objections are pressured to change their views. One of the engineers involved in the *Challenger* launching was initially opposed to the launch. Under extreme pressure from others, he changed his vote. Such conformity pressures also permeated Kennedy's decision making group. Direct pressure was placed on dissenting members to fall into line with the majority.

6. Self-Censorship   Once it appears that anyone who disagrees with the group's view will be pressured to conform, members of the group who have dissenting opinions do not speak up because of the consequences. This leads to self-censorship. After the initial opposition to the *Challenger* launching was rejected rather harshly, for example, other engineers were less likely to express doubts.

7. The Illusion of Unanimity   Because of the strong atmosphere of conformity and the self-censorship of those members who have doubts about the group decision, the group harbors the illusion that everyone is in agreement. In the *Challenger* decision, a poll was taken of management personnel (only), who generally favored the launch. The engineers were present but were not allowed to vote. What emerged was a unanimous vote to launch even though the engineers strongly disagreed. It looked as if everyone agreed to the launch.

8. Emergence of Self-appointed Mindguards   In much the same way as a person can hire a bodyguard to protect him or her, group members emerge to protect the group from damaging information. In the *Challenger* decision, managers at Morton Thiokol emerged in this role. A high-ranking Thiokol manager did not tell Arnold Aldrich about the dissension in the ranks at Thiokol. Thus, Jesse Moore was never made aware of the concerns of the Thiokol engineers.

PREVENTING GROUPTHINK   History provides us with a wonderful contrast between a bad and a good decision. After the disastrous Bay of Pigs decision, the same group had to deal with another international crisis: the Cuban missile crisis. The Soviet Union was installing offensive nuclear weapons in Cuba that could reach major U.S. cities in a matter of minutes. When John F. Kennedy found out about this, something had to be done. The same group that blundered into the Bay of Pigs now had to tackle this more serious crisis. However, the group did not operate in the same manner as it did in the Bay of Pigs decision.

Kennedy made several changes in how the group operated after the Bay of Pigs decision. Janis (1972) identified, among others, the following measures taken by Kennedy:

1. The leader of the group should assign each member the role of critical evaluator. This person is to give a high priority to expressing doubts and raising questions.

2. The leader of the group should not make his or her views known to the group and should remain impartial. This prevents the leader from biasing the group with his or her views.

3. The group should be broken up into smaller subgroups, each with its own leader, to work on specific aspects of a problem. After working on parts of the problem, the subgroups should meet together as a

whole group and work on the problem further. Furthermore, after the decision has been made, the group should have a second chance to change its mind.

4. Outside experts should be brought in, even if they do not agree with what the group's solution to the problem might be.

GROUPTHINK RECONSIDERED The groupthink hypothesis attempts to explain historical fiascos by pointing to certain flaws and failures in group dynamics. This hypothesis has had much influence in any number of fields. But, as with almost any theory, new information and ideas have led researchers to continue probing the original issues. Some social scientists have begun to look for factors other than those outlined by Janis that might lead groups to make bad decisions.

Glen Whyte (1989) suggested that group polarization, risk taking, and the possibility of fiasco all increase when a group frames a decision in terms of potential failure. As an example, consider the *Challenger* situation: If the spaceship wasn't launched, those in charge would be accused of failure, and funding for the space program might be cut off. It seemed to make more sense to the decision makers to risk the launch than to cancel it. If the O-rings failed, the launching entailed a very big risk. But, after all, the O-rings had not failed in the past, and they would fail only in cold weather. No problem, the launch site was in Florida. Unfortunately, on the morning of the launch, the temperature fell to freezing. A disaster resulted. The way the group framed the decision—both alternatives, to go or not to go, carried risks—led them to make a bad choice.

Whyte (1989) argued that if group members see all their choices as having potentially negative outcomes, they are more likely to favor the risky decisions over the more cautious ones. The risk involved in the Bay of Pigs invasion, for example, had to be balanced against the negative consequences of doing nothing. Similarly, when NASA officials decided to launch the *Challenger*, they had to balance the potential for disaster against the negative outcomes of "no go," such as falling behind on launch schedules and having funds cut.

Whyte believes that groups that have made disastrous decisions were working in an environment that actually favored a risky decision over more cautious choices. In such situations, the group is likely to become polarized around a risky decision; group members will adopt attitudes that are more extreme once they have entered into group discussion. In other words, the manner in which a group frames a problem with respect to risk may be as important as faulty group dynamics in leading to bad decisions (Whyte, 1989).

Other researchers have examined some of Janis' other conclusions. Their work suggests that group cohesiveness may not be as crucial for the emergence of groupthink as Janis believed (Cartwright, 1978; Flowers, 1977), although directive leadership may be (Flowers, 1977). Research by Philip Tetlock and associates indicates that very cohesive groups may not be any more prone to groupthink than less cohesive groups (Tetlock, Peterson, McGuire, Shi-jie Chang, & Feld, 1992). Tetlock also failed to find evidence that increasing stress levels make groupthink more likely. What he did find was that groupthink could be best predicted by faulty decision-making structures and procedures. The second best predictor was **consensus seeking**, which leads groups to become more concerned with maintaining morale and getting everybody to agree than with the quality of the group decision (Tetlock et al., 1992).

consensus seeking
A tendency in groups that leads members to be more concerned with maintaining morale and gaining unanimous agreement than with the quality of the group decision.

The Dynamics of Group Decision Making **317**

In other words, a leader who does not let group members speak freely and who controls the discussion is likely to foster a bad decision. A group that is more concerned with feelings than with quality decision making is also a prime candidate for groupthink. Groups that allow people to disagree, promote critical analysis, and have decision-making rules that help people contribute to the discussion are the least likely to fall prey to groupthink (Tetlock et al., 1992). In sum, then, this research indicates that the two most powerful factors involved in groupthink and defective decision making are procedural faults and consensus seeking.

THE *CHALLENGER* REVISITED

The space program never had an in-flight disaster. Astronauts had been killed before, but in training missions, and very early in the program's development. Despite the patently dangerous nature of space travel, the possibility of disaster had been dismissed because it simply hadn't happened. In fact, it was deemed so safe that an untrained civilian, a school teacher, was chosen to be a crew member on the *Challenger*.

When the leaders of a group have a preferred outcome and are under pressure to make decisions quickly, it becomes highly likely that information that does not conform to the favored point of view will be ignored by decision-making groups. Understanding how groups interact and influence their members is crucial to designing procedures that will provide for rational decision-making processes.

CHAPTER REVIEW

1. What is a group?

A **group** is an assemblage of two or more individuals who influence one another through social interaction. Group members share perceptions of what constitutes appropriate behavior (**group norms**), and they have formal and informal roles. Group members are interdependent; that is, they depend on one another to meet group goals, and they have emotional (affective) ties with one another. Groups can be either instrumental (existing to perform a task or reach a goal) or affiliative (existing for more general, usually social, reasons).

Groups vary in **cohesiveness**, the strength of the relationships that link the members of the group. Groups may be cohesive because the members like one another (interpersonal cohesiveness); because they are physically close to one another (propinquity); because they adhere to group norms; or because they help each other do a good job and, therefore, attain group goals (task-based cohesiveness).

2. Why do people join groups?

Groups help people meet their biological, psychological, and social needs. Groups were certainly useful in the evolutionary history of humans, aiding the species in its survival. Among the basic needs groups meet are social support; protection from loneliness; and social comparison, the process by which we compare our feelings, opinions, and behaviors with those of others in order to get accurate information about ourselves. People join groups to fulfill these needs and to enhance themselves.

3. How do groups influence their members?

In addition to fulfilling members' needs, groups also influence members' individual senses of worth, self-esteem, which, in turn, has an impact on how one group relates to other groups in a society. Self-identity theory suggests that much of our self-esteem derives from the status of the groups to which we belong or with which we identify.

Members who threaten the success of a group also threaten the positive image of the group. This leads to the **black sheep effect**, the observation that whereas an attractive in-group member is rated more highly than an attractive member of an out-group, an unattractive in-group member is perceived more negatively than an unattractive out-group member. Although groups may serve to increase our self-esteem by enhancing our social identity, groups also have power to exact painful, even dreadful punishment, social **ostracism**, which is defined by Williams (1997) as the act of excluding or ignoring other individuals or groups.

4. What effect does an audience have on performance?

The presence of other people or audiences may enhance our performance, a process known as **social facilitation**. Other times, the presence of a critical audience or an audience with high expectations decreases performance ("choking"). Research has shown that the presence of others helps when people perform a dominant, well-learned response but diminishes performance when they perform a skill not very well learned or novel (**social inhibition**). This may be due to increased effort as a result of increased arousal; or it may be due to anxiety about being judged (**evaluation apprehension**), which increases arousal; or, according to **distraction–conflict theory**, it may be due to conflicts for attention.

5. How does being in a group affect performance and other behavior?

Sometimes being in a group enhances performance. Other times, individuals performing in groups display **social loafing**, a tendency not to perform to capacity. This seems to occur when the task is not that important or when individual output cannot be evaluated. When people become **free riders,** others often work harder to make up for their lack of effort, a process known as **social compensation.**

When members of a crowd cannot be identified individually and, therefore, feel they have become anonymous, they may experience **deindividuation,** a loss of self-identity. Their sense of personal responsibility diminishes, and they tend to lose their inhibitions. This is more likely to happen if the crowd is large or if they are physically distant from a victim. Deindividuation can be a factor in mob violence. Loss of personal identity can also be positive, such as when group members act without thinking to save others' lives.

6. ***When it comes to decision making, are groups better than individuals, or are individuals better than groups?***
Groups are better than the average group member in recognizing the truth of a solution and in rejecting poor solutions. Groups are also more effective in processing information, perhaps because they use **transactive memory systems.** Memory of information becomes a transaction among group members rather than an individual process. Groups do not usually perform better than their very best individual member but recent work has shown that groups may be superior when dealing with complex problems, because they have more resources and can be more creative than can individuals.

7. ***How do groups reach decisions?***
Decision-making groups need to develop decision rules—rules about how many people must agree—in order to blend individual choices into a group outcome. Two common decision rules are majority and unanimity (consensus). Generally, majority wins is the dominant decision rule, but the selection of a decision rule often depends on the group task.

8. ***What factors affect the decision-making ability and effectiveness of a group?***
Group composition is important to the decision-making ability of a group. Groups of high-ability individuals seem to perform better than groups of low-ability individuals, but members' abilities blend and mix in unexpected ways to produce a group IQ. Groups seem to perform better when members have complementary skills but when no single member is much more talented than the others.

Group size also affects group productivity. Although increasing group size increases the resources available to the group, there is also more **process loss**; that is, it becomes harder to reach a decision. As more people are added to the group, the number of people who actually make a contribution—the group's functional size—does not increase.

Some groups and group processes offer an **illusion of efficacy**; people think they are more effective than they are. This is true of small groups, which many people erroneously think are better at solving social dilemmas than are larger groups.

Another factor in group effectiveness is group cohesiveness. When a task does not require much interaction among members, task-based cohesiveness—cohesiveness based on respect for each other's abilities—increases group productivity, but interpersonal cohesiveness—cohesiveness based on liking for each other—does not. Sometimes interpersonal cohesiveness can impede the decision-making abilities of the group, because people are afraid of hurting each other's feelings.

Leadership is also a factor in group effectiveness. **Participative leaders** can get members to bring out more unshared information and that's important because it is usually unshared information that leads to the most accurate decisions. However, a **directive leader** makes the group focus more on unshared information and therefore tends to produce fewer mistakes than do participative leaders.

9. What is group polarization?

Group decision making often results in **group polarization**, that is, the initial decision tendency of the group becomes more extreme following group discussion. It seems that the group discussion pulls the members' attitudes toward more extreme positions as a result of both social comparison and persuasive arguments.

10. What is groupthink?

Groups often make bad decisions when they become more concerned with keeping up their members' morale rather than with reaching a realistic decision. This lack of critical thinking can lead to **groupthink**, a breakdown in the rational decision-making abilities of members of a cohesive group. The group becomes driven by **consensus seeking**; members do not want to rock the boat. This was what appeared to happen to Kennedy's advisors during the Bay of Pigs fiasco.

Groupthink is favored by group cohesiveness, stress, and the persuasive strength of the leader. It is also more likely to occur when a group is insulated and homogeneous and has a leader who promotes a particular point of view. Several measures can be taken to prevent groupthink, including encouraging a critical attitude among members, discussing group solutions with people outside the group, and bringing in outside experts who don't agree with the group's solution.

Another approach suggests that group polarization, risk taking, and the possibility of a disastrous decision being reached all increase when a decision is framed in terms of potential failure. If all outcomes are seen as potentially negative, according to this view, group members will tend to favor the riskier ones over the more cautious ones. Finally, groupthink has been found to occur more often when the group process doesn't allow everyone to speak freely and fully and when group leaders become obsessed with maintaining morale.

INTERNET ACTIVITY

EXPLORING GROUP DYNAMICS

Because of the importance of groups in our culture, it is important to understand precisely how groups operate and how group decision making can sometimes go wrong. On the Internet, there are Web sites that allow you to explore various aspects of group decision making. For this activity, go to the Small Group Communication Web Site (http://www.abacon.com/commstudies/groups/group.html). Here, you will find several interactive activities (e.g., one on groupthink and one on group decision making) that you can take part in. While at the site, try to do at least two of the interactive activities and evaluate what you have learned about the group phenomenon related to the group activity. Finally, relate what you have learned to what you have learned from chapter 8 and in your social psychology class.

- What did you learn about group dynamics at this site?
- Are there any conflicts between what you found on the site and what is in your text? If so, what are they and how might you resolve them?
- Did you learn anything that you did not know from reading chapter 8? If so, what did you learn?

SUGGESTIONS FOR FURTHER READING

Feinstein, J. (1989). *Forever's team.* New York: Simon & Schuster.

This book offers an extraordinary look at how membership in a group—a college basketball team—changed the lives of its members.

Hogg, M. A., & Abrams, D. (Eds.). (1993). *Group motivation.* London: Harvester/Wheatsheaf.

This book contains enlightening and readable coverage of how groups form and function.

Janis, I. L. (1982). *Groupthink* (2nd ed.). Boston: Houghton Mifflin.

This is the classic study of why group decisions in diplomacy and war can go wrong.

Tyler, T. R. (1994). Governing amid diversity: Can fair decision-making procedures bridge competing public interests and values? *Law and Society Review, 28,* 701–722.

The leading scholar in the area presents an insightful examination of the psychology of fairness and justice in a diverse society.

Kramer, R. M. (1998). Revisiting the Bay of Pigs and Vietnam decisions twenty-five years later: How well has the groupthink hypothesis stood the test of time? *Organizational Behavior and Human Decision Processes, 73,* 236–271.

This article is a fascinating analysis of what really drove the Bay of Pigs and Vietnam policy decisions by presidents Kennedy and Johnson.

CHAPTER 9

CLOSE RELATIONSHIPS

Both had been born in California and had lived in the San Francisco Bay area. Both eventually left the United states to live in Paris. The first visit between these two people, who would be lifelong friends and lovers, did not begin well. They had become acquainted the previous night at a Paris restaurant and had arranged an appointment for the next afternoon at Gertrude's apartment. Perhaps anxious about the meeting, Gertrude was in a rage when her guest arrived a half hour later than the appointed time. But soon she recovered her good humor, and the two went walking in the streets of Paris. They found that each loved walking, and they would share their thoughts and feelings on these strolls for the rest of their lives together.

On that first afternoon, they stopped for ices and cakes in a little shop that Gertrude knew well because it reminded her of San Francisco. The day went so well that Gertrude suggested dinner at her apartment the following evening. Thus began a relationship that would last for nearly 40 years.

The one was small and dark, the other large—over two hundred pounds—with short hair and a striking roman face. Neither was physically attractive. Each loved art and literature and opera, for which they were in the right place. The Paris in which they met in the 1920s was the home to great painters (Picasso and Matisse) and enormously talented writers (Ernest Hemingway, F. Scott Fitzgerald). Gertrude knew them all.

They began to live together in Gertrude's apartment, for she was the one who had a steady supply of money. Gertrude, who had dropped out of medical school in her final year, had decided to write novels. Soon, they grew closer, their walks longer, their talks more intimate. They traveled to Italy, and it was there, outside Florence, that Gertrude proposed marriage. Both knew the answer to the proposal, and they spent the night in a 16th-century palace.

They shared each other's lives fully, enduring two wars together. In 1946, Gertrude, then 70, displayed the first signs of the tumor that would soon kill her. Gertrude handled this crisis in character, forcefully refusing any medical treatment. Not even her lifelong companion could convince her to do

otherwise. When Gertrude eventually collapsed, she was rushed to a hospital in Paris. In her hospital room before the surgery, Gertrude grasped her companion's small hand and asked, "What is the answer?" Tears streamed down Alice Toklas' face, "I don't know, Lovey."
The hospital attendants put Gertrude Stein on a cot and rolled her toward the operating room. Alice murmured words of affection. Gertrude commanded the attendants to stop, and she turned to Alice and said, "If you don't know the answer, then what is the question?" Gertrude settled back on the cot and chuckled softly. It was the last time they saw each other (Burnett, 1972; Simon, 1977; Toklas, 1963).

We have briefly recounted what was perhaps the most famous literary friendship of the last century, the relationship between Gertrude Stein and Alice B. Toklas. Stein and Toklas were not officially married. They did not flaunt their sexual relationship, for the times in which they lived were not particularly accommodating to what Stein called their "singular" preferences. Yet their partnership involved all the essential elements of a close relationship: intimacy, friendship, love, and sharing. Philosophers have commented that a friend multiplies one's joys and divides one's sorrows. This, too, was characteristic of their relationship.

In this chapter, we explore the nature of close relationships. The empirical study of close relationships is relatively new. Indeed, when one well-known researcher received a grant some years ago from a prestigious government funding agency to study love in a scientific manner, a gadfly senator held the researcher and the topic up to ridicule, suggesting that we know all we need to know about the topic.

Perhaps so, but in this chapter we ask a number of questions that most of us, at least, do not have the answers for. What draws two people together into a close relationship, whether a friendship or a more intimate love relationship? What influences attractiveness and attraction? How do close relationships develop and evolve, and how do they stand up to conflict and destructive impulses? What are the components of love relationships? And finally, what are friendships, and how do they differ from love? These are some of the questions addressed in this chapter.

KEY QUESTIONS

AS YOU READ THIS CHAPTER, FIND THE ANSWERS TO THE FOLLOWING QUESTIONS:

1. *What is a close relationship?*
2. *What are the roots of interpersonal attraction and close relationships?*
3. *How does interpersonal attraction develop?*
4. *How do close relationship form and evolve?*
5. *What are the components and dynamics of love relationships?*
6. *What is the evolutionary view of love?*
7. *What is the nature of friendships?*

THE ROOTS OF INTERPERSONAL ATTRACTION AND CLOSE RELATIONSHIPS

It is a basic human characteristics to be attracted to others, to desire to build close relationships with friends and lovers. In this section, we explore two needs that underlie attraction and relationships: affiliation and intimacy. Not everyone has the social skills or resources necessary to initiate and maintain close relationships. Therefore, we also look at the emotions of social anxiety and loneliness.

Affiliation and Intimacy

Although each of us can endure and even value periods of solitude, for most of us extended solitude is aversive. After a time, we begin to crave the company of others. People have a **need for affiliation**, a need to establish and maintain relationships with others (Wong & Csikzentmihalyi, 1991). Contact with friends and acquaintances provides us with emotional support, attention, and the opportunity to evaluate the appropriateness of our opinions and behavior through the process of social comparison. The need for affiliation is the fundamental factor underlying our interpersonal relationships.

need for affiliation
A motivation that underlies our desire to establish and maintain rewarding interpersonal relationships.

People who are high in the need for affiliation wish to be with friends and others more than do people who are low in the need for affiliation, and they tend to act accordingly. For example, in one study, college men who had a high need for affiliation picked living situations that increased the chances for social interaction. They were likely to have more housemates or to be more willing to share a room than were men with a lower need for affiliation (Switzer & Taylor, 1983). Men and women show some differences in the need for affiliation. Teenage girls, for example, spend more time with friends and less often wish to be alone than do teenage boys (Wong & Csikzentmihalyi, 1991). This is in keeping with other findings that women show a higher need for affiliation than do men.

But merely being with others is often not enough to satisfy our social needs. We also have a **need for intimacy**, a need for close and affectionate relationships (McAdams, 1982, 1989). Intimacy with friends or lovers involves sharing and disclosing personal information. Individuals with a high need for intimacy tend to be warm and affectionate and to show concern about other people. Most theorists agree that intimacy is an essential component of many different interpersonal relationships (Laurenceau, Barrett, & Pietromonaco, 1998).

need for intimacy
A motivation for close and affectionate relationships.

Intimacy has several dimensions, according to Roy Baumeister and Ellen Bratslavsky (1999). One is mutual disclosure that is sympathetic and understanding. Intimate disclosure involves verbal communication but also refers to shared experiences. Another dimension of intimacy includes having a favorable attitude toward the other person that is expressed in warm feelings and positive acts such that the person is aware of how much the other cares.

The need for affiliation and intimacy gives us positive social motivation to approach other people. They are the roots of interpersonal attraction, which is defined as the desire to start and to maintain relationships with others. But there are also emotions that may stand in the way of our fulfilling affiliation and intimacy needs and forming relationships. We look at these emotions next.

Humans have a need for affiliation which means we like to be with others. Another social motive is the need for intimacy which means that we have a need to form and maintain close personal relationships with others, such as a romantic partner.

Loneliness and Social Anxiety

loneliness

A psychological state that results when we perceive that there is an inadequacy or a deprivation in our social relationships.

Loneliness is a psychological state that results when we perceive an inadequacy in our relationships—a discrepancy between the way we want our relationships to be and the way they actually are (Peplau & Perlman, 1982). When we are lonely, we lack the high-quality intimate relationships that we need. Loneliness may occur within the framework of a relationship. For example, women often expect more intimacy than they experience in marriage, and that lack of intimacy can be a cause of loneliness (Tornstam, 1992).

Loneliness is common during adolescence and young adulthood, times of life when old friendships fade and new ones must be formed. For example, consider an 18-year-old going off to college. As she watches her parents drive away, she is likely to feel, along with considerable excitement, a sense of loneliness or even abandonment. New college students often believe that they will not be able to form friendships and that no one at school cares about them. The friendships they make don't seem as intimate as their high school friendships were. These students often don't realize that everybody else is pretty much in the same boat emotionally, and loneliness is often a significant factor when a student drops out of school.

Loneliness is a subjective experience and is not dependent on the number of people we have surrounding us (Peplau & Perlman, 1982). We can be alone and yet not be lonely; sometimes we want and need solitude. On the other hand, we can be surrounded by people and feel desperately lonely. Our feelings of loneliness are strongly influenced by how we evaluate our personal relationships (Peplau & Perlman, 1982). We need close relationships with a few people to buffer ourselves against feeling lonely.

As suggested earlier, loneliness can be associated with certain relationships or certain times of life. There are, however, individuals for whom loneliness is a lifelong experience. Such individuals have difficulty in forming relationships with others, and consequently, they go through life with few or no close relationships. What is the source of their difficulty? The problem for at least some of these people may be that they lack the basic social skills needed to form and maintain relationships. Experiences of awkward social interactions intensify these individuals' uneasiness in social settings. Lacking confidence, they become increasingly anxious about their interactions with others. Often, because of their strained social interactions, lonely people may be further excluded from social interaction, thereby increasing feelings of depression and social anxiety (Leary & Kowalski, 1995).

Social anxiety arises from a person's expectation of negative encounters with others (Leary, 1983a, 1983b). Socially anxious people anticipate uncomfortable interactions and think that other people will not like them very much. When Alice Toklas began to meet the literary and artistic notables in Gertrude Stein's circle, she often tried to make herself as inconspicuous as possible. One day, Stein told Toklas that even the great painter Picasso was nervous at these gatherings. Toklas didn't believe this at first (Stein was quite capable of exaggeration), but whether it was true or not, Toklas soon gained confidence. People who suffer from social anxiety tend to display some of the following interrelated traits (Nichols, 1974):

social anxiety
Anxiety tied to interpersonal relationships that occurs because of an individual's anticipation of negative encounters with others.

- A sensitivity and fearfulness of disapproval and criticism.

- A strong tendency to perceive and respond to criticism that does not exist.

- Low self-evaluation.

- Rigid ideas about what constitutes "appropriate" social behavior.

- A tendency to foresee negative outcomes to anticipated social interactions, which arouses anxiety.

- An increased awareness and fear of being evaluated by others.

- Fear of situations in which withdrawal would be difficult or embarrassing.

- The tendency to overestimate one's reaction to social situations (e.g., believing that you are blushing when you are not).

- An inordinate fear of the anxiety itself.

- A fear of being perceived as losing control.

Interestingly, many of these perceptions and fears are either wrong or unfounded. The research of P. Niels Christensen and Deborah Kashy (1998) shows that lonely people view their own behavior more negatively than do other people.

Of course, real events and real hurts may be the source of much of our social anxieties. Mark Leary and his colleagues examined the effects of having our feelings hurt in a variety of ways, ranging from sexual infidelity, to unreturned phone calls, to being teased (Leary, Springer, Negel, Ansell, & Evans, 1998). The basic cause of the hurt feelings and consequent anxiety is what Leary calls *relational devaluation*, the perception that the other person does not regard the relationship as important as you do. Perhaps the major source of social anxiety is the feeling that you are being excluded from valued social relations (Baumeister & Tice, 1990). Having one's feeling hurt, however, leads to more than anxiety. People experience a complex sense of being distressed, upset, angry, guilty, and wounded. Leary and colleagues (1998) examined the stories written by people who had been emotionally hurt. They found that unlike the old saying about "sticks and stones," words or even gestures or looks elicit hurt feelings, last for a long time, and do not heal as readily as broken bones. Teasing is one example of what appeared to be an innocent event—at least from the teaser's point of view—that in reality imprints long-lasting hurt feelings for many victims. The males and females in the study did not differ much in their reactions to hurt feelings or to teasing.

The people who do these nasty deeds do not realize the depth of the damage that they cause, nor do they realize how much the victims come to dislike them. Perpetrators often say that they meant no harm. No harm, indeed.

LOVE AND CLOSE RELATIONSHIPS

Psychologists and other behavioral scientists long thought that love was simply too mysterious a topic to study scientifically (Thompson & Borrello, 1992). More recently, however, psychologists have become more adventuresome, and love has become a topic of increasing interest (Hendrick & Hendrick, 1987). This is only right, because love is among the most intense of human emotions.

Love's Triangle

triangular theory of love

A theory suggesting that love comprises three components—passion, intimacy, and commitment—each of which is conceptualized as a leg of a triangle that can vary.

Robert Sternberg (1986, 1988) proposed a **triangular theory of love**, based on the idea that love has three components: passion, intimacy, and commitment. As shown in Figure 9.1, the theory represents love as a triangle, with each component defining a vertex.

Passion is the emotional component of love. The "aching" in the pit of your stomach when you think about your love partner is a manifestation of this component. Passion is "a state of intense longing for union with the other" (Hatfield & Walster, 1981, p. 13). Passion tends to be strongest in the early stages of a romantic relationship. It is sexual desire that initially drives the relationship. Defining passion simply as sexual desire does not do justice to this complicated emotion. It is not improbable that people may love passionately without sexual contact or in the absence of the ability to have sexual contact. However, as a rough measure, sexual desire serves to define passion (Baumeister & Bratslavsky, 1999).

Figure 9.1

Robert Sternberg's triangular theory of love. Each leg of the triangle represents one of the three components of love: passion, intimacy, and commitment.

From Sternberg (1986). Reprinted with permission.

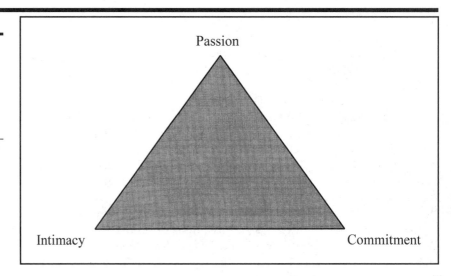

Table 9.1

Taxonomy of Kinds of Love

Kind of Love	Love Component		
	Intimacy	Passion	Commitment
Non-love	No	No	No
Liking	Yes	No	No
Infatuated love	No	Yes	No
Empty love	No	No	Yes
Romantic love	Yes	Yes	No
Companionate love	Yes	No	Yes
Fatuous love	No	Yes	Yes
Consummate love	Yes	Yes	Yes

From Sternberg (1986).

Intimacy is the component that includes self-disclosure—the sharing of our innermost thoughts—as well as shared activities. Intimate couples look out for each other's welfare, experience happiness by being in each other's company, are able to count on each other when times are tough, and give each other emotional support and understanding (Sternberg & Gracek, 1984).

The third vertex of the triangle, *commitment*, is the long-term determination to maintain love over time. It is different from the decision people make, often in the heat of passion, that they are in love. Commitment does not necessarily go along with a couple's decision that they are in love. Sternberg defined various kinds of love, based on the presence or absence of intimacy, passion, and commitment. Table 9.1 shows each of these kinds of love and the component or components with which it is associated.

According to Sternberg (1986), the components of love need not occur in a fixed order. There is a tendency for passion to dominate at the start, for intimacy to follow as a result of self-disclosure prompted by passion, and for commitment to take the longest to fully develop. However, in an arranged marriage, for example, commitment occurs before intimacy, and passion may be the laggard.

Baumeister and Bratslavsky (1999) studied the relationship between passion and intimacy and suggested that one may be a function of the other. These scholars argued that rising intimacy at any point in the relationship will create a strong sense of passion. If intimacy is stable, and that means it may be high or low, then passion will be low. But when intimacy rises, so does passion. Passion, then, is a function of change in intimacy over time (Baumeister & Bratslavsky, 1999). Research generally shows that passion declines steadily in long-term relationships, particularly among women, but intimacy does not and may increase in the late stages of the relationship (Acker & Davis, 1992). Positive changes in the amount of intimacy—self-disclosures, shared experiences—lead to increases in passion at any stage of a relationship.

Types of Love

What, then, are Sternberg's types of love? Probably the most fascinating is **romantic love**, which involves passion and intimacy but not commitment. Romantic love is reflected in that electrifying yet conditional statement, "I am in love with you." Compare this with the expression reflecting consummate love, "I love you."

Romantic love can be found around the world and throughout history. Romantic love doesn't necessarily mean marriage, however, for two main reasons. First, whereas marriage is almost universally heterosexual, romantic love need not be. Second, it is still an alien idea in most cultures that romance has anything to do with the choice of a spouse. Even in our own culture, the appeal of marrying for love seems to have increased among women in recent years, perhaps because women's roles have changed, and they no longer have so great a need to find a "good provider" (Berscheid, Snyder, & Omoto, 1989).

The importance of passion in romantic love is clear. Romantic lovers live in a pool of emotions, both positive and negative—sexual desire, fear, exultation, anger—all experienced in a state of high arousal. Intense sexual desire and physical arousal are the prime forces driving romantic love (Berscheid, 1988). Passionate lovers soon begin to share their innermost thoughts and desires and thereby foster the second component of romantic love, intimacy.

Tennov (1979) distinguished a particular type of romantic love, which she called **limerence** and characterized as occurring when "you suddenly feel a sparkle (a lovely word) of interest in someone else, an interest fed by the image of returned feeling" (p. 27). Limerence is not driven solely or even primarily by sexual desire. It occurs when a person anxious for intimacy finds someone who seems able to fulfill all of his or her needs and desires. For limerent lovers, all the happiness one could ever hope for is embodied in the loved one. Indeed, one emotional consequence of limerent love is a terror that all hope will be lost if the lover leaves us (S. Brehm, 1988).

Consummate love combines all three vertices of love's triangle: passion, intimacy, and commitment. These couples have it all; they are able to maintain their passion and intimacy along with a commitment to a lifetime together.

Although we may fantasize about romantic love and view consummate love as a long-term ideal, other types of love can also bring happiness. Many couples are perfectly happy with companionate love, which has little or no passion but is infused with intimacy and commitment. Such partners are "friends for life" and generally have great trust in and tolerance for each other. Although they may regret the lack of passion, they are pragmatic and are able to live happily within the rules or limits of the relationship (Duck, 1983).

UNREQUITED LOVE A special and very painful kind of infatuated love is love that is unfulfilled. **Unrequited love** occurs when we fall deeply and passionately in love and that love is rejected. Almost all of us have had some experience with unrequited love. In one study, 98% of the subjects had been rejected by someone they loved intensely (Baumeister, Wotman, & Stillwell, 1993).

What makes unrequited love so painful is that both individuals feel victimized (Aron, Aron, & Allen, 1998). Very often, unrequited love ostensibly starts as a platonic friendship, but then one of the individuals admits that it was

---

romantic love

Love involving strong emotion and having the components of passion and intimacy but not commitment.

limerence

Limerence occurs when a person anxious for intimacy finds someone who seems able to fulfill all of his or her needs and desires. For limerent lovers, all the happiness one could ever hope for is embodied in the loved one.

consummate love

Love that includes all three components: passion, intimacy, and commitment.

unrequited love

Love expressed by one person that is rejected and not returned by the other.

never just friendship, that he or she was always secretly in love with the other (Baumeister et al., 1993). In many cases, the object of the unrequited love is often unable to express lack of interest in terms that are sufficiently discouraging. The unrequited lover takes anything as encouragement, sustains hope, and then finds the final rejection devastating. The object of unwanted love, after the initial boost to the ego, feels bewildered, guilty, and angry.

In a typical case of spurned love, a college woman took pity on a young man whom no one liked, and one night invited him to join her and some friends in a game of Parcheesi. He thought the invitation signaled something more than she intended. Much to her horror, he began to follow her around and told her how much he loved her. She wanted this to stop, but she was unable to tell him how upset she was, because she was afraid of hurting his feelings. He interpreted her silence as encouragement and persisted (Baumeister et al., 1993).

Men are more likely than women to experience unrequited love (Aron et al., 1998). This is because men are more beguiled by physical attractiveness than are women. Men tend to fall in love with someone more desirable than they are. Interestingly, people report that they have been the object of unrequited love twice as many times as they have been rejected by another. We prefer to believe that we have been loved in vain rather than having loved in vain.

SECRET LOVE   If unrequited love is the most painful kind of love, then **secret love** may be the most exciting. In this form of love, individuals have strong passion for one another, but cannot or will not make those feelings publically known. Secrecy seems to increase the attraction of a relationship. Researchers have found that people continued to think more about past relationships that had been secret than about those that had been open (Wegner, Lane, & Dimitri, 1994). In fact, many individuals were still very much preoccupied with long-past secret relationships. In a study of secrecy and attraction, subjects paired as couples were induced to play "footsie" under the table while they were involved in a card game with another couple (Wegner et al., 1994). The researchers found that when the under-the-table game was played in secret, participants reported greater attraction for the other person than when it was not played in secret.

Why does secrecy create this strong attraction? Perhaps it is because individuals involved in a secret relationship think constantly and obsessively about each other. After all, they have to expend a lot of energy in maintaining the relationship. They have to figure out how to meet, how to call each other so that others won't know, and how to act neutrally in public to disguise their true relationship. Secrecy creates strong bonds between individuals; it can also be the downfall of ongoing relationships. The sudden revelation of a secret infidelity will often crush an ongoing relationship and further enhance the secret one (Wegner et al., 1994).

secret love
Love in which individuals have strong passion for one another but cannot or will not make those feelings publically known, increasing the attraction of a relationship.

THE FORMATION OF INTIMATE RELATIONSHIPS

The habits of the heart may be shaped by our earliest relationships. Developmental psychologists have noted that infants form attachments with their parents or primary caregivers based on the kinds of interactions they have (Ainsworth, 1992). These patterns of attachment, or attachment styles, evolve into working models, mental representations of what the individual expects to happen in close relationships (Shaver, Hazan, & Bradshaw, 1988). Attachment theory suggests that attachment styles developed in early childhood govern the way individuals form and maintain close relationships in adulthood. Three attachment styles have been identified: secure, anxious–ambivalent, and avoidant. Statements describing each style are shown in Table 9.2.

According to research, people who identified their attachment style as secure characterized their lovers as happy, friendly, and trusting and said that they and their partner were tolerant of each other's faults (Shaver et al., 1988). Avoidant lovers were afraid of intimacy, experienced roller-coaster emotional swings, and were constantly jealous. Anxious–ambivalent lovers experienced extreme sexual attraction coupled with extreme jealousy. Love is very intense for anxious lovers, because they strive to merge totally with their mate; anything less increases their anxiety. This experience of love for anxious lovers is a strong desire for union and a powerful intensity of sexual attraction and jealousy. It is no accident that anxious lovers, more than any other style, report love at first sight (Shaver et al., 1988).

An attachment style can be seen as a kind of **working model** we carry around that contains our ideas about how close relationships work. Given the working model of a partner and the expectations that anxious lovers have, it will not come as a surprise to you that individuals with this style tend to have

working model
Mental representations of what an individual expects to happen in close relationships.

Table 9.2

Adult Attachment Styles, as Indicated by Responses to the Question, Which of the Following Best Describes Your Feelings?

Answers and Percentages		
	Newspaper Sample	*University Sample*
Secure		
I find it relatively easy to get close to others and am comfortable depending on them and having them depend on me. I don't worry about being abandoned or about someone getting too close to me.	56%	56%
Avoidant		
I am somewhat uncomfortable being close to others; I find it difficult to trust them completely, difficult to allow myself to depend on them. I am nervous when anyone gets too close, and often, love partners want me to be more intimate than I feel comfortable about.	25%	23%
Anxious/Ambivalent		
I find that others are reluctant to get as close as I would like. I often worry that my partner doesn't really love me or won't want to stay with me. I want to merge completely with another person, and this desire sometimes scares people away.	19%	20%

From Shaver, Hazan, and Bradshaw (1988).

rather turbulent relationships (Simpson, Ickes, & Grich, 1999). Research shows that anxious–ambivalents have relationships that are filled with strong conflicts. One reason for this, apparently, is that anxious—ambivalent individuals have *empathic accuracy*, the ability to correctly infer their partner's thoughts and feelings. Because of this ability, they are more threatened than are other individuals and feel much more anxious (Simpson et al., 1999). This is a case of knowing too much or, at least, placing too much emphasis on their partners' present moods and feelings that may or may not tell where the relationship is going. As you might imagine, Simpson and colleagues found that of all the couples they studied, the highly anxious–ambivalent partners were much more likely to have broken up within months.

Attachment Styles and Adult Love Relationships

R. Chris Fraley and Philip Shaver (1998) showed that the ways in which we respond to our earliest caregivers may indeed last a lifetime and are used when we enter adult romantic relationships. Where better to observe how adult individuals respond to the potential loss of attachment than at an airport? The researchers had observers take careful notes on the behavior of couples when one of the members was departing. After the departure, the remaining member of the couple was asked to complete a questionnaire determining his or her attachment style.

Those with an anxious working model showed the greatest distress at the impending separation and tended to engage in actions designed to delay or stop the departure, although in reality that was not going to happen. The anxious individual would hold on to, follow, and search for their partner, not unlike a child would for a parent under similar circumstances. So attachment styles tend to be engaged particularly when there is threat (departure in this case) to the relationship. The effects seemed stronger for women than for men (Fraley & Shaver, 1998).

It is quite likely that the behavior of those airport visitors with an anxious working model was determined in great part by the level of trust they had in their partners. Mario Mikulincer (1998) examined the association between adult attachment style and feelings of trust in close relationships. The results of this research suggest that those with a secure working model showed and felt more trust in their partners, and even when trust was violated, secure individuals found a constructive way to deal with it. For secure individuals, the main goal of the relationship was to maintain or increase intimacy.

In contrast, anxious working model individuals, although also desiring greater intimacy, were very concerned with achieving a greater sense of security in their relationships. Avoidant individuals wanted more control. But clearly, level of trust differs significantly among the three types of attachment styles. Anxious-style individuals continually have their sense of trust undermined, because they tend to fail at relationships. Sometimes, these individuals try to start relationships that are bound to fail. As you might suspect, the likelihood of someone falling in love with another who does not love them in return is dependent on one's attachment style. Arthur and Elaine Aron found that individuals with an anxious attachment style were more likely to have experienced unreciprocated love (Aron et al., 1998). Secure individuals had been successful in the past in establishing relationships, and avoidants were unlikely to fall in love at all. Anxious individuals place great value in establishing a relationship with someone who is very desirable but are unlikely to be able to do so. They tend to fail at close relationships and, therefore, they should experience more incidents of unrequited love; indeed, that is exactly what the research findings show (Aron et al., 1998).

Are attachment styles a factor in long-term relationships? A study of 322 young married couples all under age 30, found a tendency for those with similar attachment styles to marry one another (Senchak & Leonard, 1992). Attachment style is not destiny, however, as shown by the observation that people may display different attachment styles in different relationships (Bartholomew & Horowitz, 1991). None of these findings, however, come from long-term studies on the effects of attachment styles beyond childhood. Longitudinal research that follows individuals from infancy at least until early adulthood would give us more definitive information about whether early attachment styles really influence the way we respond in adult love relationships.

Determinants of Interpersonal Attraction

What determines why we are attracted to some individuals but not others? Social psychologists have developed a number of models addressing this question. Some specific factors identified by these models that play a role in attraction are physical proximity, similarity, and physical attractiveness.

PHYSICAL PROXIMITY: BEING IN THE RIGHT PLACE How did you and your best friend first meet? Most likely, you met because you happened to be physically close to each other at some point in your life. For example, you might have been neighbors or sat next to each other in elementary school. Physical proximity, or physical immediacy, is an important determinant of attraction, especially at the beginning of a relationship.

physical proximity effect

The fact that we are more likely to form a relationship with someone who is physically close to us; proximity affects interpersonal attraction, mostly at the beginning of a relationship.

The importance of the **physical proximity effect** in the formation of friendships was shown in a study of the friendship patterns that developed among students living in on-campus residences for married students (Festinger, Schachter, & Back, 1959). As the distance between units increased, the number of friendships decreased. Students living close to one another were more likely to become friends than were those living far apart.

Physical proximity is such a powerful determinant of attraction that it may even overshadow other, seemingly more important, factors. One study looked at friendship choices among police recruits in a police academy class (Segal, 1974). Recruits were assigned to seats alphabetically, and the single best predictor of interpersonal attraction turned out to be the letter with which a person's last name began. Simply put, those whose names were close in the alphabet and were thus seated near each other were more likely to become friends than those whose names were not close in the alphabet and were thus seated apart. The proximity effect proved more important than such variables as common interests and religion.

Why is proximity so important at the beginning stages of a friendship? The answer seems to have two parts: familiarity and the opportunity for interaction. To understand the role of familiarity, think about this common experience. You buy a new tape or compact disc, but when you first listen to it, you don't like it very much. However, after repeated exposure it "grows on you." That is, exposure to the new music seems to increase your appreciation of it. A similar effect occurs with people we encounter. These are examples of the *mere exposure effect*, in which repeated exposure to a neutral stimulus enhances one's positive feeling toward that stimulus. Since it was first identified in 1968 by Robert Zajonc, there have been over 200 studies of the mere exposure effect (Bornstein, 1989). These studies used a wide range of stimuli and, in virtually every instance, repeated exposure to a stimulus produced liking.

Physical proximity, in addition to exposing us to other people also increases the chances that we will interact with them. That is, proximity also promotes liking, because it gives us an opportunity to find out about each other. Physical proximity and the nature of the interaction combine to determine liking (Schiffenbauer & Schavio, 1976). If we discover that the other person has similar interests and attitudes, we are encouraged to pursue the interaction.

SIMILARITY The importance of the **similarity effect** as a determinant of interpersonal attraction is suggested by all three models we looked at. Similarity in attitudes, beliefs, interests, personality, and even physical appearance strongly influence the likelihood of interpersonal attraction. This results in a **similarity effect** in which we are more likely to form a relationship with a similar other than a dissimilar other. And the more serious the relationship with another person, the more we search for similarity across a variety of areas.

Clearly, there are many possible points of similarity between people. Attitude similarity, for example, might mean that two people are both Democrats, are both Catholics, and in addition to their political and religious beliefs, have like views on a wide range of other issues. However, it is not the absolute number of similar attitudes between individuals that influences the likelihood and strength of attraction. Far more critical are the proportion

similarity effect
The fact that we are more likely to form a relationship with a similar than a dissimilar other.

One of the most powerful factors determining attraction is similarity. Individuals who share common attitudes and interests are often attracted to one another and form interpersonal relationships. Undoubtedly, these motorcyclists have a great deal in common with one another and consequently have forged friendships.

and importance of similar attitudes. It does little good if someone agrees with you on everything except for the one attitude that is central to your life (Byrne & Nelson, 1965).

What about the notion that in romantic relationships, opposites attract? This idea is essentially what Newcomb called *complementarity*. Researchers have found little evidence for complementarity (Duck, 1988). Instead, a **matching principle** seems to apply in romantic relationships. People tend to become involved with a partner with whom they are usually closely matched in terms of physical attributes or social status (Schoen & Wooldredge, 1989).

Different kinds of similarity may have different implications for attraction. If you and someone else are similar in interests, then liking results. Similarity in attitudes, on the other hand, leads to respect for the other person. In a study of college freshmen, similarity in personality was found to be the critical factor determining the degree of satisfaction in friendships (Carli, Ganley, & Pierce-Otay, 1991). This study found similarity in physical attractiveness to have some positive effect on friendships but not a large one.

Why does similarity promote attraction? Attitude similarity promotes attraction in part because of our need to verify the "correctness" of our beliefs. Through the process of social comparison we test the validity of our beliefs by comparing them to those of our friends and acquaintances (Hill, 1987). When we find that other people believe as we do, we can be more confident that our attitudes are valid. It is rewarding to know that someone we like thinks the way we do; it shows how smart we both are. Similarity may also promote attraction because we believe we can predict how a similar person will behave (Hatfield, Walster, & Traupmann, 1978).

Taking a somewhat different view of the effect of similarity, Milton Rosenbaum (1986) argued that it is not so much that we are attracted to similar others as that we are repulsed by people who are dissimilar. Further examination of this idea that dissimilarity breeds repulsion suggests that dissimilarity serves as an initial filter in the formation of relationships. Once a relationship begins to form, however, similarity becomes the fundamental determinant of attraction (Byrne, Clore, & Smeaton, 1986; Smeaton, Byrne, & Murnen, 1989). Thus, the effect of similarity on attraction may be a two-stage process, with dissimilarity and other negative information leading us to make the initial "cuts," and similarity and other positive information then determining with whom we become close.

PHYSICAL ATTRACTIVENESS   Physical attractiveness is an important factor in the early stages of a relationship. Research shows, not surprisingly, that we find physically attractive people more appealing than unattractive people, at least on initial contact (Eagly, Ashmore, Makhijani, & Longo, 1991). Moreover, our society values physical attractiveness, so a relationship with an attractive person is socially rewarding to us.

In their now classic study of the effects of physical attractiveness on dating, Elaine Hatfield and her colleagues led college students to believe that they had been paired at a dance based on their responses to a personality test, but in fact the researchers had paired the students randomly (Hatfield, Aronson, Abrahams, & Rottman, 1966). At the end of the evening, the couples evaluated each other and indicated how much they would like to date again. For both males and females, the desire to date again was best predicted by the physical attractiveness of the partner. This is not particularly surprising, perhaps, because after only one brief date the partners probably had little other information to go on.

Physical attractiveness affects not only our attitudes toward others but also our interactions with them. A study of couples who had recently met found that, regardless of gender, when one person was physically attractive, the other tried to intensify the interaction (Garcia, Stinson, Ickes, Bissonette, & Briggs, 1991). Men were eager to initiate and maintain a conversation no matter how little reinforcement they got. Women tried to quickly establish an intimate and exclusive relationship by finding things they had in common and by avoiding talk about other people.

There are, however, gender differences in the importance of physical attractiveness. Generally, women are less impressed by attractive males than are men by attractive females (Buss, 1988a). Women are more likely than men to report that attributes other than physical attractiveness, such as a sense of humor, are important to them.

Dimensions of Physical Attractiveness

What specific physical characteristics make someone attractive? Facial appearance has been shown to strongly affect our perceptions of attractiveness through much of our life span (McArthur, 1982; Zebrowitz, Olson, & Hoffman, 1993). Moreover, various aspects of facial appearance have specific effects. One group of researchers suspected that people find symmetrical faces more attractive than asymmetrical faces (Thornhill & Gangestad, 1994). They took photographs of males and females, fed those photos into a computer, created computer versions of the faces, and made precise measurements of the symmetry of the faces. They then asked subjects to rate the computer-generated images for attractiveness. They found that people do judge symmetrical faces to be more attractive than asymmetrical ones.

The researchers also asked the photographed students to fill out questionnaires about their sex and social lives. Those with symmetrical faces reported that they were sexually active earlier than others and had more friends and lovers. Why should symmetry and facial features in general be so important? The answer may lie more in our biology than in our psychology, an issue we explore later in the chapter.

There is a growing body of research that suggests that people's facial appearance plays a role in how others treat them (Berry, 1991; Zebrowitz, Collins, & Dutta, 1998; Zebrowitz & Lee, 1999). Zebrowitz and her coworkers (1998) noted that there is a **physical attractiveness bias**, a "halo," whereby individuals who are physically attractive are thought to also have other positive attributes. One cultural stereotype is that what is beautiful is good. That is, we tend to believe that physically attractive individuals possess a wide range of desirable characteristics and that they are generally happier than unattractive individuals (Dion, Berscheid, & Walster, 1972) Not only do we find attractive individuals more appealing physically, but also we also confer on them a number of psychological and social advantages. We think that they are more competent and socially appealing than the average-appearing person. Moreover, unattractive individuals may experience discrimination because of their appearance.

Much of this attractiveness bias is probably learned. However, there is some evidence that the attractiveness bias may have a biological component as well. In one experiment, infants 2 or 3 months old were exposed to pairs of

physical attractiveness bias
The tendency to confer a number of psychological and social advantages to physically attractive individuals.

adult faces and their preferences were recorded (Langlois, Roggman, Casey, Riesner-Danner, & Jenkins, 1987). Preference was inferred from a measure known as *fixation time*, or the amount of time spent looking at one face or the other. If the infant prefers one over the other, the infant should look at that face longer. As shown in Figure 9.2, when attractive faces were paired with unattractive faces, infants displayed a preference for the attractive faces. It is therefore quite unlikely that infants learned these preferences.

Furthermore, a number of distinctly different cultures seem to have the same biases. This doesn't necessarily mean that these biases aren't learned; various cultures may simply value the same characteristics. Studies comparing judgments of physical attractiveness in Korea and in the United States found agreement on whether a face was attractive and whether the face conveyed a sense of power. In both countries, for example, faces with broad chins, thin lips, and receding hairlines were judged to convey dominance (Triandis, 1994).

Leslie Zebrowitz and her coworkers showed that appearance of both attractive people and people with baby faces (round faces, large eyes, small nose and chin, high eyebrows) affect how others treat them (Zebrowitz & Lee, 1999; Zebrowitz et al., 1998). Whereas attractive people are thought to be highly competent both physically and intellectually, baby-faced individuals are viewed as weak, submissive, warm, and naive. What happens when baby-faced individuals do not conform to the stereotype that they are harmless? In a study of delinquent adolescent boys, Zebrowitz and Lee (1999) showed that baby-faced boys, in contrast to more mature-looking delinquents, were punished much more severely. This is a contrast effect: Innocent looking people who commit antisocial actions violate our expectations.

Although attractiveness and baby-facedness may have a downside when these individuals run afoul of expectations, the upside is, as you might expect, that the positive expectations and responses of other people shape the

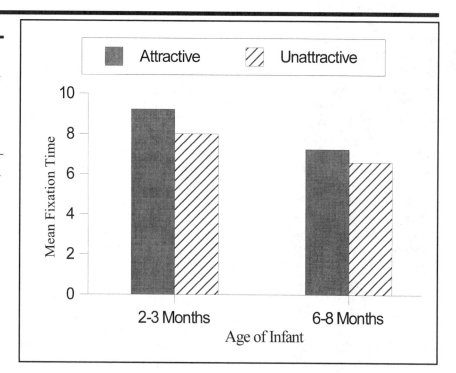

Figure 9.2

Infant fixation time as a function of the attractiveness of a stimulus face. Infants as young as 2- or 3-months-old showed a preference for an attractive face over an unattractive face.

From Langlois and colleagues (1987). Reprinted with permission.

personalities of attractive individuals across their life (Zebrowitz et al., 1998). This is self-fulfilling prophecy, whereby attractive men who are treated positively because of their appearance become more socially secure as they get older. Similarly, Zebrowitz found that a man who had an "honest " face in his youth tended to be more honest as he got older.

For baby-faced individuals, the effect over time was somewhat different. These individuals become more assertive and aggressive over time, probably as a way of compensating for the stereotype of a baby-faced individual as submissive and weak,

However, Zebrowitz and colleagues (1998) did not observe such a self-fulfilling prophecy for women. That is, attractive young women do not become more attractive and competent socially as they age. Zebrowitz suggested further that less attractive women may learn to compensate by becoming more socially able to counteract the negative image held of less attractive women. This would explain the lack of significant differences in socially valued personality attributes between younger attractive and less attractive women as they age into their fifties. Interestingly, women who had an attractive personality in their youth developed high attractiveness in their fifties suggesting, according to Zebrowitz, that women manipulated their appearance and presentation (makeup, etc.) more then men did. It may be that this is due to women's greater motivation to present an attractive appearance because they have less power to achieve their social goals in other ways (Zebrowitz et al., 1998).

Physique and the Attractiveness Bias

Physique also profoundly affects our perceptions of attractiveness. David Buss (1994) observed that the importance of physical attractiveness has increased in the United States in every decade since the 1930s. This is true for both men and women, although men rate physical attractiveness as much more important than do women. Our society has widely shared notions of which bodily attributes are attractive. We have positive perceptions of people who fit these notions and negative perceptions of those who do not. We sometimes even display discriminatory behavior against those who deviate too far from cultural standards.

People can be categorized by body type into *ectomorphs* (thin, perhaps underweight), *mesomorphs* (athletic build), and *endomorphs* (overweight). Positive personality traits tend to be attributed to mesomorphs and negative ones to people with the other body types (Ryckman et al., 1991). There is some ambivalence about ectomorphs, especially as societal attitudes toward thinness seem to shift, influenced by such factors as an increasing health consciousness and an association of excessive thinness with acquired immunodeficiency syndrome (AIDS). Perceptions of endomorphs, in contrast, remain consistently negative. Of course, some people are more intensely attuned to physical appearance than are others. It appears that those people who are most conscious of their own appearance are the most likely to stereotype others on the basis of physique.

Certainly this is the case with regard to overweight individuals. Research confirms that obese individuals are subject to negative stereotyping in our society. In one study (Harris, 1990), subjects judged a stimulus person who was depicted as either normal weight or (with the help of extra clothing) obese. They evaluated "Chris," the stimulus person, along several dimensions including the likelihood that Chris was dating or married, her self-esteem, and her ideal romantic partner. The results, almost without exception, reflected negative stereotyping of an obese Chris compared to a normal-weight Chris. Subjects judged that the obese Chris was less likely to be dating or married compared to the normal-weight Chris. They also rated the obese Chris as having lower self-esteem than the normal-weight Chris and felt that her ideal love partner should also be obese.

Studies also show the practical consequences of these attitudes. For example, it has been shown that overweight college students are less likely than other students to get financial help from home (Crandall, 1991). This effect was especially strong with respect to female students and was true regardless of the resources the student's family had, the number of children in the family, or other factors that could affect parents' willingness to provide financial help. The researchers suggested that the finding might be largely explained by parents' negative attitudes toward their overweight children and consequent lack of optimism about their future. In a related domain, there is evidence that businesspeople sacrifice $1,000 in annual salary for every pound they are overweight (Kolata, 1992).

One reason obese individuals are vilified is that we believe that their weight problem stems from laziness and a lack of discipline. If we know that an individual's weight problem is the result of a biological disorder and thus beyond his or her control, we are less likely to make negative judgments of that individual (DeJong, 1980). What we fail to realize is that most obese people cannot control their weight. There is a genetic component in obesity, and this tendency can be exacerbated by social and cultural factors, such as lack of information and an unhealthy lifestyle.

Attractiveness judgments and stereotyping in everyday life may not be as strong as they are in some laboratory studies. In these studies, we make "pure" attraction judgments: We see only a face or a physique. When we deal with people, we evaluate an entire package even if much of what we see initially is only the wrapping. The entire package includes many attributes. A person may be overweight but may also have a mellifluous voice and a powerful personality. In a laboratory study in which subjects were exposed to a person's face and voice, the perception of the person's physical attractiveness was affected by judgments about that person's vocal attractiveness and vice versa (Zuckerman, Miyake, & Hodgins, 1991). Gertrude Stein was a woman many people found attractive even though she weighed over 200 pounds. Her striking face and her powerful personality were the main attributes that people remembered after meeting her.

Beauty and the View from Evolutionary Psychology

It is obvious that we learn to associate attractiveness with positive virtues and unattractiveness with vice, even wickedness. Children's books and movies often portray the good characters as beautiful and the villains as ugly. In the Walt Disney movie *The Little Mermaid*, the slender, beautiful mermaid, Ariel, and the evil, obese sea witch are cases in point. Such portrayals are not limited to works for children. The hunchback of Notre Dame, the phantom of the opera, and Freddy Kruger are all physically unattractive evildoers.

Evolutionary psychologists suggest that perhaps beauty is more than skin deep. Recall the research on the attractiveness of symmetrical faces. It seems that it is not only humans who value symmetry but also a variety of other species. For example, Watson and Thornhill (1994) reported that female scorpion flies can detect and prefer as mates males with symmetrical wings. Male elks with the most symmetrical racks host the largest harems.

MATE SELECTION: GOOD GENES OR GOOD GUYS? Proponents of evolutionary psychology, a subfield of both psychology and biology, employ the principles of evolution to explain human behavior, and believe that symmetry is reflective of underlying genetic quality. Lack of symmetry is thought to be caused by various stresses, such as poor maternal nutrition, late maternal age, attacks by predators, or disease, and may therefore reflect bad health or poor genetic quality. Thus, the preference for symmetry in potential mates, whether human or animal, may be instinctive (Watson & Thornhill, 1994). Indeed, even small differences matter. Twins with lower levels of symmetry are reliably rated as less attractive than their slightly more symmetrical counterpart (Mealey, Bridgstock, & Townsend, 1999).

The degree to which biology may control human mating preferences can be underscored by the finding that the type of face a woman finds attractive varies with her menstrual cycle. Perret and Penton-Voak (1999) reported a study that showed that when a woman is ovulating she is more likely to prefer men with highly masculine features. In contrast, during other times, men with softer, feminine features are preferred. The researchers had numerous women from various countries—Japan, Scotland, England—judge male faces during different parts of their menstrual cycles. The researchers believe that these results are explained by the observation that masculine looks, in all of the animal kingdom, denote virility and the increased likelihood for healthy offspring. In a related finding, Gangestad & Thornhill (1998) reported a study that showed that females preferred the smell of a "sweaty" T-shirt worn by the most symmetrical males but only if the women were ovulating.

Of course, it is likely that more choice is involved in mate selection than would be indicated by these studies. In any event, most people do rebel against the notion that decisions about sex, marriage, and parenthood are determined by nothing more than body odor (Berreby, 1998).

Certainly we would expect those with symmetrical appearances to become aware of their advantages in sexual competition. For example, consider the following study by Jeffry Simpson and his coworkers. Heterosexual men and women were told that they would be competing with another same-sex person for a date with an attractive person of the opposite sex. The experimenters videotaped and analyzed the interactions among the two competitors and the potential date. Men who had symmetrical faces used direct competition tactics. That is, when trying to get a date with the attractive woman, symmetrical men simply and baldly compared their attractiveness (favorably) with the competitor. Less attractive (read as less symmetrical faced) men used indirect competitive methods, such as emphasizing their positive personality qualities (Simpson, Gangestad, Christensen, & Leck, 1999).

Gangestad and Thornhill (1998) have argued that physical appearance marked by high symmetrical precision reveals to potential mates that the individual has good genes and is, therefore, for both men and women, a highly desirable choice. These individuals, especially men, should have fared very well in sexual competition during evolutionary history. Why? Research suggests that greater symmetry is associated with higher survival rates as well as higher reproductive rates in many species (Simpson et al., 1999). In men, it seems that certain secondary sexual attributes that are controlled by higher levels of testosterone, such as enlarged jaws, chins and so forth, may project greater health and survival capability (Mealey, Bridgstock, & Townsend, 1999). Indeed, symmetrical men and women report more sexual partners and have sex earlier in life than less symmetrical individuals. The more symmetrical the individual—again, especially males—the more probable the person will have the opportunity for short-term sexual encounters, and the more likely, as Simpson and colleagues (1999) found, they will use direct competitive strategies to win sexual competitions.

Of course, good genes are not enough. Raising human offspring is a complicated, long-term—some might say never-ending—affair, and having a good partner willing to invest in parenthood is important. Indeed, theorists have developed what are called "good provider" models of mate selection that emphasize the potential mate's commitment to the relationship and ability to provide resources necessary for the long-term health of that relationship (Trivers, 1972; Gangestad & Thornhill, 1997).

HOW TO ATTRACT A MATE David Buss, a prominent evolutionary social psychologist, suggested that to find and retain a reproductively valuable mate, humans engage in love acts—behaviors with near-term goals, such as display of resources the other sex finds enticing. The ultimate purpose of these acts is to increase reproductive success (Buss, 1988a, 1988b). Human sexual behavior thus can be viewed in much the same way as the sexual behavior of other animal species. Figure 9.3 shows different love acts and how they are associated with various near-term (proximate) goals, with the ultimate goal of successful reproduction.

The love acts in Figure 9.3 were identified in studies of college students. Subjects in one study (Buss, 1988b) listed some specific behaviors they used to keep their partner from getting involved with someone else. Buss found that males tended to use display of resources (money, cars, clothes, sometimes even brains), whereas females tried to look more attractive and threatened to be unfaithful if the males didn't shape up. Buss argued that these findings support an evolutionary interpretation of mate retention: The tactics of females focus on their value as a reproductive mate and on arousing the jealousy of the male who needs to ensure they are not impregnated by a rival.

Jealousy is evoked when a threat or loss occurs to a valued relationship due to the partner's real or imagined attention to a rival (Dijkstra & Buunk, 1998). Men and women respond differently to infidelity, according to evolutionary psychologists, due to the fact that women bear higher reproductive costs than do men (Harris & Christenfeld, 1996). Women are concerned with having a safe environment for potential offspring, so it would follow that sexual infidelity would not be as threatening as emotional infidelity, which could signal the male's withdrawal from the relationship. Men, however, should be most concerned with ensuring the prolongation of their genes and avoid investing energy in safeguarding some other male's offspring. Therefore, males are most threatened by acts of sexual infidelity and less so by emotional ones. Thus, males become most jealous when their mates are sexually unfaithful, whereas women are most jealous when their mates are emotionally involved with a rival (Buss, 1994; Harris & Christenfeld, 1996).

According to the evolutionary psychology view, males ought to be threatened by a rival's dominance, the ability to provide resources (money,

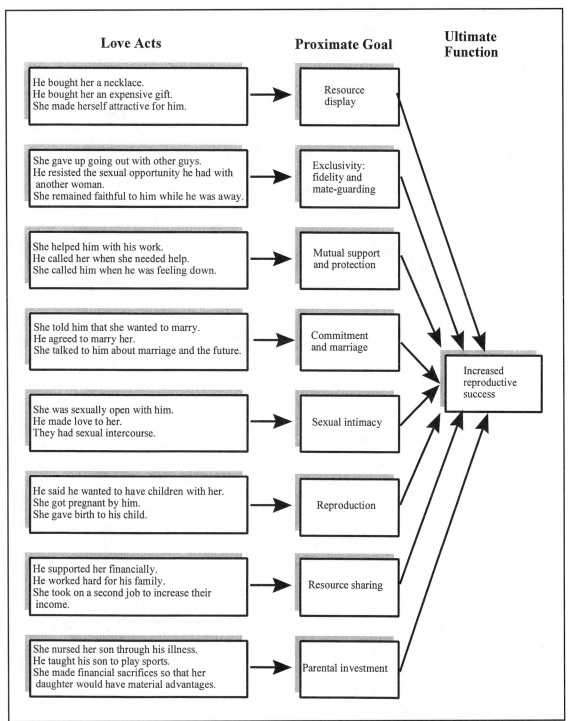

Figure 9.3 *Proximate and ultimate goals of love acts. According to the sociobiological view of love, individuals engage in various interpersonal behaviors designed to attract and keep mates (love acts). The ultimate goal of these love acts is to increase reproductive success.*

From Buss (1988b). Reprinted with permission.

status, power) to the female in question, whereas women ought to be most threatened by a rival who is physically attractive, because that attribute signals the potential for viable offspring. Indeed, a clever experiment by Dijkstra and Buunk (1998), in which participants judged scenarios in which the participant's real or imagined mate was flirting with a person of the opposite sex, showed that dominance in a male rival and attractiveness in a female rival elicited the greatest amount of jealousy for men and women, respectively.

Many of Buss's findings about human mating behavior are disturbing because both men and women in pursuit of the sexual goals cheat and frustrate their mates and derogate their rivals. However, some of his findings are kinder to our species. For example, he points out that the most effective tactics for men who wish to keep their mates are to provide love and kindness, to show affection, and to tell their mates of their love. That sounds rather romantic.

Indeed, evidence suggests that women are driven, at least in long-term mate selection strategies, by behavior and traits represented by the good provider models. Although men are strongly influence by traits such as youth and attractiveness, women tend to select partners on the basis of attributes such as social status and industriousness (Ben Hamida, Mineka, & Bailey, 1998). Note the intriguing differences between traits that men find attractive in women and those that women find attractive in men. The obvious one is that men seem to be driven by the "good genes" model, whereas women's preferences seem to follow the good provider models. The other difference, however, is that traits that make women attractive are in essence uncontrollable: Either you are young or you are not; either you are attractive or you are not. Modern science can help, but not much. Therefore, a woman who desires to increase her value has the problem of enhancing attributes that are really not under her control (Ben Hamida et al., 1998). Male-related attributes—status, achievement—are all, to a greater or lesser extent, under some control and may be gained with effort and motivation. Ben Hamida and his colleagues argue that the uncontrollability of the factors that affect a woman's fate in the sexual marketplace may have long-term negative emotional consequences.

Before we conclude that there is an unbridgeable difference between men and women and that men only follow the good genes model and women only the good provider model, we should consider the possibility that what one wants in the sexual marketplace depends on what one's goals are and what one can reasonably expect to get. In fact, it appears that when looking for a casual sexual partner, both men and women emphasize attractiveness, and when searching for a long-term relationship both look for a mate with good interpersonal skills, an individual who is attentive to the partner's needs, has a good sense of humor, and is easy-going (Regan, 1998). In fact, Geoffrey Miller (2000), an evolutionary psychologist, argued that the most outstanding features of the human mind—consciousness, morality, sense of humor, creativity—were shaped not so much by natural selection but rather by sexual selection. Miller suggested that being funny and friendly and a good conversationist serves the same purpose for humans as an attractive tail serves peacocks: It helps attract mates.

Pamela Regan (1998) reported women were less willing to compromise on their standards. For example, although women wanted an attractive partner for casual sex, they also wanted a male who was older and more interpersonally responsive. Men wanted attractiveness and would compromise on everything else. In fact, a woman's attractiveness seems to overcome a male potential partner's common sense as well. Agocha and Cooper (1999) reported that when men knew a potential partner's sexual history and also knew that she was physically attractive, they weighed attractiveness as much more important in the decision to engage in intercourse than the probability of contracting a sexually transmitted disease as suggested by that sexual history. However, women and men are less willing to compromise when it comes to long-term relationships. The results conform to the idea that causal sex affords men a chance to advertise their sexual prowess and gain favor with their peer group but that long-term relationships are driven by quite different needs (Regan, 1998).

DYNAMICS OF CLOSE RELATIONSHIPS

We have discussed why people form close relationships and why they form them with the people they do. We turn now to the dynamics of close relationships—how they develop and are kept going and how in some cases conflict can lead to their dissolution.

But what exactly are close relationships? What psychological factors define them? There appear to be three crucial factors, all of which we saw in the relationship between Gertrude Stein and Alice Toklas. The first factor is emotional involvement, feelings of love or warmth and fondness for the other person. The second is sharing, including sharing of feelings and experiences. The third is interdependence, which means that one's well-being is tied up with that of the other (Kelley et al., 1983). As is clear from this definition, a close relationship can be between husband and wife, lovers, or friends. Note that even when research focuses on one type of close relationship, it is usually also applicable to the others.

Relationship Development

Models of how relationships develop emphasize a predictable sequence of events. This is true of both models we examine in this section, the stage model of relationship development and social penetration theory. According to the stage model of relationship development, proposed by George Levinger and J. D. Snoek (1972), relationships evolve through the following stages:

Stage 0, no relationship.   This is a person's status with respect to virtually all other people in the world.

Stage 1, awareness.   We become conscious of another's presence and feel the beginning of interest. When Stein and Toklas first met in the company of friends, their conversation suggested to each of them that they might have much in common.

Stage 2, surface contact.   Interaction begins but is limited to topics such as the weather, politics, and mutual likes and dislikes. Although the contact is superficial, each person is forming impressions of the other. Stein and Toklas moved into this stage the day after their first meeting and soon moved beyond it.

Stage 3, mutuality.   The relationship moves, in substages, from lesser to greater interdependence. The first substage is that of involvement, which is characterized by a growing number of shared activities (Levinger, 1988). A subsequent substage is commitment, characterized by feelings of responsibility and obligation each to the other. Although not all close relationships involve commitment (Sternberg, 1988), those that have a serious long-term influence on one's life generally do. We noted how Stein and Toklas began by sharing activities, then feelings, and then an increasing commitment to each other.

social penetration theory

A theory that relationships vary in breadth, the extent of interaction, and depth, suggesting they progress in a an orderly fashion from slight and superficial contact to greater and deeper involvement.

A second model of relationship development, **social penetration theory**, developed by Irwin Altman and Dalmas Taylor (1973), centers on the idea that relationships change over time in both breadth—the range of topics people discuss and activities they engage in together—and depth—the extent to which they share their inner thoughts and feelings. Relationships progress in a predictable way from slight and superficial contact to greater and deeper involvement. First the breadth of a relationship increases. Then there is an increase in its depth, and breadth may actually decrease. Casual friends may talk about topics ranging from sports to the news to the latest rumors at work. But they will not, as will more intimate friends, talk about their feelings and hopes. Close friends allow each other to enter their lives—social penetration—and share on a deeper, more intimate level, even as the range of topics they discuss may decrease.

Evidence in support of social penetration theory comes from a study in which college students filled out questionnaires about their friendships several times over the course of a semester and then again 3 months later (Hays, 1985). Over 60% of the affiliations tracked in the study developed into close relationships by the end of the semester. More important, the interaction patterns changed as the relationships developed. As predicted by social penetration theory, interactions of individuals who eventually became close friends were characterized by an initial increase in breadth followed by a decrease in breadth and an increase in intimacy, or depth.

self-disclosure

The ability and willingness to share intimate areas of one's life with another person in a relationship.

An important contributor to increasing social penetration—or to the mutuality stage of relationship development—is **self-disclosure**, the ability and willingness to share intimate areas of one's life. College students who kept diaries of their interactions with friends reported that casual friends provided as much fun and intellectual stimulation as close friends but that close friends provided more emotional support (Hays, 1988b). Relationship development is fostered by self-disclosure simply because we often respond to intimate revelations with self-disclosures of our own (Jourard, 1971).

Evaluating Relationships

Periodically we evaluate the state of our relationships, especially when something is going wrong or some emotional episode occurs. Ellen Berscheid (1985) observed that emotion occurs in a close relationship when there is an interruption in a well-learned sequence of behavior. Any long-term dating or marital relationship develops sequences of behavior—Bercheid called these interchain sequences—that depend on the partners coordinating their actions. For example, couples develop hints and signals that show their interest in lovemaking. The couple's lovemaking becomes organized, and the response of one partner helps coordinate the response of the other. A change in the frequency or pattern of this behavior will bring about a reaction, positive or negative, from the partner. The more intertwined the couples are, the stronger are their interchain sequences; the more they depend on each other, the greater the impact of interruptions of these sequences.

EXCHANGE THEORIES One perspective on how we evaluate relationships is provided by **social exchange theory** (Thibaut & Kelley, 1959) that suggests that people make assessments according to rewards and costs, which correspond to all the positive and all the negative factors derived from a relationship. Generally, rewards are high if a person gets a great deal of gratification from the relationship, whereas costs are high if the person either must exert a great deal of effort to maintain the relationship or experiences anxiety about the relationship. According to this economic model of relationships, the outcome is decided by subtracting costs from rewards. If the rewards are greater than the costs, the outcome is positive; if the costs are greater than the rewards, the outcome is negative.

This doesn't necessarily mean that if the outcome is positive, we will stay in the relationship, or that if the outcome is negative, we will leave it. We also evaluate outcomes against comparison levels. One type of comparison level is our expectation of what we will obtain from the relationship. That is, we compare the outcome with what we think the relationship should be giving us. A second type is a comparison level of alternatives, in which we compare the outcome of the relationship we are presently in with the expected outcomes of possible alternative relationships. If we judge that the alternative outcomes would be not better, or even worse, than the outcome of our present relationship, we will be less inclined to make a change. If, on the other hand, we perceive that an alternative relationship promises a better outcome, we are more likely to make a change.

A theory related to exchange theory, **equity theory**, like social exchange theory, says that we evaluate our relationships based on their rewards and costs, but it also focuses on our perception of equity, or balance, in relationships (Hatfield, Traupmann, Sprecher, Utne, & Hay, 1985). Equity in a relationship occurs when the following equation holds:

$$\frac{\text{Person A's Benefits [rewards} - \text{costs]}}{\text{B's Contributions}} = \frac{\text{Person B's Benefits [rewards} - \text{costs]}}{\text{A's Contributions}}$$

Rewards may include, but are not limited to, companionship, sex, and social support. Costs may include loss of independence and increases in financial obligations. The contributions made to the relationship include earning power or high social status. The rule of equity is simply that person A's benefits should equal person B's if their contributions are equal. However, fairness requires that if A's contributions are greater than B's, A's benefits should also be greater.

Thus, under equity theory, the way people judge the fairness of the benefits depends on their understanding of what each brings to the relationship. For example, the spouse who earns more may be perceived as bringing more to the marriage and, therefore, as entitled to higher benefits. The other spouse may, as a result, increase her costs, perhaps by taking on more of the household chores.

In actual relationships, of course, people differ, often vigorously, on what counts as contributions and on how specific contributions ought to be weighed. For example, in business settings, many individuals believe that race or gender should count as a contribution when hiring. Others disagree strongly with that position.

Has the fact that most women now work outside the home altered the relationship between wives and husbands as equity theory would predict? It appears, in keeping with equity theory, that the spouse who earns more,

social exchange theory
A theory of how relationships are evaluated suggesting that people make assessments according to the rewards (positive things derived from a relationship) and costs (negative things derived from a relationship).

equity theory
An interpersonal relationship theory suggesting that we strive to maximize fairness in our social relationships with others; when inequity is perceived we are motivated to change a relationship.

regardless of gender, often has fewer child-care responsibilities than the spouse who earns less (Steil & Weltman, 1991, 1992).

However, it also appears that cultural expectations lead to some inequity. Husbands tend to have more control over financial matters than wives do regardless of income (Biernat & Wortman, 1991). Moreover, a study of professional married couples in which the partners earned relatively equal amounts found that although the wives were satisfied with their husbands' participation in household chores and childrearing, in reality there was considerable inequity (Biernat & Wortman, 1991). Women were invariably the primary caregivers for the children. Men spent time with their children and did many of the household chores, but they were not the primary caregivers. This may reflect a lack of equity in these relationships, or it may mean that women simply do not fully trust their husbands to do a competent job of taking care of the children.

What happens when people perceive inequity in a relationship? As a rule, they will attempt to correct the inequity and restore equity. If you realize that your partner is dissatisfied with the state of the relationship, you might try, for example, to pay more attention to your partner and in this way increase the rewards he or she experiences. If equity is not restored, your partner might become angry or withdraw from the relationship. Inequitable relationships are relationships in trouble.

In one study, researchers measured the level of perceived equity in relationships by means of the following question and scale (Hatfield, Walster, & Berscheid, 1978, p. 121). Comparing what you get out of this relationship with what your partner gets out of it, how would you say the relationship stacks up?

+3 I am getting a much better deal than my partner.

+2 I am getting a somewhat better deal.

+1 I am getting a slightly better deal.

 0 We are both getting an equally good — or bad — deal.

−1 My partner is getting a slightly better deal.

−2 My partner is getting a somewhat better deal.

−3 My partner is getting a much better deal than I am.

Respondents were grouped into three categories: those who felt that their relationship was equitable; those who felt that they got more out of the relationship than their partners and, therefore, were overbenefited; and those who felt that they got less than their partners and, therefore, were underbenefited.

The researchers then surveyed 2,000 people and found, as expected, that those individuals who felt underbenefited were much more likely to engage in extramarital sex than those who thought that their relationship was equitable or felt overbenefited (Hatfield, Walster, & Traupmann, 1978). Figure 9.4 shows how eager people are to engage in extramarital affairs based on their evaluation of the relationship. Note that those who feel deprived, for example, evaluate their status as underbenefited, have many extramarital partners, and engage in affairs sooner than individuals who judge themselves to be equitably treated or overbenefited in the relationship. Generally, couples who feel that they are in an equitable relationship are more likely to maintain the relationship than those who were less equitably matched (Hill, Rubin, & Peplau, 1976).

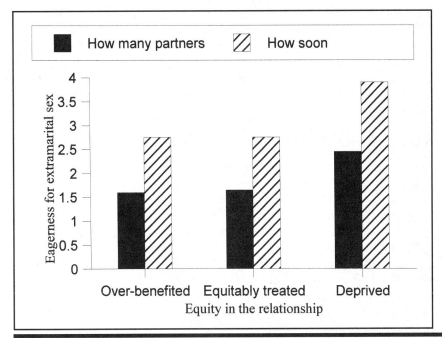

Figure 9.4

Interest in having an extramarital affair as a function of equity in a marriage. Individuals who feel underbenefited in a relationship are more likely to express the desire for an extramarital affair than those who are equitably treated or overbenefited.

From Hatfield, Traupmann, and Walster (1978). Reprinted with permission.

COMMUNAL RELATIONSHIPS Although the research just reviewed suggests that people make rather cold-blooded, marketplace judgments about the quality of their relationships, it is likely that they also have other ways of evaluating relationships. For example, a distinction has been made between relationships governed by exchange principles—in which, as we have seen, people benefit each other with the expectation of receiving a benefit in return—and relationships governed by communal principles—in which individuals benefit each other in response to the other's needs (Clark, 1986). In **communal relationships**, if one partner can put put more into the relationship than the other, so be it. That is, people may deliberately underbenefit themselves for the sake of the relationship.

Love relationships are often governed by communal principles. Clark and Grote reviewed the research concerning how couples evaluate their relationships and although some of the results show that costs are negatively related to satisfaction as exchange theories would predict, sometimes, however, costs are positively related to satisfaction. That is, Clark and Grote (1998) found evidence that sometimes the more costs a partner incurs, the higher the satisfaction. How might we explain this? Well, if we consider the communal norm as one that rewards behavior that meets the needs of one's partner, then we might understand how costs could define a warm, close, and affectionate relationship. As Clark and Grote noted, it may be admirable, and one may feel good about oneself if, having helped one's partner, one has also lived up to the communal ideal. By doing so, the helping partner gains the gratitude of the other, feel good about oneself, and these positive feelings then become associated with the relationship.

One way to reconcile the different findings concerning the relationship between costs and satisfaction is to note the costs one bears in a communal relationship are qualitatively different than those we bear in an purely exchange relationship that may be deteriorating. For example, consider the

communal relationship

An interpersonal relationship in which individuals benefit each other in response to each others' needs.

following costs borne in an exchange relationship: "She told me I was dumb." This is an intentional insult (and cost) that suggests a relationship that may be going badly. Compare this to a communal cost: "I listened carefully to what he said when a problem arose even though I was quite busy and had other things to get done." This communal cost served to strengthen the relationship (Clark & Grote, 1998). To state the obvious, there are costs and then there are costs.

Love Over Time

We have talked about how relationships get started and how the partners evaluate how that relationship is going. Now let's consider what happens to relationships over time. What factors keep them together and what drives them apart? Susan Sprecher (1999) studied partners in romantic relationships over a period of several years. The measures of love, commitment, and satisfaction taken several times over the period of the research show that couples who maintained their relationship increased on all measures of relationship satisfaction. Couples who broke up showed a decrease in measures of relationship health just before the breakup. The collapse of the relationship did not mean that love was lost. In fact, the splintered partners continued to love each other, but everything else had gone wrong.

Sprecher's work as well as that of others suggests that intact relationships are perceived by the partners in idealistic ways and that the partners truly feel that their love and commitment grows stronger as time goes on. Intact, long-term couples are very supportive of each other and that makes it easier for them to weather difficult personal or financial problems (Gottman, Coan, Carrere, & Swanson, 1998). For example, couples who support each other during times of stress are much better able to survive periods of economic pressure that tend to cause much emotional distress in a relationship (Conger, Rueter, & Elder, Jr., 1999).

Some individuals are especially idealistic and affirm a belief that they have met the person that destiny provided. Raymond Knee (1998) examined the relationships of those romantic partners who believed in romantic destiny and those who did not. He found that he could predict the longevity of the relationship by two factors: One was belief in romantic destiny and the other was whether the initial interaction was very positive. As Figure 9.5 shows, individuals who believed in romantic destiny and had that confirmed by initial satisfaction tended to have longer relationships than those who did not believe in destiny. But if things don't go quite so well at first, those who believe in destiny tend to bail out quite quickly and do not give the relationship a chance (Knee, 1998).

Sculpting a Relationship

So we see that strong relationships are idealized and are able to withstand stresses because the partners support each other rather than work at cross purposes. How do such relationships develop? Stephen Drigotas and his co-experimenters found that successful couples have an obliging interdependence in which each, in essence, sculpts the other, much as Michelangelo carved David out of the embryonic stone. This Drigotas aptly called the *Michelangelo phenomenon* (Drigotas, Rusbult, Wieselquist, & Whitton, 1999). In a series of four studies, these researchers showed that each partner tended to become more like the ideal self that their partner envisioned for them. In

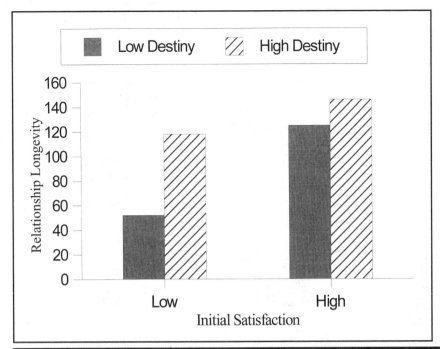

Figure 9.5

Relationship longevity as a function of belief in destiny and initial satisfaction with a relationship. Individuals who believed in romantic destiny and had initial satisfaction with the relationship tended to have longer relationships then those who did not. However, when initial satisfaction was low, individuals who believed in destiny tended not to give the relationship a chance and exited the relationship after a short time.

From Knee (1998). Reprinted with permission.

other words, each partner supports the other's attempts to change. This partner affirmation of each other is strongly associated with ongoing well-functioning couples.

Of course, one reason that successful couples have similar views of each other is that individuals tend to search for people who are similar to them. For example, Klohnen and Mendelsohn (1998) reported research that showed that individuals pair up with partners of approximately equal value and attributes. Note this is in line with exchange theories discussed earlier. Therefore, people with positive self-images tend to have more positive descriptions of their ideal partner as compared to those with lesser self-images. Klohnen and Mendelsohn reported a significant similarity between one partner's description of the ideal self and his or her description of the partner. In fact, individuals tended to bias their views of their partner in the direction of the ideal self-concepts.

It appears then that successful relationships require that each partner work to affirm his or her beliefs about the other partner. What happens when one partner, say, gets a nasty surprise and learns that her spouse, a competent individual in social situations with people he does not know, is a awkward mutterer with close family members? Certainly, she may be upset and disillusioned. Past research by Swann (1996) has shown that when individuals confront evidence that goes against their firmly held views of themselves, they work very hard to refute or downgrade that evidence. Similarly, Chris De La Ronde and William Swann (1998) found that partners work hard to verify their views of their spouses. As Drigotas and colleagues (1999) suggested, we often enter into relationships with people who view us as we view ourselves. Therefore, we and our partners are motivated to preserve these impressions. Therefore, our surprised spouse will be motivated to see her husband as competent in social situations, as he sees himself, by suggesting perhaps that there is something about family gatherings that makes him act out of character.

There seems, then, to be a kind of unspoken conspiracy among many intact couples to protect and conserve the social world that the couple inhabits. The downside of this, of course, is when one of the partners changes in a way that violates the expectations of the other partner. For example, as De La Ronde and Swann (1998) suggested, if one partner, because of low self-esteem goes into therapy and comes out with a more positive self-image, the spouse holding the other in low regard in the first place is motivated, according to the notion of partner verification, to maintain that original negative image. Clearly, that does not bode well for the relationship.

Of course, having negative views of one's partner, as you might expect, is associated with decreased relationship well-being (Ruvolo & Rotondo, 1998). In fact, some people have a strong belief that people can change and, to go back to the example used here, that someone with a negative self-image can change for the better. Ann Ruvulo and Jennifer Rotondo (1998) measured the extent to which people involved in relationships believed that people can change. They found when individuals had strong beliefs that individuals can change, then the views that they had of their partner were less likely to be related to the current well-being of the relationship. This means that if you saw that your partner had a negative self-image, but you were convinced that he or she could change for the better, that current image was not crucial to how you viewed the status of the relationship. However, for those individuals who did not feel that it was possible for people to change, the views of their partners was crucial to how they evaluated their relationships. So, if you believed that your partner's attributes and feelings were forever fixed, it makes sense that those views would be crucial to how you felt about the relationship. But, if things could change, probably for the better, well then these negative views won't last forever. Therefore, many successful couples behave in a manner that verifies initial images of each other.

Responses to Conflict

When relationships are deemed to be unfair, or inequitable, the result almost inevitably will be conflict. Conflict also can occur when a partner behaves badly, and everyone behaves badly at one time or another. The mere passage of time also makes conflict more likely. Couples are usually more affectionate and happier as newlyweds than they are 2 years later (Huston & Vangelisti, 1991). What happens, then, when conflicts arise? How do people in a relationship respond to conflicts?

Satisfied couples bias their impressions of their partner in ways that cause idealization of the partner and increases satisfaction in the relationship (McGregor & Holmes, 1999). Researchers have discovered that when satisfied couples confront a threat in the marriage due to something the partner has done (say, had a drink with another man or woman on the sly), individuals devise stories that work to diminish that threat. They construct a story to explain the event in a way that takes the blame away from their partner. The story puts the partner in the best light possible. McGregor and Holmes (1999) suggested that the process of devising a story to explain a behavior convinces the storyteller of the truth of that story. Constructing the motives of the characters in the story (the partner and others) and making the story come to a desired conclusion—all of this cognitive work is convincing to the story's author, who comes to believe in its conclusions.

Conflict is a part of any relationship. How a couple like this responds to the conflict will have an impact on whether the relationship continues. Couples who begin to view each other negatively are likely to split. Couples who engage in an accommodation process which involves doing things to maintain and enhance a relationship in times of conflict, are more likely to continue their relationship.

When reality is complicated, a story that is charitable, apparently, can go far in soothing both the offending partner and the story-telling partner (McGregor & Holmes, 1999).

Sometimes, instead of escalating the conflict, couples find ways to accommodate each other, even when one or both have acted in a negative or destructive manner (Rusbult, Verette, Whitney, Slovik, & Lipkus, 1991). Typically, our initial impulse in response to a negative act such as our partner embarrassing us in front of other people is to be hurtful in return. That is, we tend toward the primitive response of returning the hurt in kind.

Then other factors come into play. That initial impulse gets moderated by second thoughts: If I react this way, I'm going to hurt the relationship and I will suffer. What should I do? Should I lash back, or should I try to be constructive? Do I satisfy the demands of my ego, or do I accommodate for the good of the relationship?

These second thoughts, therefore, might lead to an **accommodation process**, which means that in interactions in which there is conflict, a partner does things that maintain and enhance the relationship (Rusbult et al., 1991). Whether a partner decides to accommodate will depend largely on the nature of the relationship. To accommodate, a person must value the relationship above his or her wounded pride. If the relationship is happy, if the partners are committed to each other, then they will be more likely to accommodate. People are also more likely to accommodate when they have no alternatives to the relationship.

Accommodation does not always mean being positive. Consistently reacting to a partner's negative behavior in positive ways may lessen the power that constructive comments can have under really serious circumstances. At

accommodation process
Interacting in such a way that, despite conflict, a relationship is maintained and enhanced.

times, it may be better to say nothing at all than to respond in a positive way. More important than being positive and agreeing with one's partner is to avoid being unduly negative (Montgomery, 1988). The health of a relationship depends less on taking good, constructive actions than on carefully avoiding insulting, destructive actions (Rusbult et al., 1991).

The way people in a committed relationship handle conflict, in short, is an excellent predictor of the health of the relationship. Relationship health correlates with handling conflict through accommodation rather than ignoring conflict or focusing on negatives. Research shows a positive association between happiness in a relationship and a couple's commitment to discuss and not ignore conflicts (Crohan, 1992). Those couples who ignore conflicts report less happiness in their relationship.

Couples who tend to focus on negatives when dealing with conflict are more likely to end their relationship. An initial study showed that couples whose relationship was in difficulty tended to express negative feelings, sometimes even in anticipation of an interaction, and to display high levels of physiological arousal, whereas couples whose relationship was not in difficulty expected interactions to be constructive and were able to control their emotions (Levenson & Gottman, 1983). A follow-up study of most of the couples revealed that those couples who had recorded high physiological arousal were likely to have separated or ended the relationship (Gottman & Levenson, 1986).

As should be clear, conflict is not the cause of relationship breakup, nor is the lack of overt conflict a sign that a relationship is well. Rather, it is the way couples handle conflict that counts. Mark Twain mused that people may think of perhaps 80,000 words a day but only a few will get them into trouble. So it is with relationships. Just a few "zingers"—contemptuous negative comments—will cause great harm (Notarius & Markman, 1993). Consider the husband who thinks of himself as an elegant dresser, a person with impeccable taste in clothes. If, one day, his wife informs him during a heated exchange that she finds his clothing vulgar and is often embarrassed to be seen with him, she has struck a sensitive nerve. Her comment, perhaps aimed at damaging his self-esteem, may provoke an even more hurtful response and lead to growing ill will between the two—or to defensiveness and withdrawal. One zinger like this can undo a whole week's worth of loving and supportive interchanges.

Love in the Lab

John Gottman has studied marriages in a systematic and scientific manner by using a variety of instruments to observe volunteer couples who agree to live in an apartment that is wired and to have their behavior observed and recorded. Results of research from what is known as the "love lab" suggest that there are three kinds of stable marriages (Gottman, 1995). The first type is the *conflict avoiding couple*, who survive by accentuating the positive and simply ignoring the negative; the second type is the *volatile couple*, who are passionate in everything they do, even fighting. Last is the *validating couple*, who listen carefully to each other, compromise, and reconcile differences (Gottman, 1995). All these styles work, because the bottom line is that each style promotes behavior that most of the time is positive.

Gottman has been able to predict with uncanny accuracy the couples that are headed for divorce. He has identified four factors he refers to as the

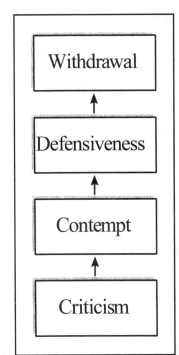

Figure 9.6

John Gottman's four horsemen of the apocalypse: complaining–criticizing, contempt, defensiveness, and withdrawal from social interaction (stonewalling).

From Gottman (1995). Reprinted with permission.

four horsemen of the apocalypse (see Figure 9.6). These four factors are: complaining–criticizing, contempt, defensiveness, and withdrawal from social interaction (stonewalling). The last factor is the most destructive to a relationship and is a very reliable predictor of which couples divorce. There is no answer to stonewalling, but it means that communication has ceased and one partner is in the process of ostracizing the other by refusing to talk. Gottman suggested, as shown in Figure 9.6, that there is a cascading relationship between the four horsemen of the apocalypse. Criticism may lead to contempt, which may lead to defensiveness and finally to stonewalling.

Most happy couples do not refuse to talk. Indeed, Gottman's observations in the love lab suggest that these partners make lots of attempts to repair a dispute to make sure the argument does not spiral out of control. These repair attempts, reaching out to the other, also include humor that works to defuse anger. Gottman (1995) noted that most marital problems are not easy to resolve. But happy couples realize that their relationship is more important than satisfying their own preferences and idiosyncrasies. For example, one spouse may be a "morning" person and the other is not. So when this couple goes on trips, they compromise. The "morning" person is willing to wait a bit later to start the day and the "night" person is willing to wake up a bit earlier.

four horsemen of the apocalypse
Four factors identified as important in relationship dissolution: complaining–criticizing, contempt, defensiveness, and withdrawal from social interaction (stonewalling).

Friendships

According to Sternberg's definition mentioned earlier, liking involves intimacy without passion. Given that liking involves intimacy, does liking lead to romantic loving? The answer to this question appears to be no. Liking evidently leads only to liking. It is as if the two states—liking and loving—are on different tracks (Berscheid, 1988). People may be fond of each other and may go out together for a long time without their affection ever quite ripening into romantic love. Can we say, then, that liking and loving are basically different?

Zick Rubin (1970, 1973) thought that liking and loving were indeed essentially different. He constructed two separate measures, a liking scale and a loving scale, to explore the issue systematically. He found that although both friends and lovers were rated high on the liking scale, only lovers were rated high on the loving scale. Moreover, separate observations revealed that dating couples who gave each other high scores on the loving scale tended more than others to engage in such loving actions as gazing into each other's eyes and holding hands. A follow-up study found that these couples were more likely to have maintained the relationship than were those whose ratings on the loving scale were lower. Therefore, according to Rubin, we may like our lovers, but we do not generally love those we like, at least with the passion we feel toward our lovers.

However, even if liking and (romantic) loving are conceptually different, this does not necessarily mean that friendship does not involve love or that some of the same motives that drive romantic relationships are absent in long-term friendships. The friendships that we form during our lives can be loving and intimate and passionate. Baumeister and Bratslavsky (1999) suggested that passion can be just as strong in friendships except that the sexual component may be absent for a variety of reasons, the most obvious one being that the gender of the friend is wrong. The history of a friendship ought not to differ very much from that of a romantic relationship. When two individuals become friends, they experience attraction and affection and share disclosures and experiences. This rising intimacy leads to an increase in the passion of the friends, absent the sexual component (Baumeister & Bratslavsky, 1999).

GENDER DIFFERENCES IN FRIENDSHIPS Female same-sex friendships and male same-sex friendships show somewhat different patterns (S. Brehm, 1985). Males tend to engage in activities together, whereas females tend to share their emotional lives. Richard and Don may play basketball twice a week, and while playing, they may talk about their problems and feelings, but that is not their purpose in getting together. Karen and Terri may have lunch twice a week with the express purpose of sharing their problems and feelings. Men live their friendships side by side; women live them face to face (Hendrick 1988; Wright, 1982).

The degree of this difference may be diminishing. In the last few decades, there appears to have been a marked increase in the importance both men and women assign to personal intimacy as a source of fulfillment (McAdams, 1989). Some recent research suggests that men and women self-disclose with equal frequency and perhaps intensity (Prager, Fuller, & Gonzalez, 1989).

Men and women report having about the same number of close friends. Women tend to view their close friends as more important than men do, but men's close friendships may last longer than women's (Fiebert & Wright, 1989). Men typically distinguish between same-sex and cross-sex friendships. For men, cross-sex bonds offer the opportunity for more self-disclosure and emotional attachment. Men, generally, obtain more acceptance and intimacy from their female friends than from their male friends (Duck, 1988). However, for heterosexual men, cross-sex relationships are often permeated with sexual tension (Rawlins, 1992).

Women, in comparison, do not sharply distinguish among their friendships with males and females. They also see differences in their feelings for the various men in their lives. Some of their relationships with men are full of sexual tension, whereas other men may be liked, even loved, but sexual tension may be absent in those relationships.

Greater levels of interaction with females are associated with fewer episodes of loneliness for both men and women. Why? Interactions with women are infused with disclosure, intimacy, and satisfaction, and all these act as buffers against loneliness (Wheeler, Reis, & Nezlek, 1983). Women seem to make better friends than men do. It is telling that married men, when asked to name their best friend, are likely to name their wives. The expectations women have for friendship are often not satisfied by their spouse, and they tend to have at least one female friend in whom they confide (Oliker, 1989).

FRIENDSHIPS OVER THE LIFE CYCLE   Friendships are important throughout the life cycle. But they also change somewhat in relation to the stage of the life cycle and to factors in the individual's life. Sharing and intimacy begin to characterize friendships in early adolescence, as a result of an increasing ability to understand the thoughts and feelings of others. Girls have more intimate friendships in their early adolescent years than boys do, and this tends to remain true throughout life (Rawlins, 1992).

Why are boys less intimate than girls with same-sex friends? The reason might be that girls trust their friends more than boys do (Berndt, 1992). Girls tend to listen to their friends and protect their friends' feelings, whereas boys tend to tease or embarrass their friends when the opportunity arises. The more intimate the adolescent friendships, the more loyal and supportive they are. However, disloyalty and lack of support can sometimes result from pressure to conform to the peer group. Of course, these issues are not unique to adolescent friendships. Conflicts between intimacy and social pressure simply take on different forms as people get older (Berndt, 1992).

As individuals move into early and middle adulthood, the end of a marriage or other long-term intimate relationship can profoundly affect the pattern of a couple's friendships. When a woman experiences the breakup of a relationship, her friends rally around and support her (Oliker, 1989). Often, the couple's close friends will have already guessed that the relationship was in trouble. When the breakup occurs, they tend to choose one partner or the other, or to simply drift away, unable to deal with the new situation.

In later adulthood, retirement affects our friendships. We no longer have daily contact with co-workers and, thus, lose a source of potential friends. With increasing age, new issues arise. The death of a spouse affects friendships perhaps as much as the breakup of a marriage. People who are recently widowed can often feel like "fifth wheels" (Rawlins, 1992). The physical problems often associated with old age can lead to a conflict between a need for independence and a need for help (Rawlins, 1992). As a result, older friends might have to renegotiate their relationships to ensure that both needs are met. Whatever the problems, friendships among the elderly are often uplifting and vital. This is well illustrated by the following statement from a 79-year-old widower: "I don't know how anyone would ever live without friends, because to me, they're next to good health, and all your life depends on friendship" (quoted in Rawlins, 1992).

GERTRUDE AND ALICE REVISITED

Stein and Toklas are important because of their role in the vibrant literary world of Paris just after the end of World War I, a period that lasted well into the 1930s. However, aside from their historical importance, the relationship of these two individuals reflects and exemplifies the basic characteristics of close relationships. We saw how the need for intimacy overcame Alice's very strong feelings of social anxiety. Their relationship changed over time, of course, ending, finally, in a companionate one. However, they touched all the vertices of Sternberg's triangle of love: intimacy, passion, and commitment.

CHAPTER REVIEW

1. **What is a close relationship?**

   The essence of a close relationship is intimacy, friendship, sharing, and love between two people.

2. **What are the roots of interpersonal attraction and close relationships?**

   Human beings possess positive social motives, the **need for affiliation**—the desire to establish and maintain rewarding interpersonal relationships—and the **need for intimacy**—the desire for close and affectionate relationships, which influence us to seek fulfilling relationships. There are, however, motives that may inhibit the formation of social relationships, particularly **loneliness** and **social anxiety**, which arise because of a person's expectation of negative encounters with and evaluations from others. Another important factor in interpersonal attraction and close relationships is our earliest interaction with our primary caregiver, which shapes our particular attachment style. Attachment styles are patterns of interacting and relating that influence how we develop affectional ties with others later in life. Each of these styles evolve into a **working model**, a mental representation of what we as individuals expect to happen in a close relationship.

3. **How does interpersonal attraction develop?**

   Several factors influence the development of interpersonal attraction. The **physical proximity effect** is an initially important determinant of potential attraction. The importance of proximity can be partly accounted for by the mere exposure effect, which suggests that repeated exposure to a person increases familiarity, which in turn increases attraction. Proximity is also important because it increases opportunities for interaction, which may increase liking.

   Another factor affecting attraction is the **similarity effect**. We are attracted to those we perceive to be like us in interests, attitudes, personality, and physical attractiveness. We tend to seek out partners who are at the same level of attractiveness as we are, known as the **matching principle**. Matching becomes more important as a relationship progresses.

   We also tend to be more attracted to people who are physically attractive, which is a third factor in interpersonal attraction. Generally, males are more overwhelmed by physical attractiveness than are females. Facial appearance, body appearance, and the quality of one's voice contribute to the perception of physical attractiveness. We tend to ascribe positive qualities to physically attractive people.

   The downside to the **physical attractiveness bias** is that we tend to stigmatize those who are unattractive and ascribe negative qualities to them. In our society, obese people are particularly stigmatized and are portrayed negatively in art, literature, and films.

   There is research evidence that the physical attractiveness bias is rooted in our biology: Even at 2 months, infants attend more to an attractive than an unattractive face. A new theory suggests that attractiveness, in the form of facial and body symmetry, may reflect genetic soundness. The physical attractiveness bias would thus have survival value for the species.

4. **How do close relationships form and evolve?**

   Most theories of relationship development emphasize an initial increase in shared activities followed by an increase in mutuality. That is, friends or lovers begin to share more intimate thoughts and feelings and become more and more interdependent.

Social penetration theory emphasizes that relationships change over time in both breadth—the range of topics people discuss and activities they engage in together—and depth—the extent to which they share their inner thoughts and feelings. Relationships progress in a predictable way from slight and superficial contact to greater and deeper involvement. An important contributor to increasing social penetration is **self-disclosure**, the ability and willingness to share intimate areas of one's life.

At some point, individuals begin to evaluate the status of their relationships according to the rewards and costs derived from them. According to **social exchange theory**, people evaluate a relationship against two comparison levels: what they think they should be getting out of a relationship and how the present relationship compares with potential alternatives. **Equity theory** maintains that people evaluate relationships according to the relative inputs and outcomes for each party in the relationship. If inequity exists, the relationship may be in trouble. However, many love relationships are governed by communal principles, in which individuals benefit each other in response to the other's needs. In communal relationships, one partner can put more into the relationship than the other. That is, people may deliberately underbenefit themselves for the sake of the relationship.

5. What are the components and dynamics of love?

In Sternberg's **triangular theory of love**, love has three components: passion, intimacy, and commitment. Different mixes of these three components define different types of love. **Romantic love**, for example, has passion and intimacy; it involves strong emotion and sexual desire. Companionate love has intimacy and commitment; it is based more on mutual respect and caring than on strong emotion. **Consummate love** has all three components. **Limerence** is an exaggerated form of romantic love that occurs when a person anxious for intimacy finds someone who seems able to fulfill all his or her needs. **Unrequited love**—love that is not returned—is the most painful kind of love. **Secret love** seems to have a special quality. Secrecy makes a partner more attractive and creates a bond between individuals.

6. What is the evolutionary view of love?

Sociobiologists suggest that the three components may have evolved because of the need of human infants for protection, the need of parents to protect their child, and the sexual instinct. Passion, intimacy, and commitment are seen as important to the survival of the species. An implication of sociobiological theory is that males, seeking to reproduce their genes as widely as possible, will prefer many short-term sexual encounters or relationships and that females, seeking to protect the children they bear, will prefer long-term relationships. Ultimately, however, males do participate in long-term relationships, partly because such relationships have more survival value for the species.

7. What is the nature of friendships?

According to Sternberg, friendships are characterized by liking and involve intimacy but not passion or commitment. Friendships are based on an ongoing interdependence between people. There are some gender differences in friendships, although these differences may have decreased in recent years. Both males and females need the intimacy offered by friendships. However, females still seem to view friends as more important than males do, and females make better friends. Interactions with females are more likely to be characterized by disclosure, intimacy, and satisfaction, all of which act as buffers against loneliness.

WHAT DO MEN AND WOMEN LOOK FOR IN A MATE?

We have all probably heard about how men and women differ. After all, aren't "men from Mars and women from Venus?" Is it true that men and women look for different qualities in a mate? One way that this question has been addressed is to look at what men and women place in personal advertisements. There are studies showing that men look more for attractiveness and women for economic security. For this exercise, use the Internet personal advertisements (e.g., Yahoo Personals) to see if this is so. Get to some online personal advertisements, and analyze some placed by men and some placed by women (you might want to analyze every 10th or 15th advertisement). Use the categories indicated for your analysis (these are based on a study done by Davis, 1990), and note the number of males and females who mention that attribute in their personal advertisement.

ATTRIBUTE	DESCRIPTION: LOOKING FOR A PARTNER WHO IS
Attractiveness	"cute," "pretty," "attractive," etc.
Physical appearance	"in shape," "fit," "has a good figure," etc.
Sexuality	"sensual," "high sex drive," "erotic," etc.
Professional	"a professional" (e.g., a doctor, lawyer, etc.)
Educational level	"highly educated," "college graduate," "well read," etc.
Financial security	"financially secure," "financially independent," etc.
Intelligence	"intelligent," "smart," "bright," etc.
Commitment	"looking for committed relationship," "looking for a long-term relationship," "looking for a relationship leading to marriage," etc.
Emotionality	"warm," "romantic," "sensitive," "emotionally responsive," etc.

Use the following tally sheet to analyze the personal advertisements you find.

ATTRIBUTE	MALE SEEKING FEMALE	FEMALE SEEKING MALE
Attractiveness		
Physical appearance		
Sexuality		
Professional		
Educational level		
Financial security		
Intelligence		
Commitment		
Emotionality		

On which, if any, of the attributes sought did males and females appear to differ? You might want to compare your results to those of Davis (1990). Here is the reference:

Davis, S. (1990). Men as success objects and women as sex objects: A study of personal advertisements. *Sex Roles, 23,* 43–50.

SUGGESTIONS FOR FURTHER READING

Austen, J. (1980). *Pride and prejudice.* New York: New American Library. (Originally published 1813)

Jane Austen's intricate and wonderfully crafted novel of the relationship between two prideful and opinionated young people in early 19th-century England is a classic. It teaches much about character and relationships and the role of love and affection in an ordered and class-conscious society.

Baumeister, R., & Bratslavsky, E. (1999). Passion, intimacy, and time: Passionate love as a function of change in intimacy. *Personality and Social Psychology Review, 3,* 49–67.

This is a well-written and insightful review of theory and literature examining the relationship between passion and intimacy.

Buss, D. M. (1994). *The evolution of desire: Strategies of human mating.* New York: Basic Books.

Everything you wanted to know about sex and love is written with clarity, humor, and sensitivity by one of the foremost evolutionary psychologists. Buss is convincing in his argument that in order for us to truly understand love, we must first understand our evolutionary past. This is a novel look to the sexiest organ: the human brain.

CHAPTER 10

INTERPERSONAL AGGRESSION

Matthew Wayne Shepard was a 21-year-old student at the University of Wyoming in Laramie, who was described by those who knew him as gentle and giving and as having a passion for human rights. He was a small man, standing only 5 feet 2 inches tall and weighing 110 pounds. There was another thing about Shepard, which may have cost him his life: He was gay.

On the night of October 7, 1998, Shepard was at a local bar. Two men who would play a key role in Shepard's fate were also at the Fireside Bar that night. Russell Henderson and Aaron McKinney were drinking beer and shooting pool. Shepard allegedly made a pass at the two men, which enraged McKinney. Henderson and McKinney hatched a plan to lure Shepard out of the bar by posing as gay men themselves and offering Shepard a ride home. The three of them left the bar and

drove off in a pickup truck, heading west, out of town. It was an ill-fated ride for Matthew Shepard.

Once inside the truck, McKinney told Shepard that he and Henderson were not gay, and he was being "jacked." McKinney then pulled out a .357-Magnum handgun and demanded Shepard's wallet. McKinney then began to beat Shepard with the butt of the gun. Henderson and McKinney drove Shepard to a deserted field where they pulled him out of the truck as they continued to hit him. McKinney told Henderson to get some rope out of the truck, and the two men tied Shepard to a fence rail. Henderson and McKinney beat and tortured Shepard while shouting antigay epithets. Shepard pleaded for his life, but his pleas went unheeded. At one point, McKinney became concerned that Shepard could read the license plate on his truck and asked him as much. Shepard said he could and read off the plate number. This further enraged McKinney, who again began beating Shepard savagely. Shepard lost consciousness; his face was red with his own blood. The only white skin showing through the blood was where his tears washed his blood away.

Henderson and McKinney left Shepard for dead, his naked, battered body tied to the fence. But Shepard did not die that night. He remained tied to the fence in freezing temperatures for the next 12 hours, until a bicyclist found him. The cyclist couldn't believe what he saw; at first, he thought Shepard was a scarecrow. Shepard was taken to Poudre Valley Hospital in Fort Collins, Colorado. He was unconscious, his skull was fractured, he was suffering from hypothermia, and there were burn marks on his body. For the next several days he lay in a coma, and on Monday, October 12, 1998, Matthew Wayne Shepard died.

His assailants were caught and faced the bar of justice. Henderson accepted a plea agreement to avoid the death penalty. The agreement gave him a sentence of two consecutive life sentences with no chance of parole. McKinney went to trial and was convicted of murder. Before the jury began to deliberate on whether McKinney should receive the death penalty, Shepard's parents brokered a deal with the prosecution and defense that handed McKinney two consecutive life sentences with no chance for parole.

What possessed Henderson and McKinney to so savagely murder Matthew Shepard?

Were they disturbed individuals, or were they a product of their environment? Were they angry, frustrated? Had they learned that this was a socially acceptable method of dealing with people who are different from them? Or, was it, as the defense contended, a case of "gay panic" that awakened in McKinney deeply repressed memories?

Shepard's brutal murder also raises other important questions. For example, what can be done to lessen the use of violence and aggression as a form of conflict resolution? What steps can we as individuals and as a society take to prevent such a tragic event from occurring again? These are some of the questions addressed in this chapter.

In this chapter, we explore how social psychologists have looked for and found answers to these questions. We explore the related concepts of prejudice, stereotyping, and discrimination. We then look at the explanations that social psychologists have developed for prejudicial attitudes and behavior. Finally, we explore the impact of prejudice on its targets and what can be done to reduce prejudice.

KEY QUESTIONS

AS YOU READ THIS CHAPTER, FIND THE ANSWERS TO THE FOLLOWING QUESTIONS:

1. *How do social psychologists define aggression?*
2. *What are the different types of aggression?*
3. *What are the gender differences in aggression?*
4. *How can we explain aggression?*
5. *What are the ethological and sociobiological explanations for aggression?*
6. *What role do brain mechanisms play in aggression?*
7. *How does alcohol consumption relate to aggression?*
8. *What is the frustration–aggression hypothesis?*
9. *How does anger relate to frustration and aggression, and what factors contribute to anger?*
10. *How does social learning theory explain aggression?*
11. *What are aggressive scripts, and how do they relate to aggression?*

12. How does the family socialize a child into aggression?
13. What is the role of culture in aggression?
14. What role does the media play in aggression?
15. What is the link between sexual violence portrayed in the media and sexual aggression directed toward women?
16. How can aggression be reduced?

WHAT IS AGGRESSION?

What exactly is aggression? The term tends to generate a certain amount of confusion, because a layperson's concept of aggression differs somewhat from what social psychologists study. In day-to-day life we hear about the aggressive salesperson who will not take no for an answer and the aggressive businessperson who stops at nothing to win a promotion. These usages convey forceful, overbearing, or overly assertive behavior.

aggression
Any behavior intended to inflict either psychological or physical harm on another organism or object.

Social psychologists, however, define **aggression** as any behavior that is intended to inflict harm (whether psychological or physical) on another organism or object. There are several important things to note about this definition. First, a crucial element of the definition is *intent*: A person must have intended to harm in order for the act to be classified as aggressive. If someone deliberately hits a neighbor with a baseball bat during an argument, it is considered aggressive. If the person accidentally hits the neighbor with a baseball bat while playing ball in the yard, it is not considered aggressive.

Note, too, that the harm intended by an aggressive act need not be physical. A navy commander who continually sexually harasses a female subordinate, causing stress, anxiety, and depression, may not be doing her any overt physical harm; he is, however, causing her psychological harm. Third, aggression is not limited to actions directed toward living organisms. Aggression also can be directed toward inanimate objects. A person might smash the window of a neighbor's car in retaliation for some real or imagined conflict with that neighbor.

This broad definition covers a great deal of ground, but it requires further elaboration. Using this definition, we would be tempted to liken the actions of a police officer who kills a murder suspect in the line of duty with those of a paid assassin who kills for profit. Because such a wide range of behavior can be called aggressive, psychologists have defined several different types of aggression, which we look at next.

Levels and Types of Aggression

Clearly, aggression exists on many different levels and is made up of several types of behavior. All aggression, for example, does not stem from the same underlying motives and intentions. Some, referred to as **hostile aggression**, stems from angry and hostile impulses (Feshbach, 1964), and its primary goal is to inflict injury on some person or object. For example, Aaron McKinney was apparently seethingly angry over a purported "pass" made by Matthew Shepard. Acts of aggression that stem from such emotional states are examples of hostile aggression. **Instrumental aggression** stems from the desire to achieve a goal. For example, such aggression could be involved in the desire to get rid of a rival.

hostile aggression
Aggressive behavior stemming from angry or hostile impulses, with a primary goal to inflict injury to some person or object.

instrumental aggression
Aggressive behavior stemming from a desire to achieve a goal.

Hostile aggression and instrumental aggression are not mutually exclusive. One can commit an aggressive act having both underlying motives. In 1994, when Baruch Goldstein killed over 30 Palestinians in a mosque in Hebron, he had two motives. He was motivated by intense hatred of Palestinians, whom he perceived as trying to take away land that rightfully belonged to Jews. He also was motivated by the hope of derailing the fragile peace talks between the Palestine Liberation Organization and the Israeli government. His act, thus, had a hostile component (hatred) and an instrumental component (derailing the peace talks).

Aggression comes in many forms. Instrumental aggression is used to obtain a goal, whereas hostile aggression stems from anger. Often, acts of terrorism have both an instrumental and hostile basis.

Some forms of aggression don't inflict physical harm. Instead, the victim is harmed verbally through gossip, character assassination, damage to the victim's property (Moyer, 1987), or interference with the victim's advancement toward a goal. This form of aggression is called **symbolic aggression**. For example, if a person spreads rumors about a co-worker in order to keep her from getting promoted, the person has used symbolic aggression. Although no physical harm was done, the co-worker was blocked from achieving a goal.

symbolic aggression
Aggressive behavior that interferes with a victim's advancement toward a goal.

Symbolic aggression can be either hostile or instrumental. The office worker may have spread the rumor because she was angry at her co-worker—a case of hostile aggression. Alternatively, she may have spread the rumor to secure the promotion for herself at her co-worker's expense—a case of instrumental aggression.

Yet another form of aggression is **sanctioned aggression**. A soldier taking aim and killing an enemy soldier in battle engages in sanctioned aggression. Self-defense, which occurs when a person uses aggression to protect himself or herself or others from harm, is another example of sanctioned aggression. Society declares that in certain situations, aggression is acceptable, even mandatory. A soldier who refuses to engage in aggressive behavior may be subject to disciplinary action or even have his or her military service abruptly ended. Typically, sanctioned aggression is instrumental in nature. Soldiers kill each other to save their own lives, to follow orders, to help win a war. There need not be anger among enemy soldiers for them to try to kill one another.

sanctioned aggression
Aggressive behavior that society accepts or encourages.

Gender Differences in Aggression

One of the most striking features of aggression is the difference in its expression by males and females. Certainly females can be aggressive, but males show higher levels of physical aggression (Archer, Pearson, & Westeman, 1988). This is true among humans (Eagly & Steffen, 1986) as well as animals (Vallortigara, 1992). Interestingly, the difference between the sexes in their expression of aggression is greater among children than among adults (Hyde,

1984). Additionally, males tend to favor aggression, verbal or physical, as a method of conflict resolution (Bell & Forde, 1999; Reinisch & Sanders, 1986). They also are more likely to be the target of physical aggression (Archer et al., 1988).

Additionally, whereas males are more physically aggressive than females, females are more verbally aggressive than males (Archer et al., 1988; Eagly & Steffen, 1986). Females also are more likely to use indirect aggression (e.g., manipulating social relationships); males tend to favor more direct (physical) forms of aggression (Lagerspetz, Bjorkqvist, & Peltonen, 1988).

There are further gender differences in the cognitive aspects of using aggression. Females report more guilt over using aggression than do males and are more concerned about the harm their aggression may inflict on others (Eagly & Steffen, 1986). This difference is especially pronounced when physical aggression is used.

Why do these differences exist? Possible causes fall into two major areas: biological factors and social factors. Biological factors include both brain mechanisms and hormones. Most research in this area centers on the male hormone testosterone. Higher levels of this hormone are associated with heightened aggression in both humans and animals. We explore this topic more fully in the next section.

Despite hormonal differences between males and females, differences in aggressive tendencies and expression may relate more closely to gender roles than to biology (Eagly & Steffen, 1986). Both boys and girls are encouraged to engage in gender-typed activities, and activities deemed appropriate for boys are more aggressive than those for girls (Lytton & Romney, 1991). For example, parents, especially fathers, encourage their sons to play with war toys such as GI Joe figures and their daughters to play with Barbie dolls. Socialization experiences probably further reinforce the inborn male push toward being more aggressive.

Yet another possible reason for the observed differences in aggression between males and females is that females tend to be more sympathetic and empathic (Carlo, Raffaelli, Laible, & Myer, 1999). Carlo and colleagues studied the relationship between sympathy, parental involvement, and aggression (Carlo et al., 1999). They found that individuals with high levels of sympathy and empathy were less likely to be aggressive. Males scored lower on these dimensions but higher on aggressiveness. Additionally, if an individual perceived that his or her parents were highly involved in childrearing, aggression was lower for both males and females. Thus, prosocial motives (on which females tend to outscore males) and level of parental involvement are important mediators of physical aggression.

It is important to note that although social psychological research (both in the laboratory and in the field) shows a consistent difference between males and females in aggression, this difference is very small (Eagly & Steffen, 1986; Hyde, 1984). Males are more aggressive than females when they are unprovoked, but males and females show equivalent levels of aggression when provoked (Bettencourt & Miller, 1996). Males and females also respond differently to different types of provocation. B. Ann Bettencourt and Norman Miller (1996) report a large gender difference when different forms of provocation are used. If provocation involves an attack on one's intellectual ability then males are much more aggressive than females. However, if provocation takes the form of a physical attack or a negative evaluation of one's work, males and females respond similarly. In other words, although males and females differ in levels of aggression, we should not conclude that gender is the only—or even a predominant—factor in aggression. It is evident that the relationship between gender and aggression is more complex than meets the eye.

Nevertheless, we must also note that there are relatively large gender differences in real-life expressions of aggression. Statistics for violent crimes show that males are far more likely to commit violent offenses than females by a wide margin. According to statistics compiled by the U.S. Department of Justice for 1996, for example, males commit 91% of murders (including nonnegligent manslaughter), 93% of robberies, and 89% of aggravated assaults. With respect to murder, the gap between males and females has widened over the years. In 1976, males committed 83.4% of murders compared to 16.6% for females, and in 1988, males committed 88% of murders compared to 12% for females (Flanagan & Maguire, 1992). So, even though the difference between the genders in measurable acts of aggressiveness is small, in any specific real-world situation, this difference is magnified and elaborated.

FACTORS THAT CONTRIBUTE TO AGGRESSION   We turn now to the broad question, What causes aggression? As suggested here, both biological and social factors contribute to aggressive behavior. Additionally, research shows that frustration often leads to aggression. These factors are considered in the next section.

BIOLOGICAL EXPLANATIONS FOR AGGRESSION

Biological explanations for aggression occur on two levels, the *macro* and the *micro*. On the macro level, aggression is considered for its evolutionary significance, its role in the survival of the species. On the micro level, aggression is investigated as a function of brain and hormonal activity. We consider here two theories of aggression on the macro level—the ethological and sociobiological approaches—and then turn to the physiology of aggression. We also consider the effects of alcohol on agression.

Ethology

Ethology is the study of the evolution and functions of animal behavior (Drickamer & Vessey, 1986). Ethological theory views behavior in the context of survival; it emphasizes the role of instincts and genetic forces in shaping how animals behave (Lorenz, 1963). From an ethological perspective, aggression is seen as behavior that evolved to help a species adapt to its environment. Aggression is governed by innate, instinctual motivations and triggered by specific stimuli in the environment. Aggressive behavior helps establish and maintain social organization within a species.

For example, many species mark and defend their territories, the space they need to hunt or forage. If they didn't do this, they wouldn't survive. Territorial defense occurs when one member of a species attacks another for crossing territorial boundaries. The intruder is driven off by aggressive displays or overt physical attacks—or loses his territory to the intruder. Aggression also is used to establish dominance hierarchies within groups of animals. Within a troop of baboons, for example, the dominant males enjoy special status, ascending to their positions of power by exercising physical aggression.

ethology
A theoretical perspective that views behavior within the context of survival and emphasizes the role of instincts and genetic forces.

Although animals use aggression against each other, few species possess the power to kill a rival with a single blow (Lorenz, 1963). In most species, furthermore, there are biological inhibitions against killing another member. When a combatant makes a conciliatory gesture, such as rolling over and exposing its neck, the aggressive impulse in the other animal is automatically checked. Thus, aggression may involve merely exchanging a few violent actions; the fight soon ends with no major harm done.

How does ethological theory relate to the human animal? First of all, humans display territorial behavior just as animals do. Konrad Lorenz, the foremost ethologist of the century, believed that aggression had little to do with murderous intent and a lot to do with territory (Lorenz, 1963). Ethologists, for example, see aggressive behaviors among gang members as a matter of protecting one's turf such as when members of urban street gangs physically attack members of rival gangs who cross territorial boundaries (Johnson, 1972).

Second, there is evidence that aggression plays a role in the organization of dominance hierarchies in human groups just as it does among animals. In one study, researchers organized first- and third-grade children into play groups and observed the development of dominance hierarchies within those groups (Pettit, Bakshi, Dodge, & Coie, 1986). Aggression was found to play a significant role in establishing dominance among both groups. Interestingly, however, among the older children another variable emerged as important in establishing dominance: leadership skills. Leaders did not always have to use aggression to control the group.

Finally, ethological theory points out that humans still possess the instinct to fight. Unlike most animals, however, humans can make the first blow the last. Technology has given us the power to make a single-blow kill (Lorenz, 1963). Aaron McKinney and Russell Henderson, for example, had the means to intimidate Matthew Shepard and force him to do what they said. Facing down a .357-Magum handgun is a harrowing and terrifying experience. According to Lorenz (1963), human technological evolution has outpaced biological evolution. We have diminished the importance of conciliatory cues; bombs dropped from 30,000 feet cannot respond to a conciliatory gesture.

Sociobiology

sociobiology

A theoretical perspective that views social behavior as helping groups of organisms within a species survive.

Like ethology, **sociobiology** is the study of the biological basis of behavior. Sociobiologists, however, focus on the evolution and function of social behavior (Drickamer & Vessey, 1986; Reiss, 1984). Like ethological theory, sociobiology emphasizes the biological origins and causes of behavior and views aggression as a behavior with survival value for members of a species. For sociobiologists, aggression, like many other behaviors, plays a natural role in the intricate balance that keeps species alive and growing.

Sociobiologist E. O. Wilson (1975) suggested that the principal function of aggression within and between species is to resolve disputes over a common limited resource. Competition can be divided into two categories: sexual competition and resource competition. Sexual competition occurs when males compete for females at mating time. The stronger male drives the weaker male off and then mates with the female. As a result, the species becomes stronger. Resource competition occurs when animals must vie for environmental resources such as food, water, and shelter. Again, the stronger animals are able to win these competitive situations with the use of aggression.

Aggression, then, is one of many behaviors that are genetically programmed into a species and passed along from generation to generation, according to sociobiologists. Patterns of aggression (often mere displays of pseudoaggression) steer the course of natural selection. Also programmed into a species are behaviors and gestures of submission. An animal can choose not to fight or to withdraw from a competitive situation. There is, thus, a natural constraint on aggression within a species. It is kept at an "optimal level," allowing the species to secure food and shelter and to resolve disputes over mating partners. Aggression, a potentially destructive behavior, actually contributes to the biological health of a species, according to sociobiologists (Wilson, 1975).

In both ethology and sociobiology, then, aggression is viewed as a genetically programmed behavior with evolutionary significance. Human beings display aggression under various circumstances because it is part of their biological heritage. However, as noted earlier, biology plays another role in aggression. We consider another biological approach to aggression that focuses on physiological forces within the individual that cause aggressive behavior.

The Physiology of Aggression

The brain and endocrine systems of humans and animals play an intricate role in mediating aggression. Research on the physiology of aggression has focused on two areas: brain mechanisms and hormonal influences. The sections that follow explore each of these.

BRAIN MECHANISMS   Research on brain mechanisms has focused on the brain structures that mediate aggressive behavior. Researchers have found, for example, that aggressive behavior is elicited when parts of the hypothalamus are stimulated. The **hypothalamus** is part of the *limbic system*, a group of brain structures especially concerned with motivation and emotion. Stimulation of different parts of the hypothalamus (called nuclei) produce different forms of aggressive behavior.

hypothalamus
A structure in the limbic system of the brain associated with aggressive behavior.

In one study, researchers implanted electrodes in the brains of cats in various parts of the hypothalamus (Edwards & Flynn, 1972). A small electric current was then passed through these structures. When one part of the hypothalamus was stimulated, the cats displayed the characteristic signs of anger and hostile aggression: arched back, hissing and spitting, fluffed tail. This reaction was nondiscriminating; the cats attacked anything placed in their cage, whether a sponge or a live mouse. When another part of the hypothalamus was stimulated, the cats displayed selective predatory aggression. They went through the motions of hunting; with eyes wide open, they stalked and pounced on a live animal, but they ignored the sponge.

Research shows that other parts of the brain are also involved in aggression. There is a neural circuit in the brain, including parts of the limbic system and the cortex, that organizes aggressive behavior. No single brain structure is the master controller of aggression.

Furthermore, brain stimulation does not inevitably lead to aggression. In one study, brain stimulation led to an aggressive response if a monkey was restrained in a chair (Delgado, 1969). But if the monkey was placed in a cage with another docile monkey, the same brain stimulation produced a different behavior: The monkey ran across the cage making repeated high-pitched vocalizations. The expression of aggressive behavior also depended on a monkey's status within a group. If a more dominant monkey was present, brain stimulation did not lead to aggression. If a less dominant monkey was present, stimulating the same part of the brain did lead to aggression. Thus, even with brain stimulation, aggressive behavior occurred only under the "right" social conditions.

HORMONAL INFLUENCES   Researchers also have investigated the role of hormones in aggressive behavior. As mentioned earlier, high levels of the male hormone testosterone are generally associated with increased aggression (Christiansen & Knussmann, 1987). However, the influence of testosterone on aggressive behavior—like the effect of brain stimulation—is complex.

Hormones come into play twice during the normal course of development in humans: first, during prenatal development, and later, at puberty. Prenatally, testosterone influences the sex organs and characteristics of the unborn child. Testosterone levels are higher for a genetic male than for a genetic female. The hormone permeates the entire body, including the brain, making it possible that the male brain is "wired" for greater aggression. Early in life, testosterone exposure serves an organization function, influencing the course of brain development. Later in life, it serves an activation function (Carlson, 1991), activating behavior patterns, such as aggression, that are related to testosterone levels.

These two effects were shown clearly in an experiment conducted by Robert Conner and Seymour Levine (1969). Conner and Levine castrated rats either neonatally (immediately after birth) or as weanlings (about 3 weeks after birth). (In rats, the critical period for exposure to testosterone is within a day or so after birth. Castrating males immediately after birth effectively prevents exposure to the necessary levels of testosterone for normal masculinization. The rats castrated as weanlings were exposed to the early necessary levels of testosterone and were masculinized normally.) Other rats were not castrated. Later, as adults, the castrated rats were exposed either to testosterone or to a placebo. The design of this experiment is shown in Figure 10.1.

Figure 10.1

Design of Conner and Levine's (1969) experiment on the effects of testosterone exposure on aggression. Rats were castrated either as neonates or as weanlings and were exposed to testosterone or a placebo as adults.

Adapted from Carlson (1991).
Reprinted with permission.

		Time of castration	
		Neonatal	**Weanling**
Treatment as an adult	**Testosterone**	No early testosterone exposure Testosterone exposure as an adult	Natural, early testosterone exposure Testosterone exposure as an adult
	Placebo	No early testosterone exposure No testosterone exposure as an adult	Natural, early testosterone exposure No testosterone exposure as an adult

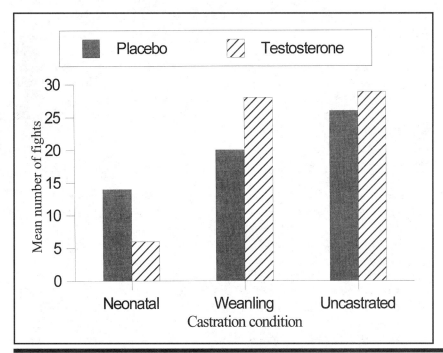

Figure 10.2

Results from Conner and Levine's (1969) experiment on testosterone exposure. Results show that when there was no neonatal castration, adult exposure to testosterone did not increase aggression. When there was early testosterone exposure (weanling castration), adult exposure to testosterone increased aggression.

Adapted from Conner and Levine (1969). Reprinted with permission.

The experiment showed that for the rats castrated neonatally, the levels of aggression displayed after exposure to testosterone as adults did not differ significantly from the levels displayed after exposure to a placebo (Figure 10.2). For the weanling rats, exposure to testosterone as adults increased the level of aggression compared to that of the rats receiving the placebo. The levels of aggression after exposure to the testosterone or placebo did not differ for noncastrated rats.

This study showed that early exposure to male hormones is necessary in order for later exposure to a male hormone to increase aggression. Those rats castrated at birth missed the "organizing function" of the male hormone; the normal process of masculinization of the brain did not occur. Later injections of testosterone (activation function) thus had little effect. Rats castrated as weanlings were subjected to the organization function of the male hormone. Their brains were normally masculinized and more receptive to the activation function of the testosterone injections received later in life. We can conclude that high testosterone levels are effective in elevating levels of aggression only if there is normal exposure to male hormones early in life.

Another experiment demonstrated that hormonal influences interact with social influences to affect aggression. In this experiment, male rats were castrated and then implanted with a capsule (Albert, Petrovic, & Walsh, 1989a). For some rats the capsule was empty, for others it contained testosterone. These rats were then housed with another rat under one of two conditions. Half the rats were housed with a single feeding tube, requiring the animals to compete for food. The other half were housed with two feeding tubes, so no competition was necessary. The treated rats were then tested for aggression. The results were striking. Testosterone increased aggression only if the rats competed for food. If the rats were not required to compete, the levels of aggression were quite low, about the same as those for the rats implanted with the empty capsule.

Female aggression may also be mediated by hormones. In another study, the ovaries were removed from some female rats but not from others (Albert, Petrovic, & Walsh, 1989b). The rats were then housed with a sterile yet sexually active male rat. Weekly, the male rat was removed and an unfamiliar female rat was introduced into the cage. Female rats whose ovaries had been removed displayed less aggression toward the unfamiliar female than those whose ovaries had not been removed, suggesting a role of female hormones in aggression among female rats.

The Effects of Alcohol on Aggression

There is ample evidence showing a connection between alcohol consumption and aggression (Quigley & Leonard, 1999; Bushman & Cooper, 1990). What is it about alcohol that increases violent behavior? Is there something about the drug effects of alcohol, or is it a function of the social situations in which alcohol is used?

There is no question that alcohol has pharmacological (drug-related) effects on the body, especially on the brain. Alcohol becomes concentrated in organs with a high water content, and the brain is one such organ. Alcohol lowers reaction time, impairs judgment, and weakens sensory perception and motor coordination. Under the influence of alcohol, people focus more on external cues, such as people or events in the situation that seem to encourage them to take action, and less on internal ones, such as thoughts about risks and consequences.

Although alcohol is a central nervous system depressant, it initially seems to act as a stimulant. People who are drinking at first become more sociable and assertive. This is because alcohol depresses inhibitory brain centers (Insel & Roth, 1994). As more alcohol is consumed, however, the effects change. Drinkers often become irritable and are easily angered. Levels of hostility and aggressiveness increase. Considering all the effects of alcohol, it is not surprising that it is a major factor not only in automobile crashes and fatal accidents of other kinds (such as drownings, falls, and fires) but also in homicides, suicides, assaults, and rapes.

Research confirms that levels of aggression increase with the amount of alcohol consumed (Kreutzer, Schneider, & Myatt, 1984; Pihl & Zacchia, 1986; Shuntich & Taylor, 1972). In one study, participants who consumed 1.32 mg/kg of 95% alcohol were more aggressive than participants receiving a placebo (nonalcoholic) drink or no drink at all (Pihl & Zacchia, 1986). The type of beverage consumed affects aggression as well (Pihl, Smith, & Farrell, 1984). Participants who consumed a distilled beverage gave longer shocks to a target than those who consumed beer. In another experiment, participants in a bar were approached and asked a series of annoying questions. In this natural setting, bar patrons drinking distilled beverages displayed more verbal aggression toward the interviewer than those drinking beer (Murdoch & Pihl, 1988).

How does alcohol increase aggression? Most likely, alcohol has an indirect effect on aggression by reducing a person's ability to inhibit behaviors that are normally suppressed by fear, such as aggression (Pihl, Peterson, & Lau, 1993). Although the precise brain mechanisms that are involved in this process are not fully known, there is evidence that alcohol is associated with a significant drop in the amount of brain serotonin (a neurotransmitter), which makes individuals more likely to engage in aggression in response to external stimuli (Badaway, 1998; Pihl & Lemarquand, 1998). Serotonin, when it is operating normally, inhibits antisocial behaviors such as aggression through the arousal of anxiety under threatening conditions (Pihl & Peterson, 1993). When serotonin levels are reduced, anxiety no longer has its inhibitory effects, but intense emotional arousal remains, resulting in increased aggression under conditions of threat (Pihl & Peterson, 1993).

Alcohol has also been found to influence the functioning of the prefrontal cortex of the brain, disrupting *executive cognitive functioning (ECF)*, or functions that help one use higher cognitive processes such as attention, planning, and self-monitoring (Hoaken, Giancola, & Pihl, 1998). These executive functions play a major role in one's ability to effectively regulate goal-directed behavior (Hoaken et al., 1998). In individuals with low-functioning ECF, aggression is more likely than among individuals with high-functioning ECF, regardless of alcohol consumption (Hoaken et al., 1998). The inhibitory effect of alcohol on ECF is one factor contributing to increased aggression after alcohol consumption. Interestingly, however, even in an intoxicated state, one can override the effects of alcohol if properly motivated (Hoaken, Assaad, & Pihl, 1998). Peter Hoaken and his associates (1998) placed intoxicated and sober individuals into a situation where they could deliver electric shocks to another person. Half the participants in each group received an incentive to deliver low levels of shocks (the promise of money). The results showed that intoxicated participants were just as able as their sober counterparts to reduce the severity of shocks delivered when the incentive was provided. However, when no incentive was provided, intoxicated participants delivered higher shock levels than the sober participants.

Although the amount and type of alcohol consumed affect aggression, research shows that one's expectations about the effects of alcohol also have an impact on aggression (Kreutzer, Schneider, & Myatt, 1984; Lang, Goeckner, Adesso, & Marlatt, 1975; Rohsenow & Bachorowski, 1984). Generally, participants in experiments who believe they are drinking alcohol display elevated levels of aggression, even if in reality they are drinking a nonalcoholic placebo. The mere belief that one has consumed alcohol is enough to enhance aggression. In fact, even the experimenter's knowledge of who has consumed alcohol can affect the level of aggression observed in experiments like this. An analysis of the literature shows that the effects of alcohol on aggression are smaller when the experimenter is blind to the conditions of the experiment (Bushman & Cooper, 1990).

Expectations cannot account for the entire effect of alcohol, however. In some cases even when there is an expectation that alcohol may lead to aggression, such an expectation does not increase aggression, whereas actual alcohol consumption does (Quigley & Leonard, 1999). Social cues, expectations, and attitudes play some part in mediating alcohol-induced aggression, However, the pharmacological effects of alcohol on the body and brain are real. Probably through a combination of reducing inhibitions and increasing irritability and hostility on the one hand, and giving the drinker "permission" to act out in social situations on the other, alcohol has the net effect of enhancing aggressive behavior.

Finally, the alcohol–aggression link is mediated by individual characteristics and the social situation. Jeewon Cheong and Craig Nagoshi (1999) had participants engage in a competitive game with a bogus participant. The game was played under one of three conditions. In one condition, the real participant was told that his opponent could deliver a loud noise in an attempt to disrupt his performance (aggression). In the second condition, the real participant was told that his opponent would use the loud noise to keep the real participant alert during the boring task (altruism). In the third condition, the real participant was given ambiguous information about his opponent's motives (maybe aggression or maybe altruism). Furthermore, before engaging in the task, participants consumed either alcoholic drinks or a placebo. One half the placebo participants were told they were consuming an alcoholic beverage (expectancy for alcohol) and the other half were told their drinks were placebos. Finally, participants completed a personality measure of their impulsiveness and sensation-seeking tendencies.

The results of this experiment showed that alcohol-mediated aggression depended on the nature of the situation (aggression v. altruism), personality, and alcohol consumption. Specifically, participants who scored highly on the measure of impulsiveness–sensation-seeking were the most aggressive after consuming alcohol, but only when they believed their opponent was using the loud noise aggressively. When the opponent's motive was either altruistic or ambiguous, this effect did not occur. Thus, whether an individual behaves aggressively after consuming alcohol depends on the nature of the situation and one's predisposition toward impulsive behavior or sensation seeking.

What can we learn from this research on the physiological aspects of aggression in animals? How much of it can be applied to human beings? Not many people would attribute Aaron McKinney's and Russell Henderson's murderous behavior to an overabundance of testosterone or abnormal brain circuitry. Research with animals supports the general conclusion that aggression does have a physiological component. However, in humans, biological forces cannot account for all, or even most, instances in which aggression is displayed (Huesmann & Eron, 1984). The human being is a profoundly cultural animal. Although aggression is a basic human drive, the expression of that drive depends on forces operating in a particular society at a particular time. McKinney and Henderson's behavior was the product not only of their biology but also of their social world, which included playing violent video games and hanging around with a group that supported violence. Laws and social and cultural norms serve as powerful factors that can inhibit or facilitate aggressive behavior.

THE FRUSTRATION–AGGRESSION LINK

Imagine for a moment that you are standing in front of a soda machine, the kind that pours you a drink in a cup. You dig into your pocket and come up with your last 50 cents. You breathe a sigh of relief. You are very thirsty and have just enough money to get a soda. You put your money into the machine and press the button. You watch and wait for the cup to drop, but no cup appears. Instead, the soda begins to pour out, draining through the grate where the cup should have been. After the soda stops pouring, the cup finally comes down. You mutter a few choice words, kick the machine, crumple the cup, and throw it across the room.

frustration–aggression hypothesis
A hypothesis that frustration and aggression are strongly related suggesting that aggression is always the consequence of frustration and frustration leads to aggression.

Analysis of this incident gives us some insight into a factor that social psychologists believe instigates aggression. In the example, a goal you wished to obtain—quenching your thirst—was blocked. This produced an emotional state that led to aggression. Your reaction to such a situation illustrates the general principles of a classic formulation known as the **frustration–aggression hypothesis** (Dollard, Doob, Miller, Mowrer, & Sears, 1939).

In its original form, the frustration–aggression hypothesis stated that "aggression is always a consequence of frustration . . . the occurrence of aggressive behavior always presupposes the existence of frustration and, contrariwise . . . the existence of frustration leads to some form of aggression" (Dollard et al., 1939, p. 1). In other words, according to the frustration–aggression hypothesis, when we are frustrated, we behave aggressively.

Components of the Frustration–Aggression Sequence

What are the components of the frustration–aggression sequence? An assumption of the frustration–aggression hypothesis is that emotional arousal occurs when goal-directed behavior is blocked. Frustration occurs, then, when two conditions are met. First, we expect to perform certain behaviors, and second, those behaviors are blocked (Dollard et al., 1939).

Frustration can vary in strength, depending on three factors (Dollard et al., 1939). The first is the strength of the original drive. If you are very thirsty, for example, and are deprived of a soda, your frustration will be greater than if you are only slightly thirsty. The second factor is the degree to which the goal-directed behavior is thwarted. If the machine filled your cup halfway, for example, you would be less frustrated than if you received no soda at all. The third factor is the number of frustrated responses. If your thwarted attempt to get a soda came on the heels of another frustrating event, your frustration would be greater.

Once we are frustrated, what do we choose as a target? Our first choice is the source of our frustration (Dollard et al., 1939)—the soda machine, in our example. But sometimes aggression against the source of frustration is not possible. The source may be a person in a position of power over us, such as our boss. When direct aggression against the source of aggression is blocked, we may choose to vent our frustration against another safer target, a son perhaps. If we have a bad day at work or school, we may take it out on an innocent roommate or family member when we get home. This process is called **displaced aggression** (Dollard et al., 1939).

displaced aggression
Aggressive behavior used when direct aggression against a source is not possible or is blocked; frustration may be vented against another, safer target.

Although the original frustration–aggression hypothesis stated categorically that frustration always leads to aggression, acts of frustration-based aggression can be inhibited (Dollard et al., 1939). If there is a strong possibility that your aggressive behavior will be punished, you may not react aggressively to frustration. If a campus security guard were standing beside the soda machine, for example, you probably wouldn't kick it for fear of being arrested.

Factors Mediating the Frustration–Aggression Link

The frustration–aggression hypothesis stirred controversy from the moment it was proposed. Some theorists questioned whether frustration inevitably led to aggression (Miller, 1941). Others suggested that frustration leads to aggression only under specific circumstances, such as when the blocked response is important to the individual (Blanchard & Blanchard, 1984).

As criticisms of the original theory mounted, modifications were made. For example, Berkowitz (1989) proposed that frustration is connected to aggression by negative affect, such as anger. If, as shown in Figure 10.3 on

Figure 10.3

*The relationship among
frustration, anger, and
aggression. Frustration
leads to aggression only if it
arouses negative affect,
such as anger.*

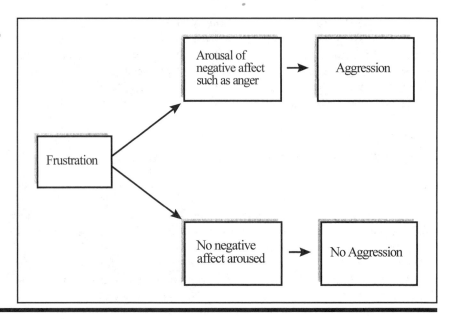

p. 378, the frustration of goal-directed behavior leads to anger, then aggression will occur. If no anger is aroused, no aggression will result. If anger mediates frustration, we must specify which frustrating conditions lead to anger. Theoretically, if the blocking of goal-directed behavior does not arouse anger, then the frustrated individual should not behave aggressively. Let's consider other factors that mediate the frustration–aggression link.

ATTRIBUTIONS ABOUT INTENT   Recall from chapter 4 that we are always interpreting people's behavior, deciding that they did something because they meant it (an internal attribution) or because of some outside, situational factor (an external attribution). The type of attribution made about a source of frustration is one important factor contributing to aggression. If someone's behavior frustrates us and we make an internal attribution, we are more likely to respond with aggression than if we make an external attribution.

Research shows that the intent behind an aggressive act is more important in determining the degree of retaliation than the actual harm done (Ohbuchi & Kambara, 1985). Individuals who infer negative intent on the part of another person are most likely to retaliate. The actual harm done is not so important as the intent behind the aggressor's act (Ohbuchi & Kambara, 1985).

There is additional evidence about the importance of attributions for aggression. Research shows that if we are provided with a reasonable explanation for the behavior of someone who is frustrating us, we will react less aggressively than if no explanation is given (Johnson & Rule, 1986; Kremmer & Stephens, 1983). Moreover, if we believe that aggression directed against us is typical for the situation in which it occurs, we are likely to attribute our attacker's actions to external factors. Thus, we will retaliate less than if we believe the attacker was choosing atypical levels of aggression (Dyck & Rule, 1978). In this case, we would be more likely to attribute the attacker's aggression to internal forces and to retaliate in kind if given the opportunity.

PERCEIVED INJUSTICE AND INEQUITY   Another factor that can contribute to anger and ultimately to aggression is the perception that we have been treated unjustly. The following account of a violent sports incident illustrates the power of perceived injustice to incite aggression (Mark, Bryant, & Lehman, 1983, pp. 83–84):

In November 1963, a riot occurred at Roosevelt Raceway, a harness racing track in the New York metropolitan area. Several hundred fans swarmed onto the track. The crowd attacked the judges' booth, smashed the tote board, set fires in program booths, broke windows, and damaged cars parked in an adjacent lot. Several hundred police officers were called to the scene. Fifteen fans were arrested, 15 others hospitalized.

What incited this riot? The sixth race was the first half of a daily double, in which bettors attempt to select the winners of successive races, with potentially high payoffs. During the sixth race, six of the eight horses were involved in an accident and did not finish the race. In accordance with New York racing rules, the race was declared official. All wagers placed on the six nonfinishing horses were lost, including the daily double bets. Many fans apparently felt that they were unjustly treated, that the race should have been declared "no contest."

This incident is not unique. Frequently, we read about fans at a soccer match who riot over a "bad call" or fans at a football game who pelt officials with snowballs or beer cans following a call against a home team. In each case, the fans are reacting to what they perceive to be an injustice done to the home team.

Aggression is often seen as a way of restoring justice and equity in a situation. The perceived inequity in a frustrating situation, as opposed to the frustration itself, leads to aggression (Sulthana, 1987). For example, a survey of female prison inmates who had committed aggravated assault or murder suggested that an important psychological cause for their aggression was a sense of having been treated unjustly (Diaz, 1975). This perception,

Frustration often leads to aggression when the frustration gives rise to anger. Anger is aroused when one feels that there is injustice or inequity in a situation. Sports fans who believe that their team was "robbed" of a victory because of bad officiating may vent their frustration and anger through violence. The history of sport has shown us many times how perceived injustice and inequity give rise to fan violence.

apparently rooted in an inmate's childhood, persisted into adulthood and resulted in aggressive acts.

Of course, not all perceived injustice leads to aggression. Not everyone rioted at the New York race track, and most sports fans do not assault referees for bad calls. There may be more of a tendency to use aggression to restore equity when the recipient of the inequity feels particularly powerless (Richardson, Vandenbert, & Humphries, 1986). In one study, participants with lower status than their opponents chose higher shock levels than did participants with equal or higher status than their opponents (Richardson et al., 1986). We can begin to understand from these findings why groups who believe themselves to be unjustly treated, who have low status and feel powerless, resort to aggressive tactics, especially when frustrated, to remedy their situation. Riots and terrorism are often the weapons of choice among those with little power.

THE SOCIAL LEARNING EXPLANATION FOR AGGRESSION

The frustration–aggression hypothesis focuses on the responses of individuals in particular, frustrating situations. But clearly, not all people respond in the same ways to frustrating stimuli. Some respond with aggression, whereas others respond with renewed determination to overcome their frustration. It appears that some people are more predisposed to aggression than others. How can we account for these differences?

Although there are genetically based, biological differences in aggressiveness among individuals, social psychologists are more interested in the role of socialization in the development of aggressive behavior (Huesmann, 1988; Huesmann & Malamuth, 1986). *Socialization,* as mentioned earlier, is the process by which children learn the behaviors, attitudes, and values of their culture. Socialization is the work of many agents, including parents, siblings, schools, churches, and the media. Through the socialization process, children learn many of the behavior patterns, both good and bad, that will stay with them into adulthood.

Aggression is one behavior that is developed early in life via socialization and persists into adulthood (Huesmann, Eron, Lefkowitz, & Walder, 1984). In fact, a long-term study of aggressive behavior found that children who were rated by their peers as aggressive at age 8 were likely to be aggressive as adults, as measured by self-ratings, ratings by participants' spouses, and citations for criminal and traffic offenses (Huesmann et al., 1984).

The stability of aggression over time applies to both males and females (Pulkkinen & Pitkanen, 1993). However, the age at which early aggressiveness predicts later aggressive behavior differs for males and females. In one study, researchers investigated the relationship between Swedish children's aggressiveness (measured by teacher ratings) at two ages (10 and 13) and crime rates through age 26 (Stattin & Magnusson, 1989). For males, aggressiveness ratings at both age levels were significant predictors of serious crimes committed later in life. However, for females, only aggressiveness ratings at age 13 predicted later criminal behavior. For males and females, early aggressiveness was most closely related to crimes of the "acting out" type, such as violent crimes against property and other people, rather than drug offenses, traffic offenses, or crimes committed for personal gain (Stattin & Magnusson, 1989).

Taken together, these studies show a clear pattern of early aggression being significantly related to aggression later in life (as measured by crime statistics). Although there is some difference between males and females (at least in terms of the age at which the relationship between early aggression and later aggression begins), it is clear that the relationship between childhood aggression and adulthood aggression is true for both males and females.

What happens during these early years to increase aggression among some children? In the sections that follow, we look at how socialization relates to the development of aggressive behavior patterns.

The Socialization of Aggression

Unlike the biological approaches to aggression, Albert Bandura's **social learning theory** (1973) maintains that aggression is learned, much like any other human behavior. Aggression can be learned through two general processes: direct reinforcement and punishment, and observational learning. Often, individuals who commit violent acts grow up in a neighborhood where violence was commonplace. These individuals see that aggression was a method of getting one's way. They probably even tried it for themselves and obtained some goal. If aggression pays off, one is then more likely to use aggressive behavior again, learning through the process of direct reinforcement. If the aggression fails, or one is punished for using aggression, aggression is less likely to be used in the future.

Although the processes of direct reinforcement and punishment are important, social learning theory maintains that its primary channel is through **observational learning**, or modeling. This occurs when, for example, a young man standing in a playground sees a person get money by beating up another person. People quickly learn that aggression can be effective. By watching others, they learn new behaviors, or they have existing behaviors encouraged or inhibited.

Bandura (1973) and his colleagues (Bandura, Ross, & Ross, 1963) provided powerful evidence in support of the transmission of aggression through observational learning. They showed that children who watch an aggressive model can learn new patterns of behavior and will display them when given the opportunity to do so. Bandura and his colleagues designed an ingenious experiment to test this central principle of social learning theory.

In this experiment, children were exposed to a model who behaved aggressively against a "bobo doll," a large, inflatable plastic punching doll. The model engaged in some specific behavior, such as kicking and punching the doll while screaming, "Sock him in the nose" (Bandura, Ross, & Ross, 1961). After the child observed the model engage in this behavior, he or she was taken to a room with several toys. After a few minutes, the experimenter went in and told the child that he or she could not play with the toys because they were being saved for another child (this was to frustrate the child). The child was then taken to another room with several other toys, including the bobo doll.

Bandura performed a number of variations on this basic situation. In one experiment, for example, the children saw the model being rewarded, being punished, or receiving no consequences for batting around the bobo doll (Bandura, 1965). In another, children observed a live model, a filmed model,

social learning theory
A theory that social behavior is acquired through direct reinforcement or punishment of behavior and observational learning.

observational learning
Attitude formation learning through watching what people do and whether they are rewarded or punished and then imitating that behavior.

or a cartoon model (Bandura, Ross, & Ross, 1963). In all the variations, the dependent variable was the same—the number of times the child imitated the aggressive behaviors the model displayed.

Bandura found that when the children saw aggression being rewarded, they showed more imitative responses than when it was punished. Live models evoked the most imitative responses, followed by film models and then cartoon models, but any aggressive model increased imitative responses over the nonaggressive or no-model conditions. Exposure to the aggressive model elicited other aggressive responses that the child had not seen from the model (Bandura et al., 1963). Apparently, an aggressive model can motivate a child to behave aggressively in new, unmodled ways.

Bandura concluded that observational learning can have the following effects (1973). First, a child can learn totally new patterns of behavior. Second, a child's behavior can be inhibited—if the model is punished—or disinhibited—if the model is rewarded. *Disinhibition* in this context means that a child already knows how to perform a socially unacceptable behavior (such as hitting or kicking) but is not doing it for a reason. Seeing a model rewarded removes inhibitions against performing the behavior. Bandura calls this process *vicarious reinforcement*. And third, a socially desirable behavior can be enhanced by observing models engaged in prosocial activities.

Bandura's findings have been observed across cultures. Eva McHan (1985) replicated Bandura's basic experiment in Lebanon. Children were exposed either to a film showing a child playing aggressively with a bobo doll or to a film showing the boy playing nonaggressively with some toys. McHan found that the children who were exposed to the aggressive film were more aggressive in a subsequent play situation. They also exhibited more novel aggressive behaviors than children who had seen the nonaggressive film. These results exactly replicate Bandura's original findings and offer additional support for the social learning approach to aggression.

We have established that exposing children to filmed aggressive models contributes to increased physical aggression. Is there any evidence that exposure to violence in naturalistic settings relates to levels of aggression? According to a study by Deborah Gorman-Smith and Pactrick Tolan (1998), the answer to this question is yes. Gorman-Smith and Tolan investigated the relationship between exposure to community violence and aggression in a sample of minority males growing up in high-crime neighborhoods. Their results showed that exposure to violence in the community was related to an increase in aggression and feelings of depression. They also reported that the increase in aggression is specific to exposure to violence in the neighborhood and not to general levels of stress. Finally, Gorman-Smith and Tolan reported that the number of people who are exposed to community violence does not relate significantly to parental discipline practices but may relate more strongly to peer influences and other community-related factors.

Aggressive Scripts: Why and How They Develop

aggressive script
An internalized representation of an event that leads to increased aggression and the tendency to interpret social interactions aggressively.

One mechanism believed to underlie the relationship between observation and aggression is the formation of **aggressive scripts** during the socialization process. Scripts are internalized representations of how an event should occur. Recall from chapter 3 that another term for a script is event *schema*. You may, for example, have a script about what goes on at a college basketball game: You go to the arena, sit in your seat, and cheer for your team. Such scripts influence how people behave in a given social situation.

Exposing a child to aggressive models—parents, peers, television characters, video games—during socialization contributes to the development of aggressive scripts (Huesmann, 1986; Huesmann & Malamuth, 1986). These scripts, in turn, lead to increased aggression and a tendency to interpret social interactions aggressively. And they can persist, greatly influencing levels of aggression in adulthood.

Aggressive scripts develop through three phases (Huesmann & Malamuth, 1986). During the *acquisition and encoding phase*, the script is first learned and placed into the child's memory. Much like a camcorder, a child who sees violence—or is reinforced directly for violence—records the violent scenes into memory. A script will be most easily encoded into memory if the child believes the script-related behavior is socially acceptable (Huesmann, 1988). When one grows up in a violent neighborhood, for example, one will undoubtedly acquire and encode an aggressive script based on his or her experiences.

The stored script is strengthened and elaborated on during the *maintenance phase*. Strengthening and elaboration occur each time a child thinks about an aggressive event, watches an aggressive television show, plays aggressively, or is exposed to violence from other sources (Huesmann, 1988; Huesmann & Malamuth, 1986). Research shows, for example, that children who are exposed to high levels of violence in their communities tend to develop aggressive behaviors (Gorman-Smith & Tolan, 1998).

Finally, during the *retrieval and emission phase*, the internalized script guides the child's behavior whenever a situation similar to the one in the script occurs. If the child has watched too many Clint Eastwood movies, for example, competition with another child for a toy may lead to a "make my day" scenario. The script may suggest to young Clint that competition is best resolved using aggression. Often aggressive behavior certainly fits with this model. Those who are exposed to violence on a day-to-day basis and feel threatened may turn to violence as a way to resolve conflicts. Aggressive scripts are played out to their bloody conclusions.

The Role of the Family in Developing Aggressive Behaviors

Although children are exposed to many models, the family provides the most immediate environment and is the most influential agent of socialization. It makes sense, then, that aggressive behavior is closely linked with family dynamics.

One developmental model proposed to explain the evolution of aggressive behavior is the **social-interactional model** (Patterson, DeBaryshe, & Ramsey, 1989). According to this model, antisocial behavior (such as aggression) arises early in life as a result of poor parenting, such as harsh, inconsistent discipline and poor monitoring of children. Poor parenting leads to a child's behavior problems, which in turn contribute to rejection by peers and academic problems in school. Such children often become associated with deviant peer groups in late childhood and adolescence. In many cases, delinquency results.

social-interactional model

A model suggesting that antisocial behavior arises early in life and is the result of poor parenting, leading a child to develop conduct problems that affect peer relations and academic performance.

AGGRESSIVE PARENTING Key to the social-interactional model is the disciplinary style adopted by parents and the parent–child interaction style that results. Some parents have an antisocial parenting style, according to the model. Several factors contribute to such parental behavior. As shown in Figure 10.4, these factors include antisocial behavior and poor family management by their own parents, family demographics, and family stressors. Parents' antisocial behavior contributes to disruptions in their family management practices and ultimately to antisocial behavior from the child.

Parents who fall into a harmful cycle of parenting generally rely heavily on the use of power, or harsh measures designed to control the child's behavior. They also use physical and/or verbal punishment. Do these techniques encourage children to act aggressively themselves? The answer is a firm yes! Although parents use power assertion and punishment with their children to make them comply, research shows that it actually reduces children's compliance (Crockenberg & Litman, 1986). This noncompliance may, in turn, cause parents to adopt an even more coercive disciplinary style.

Murray Straus conducted a series of correlational studies (summarized in Straus, 1991) on the relationship between the use of physical punishment and aggressive behavior. Straus obtained information from adolescents and adults about the frequency with which they experienced physical punishment while they were children. Straus reported, first, that almost 90% of U.S. parents of children aged 3 to 4 used some form of physical punishment. The rate of physical punishment declined slowly after age 4 but remained at a relatively high level—60% or above—until the child was 13 years old. Thus, physical punishment as a parenting technique is widespread in our society.

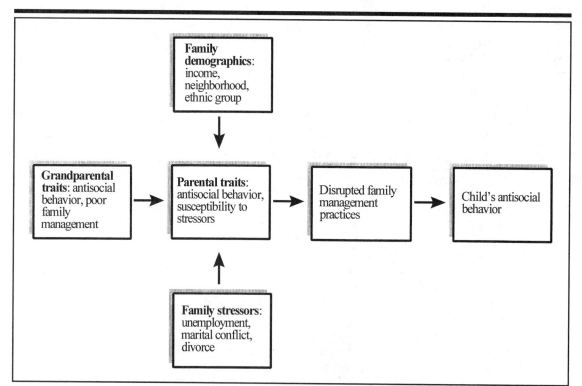

Figure 10.4 *The social-interaction model of antisocial behavior. According to this model, antisocial parenting gives rise to disrupted family management and an increase in a child's antisocial behavior. Antisocial parenting relates to three factors: family demographics, grandparental traits, and family stressors.*

From Patterson, DeBaryshe, and Ramsey (1989). Reprinted with permission.

Straus also found that as the frequency of physical punishment used during socialization increased, so did the rate of physical aggression used outside the family later on in adulthood. More ominously, as the frequency of physical punishment increased, so did homicide rates.

Physical punishment is not the only form of parental behavior associated with heightened aggression. Parents also subject their children to verbal and symbolic aggression, which can include these behaviors (Vissing, Straus, Gelles, & Harrop, 1991, p. 228):

- Insulting or swearing at the child.
- Sulking or refusing to talk about a problem.
- Stomping out of the room or house.
- Doing or saying something to spite the child.
- Threatening to throw something at or hit the child.
- Throwing, smashing, hitting, or kicking something.

Like physical aggression, verbal or symbolic aggression is commonly directed at children and can contribute to "problems with aggression, delinquency, and interpersonal relationships" on the part of the children (Vissing et al., 1991, p. 231). This relationship holds even when the effects of other variables—such as physical aggression, age and gender of the child, socioeconomic status, and psychosocial problems of the child—are held constant. Moreover, parent's use of verbal or symbolic aggression as part of their parenting style is more highly associated with aggression in children than is physical aggression.

Supporting evidence comes from a 22-year study of the relationship between the parental behaviors of rejection, punishment, and low identification with their children and aggression in children (Eron, Huesmann, & Zelli, 1991). This study suggests that parental rejection and punitiveness are significantly correlated with aggression in childhood and later in adulthood. Children whose parents rejected them at age 8, for example, showed a greater tendency toward aggression as adults than nonrejected children, and harsh parental punishment, particularly for girls, led to increased aggression. Generally, parental rejection and punitiveness were found to have their most enduring relationship with aggression if the rejection and punitiveness began before age 6.

The picture, however, is quite complex. For example, rejected children tend to behave in ways that lead parents to reject them (Eron et al., 1991). So, parental rejection that is related to aggression later in life may be partly caused by the child's behavior—a vicious cycle.

Exposure to high levels of family aggression also relates to aggression used in a wide variety of relationships. For example, Stephen Chermack and Maureen Walton (1999) studied the relationship between family aggression (parent-to-parent aggression, parent-to-child aggression) and the use of aggression in several types of relationships (dating, marital, etc.). They found if participants saw their parents behaving aggressively toward each other and were the recipients of parental aggression themselves, the participants were more likely to use aggression in their own dating relationships. Interestingly, general aggression related positively only to being the actual target of parental aggression. Additionally, seeing one's parents behave aggressively also contributes to heightened feelings of psychological stress among both men and women (Julian, McKenry, Gavazzi, & Law, 1999). However, the psyhological stress was most likely to be transformed into verbal or physical aggression among men as opposed to women (Julian et al., 1999). Thus, exposure to aggression in the family appears to influence adult aggression through the arousal of negative psychological symptoms. In any event, the evidence is clear: Exposure to family violence as a child contributes significantly to aggression later in life.

ROLE MODELING OF AGGRESSIVE BEHAVIOR   What is the link between parental aggression and child aggression? The most likely explanation is role modeling. Whenever parents use physical or verbal aggression, they are modeling that behavior for their children. This is a special case of observational learning. Children observe their parents behaving aggressively; they also see that the aggressive behavior works, because ultimately the children are controlled by it. Because the behavior is reinforced, both parents and children are more likely to use aggression again. The message sent to the child is loud and clear: You can get your way by using physical or verbal aggression. Through these processes of learning, children develop aggressive scripts (Eron et al., 1991), which organize and direct their aggressive behavior in childhood and in adulthood.

Child Abuse and Neglect

Parental discipline style is not the only family-related factor related to increases in aggression. Child abuse has also been linked to aggressive behavior later in life, especially among children who also have intrinsic vulnerabilities, such as cognitive, psychiatric, and neurological impairments (Lewis, Lovely, Yeager, & Della Femina, 1989). Research shows that being abused or witnessing abuse is strongly related to highly violent behavior patterns. But physical abuse is not the only kind of abuse that contributes to increased aggressive behavior. Abused and neglected children are more likely to be arrested for juvenile (26%) and adult (28.6%) violent criminal behavior compared to a nonabused, nonneglected control group (16.8% and 21.1% arrest rates for juvenile and adult violent crime, respectively; Widom, 1992). Children who were only neglected had a higher arrest rate for violent crime (12.5%) than nonneglected children had (7.9%).

Being the victim of child abuse has another pernicious effect. Exposure to abusive situations desensitizes one to the suffering of others. In one study (Main & George, 1985), for example, abused and nonabused children were exposed to a peer showing distress. Nonabused children showed concern and empathy for the distressed peer. Abused children showed a very different pattern. These children did not respond with concern or empathy but rather with anger, including physical aggression. Thus, child abuse and neglect are major contributors not only to aggressive behavior later in life but also to an attitude of less caring for another person's suffering.

Family Disruption

Yet another family factor that contributes to aggressive behavior patterns is family disruption, for example, disruption caused by an acrimonious divorce. Research shows that disruption of the family is significantly related to higher rates of crime (Mednick, Baker, & Carothers, 1990; Sampson, 1987). One study investigated the relationship between several family variables, such as family income, male employment, and family disruption (defined as a female-headed household with children under age 18), and homicide and robbery rates among blacks and whites (Sampson, 1987). The study found that the single best predictor of African-American homicide was family disruption. A similar pattern emerged for black and white robbery. Family disruption, which was strongly related to living under economically deprived conditions, was found to have its greatest effect on juvenile crime, as opposed to adult crime. It was found that, at least for robbery, the effects of family disruption cut across racial boundaries. Family disruption was equally harmful to blacks and whites.

Another study looked at family disruption from a different perspective: the impact of divorce on children's criminal behavior (Mednick, Baker, & Carothers, 1990). The study examined Danish families that had divorced but were stable after the divorce (the divorce solved interpersonal problems between the parents); divorced but unstable after the divorce (the divorce failed to resolve interpersonal problems between the parents); and not divorced. The study showed the highest crime rates among adolescents and young adults who came from a disruptive family situation. The crime rate for those whose families divorced but still had significant conflict was substantially higher (65%) than for those whose families divorced but were stable afterward (42%) or for families that did not divorce (28%).

Clearly, an important contributor to aggression is the climate and structure of the family in which a child grows up. Inept parenting, in the forms of overreliance on physical or verbal punishment, increases aggression. Child abuse and neglect, as well as family disruption, also play a role in the development of aggressive behavior patterns. Children learn their aggressive behavior patterns early as a result of being in a family environment that supports aggression. And, as we have seen, these early aggressive behavior patterns are likely to continue into adolescence and adulthood.

The Role of Culture in Violent Behavior

In addition to the influence of the immediate family on the socialization of aggression, social psychologists have also investigated the role that culture plays. Richard Nisbett and his colleagues have been studying this issue by comparing southern and northern regions of the United States. In a series of studies that include examining homicide statistics (Nisbett, 1993), field experiments (Nisbett, Polly, & Lang, 1995), and laboratory experiments (Cohen, 1998), a clear trend toward greater violence among southern than northern Americans emerges.

To what can we attribute the regional differences in violence? Nisbett (1993) suggested that there are a variety of explanations for regional differences. These include traditional explanations suggesting that the South has more poverty, higher temperatures, and a history of slavery as well as the possibility that whites have imitated aggressive behavior seen among the black population. Nisbett suggested that there is another more plausible explanation for the regional differences observed. He hypothesized that in the South (and to some extent in the frontier West) a **culture of honor** has evolved in which violence is both more widely accepted and practiced than in the North where no such culture exists. Nisbett suggested that this culture of honor arose because of the different peoples who settled in the North and South in the 17th and 18th centuries.

culture of honor
An evolved culture in the southern and western U.S. in which violence is more widely accepted and practiced than in the northern and eastern U.S. where no such culture exists.

Research has shown that individuals from southern and western regions of the United States display aggression when honor is on the line to a greater extent than individuals from the north. Researchers believe this is because of a culture of honor that developed in the southern United States. Defending one's honor, as this Civil War soldier may have done, contributes to culture-based aggression.

The South was largely settled by people who came from herding economies in Europe, most notably from borderlands of Scotland and Ireland (Nisbett, 1993). The North, in contrast, was settled by Puritans, Quakers, and Dutch farmers, who developed a more agriculturally based economy (Nisbett, 1993). According to Nisbett, violence is more endemic to herding cultures, because it is important to be constantly vigilant for theft of one's livestock. It was important in these herding economies to respond to any threat to one's herd or grazing lands with sufficient force to drive away intruders or potential thieves. Nisbett maintains that from this herding economy arose the culture of honor that persists in the South to this day. This culture of honor primes southern individuals for greater violence than their northern counterparts.

What evidence do we have that such a culture of honor exists and that it affects violence levels in the South? Nisbett (1993) reported that when southern and northern cities of equal size and demographic make up are compared, there is a higher homicide rate among southern white males than among northern white males. This difference is only true for argument-related homicides, not for homicides resulting from other felonies (e.g., robbery; Cohen, Nisbett, Bowdle, & Schwartz, 1996). Interestingly, this regional difference holds only for white males and not African-American males (Nisbett, Polly, & Lang, 1995). Additionally, Nisbett found a greater acceptance of violence to solve interpersonal conflicts and to respond to a perceived insult among southern than among northern white males.

These findings, based on homicide rates, were verified by Nisbett and his colleagues in a series of experiments. In a field experiment (Cohen & Nisbett, 1997), employers in various parts of the United States were sent a letter from a potential job applicant who committed either an honor-based homicide (killing someone who was having an affair with his fiancé) or an auto theft. Each response was analyzed for whether an application was sent to the potential employee and the tone of the return letter. Cohen and Nisbett found that more southern-based companies sent a job application to the employee convicted of manslaughter than did northern-based companies. However, there was no difference between southern and northern companies in the rate of compliance to the employee who stole a car. Additionally, the tone of the letters coming from southern companies were warmer and more understanding of the homicide than were the letters from northern companies. Again, there was no difference in warmth or understanding between northern and southern companies for the theft letter.

Regional differences in violence between the North and South have been well documented. But is the culture of honor responsible? Are southern males more likely to react negatively to insults than northern males? In a series of interesting laboratory experiments (Cohen, Nisbett, Bowdle, & Schwartz, 1996), southern and northern white males were insulted or not insulted by a male confederate of the experimenter. In one experiment, Cohen and colleagues (1996) were interested in whether there was a difference between southerners and northerners in their physiological responses to the insult. Participants were told that they were going to take part in an experiment that required monitoring of blood sugar levels. Saliva samples were obtained from participants before and after the insult (or no insult). The saliva samples were analyzed for cortisol and testosterone levels. (Cortisol is a stress-related hormone that increases when one is aroused or under stress.)

The results from this experiment are shown in Figure 10.5 (testosterone levels) and Figure 10.6 on p. 390 (cortisol levels). As you can see, there was no difference between insulted and noninsulted northern participants for both cortisol and testosterone levels. However, for southern participants, there was a significant rise in both cortisol and testosterone levels for insulted southern participants (compared to the noninsulted southerners). Thus, in response to an insult, southern white males are more "primed" physiologically for aggression than their northern counterparts (Cohen et al., 1996). In another experiment, Cohen and colleagues (1996) found that after being publically in-

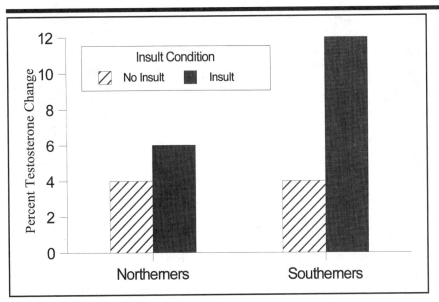

Figure 10.5

Percentage testosterone change as a function of culture and insult. Northerners did not show a significant increase in testosterone levels after being insulted. Southerners, on the other hand, showed substantial increases in testosterone levels after being insulted.

Figure 10.6

Percentage cortisol change as a function of culture and insult. Northerners did not show a significant increase in cortisol levels after being insulted. In contrast, southerners showed an increase in cortisol levels after being insulted.

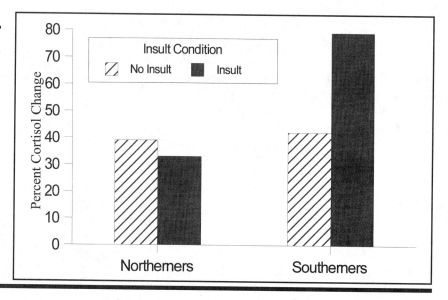

sulted (compared to being privately insulted or not insulted), southern white males were more likely to experience a drop in perceived masculinity. No such difference was found for northern white males.

Cohen (1998) investigated those aspects of southern and western culture that relate most closely to the acceptance and use of violence. Cohen looked at the role of community and family stability in explaining honor-based violence. Cohen hypothesized that among more stable communities, reputations and honor would have more meaning than in less stable communities. As a consequence, more honor-based violence was expected in stable than in unstable communities. Homicide rates among stable and unstable communities in the North, South, and West were compared. Cohen found a higher honor-based homicide rate among stable southern and western communities than among unstable southern and western communities. No such difference existed for stable and unstable northern communities. Cohen also found that the rate of felony-related homicides (not related to honor) were lower among stable than among unstable communities in the South and West, but not in the North. Additionally, Cohen found that honor-related homicides were higher among communities in the South and West in which traditional families (i.e., intact nuclear families) were more common than less common. The opposite was true for northern communities. Thus, the manner in which cultures evolve, with respect to stability and adherence to traditional family structures, relates closely to patterns of violence. In the South and West, evolution toward community stability (in which honor and reputation in the South and West are important) and adherence to more traditional family structures gives rise to higher levels of violence. Such is not the case for northerners, for whom honor and reputation appear to be less important.

Further evidence for a unique southern culture of honor is provided in another study by Cohen (1996). Cohen compared northern and southern (and western) states with respect to gun-control laws, self-defense laws, treatment of violence used in defense of one's property, laws concerning corporal punishment, capital punishment laws, and stances taken by legislators on using military responses to threats to U.S. national interests. Cohen found that compared to northern states, southern (and western) states had more lax gun-control laws, more lenient laws concerning using violence for self-defense and protection of property, more lenient laws for domestic violence offenders (where disciplining one's wife is used as a justification for male perpetrators of domestic violence), and a greater tolerance for the use of corporal punishment. Southern states were more likely to execute condemned prisoners than northern or western states. Finally, southern legislators were more likely to endorse the use of military force than northern (or western) states. These findings support the conclusion that cultural differences, embodied in regional laws, exist between the North and South (and to a lesser extent between the West and the North). More lenient laws in the South tend to sanction and support the use of violence.

The Role of Television in Teaching Aggression

Although parents play the major role in the socialization of children and probably contribute most heavily to the development of aggressive scripts, children are exposed to other models as well. Over the years, considerable attention has focused on the role of television in socializing aggressive behaviors. Generally, most research on this topic suggests that there is a link (though not necessarily a causal link) between exposure to television violence and aggressive behavior (Huesmann, 1988; Huesmann, Lagerspetz, & Eron, 1984; Josephson, 1987).

One factor contributing to aggression among children is exposure to media violence. Children who are heavy viewers of televised violence or play violent video games excessively are often more aggressive than children who do not watch violent television or play violent video games. However, this relationship is relatively small, but consistent.

Some early research in the area showed that males are more influenced than females by violent television (Liebert & Baron, 1972). More recent research suggests that gender may not be important in understanding the relationship between exposure to televised violence and aggression (Huesmann et al., 1984). The correlations between watching television violence and aggression are about the same for male and female children. However, one interesting gender difference exists. Children, especially males, who identify with television characters (that is, want to be like them) are most influenced by television violence.

Watching television violence may also have some subtle effects. People who watch a lot of violence on television tend to become desensitized to the suffering of others, as we saw was the case with abused children (Rule & Ferguson, 1986). Furthermore, children who watch a lot of violent television generally have a more favorable attitude toward aggressive behavior than do children who watch less.

Even sanctioned aggression can increase the incidence of aggressive behavior among those who view it on television. The impact of well-publicized heavyweight championship fights on aggression has been documented (Phillips, 1983). Among adults, homicide rates were found to increase for 3 days after these boxing matches (Miller, Heath, Molcan, & Dugoni, 1991). When a white person loses the match, homicides of whites increase; when an African American loses the match, homicides of African Americans increase. A similar effect can be seen with suicide rates. The number of suicides increases during the month in which a suicide is reported in the media compared to the month before the report appears (Phillips, 1986). Interestingly, the rate remains high (again compared to the month before the report) a month after the report.

Although most studies support the general conclusion that there is a relationship between watching media portrayals of violence and aggression, a few words of caution are appropriate (Freedman, 1984):

- The relationship may not be strong. Correlational studies report relatively low correlations between watching media violence and aggression, and experimental studies typically show weak effects.

- Although watching violence on television is associated with increased aggression, there is some evidence that watching television is also associated with socially appropriate behavior, such as cooperative play or helping another child (Gadow & Sprafkin, 1987).

- Other variables, such as parental aggressiveness and socioeconomic status, also correlate significantly with aggression (Huesmann et al., 1984). One 3-year study conducted in the Netherlands found that the small correlation between violent television viewing and aggression ($r = .23$ and $.29$ for boys and girls, respectively) virtually disappeared when children's preexisting levels of aggression and intelligence were taken into account (Wiegman, Kuttschreuter, & Baarda, 1992).

- Many studies of media violence and aggression are correlational and, as explained in chapter 1, cannot be used to establish a causal relationship between these two variables. Other variables, such as parental aggressiveness, may contribute causally to both violent television viewing and aggression in children.

Exposure to media violence, then, is one among many factors that can contribute to aggression (Huesmann et al., 1984). Available research shows a consistent but sometimes small relationship between media violence and aggression. But interpersonal aggression probably can best be explained with a multiprocess model, one that includes media violence and a wide range of other influences (Huesmann et al., 1984). In all likelihood, media violence interacts with other variables in complex ways to produce aggression.

Viewing Sexual Violence: The Impact on Aggression

Television is not the only medium that has come under fire for depicting violence. Many groups have protested the depiction of violence against women in pornographic magazines and in movies. These groups claim that such sexually explicit materials influence the expression of violence, particularly sexual violence, against women in real life.

In the debate about pornographic materials, researchers have made a distinction between sexually explicit and sexually violent materials (Linz, Penrod, & Donnerstein, 1987). Sexually explicit materials are those specifically created to produce sexual arousal. A scene in a movie depicting two nude people engaging in various forms on consensual sex is sexually explicit. Sexually violent material includes scenes of violence within a sexual context that are degrading to women. These scenes need not necessarily be sexually explicit (e.g., showing nudity). A rape scene (with or without nudity) is sexually violent. Of course, materials can be both sexually explicit and sexually violent.

Although the causes of rape are complex (Groth, 1979; Malamuth, 1986), some researchers and observers have focused on pornography as a factor that contributes to the social climate in which sexual violence against forms of erotica, such as pictures from *Playboy* magazine or scenes of sex between consenting couples, may inhibit sexual violence against women (Donnerstein, Donnerstein, & Evans, 1975, p. 175).

In another study reported by Denise Donnelly and James Fraser (1998), 320 college students responded to a questionnaire concerning arousal to sadomasochistic fantasies and acts. The results showed that males were significantly more likely to be aroused by fantasizing about and engaging in sadomasochistic sexual acts. Specifically, males scored higher than females on measures of being dominant during sex, participating in bondage and discipline, being restrained, and being spanked. In terms of arousal to behaviors, males scored higher than females on watching bondage and discipline, being dominant during sex, and taking part in discipline and bondage.

Of course, sexual arousal does not usually lead to aggression. Most males can easily control their sexual and aggressive impulses. A wide range of social norms, personal ethics, and moral beliefs act to moderate the expression of violence toward women, even when conditions exist that, according to research, lead to increased violence.

THE IMPACT OF SEXUALLY VIOLENT MATERIAL ON ATTITUDES Besides increasing violence against women, exposure to sexually violent material has another damaging effect. It fosters attitudes, especially among males, that tacitly allow rape to continue. There is a pervasive rape myth in U.S. society, which fosters such beliefs as "only bad girls get raped," "if a woman gets raped, she must have asked for it," "women 'cry rape' only when they've been jilted or have something to cover up," and "when a woman says no, she really means yes" (Burt, 1980, p. 217; Groth, 1979). Men are more likely than women to accept the rape myth (Muir, Lonsway, & Payne, 1996). Additionally, such beliefs are most common among men who believe in stereotyped sex roles, hold adversarial sexual beliefs, and find interpersonal aggression an acceptable form of behavior. Thus, the rape myth is integrally tied to a whole set of related attitudes (Burt, 1980). Interestingly, research shows that the rape myth may be stronger in U.S. culture than in other cultures. Grant Muir, Kimberly Lonsway, and Diana Payne (1996) compared U.S. and Scottish individuals for acceptance of the rape myth. They found that the rape myth was more pervasive among Americans that Scotts.

Do media portrayals of sexual violence contribute to rape myths and attitudes? Research suggests that they do (Malamuth & Check, 1981, 1985). In these studies, viewing sexually explicit, violent films increased male (but not female) participants' acceptance of violence against women. Such portrayals also tended to reinforce rape myths. Media portrayals of a woman enjoying sexual violence had their strongest impact on males who were already predisposed to violence against women (Malamuth & Check, 1985). Men who are likely to commit rape also have beliefs that support the rape myth, such as a belief that rape is justified and the perception that the victim enjoyed the rape (Linz, Penrod, & Donnerstein, 1987; Malamuth & Check, 1981).

Neil Malamuth and James Check, for example, had some participants watch films widely distributed in mainstream movie theaters that depicted sexual violence against women (e.g., *The Getaway*). In these films, the sexual violence was portrayed as justified and having positive consequences. Other participants watched films with no sexual violence (e.g., *Hooper*). After viewing the films, participants (both male and female) completed measures of rape-myth acceptance and acceptance of interpersonal violence. The results showed that for male participants, exposure to the films with sexual violence against women increased acceptance of the rape myth and acceptance of interpersonal violence against women. Female participants showed no such increase in acceptance of the rape myth or in violence against women. In fact, there was a slight trend in the opposite direction for female participants.

These "softer" portrayals of sexual violence with unrealistic outcomes in films and on television (e.g., the raped woman marrying her rapist) may have a more pernicious effect than hard-core pornography. Because they are widely available, many individuals see these materials and may be affected by them. The appetite for such films has not subsided since Malamuth and Check's 1981 experiment, and films depicting violence against women are still made and widely distributed.

Finally, one need not view sexually explicit or violent materials in order for one's attitudes toward women and sexual violence to be altered. Natalie McKay and Katherine Covell (1997) reported that male students who looked at magazine advertisements with sexual images (compared to those who saw more "progressive" images) expressed attitudes that showed greater acceptance of interpersonal violence and the rape myth. They were also more likely to express adversarial sexual attitudes and less acceptance of the women's movement.

MEN PRONE TO SEXUAL AGGRESSION: PSYCHOLOGICAL CHARACTERISTICS We have seen that male college students are aroused

by depictions of rape and can be instigated to aggression against women through exposure to sexually explicit, violent materials. Does this mean that all, or at least most, males have a great potential for sexual aggression, given the appropriate circumstances? No, apparently not. Psychological characteristics play a part in a man's inclination to express sexual aggression against women (Malamuth, 1986).

In one study, six variables were investigated to see how they related to self-reported sexual aggression. The six *predictor variables* were:

1. Dominance as a motive for sexual behavior.
2. Hostility toward women.
3. Accepting attitudes toward sexual aggression.
4. Antisocial characteristics or psychoticism.
5. Sexual experience.
6. Physiological arousal to depictions of rape.

Participants' sexual aggression was assessed by a test that measured whether pressure, coercion, force, and so on were used in sexual relationships.

Positive correlations were found between five of the six predictor variables and sexual aggression directed against women. Psychoticism was the only variable that did not correlate significantly with aggression. However, the presence of any one predictor alone was not likely to result in sexual aggression. Instead, the predictor variables tended to interact to influence sexual aggression. For example, arousal to depictions of rape is not likely to translate into sexual aggression unless other variables are present. So, just because a man is aroused by depictions of rape, he will not necessarily be sexually violent with women. In other words, several variables interact to predispose a man toward sexual aggression.

In another study, Leandra Lackie and Anton de Man (1997) investigated the relationship between several variables including sex-role attitudes, physical aggression, hostility toward women, alcohol use, and fraternity affiliation and sexual aggression. Their findings showed that sexually aggressive males tended to be physically aggressive in general. Furthermore, they found stereotyped sex-role beliefs, acceptance of interpersonal violence, masculinity, and fraternity membership were positively related to self-reported sexual aggression. They also found that the most important predictors of sexual aggression were the use of physical aggression, stereotyped sex-role beliefs, and fraternity membership.

So, whether an individual will be sexually aggressive is mediated by other factors. For example, Dean and Malamuth (1997) found that males who are at risk for sexual violence against women were most likely to behave in a sexually aggressive way if they were also self-centered. A high-risk male who is not self-centered but rather is sensitive to the needs of others is not likely to behave in a sexually aggressive way. However, regardless of whether a high-risk male is self-centered, he is likely to fantasize about sexual violence (Dean & Malamuth, 1997). Additionally, feelings of empathy also appear to mediate sexual aggression. Malamuth, Heavey, and Linz found that males who are high in empathy are less likely to show arousal to scenes of sexual violence than males who are low in empathy (cited in Dean & Malamuth, 1997).

What do we know, then, about the effects of exposure to sexual violence on aggression? The research suggests the following conclusions:

- Exposure to mild forms of nonviolent erotica tends to decrease sexual aggression against women.

- Exposure to explicit or sexually violent erotica tends to increase sexual aggression against women but not against men.

- Individuals who are angry are more likely to be more aggressive after viewing sexually explicit or violent materials than are individuals who are not angry.

- Male college students are aroused by depictions of rape. However, men who show a greater predisposition to rape are more aroused, especially if the woman is portrayed as being aroused.

- Exposure to media portrayals of sexual aggression against women increases acceptance of such acts and contributes to the rape myth. Thus, sexually explicit, violent materials contribute to a social climate that tolerates rape.

- No single psychological characteristic predisposes a man to sexual aggression. Instead, several characteristics interact to increase the likelihood that a man will be sexually aggressive toward women.

REDUCING AGGRESSION

We have seen that interpersonal aggression comes in many different forms, including murder, rioting, and sexual violence. We also have seen that many different factors can contribute to aggression, including innate biological impulses, situational factors such as frustration, situational cues such as the presence of weapons, and aggressive scripts internalized through the process of socialization. We turn now to a more practical question: What can be done to reduce aggression? Although aggression can be addressed on a societal level, such as through laws regulating violent television programming and pornography, the best approach is to undermine aggression in childhood, before it becomes a life script.

Reducing Aggression in the Family

According to the social-interactional model described earlier in this chapter, antisocial behavior begins early in life and results from poor parenting. The time to target aggression, then, is during early childhood, when the socialization process is just under way. Teachers, health workers, and police need to look for signs of abuse and neglect and intervene as soon as possible (Widom, 1992). Waiting until an aggressive child is older is not the best course of action (Patterson et al., 1989). Intervention attempts with adolescents produce only temporary reductions in aggression, at best.

One way to counter the development of aggression is to give parents guidance with their parenting. Parents who show tendencies toward inept parenting can be identified, perhaps through child-welfare agencies or schools, and offered training programs in productive parenting skills. Such training programs have been shown to be effective in reducing noncompliant and aggressive behavior in children (Forehand & Long, 1991). Children whose parents received training in productive parenting skills were also less likely to show aggressive behavior as adolescents.

What types of parenting techniques are most effective in minimizing aggression? Parents should avoid techniques that provide children with aggressive role models. Recommended techniques include positive reinforcement of desired behaviors and time-outs (separating a child from activities for a time) for undesired behaviors. Also, parenting that involves inductive techniques, or giving age-relevant explanations for discipline, is related to lowered levels of juvenile crime (Shaw & Scott, 1991). Parents can also encourage prosocial behaviors that involve helping, cooperating, and sharing. It is a simple fact that prosocial behavior is incompatible with aggression. If a child learns to be empathic and altruistic in his or her social interactions, aggression is less likely to occur. To support the development of prosocial behaviors, parents can take four specific steps (Bee, 1992, pp. 331–443):

1. Set clear rules and explain to children why certain behaviors are unacceptable. For example, tell a child that if he or she hits another child, that other child will be hurt.

2. Provide children with age-appropriate opportunities to help others, such as setting the table, cooking dinner, and teaching younger siblings.

3. Attribute prosocial behavior to the child's internal characteristics; for example, tell the child how helpful he or she is.

4. Provide children with prosocial role models who demonstrate caring, empathy, helping, and other positive traits.

Reducing Aggression with Cognitive Intervention

Reducing aggression through better parenting is a long-term, global solution to the problem. Another more direct approach to aggression in specific individuals makes use of cognitive intervention. We have seen that children who are exposed to violence develop aggressive scripts. These scripts increase the likelihood that a child will interpret social situations in an aggressive way. Kenneth Dodge (1986) suggested that aggression is mediated by the way we process information about our social world. According to this **social information-processing view of aggression**, there are five important steps involved in instigating aggression (as well as other forms of social interaction). These are (as cited in Kendall, Ronan, & Epps, 1991):

1. We perceive and decode cues from our social environment.

2. We develop expectations of others' behavior based on our attribution of intent.

3. We look for possible responses.

4. We decide which response is most appropriate.

5. We carry out the chosen response.

social information-processing view of aggression
A view emphasizing how a person processes information about one's social world mediates aggression.

Individuals with aggressive tendencies see their own feelings reflected in the world. They are likely to interpret and make attributions about the behaviors of others that center on aggressive intent. This leads them to respond aggressively to the perceived threat. Generally, aggressive individuals interpret the world as a hostile place, choose aggression as a desired way to solve conflict, and enact those aggressive behaviors to solve problems (Kendall et al., 1991).

Programs to assess and treat aggressive children have been developed using cognitive intervention techniques. Some programs use behavior management strategies (teaching individuals to effectively manage their social behavior) to establish and enforce rules in a nonconfrontational way (Kendall et al., 1991). Aggressive children (and adults) can be exposed to positive role models and taught to consider nonaggressive solutions to problems.

Other programs focus more specifically on teaching aggressive individuals new information-processing and social skills that they can use to solve interpersonal problems (Pepler, King, & Byrd, 1991). Individuals are taught to listen to what others say and, more important, think about what they are saying. They are also taught how to correctly interpret others' behaviors, thoughts, and feelings and how to select nonaggressive behaviors to solve interpersonal problems. These skills are practiced in role-playing sessions where various scenarios that could lead to aggression are acted out and analyzed. In essence, the aggressive child (or adult) is taught to reinterpret social situations in a less threatening, hostile way.

These cognitively based therapy techniques have produced some encouraging results. It appears that they can be effective in changing an individual's perceptions of social events and in reducing aggression. However, the jury is still out on these programs. It may be best to view them as just one technique among many to help reduce aggression.

MATTHEW SHEPARD REVISITED

The fate that befell Matthew Shepard on that fateful night in October of 1998 was the result of brutal aggression directed against him. We would classify the type of aggression directed at Matthew as hostile aggression. The level of brutality and the fact that Matthew was left to die hanging on a fence suggests a high level of anger behind the aggression. His killers were evidently angered over Matthew's sexual orientation. However, there was also an instrumental nature to the aggression. Recall that McKinney became concerned that Matthew would be able to read the license plate number on his truck. Killing Matthew served the instrumental purpose of preventing him from being a witness.

Although it would be difficult to pinpoint an exact cause for the aggression directed against Matthew Shepard, it is fairly clear that there were no physiological causes for the aggression (e.g., no damage to the hypothalamus). The best explanations for the violence directed at Matthew Shepard probably rest in learning processes and frustration. Was there something in McKinney's past that contributed to this brutal crime? Apparently so. At age 15, McKinney was forced to perform oral sex on a neighborhood bully, and later had a homosexual experience with his cousin (Gierhart, 1999). Recall from the social interaction model of aggression how family experiences can shape a person's tendencies toward aggressive behavior. Shepard's sexual orientation may have angered McKinney, leading to the brutal aggression perpetrated on Shepard. Finally, recall that McKinney and his friend Russell Henderson were drinking that night. We have seen how alcohol may increase aggression by suppressing inhibitions against aggression. Most likely no one factor can explain the aggression directed at Matthew Shepard. A confluence of factors including early experience, anger, and alcohol consumption came together that night.

CHAPTER REVIEW

1. How do social psychologists define aggression?

For social psychologists, the term **aggression** carries a very specific meaning, which differs from a layperson's definition. For social psychologists, aggression is any behavior intended to inflict harm (whether psychological or physical) on another organism or object. Key to this definition are the notions of intent and the fact that harm need not be limited to physical harm but can also include psychological harm.

2. What are the different types of aggression?

Social psychologists distinguish different types of aggression, including **hostile aggression** (aggression stemming from emotions such as anger or hatred) and **instrumental aggression** (aggression used to achieve a goal). **Symbolic aggression** involves doing things that block another person's goals. **Sanctioned aggression** is aggression that society approves, such as a soldier killing in war or a police officer shooting a suspect in the line of duty.

3. What are the gender differences in aggression?

Research has established that there are, in fact, differences in aggression between males and females. One of the most reliable differences between males and females is the male's greater predisposition toward physical aggression, most evident among children. Males tend to favor physical aggression as a way to settle a dispute and are more likely than females to be the target of aggression. Females, however, tend to use verbal aggression more than males. Males and females also think differently about aggression. Females tend to feel guiltier than males about using aggression and show more concern for the harm done by aggression. The observed gender differences are most likely a result of the interaction between biological and social forces.

Laboratory research on gender differences in aggression suggest that the difference between males and females is reliable but quite small. However, crime statistics bear out the commonly held belief that males are more aggressive than females. Across three major categories of violent crime (murder, robbery, and assault), males commit far more violent crimes than females.

4. How can we explain aggression?

As is typical of most complex behaviors, aggression has multiple causes. Several explanations for aggression can be offered, including both biological and social factors.

5. What are the ethological and sociobiological explanations for aggression?

Biological explanations include attempts by ethologists and sociobiologists to explain aggression as a behavior with survival value for individual and groups of organisms. **Ethology** theory suggests that aggression is related to the biological survival and evolution of an organism. This theory emphasizes the roles of instincts and genetics. **Sociobiology**, like ethology, looks at aggression as having survival value and resulting from competition among members of a species. Aggression is seen as one behavior biologically programmed into an organism.

6. What role do brain mechanisms play in aggression?

The roles of brain mechanisms and hormonal influences in aggression have also been studied. Stimulation of certain parts of the brain elicits aggressive behavior. The hypothalamus is one part of the brain that has been implicated in aggression. Stimulation of one part of the **hypothalamus** in a cat leads to emotional aggression, whereas stimulation of another elicits predatory aggression. Interacting with social factors, these neurological factors increase or decrease the likelihood of aggression. The male hormone testosterone has also been linked to aggressive behavior. Higher concentrations of testosterone are associated with more aggression. Like brain mechanisms, hormonal influences interact with the social environment to influence aggression.

7. How does alcohol consumption relate to aggression?

Although alcohol is considered a sedative, it tends to increase aggression. Research shows that individuals who are intoxicated behave more aggressively than those who are not. Furthermore, it is not only the pharmacological effects of alcohol that increase aggression. An individual's expectations about the effects of alcohol also can increase aggression after consuming a beverage believed to be alcoholic. Alcohol appears to operate on the brain to reduce levels of the neurotransmitter serotonin. This reduction is serotonin is related to increased aggression. Furthermore, alcohol tends to suppress the executive cognitive functions that normally operate to mediate aggressive responses.

8. What is the frustration–aggression hypothesis?

The **frustration-aggression hypothesis** suggests that aggression is caused by frustration resulting from blocked goals. This hypothesis has raised much controversy. Once frustrated, we choose a target for aggression. Our first choice is the source of the frustration, but if the source is an inappropriate target, we may vent our frustration against another target. This is called **displaced aggression**.

9. How does anger relate to frustration and aggression, and what factors contribute to anger?

A modified version of the frustration–aggression hypothesis suggests that frustration does not lead to aggression unless a negative affect such as anger is aroused. Anger may be aroused under several conditions. Cognitive mediators, such as attributions about intent, have been found to play a role in the frustration–aggression link as well. If we believe that another person intends to harm us, we are more likely to react aggressively. If we are given a good reason for why we are frustrated, we are less likely to react aggressively.

Another social psychological mechanism operating to cause aggression is perceived injustice. Aggression can be used to restore a sense of justice and equity in such situations. Research suggests that a perceived inequity in a frustrating situation is a stronger cause for aggression than frustration itself.

10. How does social learning theory explain aggression?

According to **social learning theory**, aggression is learned, much like any other human behavior. The primary means of learning for social learning theorists is **observational learning**, or modeling. By watching others we learn new behaviors or have preexisting behaviors inhibited or disinhibited.

11. What are aggressive scripts, and how do they relate to aggression?

One mechanism believed to underlie the relationship between observation and aggression is the formation of an **aggressive script** during the socialization process. These aggressive scripts lead a person to behave more aggressively and to interpret social situations in aggressive terms. During the socialization process, children develop aggressive scripts and behavior patterns because they are exposed to acts of aggression, both within the family and in the media.

12. How does the family socialize a child into aggression?

Research shows that aggressive behavior patterns develop early in life. Research also shows that there is continuity between childhood aggression and aggression later in life; that is, an aggressive child is likely to grow into an aggressive adult.

According to the **social-interactional model**, antisocial behavior such as aggression results from inept parenting. Parental use of physical or verbal aggression is related to heightened aggressiveness among children, with verbal aggression being particularly problematic. Parents who use physical and verbal aggression with their children provide them with aggressive role models.

Child abuse and neglect also have been found to lead to increases in aggression (as measured by violent crime). In addition, child abuse leads to a desensitization to the suffering of others. An abused child is likely to respond to an agemate in distress with anger and physical abuse, rather than concern or empathy (as would a nonabused child). Child abuse, then, leads to a callous attitude toward others as well as increases in aggression.

Finally, family disruption also relates to increases in aggression. Children from disrupted homes have been found to engage in more criminal behavior as adults than children from nondisrupted homes.

13. *What is the role of culture in aggression?*

An individual's level of aggressiveness relates to the cultural environment within which he or she is reared. Research comparing individuals from the American South with the American North has shown differences in attitudes toward using aggression. Generally, individuals from the South are more favorable toward using aggression than individuals from the North. One explanation for this is that a **culture of honor** has developed in the South (and the West) because different people settled these regions during the 17th and 18th centuries. The south was settled by people from herding economies, and these people were predisposed to be constantly vigilant for theft on one's stock and react with force to drive intruders away to protect one's property. From this the culture of honor emerged.

14. *What role does the media play in aggression?*

One important application of social learning theory to the problem of aggression is the relationship between media portrayals of aggression and aggressive behavior. Research suggests that children who watch aggressive television programs tend to be more aggressive. Although some early research suggested that males were more affected by television violence than were females, more recent research suggests that there is no reliable, general difference between males and females. One gender difference that does emerge is that children, especially males, who identify with television characters are most affected by television violence. Additionally, heavy doses of television violence desensitize individuals to violence.

Although many studies have established a link between watching media violence and aggression, the observed effects are small and some studies show just the opposite effect. We should be cautious about overplaying the role of media violence in aggressive behavior.

15. *What is the link between sexual violence portrayed in the media and sexual aggression directed toward women?*

The research on the link between violent sexual media portrayals and violence directed at women leads to six conclusions: (1) Exposure to mild forms of erotica tends to decrease sexual violence against women. (2) Exposure to explicit or sexually violent erotica increases aggression against women but not against men. (3) Individuals who are angry are more likely to be more aggressive after viewing sexually explicit or violent materials than individuals who are not angry. (4) Male college students are aroused by depictions of rape. However, individuals who show a greater predisposition to rape are more aroused, especially if the victim is shown being aroused by sexual violence. (5) Exposure to media portrayals of sexual violence increases acceptance of violence against women and contributes to the rape myth. Thus, sexually explicit, violent pornography contributes to a social climate that tolerates rape. (6) There is no single psychological characteristic that predisposes a man to sexual violence. Instead, several characteristics interact to increase the likelihood that a man will be sexually violent.

Finally, research suggests that males with certain characteristics may be at particular risk for committing sexual violence against women. Men who show dominance as a motive for sexual behavior, display hostility toward women, have accepting attitudes toward sexual aggression, are sexually experienced, and show physiological arousal to depictions of rape are more likely to commit sexual violence against women. However, no one of these factors alone can reliably predict sexual violence against women.

16. How can aggression be reduced?

Many factors contribute to aggression, including biological predispositions, frustration, the presence of aggressive cues, the media, and family factors. The most fruitful approach to reducing aggression is to target family factors that contribute to aggression. Aggression can be reduced if parents change inept parenting styles, do not abuse or neglect their children, and minimize family disruption. Parents should reduce or eliminate their use of physical and verbal aggression directed at children. Positive reinforcement for desired behavior and time-out techniques should be used more often. Socializing children to be altruistic and caring can also help reduce aggression.

According to the cognitive approach, children are encouraged to reinterpret situations as nonaggressive. The **social information-processing view of aggression** maintains that there are five important steps involved in the instigation to aggression: We perceive and decode cues from our social environment, we develop expectations of others' behavior based on our attribution of intent, we look for possible responses, we decide which response is most appropriate, and we carry out the chosen response. The cognitive approach suggests that aggressive individuals need to change their view of the world as a hostile place, to manage their aggressive impulses, and to learn new social skills for managing their interpersonal problems.

INTERNET ACTIVITY

ARE YOU PRONE TO ROAD RAGE?

One type of aggression that has been on the rise in recent years is road rage. *Road rage* is defined as the situation in which one or more drivers uses his or her vehicle as a weapon intending to commit harm on another driver or escalates a driving incident into another form of violence. For this exercise, evaluate yourself for the tendency toward aggressive driving and road rage. Use an Internet search engine to find a Web site with a self-test for road rage (one can be found at: http://www.aloha.net/~dyc/testimony.html). Use other Internet resources to more fully explore road rage. Specifically, you could explore:

- The formal definitions of road rage.
- The frequency of road rage incidents.
- The severity of road rage incidents.
- What can be done if you are prone to road rage.
- What you can do to prevent becoming a victim of road rage.

SUGGESTIONS FOR FURTHER READING

Baron, R. A., & Richardson, D. R. (1994). *Human aggression* (2nd ed.). New York: Plenum.

This is an update of a classic book on human aggression that is clearly written and covers the latest research and theories. Furthermore, it also examines aggression in natural settings, such as the effects of pornography on aggression, aggression in sport, and the effects of alcohol and drugs on aggression.

Berkowitz, L. (1989). Frustration–aggression hypothesis: Examination and reformation. *Psychological Bulletin, 106,* 59–73.

In this article, Berkowitz reviews the frustration–aggression hypothesis in its original form. He then goes on to develop the hypothesis further, suggesting that frustration will lead to aggression only if the frustration arouses negative affect, such as anger or fear. It provides a good, one-source overview of the frustration–aggression hypothesis.

Brewer, J. D. (1994). *The danger from strangers.* New York: Plenum.

Brewer explores what makes an individual vulnerable to violent crime. The vividness of the interviews with victims lend power to the book. Brewer advises the reader on such matters as carrying weapons and precautions one should take to avoid violent confrontations.

Liebert, R. M., & Sprafkin, J. (1988). *The early window.* New York: Pergamon Press.

This book summarizes the issues concerning the effects of television on children. In addition to covering the issue of the effects of television violence on children, it addresses more general issues surrounding the impact of television on children, including advertising and prosocial programs.

Lorenz, K. (1963). *On aggression.* London: Methuen.

In this classic work, Lorenz presents the ethological perspective on aggression. The book reviews years of research with animals on aggression and concludes with chapters that address the applicability of the animal research findings to human aggression.

Nisbett, R. E., & Cohen, D. (1995). *Culture of honor: The psychology of violence in the South.* Boulder, CO: Westview Press.

In this book, Nisbett and Cohen further develop their theory that there are regional differences in the causes for honor-related violence. The book provides several explanations for the regional differences observed.

Rule, J. B. (1988). *Theories of civil violence.* Berkeley, CA: University of California Press.

In this book, Rule explores the roots of civil unrest as well as the social and psychological roots of civil unrest.

CHAPTER 11

ALTRUISM

When Peter Still was 6 years old and living in Philadelphia, Pennsylvania, he was kidnaped and taken into slavery in the South. For the next 40 years, Still remained a slave in Alabama, not knowing the fate of his parents and brothers and sisters. He never gave up hope that he would someday be free. Over a period of years, he saved enough money to buy his freedom. He did not have enough money to buy the freedom of his wife and two sons, however. He decided to leave them in Alabama, travel to the North, and arrange to obtain their freedom after he arrived. He made his way back to Philadelphia and tried to find his parents and siblings. He contacted William Still, a prominent businessman and abolitionist, who, unknown to Peter, was his long-lost brother.

The *Pennsylvania Freeman*, a local newspaper, decided to report Still's plight for its human interest. Seth Conklin, a white man, read about Still in the paper. He was so moved by the story that he felt it was his humanitarian duty to help Still recover the family he had left behind in Alabama. Conklin

contacted Still and offered his help, asking nothing in return. At first, Still refused Conklin's help. Instead, Still went to Alabama with the intention of buying his family's freedom. Unfortunately, he did not have enough money, and even if he had, strict Alabama laws concerning buying slaves into freedom may have prevented him.

Returning to Philadelphia, Still decided to take Seth Conklin up on his offer. Conklin laid out a plan to go to Alabama and bring back Still's family, an extremely dangerous decision because, at the time, black slaves were legally the property of their owners. Fugitive slave laws, newly passed by the U.S. Congress, made it a crime to help fleeing slaves. Those who helped slaves escape were commonly arrested, jailed, or even killed. Conklin was risking his life for a family of blacks he did not know.

Conklin set out for Alabama with a few articles of clothing and a small sum of money. Once he located Still's family, he befriended the slave master and then spirited Still's wife and children out of the state to freedom. His trip back North was difficult and dangerous. He found no help; there were no good Samaritans along the way. Quite the contrary. He wrote in a letter dated February 3, 1851,

405

mailed from Eastport, Mississippi, that "the whole country for miles around is inhabited by 'Christian wolves.'" These "wolves" were church-going Christians who would abduct any unknown black and turn him or her in for a reward.

Because of the irregularity of the steamboat schedules, Conklin and his charges had to find alternative means of transportation. Often traveling at night over land and water, they made the slow, dangerous trip northward. Once, while traveling over water in a small rowboat, they came under gunfire from shore.

In March 1851, Conklin and Still's family arrived in Indiana. Conklin wrote to Still seeking to arrange a reunion within a few days. Unfortunately, no such reunion ever occurred. Conklin and Still's family were apprehended. Conklin tried to free Still's family through legal means, but his efforts were futile. Eventually, Conklin was arrested, and in chains, both he and Still's family were returned to Alabama. Not too long afterward a white man's body was found "drowned, with his hands and feet in chains, and his skull fractured" (Still, 1872/1968). The body was later positively identified as that of Seth Conklin.

What motivated Seth Conklin? Why would a man forgo his comfortable existence and risk all for people who previously had meant nothing to him? Why do we care about the fate of other people? Indeed, do we care at all? These are fundamental questions about human nature. Theologians, philosophers, evolutionary biologists, and novelists all have suggested answers. Social psychologists have suggested answers, too, contributing their empirical findings to the discussion.

Conklin's behavior was clearly out of the ordinary. Not many whites left their firesides in the North to rescue families of former slaves. The most notable aspect of Conklin's behavior was that he expected nothing in return, neither material nor psychological rewards. His actions were purely altruistic. So Conklin was an unusual human being—but not unique. Others have performed equally selfless acts.

In this chapter we consider why people help others, when they help, and what kinds of people help. We ask, What lies behind behavior such as Seth Conklin's? Does it spring from compassion for our fellow human beings? Does it come from a need to be able to sleep at night, to live with ourselves? Or is there some other motivation? What circumstances led Conklin to offer the help he did, and what process did he go through to arrive at his decision? Or was his decision more a function of his character, his personal traits? Was he perhaps an example of an altruistic personality? And what about Peter Still? How did receiving Conklin's help affect him? What factors determined how he responded to that help? These are some of the questions addressed in this chapter.

KEY QUESTIONS

AS YOU READ THIS CHAPTER, FIND THE ANSWERS TO THE FOLLOWING QUESTIONS:

1. *What is altruism and how is it different from helping behavior? Why is the difference important?*
2. *What are empathy and egoism, and how do they relate to altruism?*
3. *What about the idea that we may help to avoid guilt or shame?*
4. *Does biology play any role in altruism?*

5. How do social psychologists explain helping in emergency situations?
6. What other factors affect the decision to help?
7. If I need help, how can I increase my chances of getting it?
8. How do personality characteristics influence helping?
9. What situational and personality variables played a role in the decision to help Jews in Nazi-occupied Europe?
10. What factors contribute to a person's developing an altruistic personality?
11. What is the interactionist view of altruism?
12. How does long-term helping relate to models of emergency helping?
13. What factors influence a person's likelihood of seeking and receiving help?
14. What reactions do people show to receiving help?

WHY DO PEOPLE HELP?

There are two types of motives for behaviors such as Seth Conklin's. Sometimes we help because we want to relieve a person's suffering. Behavior motivated by the desire to relieve a victim's suffering is called **altruism**. Other times we help because we hope to gain something from it for ourselves. We may give to a charity to get a tax deduction, for example, or we may give because we think it makes us look good. Often, we experience personal satisfaction and increased self-esteem after helping. When we give help with an eye on the reward we will get, our behavior is not really altruistic. It falls into the category of behaviors known simply as **helping behavior**.

Notice that the distinction between altruism and helping behavior lies in the motivation for performing the behavior, not the outcome. A person who is motivated purely by the need to relieve the suffering of the victim may receive a reward for his or her actions. However, he or she didn't perform the actions with the expectation of receiving that reward. This marks the behavior as altruistic.

The distinction between altruism and helping behavior may seem artificial, because the outcome in both cases is that someone in need receives help. Does it matter what motivates the behavior? Yes, it does. The quality of the help given may vary according to the motivation behind the behavior. For example, there were others besides Conklin who helped slaves escape in pre-Civil War days, but some of them were paid for their efforts. The slaves who paid their helpers were not necessarily treated very well. In one case, a ship captain agreed to ferry some escaped slaves to freedom. Once they reached the shores of freedom, the captain turned the slaves in and kept the money. Similarly, Christians in Nazi-occupied Europe who helped hide Jews for pay did not extend the same level of care as those who were not paid. Jews hidden by "paid helpers" were more likely to be mistreated, abused, and turned in than were those hidden by the more altruistic "rescuers" (Tec, 1986).

The question posed by social psychologists about all of these acts is, What motivates people to help? Is there really such a thing as altruism, or are people always hoping for some personal reward when they help others? Researchers have proposed a number of hypotheses to answer this question.

Empathy: Helping in Order to Relieve Another's Suffering

Social psychologist C. Daniel Batson (1987, 1990a, 1990b) suggested that we may help others because we truly care about them and their suffering. This caring occurs because humans have strong feelings of **empathy**, compassionate understanding of how the person in need feels. Feelings of empathy encompass sympathy, pity, and sorrow (Eisenberg & Miller, 1987).

What cognitive and/or emotional experience underlies empathy? Daniel Batson, Shannon Early, and Giovanni Salvarani (1997) suggested that *perspective taking* is at the heart of helping acts. According to Batson and colleagues, there are two perspectives that are relevant to helping situations: *imagine other* and *imagine self*. An imagine-other perspective operates when you think about how the person in need of help perceives the helping situation and the feelings that are aroused in that situation. An imagine-self perspective operates when you imagine how you would think and feel if you were in the victim's situation. Batson and colleagues predicted that the perspective taken affects the arousal of empathy or personal distress.

Batson and colleagues (1997) conducted an experiment in which participants were told to adopt one of three perspectives while listening to a story about a person in need (Katie). In the *objective-perspective* condition, participants were instructed to be as objective as possible and not to imagine what the person had been through. In the *imagine-other* condition, participants were instructed to try to imagine how the person in need felt about what had happened. In the *imagine-self* condition, participants were told to imagine how they themselves would feel in the situation. Batson and colleagues measured the extent to which the manipulation produced feelings of empathy or personal distress.

Batson and colleagues (1997) found that participants in both imagine conditions felt more empathy for Katie than did those in the objective condition. Furthermore, they found that participants in the imagine-other condition felt more empathy than did those in the imagine-self condition. Participants in the imagine-self condition were more likely to experience personal distress than empathy. Thus, two emotional experiences were produced depending on which perspective a person took.

How does empathy relate to altruism? Although attempts to answer this question have been somewhat controversial, it appears that empathy, once aroused, increases the likelihood of an altruistic act. This is exactly what is predicted from Batson and colleagues' (1997) **empathy–altruism hypothesis.** Psychologists, however, have never been comfortable with the idea that people may do selfless acts. The idea of a truly altruistic act runs contrary to the behavioristic tradition in psychology. According to this view, behavior is under control of overt reinforcers and punishers. Behavior develops and is maintained if it is reinforced. Thus, the very idea of a selfless, nonrewarded act seems farfetched.

empathy–altruism hypothesis
An explanation suggesting that the arousal of empathy leads to altruistic acts.

Empathy and Egoism: Two Paths to Helping

When we see or hear about someone in need, we often experience personal distress. Now, distress is an unpleasant emotion, and we try to avoid it. After all, most of us do not like to see others suffer. Therefore, we may give help not out of feelings of empathy for victims but in order to relieve our own personal distress. This motive for helping is called **egoism.** For example, if you saw the suffering in Bosnia or Somalia and thought, "If I don't do something, I'll feel terrible all day," you would be focused on your own distress rather than on the distress of the victims. Generally, egoistic motives are more self-centered and selfish than empathic motives (Batson, Fultz, & Schoenrade, 1987). Thus, there are different paths to helping, one involving empathy and the other personal distress. These two competing explanations of helping are shown in Figure 11.1 on p. 410.

egoism
The idea that helping a person in need occurs to relieve personal distress.

How can we know which of these two paths better explains helping behavior? Note that when the motivation is to reduce personal distress, helping is only one solution. Another is to remove ourselves from the situation. But when the motivation is altruistic, only one solution is effective: helping the victim. The egoist, motivated by reducing personal distress, is more likely to respond to someone in need by escaping the situation if possible. The altruist, motivated by empathy for the victim, is not.

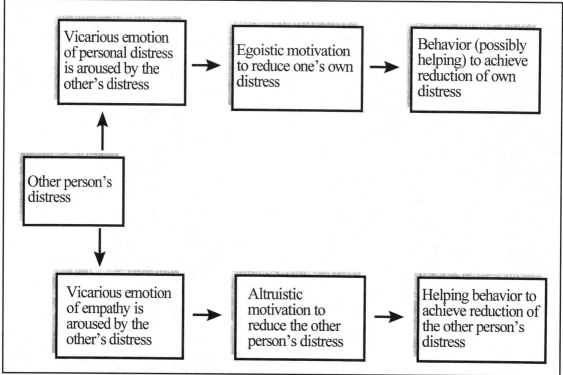

Figure 11.1 *Two paths to helping. The empathy–altruism hypothesis suggests that helping is related to feelings of empathy aroused by the suffering of another (lower path). The personal distress hypothesis proposes that helping occurs to reduce one's own negative feelings generated by seeing another person in need of help.*

From Batson, Fultz, and Schoenrade (1987). Reprinted with permission.

Batson designed some experiments to test the relative merits of the personal distress versus the empathy–altruism explanations by varying the ease with which subjects could avoid contact with the person in need. In one study, subjects watched someone (apparently) experiencing pain in response to a series of electric shocks (Batson, 1990a). Some subjects were told that they would see more of the shock series—the difficult-escape condition. Others were told that they would see no more of the shock series, although the victim would still get shocked—the easy-escape condition.

The personal distress reduction explanation predicts that everyone will behave the same in this situation. When escape is easy, everyone will avoid helping—we all want to relieve our feelings of personal distress. When escape is difficult, everyone will help—again, we all want to relieve our feelings of personal distress. The empathy–altruism explanation, on the other hand, predicts that people will behave differently, depending on their motivation. This will be particularly apparent when it is easy to escape. Under these conditions, those motivated by egoistic concerns will escape. Those motivated by empathy will help even though they easily could have escaped.

Batson's research confirmed the empathy hypothesis, which predicts that empathic feelings matter very much. Some people chose to help even when escape was easy, indicating that it was their caring about the victim, not their own discomfit, that drove their behavior (Figure 11.2). Other research shows that it is the helper's empathic feelings for the person in need that is the prime motivator for helping (Dovidio, Allen, & Schroeder, 1990).

In a different test of the empathy–altruism hypothesis, Batson and Weeks (1996) reasoned that if a person aroused to empathy tries to help a person in distress and fails, there should be a substantial change in the helper's state of mind to a negative mood. They reasoned further that less negative mood change would result when little or no empathy was aroused. The results of their experiment confirmed this. Participants in the high-empathy condition experienced greater negative mood shifts after failed help than participants in the low-empathy condition.

Interestingly, empathy does not always lead to an increase in altruism. Batson and colleagues (1999) demonstrated that both egoism and empathy can lead to reduced helping or, what they called a "threat to the common good." Batson and colleagues gave participants the opportunity to divide resources among a group or keep themselves (egoism). In one group-allocation condition, one of the group members aroused the empathy of the participants. In a second group-allocation condition, there was no group member who aroused empathy. In both group conditions, participants could choose to allocate resources to the group as a whole or to an individual member of the group. Batson and colleagues found that when a participant's allocation scheme was private, he or she allocated fewer resources to the group than the self. This was true regardless of whether the empathy-arousing victim was present. Conversely, when allocation strategies were public, participants allocated fewer resources to the group as a whole only when the empathy-arousing victim was present. The research from Batson and colleagues suggests that both egoism and empathy can threaten the common good. However, potential evaluation by others (the public condition) strongly inhibits those motivated by egoism but not empathy.

Challenging the Empathy–Altruism Hypothesis

Everett Sanderson was standing on a subway platform one day when a woman fell onto the tracks. Sanderson leapt down onto the tracks and pulled the woman to safety just moments before a train rushed into the station. When asked why he went to a stranger's aid, he replied that he would not have been able to live with himself had he not helped.

Perhaps a similar thought motivated Seth Conklin some 150 years

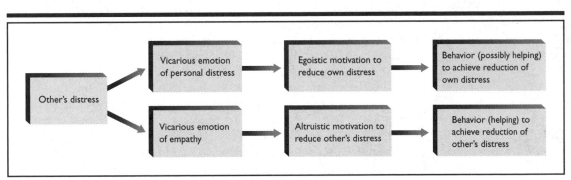

Figure 11.2   *Helping as a function of ease of escape and empathy. Participants high in empathy are likely to help a person in need, even if escape is easy. Participants low in empathy help only if escape is difficult.*

ago. Perhaps people help because not helping would violate their view of themselves as moral and altruistic and would make them feel guilty. Or, perhaps they are concerned with what others may think if they do not help, and they would experience shame. The notion that people may help because of the shame and guilt they will feel if they do not help—known as the **empathy–punishment hypothesis**—is another challenge to the empathy–altruism hypothesis.

Batson accepted the challenge of this hypothesis. He thought that people who help to avoid guilt or shame should help less when provided with a good justification for not helping. After all, if you can plausibly justify not helping to other people (avoid shame) and to yourself (avoid guilt), then no punishment occurs. If, however, your motive for helping is purely altruistic, then reduction of the victim's distress is the issue, not good rationalizations for not helping.

Batson and his colleagues (1988) designed research to pit the empathy–altruism hypothesis against the empathy–punishment explanation. There were two variables in this experiment: the subject's level of empathy for the victim (high or low) and the strength of the justification for not helping (strong or weak). Subjects listened to a simulated news interview in which a college senior (Katie) was interviewed about her parents' and sister's recent deaths in an automobile accident and her current role as sole supporter of her younger brother and sister. Empathy was manipulated by instructing subjects either to pay attention to the "technical aspects" of the news program (low empathy) or to "try to imagine how the person who is being interviewed feels" (Batson et al., 1988, p. 61).

After hearing the news program, the subjects read two letters left by the professor in charge of the experiment. The first letter thanked the subjects for participating and indicated that it occurred to him that some subjects might want to help Katie. The second letter was from Katie herself, outlining ways that the subjects could help her (e.g., babysitting, helping around the house, helping with fundraising projects). Subjects indicated their willingness to help on a response form that was used for the justification manipulation. The response form had eight spaces for individuals to indicate whether they would help Katie. In all cases, seven of the eight spaces were already filled in with fictitious names. In the low justification for not helping condition, five of the seven individuals on the list had agreed to help Katie. In the high justification for not helping condition, only two of the seven agreed to help.

The empathy–punishment explanation predicts that when there is a strong justification for not helping, the amount of empathy aroused won't matter. The empathy–altruism hypothesis predicts that empathic motivation matters most when justification for not helping and empathy are high. Only when people fail to empathize with the person in need does high justification for not helping have an effect on helping. The results of the research support the empathy–altruism hypothesis (Batson, 1990a; Batson et al., 1988). If a person has empathic feelings and truly cares about the person in need, rationalizations, however strong, do not stop him or her from helping.

Yet another challenge to the empathy–altruism hypothesis comes from research by Robert Cialdini and his colleagues. Cialdini suggested that the data supporting the empathy–altruism hypothesis can be reinterpreted with changes in one's sense of self that occur in empathy situations. Cialdini and colleagues argued that in addition to arousing empathic concern about a person in distress, helping situations also arouse a greater sense of self–other overlap. Specifically, the helper sees more of himself or herself in the person

---

empathy–punishment hypothesis

A hypothesis suggesting that helping occurs because individuals are motivated to avoid the guilt or shame brought about by failure to help.

in need (Cialdini, Brown, Lewis, Luce, & Neuberg, 1997). When this occurs, the helper may engage in helping because of a greater sense of closeness with the victim than with the arousal of empathic concern alone.

Cialdini and colleagues (1997) conducted three experiments to test the self–other oneness hypothesis. They found that when the self–other oneness dimension was considered along with empathy arousal, the relationship between empathy and altruism was weakened substantially. Furthermore, they found that empathy increases altruism only if it results in an increase in self–other oneness. According to Cialdini and colleagues empathic concern for a victim serves as an emotional cue for the increase in self–other oneness. Additionally, as suggested by Steven Neuberg and colleagues, because empathy is an emotion, it may only be important in deciding between not helping or providing minimal or superficial help (Newberg, Cialdini, Brown, Luce, & Sagarin, 1997).

However, the matter was not resolved, because Batson (1997) pointed out that the methods used by Cialdini and colleagues were questionable. In fact, Batson and colleagues (1997) found that when more careful procedures were used, there was little evidence that self–other oneness was critical in mediating the empathy–altruism link. As to whether empathy arousal leads only to superficial helping, Batson pointed out that the empathy–altruism hypothesis only states that empathy arousal is often associated with an altruistic act and does not specify the depth of the act. Batson, however, does acknowledge that there may be limits to the empathy–altruism relationship.

Where do we stand currently on these hypotheses about helping? Although the research of Batson and others supports the empathy–altruism hypothesis (Batson et al., 1988; Dovidio et al., 1990), other research does not. For example, a strong relationship has been found between feeling and giving help, a finding that does not support the empathy–altruism hypothesis (Cialdini & Fultz, 1990). If we give help when we feel sad, it seems more likely that we are helping to relieve personal distress than out of pure altruism.

It is apparent that the empathy–altruism hypothesis remains a point of controversy in social psychology. Batson (1997) suggested that the controversy exists mainly over whether there is enough clear evidence to justify acceptance of the empathy–altruism hypothesis. There is agreement, according to Batson, that empathy can be a factor in altruistic behavior. At this point, it is probably best to adopt a position between the competing hypotheses. People may be motivated by empathic altruism, but they seem to need to know that the victim benefitted from their help (Smith, Keating, & Stotland, 1989). This allows them to experience *empathic joy* for helping the victim. Empathic joy simply means that helpers feel good about the fact that their efforts helped someone and that there was a positive outcome for that person. Helpers get a reward, the knowledge that someone they helped benefitted. Additionally, helping situations may arouse a greater sense of closeness or oneness with the helper and the victim. In any event, empathy does appear to be an important emotion involved in altruism.

Biological Explanations: Helping in Order to Preserve Our Own Genes

As mentioned earlier, some psychologists have been skeptical about the existence of purely altruistic behavior, because they believe behavior is shaped and regulated by rewards and punishments. But there is another reason psychologists have been skeptical about the existence of pure altruism, and that reason is biological: People or animals who carry altruism involving personal danger to its logical conclusion, as Conklin did, die. Because self-preservation, or at least the preservation of one's genes (i.e., one's children or relatives), is a fundamental rule of evolutionary biology, pure altruism stands on some shaky grounds (Wilson, 1978). Self-sacrificing behavior is very rare. When it occurs, we reward it extravagantly. The Medal of Honor, for example, is given for extraordinary bravery, behavior that goes beyond the call of duty.

Evolutionary biologists find altruistic behavior fascinating, because it presents a biological paradox: In light of the principle of survival of the fittest, how can a behavior have evolved that puts the individual at risk and makes survival less likely (Wilson, 1975)? The principle of natural selection favors selfish behavior. Those animals that take care of themselves and do not expend energy on helping others are more likely to survive and reproduce their genes. The basic measure of biological fitness is the relative number of an individual's offspring that survive and reproduce (Wilson, 1975).

The evolutionary biologist's answer to the paradox is to suggest that there are no examples of purely altruistic, totally selfless behavior in nature. Instead, there is behavior that may have the effect of helping others but also serves some selfish purpose. For example, consider the white-fronted bee eater, a bird living in eastern and southern Africa (Goleman, 1991b). These birds live in complex colonies consisting of 15 to 25 extended families. Family units consist of about four overlapping generations. When breeding time arrives, some family members do not breed. Instead, they serve as helpers, who devote themselves to constructing nests, feeding females, and defending the young. This helping is called *alloparenting*, or cooperative breeding.

How could such behavior have evolved? The bee eaters who do not breed lose the opportunity to pass on their genes to offspring. However, their behavior does help to ensure the survival of the whole colony and, specifically, the family members with whom they share genes. This conclusion is supported by the fact that the bee eater helpers provide cooperative help only to their closest relatives. Birds that could have provided help but do not turn out to be "in-laws"—birds that have no genetic connection with the mating pairs. Although the helping behavior does not further the survival of the individual's genes, it serves to preserve the individual's gene pool.

Do humans differ significantly from animals when it comes to altruism? According to sociobiologists, human social behavior is governed by the same rules that order all animal behavior. A central problem of sociobiology is to explain how altruism can exist even though such behavior endangers individual fitness and survival (Wilson, 1975, 1978). However, there is ample evidence that altruism among humans flourishes and endures.

One possible resolution to this apparent paradox lies in the idea that human survival, dating to the beginnings of human society, depends on cooperation. Human beings, smaller, slower, and weaker than many other animal species, needed to form cooperative groups to survive. In such groups *reciprocal altruism* may be more important than *kin altruism*. In reciprocal altruism, the costs of behaving altruistically are weighed against the benefits. If there is greater benefit than cost, an altruistic response will occur. Also, reciprocal altruism involves a kind of tit-for-tat mentality. You help me, and I'll help you.

Cooperation and reciprocal altruism (helping one another) would have been selected for, genetically, because they increased the survival of human beings (Hoffman, 1981). Unlike animals, humans do not restrict their helping to close genetic relatives. Instead, humans can maintain the gene pool by helping those who share common characteristics, even if they are not close kin (Glassman, Packel, & Brown, 1986). Helping nonkin may help one preserve one's distinguishing characteristics in the gene pool in a manner analogous to helping kin.

Social psychologists acknowledge that biology plays a role in altruistic behavior. Altruism does not occur as often or as naturally as aggression, but it does occur. However, social psychology also points out that altruistic behavior in humans is determined by more than the biological dimension of our nature.

Reprise: Why Do We Help?

Why did Seth Conklin go to such extraordinary lengths to help Peter Still and his family? Still was not his kin, so Conklin was not motivated by the urge to protect his gene pool. Nor was he motivated simply by a desire to reduce his own personal distress on reading about Still's predicament, although we can be sure that Conklin felt emotional pain. He could have relieved his distress by putting the paper down and going on about his life. He probably wasn't motivated by what his neighbors would say either, because most of them were able to live with Still's story.

No, Conklin must have been motivated by altruistic empathy, by compassionate understanding of how Still felt. Conklin simply knew that he had to help. Altruistic behavior, as noted earlier, does occur. But the extraordinary long-term helping exemplified by Conklin needs further explanation. We return to this issue a bit later in the chapter.

HELPING IN EMERGENCIES: A FIVE-STAGE DECISION MODEL

Conklin's decision to help Still's family is an example of helping involving a long-term commitment to a course of action. We refer to this as long-term helping. Conklin's help involved a commitment that was extended over a period of months and required a great investment of effort and resources. However, there are many other situations that require quick action involving a short-term commitment to helping. For example, if you saw a child fall into a pond, you probably would rescue that child. We refer to this type of helping as situation-specific helping. This helping, most likely in response to an emergency, does not require a long-term investment of effort and resources.

Emergency situations in which bystanders give help occur quite often. But there are also many instances in which bystanders remain passive and do not intervene, even when a victim is in clear need of help. One such incident captured the attention not only of the public but also of social psychologists: the tragic death of Kitty Genovese on March 13, 1964.

Genovese, a 24-year-old waitress, was coming home from work in Queens, New York, late one night. As she walked to her apartment building, she was attacked by a man wielding a knife. She screamed for help; 38 of her neighbors took notice from their apartments. One yelled for the man to stop. The attacker ran off, only to return when it was obvious that nobody was coming to her aid. He stabbed Genovese repeatedly, eventually killing her. The attack lasted 40 minutes. When the police were called, they responded within 2 minutes. More than 35 years later, this tragedy continues to raise questions about why her neighbors did not respond to her cries for help.

The Genovese tragedy and similar incidents that occur all too frequently have raised many questions among the public and among social scientists. Dissatisfied with explanations that blamed life in the big city ("urban apathy"), social psychologists John Darley and Bibb Latané began to devise some explanations about why the witnesses to Genovese's murder did nothing to intervene. Darley and Latané sketched out a social psychological model to explain the bystanders' behavior.

The model proposed that there are five stages a bystander must pass through, each representing an important decision, before he or she will help a person in need (Latané, & Darley, 1968). In their original formulation of the model, Latané and Darley (1968) suggested that a bystander must notice the situation, label the situation correctly as an emergency, and assume responsibility for helping. Darley and Latané proposed that there is a factor even beyond assuming responsibility: The individual must decide how to help. Help, according to these researchers, could take the form of direct intervention (Conklin's behavior) or indirect intervention (calling the police). The general model proposed by Latané and Darley (1968; Darley & Latané, 1968) along with an additional stage, is shown in Figure 11.3.

At each stage of the model, the individual must assess the situation and make a yes or no decision. At any point in the decision process, a no decision

Figure 11.3

The five-stage model of helping. The path to helping begins with noticing an emergency situation. Next, a potential helper must label the situation correctly as an emergency and then assume responsibility for helping. A negative decision at any point will lead to nonhelping.

Based on Darley and Latane (1968) and Latane and Darley (1968). Reprinted with permission.

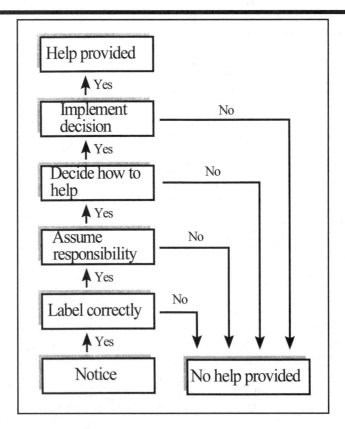

will lead to failure to help. A yes decision itself does not guarantee intervention; it simply allows the person to move to the next stage of the model. According to the model, help will be given only if a yes decision is made at each stage. Let's consider each of the five stages.

1. Noticing the Situation

Before we can expect a person to intervene in a situation, that person must have noticed that an emergency exists. In general, we are particularly likely to notice a stimulus that is brightly colored, noisy, or somehow stands out against a background. This is also true when noticing an emergency. Our chances of noticing an emergency increase if it stands out against the background of everyday life. For example, we are more likely to notice an automobile accident if there is a loud crash than if there is little or no sound. Anything that makes the emergency more conspicuous will increase the probability that we will attend to it.

2. Labeling the Situation as an Emergency

If a person notices the situation, the next step is to correctly label it as one that requires intervention. One very important factor at this stage is whether there is ambiguity or uncertainty about what has happened. For example, imagine that you look out the window of your second-floor apartment one day and notice immediately below the window a car with its driver's side door open and a person lying half in and half out of the car. Has the person collapsed, perhaps of a heart attack or a stroke? Or is the person changing a fuse under the dashboard or fixing the radio? If you decide on the latter explanation, you will turn away and not give it another thought. You have made a no decision in the labeling stage of the model.

Recognizing in emergency situation can be highly ambiguous because there is often more than one interpretation for a situation. Is the woman upstairs beating her child or merely disciplining her? Is the man staggering down the street sick or drunk? Is that person slumped in the doorway injured or a drunken derelict? These questions must be resolved if we are to correctly label a situation as an emergency requiring our intervention.

When two 10-year-old boys abducted a 2-year-old from a shopping center in Liverpool, England in 1993 and subsequently killed him, they walked together $2\frac{1}{2}$ miles along a busy road congested with traffic. Thirty-eight people remembered seeing the three children, and some said later that the toddler was being dragged or appeared to be crying. Apparently, the situation was ambiguous enough—were they his older brothers, trying to get him home for dinner?—that no one stopped. A driver of a dry-cleaning van said he saw one of the older boys aim a kick at the toddler, but it looked like a "persuading" kind of kick such as one might use on a 2-year-old (Morrison, 1994). The driver failed to label the situation correctly.

THE AMBIGUITY OF THE SITUATION   Research confirms that situational ambiguity is an important factor in whether people help. In one study, subjects were seated in a room and asked to fill out a questionnaire (Yakimovich & Salz, 1971). Outside the room, a confederate of the experimenter was washing windows. When the experimenter signaled, the confederate knocked over his ladder and pail, fell to the pavement, and grabbed his ankle. In one condition (the verbalization condition), the confederate

Emergency situations are often unclear. How one labels a situation is important in determining whether someone in need will get help. Is this man taking a nap? Is he drunk? Or, has he had a heart attack? If you label this situation as the person "taking a nap," you are less likely to render assistance than if you label the situation as a possible "heart attack."

screamed and cried for help. In the other condition (the no-verbalization condition), the confederate moaned but didn't cry for help.

In both conditions, subjects jumped up and went to the window when they heard the sound of the crash. Therefore, all subjects noticed the emergency. In the verbalization condition, 81% (13 of 16) tried to help the victim. In the no-verbalization condition, however, only 29% (5 of 17) subjects tried to help. The clear cry for help, then, increased the probability that people would help. Without it, it wasn't clear that the man needed help.

Note also that the potential helpers had all seen the victim before his accident. He was a real person to them. Recall in the Genovese case that the witnesses had not seen her before she was stabbed. Given this fact and that the murder took place in the fog of the early morning hours, ambiguity must have existed, at least for some witnesses.

THE PRESENCE OF OTHERS The presence of other bystanders also may affect the labeling process. Reactions of other bystanders often determine the response to the situation. If bystanders show little concern over the emergency, individuals will be less likely to help. When we are placed in a social situation (especially an ambiguous one), we look around us to see what others are doing (the process of social comparison). If others are not concerned, we may not define the situation as an emergency, and we probably will not offer to help.

In one study, increasing or decreasing the availability of cues from another bystander affected helping (Darley, Teger, & Lewis, 1973). Subjects were tested either alone or in groups of two. Those participating in groups were either facing each other across a table (face-to-face condition) or seated back-to-back (not-facing condition). An emergency was staged (a fall) while the subjects worked on their tasks. More subjects who were alone helped (90%) than subjects who were in groups. However, whether subjects were facing each other made a big difference. Subjects who were facing each other were significantly more likely to help (80%) than subjects not facing each other (20%). Consider what happens when you sit across from someone and you both hear a cry for help. You look at her, she looks at you. If she then goes back to her work, you probably will not define the situation as an emergency. If she says, "Did you hear that?" you are more likely to go investigate.

Generally, we rely on cues from other bystanders more and more as the ambiguity of the situation increases. Thus, in highly ambiguous emergency situations, we might expect the presence of others who are passive to suppress helping. The fact that the witnesses to Genovese's murder were in their separate apartments and did not know what others were doing and thinking operated to suppress intervention.

3. Assuming Responsibility to Help: The Bystander Effect

Noticing and correctly labeling a situation as an emergency are not enough to guarantee that a bystander will intervene. It is certain that the 38 witnesses to Genovese's murder noticed the incident and probably labeled it as an emergency. What they did not do is conclude that they had a responsibility to help. Darley and Latané (1968), puzzled by the lack of intervention on the part of the witnesses, thought that the presence of others might inhibit rather than increase helping. They designed a simple yet elegant experiment to test for the effects of multiple bystanders on helping. Their experiment demonstrated the power of the **bystander effect,** in which a person in need of help is less likely to receive help as the number of bystanders increases.

bystander effect
The social phenomenon that helping behavior is less likely to occur as the number of witnesses to an emergency increases.

Subjects in this experiment were told it was a study of interpersonal communication. They were asked to participate in a group discussion of their current problems. To ensure anonymity, the discussion took place over intercoms. In reality, there was no group. The experimenter played a tape of a discussion to lead the subject to believe that other group members existed.

Darley and Latané (1968) varied the size of the group. In one condition, the subject was told that there was one other person in the group (so the

One would think that help would be more likely in a crowded place, like this train station, than in a place with few people. However, what really happens is help is less likely when there are many bystanders around than if there is only one. This is known as the bystander effect.

group consisted of the subject and the victim); in a second condition, there were two other people (subject, victim, and four others). The discussion went along uneventfully until it was the victim's turn to speak. The actor who played the role of the victim on the tape simulated a seizure. Darley and Latané noted the number of subjects who tried to help and how long it took them to try to help.

The study produced two major findings. First, the size of the group had an effect on the percentage of subjects helping. When the subject believed that he or she was alone in the experiment with the victim, 85% of the subjects helped. The percentage of subjects offering help declined when the subject believed there was one other bystander (62%) or four other bystanders (31%). In other words, as the number of bystanders increased, the likelihood of the subject helping the victim decreased.

The second major finding was that the size of the group had an effect on time between the onset of the seizure and the offering of help. When the subject believed he or she was alone, help occurred more quickly than when the subject believed other bystanders were present. In essence, the subjects who believed they were members of a larger group became "frozen in time" by the presence of others. They had not decided to help or not to help. They were distressed but could not act.

WHY DOES THE BYSTANDER EFFECT OCCUR?

diffusion of responsibility
An explanation suggesting that each bystander assumes another person will take responsibility to help.

The best explanation offered for the bystander effect is **diffusion of responsibility** (Darley & Latané, 1968). According to this explanation, each bystander assumes that another bystander will take action. If all the bystanders think that way, no help will be offered. This explanation fits quite well with Darley and Latané's findings in which the bystanders could not see each other, as was the case in the Genovese killing. Under these conditions, it is easy to see how a bystander (unaware of how other bystanders are acting) might assume that someone else has already taken or will take action.

pluralistic ignorance
An explanation suggesting that an individual who is uncertain about what to do in an emergency situation notes how others are reacting; if others act as though no emergency exists, the bystander will not intervene to help the victim.

What about emergency situations in which bystanders can see one another? In this case, the bystanders could actually see that others were not helping. Diffusion of responsibility under these conditions may not explain bystander inaction (Latané & Darley, 1968). Another explanation has been offered for the bystander effect that centers on **pluralistic ignorance,** which occurs when a group of individuals acts in the same manner despite the fact that each person has different perceptions of an event (Miller & McFarland, 1987). In the bystander effect, pluralistic ignorance operates when the bystanders in an ambiguous emergency situation look around and see each other doing nothing; they assume that the others are thinking that the situation is not an emergency (Miller & McFarland, 1987). In essence, the collective inaction of the bystanders leads to a redefinition of the situation as a nonemergency.

Latané and Darley (1968) provided evidence for this explanation. Subjects filled out a questionnaire alone in a room, with two passive bystanders (confederates of the experimenter) or with two other actual subjects. While the subjects were filling out the questionnaire, smoke was introduced into the room through a vent. The results showed that when subjects were alone in the room, 75% of the subjects reported the smoke, many within 2 minutes of first noticing it. In the condition in which the subject was in the room with two passive bystanders, only 10% reported the smoke. In the last condition, in which the subject was with two other subjects, 38% reported the smoke. Thus, the presence of bystanders once again suppressed helping. This occurred despite the fact that subjects in the bystander conditions denied that the other people in the room had any effect on them.

In postexperimental interviews, Latané and Darley (1968) searched for the underlying cause for the observed results. They found that subjects who reported the smoke felt that the smoke was unusual enough to report, although they didn't feel that the smoke was dangerous. Subjects who failed to report the smoke, which was most likely to occur in the two-bystander conditions, developed a set of creative reasons why the smoke should not be reported. For example, some subjects believed that the smoke was smog piped into the room to simulate an urban environment, or that the smoke was truth gas designed to make them answer the questionnaire truthfully. Whatever reasons these subjects came up with, the situation was redefined as a nonemergency.

EXCEPTIONS TO THE BYSTANDER EFFECT Increasing the number of bystanders does not always suppress helping; there are exceptions to the bystander effect. One group of researchers staged a rape on a college campus and measured how many subjects intervened (Harari, Harari, & White, 1985). The subjects had three options in the experimental situation: fleeing without helping, giving indirect help (alerting a police officer who is out of view of the rape), or giving direct help (intervening directly in the rape). Figure 11.4 on p. 422 shows the experimental situation and the various paths available to subjects.

Male subjects were tested as they walked either alone or in groups. (The groups in this experiment were simply subjects who happened to be walking together and not interacting with one another.) As the subjects approached a certain point (see Figure 11.4 on p. 422), two actors staged the rape. The woman screamed, "Help! Help! Please help me! You bastard! Rape! Rape!" (Harari et al., 1985, p. 656). The results of this experiment did not support the bystander effect. Subjects walking in groups were more likely to help (85%) than subjects walking alone (65%). In this situation—a victim is clearly in need and the helping situation is dangerous—it seems that bystanders in groups are more likely to help than solitary bystanders (Clark & Word, 1974; Harari et al., 1985).

The bystander effect also seems to be influenced by the roles people take. In another study, some subjects were assigned to be the leaders of a group discussion and others to be assistants (Baumeister, Chesner, Senders, & Tice, 1988). When a seizure was staged, subjects assigned the role of leader were more likely to intervene (80%) than those assigned the role of assistant (35%). It appears that the responsibility inherent in the leadership role on a specific task generalizes to emergencies as well.

4. Deciding How to Help

The fourth stage of the five-stage model of helping is deciding how to help. In the staged rape study, for example, subjects had a choice of directly intervening to stop the rape or aiding the victim by notifying the police (Harari, Harari, & White, 1985). What influences decisions like this?

There is considerable support for the notion that people who feel competent, who have the necessary skills, are more likely to help than those who

Figure 11.4

The setup for a field experiment on helping. A rape was staged in front of participants either walking alone or in noninteracting groups. The results showed that more participants helped when walking in a group than when alone.

From Harari, Harari, and White (1985). Reprinted with permission.

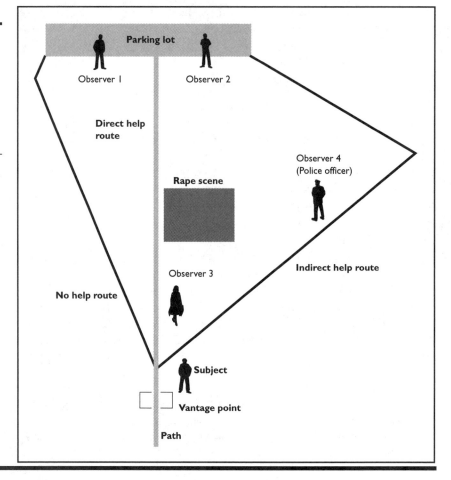

feel they lack such competence. In a study in which subjects were exposed to a staged arterial bleeding emergency, the likelihood of providing effective help was determined only by the expertise of the subjects (some had Red Cross training; Shotland & Heinhold, 1985).

There are two reasons why greater competence may lead to more helping. First, feelings of competence increase confidence in one's ability to help and knowledge of what ought to be done (Cramer, McMaster, Bartell, & Dragna, 1988). Second, feelings of competence increase sensitivity to the needs of others and empathy toward victims (Barnett, Thompson, & Pfiefer, 1985). People who feel like leaders are probably also more likely to help because they feel more confident about being able to help successfully.

Many emergencies, however, do not require any special training or competence. Conklin had no more competence in rescuing slave families than anyone else in Philadelphia. In the Genovese case, a simple telephone call to the police was all that was needed. Clearly, no special competence was required.

5. Implementing the Decision to Help

Having passed through these four stages, a person may still choose not to intervene. To understand why, imagine that as you drive to campus you see a fellow student standing next to his obviously disabled car. Do you stop and offer to help? Perhaps you are late for your next class and you feel that you do not have the time. Perhaps you are not sure it is safe to stop on the side of the highway. Or perhaps the student strikes you as somehow undeserving of help (Bickman & Kamzan, 1973). These and other considerations influence your decision whether to help.

ASSESSING REWARDS AND COSTS FOR HELPING   Social psychologists have found that people's evaluation of the rewards and costs involved in helping affect their decision to help or not to help. There are potential rewards for helping (gratitude from the victim, monetary reward, recognition by peers) and for not helping (avoiding potential danger, arriving for an appointment on time). Similarly, there are costs for helping (possible injury, embarrassment, inconvenience) and for not helping (loss of self-esteem). Generally, research indicates that the greater the cost of helping, the less likely people are to help (Batson, O'Quin, Fultz, & Vanderplas, 1983; Darley & Batson, 1973; Piliavin & Piliavin, 1972; Piliavin, Piliavin, & Rodin, 1975).

In a study of this relationship, Darley and Batson (1973) told seminarians taking part in an experiment at Princeton University that a high school group was visiting the campus and had requested a seminarian speaker. Half the subjects were told they had little time to get across campus to speak to the high school group, and the other half were told they had plenty of time. Additionally, some subjects were asked to speak about the meaning of the parable of the good Samaritan. The seminarians then left the building to give their talk, and lo and behold, while walking down a narrow lane, they saw a young man collapse in front of them. What did they do?

Now, do you recall the story of the good Samaritan? A traveler is set on by robbers and left by the side of the road. A priest and a Levite, people holding important positions in the clergy of the time, walked by swiftly without helping. But a Samaritan, passing along the same road, stopped and helped. We might say that, for whatever reasons, helping was too costly for the priest and the Levite but not too costly for the Samaritan.

What about the seminarians? The "costly" condition in this experiment was the tight schedule: Stopping to help would make them late for their talk. Was helping too costly for them? Yes, it was. Subjects who were in a hurry, even if they were thinking about the story of the good Samaritan, were less likely to stop and help than were subjects who were not in a hurry.

THE EFFECT OF MOOD ON HELPING   Likelihood of helping can even be affected by the bystander's mood. The research of Alice Isen (1987) and her co-workers has shown that adults and children who are in a positive mood are more likely to help others than people who are not. People who had found a dime in a phone booth in a shopping mall were more likely to pick up papers dropped by a stranger than people who had not found a coin. Students who had gotten free cookies in the library were more likely to volunteer to help someone and were less likely to volunteer to annoy somebody else when asked to do so as part of an experiment.

Although positive mood is related to an increase in helping, it does not lead to more helping if the person thinks that helping will destroy the good mood (Isen & Simmonds, 1978). Good moods seem to generate good thoughts about people, and this increases helping. People in good moods also are less concerned with themselves and more likely to be sensitive to other people, making them more aware of other people's needs and therefore more likely to help (Isen, 1987).

CHARACTERISTICS OF THE VICTIM   A decision to help (or not to help) also is affected by the victim's characteristics. For example, males are more likely to help females than to help other males (Eagly & Crowley, 1986; West, Whitney, & Schnedler, 1975). Females, on the other hand, are equally likely to help male and female victims (Early & Crowley, 1986). Physically attractive people are more likely to receive help than unattractive people (Benson, Karabenick, & Lerner, 1976). In one study, a pregnant woman, whether alone or with another woman, received more help than a nonpregnant woman or a facially disfigured woman (Walton et al., 1988).

Just-World Hypothesis   Potential helpers also make judgments about whether a victim deserves help. If we perceive that a person got into a situation through his or her own negligence and is therefore responsible for his or her own fate, we tend to generate "just-world" thinking (Lerner & Simmons, 1966). According to the **just-world hypothesis,** people get what they deserve and deserve what they get. This type of thinking often leads us to devalue a person whom we think caused his or her own misfortune (Lerner & Simmons, 1966). Generally, we give less help to victims we perceive to have contributed to their own fate than to those we perceive as needy through no fault of their own (Berkowitz, 1969; Schopler & Matthews, 1965).

However, we may relax this exacting standard if we perceive that the person in need is highly dependent on our help. In one experiment, subjects received telephone calls at home in which the caller mistook them for the owner of "Ralph's Garage" and told them that her car had broken down (Gruder, Romer, & Korth, 1978). The caller says either that she meant to have the car serviced but forgot (help needed due to victim's negligence) or that the car was just serviced (no negligence). In one condition, after the subject informs the caller that she has not reached Ralph's Garage, the caller says that she has no more change to make another call (high dependency). In another condition, no mention is made of being out of change. In all conditions the caller asks the subject to call Ralph's Garage for her. The researchers found that subjects were more likely to help the negligent victim who had no more change than the negligent victim who presumably had other ways to get help (Figure 11.5). It seems that high dependence mediates just-world thinking. Regardless of whether the victim deserves what she gets, we can't help but take pity on her.

Just-world thinking also comes into play when we consider the degree to which a victim contributed to his or her own predicament. If you, as a helper, attribute a victim's suffering to his or her own actions (i.e., make an internal attribution), you will be less likely to help than if you attribute the suffering to some external cause (Schmidt & Weiner, 1988). When making judgments about individuals in need of help, we take into account the degree to which the victim had control over his or her fate (Schmidt & Weiner, 1988). For example, Greg Schmidt and Bernard Weiner (1988) found that subjects expressed less willingness to help a student in need of class notes if he needed the notes because he went to the beach instead of class (a controllable situation) than if he had medically related vision problems that prevented him from taking notes (uncontrollable situation).

just-world hypothesis
A hypothesis that we believe people get what they deserve and deserve what they get.

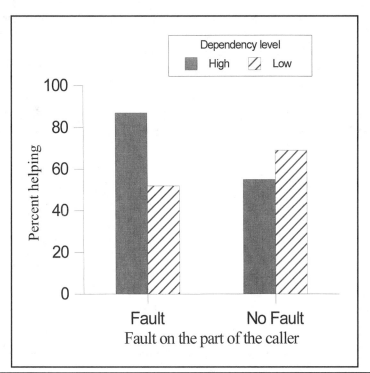

Figure 11.5

The effect of dependency and victim fault on helping. In Gruder's "Ralph's Garage" experiment, participants were more likely to help a victim high in dependency who was at fault for his predicament.

Based on data from Gruder, Romer, and Kroth (1974).

Why do perceptions of controllability matter? Schmidt and Weiner (1988) reported that the emotions aroused are important factors in one's reaction to a person in need. If a victim's situation arouses anger, as in the controllable situation, we are less likely to give help than if the victim's situation arouses sympathy (as in the uncontrollable situation). Apparently, we are quite harsh when it comes to a victim whom we perceive as having contributed to his or her own plight. We reserve our sympathy for those victims who had little or no control over their own fates.

In an interesting application of this effect, Bernard Weiner and his colleagues (Graham, Weiner, Giuliano, & Williams, 1993; Weiner, 1993; Weiner, Perry, & Magnusson, 1988) have applied this analysis to victims of various illnesses. Subjects tended to react with pity (and less anger) toward victims of conditions over which the victims had little control (Alzheimer's disease, cancer). Conversely, subjects tended to react with anger (and less pity) for victims of supposedly controllable conditions (AIDS, obesity; Weiner, 1993; Weiner et al., 1988). The emotion tied to the victim's situation (pity versus anger) mediated willingness to help. Subjects indicated less willingness to help victims with controllable problems than those with uncontrollable problems (Weiner et al., 1988). Additionally, subjects assigned greater responsibility to a person with a disease (AIDS) if the victim's behavior was perceived to have contributed to his or her disease than if the victim's behavior was not perceived to have contributed. For example, if a person with AIDS contracted the disease via a blood transfusion, less responsibility is assigned to the victim than if the person contracted the disease via a sexual route (Graham et al., 1993).

Does this concept of the deserving versus the nondeserving victim hold across cultures? In an interesting study conducted by Elizabeth Mullen and

Linda Stitka (2000), U.S. and Ukranian participants were compared. Participants read profiles about individuals who needed organ transplants. Half the individuals were portrayed as having contributed to their own problems (practicing poor health behaviors), whereas the other half were said to have their condition because of a genetic disorder. Two other variables were manipulated. One was the degree to which the individual needing the transplant contributed to society (high or low), and the other was the degree of need for the new organ (i.e., 95% versus 80% chance of dying if a transplant was not performed). Mullen and Stitka found clear evidence for a cultural difference in the variables that mediate helping. United States participants mainly based their helping decisions on the degree to which an individual contributed to his or her own problems. That is, less help is likely to be given to the person who practiced poor health habits than to the person who suffers from a genetic disorder. Ukranian participants, on the other hand, placed more weight on one's contributions to society than to the other factors. However, both American and Ukranian participants were influenced by the other variables. United States participants were influenced by contribution to society and need, in that order, following personal responsibility. Ukranian participants also were influenced by personal responsibility and need, in that order, after contributions to society.

Finally, there is evidence that characteristics of the helper may interact with perceived controllability in determining affective responses to victims and helping behavior. In an analysis of reactions to individuals living in poverty, Gail Zucker and Bernard Weiner (1993) found that politically conservative individuals were likely to blame the victim for being in poverty, attributing poverty to characteristics of the victim. Consequently, these individuals tend to react with anger and are less willing to help. On the other hand, more liberal individuals see poverty as driven by societal forces, not under control of the victim, and react with pity and are more willing to help.

Race and helping behavior   Another characteristic of the victim investigated by social psychologists is race. Are blacks more or less likely than whites to receive help when they need it? If you base your answer on stories on television and in the newspapers, you might think that blacks and whites in our society never help each other. But this is simply not true. Recall from chapter 1 that many blacks risked their lives to save whites during the Los Angeles riots in 1992. A group of African-American residents of South Central Los Angeles helped get Reginald Denny to the hospital, saving his life. Interracial helping does occur. What does the social psychological research say about this issue?

Numerous studies have been conducted to investigate aspects of interracial helping (Benson, Karabenick, & Lerner, 1976; Dovidio & Gaertner, 1981; Gaertner, Dovidio, & Johnson, 1982) In one, for example, white subjects, assessed as either high or low in prejudice, were given an opportunity to help either a black or a white victim (Gaertner et al., 1982). The subjects were either alone (subject and victim) or with four others (three bystanders and the victim). The researchers recorded the amount of time subjects took to give the victim aid. Their results showed that white victims were helped more quickly than black victims, especially by prejudiced subjects, when bystanders were present. Blacks and whites were helped equally quickly when no bystanders were present. Thus, the bystander effect is stronger for black than for white victims (Gaertner & Dovidio, 1977; Gaertner et al., 1982).

Given the opportunity to diffuse responsibility, bystanders will avail themselves of the opportunity more with black than with white victims (Gaertner & Dovidio, 1977) This may occur because when multiple by-standers are present, a black victim is seen as less severely injured than a white victim (Gaertner, 1975). When there is a single bystander, there is no such differential assessment of injury severity (Gaertner, 1975).

Other factors also influence the help given to black versus white victims. In another study, white subjects were given an opportunity to help either a black or white male (Dovidio & Gaertner, 1981). This person was introduced as the subject's "supervisor" or "subordinate" and was said to be of either higher or lower cognitive ability than the subject. When given an opportunity to help, white subjects helped the black subordinate (lower status) more than the black supervisor (higher status), regardless of the ability level. However, African American subjects gave help based more on ability than on status. According to this study, status is relevant in whites' decision to help blacks, with more help given to lower-status blacks (Dovidio & Gaertner, 1981). Ability is more relevant in blacks' decision to help whites, with more help given to high-ability than low-ability whites.

The relationship between race and helping behavior is complex and involves numerous situational factors as well as racial attitudes. A review of the literature by Crosby, Bromley, and Saxe (1980) found mixed results. These researchers drew three conclusions:

1. Bias exists against African-American victims, but the bias is not extreme. Clear discrimination against African-American victims was reported in 44% of the studies reviewed; 56% showed no discrimination or reverse discrimination.

2. Whites and blacks discriminate against the opposite race at about the same level.

3. Whites discriminate against black victims more under remote conditions (over the telephone) than in face-to-face situations.

In another study, researchers investigated race differences in the level of help given to elderly individuals who lived at home (Morrow-Howell, Lott, & Ozawa, 1990). They analyzed a program in which volunteers were assigned to help elderly clients shop and to provide them with transportation, counseling, and telephone social support. This study found very few differences between black and white volunteers. For example, both black and white volunteers attended training sessions at equal rates and were evaluated equally by their supervisors.

There was, however, one interesting difference between black and white volunteers when the race of the client was considered. According to client reports, volunteers who were of a different race than the client spent less time with clients than did volunteers of the same race. Additionally, when the volunteer and client were of the same race, the client reported that there were more home visits and that the volunteer was more helpful than if the volunteer and client differed in race.

A few cautions are in order here, however. There was no independent measure of the amount of time volunteers spent with clients or the quality of service rendered. The data on the volunteers' performance were based on client reports. It could be that same-race clients were simply more inclined to rate their volunteers positively than were different-race clients. Nevertheless, the study documented a program of helping in which altruistic tendencies transcended racial barriers.

Sexual orientation and helping behavior   Finally, the sexual orientation of a person in need influences willingness to help (Gore, Tobiasen, & Kayson, 1997; Shaw, Bourough, & Fink, 1994). For example, Gore and colleagues (1997) had either a male or female victim make a telephone call to participants. When the participant answered, the victim made it clear that he or she had dialed the wrong number. Implied sexual orientation was manipulated by having the victim tell the participant that he or she was trying to reach his or her boyfriend or girlfriend. They also told the participant that they had either used their last quarter (high urgency) or had no more change (low urgency). Participants were asked to call a number to report the emergency (which was actually the experimenter's number.) The proportion of participants who returned the victim's call to the experimenter within 60 seconds was the measure of helping. The results showed that heterosexuals were more likely to get help (80%) than homosexuals (48%). Additionally, even when homosexuals were helped, it took longer for the participants to call back than when the victim was heterosexual.

INCREASING THE CHANCES OF RECEIVING HELP

We have been looking at helping behavior from the point of view of the potential helper. But what about the person in need of help? Is there anything a victim can do to increase the chances of being helped? Given all the obstacles along the path of helping, it may seem a small miracle that anyone ever receives any help. If you are in a position of needing help, however, there are some things you can do.

First, make your plea for help as loud as possible. Yelling and waving your arms increase the likelihood that others will notice your plight. Make your plea as clear as possible. You do not want to leave any room for doubt that you need help. This will help bystanders correctly label the situation as an emergency.

Next, you want to increase the chances that a bystander will assume responsibility for helping you. Don't count on this happening by itself. Anything you can do to increase a bystander's personal responsibility for helping will increase your chances of getting help. Making eye contact is one way to do this; making a direct request is another.

The effectiveness of the direct-request approach was graphically illustrated in a field experiment in which a confederate of the experimenter approached subjects on a beach (Moriarty, 1975). In one condition, the confederate asked the subject to watch his things (a blanket and a radio) while the confederate went to the boardwalk for a minute (the subject is given responsibility for helping). In another condition, the confederate simply asked the subject for a match (social contact, but no responsibility). A short time after the confederate left, a second confederate came along and took the radio and ran off. More subjects helped in the personal-responsibility condition (some actually ran the second confederate down) than in the nonresponsibility condition. Thus, making someone personally responsible for helping increases helping.

HELPING IN NONEMERGENCIES: SITUATIONAL AND PERSONALITY INFLUENCES

Much of the research on helping behavior that we have discussed suggests that whether people help depends on situational factors. For example, research shows that the costs of helping, the degree of responsibility for helping, the assumed characteristics of the victim, and the dangerousness of the situation all affect helping behavior. None of these factors are under the control of the potential helper; they are part of the situation.

Situational factors seem to be crucial in situations that require spontaneous helping (Clary & Orenstein, 1991). The situations created in the laboratory, or for that matter in the field, are analogous to looking at a single frame in a motion picture. Recall the seminarians. They were in a hurry, and although thinking of the parable of the good Samaritan, they practically leapt over the slumped body of a person in need of their help. Is this unexpected event a fair and representative sample of their behavior? It was for that particular situation. But, unless we look at what comes before and after, we cannot make judgments about how they would behave in other situations. Looking at these single-frame glimpses of helping can lead us to overlook personality variables.

Although personality factors come into play in all forms of altruism, they may be more likely to come to the fore in long-term helping situations. Helping on a long-term basis, whether it involves volunteering at a hospital or Seth Conklin helping the Still family, requires a degree of planning. This planning might take place before the help begins, as was the case for Conklin. Or it may occur after help begins. For example, rescuers of Jews in Nazi-occupied Europe often did not plan their initial helping acts (Tec, 1986). However, their continued helping required thought and planning. During planning, helpers assess risks, costs, and priorities, and they match personal morals and abilities with victims' needs. This is the kind of planned helping Conklin had to do.

History teaches us that in times of great need, a select few individuals emerge to offer long-term help. What is it about these people that sets them apart from others who remain on the sidelines? Perhaps some individuals possess an **altruistic personality,** or a cluster of personality traits, including empathy, that predispose them to great acts of altruism. Although there is evidence for the existence of such a personality cluster (Oliner & Oliner, 1988), we also must remain mindful that situational forces still may be important, even in long-term helping situations. In the sections that follow, we explore how situational factors and personality factors combine to influence altruism. We begin by considering the factors that influenced a relatively small number of individuals to help rescue Jews from the Nazis during their World War II occupation of Europe.

altruistic personality
A cluster of personality traits that predispose a person to acts of altruism.

Righteous Rescuers in Nazi-Occupied Europe

As Hitler's final solution (the systematic extermination of European Jews) progressed, life for Jews in Europe became harder and more dangerous. Although most of Eastern Europe's and many of Western Europe's Jews were murdered, some did survive. Some survived on their own by passing as Christians or leaving their homes ahead of the Nazis. Many, however, survived with the help of non-Jews who risked their lives to help them. The state of Israel recognizes a select group of those who helped Jews for their heroism and designates them **righteous rescuers** (Tec, 1986).

Sadly, not as many individuals emerged as rescuers as one might wish. The number of rescuers is estimated to have been between 50,000 and 500,000, a small percentage of those living under Nazi rule (Oliner & Oliner, 1988). In short, only a minority of people were willing to risk their lives to help others.

It should not be too surprising that the majority did not help the Jews. Those caught helping Jews, even in the smallest way, were subjected to punishment, death in an extermination camp, or summary execution. In other cases, especially in Poland, rescuing Jews amounted to flying in the face of centuries of anti-Semitic attitudes and religious doctrine that identified Jews as the killers of Jesus Christ (Oliner & Oliner, 1988; Tec, 1986). The special problems facing Polish rescuers are illustrated in the following quotation from one: "My husband hated Jews. . . . Anti-Semitism was ingrained in him. Not only was he willing to burn every Jew but even the earth on which they stood. Many Poles feel the way he did. I had to be careful of the Poles" (Tec, 1986, p. 54)

Because Polish rescuers violated such powerful social norms, some social psychologists have suggested that their behavior is an example of **autonomous altruism,** selfless help that society does not reinforce (Tec, 1986). In fact, such altruism may be discouraged by society. Rescuers in countries outside Poland may have been operating from a different motive. Most rescuers in Western Europe, although acting out of empathy for the Jews, may have had a *normocentric motivation* for their first act of helping (Oliner & Oliner, 1988). A normocentric motivation for helping is oriented more toward a group (perhaps society) with whom an individual identifies than toward the individual in need. In small towns in southern France, for example, rescuing Jews became normative, the accepted and expected thing to do. This type of altruism is known as **normative altruism,** altruism that society supports and encourages (Tec, 1986).

The Oliners and the Altruistic Personality Project

One family victimized by the Nazis in Poland was that of Samuel Oliner. One day in 1942, when Samuel was 12 years old and living in the village of Bobawa, he was roused by the sound of soldiers' boots cracking the predawn silence. He escaped to the roof and hid there in his pajamas until they left. When he dared to come down from his rooftop perch, the Jews of Bobawa lay buried in a mass grave. The village was empty.

Two years earlier, Samuel's entire family had been killed by the Nazis. Now he gathered some clothes and walked for 48 hours until he reached the farm of Balwina Piecuch, a peasant woman who had been friendly to his family in the past. The 12-year-old orphan knocked at her door. When Piecuch saw Samuel, she gathered him into her house. There she harbored him against the Nazis, teaching him what he needed to know of the Christian religion to pass as a Polish stable boy.

---

righteous rescuers
The designation bestowed by Israel on non-Jews who helped save Jews from the Nazis during World War II.

autonomous altruism
Selfless altruism that society does not support or might even discourage.

normative altruism
Altruism that society supports and encourages.

Oliner survived the war, immigrated to the United States, and went on to teach at Humboldt State University in Arcata, California. One of his courses was on the Holocaust. In it, he examined the fate of the millions of Jews, Gypsies, and other Europeans who were systematically murdered by the Nazis between 1939 and 1945. In 1978, one of his students, a German woman, became distraught, saying she couldn't bear the guilt over what her people had done.

At this point, Oliner realized that the history of the war, a story of murder, mayhem, and sadism, had left out a small but important aspect: the accomplishments of the many altruistic people who acted to help Jews and did so without expectation of external rewards (Goldman, 1988; Oliner & Oliner, 1988). Oliner and his wife, Pearl, established the Altruistic Personality Project to study the character and motivations of those altruists, whom the Oliners rightly call heroes.

Situational Factors Involved in Becoming a Rescuer

Oliner and Oliner (1988) and Nechama Tec (1986) investigated the situational forces that influence individuals to become rescuers. These situational factors can be captured in the five questions for which the Oliners wanted to find answers:

1. Did rescuers know more about the difficulties the Jews faced than nonrescuers?
2. Were rescuers better off financially and therefore better able to help?
3. Did rescuers have social support for their efforts?
4. Did rescuers adequately evaluate the risks, the costs of helping?
5. Were rescuers asked to help, or did they initiate helping on their own?

The Oliners interviewed rescuers and a matched sample of nonrescuers over the course of a 5-year study and compared the two groups. The Oliners used a 66-page questionnaire, translated into Polish, German, French, Dutch, Italian, and Norwegian and used 28 bilingual interviews. Results indicate that the situational differences between rescuers and nonrescuers were not as significant as expected. For example, rescuers were not wealthier then nonrescuers. Tec (1986) reported that the greatest number of Polish helpers came from the peasant class, not the upper class of Poles. Additionally, rescuers and nonrescuers alike knew about the persecution of the Jews and knew the risks involved in going to their aid (Oliner & Oliner, 1988).

Only two situational variables are relevant to the decision to rescue. First, family support was important for the rescue effort (Tec, 1986). Sixty percent of the rescuers in Tec's sample reported that their families supported the rescue effort, compared to only 12% who said that their families opposed rescue efforts, a finding mirrored in Oliner and Oliner's study. Evidence suggests that rescue was made more likely by the rescuers' being affiliated with a group that supported the rescue effort (Baron, 1986). We can conclude that support from some outside agency, be it the family or another support group, made rescue more likely.

The second situational factor was how the rescuer first began his or her efforts. In most cases (68%), rescuers helped in response to a specific request to help; only 32% initiated help on their own (Oliner & Oliner, 1988). Tec reported a similar result. For most rescuers the first act of help was unplanned. But once a rescuer agreed to help that first time, he or she was likely to help again. Help was refused in a minority of instances (about 15%), but such refusal was related to specific risks involved in giving help. Most rescuers (61%) helped for 6 months or more (Tec, 1986). And 90% of the people rescuers helped were strangers (Goldman, 1988).

These situational factors—the costs of helping, a request for help, and the support of other bystanders in a group of which the rescuer was a member—also have been identified in research as important in influencing the decision to help.

Personality Factors Involved in Becoming a Rescuer

The results of the work by Oliner and Oliner (1988) suggest that rescuers and nonrescuers differed from each other less by circumstances than by their upbringing and personalities. The Oliners found that rescuers exhibited a strong feeling of personal responsibility for the welfare of other people and a compelling need to act on that felt responsibility. They were moved by the pain of the innocent victims, by their sadness, helplessness, and desperation. Empathy for the victim was an important factor driving this form of altruism. Interestingly, rescuers and nonrescuers did not differ significantly on general measures of empathy. However, they did differ on a particular type of empathy called *emotional empathy*, which centers on one's sensitivity to the pain and suffering of others (Oliner & Oliner, 1988). According to the Oliners, this empathy, coupled with a sense of social responsibility, increased the likelihood that an individual would make and keep a commitment to help.

Beyond empathy, rescuers shared several other characteristics (Tec, 1986). First, they showed an inability to blend in with others in the environment. That is, they tended to be socially marginal, not fitting in very well with others. Second, rescuers exhibited a high level of independence and self-reliance. They were likely to pursue their personal goals even if those goals conflicted with social norms. Third, rescuers had an enduring commitment to helping those in need long before the war began. The war did not make these people altruists; rather, it allowed these individuals to remain altruists in a new situation.

Fourth, rescuers had (and still have) a matter-of-fact attitude about their rescue efforts. During and after the war, rescuers denied that they were heroes, instead saying that they did the only thing they could do. Finally, rescuers had a universalistic view of the needy. That is, rescuers were able to put aside the religion or other characteristics of those they helped. Interestingly, some rescuers harbored anti-Semitic attitudes (Tec, 1986). But they were able to put those prejudices aside and help a person in need. These characteristics, along with high levels of empathy, contributed to the rescuers' decision to help the Jews.

The research on rescuers clearly shows that they differed in significant ways from those who were nonrescuers (Oliner & Oliner, 1988) or paid helpers (Tec, 1986). How can we account for these differences? To answer this question we must look at the family environments in which rescuers were socialized.

Altruism as a Function of Child-Rearing Style

In chapter 10, we established that inept parenting contributes to the development of antisocial behaviors such as aggression. Oliner and Oliner (1988) found that the child-rearing styles used by parents of rescuers contributed to the development of prosocial attitudes and behaviors. The techniques used by parents of rescuers fostered empathy in the rescuers.

Research shows that a parental or adult model who behaves altruistically is more likely to influence children to help than are verbal exhortations to be generous (Bryan & Walbek, 1970). Additionally, verbal reinforcement has a different effect on children's helping, depending on whether a model behaves in a charitable or selfish manner (Midlarsky, Bryan, & Brickman, 1973). Verbal social approval from a selfish model does not increase children's donations. However, social approval from a charitable model does.

Models obviously have a powerful effect on both aggressive and prosocial behaviors. Why, however, do you think that a prosocial model has more effect on younger children than older children? What factors can you think of to explain the fact that a model's behavior is more important than what the model says? Based on what you know about the effect of prosocial models on children's altruism, if you were given the opportunity to design a television character to communicate prosocial ideals, what would that character be like? What would the character say and do to foster prosocial behavior in children? Similarly, what types of models should we be exposing adults to in order to increase helping? Parents of rescuers provided role models for their children that allowed them to develop the positive qualities needed to become rescuers later in life. For example, rescuers (more than nonrescuers) came from families that stressed the universal similarity of all people, despite superficial differences among them (Oliner & Oliner, 1988). Families stressed the aspect of religion that encouraged caring for those in need. Additionally, families of rescuers did not discuss negative stereotypes of Jews, which was more common among families of nonrescuers. As children, then, rescuers were exposed to role models that instilled in them many positive qualities.

It is not enough for parents simply to embrace altruistic values and provide positive role models, however (Staub, 1985); they must also exert firm control over their children. Parents who raise altruistic children coach them to be helpful and firmly teach them how to be helpful (Goleman, 1991a; Stab, 1985). Parents who are warm and nurturant and use reasoning with the child as a discipline technique are more likely to produce an altruistic child than cold, uncaring, punitive parents (Eisenberg & Mussen, 1989). This was certainly true of families of rescuers. Parents of rescuers tended to avoid using physical punishment, using an inductive style that focused on verbal reasoning and explanation.

As important as the family is in the socialization of altruism, it cannot alone account for a child growing up to be an altruistic individual. The child's cognitive development, or his or her capacity to understand the world, also plays a role.

Altruism as a Function of Cognitive Development

As children grow, their ability to think about and understand other people and the world changes. The cognitive perspective focuses on how altruistic behavior develops as a result of changes in the child's thinking skills. To study altruism from this perspective, Nancy Eisenberg presented children with several moral dilemmas that pit one person's welfare against another person's welfare. Here is one example: Bob, a young man who was very good at swimming, was asked to help young crippled children who could not walk to learn to swim so that they could strengthen their legs for walking. Bob was the only one in his town who could do this job well, because only he had both life-saving and teaching experiences. But helping crippled children took much of Bob's free time left after work and school, and Bob wanted to practice hard as often as possible for an upcoming series of important swimming contests. If Bob did not practice swimming in all his free time, his chances of winning the contests and receiving a paid college education or sum of money would be greatly lessened (Eisenberg & Mussen, 1989, p. 124).

The dilemma pits Bob's needs against those of other people. The children in Eisenberg's study were asked several questions about what Bob should do. For example, "Should Bob agree to teach the crippled children? Why?" Based on their responses, children were classified according to Eisenberg's levels of prosocial reasoning. Eisenberg's findings show that as children get older, they are more likely to understand the needs of other people and are less focused on their own selfish concerns. The research suggests that this is a continual process and that people's altruistic thinking and behavior can change throughout life.

The idea that the development of altruism is a lifelong process is supported by the fact that rescuers did not magically become caring and empathic at the outset of the war. Instead, the ethic of caring grew out of their personalities and interpersonal styles, which had developed over the course of their lives. Rescuers were altruistic long before the war (Huneke, 1986; Oliner & Oliner, 1988; Tec, 1986) and tended to remain more altruistic than nonrescuers after the war (Oliner & Oliner, 1988).

Becoming an Altruistic Person

Altruism requires something more than empathy and compassionate values (Staub, 1985). It requires the psychological and practical competence to carry those intentions into action (Goleman, 1991). Goodness, like evil, begins slowly, in small steps. Recall from chapter 7 on social influence that we are often eased into behaviors in small steps (i.e., through the foot-in-the-door technique). In a similar manner, many rescuers eased themselves into their roles as rescuers gradually. People responded to a first request for help and hid someone for a day or two. Once they took that first step, they began to see themselves differently, as the kind of people who rescued the desperate. Altruistic actions changed their self-concept: Because I helped, I must be an altruistic person. As we saw in chapter 2, one way we gain self-knowledge is through observation of our own behavior. We then apply that knowledge to our self-concept.

This is how Swedish diplomat Raoul Wallenberg got involved in rescuing Hungarian Jews during World War II (Staub, 1985). The first person he rescued was a business partner who happened to be a Hungarian Jew. Wallenberg then became more involved and more daring. He began to manufacture passes for Jews, saying that they were citizens of Sweden. He even handed out passes to Jews who were being put in the cattle cars that would take them to the death camps. Wallenberg disappeared soon after, and his fate is still unknown. Apparently, there is a unique type of person who is likely to take that very first step to help and to continue helping until the end (Goleman, 1991). Wallenberg and the other rescuers were such people.

A Synthesis: Situational and Personality Factors in Altruism

We have seen that both situational and personality factors influence the development and course of altruism. How do these factors work together to produce altruistic behavior? Two approaches provide some answers: the interactionist view and the application of the five-stage decision model to long-term helping situations.

The Interactionist View

The **interactionist view of altruism** argues that an individual's internal motives (whether altruistic or selfish) interact with situational factors to determine whether a person will help (Callero, 1986). D. Romer and his colleagues (Romer, Gruder, & Lizzadro, 1986) identified four altruistic orientations based on the individual's degree of nurturance (the need to give help) and of succorance (the need to receive help):

interactionist view of altruism
The view that an individual's altruistic or selfish internal motives interact with situational factors to determine whether help is given.

1. *Altruistic.* Those who are motivated to help others but not to receive help in return.

2. *Receptive giving.* Those who help to obtain something in return.

3. *Selfish.* Those who are primarily motivated to receive help but not give it.

4. *Inner-sustaining.* Those who are not motivated to give or receive help.

In their study, Romer and colleagues (1986) led people to believe that they either would or would not be compensated for their help. On the basis of the four orientations just described, these researchers predicted that individuals with an altruistic orientation would help even if compensation was not expected; receptive givers would be willing to help only if they stood to gain something in return; selfish people would not be oriented toward helping, regardless of compensation; and those described as inner-sustaining would neither give nor receive, no matter what the compensation.

Romer's (1986) results confirmed this hypothesis. Figure 11.6 on p. 436 shows the results on two indexes of helping: the percentage of subjects who agree to help and the number of hours volunteered. Notice that altruistic people were less likely to help when compensation was offered. This is in keeping with the reverse-incentive effect described in chapter 6. When people are internally motivated to do something, giving them an external reward decreases their motivation and their liking for the activity. There is also evidence that personality and the situation interact in a way that can reduce the bystander effect. In one study, researchers categorized subjects as either "esteem oriented" or "safety oriented" (Wilson, 1976). Esteem-oriented

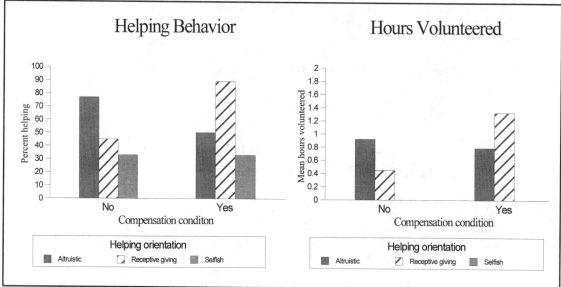

Figure 11.6 *Helping behavior and hours volunteered as a function of helping orientation and compensation. Participants whose orientation was receptive giving were more likely to help when they received compensation. Altruistic participants were willing to help regardless of whether they were compensated.*

From Romer, Gruder, and Lizzardo (1986). Reprinted with permission.

individuals are motivated by a strong sense of personal competency rather than by what others do. Safety-oriented individuals are more dependent on what others do. Subjects were exposed to a staged emergency (a simulated explosion that supposedly hurt the experimenter), either while alone, in the presence of a passive bystander (who makes no effort to help), or in the presence of a helping bystander (who goes to the aid of the experimenter).

The study showed that esteem-oriented subjects were more likely to help than safety-oriented subjects in all cases (Figure 11.7). Of most interest, however, is the fact that the esteem-oriented subjects were more likely to help when a passive bystander was present than were the safety-oriented subjects. Thus, subjects who are motivated internally (esteem oriented) are not just more likely to help than those who are externally motivated (safety oriented); they are also less likely to fall prey to the influence of a passive bystander. This suggests that individuals who helped in the classic experiments on the bystander effect may possess personality characteristics that allow them to overcome the help-depressing effects of bystanders.

We might also expect that the individual's personality will interact with the costs of giving help. Some individuals help even though the cost of helping is high. For example, some subjects in Batson's (1990a) research described earlier in this chapter helped by offering to change places with someone receiving electric shocks even though they could have escaped the situation easily. And rescuers helped despite the fact that getting caught helping Jews meant death. In contrast, there are those who will not help even if helping requires minimal effort.

The degree to which the personality of the helper affects helping may depend on the perceived costs involved in giving aid. In relatively low-cost situations, personality will be more important than the situation. However, in high-cost situations, personality will be more important than the situation. As the perceived cost of helping increases, personality exerts a stronger effect on the decision to help. This is represented in Figure 11.8 on p. 438. The base of the triangle represents very low-cost behaviors. As you move up the triangle, the cost of helping increases. The relative size of each division of the triangle represents the number of people who would be willing to help another in distress.

An extremely low-cost request (e.g., giving a stranger directions to the campus library) would result in most people's helping. People's personalities matter little when it costs almost nothing to help. In fact, probably more effort is spent on saying no than on directing the passerby to the library. When the cost of helping becomes high, even prohibitive, as in the case of rescuing Jews from the Nazis, fewer people help. However, there are those who successfully overcome the situational forces working against helping, perhaps due to their altruistic personalities, and offer help.

APPLYING THE FIVE-STAGE DECISION MODEL TO LONG-TERM HELPING

Earlier in this chapter we described a five-stage decision model of helping. That model has been applied exclusively to the description and explanation of helping in spontaneous emergencies. Now that we have explored some other aspects of helping, we can consider whether that model may be applied to long-term and situation-specific spontaneous helping. Let's consider how each stage applies to the actions of those who rescued Jews from the Nazis.

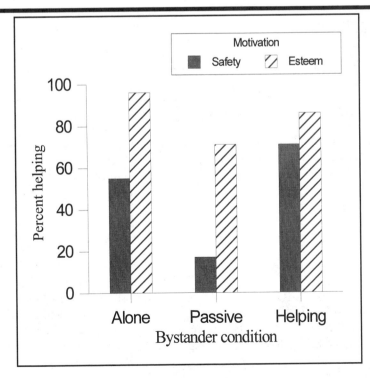

Figure 11.7

The relationship between personality characteristics, presence, and type of bystander on the likelihood of helping. Esteem-oriented participants were most likely to help, regardless of bystander condition. Safety-oriented participants were most likely to help if they were alone or if there was a helping bystander present.

Based on data from Wilson (1976).

Figure 11.8

The relationship between personality and likeliness of helping in different helping situations. Nearly everyone would help if cost were very low. As the cost of the helping act increases, fewer and fewer individuals are expected to help. Only the most altruistic individuals are expected to help in very high cost situations.

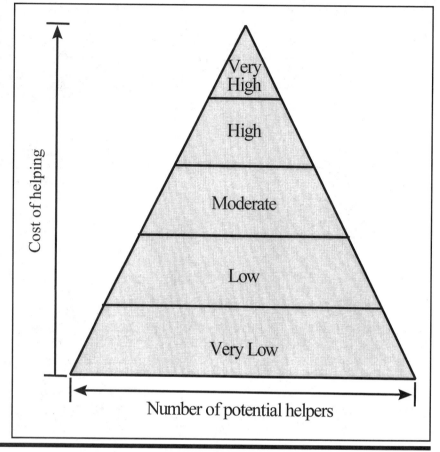

Noticing the Situation

For many rescuers, seeing the Nazis taking Jews away provoked awareness. One rescuer, Irene Gut Opdyke, first became aware of the plight of the Jews when she happened to look through a hotel window and saw Jews being rounded up and taken away (Opdyke & Elliot, 1992). Oliner and Oliner (1988) reported that rescuers were motivated to action when they witnessed some external event such as the one Opdyke had witnessed. Of course, however, many nonrescuers also saw the same events yet did not help.

Labeling the Situation as an Emergency

A critical factor in the decision to rescue Jews was to label the situation as one serious enough to require intervention. Here, the differences between rescuers and nonrescuers became important. Apparently, rescuers were more likely to see the persecution of the Jews as something serious that required intervention. The persecutions appeared to insult the sensibilities of the rescuers. Nonrescuers often decided that Jews must truly have done something to deserve their awful fate. They tended to blame the victim and by so doing relieved themselves of any responsibility for helping.

Rescuers also had social support to help because they belonged to groups that valued such action. This is consistent with the notion that encouragement from others may make it easier to label a situation as one requiring intervention (Dozier & Miceli, 1985).

Assuming Responsibility to Help

The next step in the process is for the rescuer to assume responsibility to help. For rescuers, the universalistic view of the needy, ethics of justice and caring, and generally high levels of empathy made assuming responsibility probable. In fact, many rescuers suggested that after they noticed the persecution of Jews they had to do something. Their upbringing and view of the world made assumption of responsibility almost a given rather than a decision. The main difference between the rescuers and the nonrescuers who witnessed the same events was that the rescuers interpreted the events as a call to action (Oliner & Oliner, 1988). For the rescuers, the witnessed event connected with their principles of caring (Oliner & Oliner, 1988) and led them to assume responsibility.

Another factor may have come into play when the rescuers (or a bystander to an emergency situation) assumed responsibility. Witnessing maltreatment of the Jews may have activated the *norm of social responsibility* in these individuals. This norm involves the notion that we should help others without regard to receiving help or a reward in exchange (Berkowitz, 1972; Schwartz, 1975).

Deciding How to Help

Rescuers helped in a variety of ways (Oliner & Oliner, 1988). They had to assess the alternatives available and decide which was most appropriate. Alternatives included donating money to help Jews, providing false papers, and hiding Jews. It appears that, at least sometimes, perceived costs were not an issue. For example, Opdyke hid several Jews in the basement of a German major's house in which she was the housekeeper, even after she witnessed a Polish family and the family of Jews they were hiding hanged by the Nazis in the town marketplace.

Implementing the Decision to Help

The final stage, implementing the decision to help, includes assessing rewards and costs for helping and potential outcomes of helping versus not helping. When Everett Sanderson rescued someone who had fallen onto the subway tracks, he said he could not have lived with himself if he had not helped. This is an assessment of outcomes. For Sanderson, the cost for not helping outweighed the cost for helping, despite the risks.

It is quite probable that the altruistic personalities we have been studying made similar assessments. Because of their upbringing and the events of their lives that defined them as altruistic people, they decided that helping was less costly to them than not helping. Most of them engaged in long-term helping. This suggests that they assessed the outcome of their initial decision to help and decided that it was correct. This was certainly true of Seth Conklin and

Balwina Piecuch. It was also true of the Polish woman in the following example, which illustrates the interactionist nature of helping—the interplay of situational and personality factors and the combination of spontaneous and long-term events:

A woman and her child were being led through Cracow, Poland, with other Jews to a concentration station. The woman ran up to a bystander and pleaded, "Please, please save my child." A Polish woman took the young boy to her apartment, where neighbors became suspicious of this sudden appearance of a child and called the police. The captain of the police department asked the woman if she knew the penalty for harboring a Jewish child. The young woman said, with some heat, "You call yourself a Pole . . . a gentleman . . . a man of the human race?" She continued her persuasive act, claiming that one of the police in the room had actually fathered the child "and stooped so low as to be willing to have the child killed" (Goldman, 1988, p. 8). Both the woman and the young boy survived the war.

ALTRUISTIC BEHAVIOR FROM THE PERSPECTIVE OF THE RECIPIENT

Our discussion of altruism to this point has centered on the helper. But helping situations, of course, involve another person: the recipient. Social psychologists have asked two broad questions that relate to the recipient of helping behavior: What influences an individual's decision to seek help? What reactions do individuals have to receiving help?

Seeking Help from Others

The earlier discussion of helping in emergencies may have suggested that helping behavior occurs when someone happens to stumble across a situation in which help is needed. Although this does happen, there are also many situations in which an individual actively seeks out help from another. Peter Still actively sought his brother William's help in rescuing his family from slavery. But he also refused Seth Conklin's initial offer of help, believing he could rescue his family on his own. Many Jews in the Nazi-occupied Europe approached potential helpers and asked for help. And today, we see many examples of people seeking help: refugees seeking entrance to other countries, the homeless seeking shelter, the uninsured seeking health care.

Seeking help has both positive and negative aspects. On the positive side, the help a person needs will often be forthcoming. For example, medical care may be given for a life-threatening condition. On the negative side, a person may feel threatened or suffer loss of self-esteem by asking for help (Fisher, Nadler, & Whitcher-Algana, 1982). In our society, a great premium is placed on being self-sufficient and taking care of oneself. There is a social stigma attached to seeking help, along with potential feelings of failure. Generally, seeking help generates costs, as does helping (DePaulo & Fisher, 1980).

A Decision Model for Seeking Help

Researchers have suggested that a person deciding whether to seek help may go through a series of decisions, much like the helper does in Darley and

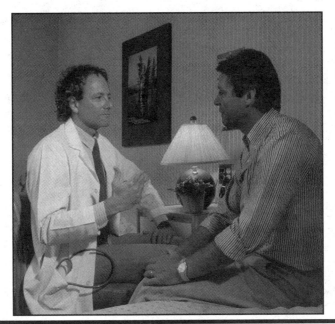

Seeking help from another is a complex affair, having both positive and negative consequences. On the positive side, seeking help (such as seeing a doctor) can help remedy a severe situation. On the negative side, seeking help may be threatening (what if the doctor diagnoses you with cancer?). When considering seeking help, we ask ourselves whether the help will alleviate the problem, whether we should seek help, and who is the most capable person to provide the help.

Latané's five-stage decision model. According to Allen Gross and Peg Mc-Mullen (1982, p. 308), a person asks three questions before seeking help:

1. Do I have a problem that help will alleviate?
2. Should I seek help?
3. Who is most capable of providing the kind of help I need?

Gross and McMullen (1982) developed a model to describe the process of help seeking. The model works in the following way: Imagine that you have begun to have trouble falling asleep at night. Before you will seek help, you must first become aware that there is a problem. If you had trouble falling asleep only a few times, you probably will not identify it as a problem, and you will not seek help. But if you have trouble falling asleep for a few weeks, you may identify it as a problem and move to the next stage of help seeking.

Now you must decide if the situation is one that requires help. If you decide that it is not (the problem will go away by itself), you will not seek help. If you decide that it is, you move on to the next stage, deciding on the best way to alleviate the problem. Here you can opt for self-help (go to the drug-store and buy some over-the-counter drug) or help from an outside party (a physician or psychologist). If you choose self-help and it is successful, the problem is solved and no further help is sought. If the self-help is unsuccessful, you could then seek help from others or resign yourself to the problem and seek no further help.

The likelihood that you may ask for and receive help may also depend on the nature of the groups (and society) to which you belong. Members of groups often behave altruistically toward one another (Clark, Mills, & Powell, 1986) and are often governed by communal relationships. Members benefit one another in response to each other's needs (Williamson & Clark, 1989). These relationships are in contrast to exchange relationships, in which people benefit one another in response to, or with the expectation of, receiving a benefit in return. Communal relationships are characterized by helping even when people cannot reciprocate each other's help (Clark, Mills, & Powell, 1986).

Factors Influencing the Decision to Seek Help

Clearly, the decision to seek help is just as complex as the decision to give help. What factors come into play when a person is deciding whether to seek help?

For one, individuals may be more likely to ask for help when their need is low than when it is high (Krishan, 1988). This could be related to the perceived "power" relationship between the helper and the recipient. When need is low, people may perceive themselves to be on more common footing with the helper. Additionally, when need is low there is less cost to the helper. People may be less likely to seek help if the cost to the helper is high (DePaulo & Fisher, 1980).

Another variable in this decision-making process is the person from whom the help is sought. Are people more willing to seek help from a friend or from a stranger? In one study, the relationship between the helper and the recipient (friends or strangers) and the cost to the helper (high or low) were manipulated (Shapiro, 1980). Generally, subjects were more likely to seek help from a friend than from a stranger (Figure 11.9). When help was sought from a friend, the potential cost to the helper was not important. When the helper was a stranger, subjects were reluctant to ask when the cost was high.

There are several possible reasons for this. First, people may feel more comfortable and less threatened asking a friend rather than a stranger for

Figure 11.9

Help seeking as a function of the cost of help and the nature of the potential helper. Participants were likely to seek help from a friend in both low-cost and high-cost helping situations. However, help was more likely to be sought from a stranger if the cost of help were low.

Based on data from Shapiro (1980).

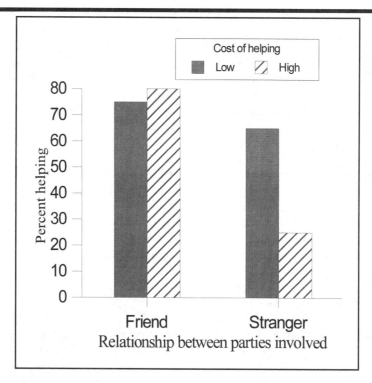

costly help. Second, the norm of reciprocity (see chapter 7) may come into play in a more meaningful way with friends (Gouldner, 1960). People may reason that they would do it for their friends if they needed it. Thus, the expectation of reciprocity may make it easier to ask for high-cost help from a friend. Third, people may perceive that they will have more opportunities to reciprocate a friend's help. They may never see a stranger again.

A final variable that comes into play in deciding to seek help is the type of task on which the help is needed. If someone is doing something easy (but needs help), the person is less likely to seek help than if the task is hard (DePaulo & Fisher, 1980). And if the task is something in which the person has ego involvement, he or she is also less likely to seek help. So, for example, an accountant would be unlikely to seek help preparing his or her own taxes even if he or she needed the help.

Reacting to Help When It Is Given

Receiving help is thus a double-edged sword. On the one hand, people are grateful for receiving help. On the other hand, they may experience negative feelings when they are helped, feelings of guilt, lowered self-esteem, and indebtedness. Jews who were hidden by rescuers, for example, probably were concerned about the safety of their benefactors; they also may have been disturbed by the thought that they could never reciprocate the help they received.

Generally, there are four potentially negative outcomes of receiving help. First, an inequitable relationship may be created. Second, those who are helped may experience psychological reactance; that is, they may feel their freedom is threatened by receiving help. Third, those who receive help may make negative attributions about the intent of those who have helped them. Fourth, those who receive help may suffer a loss of self-esteem (Fisher et al., 1982). Let's look at two of these outcomes: inequity and threats to self-esteem.

THE CREATION OF AN INEQUITABLE RELATIONSHIP Recall from chapter 9 that we strive to maintain equity in our relationships with others. When inequity occurs, we feel distress and are motivated to restore equity. Helping someone creates inequity in a relationship (Fisher et al., 1982), because the recipient feels indebted to the helper (Leventhal, Allen, & Kemelgor, 1969). The higher the cost to the helper, the greater the inequity and the greater the negative feelings (Gergen, 1974).

Inequity can be reversed when the help is reciprocated. Generally, a recipient reacts more negatively to that help and likes the helper less if he or she does not have the ability to reciprocate (Castro, 1974). Recipients are also less likely to seek help in the future when they have not been able to reciprocate, especially if the cost to the helper was high.

The relationship between degree of indebtedness and need to reciprocate is a complex one. For example, if someone helps you voluntarily, you will reciprocate more than if someone is obliged to help you as part of a job (Goranson & Berkowitz, 1966). You also are likely to reciprocate when the cost to the donor is high. (Pruitt, 1968). Interestingly, the absolute amount of help given is less important than the cost incurred by the helper (Aikwa, 1990; Pruitt, 1968). For example, if a person who makes $100,000 per year gave you $1,000 (1% of the income), you would feel less indebted to that person than if you received the same $1,000 from someone who makes $10,000 per year (10% of the income).

THREATS TO SELF-ESTEEM   Perhaps the strongest explanation for the negative impact of receiving help centers on threats to self-esteem. When people become dependent on others, especially in our society, their self-esteem and self-worth come into question (Fisher et al., 1982). Under these conditions, receiving help may be a threatening experience.

threat to self-esteem model

A model explaining the reactions of victims to receiving help suggesting that they might refuse help because accepting it is a threat to their self-esteem.

There is considerable support for the **threat to self-esteem model.** In one study, subjects who received aid on an analogy task showed greater decrements in situational self-esteem (self-esteem tied to a specific situation) than subjects not receiving help (Balls & Eisenberg, 1986). In another study, researchers artificially manipulated subjects' situational self-esteem by providing them with either positive or negative information about themselves (Nadler, Altman, & Fisher, 1979). The researchers then created a situation in which the individual either received or did not receive aid. Subjects who received self-enhancing information (positive self-information) showed more negative affect when aid was offered than when no aid was offered. Subjects who received negative self-information showed positive affect when they were helped.

Thus, subjects who had positive thoughts about themselves were more negatively affected by help than those who had negative thoughts about themselves. The offer of help was a greater threat to those with high self-esteem than to those with low self-esteem. In other words, not only does receiving help threaten self-esteem but also the higher a person's self-esteem is, the more threatened that person is by offers of help. For example, if you consider yourself the world's best brain surgeon, asking for assistance on a case would be more disturbing to you than if you saw yourself as an average brain surgeon.

When someone with high self-esteem fails at a task, that failure is inconsistent with his or her positive self-image (Nadler, Fisher, & Streufert, 1976). Help offered in this situation is perceived as threatening, especially if it comes from someone who is similar (Fisher & Nadler, 1974; Nadler et al., 1979). Receiving help from someone similar may be seen as a sign of relative inferiority and dependency (Nadler et al., 1979).

Conversely, when a person with high self-esteem receives help from a dissimilar person, he or she experiences an increase in situational self-esteem and self-confidence. When a person with low self-esteem receives help from a similar other, that help is more consistent with the individual's self-image. For these individuals, help from a similar other is seen as an expression of concern, and they respond positively (Nadler et al., 1979).

A model to explain the complex relationship between self-esteem and receiving help was developed by Nadler, Fisher, and Ben Itchak (1983). The model suggests that help from a friend is more psychologically significant than help from a stranger. This greater significance is translated into negative affect if failure occurs on something that is ego involving (losing a job). Here, help from a friend is seen as a threat to one's self-esteem, and a negative reaction follows.

There are also gender differences in how people react to receiving help. In one study, males and females were paired with fictitious partners of comparable, superior, or inferior ability and were offered help by that partner (Balls & Eisenberg, 1986). Females paired with a partner of similar ability showed greater reductions in situational self-esteem than males paired with a similar partner. Thus, females perceived help as more threatening to self-esteem than did males. Females, however, were more satisfied than males with the help they received. Females were also more likely than males to express a need for help.

Reactions to receiving help, then, are influenced by several factors, including the ability to reciprocate, the similarity or dissimilarity of the helper, self-esteem, and gender. Other factors can play a role as well. For example, if the helper has positive attributes and is seen as having good motives, the person receiving help is more likely to feel positive about the experience. A positive outcome is also more likely if the help is offered rather than requested, if the help is given on an ego-relevant task, and if the help does not compromise the recipient's freedom (e.g., with a very high obligation to repay the helper). Overall, we see that an individual's reaction to receiving help is influenced by an interaction between situational variables (for example, the helper's characteristics) and personality variables (Fisher et al., 1982).

SETH CONKLIN REVISITED

Seth Conklin offered help to perfect strangers and ultimately lost his life for his efforts. Conklin was undoubtedly an empathic person who felt the suffering of Peter Still's family. In deciding to help, he must have gone through something similar to the process described in this chapter. He noticed the situation requiring help when he read about the Still family in the newspaper. He labeled the situation as one that required help, and he assumed responsibility for helping. He knew what he had to do to help: go south and bring the Still family north. Finally, he implemented his decision to help. Conklin's behavior fits quite well with the five-stage decision model to helping.

Conklin's decision is also similar to the decisions made by hundreds of rescuers of Jews. In both types of situations, individuals put their lives on the line to save others. Although we do not know much about what kind of person Conklin was, we can safely assume that he had emotional empathy and a strong sense of social responsibility. Most likely, Conklin came from a family with characteristics similar to the characteristics of rescuers' families. Like the rescuers, Conklin left us with an inspiring example of an altruistic person who put the welfare of others above his own.

1. What is altruism and how is it different from helping behavior? Why is the difference important?

Altruism is behavior that helps a person in need that is focused on the victim and is motivated purely by the desire to help the other person. Other, similar behaviors may be motivated by relieving one's personal distress or to gain some reward. These behaviors are categorized as **helping behavior**. The motivation underlying an act of help is important because it may affect the quality of the help given.

2. What are empathy and egoism, and how do they relate to altruism?

Empathy refers to compassionate understanding of how a person in need feels. Some acts of helping are focused on and motivated by our desire to relieve the suffering of the victim rather than our own discomfort. Empathy for a person in need is rooted in perspective taking. A person who focuses on how a person in distress feels is more likely to experience empathy. The **empathy–altruism hypothesis** proposes that arousal of empathy increases the likelihood of altruism. This hypothesis has received research support, it remains a controversial hypothesis. In contrast, **egoism** refers to a motive for helping that is focused on relieving our own discomfort rather than on relieving the victim's suffering.

3. What about the idea that we may help to avoid guilt or shame?

This has been raised as a possibility in the **empathy–punishment hypothesis**, which states that people help to avoid the guilt and shame associated with not helping. Research pitting this hypothesis against the empathy–altruism hypothesis has fallen on the side of empathy–altruism. However, the book is still open on the validity of the empathy–altruism hypothesis.

4. Does biology play any role in altruism?

There is evidence that helping has biological roots, as suggested by sociobiologists. According to this view, helping is biologically adaptive and helps a species survive. The focus of this explanation is on survival of the gene pool of a species rather than on survival of any one member of a species. According to evolutionary biologists, animals are more likely to help members of their own family through alloparenting. For humans, a similar effect occurs: We are more likely to help others who are like us and who thus share genetic material.

Although this idea has some merit, it cannot account for the complexity of animal or human altruism. We might have predicted, based on the biological explanation, that Seth Conklin would not have been motivated to help Peter Still's family because he and Still were not closely related and were from different racial groups.

5. How do social psychologists explain helping in emergency situations?

To explain helping (or nonhelping) in emergencies, social psychologists Darley and Latané developed a decision model with five stages: noticing the emergency, labeling the emergency correctly, assuming responsibility to help, knowing what to do, and implementing the decision to help. At each stage, many variables influence an individual's decision to help.

At the noticing stage, anything that makes the emergency stand out increases the likelihood of help being offered. However, interpreting a situation as an emergency can be ambiguous, and we may mislabel it, in which case we do not give help.

Next, we must assume personal responsibility for helping. This is known as the **bystander effect**. Two reasons for this failure to help when bystanders are present are **diffusion of responsibility** (assuming that someone else will help) and **pluralistic ignorance** (responding to the inaction of others). Although the bystander effect is a powerful, reliable phenomenon, there are exceptions to it. Research shows that when help requires potentially dangerous intervention, people are more likely to help when in groups than when alone.

Even if we assume responsibility, we may not help because we do not know what to do or lack skills, or we may think that someone else is more qualified to help. Finally, we may fail to help because the costs of helping are seen as too high. Costs are increased when we might be injured or otherwise inconvenienced by stopping to help.

6. What other factors affect the decision to help?

Mood makes a difference. Bystanders who are in a positive (good) mood are more likely to help others. However, people may not help if they think helping will spoil their good mood. Characteristics of the victim also play a role. Females are more likely to be helped if the helper is male. Physically attractive people are more likely to be helped than unattractive people. We also take into account whether we feel that the victim deserves help. If we believe the victim contributed to his or her own problems, we are less likely to help than if we believe the victim did not contribute. This fits with the **just-world hypothesis,** the idea that people get what they deserve and deserve what they get. We may relax this standard if we believe the victim strongly needs our help.

7. If I need help, how can I increase my chances of getting it?

You need to help people come to the right decision at each stage of the decision model. To ensure that you get noticed, make any plea for help as loud and as clear as possible. This will also help bystanders correctly label your situation as an emergency. To get someone to assume responsibility, make eye contact with a bystander. Better yet, make a direct request of a particular bystander for help. Research shows that making such a request increases a bystander's sense of responsibility for helping you and increases the likelihood of helping.

8. How do personality characteristics influence helping?

Although situational factors play an important role in helping, especially spontaneous helping, they may not give us a true picture of the helper and how he or she might behave across helping situations. Personality characteristics may become more relevant when nonspontaneous, long-term helping is considered. In this case, more planning and thought are required. Some individuals might possess an **altruistic personality**, or a cluster of traits, including empathy, that predispose a person to helping.

Research on rescuers of Jews in Nazi-occupied Europe—who have been designated **righteous rescuers** by Israel—provides evidence for the existence of an altruistic personality. Rescuers from Eastern Europe (especially Poland) displayed **autonomous altruism**, altruism that is not supported by social norms. Rescuers from Western Europe were more likely to display **normative altruism**, altruism that society supports and recognizes.

9. What situational and personality variables played a role in the decision to help Jews in Nazi-occupied Europe?

Although situational factors did not exert as strong an influence on the decision to help as one might expect, two have been found to be significant: the presence of family or group support and the initiation of rescue efforts as a result of a specific request for help. After rescuers began helping, they were likely to continue helping.

There were also personality variables that related to the decision to become a rescuer. Compared to nonrescuers, rescuers were higher in emotional empathy (sensitivity to the suffering of others) and had a strong sense of social responsibility. Other characteristics of rescuers included an inability to blend with others, a high level of independence and self-reliance, a commitment to helping before the war, a matter-of-fact attitude about their helping, and a universalistic view of the needy.

10. What factors contribute to a person's developing an altruistic personality?

Oliner and Oliner found that families of rescuers of Jews in Nazi-occupied Europe and families of nonrescuers differed in their styles. Families of rescuers provided role models for helping and stressed the universal nature of all people. They emphasized aspects of religion that focus on caring for others, and they were less likely to discuss negative stereotypes of Jews. Parents of altruistic individuals tended to be warm and nurturing in their parenting style. Parents of rescuers used less physical punishment than parents of nonrescuers, relying instead on induction.

Cognitive development also contributes to the development of an altruistic personality. As children get older, they are more likely to understand the needs of others. This development is a lifelong process.

Rescuers did not magically become altruists when World War II broke out. Instead, they tended to be helpers long before the war. Becoming a rescuer involved a series of small steps. In many cases, rescuers started with a small act and then moved to larger ones.

11. What is the interactionist view of altruism?

According to the **interactionist view of altruism,** personality and situational factors interact to influence helping. Research has identified four altruistic orientations: altruistic (those who are motivated to help others but not to receive help in return), receptive giving (those who help to obtain something in return), selfish (those who are primarily motivated to receive help but not give it), and inner-sustaining (those who are not motivated to give or receive help).

Research shows that individuals with an altruistic orientation are less likely to help if compensation is offered. There is also evidence that personality factors can help a person overcome the bystander effect. Esteem-oriented individuals (who are motivated internally) are more likely to help than safety-oriented individuals (who are externally motivated) when a passive bystander is present. Additionally, personality and cost of help might interact. For low-cost behaviors, we would expect personality factors to be less important than for high-cost behaviors.

12. How does long-term helping relate to models of emergency helping?

With slight modification, Latané and Darley's five-stage model applies to long-term helping. Noticing, labeling, accepting responsibility, deciding how to help, and implementing the decision to help are all relevant to acts of long-term help. Additionally, at the assuming responsibility stage, the norm of social responsibility may have been activated. This norm suggests that we should help those in need without regard to reward.

13. What factors influence a person's likelihood of seeking and receiving help?

Seeking help from others is a double-edged sword: The person in need is more likely to receive help but also incurs a cost. Helping also involves costs for the helper. A person in need of help weighs these costs when deciding whether to ask for help, progressing through a multistage process. A person is more likely to seek help when his or her needs are low and from a friend, especially if the cost to the helper is high. A person is less likely to seek help with something easy than with something hard.

14. What reactions do people show to receiving help?

Receiving help is also a double-edged sword. The help relieves the situation but leads to negative side effects, including feelings of guilt, lowered self-esteem, and indebtedness to the helper. Generally, there are four negative reactions to receiving aid: the creation of inequity between the helper and the recipient, psychological reactance, negative attributions about the helper, and threats to one's self-esteem. There is considerable support for the **threat to self-esteem model** of reactions to receiving help. How much a person's self-esteem is threatened depends on several factors, including the type of task and the source of the help. Males and females differ in their responses to receiving help. Females react more negatively to receiving help but are more satisfied than males with the help they received.

INTERNET ACTIVITY

LEARNING MORE ABOUT RESCUERS

Steven Spielberg's Oscar-winning film *Schindler's List* made Oskar Schindler a household word. Schindler was directly responsible for saving hundreds of Jews during the Holocaust. Rescuers such as Oskar Schindler and Raul Wallenberg are well known, and their efforts are widely publicized. However, there were thousands who risked and sometimes lost their lives trying to help rescue victims of the Holocaust. Following is a list of rescuers of whom you may not have heard. Use an Internet search engine (e.g., Yahoo or Infoseek) to find information about one or more of these rescuers. Consider and answer the following questions:

- What did the rescuer do to help during the Holocaust?
- Was their altruism normative or autonomous and why?
- What personal characteristics did the rescuer have that may have motivated him or her to become a rescuer?
- Is there anything in the rescuer's family history that relates to the individual's becoming a rescuer?

RESCUERS

Per Anger

Pierre-Marie Benoît

Camille Ernst

Maximilian Kolbe

Irene Opdyke

Hannah Szenes

Chiune and Yukiko Sugihara

SUGGESTIONS FOR FURTHER READING

Batson, C. D. (1990). How social an animal? The human capacity for caring. *American Psychologist, 45,* 336–346.
In this article, Batson presents an overview and arguments for the empathy–altruism hypothesis. A history of the concepts of egoism and altruism is offered along with a discussion of the importance and limitations of our capacity for empathy for others.

Dozier, J. B., & Miceli, M. P. (1985). Potential predictors of whistle-blowing: A prosocial behavior perspective. *Academy of Management Review, 10,* 823–836.

In this article, Darley and Latané's five-stage model of helping is adapted and applied to a specific example of long-term helping: whistle-blowing. Whistle-blowers are individuals who risk their jobs, and perhaps their lives, to bring to the public eye dangerous actions taken by businesses or government. Dozier and Miceli show how whistle-blowers go through the same stages when deciding to help as an individual facing an emergency.

Opdyke, I. G., & Elliot, J. M. (1992). *Into the flames: The life story of a righteous rescuer.* San Bernardino, CA: Borgo Press.

This book is an autobiography of Irene Gut Opdyke, a righteous rescuer. Opdyke describes how she came to hide a group of Jews in the basement of the house in which she worked as a housekeeper for a German major. In vivid detail, she describes her first experience with the persecution of the Jews and why she decided to risk her life to help those persecuted by the Nazis. In an ironic twist of fate, Opdyke describes what happens after the major discovered her secret.

Tec, N. (1986). *When light pierced the darkness.* New York: Oxford University Press.

This book details Tec's study of Christian rescuers in Poland. In the first part of the book, Tec describes the social climate within Poland during World War II and how rescuers had to overcome centuries of anti-Semitic attitudes. The study also compares rescuers with paid helpers and shows how the quality of care Jews received was influenced by the underlying motives of the person helping (altruism or money).

Weiner, B. (1993). On sin versus sickness: A theory of perceived responsibility and social motivation. *American Psychologist, 48,* 957–965.

In this article, Weiner gives an overview of his research on the relationship among attributions, affective responses to victims, and helping. He develops a theory suggesting that if we perceive that a victim had control over his or her fate, we experience negative affect (anger) and are less willing to help than if we perceive that a victim is in distress because of uncontrollable factors.

NEW REFERENCES

Batson, C. D. Nadia, A., Jodi, Y., Bedell, S. J., & Johnson, J. W. (1999). Two threats to the common good: Self-interest and empathy and empathy-induced altruism. *Personality and Social Psychology Bulletin, 25,* 3–16.

Batson, C. D. (1997). Self-other merging and the empathy-altruism hypothesis: Reply to Neuberg et al. (1997). *Journal of Personality and Social Psychology, 73,* 517–522.

Batson, C. D., Early, S., & Salvarani, G. (1997). Perspective taking: Imagining how another feels versus imagining how you would feel. *Personality and Social Psychology Bulletin, 23,* 751–758.

Batson, C. D., Sager, K., Garst, E., Kang, M., Rubchinsky, K., & Dawson, K. (1997). Is empathy-induced helping due to self-other merging?. *Journal of Personality and Social Psychology, 73,* 495–509.

Batson, C. D., & Weeks, J. L. (1996). Mood effects of unsuccessful helping: Another test of the empathy–altruism hypothesis. *Personality and Social Psychology Bulletin, 22,* 148–157.

Cialdini, R. B., Brown, S. L., Lewis, B. P., Luce, C., & Neuberg, S. (1997). Reinterpreting the empathy–altruism relationship: When one into one equals oneness. *Journal of Personality and Social Psychology, 73,* 481–494.

Gore, K. Y., Tobiasen, M. A., & Kayson, W. A. (1997). Effects of sex of caller, implied sexual orientation, and urgency on altruistic response using the wrong number technique. *Psychological Reports, 80,* 927–930.

Neuberg, S. L., Cialdini, R. B., Brown, S. L., Luce, C., & Sagarin, B. J. (1997). Does empathy lead to anything more than superficial helping? Comment on Batson et al. (1997). *Journal of Personality and Social Psychology, 73,* 510–516.

GLOSSARY

A

accommodation process   Interacting in such a way that, despite conflict, a relationship is maintained and enhanced.

actor–observer bias   An attribution bias showing that we prefer external attributions for our own behavior, especially if outcomes are negative, whereas observers tend to make internal attributions for the same behavior performed by others.

actual self   A person's current self-concept.

agentic state   A factor that may mediate obedience to authority. In the agentic state, the individual becomes focused on the source of authority, tuning in to the instructions issued. The individual becomes an agent of the authority source in carrying out the instructions.

aggression   Any behavior intended to inflict either psychological or physical harm on another organism or object.

aggressive script   An internalized representation of an event that leads to increased aggression and the tendency to interpret social interactions aggressively.

altruism   Helping behavior motivated purely by the desire to relieve a victim's suffering and not the anticipation of reward.

altruistic personality   A cluster of personality traits that predispose a person to acts of altruism.

applied research   Research that has a principal aim to address a real-world problem.

attitude   A mental and neural state of readiness, organized through experience, exerting a directive or dynamic influence on the individual's response to all objects and situations with which it is related.

attitude structure   The fact that attitudes comprise a cognitive, affective, and behavioral component in their basic structure.

attitude survey   A self-report method of measuring attitudes that involves a researcher's mailing a questionnaire to a potential respondent, conducting a face-to-face interview, or asking a series of questions on the telephone.

attribution   The process of assigning causes of behavior, both your own and that of others.

authoritarianism   A personality characteristic that relates to a person's unquestioned acceptance of and respect for authority.

authoritarian personality   A personality dimension characterized by submissive feelings toward authority, rigid and unchangeable beliefs, and a tendency toward prejudicial attitudes.

autobiographical memory   Memory for information relating to the self that plays a powerful role in recall of events.

automatic processing   The idea that because of our limited information processing capacity we construct social impressions without much thought or effort, especially when we lack the motivation for careful assessment or when our initial impressions are confirmed. See also controlled processing.

autonomous altruism   Selfless altruism that society does not support or might even discourage.

availability heuristic   A shortcut used to estimate the frequency or likelihood of an event based on how quickly examples of it come to mind.

B

badge value   The aspect of attitude that provides an up-front statement about who a person is or would like others to think he or she is.

basic research   Research that has the principal aim of empirically testing a theory or a model.

behavioral confirmation   A tendency for perceivers to behave as if their expectations are correct and the targets then to respond in ways that confirm the perceivers' beliefs.

belief perseverence   The tendency for initial impressions to persist despite later conflicting information, accounting for much of the power of first impressions.

black sheep effect   The phenomenon in which an attractive in-group member is rated more highly than an attractive member of an out-group and an unattractive in-group member is perceived more negatively than an unattractive out-group member.

bystander effect   The social phenomenon that helping behavior is less likely to occur as the number of witnesses to an emergency increases.

C

central route processing   In the ELM, some information may be processed by effortful, controlled mechanisms involving attention to and understanding and careful processing of the content of a persuasive message.

classical conditioning   A form of learning that occurs when a stimulus comes to summon a response that it previously did not evoke to form an attitude.

cognitive dissonance theory   A theory of attitude change proposing that if inconsistency exists among our attitudes, or between our attitudes and our behavior, we experience an unpleasant state of arousal called cognitive dissonance, which we will be motivated to reduce or eliminate.

cognitive miser   The idea suggesting that because humans have a limited capacity to understand information, we deal only with small amounts of social information and prefer the least effortful means of processing it.

cohesiveness   The strength of the relationships that link members of a group together and is essentially what keeps people in a group or causes them to stick together.

collective self   The part of our self-concept that comes from our membership in groups.

communal relationship   An interpersonal relationship in which individuals benefit each other in response to each others' needs.

compliance   Social influence process which involves modifying behavior after accepting a direct request.

confirmation bias   A tendency to engage in a search strategy that confirms rather than disconfirms our hypothesis.

conformity   A social influence process that involves modifying behavior in response to real or imagined pressure from others.

confounding variable   An extraneous variable in an experiment that varies systematically with the independent variable, making it difficult or impossible to establish a causal connection between the independent and dependent variables.

consensus seeking   A tendency in groups that leads members to be more concerned with maintaining morale and gaining unanimous agreement than with the quality of the group decision.

consummate love   Love that includes all three components: passion, intimacy, and commitment.

contact hypothesis   A hypothesis that contact between groups will reduce hostility, which is most effective when members of different groups have equal status and a mutual goal.

control group   A group in an experiment comprising participants who do *not* receive the experimental treatment.

controlled processing   An effortful and careful processing of information that occurs when we are motivated to accurately assess information or if our initial impressions or expectations are disconfirmed.

correlation coefficient (r)   A measure of association between two variables that provides two important pieces of information: the degree of relationship between variables (indicated by the size of the coefficient) and the direction of the relationship (indicated by the sign of the coefficient).

correlational research   Research that measures two or more dependent variables and looks for a relationship between them; causal relationships among variables cannot be established.

correspondent inference   An inference that occurs when we conclude that a person's overt behavior is caused by or corresponds to the person's internal characteristics or beliefs.

counterfactual thinking   The tendency to create positive alternatives to a negative outcome that actually occurred, especially when we can easily imagine a more positive outcome.

covariation principle   The rule that if a response is present when a situation (person, object, or event) is present and absent when that same situation is absent, the situation is presumed to be the cause of the response.

credibility   The believability (expertise and trustworthiness) of the communicator of a persuasive message.

culture of honor   An evolved culture in the southern and western U.S. in which violence is more widely accepted and practiced than in the northern and eastern U.S.

D

deindividuation   A phenomenon that occurs in large-group (crowd) situations in which individual identity is lost within the anonymity of the large group, perhaps leading to a lowering of inhibitions against negative behaviors.

dependent variable   The measure the researcher assesses to determine the influence of the independent variable on the participants' behavior.

diffusion of responsibility   An explanation suggesting that each bystander assumes that another person will take responsibility to help.

directive leader   A leadership style involving a leader who gives less value to participation, emphasizes the need for agreement, and tends to prefer his or her own solution.

discrimination   Overt behavior — often negatively directed toward a particular group — often tied to prejudicial attitudes, which involves behaving in different ways toward members of different groups.

displaced aggression   Aggressive behavior used when direct aggression against a source is not possible or is blocked; frustration may be vented against another, more appropriate target.

distinctiveness theory   The theory suggesting that individuals think of themselves in terms of those attributes or dimensions that make them different — rather than in terms of attributes they have in common with others.

distraction – conflict theory   A theory of social facilitation suggesting that the presence of others is a source of distraction that leads to a decrease in performance.

door-in-the-face technique (DITF)   A social influence process in which a person is first asked to perform a large task, and then a smaller one.

Compliance is more likely on the second, smaller task following the first, larger one than if the smaller task was the only one requested.

E

ego depletion   The loss of self-energy that occurs when a person has to contend with a difficult cognitive or emotional situation.

egoism   The idea that helping a person in need occurs to relieve personal distress.

egotistical bias   The tendency to present oneself as responsible for success, whether you are or not, and the tendency to believe these positive presentations.

Eichmann's fallacy   The belief that evil deeds are done only by evil people.

elaboration likelihood model (ELM)   A cognitive model of persuasion suggesting that a target's attention, involvement, distraction, motivation, self-esteem, education, and intelligence all influence central and/or peripheral reception to a persuasive attempt.

empathy   The compassionate understanding of how a person in need feels.

empathy–altruism hypothesis   An explanation suggesting that the arousal of empathy leads to altruistic acts.

empathy–punishment hypothesis   A hypothesis suggesting that helping occurs because individuals are motivated to avoid the guilt or shame brought about by failure to help.

equity theory   An interpersonal relationship theory suggesting that we strive to maximize fairness in our social relationships with others; when inequity is perceived we are motivated to change a relationship.

ethology   A theoretical perspective that views behavior within the context of survival and emphasizes the role of instincts and genetic forces.

evaluation apprehension   An explanation for social facilitation suggesting that the presence of others will cause arousal only when they can reward or punish the performer.

everyday prejudice   Prejudice that comprises recurrent and familiar events considered to be commonplace.

experimental group   A group comprising participants who receive the experimental treatment in an experiment.

experimental research   Research involving manipulating a variable suspected of influencing behavior to see how that change affects behavior; results show **causal relationships** among variables.

expertise   A component of communicator credibility that refers to the communicator's credentials and stems from the individual's training and knowledge.

explicit attitude   An attitude that operates on a conscious level via controlled processing.

external attribution   The process of assigning the cause of behavior to some situation or event outside a person's control rather than to some internal characteristic.

extraneous variable   Any variable not controlled by the researcher that could affect the results of a study.

F

factorial experiment   An experimental design in which two or more independent variables are manipulated, allowing for the establishment of a causal connection between the independent and dependent variables.

false consensus bias   The tendency to believe that our own feelings and behavior are shared by everyone else.

field experiment   A research setting in which the researcher manipulates one or more independent variable and measures behavior in the participant's natural environment.

field study   A descriptive research strategy in which the researcher makes unobtrusive observations of the participants without making direct contact or interfering in any way.

field survey   A descriptive research strategy in which the researcher directly approaches participants and asks them questions.

flexible correction model (FCM)   A model stating that individuals using central route processing are influenced by biasing variables, because they are not aware of the potential impact of the biasing variable.

foot-in-the-door technique (FITD)   A social influence process in which a person is first asked to perform a small task, and then a larger one. Compliance is more likely on the second, larger task if it follows the first, smaller task than if it were the task requested.

four horsemen of the apocalypse   Four factors identified as important in relationship dissolution: complaining–criticizing, contempt, defensiveness, and withdrawal from social interaction (stonewalling).

free riders   Group members who do not do not do their share of the work in a group.

frustration–aggression hypothesis   A hypothesis that frustration and aggression are strongly related suggesting that aggression is always the consequence of frustration and frustration leads to aggression.

fundamental attribution error   The tendency to automatically attribute the causes for another person's behavior to internal rather than situational forces.

G

group   An aggregate of individuals who interact with and influence one another.

group norms   Expectations concerning the kinds of behaviors required of group members.

group polarization   The tendency for individual, prediscussion opinion to become more extreme following group discussion.

groupthink   A group-process phenomenon that may lead to faulty decision making by highly cohesive group members more concerned with reaching consensus than with carefully considering alternative courses of action.

H

helping behavior   Helping partially motivated by personal gain rather than relieving the suffering of a victim.

heritability   An indicator of the degree to which genetics accounts for differences among people for any given behavior or characteristic.

heuristic and systematic information processing model (HSM)   A cognitive model of persuasion suggesting that of the two routes to persuasion, systematic and heuristic, people choose to use heuristics or peripheral cues more often.

heuristics   Handy rules of thumb that serve as shortcuts to organizing and perceiving social reality.

hindsight bias   Also known as the "I-knew-it-all-along" phenomenon; shows that with the benefit of hindsight, everything looks obvious.

hostile aggression   Aggressive behavior stemming from angry or hostile impulses, with a primary goal to inflict injury to some person or object.

hypothalamus   A structure in the limbic system of the brain associated with aggressive behavior.

hypothesis   A tentative and testable statement about the relationship between variables.

I

ideal self   The mental representation of what a person would like to be or what a significant other would like him or her to be.

ideology   A person's doctrines, opinions, or ways of thinking that characterize an overarching view of the world.

illusion of efficacy   The illusion that members of small groups think they are more effective than larger groups, which may not be the case.

illusion of transparency   The belief that observers can read our private thoughts and feelings because they somehow leak out.

illusion of unique invulnerability   A tendency to underestimate the likelihood of bad things happening to oneself.

illusory correlation   An error in judgement about the relationship between two variables in which two unrelated events are believed to covary.

implicit attitude   An attitude that affects behavior automatically, without conscious thought and below the level of awareness.

implicit personality theory   A common person-schema belief that certain personality traits are linked together and may help us make a quick impression of someone, but there is no guarantee that initial impression will be correct.

impression formation   The process by which we make judgments about others.

independent variable   The variable that the researcher manipulates in an experiment, which must have at least two levels.

individual self   The part of the self that refers our self-knowledge, including our private thoughts and evaluations of who and what we are.

informational social influence   Social influence that results from a person's responding to information provided by others.

informed consent   An ethical research requirement that participants must be informed of the nature of the study, the requirements for participation, any risks or benefits associated with participating in the study, and the right to decline or withdraw from participation with no penalty.

in-group bias   The powerful tendency of humans to favor over other groups the group to which they belong.

inoculation theory   A theory that if a communicator exposes an audience to a weakened version of an opposing argument, the audience will devise counterarguments to that weakened version and avoid persuasion by stronger arguments later.

instrumental aggression   Aggressive behavior stemming from a desire to achieve a goal.

interactionist view of altruism   The view that an individual's altruistic or selfish internal motives interact with situational factors to determine whether help is given.

internal attribution   The process of assigning the cause of behavior to some internal characteristic rather than to outside forces.

introspection   The act of examining our own thoughts and feelings to understand ourselves, which may yield a somewhat biased picture of our own internal state.

J

just-world hypothesis   A hypothesis that we believe people get what they deserve and deserve what they get.

L

latitude of acceptance   In social judgment theory, the region of an attitude into which messages that one will accept fall.

latitude of noncommitment   In social judgment theory, the region of an attitude into which messages that one will neither accept nor reject fall.

latitude of rejection   In social judgment theory, the region of an attitude into which messages that one will reject fall.

legitimacy   A group member's feeling of obligation to obey the group's leader.

limerence   A type of romantic love that occurs when you suddenly feel an interest in another person which is fed by the image of returned feeling. This happens because a lonely person anxious for intimacy finds someone who apparently matches his or her wishes or fantasies.

loneliness   A psychological state that results when we perceive that there is an inadequacy or a deprivation in our social relationships.

low-ball technique (or low-balling)   A social influence process in which a solicitor makes you an offer that seems too good to be true but then backs off and proposes a less attractive alternative.

M

matching principle   A principle that applies in romantic relationships suggesting that individuals become involved with a partner with whom they are closely matched socially and physically.

mere exposure   The phenomenon that being exposed to a stimulus increases one's feelings, usually positive, toward that object; repeated exposure can lead to positive attitudes.

metacognition   The way we think about thinking, which is primarily optimistic.

modern racism   Subtle racial prejudice, expressed in a less open manner than is traditional overt racial prejudice and characterized by an uncertainty in feeling and action toward minorities.

multiple audience problem   In persuasion, the problem that arises when a communicator directs the same message at two different audiences, wishing to communicate different meanings to each.

N

need for affiliation   A motivation that underlies our desire to establish and maintain rewarding interpersonal relationships.

need for cognition (NC)   An individual difference dimension in persuasion concerning the degree to which individuals prefer effortful processing of information.

need for intimacy   A motivation for close and affectionate relationships.

negative correlation   The direction of a correlation in which the value of one variable increases whereas the value of a second decreases.

nonrational actor   A view that humans are not always rational in their behavior and their behavior can be inconsistent with their attitudes.

norm   An unwritten social rule existing either on a wide cultural level or on a smaller, situation-specific level that suggests what is appropriate behavior in a situation.

normative altruism   Altruism that society supports and encourages.

normative social influence   Social influence in which a person modifies behavior in response to pressure to conform to a norm.

norm of reciprocity   A social norm stating that you should help those who help you and should not injure those who help you.

O

obedience   A social influence process involving modification of behavior in response to a command from an authority figure.

observational learning   Learning through watching what people do and whether they are rewarded or punished and then imitating that behavior.

operant conditioning   A method by which attitudes are acquired by rewarding a person for a given attitude in the hopes it will be maintained or strengthened.

ostracism   The widespread and universal behavior of excluding or ignoring other individuals or groups.

ought self   The mental representation of what a person believes he or she should be.

out-group homogeneity bias   The predisposition to see members of an out-group as having similar characteristics or being all alike.

P

participative leader   A leadership style characterized by a leader who shares power with the other members of the group and includes them in the decision making.

peripheral route processing   In the ELM, information may be processed using cues peripheral or marginal to the message.

personal attributes   An aspect of the self-concept involving the attributes we believe we have.

persuasion   A form of social influence that involves changing others' thoughts, attitudes, or behaviors by applying rational and emotional arguments to convince them to adopt your position.

physical attractiveness bias The tendency to confer a number of psychological and social advantages to physically attractive individuals.

physical proximity effect The fact that we are more likely to form a relationship with someone who is physically close to us; proximity affects interpersonal attraction, mostly at the beginning of a relationship.

pluralistic ignorance An explanation suggesting that an individual who is uncertain about what to do in an emergency situation notes how others are reacting; if others act as though no emergency exists, a bystander will not intervene to help the victim.

positive correlation The direction of a correlation in which the values of two variables increase or decrease in the same direction.

positive illusions Beliefs that include unrealistically optimistic notions about individuals' ability to handle a threat and create a positive outcome.

postdecision dissonance Cognitive dissonance that is aroused after you have chosen between two equally attractive, mutually exclusive alternatives.

prejudice A biased attitude, positive or negative, based on insufficient information and directed at a group, which leads to prejudgment of members of that group.

primacy effect The observation that information encountered early in the impression formation process plays a powerful role in our eventual impression of an individual.

primary compensation A method by targets of prejudice that reduces threats posed by using coping strategies that allow the targets of prejudice to achieve their goals.

process loss The loss of group efficiency that results from increased group size and generally leads to a decrement in productivity.

psychological reactance A psychological state that results when individuals feel that their freedom of action is threatened because other people are forcing them to do or say things, making them less prone to social influence attempts.

R

random assignment A method of assigning participants to groups in an experiment that involves each participant's having an equal chance of being in the experimental or control group.

reflected appraisal A source of social information involving our view of how other people react to us.

representativeness heuristic A rule used to judge the probability of an event or a person falling into a category based on how representative it or the person is of the category.

righteous rescuers The designation bestowed by Israel on non-Jews who helped save Jews from the Nazis during World War II.

role strain The discomfort one feels in an obedience situation that causes a person to question the legitimacy of the authority figure and weakens the agentic state.

romantic love Love involving strong emotion and having the components of passion and intimacy but not commitment.

S

sanctioned aggression Aggressive behavior that society accepts or encourages.

schema A set of organized cognitions that help us interpret, evaluate, and remember a wide range of social stimuli including events, persons, and ourselves.

scientific method A method of developing scientific explanations involving four steps: identifying a phenomenon to study, developing a testable research hypothesis, designing a research study, and carrying out the research study.

secondary compensation A method of handling prejudice involving attempts to change one's mode of thinking about situations to psychologically protect oneself against the outcomes of prejudice.

secret love Love in which individuals have strong passion for one another but cannot or will not make those feelings publically known, increasing the attraction of a relationship.

self-affirmation theory A theory that individuals may not try to reduce dissonance if they can maintain (affirm) their self-concept by showing they are morally adequate in other ways.

self-categorization theory (SCT) A theory suggesting people need to reduce uncertainty about whether their perceptions of the world are "correct" and seek affirmation of their beliefs from fellow group members.

self-concept All the knowledge and thoughts related to whom you believe you are, comprising the cognitive component of the self.

self-disclosure The ability and willingness to share intimate areas of one's life with another person in a relationship.

self-esteem An individual's evaluation of the self, which can be positive or negative.

self-evaluation maintenance (SEM theory) A theory explaining how the behavior of other people affects how you feel about yourself, especially when they perform some behavior that is important to your self-conception.

self-focus The extent to which one has a heightened awareness of oneself in certain situations (e.g., when a minority within a group).

self-fulfilling prophecy A tendency to expect ourselves to behave in ways that lead to confirmation of our original expectation.

self-handicapping   Self-defeating behavior engaged in when you are uncertain about your success or failure at a task to protect your self-esteem in the face of failure.

self-identity theory (SIT)   A theory proposing that a number of factors predict one group's reaction to competing groups and concerning what may arise from identifications with a social category.

self-monitoring   The degree, ranging from low to high, to which a person focuses on his or her behavior when in a given social situation.

self-perception theory   A theory suggesting that we learn about our motivations by evaluating our own behavior, useful especially in the area of attitude change.

self-regulation   A critical control mechanism used by individuals to match behavior to internal standards of the self or to the expectations of others.

self-schemas   Self-conceptions that guide us in ordering and directing our behavior involving how we represent our thoughts and feelings about our experiences in a particular area of life.

self-serving bias   Our tendency to attribute positive outcomes of our own behavior to internal, dispositional factors and negative outcomes to external, situational forces.

self-verification   A method of supporting and confirming your self-identity involving behavior that encourages others to see you as you see yourself, providing orderliness to and control over your social world.

sexual self-schema   How we think about the sexual aspects of the self, derived from past sexual knowledge and experience, and which guides future sexual activity.

similarity effect   The fact that we are more likely to form a relationship with a similar than a dissimilar other.

sinister attribution error   The tendency for certain people to overattribute lack of trustworthiness to others.

sleeper effect   A phenomenon of persuasion that occurs when a communication has more impact on attitude change after a long delay than when it is first heard.

social anxiety   Anxiety tied to interpersonal relationships that occurs because of an individual's anticipation of negative encounters with others.

social cognition   The general process we use to make sense out of social events, which may or may not include other people.

social comparison process   A source of social knowledge involving how we compare our reactions, abilities, and attributes to others'.

social compensation   The tendency to work harder in a group to make up for the weaknesses of others in the group when the task is important and motivation to perform is high.

social exchange theory   A theory of how relationships are evaluated suggesting that people make assessments according to the rewards (positive things derived from a relationship) and costs (negative things derived from a relationship).

social facilitation   The performance-enhancing effect of others on behavior; generally, simple, well-learned behavior is facilitated by the presence of others.

social identity theory (SIT)   An assumption that we all need to have a positive self-concept, part of which is conferred on us through identification with certain groups.

social impact theory   A theory proposing that social influence processes involve factors combined in the formula: $I = f(SIN)$, I is the amount of influence, S is the strength of the source of the influence, I = the immediacy (or closeness) of the source of influence, and N = the number of influence sources.

social information-processing view of aggression   A view emphasizing how a person processes information about one's social world mediates aggression.

social inhibition   The performance-detracting effect of an audience or coactors on behavior; generally, complex, not-well-learned behaviors are inhibited by the presence of others.

social-interactional model   A model suggesting that antisocial behavior arises early in life and is the result of poor parenting, leading a child to develop conduct problems that affect peer relations and academic performance.

social judgment theory   An attitude theory suggesting that the degree of personal involvement with an issue determines how a target of persuasion will judge an attempt at persuasion.

social learning theory   A theory that social behavior is acquired through direct reinforcement or punishment of behavior and observational learning.

social loafing   The performance-inhibiting effect of working in a group that involves relaxing individual effort based on the belief that others will take up the slack.

social penetration theory   A theory that relationships vary in breadth, the extent of interaction, and depth, suggesting they progress in a an orderly fashion from slight and superficial contact to greater and deeper involvement.

social perception   The social processes by which we come to comprehend the behavior, the words and actions, of other people.

social psychology   The scientific study of how individuals think about, interact with, and influence each other.

sociobiology   A theoretical perspective that views social behavior as being determined by biological forces.

spotlight effect   A phenomenon occurring when we overestimate the ability of others to read our overt behavior, how we act and dress, suggesting that we think others notice and pay attention to whatever we do.

stereotype   A set of beliefs, positive or negative, about the characteristics or attributes of a group, resulting in rigid overgeneralized images of members of that group.

stereotype threat   The condition that exists when a person is asked to perform a task for which there is a negative stereotype attached to their group and performs poorly because the task is threatening.

symbolic aggression   Nonviolent or subtle behavior that interferes with a victim's advancement toward a goal.

T

theory   A set of interrelated propositions concerning the causes for a social behavior that help organize research results, make predictions about the influence of certain variables, and give direction to future social research.

theory of planned behavior   A theory that explains attitude–behavior relationships, focusing on the relationship between the strength of our behavioral intentions and our performance of them.

theory of reasoned action   A theory of attitudes stating that people are relatively thoughtful creatures and are aware of their attitudes and behavior.

threat to self-esteem model   A model explaining the reactions of victims to receiving help suggesting that they might refuse help because accepting it is a threat to their self-esteem.

transactive memory systems   Systems within groups that are sets of individual memories that allow group members to learn about each other's expertise and to assign memory tasks on that basis.

triangular theory of love   A theory suggesting that love comprises three components—passion, intimacy, and commitment—each of which is conceptualized as a leg of a triangle that can vary.

true partner effect   The phenomenon whereby an individual's tendency to conform with a majority position is reduced if there is one other person who supports the nonconforming individual's position.

trustworthiness   A component of communicator credibility that involves our assessment of the communicator's motives for delivering the message.

U

ultimate attribution error   The tendency to give in-group—but not out-group—members the benefit of the doubt for negative behaviors.

unobtrusive measure   A method of assessing attitudes such that the individuals whose attitudes you are measuring are not aware of your interest in them.

unrequited love   Love expressed by one person that is rejected and not returned by the other.

V

value   A concept closely related to an attitude that is a standard of what is desirable for one's actions.

W

working model   Mental representations of what an individual expects to happen in close relationships.

Y

Yale communication model   A model of the persuasion process that stressed the role of the communicator (source of a message), the nature of the message, the audience, and the channel of communication.

REFERENCES

Aakker, J. L., & Maheswaran, D. (1997). The effect of cultural orientation on persuasion. *Journal of Consumer Research, 24,* 315–327.

Abelson, R. (1986). Beliefs are like our possessions. *Journal for the Theory of Social Behavior, 16,* 223–250.

Abelson, R. (1988). Conviction. *American Psychologist, 43,* 267–275.

Abelson, R. P., & Prentice, D. A. (1989). Beliefs as possessions: A functionalized perspective. In A. Pratkanis, S. Breckler, & A. G. Greenwald (Eds.), *Attitude structure and function* (pp. 361–381). Hillsdale, NJ: Erlbaum.

Acker, M., & Davis, M. H. (1992). Intimacy, passion and commitment in adult romantic relationships: A test of the triangular theory of love. *Journal of Social and Personal Relationships 9,* 21–50.

Adler, T. (1990, January 9). Happiness-health link remains questionable. *APA Monitor.*

Adorno, T. W., Frenkel-Brunswik, E., Levison, D. J., & Sanford, R. N. (1950). *The authoritarian personality.* New York: Harper.

Agocha, V. B., & Cooper, M. L. (1999). Risk perceptions and safer-sex intention: Does a partner's physical attractiveness undermine the use of risk-relevant information? *Personality and Social Psychology Bulletin, 25,* 756–759.

Aikwa, A. (1990). Determinants of the magnitude of indebtedness in Japan: A comparison of relative weight of the recipient's benefits and the donor's costs. *Journal of Psychology, 124,* 523–533.

Ainsworth, M. D. S. (1992). Epilogue. In D. Cicchetti, M., M. Greenberg, & M. Cummings (Eds.), *Attachment in the preschool years.* Chicago: University of Chicago Press.

Ajzen, I. (1985). From actions to intentions: A theory of planned behavior. In J. Kuhl & J. Beckman (Eds.), *Action control: From cognition to behavior* (pp. 11–39). New York: Springer-Verlag.

Ajzen, I. (1987). Attitudes, traits, and actions: Dispositional prediction of behavior in personality and social psychology. In L. Berkowitz (Ed.), *Advances in experimental social psychology* (Vol. 20, pp. 1–64). San Diego, CA: Academic Press.

Ajzen, I. (1989). Attitude structure and behavior. In A. R. Pratkanis, S. J. Breckler, & A. G. Greenwald (Eds.), *Attitude structure and function.* Hillsdale, NJ: Erlbaum.

Ajzen, I. (1991). The theory of planned behavior. *Organizational Behavior and Human Decision Processes, 50,* 179–211.

Ajzen, I., & Fishbein, M. (1980). *Understanding attitudes and predicting human behavior.* Englewood Cliffs, NJ: Prentice-Hall.

Albert, D. J., Petrovic, D. M., & Walsh, M. L. (1989a). Competitive experience activates testosterone-dependent social aggression toward unfamiliar males. *Physiology and Behavior, 45,* 723–727.

Albert, D. J., Petrovic, D. M., & Walsh, M. L. (1989b). Ovariectomy attenuates aggression by female rats cohabiting with sexually active sterile males. *Physiology and Behavior, 45,* 225–228.

Albright, L., Kenny, D. A., & Malloy, T. E. (1988). Consensus in personality judgments at zero acquaintance. *Journal of Personality and Social Psychology, 55,* 387–395.

Allen, J., & Howland, A. (1974). *The United States of America.* New York: Prentice-Hall.

Allen, K. M. , Blascovich, J., Tomaka, J., & Kelsey, R. M. (1991). Presence of human friends and pet dogs as moderators of autonomic responses to stress in women. *Journal of Personality and Social Psychology, 61,* 582–589.

Allport, G. (1954). *The nature of prejudice.* Reading, MA.: Addison-Wesley.

Allport, G. W. (1935). Attitudes. In C. Murchison (Ed.), *Handbook of social psychology* (pp. 173–210). Worcester, MA: Clark University Press.

Altman, I., & Taylor, D. A. (1973). *Social penetration: The development of interpersonal relationships.* New York: Holt, Rinehart & Winston.

American Psychological Association. (1998). Psychology examines the issues: Hate crimes today: An age-old foe in modern dress. American Psychological Association. Washington, DC: Retrieved January 8, 2001, from the World Wide Web: http://www.apa.org/pubinfo/hate/.

American Psychological Association [APA]. (1992). Ethical principles of psychologists. *American Psychologist, 45,* 1597–1611.

Andersen, B. L., Cyranowski, J. M., & Espindle, D. (1999). Men's sexual self-schema. *Journal of Personality and Social Psychology, 76*(4), 645–661.

Anderson, C. A. (1999). Attributional style, depression, and loneliness: A cross-cultural comparison of American and Chinese students. *Personality and Social Psychology Bulletin, 25,* 482–499.

Anderson, D. E., Ansfield, M. E., & DePaulo, B. M. (1998). Love's best habit: Deception in the context of relationships. In P. Philipott, R. S. Feldman, & E. J. Coats (Eds.), *The social context of nonverbal behavior* (pp. 372–409). Cambridge, England: Cambridge University Press.

Antidefamation League. (1999). Hate on the internet: New ADL report reveals neo-Nazis and others exploiting technology. Retrieved January 8, 2001 from the World Wide Web: http://206.3.178.10/PresRele/ASUS_12/2609_12.html.

Arbuthnot, J., & Wayner, M. (1982). Minority influence: Effects of size, conversion and sex. *Journal of Psychology, 111,* 285–295.

Archer, J., Person, N. A., & Westeman, K. E. (1988). Aggressive behaviour of children aged 6–11: Gender differences and their magnitude. *British Journal of Social Psychology, 27,* 371–384.

Ardrey, R. (1969). *The territorial imperative: A personal inquiry into the animal origins of property and nations.* New York: Atheneum.

Arendt, H. (1963). *Eichmann in Jerusalem: A report on the banality of evil.* New York: Viking.

Argote, L. (1989). Agreement about norms and work unit effectiveness: Evidence from the field. *Basic and Applied Social Psychology, 10,* 131–140.

Arkin, R. M., & Baumgardner, A. H. (1986). Self presentation and self evaluation. In R. F. Baumeister (Ed.), *Public self and private self* (pp. 75–97). New York: Springer-Verlag.

Aron A., Aron, E., & Allen, J. (1998). Motivations for unrequited love. *Personality and Social Psychology Bulletin, 21,* 787–796.

Aron, A., & Aron, E. N. (1989). *The heart of social psychology* (2nd ed.). Lexington, MA: Lexington Books.

Aronson, E., & Mills, J. (1959). The effects of severity of initiation on liking for a group. *Journal of Abnormal and Social Psychology, 59,* 177–181.

Aronson, E., Blaney, N., Stephan, C., Sikes, J., & Snapp, M. (1978). *The jigsaw classroom.* Beverly Hills, CA: Sage.

Aronson, J., Quinn, D. M., & Spencer, S. J. (1998). Stereotype threat and the academic underperformance of minorities and women. In J. K. Swim & C. Stangor (Eds.), *Prejudice: The target's perspective* (pp. 85–103). San Diego, CA: Academic Press.

Aronson, E., Turner, J., & Carlsmith, J. M. (1963). Communication credibility and communication discrepancy as determinants of opinion change. *Journal of Abnormal and Social Psychology, 67,* 31–36.

Arrington, L. J., & Bitton, D. (1980). *The Mormon experience.* New York: Vintage Books.

Asch, S. E. (1946). Forming impressions of personality. *Journal of Abnormal and Social Psychology, 41,* 1230–1240.

Asch, S. E. (1951). Effects of group pressure on the modification and distortion of judgments. In H. Guetzkow (Ed.), *Groups, leadership, and men.* Pittsburgh, PA: Carnegie Press.

Asch, S. E. (1955). Opinions and social pressures. *Scientific American, 193,* 31–35.

Asch, S. E. (1956). Studies of independence and conformity: A minority of one against a unanimous majority. *Psychological Monographs, 70.*

Averill, J. R. (1985). The social construction of emotion: With special reference to love. In K. J. Gergen & K. E. Davis (Eds.), *The social construction of the person* (pp. 112–136). New York: Springer-Verlag.

Badaway, A. (1998). Alcohol, aggression and serotonin: Metabolic aspects. *Alcohol and Alcoholism, 33,* 66–72.

Baker, J. G., & Fishbein, H. D. (1998). The development of prejudice towards gays and lesbians by adolescents. *Journal of Homosexuality, 36,* 89–100.

Ball-Rokeach, S., Rokeach, M., & Grube, J. W. (1984). *The great American values test.* New York: Free Press.

Balls, P., & Eisenberg, N. (1986). Sex differences in recipients reactions to aid. *Sex Roles, 14,* 69–79.

Banaji, M. R., Hardin, C., & Rothman, A. J. (1993). Implicit stereotyping in person judgment. *Journal of Personality and Social Psychology, 65,* 272–281.

Banaji, M. R., & Steele, C. M. (1989). The social cognition of alcohol use. *Social Cognition, 7,* 137–151.

Bandura, A. (1965). Influence of models' reinforcement contingencies on the acquisition if imitative responses. *Journal of Personality and Social Psychology, 1,* 589–595.

Bandura, A. (1973). *Aggression: A Social Learning Analysis.* Englewood Cliffs, NJ: Prentice-Hall.

Bandura, A. (1977). *Social learning theory.* Englewood Cliffs, NJ: Prentice-Hall.

Bandura, A., & Jourden, F. J. (1991). Self regulatory mechanisms governing the impact of social comparison on complex decision making. *Journal of Personality and Social Psychology, 60,* 941–951.

Bandura, A., Ross, D., & Ross, S. A. (1961). Transmission of aggression through imitation of aggressive models. *Journal of Abnormal and Social Psychology, 63,* 575–582.

Bandura, A., Ross, D., & Ross, S. A. (1963). Imitation of film-mediated aggressive models. *Journal of Abnormal and Social Psychology, 67,* 601–607.

Bargh, J. (1989). Conditional automaticity: Varieties of automatic influences in social perception and cognition. In J. S. Uleman & J. A. Bargh (Eds.), *Unintended thought* (pp. 3–51). New York: Guilford.

Bargh, J. A. (1997). The automaticity of everyday life. In R. S. Wyer, Jr. (Ed.), *Advances in social cognition* (Vol. 10, pp. 1–61). Mahwah, NJ: Erlbaum.

Bargh, J. A., & Chartrand, T. L. (1999). The unbearable automaticity of being. *American Psychologist, 54,* 462–479.

Bargh, J. A., & Thein, R. D. (1985). Individual construct accessibility, person memory, and recall–judgment link: The case of information overload. *Journal of Personality and Social Psychology, 49(5),* 1129–1146.

Barkow, J. H. (1980). Sociobiology. In A. Montagu (Ed.), *Sociobiology examined.* Oxford, England: Oxford University Press.

Barnett, M. A., Thompson, M., & Pfiefer, J. R. (1985). Perceived competence to help and the arousal of empathy. *Journal of Social Psychology, 125,* 679–680.

Barnett, R., & Marshall, N. (1990, November). *Job satisfaction as a buffer against stress.* Paper presented at conference on Work and Well Being: An Agenda for the '90's.

Baron, L., (1986). The holocaust and human decency: A review of research on the rescue of Jews in Nazi occupied Europe. *Humboldt Journal of Social Relations, 13,* 237–251.

Baron, R. A. (1974). The aggression-inhibiting influence of heightened sexual arousal. *Journal of Personality and Social Psychology, 30,* 318–322.

Baron, R. S. (1986). Distraction-conflict theory: Progress and problems. *Advances in Experimental Social Psychology* (Vol. 19, pp. 1–40). Orlando, FL: Academic Press.

Baron, R. S., Kerr, N. L., & Miller, N. (1992). *Group process, group decision, group action.* Pacific Grove, CA: Brooks/Cole.

Barsalou, L. W. (1987). The instability of graded structure: Implications for the nature of concepts. In U. Neisser (Ed.), *Concepts and conceptual development: Ecological and intellectual factors in categorization.* New York: Cambridge University Press.

Bartholomew, K., & Horowitz, L. M. (1991). Attachment styles among young adults: A test of a four category model. *Journal of Personality and Social Psychology, 61,* 226–244.

Bassili, J. N. (1981). The attractiveness stereotype: Goodness or glamour? *Basic and Applied Social Psychology, 2,* 235–252.

Bassili, J. N., & Krosnick, J. A. (2000). Do strength-related attitude properties determine susceptibility to response effects? New evidence from response latency, attitude extremity, and aggregate indices. *Political Psychology, 21,* 107–132.

Batson, C. D. (1997). Self–other merging and the empathy–altruism hypothesis: Reply to Neuberg et al. (1997). *Journal of Personality and Social Psychology, 73,* 517–522.

Batson, C. D. (1987). Prosocial motivation: Is it ever truly altruistic? In L. Berkowitz (Ed.), *Advances in Experimental Social Psychology* (Vol. 20, pp. 65–122).

Batson, C. D. (1990a). How social an animal: The human capacity for caring. *American Psychologist, 45,* 336–346.

Batson, C. D. (1990b). Good samaritans–or priests of levites? *Personality and Social Psychology Bulletin,* 758–768.

Batson, C. D., Dyck, J. L., Brandt, J. R., Batson, J. G., Powell, A. L., McMaster, M. R., & Griffitt, C. (1988). Five studies testing two egoistic alternatives to the empathy–altruism hypothesis. *Journal of Personality and Social Psychology, 55,* 52–77.

Batson, C. D., Early, S., & Salvarani, G. (1997). Perspective taking: Imagining how another feels versus imagining how you would feel. *Personality and Social Psychology Bulletin, 23*, 751–758.

Batson, C. D., Fultz, J., & Schoenrade, P. A. (1987). Distress and empathy: Two qualitatively distinct vicarious emotions with different motivational consequences. *Journal of Personality, 55*, 19–39.

Batson, C. D., Nadia, A., Jodi, Y., Bedell, S. J., & Johnson, J. W. (1999). Two threats to the common good: Self-interest and empathy and empathy-induced altruism. *Personality and Social Psychology Bulletin, 25*, 3–16.

Batson, C. D., O'Quin, K., Fultz, J., & Vanderplas, M. (1983). Influence of self-reported distress and empathy on egoistic versus altruistic motivation to help. *Journal of Personality and Social Psychology, 45*, 706–718.

Batson, C. D., Sager, K., Garst, E., Kang, M., Rubchinsky, K., & Dawson, K. (1997). Is empathy-induced helping due to self-other merging? *Journal of Personality and Social Psychology, 73*, 495–509.

Batson, C. D., & Weeks, J. L. (1996). Mood effects of unsuccessful helping: Another test of the empathy–altruism hypothesis. *Personality and Social Psychology Bulletin, 22*, 148–157.

Baucom, D. H., Sayers, S. L., & Duhe, A. (1989). Attributional style and attributional patterns among married couples. *Journal of Personality and Social Psychology, 56*, 596–607.

Baum, A., & Nesselhof-Kendall, S. (1988). Psychological research and the prevention, etiology, and treatment of AIDS. *American Psychologist, 43*, 900–908.

Baum, L. (1985). *The Supreme Court* (2nd ed.). Washington, DC: Congressional Quarterly.

Baumeister, R. (1986). *Identity.* New York: Oxford University Press.

Baumeister, R., & Tice, D. (1990). Anxiety and social exclusion. *Journal of Social and Clinical Psychology, 9*(2), 165–195.

Baumeister, R., Wotman, S., & Stillwell, A. M. (1993). Unrequited love: On heartbreak, anger, guilt, scriptlessness and humiliation. *Journal of Personality and Social Psychology, 64*, 377–394.

Baumeister, R. F. (1984). Choking under pressure: Self-consciousness and paradoxical effects of incentives on skillful performance. *Journal of Personality and Social Psychology, 46*, 610–620.

Baumeister, R. F. (1987) How the self became a problem: A psychological review of historical research. *Journal of Personality and Social Psychology, 52*, 163–176.

Baumeister, R. F. (1988). Masochism as escape from the self. *Journal of Sex Research, 25*, 28–59.

Baumeister, R. F. (1990). Suicide as escape from the self. *Psychological Review, 97*, 90–113.

Baumeister, R. F., & Bratslavsky, E. (1999). Passion, intimacy, and time: Passionate love as a function of *change of intimacy* over time. *Personality and Social Psychology Review, 3*, 49–67.

Baumeister, R. F., Bratslavsky, E. , Muraven, M., & Tice, D. M. (1998). Ego depletion: Is the active self a limited resource? *Journal of Personality and Social Psychology, 74*, 1252–1265.

Baumeister, R. F., Chesner, S. P., Senders, P. S., & Tice, D. M. (1988). Who's in charge here: Group leaders do lend help in emergencies. *Personality and Social Psychology Bulletin, 14*, 17–22.

Baumeister, R. F., & Leary, M. R. (1995). The need to belong: Desire for interpersonal attachments as a fundamental human motivation. *Psychological Bulletin, 117*, 497–529.

Baumeister, R. F., & Sher, S. J. (1988). Self-defeating behavior patterns among normal individuals: Review and analysis of common self-destructive tendencies. *Psychological Bulletin, 104*, 2–22.

Baumeister, R. F., & Sommer, K. L. (1997). Consciousness, free choice, and automaticity. In R. S. Wyer, Jr. (Ed.), *Advances in social cognition* (Vol. X, pp. 75–81). Mahwah, NJ: Erlbaum.

Baumeister, R. F., & Tice, D. (1984). Role of self-presentation and choice in cognitive dissonance under forced compliance: Necessary or sufficient causes? *Journal of Personality and Social Psychology, 46*, 5–13.

Baumgarder, A. H. (1990). To know oneself is to like oneself: Self certainty and self-affect. *Journal of Personality and Social Psycholoyg, 58*, 1062–1072.

Baumgardner, A. H., Kaufman, C. M., & Crawford, J. A. (1990). To be noticed favorably: Links between the private self and the public self. *Personality and Social Psychology Bulletin, 16*, 705–716.

Baumrind, D. (1964). Some thoughts on ethics of research: After reading Milgram's "behavioral study of obedience." *American Psychologist, 19*, 421–423.

Bazerman. M. H. (1986, June). Why negotiations go wrong. *Psychology Today, 20*, 54–58.

Bee, H. (1992). *The developing child* (6th ed.). Glenview, IL: HarperCollins.

Bell, M. L., & Forde, D. R. (1999). A factorial survey of interpersonal conflict resolution. *Journal of Social Psychology, 139*, 369–377.

Bem, D. (1967). Self-perception: An alternative interpretation of cognitive dissonance phenomena. *Psychological Review, 74*, 183–200.

Bem D. J. (1966.) Inducing belief in false confessions. *Journal of Personality and Social Psychology, 3*, 707–710.

Bem, D. J. (1972). Self-perception theory. In L. Berkowitz (Ed.), *Advances in experimental social psychology* (Vol. 6, pp. 1–62). New York; Academic Press.

Bem, S. L. (1974). The measurement of psychological androgyny. *Journal of Consulting and Clinical Psychology, 42*, 155–162.

Ben Hamida, S., Mineka, S., & Bailey, J. M. (1998). Sex differences in perceived controllability of mate value: An evolutionary perspective. *Journal of Personality and Social Psychology, 75*, 963–966.

Bennett, T. L., Silver, R. C., & Ellard, J. H. (1991). Coping with an abusive relationship: How and why do women stay? *Journal of Marriage and the Family, 13*, 118–122.

Benson, P. L., Karabenick, S. A., & Lerner, R. M. (1976). Pretty pleases: The effects of physical attractiveness, race and sex on receiving help. *Journal of Experimental Social Psychology, 12*, 409–415.

Berglas, S. & Jones, E. E. (1978). Drug choice as a self-handicapping strategy in response to noncontingent success. *Journal of Personality and Social Psychology, 36*, 405–417.

Berkowitz, L. (1969). Resistance to improper dependency relationships. *Journal of Experimental Social Psychology, 5*, 283–294.

Berkowitz, L. (1972). Social norms, feelings, and other factors affecting altruism. In L. Berkowitz (Ed.), *Advances in experimental social psychology*. New York: Academic Press.

Berkowitz, L. (1978). Whatever happened to the frustration–aggression hypothesis? *American Behavioral Scientist, 21*, 691–708.

Berkowitz, L. (1988). Introduction. In L. Berkowitz (Ed.), *Advances in experimental social psychology* (Vol. 21, pp. 1–16). New York: Academic Press.

Berkowitz, L. (1989). Frustration–aggression hypothesis: Examination and reformation. *Psychological Bulletin, 106*, 59–73.

Berkowitz, L., & LePage, A. (1967). Weapons as aggression-eliciting stimuli. *Journal of Personality and Social Psychology, 7*, 202–207.

Berndt, T. J. (1992). Friendship and friends' influence in adolescence. *Current Directions in Psychological Sciences, 1*, 156–159.

Bernieri, F. J., Gillis, J. S., Davis, J. M., & Grahe, J. E. (1996). Dyad rapport and the accuracy of its judgment across situations: A lens model analysis. *Journal of Personality and Social Psychology, 71*, 110–129.

Berreby, D. (1998, June 9). Studies explore love and the sweaty t-shirt. *The New York Times*, B14.

Berry, D. (1991). Attractive faces are not all created equal: Joint effects of facial babyishness and attractiveness on social perception. *Personality and Social Psychology Bulletin, 17*, 523–528.

Berscheid, E. (1985). Compatibility, interdependence, and emotion. In W. Ickes (Ed.), *Compatible and incompatible relationships*. New York: Springer-Verlag.

Berscheid, E. (1988). Some comments on the anatomy of love: Or what ever happened to old fashioned lust? In R. J. Sternberg & M. L. Barnes (Eds.), *The psychology of love*. New Haven, CT: Yale University Press.

Berscheid, E., Snyder, M., & Omoto, A. M. (1989). The relationship closeness inventory: Assessing the closeness of interpersonal relationships. *Journal of Personality and Social Psychology, 57*, 792–807.

Berscheid, E., & Walster, E. (1974). A little bit about love. In T. L. Huston (Ed.), *Foundations of interpersonal attraction*. New York: Academic Press.

Berscheid, E., & Walster, E. H. (1978). *Interpersonal attraction* (2nd ed.). Reading, MA: Addison-Wesley.

Bettencourt, B. A., & Miller, N. (1996). Gender differences in aggression as a function of provocation: A meta-analysis. *Psychological Bulletin, 119*, 422–447.

Bettleheim, B. & Janowitz (1950). *The dynamics of prejudice*. New York: Harper.

Bickman, L. (1974). The social power of a uniform. *Journal of Applied Social Psychology, 4*, 47–61.

Bickman, L., & Kamzan, M. (1973). The effect of race and need on helping behavior. *Journal of Social Psychology, 89*, 73–77.

Biernat, M., & Wortman, C. (1991). Sharing of home responsibilities between professionally employed women and their husbands. *Journal of Personality and Social Psychology, 60*, 844–860.

Billig, M. (1992, January 27). The baseline of intergroup prejudice. *Current Contents, 4*.

Blaine, B. E., Trivedi, P., & Eshleman, A. (1998). Religious belief and the self-concept: Evaluating the implications for psychological adjustment. *Personality and Social Psychology Bulletin, 24*, 1040–1052.

Blanchard, D. C., & Blanchard, R. J. (1984). Affect and aggression: An animal model applied to human behavior. In R. J. Blanchard & D. C. Blanchard (Eds.), *Advances in the study of aggression* (Vol. 1, pp. 1–62). New York: Academic Press.

Blanchard, F. A., Lilly, T., & Vaughn, L. A. (1991). Reducing the expression of racial prejudice. *Psychological Science, 2*, 101–105.

Blascovich, J., Ernst, J. M., Tomaka, J., Kelsey, R. M., Salomon, K. L., & Fazio, R. H. (1993). Attitude accessibility as a moderator of autonomic reactivity during decision making. *Journal of Personality and Social Psychology, 64(2)*, 165–176.

Blascovich, J., & Ginsburg, G. P. (1974). Emergent norms and choice shifts involving risks. *Sociometry, 37*, 274–276.

Blass, T. (1991). Understanding behavior in the Milgram obedience experiment: The role of personality, situations, and their interactions. *Journal of Personality and Social Psychology, 60*, 398–413.

Blass, T. (2000). The Milgram paradigm after 35 years: Some things we now know about obedience to authority. In T. Blass (Ed.), *Obedience to authority: Current perspectives on the Milgram paradigm* (pp. 35–59). Mahwah, NJ: Lawrence Erlbaum Publishers.

Bodenhausen, G. V. (1990). Stereotypes as judgmental heuristics: Evidence of circadian variations in discrimination. *Psychological Science, 1(5)*, 319–322.

Bodenhausen, G. V. (1992). In A. Combs (Ed.), *Cooperation: Beyond the age of competition*. Philadelphia: Gordon and Breach.

Bodenhausen, G. V. (1993). Emotion, arousal, and stereotypic judgment: A heuristic model of affect and stereotyping. In D. Mackie & D. Hamilton (Eds.), *Affect, cognition, and stereotyping: Interactive processes in group perception*. San Diego, CA: Academic Press.

Bodenhausen, G. V., & Lichtenstein, M. (1987). Social stereotypes and information-processing strategies: The impact of task complexity. *Journal of Personality and Social Psychology, 52(5)*, 871–880.

Bodenhausen, G. V., & Wyer, R. S. (1985). Effects of stereotypes on decision making and information processing strategies: The impact of task complexity. *Journal of Personality and Social Psychology, 48*, 267–282.

Bolger, N., & Eckenrode, J. (1991). Social relationships, personality, and anxiety during a major stressful event. *Journal of Personality and Social Psychology, 61(3)*, 440–449.

Bolt, M., & Caswell, J. (1981). Attribution of responsibility to a rape victim. *Journal of Social Psychology, 114*, 137–138.

Bordens, K. S. (1979). An investigation into the weighing and integration of legal evidence. Unpublished doctoral dissertation, University of Toledo, Ohio.

Bordens, K. S. (1984). The effects of likelihood of conviction, threatened punishment, and assumed role on mock plea bargain decisions. *Basic and Applied Social Psychology, 5*, 59–74.

Bordens, K. S., & Abbott, B. B. (1991). *Research design and methods: A process approach* (2nd ed.). Mountain View, CA: Mayfield.

Bordens, K. S., & Abbott, B. B. (1999). *Research design and methods: A process approach* (4th ed.). Mountain View, CA: Mayfield.

Bordens, K. S., & Bassett, J. (1985). The plea bargaining process from the defendant's perspective: A field investigation. *Basic and Applied Social Psychology, 6*, 93–110.

Bordens, K. S., & Horowitz, I. A. (1985). Joinder of criminal offenses: A review of the legal and psychological literature. *Law and Human Behavior, 9*, 339–353.

Borgida, E., Conner, C., & Manteufel, L. (1991). Understanding living kidney donation: A behavioral decision making prospective. In S. Spacapan & S. Oskamp (Eds.), *The social psychology of helping and being helped in the real world. Beverly Hills, CA: Sage.

Bornstein, R. F. (1989). Exposure and affect: Overview and meta-analysis of research, 1968–1987. *Psychological Bulletin, 106*(2), 265–289.

Bornstein, R. F., Leone, D. R., & Galley, D. J. (1987). The generalizability of subliminal mere exposure effects: Influence of stimuli perceived without awrness on social behavior. *Journal of Personality and Social Psychology, 53*, 1070–1079.

Bowie, C., & Ford, N. (1989). Sexual behavior of young people and the risk of HIV infection. *Journal of Epidemiology and Community Health, 43*, 61–65.

Bradbury, T. N., & Fincham, F. D. (1990). Attributions in marriage: Review and critique. *Psychological Bulletin, 107*, 3–33.

Brannon, J., & Feist, J. (1992). *Health psychology* (2nd ed.). Belmont, CA: Wadsworth.

Bray, R. M., Kerr, N. L., & Atkin, R. S. (1978). The effect of group size, problem difficulty, and sex on group performance. *Journal of Personality and Social Psychology, 36*, 1224–1240.

Bray, R. M., & Noble, A. M. (1978). Authoritarianism and decisions of mock juries: Evidence of jury bias and group polarization. *Journal of Personality and Social Psychology, 36*, 1424–1430.

Breckler, S. J., & Wiggins, E. C. (1989). On defining attitude and attitude theory: Once more with feeling. In A. R. Pratkanis, S. J. Breckler, & A. G. Greenwald (Eds.), *Attitudes structure and function* (pp. 407–428). Hillsdale, NJ: Erlbaum.

Brehm, J. (1956). Post-decision changes in the desirability of alternatives. *Journal of Abnormal and Social Psychology, 52*, 384–389.

Brehm, J. (1966). A Theory of psychological reactance. New York: Academic Press.

Brehm, J., & Cohen, A. R. (1962). *Explorations in cognitive dissonance.* New York: Wiley.

Brehm, S. (1985). *Intimate relations.* New York: Random House.

Brehm, S. (1988). Passionate love. In R. J. Sternberg & M. L. Barnes (Eds.), *The psychology of love.* New Haven, CT: Yale University Press.

Brehm, S. S., & Brehm, J. W. (1981). *Psychological reactance: A theory of freedom and control.* New York: Academic Press.

Brewer, M. (1993, August). *The social self, inclusion and distinctiveness.* Address to the American Psychological Convention, Toronto, Canada.

Brewer, M. B. (1988). A dual process model of impression formation. In T. K. Srull & R. S. Wyer (Eds.), *Advances in social cognition.* Hillsdale, NJ: Erlbaum.

Bridges, J. S., & McGrail, C. A. (1989). Attributions of responsibility for date and stranger rape. *Sex Roles, 21*, 273–286.

Brinthaupt, T. M., Moreland, R. L., & Levine J. M. (1991). Sources of optimism among prospective group members. *Personality and Social Psychology Bulletin, 17*, 36–45.

Brody, J. E. (1992, February 25). Maintaining friendships for the sake of good health. *The New York Times, B8.*

Brody, S., Rau, H., Fuehrer, N., Hellebrand, H., Rudiger, D., & Braun, M. (1996). Traditional ideology as an inhibitor of sexual behavior. *Journal of Psychology, 130*, 615–626.

Broverman, I. K., Vogel, S. R., Broverman, D. M., Clarkson, F. E., & Rosenkrantz , P. S. (1972). Sex role stereotypes: A current appraisal. *Journal of Social Issues, 28*, 59–78.

Brown, J. (1991). Staying fit and staying well: Physical fitness as a moderator of life stress. *Journal of Personality and Social Psychology, 60*, 555–561.

Brown, J., & Smart, A. (1991). The self and social conduct: Linking self-representations to prosocial behavior. *Journal of Personality and Social Psychology, 60*, 368–375.

Brown, J. A. C. (1967). *Techniques of persuasion: From propaganda to brainwashing.* New York: Pelican Books.

Brown, R. (1986). *Social psychology* (2nd ed.). New York: Free Press.

Brown, R. P., & Josephs, R. A. (1999). A burden of proof: Stereotype relevance and gender differences in math performance. *Journal of Personality and Social Psychology, 76*, 246–257.

Brownmiller, S. (1975). *Against our will: Men, women and rape.* New York: Simon & Schuster.

Brownstein, R. J., & Katzev, R. D. (1985). The relative effectiveness of three compliance techniques in eliciting donations to a cultural organization. *Journal of Applied Social Psychology, 15*, 564–574.

Bruner, H. H., Nelon, M., Breakefield, X. O., Ropers, H., & van Oost, B. A. (1993). Abnormal behavior associated with a point mutation in the structural gene for monoamine oxidase. *Science, 262*, 578–580.

Brush, S. G. (1991). Women in engineering and science. *American Scientist, 79*, 404–419.

Bryan, J., & Test, M. (1967). Models and helping: Naturalistic studies in aiding behavior. *Journal of Personality and Social Psychology, 6*, 400–407.

Bryan, J. H., & Walbek, N. (1970). Preaching and practicing self-sacrifice: Children's actions and reactions. *Child Development, 41*, 329–353.

Bulman, R., & Wortman, C. (1977). Attributions of blame and coping in the "real world": Severe accident victims react to their lot. *Journal of Personality and Social Psychology, 35*, 351–383.

Burger, J., & Burns, L. (1988). The illusion of unique invulnerability and the effective use of contraception. *Personality and Social Psychology Bulletin, 14*, 264–270.

Burger, J. M. (1986). Increasing compliance by improving the deal: The that's not all technique. *Journal of Personality and Social Psychology, 51*, 277–283.

Burger, J. M. (1991). Changes in attribution over time: The ephemeral fundamental attribution error. *Social Cognition, 9*, 182–193.

Burger, J. M., & Petty, R. E. (1981). The low-ball compliance technique: Task or person commitment? *Journal of Personality and Social Psychology, 40*, 492–500.

Burnett, A. (1972). *Gertrude Stein.* New York: Atheneum.

Burnstein, E. (1982). Persuasion as argument processing. In H. Brandstatter, J. H. Davis, & G. Stocker-Kreichgauer (Eds.), *Group decision making* (pp. 103–124). London: Academic Press.

Burnstein, E., & Sentis, K. (1981). Attitude polarization in groups. In R. E. Petty, T. M. Ostrom, & T. C. Brock (Eds.), *Cognitive responses in persuasion* (pp. 197–216). Hillsdale, NJ: Erlbaum.

Burnstein, E., & Vinokur, A. (1977). Persuasive argumentation and social comparison as determinants of attitude polarization. *Journal of Experimental Social Psychology, 13*, 315–332.

Burt, M. (1980). Cultural myths and supports for rape. *Journal of Personality and Social Psychology, 38*, 217–230.

Bushman, B. J., & Cooper, H. M. (1990). Effects of alcohol on human aggression: An integrative research review. *Psychological Bulletin, 107*, 341–354.

Buss, A., Booker, A., & Buss, E. (1972). Firing a weapon and aggression. *Journal of Personality and Social Psychology, 22,* 296–302.

Buss, D. M. (1988a) Love acts: The evolutionary biology of love. In R. J. Sternberg & M. L. Barnes (Eds.), *The psychology of love.* New Haven, CT: Yale University Press.

Buss, D. M. (1988b). From vigilance to violence: Tactics of mate retention in American undergraduates. *Ethology and Sociobiology, 9,* 291–317.

Buss, D. M. (1994). *The evolution of desire: Strategies of human mating.* New York: Basic Books.

Byrne, D. (1971). *The attraction paradigm.* New York: Academic Press.

Byrne, D., & Clore, G. L. (1970). A reinforcement model of evaluative processes. *Personality: An International Journal, 1,* 103–128.

Byrne, D., Clore, G. L., & Smeaton, G. (1986). The attraction hypothesis: Do similar attitudes affect anything? *Journal of Personality and Social Psychology, 51,* 1167–1170.

Byrne, D., & Nelson, D. (1965). Attraction as a linear function of proportion of positive reinforcements. *Journal of Personality and Social Psychology, 1 ,* 659–663.

Cacioppo, J. T., Andersen, B. L., Turnquist, D. C., Tassinary, L. G. (1989). Psychophysiological comparison theory: On the experience, description, and assessment of signs and symptoms. *Patient Education and Counseling, 14,* 177–196.

Cacioppo, J. T., & Petty, R. E. (1979). Effects of message repetition and position on cognitive response, recall, and persuasion. *Journal of Personality and Social Psychology, 37,* 97–109.

Cacioppo, J. T., & Petty, R. E. (1983). *Psychophysiology: A sourcebook.* New York: Guilford.

Cacioppo, J. T., Petty, R. E., & Morris, K. (1983). Effects of need for cognition on message evaluation, recall, and persuasion. *Journal of Personality and Social Psychology, 45,* 805–818.

Cacioppo, J. T., Petty, R. E., & Tassinary, L. G. (1989). Sociophysiology: A new look. In L. Berkowitz (Ed.), *Advances in experimental social psychology* (Vol. 22, pp. 39–91). Kent, UK: Harcourt.

Cacioppo, J. T., Uchino, B. N., Crites, S. I., Snydersmith, M. A., Smith, G., Berman, G. G., & Lang, P. J. (1992). Relationship between facial expressiveness and sympathetic activation in emotion: A critical review, with emphasis on modeling underlying mechanisms and individual differences. *Journal of Personality and Social Psychology, 62,* 110–128.

Callero, P. L. (1986). Putting the social in prosocial behavior: An interactionist approach to altruism. *Humboldt Journal of Social Relations, 13,* 15–32.

Campbell, J. T., & Fairey, P. J. (1989). Informational and normative routes to conformity: The effect of faction size as a function of norm extremity and attention to the stimulus. *Journal of Personality and Social Psychology, 57,* 457–468.

Cantrill, J. G., & Siebold, D. R. (1986). The perceptual contrast explanation of sequential request strategy effectiveness. *Human Communication Research, 13,* 253–267.

Caporael, L. R. (1997). The evolution of a truly social cognition: The core configurations model. *Personality and Social Psychology Review, 1,* 276–298.

Carduci, B. J., & Deuser, P. S. (1984). The foot-in-the-door technique: Initial request and organ donation. *Basic and Applied Social Psychology, 5,* 75–82.

Carli, L. L., Ganley, R., & Pierce-Otay, A. (1991). Similarity and satisfaction in roommate relationships. *Personality and Social Psychology Bulletin, 17,* 419–427.

Carlo, G., Raffaelli, M., Laible, D. J., & Meyer, K. A. (1999). Why are girls less physically aggressive than boys: Personality and parenting mediators of physical aggression. *Sex Roles, 40,* 711–729.

Carlson, M., Marcus-Newhall, A., & Miller, N. (1990). Effects of situational aggression cues: A quantitative review. *Journal of Personality and Social Psychology, 58,* 622–633.

Carlson, N. R. (1991). *Physiology of behavior* (4th ed.). Boston: Allyn & Bacon.

Carmelli, D., Dame, A., Swan, G., & Rosenman, R. (1991). Long term changes in type A behavior: A 27 year follow up of the Western Collaborative Group Study. *Journal of Behavioral Medicine, 14,* 593–606.

Caro, R. (1982). *The years of Lyndon Johnson: The path to power.* New York: Knopf.

Carroll, J. (1996). *An American requiem.* Boston: Houghton Mifflin.

Carver, C. S. (1975). Physical aggression as a function of objective self-awareness and attitudes toward punishment *Journal of Personality and Social Psychology, 11,* 510–519.

Castro, M. A. C. (1974). Reactions to receiving aid as a function of cost to donor and opportunity to aid. *Journal of Applied Social Psychology, 4,* 194–209.

Centers for Disease Control and Prevention (2000a). HIV/AIDS among US women: minority and young women at continuing risk. Downloaded from the World Wide Web, January 12, 2001: http://www.cdc.gov/hiv/pubs/facts/women.htm.

Centers for Disease Control and Prevention (2000b). Young people at risk: HIV/AIDS among America's youth. Downloaded from the World Wide Web, January 12, 2001: http://www.cdc.gov/hiv/pubs/facts/youth.htm.

Centers for Disease Control and Prevention (2001). Figure 9: Estimated adult/adolescent AIDS incidence by region of residence and year of diagnosis, 1997, 1998, and 1999, United States. Downloaded from the World Wide Web, January 12, 2001.

Chaiken, S. (1987). The heuristic model of persuasion. In M. P. Zanna, J. M. Olson, & C. P. Herman (Eds.), *Social influence: The Ontario symposium* (Vol. 5, pp. 3–39). Hillsdale, NJ: Erlbaum.

Chaiken, S., Liberman, A., & Eagly, A. (1989). Heuristic versus systematic information processing within and beyond the persuasion context. In J. S. Uleman & J. A. Bargh (Eds.), *Unintended thought* (pp. 212–252). New York: Guilford.

Chaiken, S., & Pilner, P. (1987). Women, but not men, are what they eat: The effect of meal size and gender on perceived femininity and masculinity. *Personality and Social Psychology Bulletin, 13,* 166–176.

Chaiken, S., & Stangor, C. (1987). Attitudes and attitude change. *Annual Review of Psychology, 38,* 575–630.

Chaiken, S., & Trope, Y. (Eds.). (1999). *Dual process theories in social psychology.* New York: Guilford.

Chamberlin, H. (1972). *A minority of members: Women in the U.S. Congress.* New York: Praeger.

Chapman, L. L., & Chapman, J. (1967). Genesis of popular but erroneous psychodiagnostic observations. *Journal of Abnormal Psychology, 72,* 193–204.

Chartrand, T. L., & Bargh, J. A. (1996). Automatic activation of impression formation and memorization goals:

Nonconscious goal priming reproduces effects of explicit task instructions. *Journal of Personality and Social Psychology, 71,* 464–478.

Chartrand, T. L., & Bargh, J. A . (1999). The chameleon effect: The perception–behavior link and social interaction. *Journal of Personality and Social Psychology, 76,* 893–910.

Chen, H., Yates, B. T., & McGinnies, E. (1988). Effects of involvement on observers' estimates of consensus, distinctiveness, and consistency. *Personality and Social Psychology Bulletin, 14,* 468–478.

Cheng, P. W., & Novick, L. R. (1990). A probabilistic contrast model of causal induction. *Journal of Personality and Social Psychology, 58,* 545–567.

Cheng, P. W., & Novick, L. R. (1991). Causes versus enabling conditions. *Cognition, 40,* 83–120.

Cheng, P. W., & Novick, L. R. (1992). Covariation in natural causal induction. *Psychological Review, 99,* 365–382.

Cheong, J., & Nagoshi, C. T. (1998). Effects of sensation seeking, instruction set, and alcohol/placebo administration on aggressive behavior. *Alcohol, 17,* 81–86.

Cheong, J., & Nagoshi C. T. (1999). Effects of sensation seeking, instruction set, and alcohol/placebo administration on aggressive behavior. *Alcohol, 17,* 81–86.

Chermack, S. T., & Walton, M, A. (1999). The relationship between family aggression history and expressed aggression among college males. *Aggressive Behavior, 25,* 255–267.

Choi, I., & Nisbett, R. E. (1998). Situational salience and cultural differences in the correspondence bias and the actor–observer bias. *Personality and Social Psychology Bulletin, 24,* 949–960.

Christiansen, K., & Knussmann, R. (1987). Androgen levels and components of aggressive behavior in men. *Hormones and Behavior, 21,* 170–180.

Christensen, P. N., & Kashy, D. (1998). Perceptions of and by lonely people in initial social interaction. *Personality and Social Psychology Bulletin, 24,* 322–329.

Cialdini, R. B. (1993). *Influence: Science and practice* (3rd ed.). New York: HarperCollins.

Cialdini, R. B., & Ascani, K. (1976). Test of a concession procedure for inducing verbal, behavioral, and further compliance with a request to give blood. *Journal of Applied Psychology, 61,* 295–300.

Cialdini, R. B., Brown, S. L., Lewis, B. P., Luce, C., & Neuberg, S. (1997). Reinterpreting the empathy–altruism relationship: When one into one equals oneness. *Journal of Personality and Social Psychology, 73,* 481–494.

Cialdini, R. B., Cacioppo, J. T., Bassett, R., & Miller, J. A. (1978). Low-ball procedure for producing compliance: Commitment then cost. *Journal of Personality and Social Psychology, 36,* 463–476.

Cialdini, R. B., & Fultz, J. (1990). Interpreting the negative mood-helping literature via "mega"-analysis: A contrary view. *Psychological Bulletin, 107,* 210–214.

Cialdini, R. B., & Schroeder, D. A. (1976). Increasing compliance by legitimizing paltry contributions: When even a penny will help. *Journal of Personality and Social Psychology, 34,* 599–604.

Cialdini, R. B., Vincent, J. E., Lewis, S. K., Catalan, J., Wheeler, D., & Darby, B. L. (1975). Reciprocal concessions procedure for inducing compliance: The door-in-the-face technique. *Journal of Personality and Social Psychology, 31,* 206–215.

Ciofi, D. (1991). Asymmetry of doubt in medical diagnosis: The ambiguity of "uncertain wellness." *Journal of Personality and Social Psychology, 61,* 969–980.

Clark, M. S. (1986). Evidence for the effectiveness of manipulations of desire for communal versus exchange relationships. *Personality and Social Psychology Bulletin, 12,* 414–425.

Clark, M. S., & Grote, N. K. (1998). Why aren't indices of relationship costs always negatively related to indices of relationship quality? *Personality and Social Psychology Review, 2,* 2–17.

Clark, M. S., Mills, J., & Powell, M. C. (1986). Keeping track of needs in exchange and communal relationships. *Journal of Personality and Social Psychology, 51,* 333–338.

Clark, R. D. (1990). The impact of AIDS on gender differences in willingness to engage in casual sex. *Journal of Applied Social Psychology, 20,* 771–782.

Clark, R. D., & Word, L. E. (1974). What is the apathetic bystander?: Situational characteristics of the emergency. *Journal of Personality and Social Psychology, 29,* 279–287.

Clary, E. G., & Orenstein, L. (1991). The amount and effectiveness of help: The relationship of motives and abilities to helping behavior. *Personality and Social Psychology Bulletin, 17,* 58–64.

Cohen, D. (1996). Law, social policy, and violence: The impact of regional cultures. *Journal of Personality and Social Psychology, 70,* 961–978.

Cohen, D. (1998). Culture, social organization and patterns of violence. *Journal of Personality and Social Psychology, 75,* 408–419.

Cohen, D., & Nisbett, R. E. (1994). Self-protection and the culture of honor: Explaining southern violence. *Personality and Social Psychology Bulletin, 20,* 551–567.

Cohen, D., & Nisbett, R. E. (1997). Field experiments examining the culture of honor: The role of institutions in perpetuating norms. *Personality and Social Psychology Bulletin, 23,* 1188–1199.

Cohen, D., Nisbett, R. E., Bowdle, B. F., & Schwartz, N. (1996). Insult, aggression, and the southern culture of honor: An "experimental ethnography." *Journal of Personality and Social Psychology, 70,* 945–960.

Cohen, D., Nisbett, R. E., Bowdle, B. F., & Schwartz, N. (1997). Field experiments examining the culture of honor: The role of institutions in perpetuating norms about violence. *Personality and Social Psychology Bulletin, 23,* 1188–1199.

Cohen, S., Kaplan, J. R., Cunnick, J. E., Manuck, S. B., & Rabin, B. S. (1992). Chronic social stress, affiliation, and cellular immune response in nonhuman primates. *Psychological Science, 3,* 310–304.

Cohen, S., & Williamson, G. M. (1991). Stress and infectious disease in humans. *Psychological Bulletin, 109*(1), 5–24.

Coleman, L. T., Jussim, L., & Isaac, J. L. (1991). *Journal of Applied Social Psychology, 21,* 460–481.

Collins, R. L., Taylor, S. E., Wood, J. V., & Thompson, S. C. (1988). The vividness effect: Elusive or illusory? *Journal of Experimental Social Psychology, 24,* 1–18.

Colvin, C. R., & Funder, D. C. (1991). Predicting personality and behavior: A boundary acquaintance effect. *Journal of Personality and Social Psychology, 60,* 884–894.

Comstock, G. A. (1986). Sexual effects of movie and TV violence. *Medical Aspects of Human Sexuality, 20,* 96–101.

Conger, R. D., Rueter, M. A., Elder, G. H., Jr. (1999). Couple resilience to economic pressure. *Journal of Personality and Social Psychology, 76*, 54–71.

Conner, R. L., & Levine, S. (1969). Hormonal influences on aggressive behavior. In S. Garattini & E. B. Sigg (Eds.), *Aggressive behavior* (pp. 150–163). New York: Wiley.

Contrada, R. J. (1989). Type A behavior, personality, hardiness, and cardiovascular responses to stress. *Journal of Personality and Social Psychology, 57*(5), 895–903.

Cook, S. W. (1984). Cooperative interaction in multiethnic contexts. In N. Miller & M. B. Brewer (Eds.), *Groups in contact: The psychology of desegregation* (pp. 155–185). Orlando, FL: Academic Press.

Cooley, C. H. (1902). *Human nature and the social order.* New York: Scribner.

Cooper, L., & Fazio, R. H. (1984). A new look at cognitive dissonance theory. In L. Berkowitz (Ed.), *Advances in experimental social psychology* (Vol. 17, pp. 229–267). New York: Academic Press.

Cooper, J. (1998). Unlearning cognitive dissonance: Toward and understanding of the development of dissonance. *Journal of Experimental Social Psychology, 34*, 562–565.

Cooper, J., & Scher, S. J. (1992). Actions and attitudes: The role of responsibility and aversive consequences in persuasion. In T. Brock & S. Shavitt (Eds.), *The psychology of persuasion.* San Francisco: Freeman.

Cottrell, N. B. (1972). Social facilitation. In C. G. McClintock (Ed.), *Experimental social psychology* (pp. 185–236). New York: Holt, Rinehart & Winston.

Cottrell, N. B., Wack, D. L., Sekerak, G. J., & Rittle, R. M. (1968). Social facilitation of dominant responses by the presence of an audience and the mere presence of others. *Journal of Personality and Social Psychology, 9*, 245–250.

Courtwright, J. (1978). A laboratory investigation of groupthink. *Communications Monographs, 45*, 229–245.

Cousins, N. (1989). *Head first: The biology of hope.* New York: Dutton.

Cramer, R. E., McMaster, M. R., Bartell, P. A., & Dragna, M. (1988). Subject competence and minimization of the bystander effect. *Journal of Applied Social Psychology, 18*, 1133–1148.

Crandall, C. S. (1988). Social contagion of binge eating. *Journal of Personality and Social Psychology, 55*, 588–598.

Crandall, C. S. (1991). Do heavy weight students have more difficulty paying for college? *Personality and Social Psychology Bulletin, 17*, 606–611.

Crano, W. D., & Sivacek, J. (1984). The influence of incentive-aroused ambivalence on overjustification effects in attitude change. *Journal of Experimental Social Psychology, 20*, 137–158.

Crockenberg, S., & Litman, C. (1986). Autonomy as competence in 2-year-olds: Maternal correlates of child defiance, compliance and self-assertion. *Developmental Psychology, 26*, 961–971.

Crocker, J., Cornwell, B., & Major, B. (1993). The stigma of overweight: Affective consequences of attributional ambiguity. *Journal of Personality and Social Psychology, 64*, 60–70.

Crocker, J., Luhtanen, R., Broadnax, S., & Blaine, B. (1999). Belief in U.S. government conspiracies against blacks among black and white college students: Powerlessness or system blame? *Personality and Social Psychology Bulletin, 25*, 941–954.

Crocker, J., & Major, B. (1989). Social stigma and self-esteem: The self-protective properties of stigma. *Psychological Review, 96*, 608–630.

Crocker, J., Voelkl, K., Testa, M., & Major, B. (1991). Social stigma: The affective consequences of attributional ambiguity. *Journal of Personality and Social Psychology, 60*, 218–228.

Crohan, S. E. (1992). Marital happiness and spousal consensus on beliefs about marital conflict: A longitudinal investigation. *Journal of Social and Personal Relationships, 9*, 89–102.

Cronin, P., & Rosa, J. (1990, May). *The effects of age differences on sexual risk-taking behaviors, attitudes and justifications.* Paper presented at Midwestern Psychological Association Meetings, Chicago.

Crosby, F., Bromley, S., & Saxe, L. (1980). Recent unobtrusive studies of black and white discrimination and prejudice: A literature review. *Psychological Bulletin, 87*, 546–563.

Crott, H., Giesel, M., & Hoffman, C. (1998). The process of inductive inference in groups: The use of positive or negative hypothesis and target testing in sequential rule-discovery tasks. *Journal of Personality and Social Psychology, 75*, 938–954.

Croyle, R. T., & Ditto, P. H. (1990). Illness cognition and behavior: An experimental approach. *Journal of Behavioral Medicine, 13*(1), 31–52.

Croyle, R. T., & Hunt, J. R. (1991). Coping with health threat: Social influence processes in reactions to medical test results. *Journal of Personality and Social Psychology, 60*, 382–389.

Croyle, R. T., & Williams, K. D. (1991). Reactions to medical diagnosis: The role of stereotypes. *Basic and Applied Psychology, 12*, 227–236.

Crutchfield, R. S. (1955). Conformity and character. *American Psychologist, 10*, 191–198.

Csikszentmihalyi, M. (1990). *Flow: The psychology of optimal experience.* New York: Harper & Row.

Cyranowski, J. M., & Andersen, B. L. (1998). Schemas, sexuality, and romantic attachment. *Journal of Personality and Social Psychology, 74*, 1364–1379.

Dallek, R. (1991). *Lone star rising: Lyndon Johnson and his times, 1908–1960.* New York: Oxford University Press.

Darley, J. M., & Batson, C. D. (1973). "From Jerusalem to Jericho": A study of situational and dispositional variables in helping behavior. *Journal of Personality and Social Psychology, 27*, 100–108.

Darley, J. M., Fleming, J. H., Hilton, J. L., & Swann, W. B., Jr. (1988). Dispelling negative expectancies: The impact of interaction goals and target characteristics on the expectancy confirmation process. *Journal of Experimental Social Psychology, 24*, 19–36.

Darley, J. M., & Gross, P. H. (1983). A hypothesis confirming bias in labelling effects. *Journal of Personality and Social Psychology, 44*, 20–33.

Darley, J. M., & Latane, B. (1968). Bystander intervention in emergencies: Diffusion of responsibility. *Journal of Personality and Social Psychology, 8*, 377–383.

Darley, J. M., Teger, A. I., & Lewis, L. D. (1973). Do groups always inhibit individuals' response to potential emergencies? *Journal of Personality and Social Psychology, 26*, 395–399.

Davis, B. O., Jr. (1991). *American.* Washington, DC: Smithsonian Institution Press.

Davis, J. H. (1969). *Group performance.* New York: Addison-Wesley.

Davis, J. H. (1973). Group decision and social interaction: A theory of social decision schemes. *Psychological Review, 80,* 97–125.

Davis, J. H. (1980). Group decision and procedural justice. In M. Fishbein (Ed.), *Progress in social psychology* (Vol. 1, pp. 234–278). Hillsdale, NJ: Erlbaum.

Davison, A. R., Yantis, S., Norwood, M., & Montano, D. E. (1985). Amount of information about the attitude object and attitude–behavior consistency. *Journal of Personality and Social Psychology, 49,* 1184–1198.

Dean, J. W. (1977). *Blind Ambition.* Pocket Books, New York.

Dean, K. E., & Malamuth, N. M. (1997). Characteristics of men who aggress sexually and men who imagine aggressing: Risk and moderating variables. *Journal of Personality and Social Psychology, 72,* 449–455.

De Angelis, T. (1991, December.) Sexual harassment common, complex. *Monitor, 8,* 16–21.

Deaux, K., & Major, B. (1987). Putting gender into context: An interactive model of gender-related behavior. *Psychological Review, 94,* 369–389.

DeJong, M. (1980). The stigma of obesity: The consequence of naive assumptions concerning the causes of physical deviance. *Journal of Health and Social Behavior, 21,* 75–87.

DeJong, W. (1979). An examination of self-perception mediation of the foot-in-the-door effect. *Journal of Personality and Social Psychology, 37,* 2171–2180.

DeLamater, J. (1974). A definition of "group." *Small Group Behavior, 5*(1), 30–44.

De La Ronde, & Swann, W. B., Jr. (1998). Partner verification: Restoring the shattered images of our intimates. *Journal of Personality and Social Psychology, 75,* 374–382.

Delgado, J. M. R. (1969). Offensive–defensive behaviour in free monkeys and chimpanzees induced by radio stimulation of the brain. In S. Garattini & E. B. Sigg (Eds.), *Aggressive behavior* (pp. 109–119). New York: Wiley.

Dennis, A. R., Valacich, J. S., & Nunamaker, J. F. (1990). An experimental investigation of the effects of group size in an electronic meeting environment. *IEEE Transactions on Systems, Man, and Cybernetics, 25,* 1049–1057.

DePaulo, B. M., Charlton, K., Cooper, H., Lindsay, J. J., & Muhlenbruck, L. (1997). The accuracy–confidence correlation in detection of deception. *Personality and Social Psychology Review, 4,* 346–357.

DePaulo, B. M., & Fisher, J. D. (1980). The costs of asking for help. *Basic and Applied Social Psychology, 1,* 23–35.

DePaulo, B. M., & Kashy, D. (1999). Everyday lies in close and casual relationships. *Journal of Personality and Social Psychology, 74,* 63–79.

DePaulo, B. M., Kenny D. A., Hoover, C., Webb, W., & Oliver, P. V. (1987). *Journal of Personality and Social Psychology, 52,* 303–315.

Derlega, V. J., Winstead, B. A., & Jones, W. H. (1991). *Personality: Contemporary theory and research.* Chicago: Nelson-Hall.

Derman, K. H., & George, W. H. (1989). Alcohol expectancy and the relationship between drinking and physical aggression. *Journal of Psychology, 123,* 153–161.

Des Pres, T. (1976). *The survivor.* New York: Oxford University Press.

Desforges, D., Lord, C. G., Ramsey, S. L., Mason, J. A., Van Leeuwen, H. M., West, S. C., & Lepper, M. R. (1991). Effects of structured cooperative contact on changing negative attitudes towards stigmatized social groups. *Journal of Personality and Social Psychology, 60,* 531–544.

Deutsch, M., & Gerrard, H. B. (1955). A study of normative and informational social influence upon individual judgment. *Journal of Abnormal and Social Psychology, 51,* 629–636.

Devine, P. G. (1989). Stereotypes and prejudice: Their automatic and controlled components. *Journal of Personality and Social Psychology, 56,* 5–18.

Devine, P. G., & Baker, S. M. (1991). Measurement of racial stereotype subtyping. *Personality and Social Psychology Bulletin, 17,* 44–50.

Devine, P. G., Monteith, M. J., Zuwerink, J. R., & Elliot, A. J. (1991). Prejudice without compunction. *Journal of Personality and Social Psychology, 60,* 817–830.

Diaz, C. R. (1975). The feeling of injustice as a cause of homicidal passion [English Abstract]. *Revista de Psicologia-Universidad de Monterrey, 4,* 41–49.

Diehl, M., & Stroebe, W. (1987). Productivity loss in brainstorming groups. *Journal of Personality and Social Psychology, 53,* 497–509.

Diehl, M., & Stroebe, W. (1991). Productivity loss in idea-generating groups: Tracking down the blocking effect. *Journal of Personality and Social Psychology, 61,* 392–403.

Diener, E., & Diener, C. (1996). Most people are happy. *Psychological Science, 7,* 181–185.

Diener, E., & Diener, M. (1995). Cross cultural correlates of life satisfaction and self-esteem. *Journal of Personality and Social Psychology, 68,* 653–663.

Diener, E., Suh, E. M., Lucas, R. E., & Smith, H. L. (1999). Subjective well-being: Three decades of progress. *Psychological Bulletin, 125,* 276–302.

Dijkstra, P., & Buunk, B. (1998). Jealousy as a function of rival charactristics: An evolutionary perspectives. *Personality and Social Psychology Bulletin, 42,* 1158–1166.

Dillard, J. P., Hunter, J. E., & Burgoon, M. (1984). Sequential-request persuasive strategies: Meta analysis of foot-in-the-door and door-in-the-face. *Human Communication Research, 10,* 461–488.

Dion, K. K., Berscheid, E., & Walster, E. (1972). What is beautiful is good. *Journal of Personality and Social Psychology, 24,* 285–290.

Dion, K. L., & Dion, K. K. (1988). Romantic love: Individual and cultural perspectives. In R. J. Sternberg & M. L. Barnes (Eds.), *The psychology of love.* New Haven, CT: Yale University Press.

Dion, K. L., & Earn, B. M. (1975). The phenomenology of being a target of prejudice. *Journal of Personality and Social Psychology, 32,* 944–950.

Ditto, P. H., & Hilton, J. L. (1990). Expectancy processes in the health care interaction sequence. *Journal of Social Issues, 46,* 97–124.

Ditto P. H., & Jemmott, J. B. (1989). From rarity to evaluative extremity: Effects of prevalence information on the evaluation of positive and negative characteristics. *Journal of Personality and Social Psychology, 57,* 16–26.

Dodge, K. A. (1986). A social information processing model of social competence in children. In M. Perlmutter (Ed.), *Minnesota symposium on child psychology* (Vol. 18). Hillsdale, NJ: Erlbaum.

Doll, J., & Ajzen, I. (1992). Accessibility and stability of predictors in the theory of planned behavior. *Journal of Personality and Social Psychology, 63,* 5, 754–765.

Dollard, J., Doob, L., Miller, N., Mowrer, O., & Sears, R. (1939). *Frustration and aggression.* New Haven, CT: Yale University Press.

Doms, M., & Van Avermaet, E. (1980). Majority influence and conversion behavior: A replication. *Journal of Experimental Social Psychology, 16,* 283–292.

Donnelly, D., & Fraser, J. (1998). Gender differences in sadomasochistic arousal among college students. *Sex Roles, 39,* 391–407.

Donnerstein, E. (1980). Aggressive erotica and violence against women. *Journal of Personality and Social Psychology, 39,* 269–277.

Donnerstein, E., & Barrett, G. (1978). Effects of erotic stimuli on male aggression toward females. *Journal of Personality and Social Psychology, 36,* 180–188.

Donnerstein, E., & Berkowitz, L. (1981). Victim reactions in aggressive erotic films as a factor in violence against women. *Journal of Personality and Social Psychology, 41,* 710–724.

Donnerstein, E., & Donnerstein, M. (1973). Variables in interracial aggression: Potential in-group censure. *Journal of Personality and Social Psychology, 27,* 143–150.

Donnerstein, E., Donnerstein, M., & Evans, R. (1975). Erotic stimuli and aggression: Facilitation or inhibition. *Journal of Personality and Social Psychology, 32,* 237–244.

Dovidio, J. F., Allen, J. L., & Schroeder, D. A. (1990). Specificity of empathy-induced helping: Evidence for altruistic motivation. *Journal of Personality and Social Psychology, 59,* 249–260.

Dovidio, J. F., & Gaertner, S. L. (1981). The effects of race, status, and ability on helping behavior. *Social Psychology Quarterly, 44,* 192–203.

Dovidio, J. F., Kawakami, K., Johnson, C., Johnson, B., & Howard, A. (1997). On the nature of prejudice: Automatic and controlled processes. *Journal of Experimental Social Psychology, 33,* 510–540.

Doyle, J. A. (1985). *Sex and gender.* Dubuque, IA: Brown.

Doyle, J. A., & Paludi, M. A. (1991). *Sex and gender* (2nd ed.). Dubuque, IA: Brown.

Dower, J. W. (1986). *War without mercy.* New York: Pantheon Books.

Dozier, J. B., & Miceli, M. P. (1985). Potential predictors of whistle-blowing: A prosocial perspective. *Academy of Management Review, 10,* 820–836.

Drickamer, L. C., & Vessey, S. H. (1986). *Animal behavior: Concepts, processes and methods* (2nd ed.). Boston: Prindle, Weber, & Schmidt.

Drigotas, S. M., Rusbult, C. E., Wieselquist, J., & Whitton, S. (1999). Close partner as sculptor of the ideal self: Behavioral affirmation and the Michelangelo phenomenon. *Journal of Personality and Social Psychology, 77,* 293–324.

Duck, S. W. (1982). A topography of relationship disengagement and dissolution. In S. W. Duck (Ed.), *Personal relationships 4: Dissolving personal relationships* (pp. 1–30). New York: Academic Press.

Duck, S. W. (1983). *Friends for life.* New York: St. Martin's Press.

Duck, S. W. (1988). *Handbook of personal relationships.* New York: Wiley.

Duck, J. , Terry, D. J., & Hogg, M. A. (1998). Perceptions of a media campaign: The role of social identity and the changing intergroup context. *Personality and Social Psychology Bulletin, 24,* 3–16.

Dunbar, E. (1995). The prejudiced personality, racism and anti-Semitism: The PR scale forty years later. *Journal of Personality Assessment, 65,* 270–277.

Dunbar, R. I. M. (1987). Sociobiological explanations and the evolution of ethnocentrism. In V. Reynolds, V. Falger, & I. Vine (Eds.), *The sociobiology of ethnocentrism.* Athens, GA: University of Georgia Press.

Dunning, D., Griffin, D. W., Milojkovic, J. D., & Ross, L. (1990). The overconfidence effect in social prediction. *Journal of Personality and Social Psychology, 58,* 568–581.

Dweck, C. (1975). The role of expectations and attributions in the alleviation of learned helplessness. *Journal of Personality and Social Psychology, 31,* 674–685.

Dweck, C., Davidson, W., Nelson, S., & Enna, B. (1978). Sex differences in learned helplessness: II. The contingencies or evaluative feedback in the classroom and III. An experimental analysis. *Developmental Psychology, 14,* 268–276.

Dweck, C., & Goetz, T. E. (1978). Attributions and learned helplessness. In J. Harvey, W. Ickes, & R. F. Kidd (Eds.), *New directions in attribution theory* (Vol. 2). Hillsdale, NJ: Erlbaum.

Dyck, R. J., & Rule, B. G. (1978). Effect on retaliation of causal attributions concerning attack. *Journal of Personality and Social Psychology, 36,* 521–529.

Eagly, A. (1987) *Sex differences in social behavior: A social role interpretation.* Hillsdale, NJ: Erlbaum.

Eagly, A. H. (1978). Sex differences in influenceability. *Psychological Bulletin, 85,* 86–116.

Eagly, A. H. (1987). *Sex differences in social behavior.* Hillsdale, NJ: Erlbaum.

Eagly, A. H. (1991). The three ironies of the McGuires' theory of thought systems. In R. S. Wyer & T. K. Srull (Eds.), The content, structure, and operation of thought systems. *Advances in social cognition* (Vol. 4, pp. 121–128). Hillsdale, NJ: Lawrence Erlbaum.

Eagly, A. H. (1992). Uneven progress: Social psychology and the study of attitudes. *Journal of Personality and Social Psychology, 63*(5), 693–710.

Eagly, A. H., Ashmore, R. D., Makhijani, M. G., & Longo, L. C. (1991). What is beautiful is good, but . . . : A meta-analytic review of research on the physical attractiveness stereotype. *Psychological Bulletin, 110,* 109–128.

Eagly, A. H., & Carli, L. L. (1981). Sex of researchers and sex-typed communications as determinants of sex differences in influenceability: A meta-analysis of social influence studies. *Psychological Bulletin, 90,* 1–20.

Eagly, A. H., & Chrvala, C. (1986). Sex differences in conformity: Status and gender role interpretations. *Sex Roles, 10,* 203–220.

Eagly, A. H., & Crowley, M. (1986). Gender and helping behavior: A meta-analytic review of the social psychological literature. *Psychological Bulletin, 100,* 309–330.

Eagly, A. H., & Johnson, B. T. (1990). Gender and leadership style. *Psychological Bulletin, 108,* 233–256.

Eagly, A. H., & Karau, S. J. (1991). Gender and the emergence of leaders: A meta-analysis. *Journal of Personality and Social Psychology, 60,* 685–710.

Eagly, A. H., & Kite, M. E. (1987). Are stereotypes of nationalities applied to both women and men? *Journal of Personality and Social Psychology, 53*(3), 451–462.

Eagly, A. H., & Steffen, V. J. (1986). Gender and aggressive behavior: A meta-analytic review of the social psychological literature. *Psychological Bulletin, 100,* 309–330.

Eagly, A. H., & Telaak, K. (1972). Width of the latitude of acceptance as a determinant of attitude change. *Journal of Personality and Social Psychology, 23,* 388–397.

Eagly, A. H., Wood, W., & Chaiken, S. (1978). Causal inferences about communicators and their effect on opinion change. *Journal of Personality and Social Psychology, 36,* 424–435.

Eagly, A. H., Wood, W., & Fishbaugh, L. (1981). Sex differences in conformity: Surveillance by the group as a determinant of male conformity. *Journal of Personality and Social Psychology, 40,* 384–394.

Early, P. (1988). *Family of spies: Inside the John Walker spy ring.* New York: Bantam.

Ebbesen, E. B., & Konecni, V. J. (1975). Decision making and information integration in the courts: The setting of bail. *Journal of Personality and Social Psychology, 35,* 805–821.

Edelman, B., Engell, D., Bronstein, P., & Hirsch, E. (1986). Environmental effects of the intake of overweight and normal weight men. *Appetite, 7,* 71–83.

Edmonds, E. M., & Cahoon, D. D. (1986). Attitudes concerning crimes related to clothing worn by female victims. *Bulletin of the Psychonomic Society, 24,* 444–446.

Edwards, S. B., & Flynn, J. P. (1972). Corticospinal control of striking in centrally elicited attack behavior. *Brain Research, 41,* 51–65.

Edwards, J. A., & Weary, G. (1998). Antecedents of causal uncertainty and perceived control: A prospective study. *European Journal of Personality, 12,* 135–148.

Edwards. J. A., Weary, G., von Hippel, W., & Jacobson, J. A. (1999). The effects of depression on impression formation: The role of trait and category diagnosticity. *Personality and Social Psychology Bulletin, 25*(11), 1350–1363.

Eisenberg, N., Fabes, R. A., Miller, P. A., Fultz, J., Shell, R., Mathy, R. M., & Reno, R. R. (1989). Relation of sympathy and personal distress to prosocial behavior: A multimethod study. *Journal of Personality and Social Psychology, 57,* 55–66.

Eisenberg, N., & Miller, P. A. (1987). The relation of empathy to prosocial and related behaviors. *Psychological Bulletin, 101,* 91–119.

Eisenberg, N., Miller, P. A., Schaller, N., & Fabes, R. A. (1989). The role of sympathy and altruistic traits in helping: A reexamination. *Journal of Personality and Social Psychology, 57,* 41–67.

Eisenberg, N., & Mussen, P. (1989). *The roots of prosocial behavior in children.* Cambridge, England: Cambridge University Press.

Eitzen, D. S. (1973). Two minorities: The Jews of Poland and the Chinese of the Philippines. In D. E. Gelfand & R. D. Lee (Eds.), *Ethnic conflicts and power: A cross-national perspective* (pp. 140–156). New York: Wiley.

Ekman, P. (1985). *Telling lies: Clues to deceit in the marketplace, politics, and marriage.* New York: Norton.

Ekman, P., O'Sullivan, M. O., Frank, M. G. (1999). A few can catch a liar. *Psychological Science, 10,* 263–266.

Elkin, R. A., & Leippe M. R. (1986). Physiological arousal, dissonance, and attitude change: Evidence for a dissonance-arousal link and a "don't remind me" effect. *Journal of Personality and Social Psychology, 51*(1), 55–65.

Ellsworth, P. C. (1991). To tell what we know or wait for Godot? *Law and Human Behavior, 15,* 77–90.

Elms, A. (1972). *Social Psychology and Social Relevance.* Boston: Little Brown.

Elms, A., & Milgram, S. (1966). Personality characteristics associated with obedience and defiance toward authoritative command. *Journal of Experimental Research in Personality, 1,* 282–289.

Emswiller, R., Deaux, K., & Willits, J. (1971). Similarity, sex and requests for small favors. *Journal of Applied Social Psychology, 1,* 284–291.

Erdley, C. A., & D'Agostino, P. R. (1988). Cognitive and affective components of automatic priming effects. *Journal of Personality and Social Psychology, 54,* 741–747.

Eron, L. D., Huesmann, L. R., Lefkowitz, M. M., & Walder, L. O. (1972). Does television violence cause aggression? *American Psychologist, 27,* 253–263.

Eron, L. D., Huesmann, L. R., & Zelli, A. (1991). The role of parental variables in the learning of aggression. In D. J. Pepler & K. H. Rubin (Eds.), *The development and treatment of childhood aggression* (pp. 169–188). Hillsdale, NJ: Erlbaum.

Etcoff, N. L., Ekman, P., & Frank, M. G. (2000, May 11). Lie detection and language loss. *Nature, 405* (6783), 139–140.

Fabrigar, L. R., Priester, J. R., Petty, R. E., & Wegener, D. T. (1998). The impact of attitude accessibility on elaboration of persuasive messages. *Personality and Social Psychology Bulletin, 24,* 339–352.

Farber, J. (1993, May 13). We're not going to take it. *Rolling Stone,* 21.

Faulkner, S., Williams, K., Sherman, B., & Williams, E. (1997, May 8–11). The "silent treatment:" Its incidence and impact. Presented at the 69th Annual Midwestern Psychological Association, Chicago, IL.

Faulkner, S. L., & Williams, K. D. (1995, May). The causes and consequences of social ostracism: A qualitative analysis. Paper presented at the Midwestern Psychological Association, Chicago, IL.

Fazio, R. H. (1986). How do attitudes guide behavior? In R. M. Sorrentino & E. T. Higgins (Eds.), *Handbook of motivation and cognition: Foundations of social behavior* (pp. 204–243). New York: Guilford.

Fazio, R. H. (1988). On the power and functionality of attitudes: The role of attitude accessibility. In A. R. Pratkanis, S. J. Breckler, & A. G. Greenwald (Eds.), *Attitude structure and function.* Hillsdale, NJ: Erlbaum.

Fazio, R. H., Chen, J., McDonel, E., & Sherman, S. J. (1982). Attitude accessibility, attitude–behavior consistency, and the strength of the object-evaluation association. *Journal of Experimental Social Psychology, 18,* 339–357.

Fazio, R. H., Sanbonmatsu, D. M., Powell, M. C., & Kardes, F. R. (1986). On the automatic activation of attitudes. *Journal of Personality and Social Psychology, 50,* 229–238.

Fazio, R. H., & Williams, C. J. (1986). Attitude accessibility as a moderator of the attitude–perception and attitude–behavior relationships. *Journal of Personality and Social Psychology, 51,* 505–514.

Feeney, J. A., & Noller, P. (1990). Attachment style as a predictor of adult romantic relationships. *Journal of Personality and Social Psychology, 58,* 281–291.

Fein, S. (1996). Effects of suspicion on attributional thinking and the correspondence bias. *Journal of Personality and Social Psychology, 70,* 1164–1184.

Fellner, C. H., & Marshall, J. R. (1981). Kidney donors revisited. In J. P. Rushton & R. M. Sorentino (Eds.), *Altruism and* helping behavior: social, personality, and developmental Perspectoves (pp. 351–365). Hillsdale, NJ: Erlbaum.

Felmlee, D., Sprecher, S., & Bassin, E. (1990). The dissolution of intimate relationships: A hazard model. *Social Psychology Quarterly, 53,* 13–30.

Felner, R. D., Rowlinson, R. T., & Terre, L. (1986). Unraveling the Gordian knot in life exchange events. In S. M. Auerbach & A. L. Stolberg (Eds.), *Children's life crises events: Prevention strategies* (pp. 39–63). New York: McGraw-Hill.

Feshbach, S. (1964). The function of aggression and the regulation of aggressive drive. *Psychological Bulletin, 71,* 257–272.

Festinger, L. (1950). A theory of social comparison. *Human Relations, 7,* 117–140.

Festinger, L. (1954). A theory of social comparison processes. *Human Relations, 7,* 117–140.

Festinger, L. (1957). *A theory of cognitive dissonance.* Stanford, CA: Stanford University Press.

Festinger, L., & Carlsmith, J. M. (1959). Cognitive consequences of forced compliance. *Journal of Abnormal and Social Psychology, 58,* 203–210.

Festinger, L., Riecken, H. W., & Schachter, S. (1982). When prophecy fails. In A. Pines & C. Maslach (Eds.), *Experiencing social psychology: Readings and projects* (pp. 69–75). New York: Knopf.

Festinger, L., Schachter, S., & Back, K. W. (1959). *Social pressures in informal groups: A study of human factors in housing.* New York: Harper & Row.

Fiebert, M. S., & Wright, K. S. (1989). Midlife friendships in an American faculty sample. *Psychological Reports, 64,* 1127–1130.

Fiedler, F. W. (1967). *A theory of leadership effectiveness.* New York: McGraw-Hill.

Fiedler, K., Walther, E., & Nickel, S. (1999). Covariation-based attribution: On the ability to assess multiple covariates of an effect. *Personality and Social Psychology Bulletin, 25,* 607–622.

Fincham, F. D., & Bradbury, T. N. (1988). The impact of attributions in marriage: An experimental analysis. *Journal of Social and Clinical Psychology, 7,* 147–162.

Finkelhor, D., & Yllo, K. (1982). Forced sex in marriage: A preliminary research report. *Crime and Delinquency, 28,* 459–478.

Fishbein, M., & Ajzen, I. (1975). *Belief, attitude, intention, and behavior: An introduction to theory and research.* Reading, MA: Addison-Wesley.

Fisher, H. (1992). *Anatomy of love.* New York: Norton.

Fisher, J. D., & Nadler, A. (1974). The effect of similarity between donor and recipient on recipient's reactions to aid. *Journal of Experimental Social Psychology, 4,* 230–243.

Fisher, J. D., Nadler, A., & Ben-Itzhak, S. (1983). With a little help from my friend: Effect of single or multiple act aid as a function of donor and task characteristics. *Journal of Personality and Social Psychology, 44,* 310–321.

Fisher, J. D., Nadler, A., & Whitcher-Algana, S. (1982). Recipient reactions to aid. *Psychological Bulletin, 91,* 27–54.

Fisher, R. J. (1983). Third party consultation as a method of intergroup conflict resolution. *Journal of Conflict Resolution, 27,* 301–334.

Fiske, A. P. (1991). The cultural relativity of selfish individualism. In M. S. Clark (Ed.), *Prosocial behavior.* Newbury Park, CA: Sage.

Fiske, A. P. (1993). Social errors in four cultures: Evidence about universal forms of social relations. *Journal of Cross Cultural Psychology, 24,* 463–494.

Fiske, A. P., & Haslam, N. (1996). Social cognition is thinking about relationships. *Current Directions in Psychological Science, 5,* 137–142.

Fiske, A. P., & Haslam, N. (1997). The structure of social substitutions: A test of relational models theory. *European Journal of Social Psychology, 27,* 725–729.

Fiske, A. P., Haslam, N., & Fiske, S. T. (1991). Confusing one person with another: What errors reveal about the elementary forms of social relationships. *Journal of Personality and Social Psychology, 60,* 656–674.

Fiske, S. T. (1982). Schema-triggered affect: Applications to social perception: In M. S. Clark & S. T. Fiske (Eds.), *Affect and cognition: The 17th annual Carnegie Symposium on Cognition* (pp. 55–78). Hillsdale, NJ: Erlbaum.

Fiske, S. T. (1992). Thinking is for doing: Portraits of social cognition from daguerreotype to laserphoto. *Journal of Personality and Social Psychology, 63*(6), 877–889.

Fiske, S. T. (1993). Social cognition and social perception. In M. R. Rosenzweig & L. W. Porter (Eds.), *Annual review of psychology* (Vol. 44, pp. 155–194). Palo Alto, CA: Annual Reviews.

Fiske, S. T., & Neuberg, S. L. (1990). A continuum of impression formation, from category based to individuating processes: Influence of information and motivation attention and interpretation. In M. Zanna (Ed.), *Advances in experimental social psychology* (Vol. 23). San Diego: Academic.

Fiske, S. T., & Taylor, S. E. (1984). *Social cognition.* Reading, MA: Addison-Wesley.

Fiske, S. T., & Taylor, S. E. (1991). *Social cognition* (2nd ed.). *New York: McGraw-Hill.*

Fitzgerald, F. (1979). *America revised: History textbooks in the twentieth century.* Boston: Little, Brown.

Fitzgerald, F. S. (1925). *The great Gatsby.* New York: Collier.

Fitzgerald. L. F., Shullman, S., Bailey, N., Richards, M., Swecker, J., Gold, Y., Ormerod, M., & Weitzman, L. (1988). The incidence and dimensions of sexual harassment in the workplace. *Journal of Vocational Behavior, 32,* 152–175.

Flanagan, T. J., & Maguire, K. (1992). *Bureau of Justice statistics: Sourcebook of criminal justice statistics–1991.* Albany, NY: Hindelong Criminal Justice Center.

Fleming, A. (1986). *Ida Tarbell.* New York: Bantam.

Fleming, J. H., & Darley, J. M. (1989). Perceiving choice and constraint. The effects of contextual and behavioral cues on attitude attribution. *Journal of Personality and Social Psychology, 56,* 27–40.

Fleming, J. H., & Darley, J. M. (1990) The purposeful-action sequence and the illusion of control. *Personality and Social Psychology Bulletin, 16,* 346–357.

Fleming, J. H., & Darley, J. M. (1991). Mixed messages: The multiple audience problem and strategic communication. *Social Cognition, 9,* 25–46.

Fleming, J. H., Darley, J. M., Hilton, J. L., & Kojetin, B. A. (1990). Multiple audience problem: A strategic communication perspective on social perception. *Journal of Personality and Social Psychology, 58,* 593–609.

Fletcher, G. J. O., & Ward, C. (1988). Attribution theory and processes: A cross cultural perspective. In M. H. Bond (Ed.), *The cross-cultural challenge to social psychology* (pp. 230–244). Newbury Park, CA: Sage.

Flohr, H. (1987). Biological bases of social prejudices. In V. Reynolds, V. Falger, & I. Vine (Eds.), *The sociobiology of ethnocentrism.* Athens, GA: University of Georgia Press.

Flowers, M. (1977). A laboratory test of some implications of Janis' groupthink hypothesis. *Journal of Personality and Social Psychology, 35,* 888–896.

Foehl, J. C., & Goldman, M. (1983). Increasing altruistic behavior by using compliance techniques. *Journal of Social Psychology, 119,* 21–29.

Forehand, R., & Long, N. (1991). Prevention of aggression and other behavior problems in the early adolescent years. In D. J. Pepler & K. H. Rubin (Eds.), *The development and treatment of childhood aggression* (pp. 317–330). Hillsdale, NJ: Erlbaum.

Forgas, J. P. (1998). On being happy and mistaken: Mood effects on the fundamental attribution error. *Journal of Personality and Social Psychology, 75,* 318–331.

Forgas, J. P., Furnham, A., & Frey, D. (1990). Cross-national differences in attributions of wealth and economic success. *The Journal of Social Psychology, 129,* 643–657.

Forsyth, D. (1990). *Group dynamics* (2nd ed.). Pacific Grove, CA: Brooks/Cole.

Foss, R. D., & Dempsey, C. B. (1979). Blood donation and the foot-in-the-door technique. *Journal of Personality and Social Psychology, 37,* 580–590.

FosterLee, L., Horowitz, I. A., & Bourgeois, M. (1993). Juror competence in civil trials: The effects of preinstruction and evidence technicality. *Journal of Applied Psychology, 78,* 14–21.

Frable, D. E. S., Platt, L., & Hoey, S. (1998). Concealable stigmas and positive self-perceptions: Feeling better around similar others. *Journal of Personality and Social Psychology, 74,* 909–922.

Fraley, R. C., & Shaver, P. R. (1998). Airport separations: A naturalistic study of adult attachment dynamics in separating couples. *Journal of Personality and Social Psychology, 75,* 1198–1212.

Frank, M. G., & Gilovich, T. (1989). Effect of memory perspective on retrospective causal attribution. *Journal of Personality and Social Psychology, 57,* 399–403.

Frank, R. G., Bouman, D. E., Cain, K., & Watts, C. (1992). Primary prevention of catastrophic injury. *American Psychologist, 47,* 1045–1049.

Frazier, P. A. (1990). Victim attributions and post-rape trauma. *Journal of Personality and Social Psychology, 59,* 298–304.

Frazier, P. A. (1991). Self-blame as a mediator of postrape depressive symptoms. *Journal of Social and Clinical Psychology, 10,* 47–57.

Freedman, J. L. (1986). Television violence and aggression: A rejoinder. *Psychological Bulletin, 3,* 372–378.

Freedman, J. L., & Fraser, S. C. (1966). Compliance without pressure: The foot-in-the-door technique. *Journal of Personality and Social Psychology, 4,* 195–202.

Freedman, J. L. (1984). Effect of television violence on aggressiveness. *Psychological Bulletin, 96,* 227–246.

Freedman, J. L., & Sears, D. O. (1965). Warning, distraction, and resistance to influence. *Journal of Personality and Social Psychology, 1,* 262–266.

Freedman, J. L., Cunningham, J. A., & Krismer, K. (1992). Inferred values and the reverse-incentive effect in induced compliance. *Journal of Personality and Social Psychology, 62,* 357–368.

French, J. R. P., Jr., & Raven, B. H. (1968). The bases of social power. In D. Cartwright & A. Zander (Eds.), *Group dynamics: Research and theory* (pp. 259–269). New York: Harper and Row.

Fridlund, A. J. (1991). Sociality of solitary smiling: Potentiation by implicit an audience. *Journal of Personality and Social Psychology, 60,* 218–229.

Fried, M., Kaplan, K. J., & Klein, K. W. (1975). Juror selection: An analysis of voir dire. In R. J. Simon (Ed.), *The jury system in America* (pp. 49–66). Beverly Hills, CA: Sage.

Friedman, M., & Rosenman, R. H. (1974). *Type A behavior and your heart.* New York: Knopf.

Friedrich, L. K., & Stein, A. H. (1975). Prosocial television and young children: The effects of verbal labeling and role playing on learning and behavior. *Child Development, 46,* 27–38.

Funk, S. C., & Houston, B. K. (1987). A critical analysis of the Hardiness Scale's validity and utility. *Journal of Personality and Social Psychology, 53,* 572–578.

Furnham, A. (1984). Studies of cross-cultural conformity: A brief critical review. *Psychologia: An International Journal of Psychology, 27,* 65–72.

Fussell, P. (1975). *The great war and modern memory.* New York: Oxford University Press.

Gadow, K. D., & Sprafkin, J. (1987). Effects of viewing high versus low aggression cartoons on emotionally disturbed children. *Journal of Pediatric Psychology, 12,* 413–427.

Gaertner, L., Sedikides, C., & Graetz, K. (1999). In search of self-definition: Motivational primacy of the collective self, or contextual primacy? *Journal of Personality and Social Psychology, 76(1),* 5–18.

Gaertner, S. L. (1975). The role of racial attitudes in helping behavior. *Journal of Social Psychology, 35,* 95–101.

Gaertner, S. L., & Dovidio, J. F. (1977). The subtlety of white racism, arousal, and helping behavior. *Journal of Personality and Social Psychology, 35,* 691–707.

Gaertner, S. L., & Dovidio, J. F. (1986). The aversive form of racism. In J. F. Dovidio & S. L. Gaertner (Eds.), *Prejudice, discrimination, and racism* (pp. 1–34). Orlando, FL: Academic Press.

Gaertner, S. L., Dovidio, J. F., & Johnson, G. (1982). Race of victim, nonresponsive bystander, and helping behavior. *Journal of Social Psychology, 117,* 69–77.

Gamson, W. A., Fireman, B., & Rytina, S. (1982). *Encounters with unjust authority.* Homewood, IL: Dorsey.

Gangestad, S. W. & Thornhill, R. (1997). Human sexual selection and developmental instability. In J. A. Simpson & D. T. Kenrick (Eds.), *Evolutionary social psychology* (pp. 169–195). Mahwah, NJ: Erlbaum.

Gangestad, S. W., & Thornhill R. (1998, May 22). Menstrual cycle variation in women's preferences for the scent of symmetrical men. *Proceedings of the Royal Society of London, 265* (1399), 927.

Garcia, S., Stinson, L., Ickes, W., Bissonette, & Briggs, S. R. (1991). Shyness and physical attractiveness in mixed-sex dyads. *Journal of Personality and Social Psychology, 61,* 35–49.

Gardner, W. L., Gabriel, S., & Lee, A.. Y. (1999). "I" value freedom, but "we" value relationships: Self-construal priming mirrors cultural differences in judgment. *Psychological Science, 10,* 321–326.

Gavanski, I., & Wells, G. L. (1989). Counterfactual processing of normal and exceptional events. *Journal of Experimental Social Psychology, 25,* 314–325.

Geen, R. G. (1989). Alternative conceptions of social facilitation. In P. B. Paulus (Ed.), *Psychology of group influence* (2nd ed., pp. 15–52). Hillsdale, NJ: Erlbaum.

Geen, R. G., & Quanty, M. (1977). The catharsis of aggression: An evaluation of a hypothesis. In L. Berkowitz (Ed), *Advances in experimental social psychology* (Vol. 10). New York: Academic Press.

Geffner, R., & Gross, M. M. (1984). Sex role behavior and obedience to authority: A field study. *Sex Roles, 10,* 973–985.

General Social Survey (1999). Retrieved January 8, 2001 from the World Wide Web: http://www.icpsr.umich.edu/GSS99/home.htm.

Gentry, C. S. (1987). Social distance regarding male and female homosexuals. *Journal of Social Psychology, 127,* 199–208

Georgopoulos, B. S. (1965). Normative structure variables and organizational behavior. *Human Relations, 18,* 155–169.

Gergen, K. J. (1974). Toward a psychology of receiving help. *Journal of Applied Social Psychology, 4,* 187–193.

Gergen, K. J., Gergen, M., & Barton H. (1973, October). Deviance in the dark. *Psychology Today,* 129–130.

Gerrard, M., Gibbons, F. X., Warner, T. D., & Smith, G. E. (1993). Perceived vulnerability to HIV infection and AIDS preventive behavior: A critical review of the evidence. In J. B. Pryor and G. D. Reeder (Eds.), *The social psychology of HIV infection.* Hillsdale, NJ: Erlbaum.

Gibbons, F. X. (1990). Self-attention and behavior: A review and theoretical update. In M. P. Zanna (Ed.), *Advances in experimental social psychology* (Vol. 12). San Diego, CA: Academic Press.

Giehart, H. (1999). Defense claims gay panic. Downloaded from the World Wide Web, January 13, 2001. http://bi.uwyo.edu/news00/defense.htm.

Gilbert, D. S., Malone, P. S. (1995). The correspondence bias. *Psychological Bulletin, 117,* 21–38.

Gilbert, D. T. (1989). Thinking lightly about others: Automatic components of the social inference process. In J. Uleman & J. A. Bargh (Eds.), *Unintended thought* (pp. 189–211). New York: Guilford.

Gilbert, D. T. (1991). How mental systems believe. *American Psychologist, 46,* 107–119.

Gilbert, D. T., & Hixon, G. J. (1991). The trouble of thinking: Activation and application of stereotypic beliefs. *Journal of Personality and Social Psychology, 60,* 509–517.

Gilbert, D. T., & Krull, D. S. (1988). Seeing less is knowing more: The benefits of perceptual ignorance. *Journal of Personality and Social Psychology, 54,* 193–202.

Gilbert, D. T., McNulty, S. E., Guiliano, T. A., & Benson, J. E. (1992). Blurry words and fuzzy deeds: Attribution of obscure behavior. *Journal of Personality and Social Psychology, 62,* 18–25.

Gilbert, D. T., Pelham, B. W., & Krull, D. S. (1988). On cognitive busyness: When person perceivers meet persons perceived. *Journal of Personality and Social Psychology, 54,* 733–740.

Gilbert, D. T., Pinel, E. C., Wilson, T. D., Blumberg, S. J., & Wheatley, T. P. (1998). Immune neglect: A source of durability bias in affective forecasting. *Journal of Personality and Social Psychology, 75,* 617–638.

Gilbert, S. J. (1981). Another look at the Milgram obedience studies: The role of the graduated series of shocks. *Personality and Social Psychology Bulletin, 7,* 600–695.

Gill, M. J., Swann, W. B., Jr., & Silvera, D. H. (1998). On the genesis of confidence. *Journal of Personality and Social Psychology, 75,* 1101–1114.

Gillis, J., Bernieri, F. J., & Wooten, E. (1995). The effects of stimulus medium and feedback on judgment of rapport. *Organizational Behavior and Human Decision Processes, 63,* 33–45.

Gilovich, T. (1981). Seeing the past in the present: The effects of associations to familiar events on judgments and decisions. *Journal of Personality and Social Psychology, 40,* 797–808.

Gilovich, T. (1991). *How we know what isn't so: The fallibility of human reason in everyday life.* New York: Free Press.

Gilovich, T., Savitsky, K., & Medvec, V. H. (1998). The illusion of transparency: Biased assessments of others' ability to read pone's emotional state. *Journal of Personality and Social Psychology, 75,* 332–346.

Glassman, R. B., Packel, E. W., & Brown, D. L. (1986). Greenbeards and kindred spirits: A preliminary mathematical model of altruism toward nonkin who bear similarities to the giver. *Ethology and Sociobiology, 7,* 107–115.

Gleicher, F., & Petty, R. E. (1992). Expectations of reassurance influence the nature of fear-stimulated attitude change. *Journal of Experimental Social Psychology, 28,* 86–100.

Goldman, M. (1986). Compliance employing a combined foot-in-the-door and door-in-the-face procedure. *Journal of Social Psychology, 126,* 111–116.

Goldman, M. (1988, January). The fate of Europe's Jews under Nazi rule. *Toledo Jewish News,* 6–14.

Goldman, M., & Creason, C. R. (1981). Inducing compliance by a two door-in-the-face procedure and a self-determination request. *Journal of Social Psychology, 114,* 229–235.

Goldman, M., Creason, C. R., & McCall, C. G. (1981). Compliance employing a two-feet-in-the-door procedure. *Journal of Social Psychology, 114,* 259–265.

Goldman, M., Seever, M., & Seever, M. (1982). Social labeling and the foot-in-the-door effect. *Journal of Social Psychology, 117,* 19–23.

Goleman, D. (1991a). *Psychology updates.* New York: HarperCollins.

Goleman, D. (1991b, October 22). Sexual Harassment: About power, not sex. *The New York Times.*

Goleman, D. (1993, February 9). Poets know how spurned lovers suffer: Science finds pain on the other side, too. *The New York Times,* B1.

Goodman, G. S., Levine, M., Melton, G. B., & Ogden, D. W. (1991). Child witnesses and the confrontation clause: The American Psychological Association brief in *Maryland v. Craig, 15,* 13–30.

Goodwin, D. K. (1976). *Lyndon Johnson and the American dream.* New York: Harper & Row.

Goranson, R. E., & Berkowitz, L. (1966). Reciprocity and responsibility reactions to prior help. *Journal of Personality and Social Psychology, 3,* 227–232.

Goranson, R. E., & Berkowitz, L. (1974). Reciprocity and responsibility reactions to prior help. *Journal of Personality and Social Psychology, 3,* 227–232.

Gore, K. Y., Tobiasen, M. A., & Kayson, W. A. (1997). Effects of sex of caller, implied sexual orientation, and urgency on altruistic response using the wrong number technique. *Psychological Reports, 80,* 927–930.

Gorman-Smith, D., & Tolan, P. (1998). The role of exposure to community violence and developmental problems among inner-city youth. *Development and Psychopathology, 10,* 101–116.

Gottman, J., & Levenson, R. W. (1986). Assessing the role of emotion in marriage. *Behavioral Assessment, 8,* 31–48.

Gottman, J. M. (1995). *Why marriages fail or succeed.* New York: Fireside.

Gottman, J. M., Coan, J., Carrere, S., & Swanson, C. (1998). Predicting marital happiness and stability from newlywed interactions. *Journal of Marriage and the Family, 60,* 5–22.

Gough, H. G. (1951). Studies of social intolerance I: Psychological and sociological correlates of anti-Semitism. *Journal of Social Psychology, 33,* 237–246

Gould, S. J. (1985). *The mismeasure of man.* New York: Norton.

Gouldner, A. W. (1960). The norm of reciprocity: A preliminary statement. *American Sociological Review, 25,* 161–178.

Graham, S., Weiner, B., Giuliano, T., & Williams, E. (1993). An attributional analysis of reactions to Magic Johnson. *Journal of Applied Social Psychology, 23,* 996–1010.

Gray, J. D., & Silver, R. C. (1990). Opposite sides of the same coin: Former spouses' divergent perspectives in coping with their divorce. *Journal of Personality and Social Psychology, 59,* 1180–1191.

Greenberg, M. A., & Stone, A. A. (1992). Emotional disclosure about traumas and its relation to health: Effects of previous disclosure and trauma severity. *Journal of Personality and Social Psychology, 63,* 75–84.

Greenberg, M. S., & Frisch, D. M. (1972). Effect of intentionality on willingness to reciprocate a favor. *Journal of Experimental Social Psychology, 8,* 99–111.

Greene, E. (1990). Media effects on jurors. *Law and Human Behavior, 14,* 439–450.

Greenwald, A. G. (1968). Cognitive learning, cognitive response to persuasion, and attitude change. In A. G. Greenwald, T. C. Brock, & T. M. Ostrom (Eds.), *Psychological foundations of attitudes* (pp. 147–170). New York: Academic Press.

Greenwald, A. G. (1980). The totalitarian ego: Fabrication and revision of personal history. *American Psychologist, 35,* 603–612.

Greenwald, A. G. (1989). Self-knowledge and self-deception. In J. S. Lockard & D. L. Paulhus (Eds.), *Self-deception: An adaptive mechanism.* New York: Prentice-Hall.

Greenwald, A. G., & Banaji, M. R. (1989). The self as a memory system: Powerful but ordinary. *Journal of Personality and Social Psychology, 57,* 41–54.

Greenwald, A. G., McGhee, D. E., & Schwartz, J-L. K. (1998). Measuring individual differences in implicit cognition: The implicit association test. *Journal of Personality and Social Psychology, 74,* 1464–1480.

Greenwald, A. G., & Pratkanis, A. R. (1984). The self. In R. S. Wyer & T. K. Srull (Eds.), *Handbook of social cognition.* Hillsdale: NJ, Erlbaum.

Greenwald, A. G., Spangerberg, E. R., Pratkanis, A. R., & Eskenazi, J. (1991). Double-blind tests of self-help audiotapes. *Psychological Science, 2,* 119–122.

Grieve, P. G., & Hogg, M. A. (1999). Subjective uncertainty and intergroup discrimination in the minimal group situation. *Personality and Social Psychology Bulletin, 25,* 926–940.

Griffin, D. W., & Ross, L. (1991). In M. P. Zanna (Ed.), *Advances in experimental social psychology, 24,* San Diego, CA: Academic Press.

Gross, A. E., & McMullen, P. A. (1982). The help seeking process. In V. J. Derlaga & J. Grezlak (Eds.), *Cooperation and helping behavior: Theories and research* (pp. 305–326). New York: Academic Press.

Groth, A. N. (1979). *Men who rape: The psychology of the offender.* New York: Plenum.

Gruder, C. L., Cook, T. D., Hennigan, K. M., Flay, B. R., Alessis, C., & Halamaji, J. (1979). Empirical tests of the absolute sleeper effect predicted from the discounting cue hypothesis. *Journal of Personality and Social Psychology, 36,* 1061–1074.

Gruder, C. L., Romer, D., & Korth, B. (1978). Dependency and fault as determinants of helping. *Journal of Experimental Social Psychology, 14,* 227–235.

Haddon, W. H., Jr., & Baker, S. P. (1987). Injury control. In D. W. Clark & B. MacMahon (Eds.), *Preventive and community medicine* (2nd ed., pp. 109–140). Boston: Little, Brown.

Hamilton, D. L., & Sherman, S. J. (1989). Illusory correlations: Implications for stereotype theory. In D. Bar-Tal, C. F. Graumann, A. W. Kruglanski, & W. Stroebe (Eds.), *Stereotypes and Prejudice.* New York, Springer-Verlag.

Hamilton, D. L., & Trolier, T. K. (1986). Stereotypes and stereotyping: An overview of the cognitive approach. In J. Dovidio & S. L. Gaertner (Eds.), *Prejudice, discrimination, & racism.* Orlando, FL, Academic Press.

Hammock, G. S., Rosen, S., Richardson, D. R., & Bernstein, S. (1989). Aggression as equity restoration. *Journal of Research in Personality, 23,* 398–409.

Haney, C. (1991). The fourteenth amendment and symbolic legality: Let them eat due process. *Law and Human Behavior, 15,* 183–204.

Hansen, C. H., & Hansen, R. D. (1988). Finding the face in the crowd: An anger superiority effect. *Journal of Personality and Social Psychology, 54,* 917–924.

Harari, H., Harari, O., & White, R. V. (1985). The reaction to rape by American male bystanders. *Journal of Social Psychology, 125,* 653–668.

Haritos-Fatouros, M. (1988). The official torturer: A learning model of obedience to the authority of violence. *Journal of Applied Social Psychology, 18,* 1107–1120.

Harkins, S. G., & Petty, R. E. (1982). Effects of task difficulty and task uniqueness on social loafing. *Journal of Personality and Social Psychology, 43,* 1214–1229.

Harkins, S. G., & Szymanski, K. (1987). Social loafing and social facilitation: New wine in old bottles. In C. Hendrick (Ed.), *Review of personality and social psychology* (Vol. 9, pp. 167–188). Newbury Park, CA: Sage.

Harris, C. R., & Christenfeld, N. (1996). Gender, jealousy, and reason. *Psychological Science, 7,* 364–366.

Harris, M. B. (1990). Is love seen as different for the obese? *Journal of Applied Social Psychology, 20,* 1209–1224.

Hartley, E. L. (1946). *Attitudes and prejudice.* New York: Crown Point Press.

Harvey, C. B., Ollila, L., Baxter, K., & Guo, S. Z. (1997). Gender-related and grade-related differences in writing topics in Chinese and Canadian children. *Journal of Research and Development in Education. 31,* 1–6.

Harvey, J. H., & Weary, G. (1981). *Perspectives on attributional processes.* Dubuque, IA: Brown.

Harvey, J. H., & Weary, G. (1984). Current issues in attribution theory and research. *Annual Review of Psychology, 35,* 427–459.

Haslam, S. A., Oakes, P. J., Reynolds, K. J., & Turner, J. C. (1999). Social identity salience and the emergence of stereotype consensus. *Personality and Social Psychology Bulletin, 25,* 809–818.

Hass, R. G., Katz, I., Rizzo, N., Bailey, J., & Eisenstadt, D. (1991). Cross-racial appraisals as related to attitude ambivalence and cognitive complexity. *Personality and Social Psychology Bulletin, 17,* 83–92.

Hastie, R., Penrod, S., & Pennington, N. (1983). *Inside the jury.* Cambridge, MA: Harvard University Press.

Hastie, R., & Rasinski, K. A. (1988). The concept of accuracy in social judgment. In D. Bar-Tal & E. Kruglanski (Eds.), *The social psychology of knowledge.* Cambridge, England: Cambridge University Press.

Hatfield, E. (1988). Passionate and companionate love. In R. J. Sternberg & M. L. Barnes (Eds.), *The psychology of love.* New Haven, CT: Yale University Press.

Hatfield, E., & Walster, G. W. (1981). *A new look at love.* Reading, MA: Addison-Wesley.

Hatfield, E. (Walster), Aronson, V., Abrahams, D., & Rottman, L. (1966). Importance of physical attractiveness in dating behavior. *Journal of Personality and Social Psychology, 4,* 508–516.

Hatfield, E., Traupmann, J., Sprecher, S., Utne, M., & Hay, J. (1985). Equity and intimate relationships: Recent research. In W. Ickes (Ed.), *Compatible and incompatible relationships* (pp. 91–117). New York: Springer-Verlag.

Hatfield, E. H, Walster, G. W., & Berscheid, E. (1978). *Equity theory and research.* Boston: Allyn & Bacon.

Hatfield, E. H., Walster, G. W., & Traupmann, J. (1978). Equity and premarital sex. *Journal of Personality and Social Psychology, 36,* 82–92.

Haugtvedt, C. P., & Petty, R. E. (1992). Personality and persuasion: Need for cognition moderates the persistence and resistance of attitude change. *Journal of Personality and Social Psychology, 63,* 308–319.

Haugtvedt, C. R., Petty, R. E., & Cacioppo, J. T. (1992). Need for cognition and advertising: Understanding the role of personality in consumer behavior. *Journal of Consumer Psychology, 1,* 239–260.

Haugtvedt, C. P., & Wegener, D. T. (1993, May 1). *Need for cognition and message order effects in persuasion.* Paper presented at the sixty-fifth annual meeting of the Midwestern Psychological Association, Chicago.

Haynes, S. G., & Matthews, K. A. (1988). The association of type A behavior with cardiovascular disease. In B. K. Houston & C. R. Snyder (Eds.), *Type A behavior pattern.* New York: Wiley.

Hays, R. B. (1985). A longitudinal study of friendship development. *Journal of Personality and Social Psychology, 48,* 261–273.

Hays, R. B. (1988a). Friendship. In S. Duck (Ed.), *Handbook of personal relationships* (pp. 391–408). New York: Wiley.

Hays, R. B. (1988b). The day to day functioning of casual versus close friendships. *Journal of Social and Personal Relationships, 5,* 261–273.

Heatherton, T., & Baumeister, R. F. (1991). Binge eating as escape from the self. *Psychological Bulletin, 110,* 86–108.

Heatherton, T. F., Herman, C. P., & Polivy, J. (1991). Effects of physical threat and ego threat on eating behavior. *Journal of Personality and Social Psychology, 60,* 138–143.

Heaton, A.W., & Sigall, H. (1991). Self-consciousness, self-presentation, and performance: Who chokes, and when? *Journal of Applied Social Psychology, 21*(3), 175–188.

Heaton, T. B., & Albrecht, S. L. (1991). Stable unhappy marriages. *Journal of Marriage and the Family, 53,* 747–758.

Hebb, D. O., & Thompson, W. R. (1968). The social significance of minimal studies. In G. Lindzey & E. Aronson (Eds.), *The handbook of social psychology* (2nd ed., Vol. 2). Reading, MA: Addison-Wesley.

Heider, F. (1944). Social perception and phenomenal causality. *Psychological Review, 51,* 258–374.

Heider, F. (1958). *The psychology of Interpersonal relations.* New York: Wiley.

Heine, S. J., & Lehman, D. R. (1999). Culture, self-discrepancies, and self-satisfaction. *Personality and Social Psychology Bulletin, 25,* 915–925.

Hendrick, C. (1988). Roles and gender in relationships. In S. Duck (Ed.), *Handbook of personal relationships* (pp. 429–448). New York: Wiley.

Hendrick, C., & Hendrick, S. S. (1989). Research on love: Does it measure up? *Journal of Personality and Social Psychology, 56,* 784–794.

Hendrick, S. S., & Hendrick, C. (1987). Love and sex attitudes: A close relationship. In W. H. Jones & D. Perlman (Eds.), *Advances in personal relationships* (Vol. 1). Greenwich, CT: JAI Press.

Herhold, S. (1994, May 24). Denny's settles bias case for $46 million. *San Jose Mercury News,* pp. 1, 16A.

Herman, C. P., Olmstead, M. P., & Polivy, J. (1983). Obesity, externality, and susceptibility to social influence: An integrated analysis. *Journal of Personality and Social Psychology, 45,* 926–934.

Hersh, S. (1970). *My Lai 4: A report on the massacre and its aftermath.* New York: Vintage Books.

Hess R. D., & Torney, J. V. (1967). *The development of political attitudes in children.* Chicago: Aldine.

Hewstone, M., Hantzi, A., & Johnston, L. (1991). Social categorization and person memory: The pervasiveness of race as an organizing principle. *European Journal of Social Psychology, 21,* 517–528.

Higgins, E. T. (1989). Self-discrepancy theory: What patterns of self-beliefs cause people to suffer? In L. Berkowitz (Ed.), *Advances in experimental social psychology* (Vol. 22, pp. 93–136). New York: Academic Press.

Higgins, E. T. (1998). Promotion and prevention: Regulatory focus as a motivational principle. In M. P. Zanna (Ed.), *Advances in experimental social psychology* (Vol. 30, pp. 1–46). New York: Academic Press.

Higgins, E. T., & Bargh, J. A. (1987). Knowledge accessibility and activation: Subjectivity and social perception. *Annual Review of Psychology, 38,* 59–69.

Higgins, E. T., Shah, J., & Friedman, R. (1997). Emotional responses to goal attainment: Strengths of regulatory focus as a moderator. *Journal of Personality and Social Psychology, 72,* 515–525.

Higgins, E. T., & Stangor, C. (1988). Context-driven social judgment and memory when "behavior engulfs the field" in reconstructive memory. In D. Bar-Tal & A.W. Kruglanski (Eds.), *The social psychology of knowledge.* Cambridge, England: Cambridge University Press.

Higgins, E. T., & Tykocinsky, O. (1992). Self-discrepancies and biographical memory: Personality and cognition at the level of psychological situation. *Personality and Social Psychological Bulletin, 18*(5), 527–535.

Hill, C. A. (1987). Affiliation motivation: People who need peo-ple...but in different ways. *Journal of Personality and Social Psychology, 52,* 1008–1018.

Hill, C. T., Rubin, Z., & Peplau, L. A. (1976). Breakups before marriage: The end of 103 affairs. *Journal of Social Issues, 32,* 147–168.

Hill, J. L., & Zautra, A. J. (1989). Self-blame attributions and unique vulnerability as predictors of post-rape demoral-ization. *Journal of Social and Clinical Psychology, 8,* 368–375.

Hilton, D. J. (1990). Conversational processes and causal expla-nation. *Psychological Review, 107,* 65–81.

Hilton, D. J., & Slugoski, B. R. (1986). Knowledge-based causal attribution: The abnormal conditions focus model. *Psycho-logical Review, 93,* 75–88.

Hilton, J. L., & Darley, J. M. (1991). The effects of interaction goals on person perception. In M. P. Zanna (Ed.), *Advances in experimental social psychology, 24.* San Diego, CA: Acad-emic Press.

Hilton, J. L., Klein, J. G., & von Hippel, W. (1991). Attention allo-cation and impression formation. *Personality and Social Psychology Bulletin, 17,* 548–559.

Hixon, J. G., & Swann, W. B., Jr. (1993). When does introspection bear fruit? Self-reflection, self-insight, and interpersonal choice. *Journal of Personality and Social Psychology, 64*(1), 35–43.

Hoaken, P. N. S., Assaad, J., & Pihl, R. O. (1998). Cognitive func-tioning and the inhibition of alcohol-induced aggression. *Journal of Studies on Alcohol, 59,* 599–607.

Hoaken, P. N. S., Giancola, P. R., & Pihl, R. O. (1998). Executive cognitive functions as mediators of alcohol-related aggres-sion. *Alcohol and Alcoholism, 33,* 47–54.

Hoeksema-van Orden, C. Y. D., Gaillard, A. W. K., & Buunk, B. (1998). Social loafing under fatigue. *Journal of Personality and Social Psychology, 75,* 1179–1190.

Hoffman, M. L. (1981). Is altruism part of human nature? *Jour-nal of Personality and Social Psychology, 40,* 121–137.

Hogg, M. A., & Abrams, D. (1990). Social motivation, self-es-teem, an social identity. In D. Abrams & M. A. Hogg (Eds.), *Social identity theory: Constructive and criti-cal advances* (pp. 28–47). New York: Harvester Wheat-sheaf.

Hogg, M. A., & Mullin, B. A. (1999). Joining groups to reduce uncertainty: Subjective uncertainty reduction and group identification. In D. Abrams & M. A. Hogg (Eds.), *Social identity and social cognition* (pp. 249–279). Oxford, Eng-land: Blackwell.

Hollander, E. P. (1985). Leadership and power. In G. Lindzey & E. Aronson (Eds.), *Handbook of social psychology* (Vol. 2, pp. 485–537). New York: Random House.

Hollingshead, A. B. (1998). Retrieval processes in transactive memory systems. *Journal of Personality and Social Psychol-ogy, 74,* 659–671.

Holtzworth-Monroe, A., & Jacobson, N. S. (1985). Causal attri-butions of married couples: When do they search for causes? What do they conclude? *Journal of Personality and Social Psychology, 48,* 1398–1412.

Homans, G. C. (1961). *Social behavior: Its elementary forms.* New York: Harcourt, Brace & World.

Hornik, J. (1988). Cognitive thoughts mediating compliance in multiple request situations. *Journal of Economic Psychology, 9,* 69–79.

Horowitz, I. A., & Bordens, K. S. (1990). An experimental inves-tigation of procedural issues in toxic tort trials. *Law and Human Behavior, 14,* 269–286.

Horowitz, I. A., ForsterLee, L., & Brolly, I. (1996). The effects of trial complexity on decision making. *Journal of Applied Psychology, 81*(6), 757–768.

Horowitz, I. A., & Willging, T. E. (1991). Changing views of jury power: The nullification debate, 1787–1988. *Law and Hu-man Behavior, 15,* 165–182.

Horwitz, M., & Rabbie, J. M. (1989). Stereotype of groups, group members, and individuals in categories: A differential analysis. In D. Bar-Tal., C. F. Graumann, A.W. Kruglanski, & W. Stoebe (Eds.), *Stereotyping and prejudice.* New York: Springer-Verlag.

House, J. S., Landis, K. R., & Umberson, D. (1988). Social rela-tionships and health. *Science, 241,* 540–545.

Houston, B. K. (1988). Cardiovascular and neuroendocrine reac-tivity, global type A, and the components of type A behav-ior. In B. K. Houston & C. R. Snyder (Eds.), *Type A behav-ior pattern.* New York: Plenum.

Hovland, C. I., Harvey, O. J., & Sherif, M. (1957). Assimilation and contrast effects in reactions to communication and at-titude change. *Journal of Abnormal and Social Psychology, 55,* 244–252.

Hovland, C. I., Janis, I. L., & Kelley, H. H. (1953). *Persuasion and communication.* New Haven, CT.: Yale University Press.

Howard, D. J. (1997). Familiar phrases as peripheral persuasion cues. *Journal of Experimental Social Psychology, 33,* 241–243

Hoxter, A. L., & Lester, D. (1994). Gender differences in preju-dice. *Perceptual and Motor Skills, 79,* 1666.

Huang, L., & Harris, M. (1973). Conformity in Chinese and Americans: A field experiment. *Journal of Cross-Cultural Psychology, 4,* 427–434.

Huesmann, L. R. (1986). Psychological processes promoting the relationship between exposure to media violence and ag-gressive behavior by the viewer. *Journal of Social Issues, 42,* 125–139.

Huesmann, L. R. (1988). An information processing model for the development of aggression. *Aggressive Behavior, 14,* 13–24.

Huesmann, L. R., & Eron, L. D. (1984). Cognitive processes and the persistence of aggressive behavior. *Aggressive Behavior, 10,* 243–251.

Huesmann, L. R., Eron, L. D., Lefkowitz, M. M., & Walder, L. O. (1984). Stability of aggression over time and generations. *Developmental Psychology, 20,* 1120–1134.

Huesmann, L. R., Lagerspetz, K., & Eron, L. D. (1984). Interven-ing variables in the TV violence-aggression relation: Evi-dence from two countries. *Developmental Psychology, 20,* 746–775.

Huesmann, L. R., & Malamuth, N. M. (1986). Media violence and antisocial behavior: An overview. *Journal of Social Is-sues, 42,* 1–6.

Huggins, N. I. (1977). *Black odyssey: The Afro-American ordeal in slavery.* New York: Pantheon.

Hull, J. G., Van Treuren, R. R., & Propson, P. M. (1988). Attribu-tional style and the components of hardiness. *Personality and Social Psychology Bulletin, 14*(3), 505–513.

Hull, J. G., Van Treuren, R. R., & Virnelli, S. (1987). Hardiness and health: A critique and alternative approach. *Journal of Personality and Social Psychology, 53,* 518–530.

Huneke, D. K. (1986). The lessons of Herman Graebe's life: The origins of a moral person. *Humboldt Journal of Social Relations, 13,* 320–332.

Huston, T. L., & Vangelisti, A. L. (1991). Socioemotional behavior and satisfaction in marital relationship: A Longitudinal study. *Journal of Personality and Social Psychology, 61,* 721–733.

Hyde, J. S. (1984). How large are gender differences in aggression? A developmental meta-analysis. *Developmental Psychology, 20,* 722–736.

Hymowitz, C., & Weismann, M. (1984). *A history of women in America.* New York: Bantam.

Ike, B. W. (1987). Man's limited sympathy as a consequence of his evolution in small kin groups. In V. Reynolds, V. Falger, & I. Vine (Eds.), *The sociobiology of ethnocentrism.* Athens, GA: University of Georgia Press.

Inbau, F. E., Reid, J. E., & Buckley, J. P. (1986). *Criminal investigation and confessions* (3rd ed.). Baltimore: Williams & Atkins.

Insel, P. M., & Roth, W. T. (1985). *Core concepts in health* (4th ed.). Palo Alto, CA: Mayfield.

Insel, P. M., & Roth, W. T. (1994). *Core concepts in health* (7th ed.). Mountain View, CA: Mayfield.

Irwin, C. J. (1987). A study in the evolution of ethnocentrism. In V. Reynolds, V. Falger, & I. Vine (Eds.), *The sociobiology of ethnocentrism.* Athens, GA: University of Georgia Press.

Isen, A. M. (1987). Positive affect, cognitive processes and social behavior. In L. Berkowitz (Ed.), *Advances in social psychology* (Vol. 20, pp. 203–253). New York: Academic Press.

Isen, A. M., & Simmonds, S. F. (1978). The effect of feeling good on helping: Cookies and kindness. *Social Psychology, 41,* 346–349.

Isenberg, D. J. (1986). Group polarization: A critical review and meta-analysis. *Journal of Personality and Social Psychology, 50,* 1141–1151.

James, W. (1890). *The principles of psychology.* New York: Dover.

Jamieson, K. H. (1992). *Dirty politics: Distraction, deception, & democracy.* New York: Oxford University Press.

Janis, I. L. (1972). *Victims of groupthink.* Boston: Houghton Mifflin.

Janis, I. L. (1982). *Groupthink* (2nd ed.). Boston: Houghton Mifflin.

Janis, I. L. (1984). Improving adherence to medical recommendations: Prescriptive hypotheses derived from recent research in social psychology. In A. Baum, S. E. Taylor, & J. E. Singer (Eds.), *Handbook of psychology and health* (Vol. 4, pp. 113–148). Hillsdale, NJ: Erlbaum.

Jankowiak, J., & Fischer, E. (1992). A cross-cultural study of romantic love. *Ethology, 24,* 121–129.

Janoff-Bulman, R. (1979). Characterological versus behavioral self-blame: Inquiries into depression and rape. *Journal of Personality and Social Psychology, 37,* 1798–1809.

Janoff-Bulman, R. (1982). Esteem and control bases of blame: "Adaptive" strategies for victims versus observers. *Journal of Personality, 50,* 180–192.

Jemmott, J. B., Croyle, R. T., & Ditto, P. H. (1988). Commonsense epidemiology: Self-based judgments from laypersons and physicians. *Health Psychology, 7,* 55–73.

Jemmott, J. B., Ditto, P. H., & Croyle, R. T. (1986). Judging health status: Effects of perceived prevalence and personal relevance. *Journal of Personality and Social Psychology, 50,* 899–905.

Jenkins, M. J., & Dambrot, F. H. (1987). The attribution of date rape: Observer's attitudes and sexual experiences and the dating situation. *Journal of Applied Social Psychology, 17,* 875–895.

Jepson, C. & Chaiken, S. (1990). Chronic issue-specific fear inhibits systematic processing of persuasive communications. *Journal of Social Behavior and Personality, 5*(2), 61–84.

Johnson, B. T., & Eagly, A. H. (1989). Effects of involvement on persuasion: A meta-analysis. *Psychological Bulletin, 106*(2), 290–314.

Johnson, R. N. (1972). *Aggression in man and animals.* Philadelphia: Saunders.

Johnson, T. E., & Rule, B. G. (1986). Mitigating circumstances, information, censure, and aggression. *Journal of Personality and Social Psychology, 50,* 537–542.

Jones, C., & Aronson, E. (1973). Attribution of fault of a rape victim as a function of respectability of the victim. *Journal of Personality and Social Psychology, 26,* 415–419.

Jones, E. E. (1990). *Interpersonal perception,* New York: Freeman.

Jones, E. E., & Davis, K. E. (1965). From acts to dispositions: The attribution process in person perception. In L. Berkowitz (Ed.), *Advances in experimental social psychology* (Vol. 2, pp. 219–266) New York: Academic Press.

Jones, E. E., & Gerard, H. B. (1967). *Foundations of social psychology.* New York: Wiley.

Jones, E. E., & Harris, V. A. (1967). The attribution of attitudes. *Journal of Experimental Social Psychology, 3,* 1–24.

Jones, E. E., Rock, L., Shaver, K. G., Goethals, G. R., & Ward, L. M. (1968). Pattern of performance and ability attribution: An unexpected primacy affect. *Journal of Personality and Social Psychology, 10,* 317–340.

Jones, E. E., & Thibaut, J. W. (1958). Interaction goals as bases of inference in interpersonal perception. In R. Taguiri & L. Petrillo (Eds.), *Person perception and interpersonal behavior.* Stanford, CA: Stanford University Press.

Jones, S. E. (1987). Judge- versus attorney-conducted voir dire: An empirical investigation of juror candor. *Law and Human Behavior, 11,* 131–146.

Josephson, W. L. (1987). Television violence and children's aggression: Testing the priming, social script, and disinhibition predictions. *Journal of Personality and Social Psychology, 53,* 882–890.

Jourard, S. M. (1971). *Self-disclosure: An experimental analysis of the transparent self.* New York: Wiley.

Jowett, G. S., & O'Donnell, V. (1986). *Persuasion and propaganda.* Beverly Hills, CA: Sage.

Jowett, G. S., & O'Donnell, V. (1992). *Propaganda and persuasion* (2nd ed.). Beverly Hills, CA: Sage.

Judd, C. M., Drake, R. A., Downing, J. W., & Krosnick, J. A. (1991). Some dynamic properties of attitude structures: Context-induced response facilitation and polarization. *Journal of Personality and Social Psychology, 60,* 195–202.

Judd, C. M., & Park, B. (1993). Definition and assessment of accuracy in social stereotypes. *Psychological Review, 100,* 109–128.

Julian, T. W., McKenry, P. C., Gavazzi, S. M., & Law, J. C. (1999). Test of family of origin structural models of male verbal and physical aggression. *Journal of Family Issues, 20,* 397–423.

Jussim, L. (1986). Self-fulfilling prophecies: A theoretical and integrative review. *Psychological Review, 93,* 429–445.

Jussim, L. (1991). Social perception and social reality: A reflection-construction model. *Psychological Review, 98*, 54–73.

Jussim, L., & Eccles, J. S. (1992). Teacher expectations II: Construction and reflection of student achievement. *Journal of Personality and Social Psychology, 63*(6), 947–961.

Jussim, L., Nelson, T. E., Manis, M., & Soffin, S. (1995). Prejudice, stereotypes, and labeling effects: Sources of bias in person perception. *Journal of Personality and Social Psychology, 68*, 228–246.

Kahneman, D., & Miller, D. T. (1986). Norm theory: Comparing reality to its alternatives. *Psychological Review, 93*, 136–153.

Kahneman, D., Slovic, P., & Tversky, A. (1982). *Judgment under uncertainty: Heuristics and biases.* New York: Cambridge University Press.

Kahneman, D., & Tversky, A. (1982). The simulation heuristic. In D. Kahneman, P. Slovic, & A. Tversky (Eds.), *Judgment under uncertainty: Heuristics and biases* (pp. 201–208). Cambridge, England: Cambridge University Press.

Kaiser Family Foundation (1999). Kids and media @ the new millennium. Retrieved January 9, 2001 from the World Wide Web: http://www.kff.org/content/1999/1535/.

Kalish, J., Hilton, J. L., & Ditto, P. H. (1988). The effects of patients' expectations and physicians communication styles on doctor-patient interactions. Unpublished manuscript, University of Michigan, Ann Arbor.

Kalven, H., & Zeisel, H. (1966). *The American jury.* Boston: Little, Brown.

Kaminer, W. (1992). Crashing the locker room. *The Atlantic, 270*, 58–71.

Kanekar, S., & Maharukh, B. K. (1980). Responsibility of a rape victim in relation to her respectability, attractiveness, and provocativeness. *Journal of Social Psychology, 112*, 153–154.

Kanekar, S., & Maharukh, B. K. (1981). Factors affecting responsibility attributed to a rape victim. *Journal of Social Psychology, 113*, 285–286.

Kanekar, S., Shaherwalla, A., Franco, B., Kunju, T., & Pinto, A. J. (1991). The acquaintance predicament of a rape victim. *Journal of Applied Social Psychology, 21*, 1524–1544.

Kaplan, M. F., & Miller, C. E. (1977). Judgments and group discussion: Effect of presentation and memory factors on polarization. *Sociometry, 40*, 337–343.

Kaplan, M. F., & Miller, C. E. (1987). Group decision making and normative and informational social influence: Effects of type of issue and assigned decision rule. *Journal of Personality and Social Psychology, 53*, 306–313.

Karau, S. J., & Williams, K. D. (1993). Social loafing: A meta-analytic review and theoretical integration. *Journal of Personality and Social Psychology, 65*, 681–706.

Kassin, S. M., & Fong, C. T. (1999). "I'm innocent!" Effects of training on judgments of truth and deception in the interrogation room. *Law and Human Behavior, 23*, 499–516.

Kassin, S. M., & McNall, K. (1991). Police interrogations and confessions: Communicating promises and threats by pragmatic implications. *Law and Human Behavior, 15*, 233–252.

Kassin, S. M., Reddy, M. E., & Tulloch, W. F. (1990). Juror interpretations of ambiguous evidence: The need for cognition, presentation order, and persuasion. *Law and Human Behavior, 14*(1), 43–56.

Katz, D. (1960). The functional approach to the study of attitudes. *Public Opinion Quarterly, 24*, 163–204.

Katz, I, Cohen, S., & Glass, D. (1975). Some determinants of cross-racial helping behavior. *Journal of Personality and Social Psychology, 32*, 964–970.

Katz, I., & Hass, R. G. (1988). Racial ambivalence and American value conflict: Correlational and priming studies of dual cognition structures. *Journal of Personality and Social Psychology, 55*, 893–905.

Katz, I., Wakenhut, J., & Hass, R. G. (1986). Racial ambivalence, value duality and behavior. In J. F. Dovidio & S. L. Gaertner (Eds.), *Prejudice, discrimination and racism.* Orlando, FL: Academic Press.

Kazdin, A. E. (1987). Treatment of antisocial behavior in children: Current status and future directions. *Psychological Bulletin, 102*, 187–303.

Kelley, H. H. (1967). Attribution theory in social psychology. *Nebraska Symposium on Motivation, 14*, 192–241.

Kelley, H. H. (1971). Attribution theory in social interaction. In E. E. Jones, D. Kanouse, & H. H. Kelley (Eds.), *Attribution: Perceiving the causes of behavior* (pp. 1–26). Morristown, NJ: General Learning Press.

Kelley, H. H., Berscheid, E., Christensen, A., Harvey, J. H., Huston, T. L., Levinger, G., McClintock, E., Peplau, L. A., & Peterson, D. R. (1983). *Close relationships.* New York: Freeman.

Kelman, H., & Hamilton, L. (1989). *Crimes of obedience: Toward a social psychology of authority and responsibility.* New Haven, CT: Yale University Press.

Kelman, H. C., & Hovland, C. I. (1953). "Reinstatement" of the communicator in delayed measurement of opinion change. *Journal of Abnormal and Social Psychology, 48*, 327–335.

Kendall, P. C., Ronan, K. R., & Epps, J. (1991). Aggression in children/adolescents: Cognitive-behavioral treatment perspectives. In D. J. Pepler & K. H. Rubin (Eds.), *The development and treatment of childhood aggression* (pp. 341–360). Hillsdale, NJ: Erlbaum.

Kennedy, P. H. (1987). *The rise and fall of the great powers: Economic change and military conflict from 1500 to 2000.* New York: Random House.

Kenny, D., & Albright, L. (1987). Accuracy in interpersonal perception: A social relations analysis. *Psychological Bulletin, 102*, 390–402.

Kerr, N. L. (1983). Motivation losses in small groups: A social dilemma analysis. *Journal of Personality and Social Psychology, 45*, 819–828.

Kerr, N. L. (1989). Illusions of efficacy: The effects of group size on perceived efficacy in social dilemmas. *Journal of Experimental Social Psychology, 25*, 287–313.

Kerr, N. L. (1992). Issue importance and group decision making. In S. Worchel, W. Wood, & J. A. Simpson (Eds.), *Group process and productivity.* Newbury Park, CA: Sage.

Kerr, N. L., Kramer, G. P., Carroll, J. S., & Alfini, J. J. (1990, May 3–6). *On the effectiveness of voir dire in criminal cases with prejudicial pretrial publicity: An empirical study.* Paper presented at Midwestern Psychological Association Meetings, Chicago, IL.

Kiesler, C. A. (1971). *The psychology of commitment: Experiments linking behavior to the belief.* New York: Academic Press.

Kihlstrom, J. F., & Cantor, N. (1984). Mental representations of the self. In L. Berkowitz (Ed.), *Advances in experimental social psychology* (Vol. 17, pp. 2–40). New York: Academic Press.

Kilham, W., & Mann, L. (1974). Level of destructive obedience as a function of transmitter and executive roles in the Milgram obedience paradigm. *Journal of Personality and Social Psychology, 29,* 696–702.

King, L. A. (1998). Ambivalence over emotional expression and reading emotions in situations and faces. *Journal of Personality and Social Psychology, 74,* 753–762.

Kitayama, S., Markus, H. R., Matsumoto, H., & Norasakkunit, V. (1997). Individual and collective processes in the construction of the self: Self-enhancement in the United States and self-criticism in Japan. *Journal of Personality and Social Psychology, 72*(6), 1245–1267.

Kite, M.. E. (1984). Sex differences in attitudes toward homosexuality: A meta-analysis. *Journal of Homosexuality, 10,* 69–81.

Kite, M. E., & Whitley, B. E., Jr. (1998). Do heterosexual women and men differ in their attitudes toward homosexuality. In G. M. Herek (Ed.), *Stigma and sexual orientation* (pp. 39–61). Thousand Oaks, CA: Sage.

Klar, Y., & Gilardi, E. E. (1999). Are most people happier than their peers, or are they just happy. *Personality and Social Psychology Bulletin, 25,* 585–594.

Klein, J. G. (1991). Negativity effects in impression formation: A test in the political arena. *Personality and Social Psychology Bulletin, 17,* 412–418.

Klein, S. B., Loftus, J., & Plog, A. (1992). Trait judgments about the self: Evidence from encoding specificity paradigm. *Personality and Social Psychology Bulletin, 18*(6), 730–735.

Klohnen, E. C., & Mendelsohn, G. A. (1998). Partner selection for personality characteristics: A couple centered-approach. *Personality and Social Psychology Bulletin, 24,* 268–278.

Knee, C. R. (1998). Implicit theories of relationship: Assessment and prediction of romantic initiation, coping, and longevity. *Journal of Personality and Social Psychology, 74,* 360–370.

Kobak, R., & Hazan, C. (1991). Attachment in marriage: Effects of security and accuracy of working models. *Journal of Personality and Social Psychology, 60,* 861–869.

Kobasa, S. C. (1979). Stressful life events, personality, and health: An inquiry into hardiness. *Journal of Personality and Social Psychology, 37,* 1–11.

Kobasa, S. C. (1984, September). How much stress can you survive. *American Health Magazine,* 64–77.

Kobasa, S. C., Maddi, S. R., & Courington, S. (1981). Personality and constitution as mediators in the stress-illness relationship. *Journal of Health and Social Behavior, 22,* 368–379.

Kobasa, S. C., Maddi, S. R., & Zola, M. A. (1983). Type A and hardiness. *Journal of Behavioral Medicine, 6,* 41–51.

Kobasa, S. C., & Puccetti, M. C. (1983). Personality and social resources in stress resistance. *Journal of Personality & Social Psychology, 45,* 839–850.

Kolata, G. (1992, November 24). After kinship and marriage, anthropology discovers love. *New York Times,* p. B9.

Koltai, D. C., & Burger, J. M. (1989). *The effects of time on attributions for relationships dissolutions.* Paper presented at the annual meetings of the Western Psychological Association, Reno, Nevada.

Kortenhaus, C. M., & Demarest, J. (1993). Gender role stereotyping in children's literature: An update. *Sex Roles, 28,* 219–232.

Krackhardt, D., & Kilduff, M. (1999). Whether close or far: Social distance effects on perceived balance in friendship networks. *Journal of Personality and Social Psychology, 76,* 770–782.

Krahe, B. (1988). Victim and observer characteristics as determinants of responsibility attributions of victims of rape. *Journal of Applied Social Psychology, 18,* 50–58.

Kramer, R. M. (1998a). Paranoid cognition in social systems: Thinking and acting in the shadow of doubt. *Personality and Social Psychology Review, 2,* 251–275.

Kramer, R. M. (1998b). Revisiting the Bay of Pigs and Vietnam decisions twenty five years later: How well has the groupthink hypothesis stood the test of time? *Organizational Behavior and Human Decision Processes, 73,* 236–271.

Krantz, D. S. (1979). A naturalistic study of social influences on meal size among moderately obese and nonobese subjects. *Psychosomatic Medicine, 41,* 19–27.

Kravitz, D. A. & Martin, B. (1986). Ringelmann rediscovered: The original article. *Journal of Personality and Social Psychology, 50,* 936–941.

Kremer, J. F., & Stevens, L. (1983). Attributions and arousal as mediators of mitigation's effect on retaliation. *Journal of Personality and Social Psychology, 45,* 335–343.

Kreutzer, J. S., Schneider, H. G., & Myatt, C. R. (1984). Alcohol, aggression, and assertiveness in men: Dosage and expectancy effects. *Journal of Studies on Alcohol, 45,* 275–278.

Krishan, L. (1988). Recipient need and anticipation of reciprocity in prosocial exchange. *Journal of Social Psychology, 128,* 223–231.

Kristiansen, C. M., & Zanna, M. P. (1988). Justifying attitudes by appealing to values: A functional perspective. *British Journal of Social Psychology, 27,* 247–256.

Krosnick, J. (1989). Attitude importance and attitude accessibility. *Personality and Social Psychology Bulletin, 15,* 297–308.

Krosnick, J. A., & Alwin, D. F. (1989). Aging and susceptibility to attitude change. *Journal of Personality and Social Psychology, 57*(3), 416–425.

Krosnick, J. A., Betz, A. L., Jussim, L. J., & Lynn, A. R. (1992). Subliminal conditioning of attitudes. *Personality and Social Psychology Bulletin, 18,* 152–163.

Kruger, J., & Dunning, D. (1999). Unskilled and unaware of it: How difficulties in recognizing one's own incompetence lead to inflated self-assessments. *Journal of Personality and Social Psychology, 77,* 1121–1134.

Kruglanski, A. W. (1977). The place of naive contents in a theory of attribution: Reflections on Calder's and Zuckerman's critiques of the endogenous–exogenous partition. *Personality and Social Psychology Bulletin, 3,* 592–605.

Kruglanski, A. W. (1989). The psychology of being "right": the problem of accuracy in social perception and cognition. *Psychological Bulletin, 106,* 396–409.

Kruglanski, A. W., & Mayseless, O. (1990). Classic and current comparison research: Expanding the perspective. *Psychological Bulletin, 108,* 195–208.

Kruglanski, A. W., & Webster, D. M. (1991). Group members' reactions to opinion deviates and conformists at varying degrees of proximity to decision deadline and of environmental noise. *Journal of Personality and Social Psychology, 61,* 212–225.

Kunda, Z. (1987). Motivation and inference: Self-serving generation and evaluation of evidence. *Journal of Personality and Social Psychology, 53,* 636–647.

Kunda, Z. (1990). The case for motivated reasoning. *Psychological Bulletin, 108,* 480–498.

Kunda, Z. (1999). *Social cognition.* Cambridge, MA: MIT Press.

Kunda, Z., Miller, D. T., & Claire, T. (1990). Combining social concepts: The role of causal reasoning. *Cognitive Science, 14,* 551–557.

Kurdek, L. A. (1991). The dissolution of gay and lesbian couples. *Journal of Social and Personal Relationships, 8,* 265–278.

Lackie, L., & de Man, A. F. (1997). Correlates of sexual aggression among male university students. *Sex Roles, 5/6,* 451–457.

LaFrance, M., & Woodzicka, J. A. (1998). No laughing matter: Women's verbal and nonverbal reactions to sexist humor. In J. K. Swim & C. Stangor (Eds.), *Prejudice: The target's perspective* (pp. 62–80). San Diego, CA: Academic Press.

Lagerspetz, K. M., Bjorkqvist, K., & Peltonen, T. (1988). Is indirect aggression typical of females? Gender differences in aggressiveness in 11- to 12-year-old children. *Aggressive-Behavior, 14,* 403–414.

Lang, A. R., Goeckner, D. J., Adesso, V. J., & Marlatt, G. A. (1975). Effects of alcohol on aggression in male social drinkers. *Journal of Abnormal Psychology, 84,* 508–518.

Langer, E. (1977). The psychology of chance. *Journal for the Theory of Social Behavior, 7,* 185–207.

Langer, E. (1989). *Mindfulness.* Reading, MA: Addison-Wesley.

Langer, E., Blank, A., & Chanowitz, B. (1978). The mindlessness of ostensibly thoughtful action: The role of placebic information in interpersonal interaction. *Journal of Personality and Social Psychology, 36,* 886–893.

Langer, E., & Rodin, J. (1976). The effects of choice and enhanced personal responsibility for the aged: A field experiment in an institutional setting. *Journal of Personality and Social Psychology, 34,* 191–198.

Langlois, J. H. (1986). From the eye of the beholder to behavioral reality: The development of social behaviors and social relations as a function of physical attractiveness. In C. P. Herman, M. P. Zanna, & E. T. Higgins (Eds.), *Physical appearance, stigma, and social behavior: The Ontario symposium* (Vol. 3, pp. 23–51). Hillsdale, NJ: Erlbaum.

Langlois, J. H., Roggman, L. A., Casey, R. J., Riesner-Danner, L. A., & Jenkins, V. Y. (1987). Infant preferences for attractive faces: Rudiments of a stereotype? *Developmental Psychology, 23,* 363–369.

LaPiere, R.T. (1934). Attitudes vs. actions. *Social Forces, 13,* 230–237.

LaPiere, R. T. (1936). Type-rationalizations of group apathy. *Social Forces, 15,* 232–237.

Larsen, K. (1974). Conformity in the Asch experiment. *Journal of Social Psychology, 94,* 303–304.

Larsen, K. (1982). Cultural conditions and conformity: The Asch effect. *Bulletin of the British Psychological Society, 35,* 347.

Larsen. R. J., & Ketelaar, T. (1991). Personality and susceptibility to positive and negative emotional states. *Journal of Personality and Social Psychology, 61,* 132–140.

Larson, J. R., Jr., Christensen, C., Franz, T. M., & Abbot, A. S. (1998). Diagnosing groups. *Journal of Personality and Social Psychology, 75,* 93–108.

Larson, J. R., Jr., Foster-Fishman, P. G., & Franz, T. M. (1998). Leadership style and the discussion of shared and unshared information in decision-making groups. *Personality and Social Psychology Bulletin, 24,* 482–495.

Lassiter, G. D., Briggs, M. A., & Bowman, R. E. (1991). Need for cognition and the perception of ongoing behavior. *Personality and Social Psychology Bulletin, 17,* 156–160.

Latané, B. (1981). The psychology of social impact. *American Psychologist, 36,* 343–356.

Latané, B., & Darley, J. M. (1968). Group inhibition of bystander intervention in emergencies. *Journal of Personality and Social Psychology, 10,* 215–221.

Latané, B., Williams, K. D., & Harkins, S. G. (1979). Many hands make light the work: The causes and consequences of social loafing. *Journal of Personality and Social Psychology, 37,* 822–832.

Latané, B., & Wolf, S. (1981). The social impact of majorities and minorities. *Psychological Review, 88,* 438–453.

Laughlin, P. R. (1980). Social combination processes of cooperative problem solving groups on verbal intellective tasks. In M. Fishbein (Ed.), *Progress in social psychology* (Vol. 1, pp. 127–156). Hillsdale, NJ: Erlbaum.

Laughlin, P. R., Bonner, B. L., & Altermatt, T. W. (1998). Collective versus individual induction with single versus multiple hypotheses. *Journal of Personality and Social Psychology, 75,* 1481–1489

Laughlin, P. R., & Ellis, A. L. (1986). Demonstrability and social combination processes on mathematical intellective tasks. *Journal of Experimental Social Psychology, 22,* 177–189.

Laughlin, P. R., VanderStoep, S. W., & Hollingshead, A. D. (1991). Collective versus individual induction: Recognition of truth, rejection of error, and collective information processing. *Journal of Personality and Social Psychology, 61,* 50–67.

Laurenceau, J. P., Barrett, L. F., & Pietromanaco, P. R. (1998). Intimacy as an interpersonal process: The importance of self-disclosure, partner disclosure, and perceived partner responsiveness in interpersonal exchanges. *Journal of Personality and Social Psychology, 74,* 1238–1251.

Lawson, R. G. (1969). The law of primacy in the criminal courtroom. *Journal of Social Psychology, 77,* 121–131.

Leary, M., & Kowalski, R. M. (1990) Impression management: A literature review and the two component model. *Psychological Bulletin, 107*(1), 34–47.

Leary, M. R. (1983a). *Understanding social anxiety: Social, personality, and clinical Perspectives* (Vol. 153, Sage Library of Social Research). Beverly Hills, CA: Sage.

Leary, M. R. (1983b). Social anxiousness: The construct and its measurement. *Journal of Personality Assessment, 47,* 66–75.

Leary, M. R., & Kowalski, R. M. (1995). *Social anxiety.* New York: Guilford.

Leary, M. R., Springer, C., Negel, L., Ansell, E., and Evans, K. (1998). The causes, phenomenology, and consequences of hurt feelings. *Journal of Personality and Social Psychology, 74,* 1225–1237.

LeDoux, J. (1996). *The emotional brain.* New York: Simon & Schuster.

Lefkowitz, M. (1991) *Women's life in Greece and Rome.* Baltimore: Johns Hopkins University Press.

Lerner, M. J., & Simmons, C. H. (1966). Observers' reactions to the "innocent victim": Compassion or rejection? *Journal of Personality and Social Psychology, 4,* 203–210.

Levenson, R. W., & Gottman, J. M. (1983). Marital interaction: Physiological linkage and affective exchange. *Journal of Personality and Social Psychology, 45,* 587–597.

Leventhal, G. S., Allen, J., & Kemelgor, B. (1969). Reducing in-equity by reallocating rewards. *Psychonomic Science, 14,* 295–296.

Leventhal, H. (1970). Findings and theory in the study of fear communication. In L. Berkowitz (Ed.), *Advances in experimental social psychology* (Vol. 5, pp. 119–186). New York: Academic Press.

Levine, J. M. (1989). Reaction to opinion deviance in small groups. In P. Paulus (Ed.), *The psychology of group influence* (2nd ed., pp. 187–232). Hillsdale, NJ: Erlbaum.

Levine, J. M., & Moreland, R. L. (1990). Progress in small group research. *Annual Review of Psychology, 41,* 585–634.

Levinger, G. (1988). Can we picture "love"? In R. J. Sternberg & M. L. Barnes (Eds.), *The psychology of love.* New Haven, CT: Yale University Press.

Levinger, G., & Snoek, J. D. (1972). *Attraction in relationships: A new look at interpersonal attraction.* Morristown, NJ: General Learning Press.

Levy, S. R., Stroessner, S. J., & Dweck, C. (1998). Stereotype formation and endorsement: The role of implicit theories. *Journal of Personality and Social Psychology, 74,* 1421–1436.

Lewin, K. (1936). *A dynamic theory of personality.* New York: Mc-Graw-Hill.

Lewis, D. O., Lovely, R., Yeager, C., & Della Femina, D. (1989). Toward a theory of the genesis of violence: A follow-up study of delinquents. *Journal of the American Academy of Child and Adolescent Psychiatry, 28,* 431–437.

Lewis, L. (1932). *Sherman, fighting prophet.* New York: Harcourt, Brace.

Lewis, L., & Johnson, K. K. (1989). Effect of dress, cosmetics, sex of subject, and causal inference on attribution of victim responsibility. *Clothing and Textiles Research Journal, 8,* 22–27.

Liebert, R. M., & Baron, R. A. (1972). Some immediate effects of televised violence on children's behavior. *Developmental Psychology, 6,* 469–475.

Liebert, R. M., & Sprafkin, J. (1988). *The early window: The effects of television on children and youth* (3rd ed.). New York: Pergamon.

Lifton, R. J. (1986). *The Nazi doctors: Medical killing and the psychology of genocide.* New York: Basic Books.

Likert, R. (1932). A technique for the measurement of attitudes. *Archives of Psychology,* No. 140:55.

Linville, P. (1985). Self-complexity and affective extremity. Don't put all your eggs in one cognitive basket. *Social Cognition, 3,* 92–120.

Linville, P. (1987). Self-complexity as a cognitive buffer against stress related illnesses and depression. *Journal of Personality and Social Psychology, 52,* 663–676.

Linville, P. W., & Fischer, G. W. (1991). Preferences for separating and combining events. *Journal of Personality and Social Psychology, 60,* 5–23.

Linville, P. W., Fischer, G. W., & Salovey, P. (1989). Perceived distributions of the characteristics of in-group and out-group members: Empirical evidence and computer simulation. *Journal of Personality and Social Psychology, 57,* 165–188.

Linz, D., Penrod, S., & Donnerstein, E. (1987, Fall). The attorney general's commission on pornography: The gaps between "findings" and facts. *American Bar Foundation Research Journal,* 713–736.

Lippmann, W. (1922). *Public opinion.* New York: Harcourt, Brace & World.

Lips, H. (1993). *Sex and gender.* Mountain View, CA: Maysfield.

Lipscomb, T. J., Larrieu, J. A., McAlister, H. A., & Bregman, N. J. (1982). Modeling children's generosity: A developmental perspective. *Merrill Palmer Quarterly, 28,* 275–282.

Locke, K. D., & Horowitz, L. M. (1990). Satisfaction in interpersonal interactions as a function of similarity in level of dysphoria. *Journal of Personality and Social Psychology, 58,* 823–831.

Logan, G. A. (1989). Automaticity and cognitive control. In J. S. Uleman & J. A. Bargh (Eds.), *Unintended thought.* New York: Guilford.

Lorenz, K. (1963). *On aggression.* London: Methuen.

Lorge, I., & Solomon, H. (1955). Two models of group behavior in the solution of Eureka-type problems. *Psychometrika, 20,* 139–148.

Luginbuhl, J., & Palmer, T. (1991). Impression management aspects of self-handicapping: Positive and negative effects. *Personality and Social Psychology Bulletin, 17,* 655–662.

Luus, C. A. E., & Wells, G. L. (1991). Eyewitness identification and the selection of distractors for lineups. *Law and Human Behavior, 15,* 43–58.

Lydon, J. E., Jamieson, D. W., & Zanna, M. (1988). Interpersonal similarity and the social and intellectual dimensions of first impressions. *Social Cognition, 6,* 269–286.

Lydon, J. E., & Zanna, M. P. (1990). Commitment in the face of adversity: A value affirmation approach. *Journal of Personality and Social Psychology, 58,* 1040–1168.

Lykken, D., & Tellegran, A. (1996). Happiness is a stochastic phenomenon. *Psychological Science, 7,* 186–189.

Lynch, D. J., & Schaffer, K. S. (1989). Type A and social support. *Behavioral Medicine, 15*(2), 72–74.

Lytton, H., & Romney, D. M. (1991). Parents' differential socialization of boys and girls: A meta-analysis. *Psychological Bulletin, 109,* 267–296.

Lyubomirsky, S., Caldwell, N. D., & Nolen-Hoeksema, S. (1998). Effects of ruminative and distracting responses to depressed mood on retrieval of autobiographical memories. *Journal of Personality and Social Psychology, 75,* 166–177.

Lyubormirsky, S., & Ross, L. (1999). Changes in attractiveness of elected, rejected, and precluded alternatives: A comparison of happy and unhappy individuals. *Journal of Personality and Social Psychology, 76,* 988–1007.

Maas, A., & Clark, R. D. (1983) Internalization versus compliance: Differential processes underlying minority influence and conformity. *European Journal of Social Psychology, 13,* 197–215.

Maas, A., West, S. G., & Cialdini, R. B. (1987). Minority influence and conversion. In C. Hendrick (Ed.), *Review of personality and social psychology* (Vol. 8, pp. 121–176). Newbury Park, CA: Sage.

MaCauley, C., & Stitt, C. L. (1978). An individual and quantitative measure of stereotypes. *Journal of Personality and Social Psychology, 36,* 929–940.

Mackie, D. M. (1986). Social identification effects in group polarization. *Journal of Personality and Social Psychology, 50,* 720–728.

Mackie, D. M., Allison, S. T., Worth, L. T., & Asuncion, A. G. (1992). The impact of outcome biases on counterstereotypic inferences about groups. *Personality and Social Psychology Bulletin, 18,* 44–51.

Mackie, D. M., & Cooper, J. (1984). Attitude polarization: Effects of group membership. *Journal of Personality and Social Psychology, 46,* 575–585.

Mackie, D. M., & Worth, L. T. (1989). Processing deficits and the mediation of positive affect in persuasion. *Journal of Personality and Social Psychology, 57*(1), 27–40.

MacMurray, V. D., & Cunningham, P. D. (1973). Mormons and Gentiles: A study in conflict and persistence. In D. E. Gelfand & R. D. Lee (Eds.), *Ethnic conflicts and power: A cross-national perspective* (pp. 205–218). New York: Wiley.

Macrae, C. N., Bodenhausen, G. V., Milne, A. B., Castelli, L., Schloerscheidt, A. M., & Greco, S. (1998). On activating exemplars. *Journal of Experimental Social Psychology, 34,* 330–354.

Macrae, C. N., Hewstone, M., & Griffiths, R. J. (1993). Processing load and memory for stereotype-based information. *European Journal of Social Psychology, 23,* 77–87.

Macrae, C. N., Milne, A. B., & Bodenhausen, G. V. (1994). Stereotypes as energy saving devices: A peek inside the cognitive toolbox. *Journal of Personality and Social Psychology, 66,* 37–47.

Macrae, C. N., Shepherd, J. W., & Milne, A. B. (1992). The effects of source credibility on the dilution of stereotype-based judgments. *Personality and Social Psychology Bulletin, 18*(6), 765–775.

Main, M., & George, C. (1985). Responses of abused and disadvantged toddlers to distress in agemates: A study in the day care setting. *Developmental Psychology, 21,* 407–412.

Major, B. (1980). Information acquisition and attribution processes. *Journal of Personality and Social Psychology, 39,* 1010–1024.

Malamuth, N. (1986). Predictors of naturalistic sexual aggression. *Journal of Personality and Social Psychology, 50,* 953–962.

Malamuth, N., & Check, J. V. P. (1980). Sexual arousal to rape and consenting depictions: The importance of the woman's arousal. *Journal of Abnormal Psychology, 89,* 763–766.

Malamuth, N., & Check, J. V. P. (1981). The effects of mass media exposure on acceptance of violence against women: A field experiment. *Journal of Research in Personality, 15,* 436–446.

Malamuth, N., & Check, J. V. P. (1983). Sexual arousal to rape depictions: Individual differences. *Journal of Abnormal Psychology, 92,* 55–67.

Malamuth, N., & Check, J. V. P. (1985). The effects of aggressive pornography on beliefs in rape myths: Individual differences. *Journal of Research in Personality, 19,* 299–320.

Malamuth, N., Haber, S., & Feshbach, S. (1980). Testing hypotheses regarding rape: Exposure to sexual violence, sex differences and the "normality" of rapists. *Journal of Research in Personality, 14,* 121–137.

Malle, B. F. (1999). How people explain behavior. A new theoretical framework. *Personality and Social Psychology Review, 3,* 23–48.

Malloy, T. E., & Albright, L. (1990). Interpersonal perception in a social context. *Journal of Personality and Social Psychology, 58,* 419–428.

Malpass, R. S. (1981). Effective size and defendant bias in eyewitness identification lineups. *Law and Human Behavior, 5,* 299–309.

Malpass, R. S., & Devine, P. G. (1981). Eyewitness identification: Lineup instructions and the absence of the offender. *Journal of Applied Psychology, 66,* 482–489.

Mann, L. (1981). The baiting crowd in episodes of threatened suicides. *Journal of Personality and Social Psychology, 41,* 703–709.

Mantell, D. M. (1971). The potential for violence in Germany. *Journal of Social Issues, 27*(4), 101–112.

Mark, M. M., Bryant, F. B., & Lehman, D. R. (1983). Perceived injustice and sports violence. In J. G. Goldstein (Ed.), *Sports violence* (pp. 83–110). New York: Springer-Verlag.

Marks, G., Graham, J. W., & Hansen, W. B. (1992). Social projection and social conformity in adolescent alcohol use: A longitudinal analysis. *Personality and Social Psychology Bulletin, 18,* 96–101.

Markus, H. (1977). Self-schemata and processing information about the self. *Journal of Personality and Social Psychology, 35,* 63–78.

Markus, H., & Kitayama, S. (1991). Culture and self: Implications for cognition, emotion, and motivation. *Psychological Review.*

Markus, H., & Kunda, Z. (1986). Stability and malleability of the self-concept. *Journal of Personality and Social Psychology, 51,* 858–866.

Markus, H., & Nurius, P. (1986). Possible selves. *American Psychologist, 41,* 954–969.

Markus, H., & Wurf, E. (1987). The dynamic self-concept: A social psychological perspective. *Annual Review of Psychology, 38,* 299–337.

Markus, H., & Zajonc, R. B. (1985). The cognitive perspective in social psychology. In G. Lindzey & E. Aronson (Eds.), *The handbook of social psychology: Vol. 1. Theory and methods.* New York: Random House.

Marques, J. M., & Paez, D. (1994). The "black sheep effect": Social categorization, rejection of ingroup deviates, and perception of group variability. In W. Stroebe & M. Hewstone (Eds.), *European review of social psychology* (Vol. 5, pp. 37–68). Chichester, England: Wiley.

Marshall, J., Marquis, K. H., & Oskamp, S. (1971). Effects of kind of question and atmosphere of interrogation on accuracy and completeness of testimony. *Harvard Law Review, 84,* 1620–1643.

Martin, R., & Hewstone, M. (1999). Minority influence and optimal problem solving. *European Journal of Social Psychology, 29,* 825–832.

Matsuda, N. (1985). Strong, quasi- and weak conformity among Japanese in the modified Asch procedure. *Journal of Cross-Cultural Psychology, 16,* 83–97.

McAdams, D. P. (1982). Intimacy motivation. In A. J. Stewart (Ed.), *Motivation and society.* San Francisco: Jossey-Bass.

McAdams, D. P. (1989). *Intimacy.* New York: Doubleday.

McArthur, L. Z. (1972). The how and what of why: Some determinants and consequences of causal attribution. *Journal of Personality and Social Psychology, 22,* 171–193.

McArthur, L. Z. (1982). Judging a book by its cover: A cognitive analysis of the relationship between physical appearance and stereotyping. In A. Hastorf & A. Isen (Eds.), *Cognitive social psychology* (pp. 149–211). New York: Elsevier/North Holland.

McAuley, E., Wraith, S., & Duncan, T. E. (1991). Self-efficacy, perceptions of success, and intrinsic motivation for exercise. *Journal of Applied Social Psychology, 21*(2), 139–155.

McCaulay, C. (1989). The nature of social influence in group-think: Compliance and internalization. *Journal of Personality and Social Psychology, 57,* 250–260.

McCauley, C., & Segal, M. (1987). Social psychology of terrorist groups. In C. Hendrick (Ed.), *Group processes and intergroup relations: Review of personality and social psychology, 9.* Newbury Park, CA: Sage.

McConahay, J. G. (1986). Modern racism, ambivalence, and the modern racist scale. In J. F. Dovidio & S. L. Gaertner (Eds.), *Prejudice, discrimination, and racism,* San Diego, CA: Academic Press.

McDougall, W. (1908). *An introduction to social psychology,* New York: Barnes & Noble.

McFarland, C., & Buehler, R. (1998). The impact of negative affect on autobiographical memories: The role of self-focused attention to moods. *The Journal of Personality and Social Psychology, 75,* 1424–1440.

McGill, A. L. (1989). Context effects in judgments of causation. *Journal of Personality and Social Psychology, 57,* 189–200.

McGregor, I., & Holmes, J. G. (1999). How storytelling shapes memory and impressions of relationships over time. *Journal of Personality and Social Psychology, 76,* 406–419.

McGuire, W. J. (1969). The nature of attitudes and attitude change. In G. Lindzey & E. Aronson (Eds.), *The handbook of social psychology* (2nd ed., Vol. 3, pp. 136–314). Reading MA: Academic Press.

McGuire, W. J. (1985). Attitudes and attitude change. In G. Lindzey & E. Aronson (Eds.), *The handbook of social psychology* (3rd ed., Vol. 2, pp. 233–346). New York: Random House.

McGuire, W. J. (1989). The structure of individual attitudes. In A. Pratkanis, S. Breckler, & A. G. Greenwald (Eds.), *Attitude structure and function* (pp. 129–151). Hillsdale, NJ: Erlbaum.

McGuire, W. J., & McGuire, C. V. (1988). Content and process in the experience of self. In L. Berkowitz (Ed.), *Advances in experimental social psychology* (Vol. 21, pp. 97–144). New York: Academic Press.

McGuire, W. J., & Papageorgis, D. (1961). The relative efficacy of various types of prior belief-defense in producing immunity against persuasion. *Journal of Abnormal and Social Psychology, 62,* 327–337.

McHan, E. (1985). Imitation of aggression by Lebanese children. *Journal of Social Psychology, 125,* 613–617.

McKay, N. J., & Covell, K. (1997). The impact of women in advertisements on attitudes toward women. *Sex Roles, 9/10,* 573–583.

McLean, A. A. (1979). *Work stress.* Reading, MA: Addison-Wesley.

McNeill, W. H. (1982). *The pursuit of power: technology, armed force, and society since A.D. 1000.* Chicago: University of Chicago Press.

Mealey, L., Bridstock, R., & Townsend, G. C. (1999). Symmetry and perceived facial attractiveness.: A monozygotic twin comparison. *Journal of Personality and Social Psychology, 76,* 151–158.

Medin, D. L. (1989). Concepts and conceptual structure. *American Psychologist, 44,* 1469–1481.

Mednick, B. R., Baker, R. L., & Carothers, L. E. (1990). Patterns of family disruption and crime: The association of timing of the family's disruption with subsequent adolescent and young adult criminality. *Journal of Youth and Violence, 19,* 201–220.

Meeus, W., & Raaijmakers, Q. (1986). Administrative obedience: Carrying out orders to use psychological–administrative violence. *European Journal of Social Psychology, 16,* 311–324.

Mendolia, M., & Kleck, R. E. (1993). Effects of talking about a stressful event on arousal: Does what we talk about make a difference? *Journal of Personality and Social Psychology, 64*(2), 283–292.

Metcalfe, J. (1998). Cognitive optimism: Self-deception or memory based processing heuristics? *Personality and Social Psychology Review, 2,* 100–110.

Meyer, A. J., Nash, J. D., McAlister, A. L., Maccoby, N., & Farquhar, J. W. (1980). Skills training in a cardiovascular health education campaign. *Journal of Consulting and Clinical Psychology, 48,* 129–142.

Meyers-Levy, J., & Peracchio, L. A. (1995). Understanding the effects of color: How the correspondence between available and required resources affects attitudes. *Journal of Consumer Research, 22,* 121–138.

Midlarsky, E., Bryan, J. H., & Brickman, P. (1973). Aversion approval: Interactive effects of modeling and reinforcement on altruistic behavior. *Child Development, 44,* 321–328.

Miell, D. E., & Duck, S. W. (1986). Strategies in developing friendships. In V. J. Derlega & B. A. Winstead (Eds.), *Friendship and social interaction.* New York: Springer-Verlag.

Milgram, S. (1961). Nationality and conformity. *Scientific American, 205,* 45–51.

Milgram, S. (1963). Behavioral study of obedience. *Journal of Abnormal Psychology, 67,* 371–378.

Milgram, S. (1974). *Obedience to authority.* New York: Harper.

Milgram, S., Bickman, L., & Berkowitz, L. (1969). Note on the drawing power of crowds of different size. *Journal of Personality and Social Psychology, 13,* 79–82.

Milgram, S. L, Mann, L., & Hartner, S. (1965). The lost letter technique: A tool of social science research. *Public Opinion Quarterly, 29,* 437–438.

Milkulincer, M. (1998). Attachment working models and the sense of trust: An exploration of interaction goals and affect regulation. *Journal of Personality and Social Psychology, 74,* 1209–1224.

Miller, C. E. (1989). The social psychological effects of group decision rules. In P. Paulus (Ed.), *Psychology of group influence* (2nd ed., pp. 327–355). Hillsdale, NJ: Erlbaum.

Miller, C. T., & Downey, K. T. (1999). A meta-analysis of heavyweight and self-esteem. *Personality and Social Psychology Review, 3,* 68–84.

Miller, C. T., & Myers, A. M. (1998). Compensating for prejudice: How heavyweight people (and others) control outcomes despite prejudice. In J. K. Swim & C. Stangor (Eds.), *Prejudice: The target's perspective* (pp. 191–218). San Diego, CA: Academic Press.

Miller, D. T., & McFarland, C. (1987). Pluralistic ignorance: When similarity is interpreted as dissimilarity. *Journal of Personality and Social Psychology, 53,* 298–305.

Miller, D. T., & Ross, M. (1975). Self-serving biases in the attribution of causality: Fact or fiction? *Psychological Bulletin, 82,* 213–225.

Miller, D. T., Turnbull, W., & McFarland, C. (1989). When a coincidence is suspicious: The role of mental simulation. *Journal of Personality and Social Psychology, 57,* 581–589.

Miller, D. T., Turnbull, W., & McFarland, C. (1990). Counterfactual thinking and social perception: Thinking about what might have been. In M. P. Zanna (Ed.), *Advances in experimental social psychology, 23.* San Diego, CA: Academic press.

Miller, G. (2000). Evolution of human music through sexual selection. In N. L. Wallin, B. Merker, & S. Brown (Eds.), *The origins of music* (pp. 329–360). Cambridge, MA: MIT Press.

Miller, J. (1984). Culture and the development of everyday social explanation. *Journal of Personality and Social Psychology, 46,* 961–978.

Miller, N. & Brewer, M. B. (1984). The social psychology of desegregation: An introduction. In N. Miller & M. B. Brewer (Eds.), *Groups in contact: The psychology of desegregation.* New York: Academic Press.

Miller, N. E. (1941). The frustration–aggression hypothesis. *Psychological Review, 48,* 337–342.

Miller, R. L., Seligman, C., Clark, N. T., & Bush, M. (1976). Perceptual contrast versus reciprocal concessions as mediators of induced compliance. *Canadian Journal of Behavioural Science, 8,* 401–409.

Miller, T. Q., Heath, L., Molcan, J. R., & Dugoni, B. L. (1991). Imitative violence in the real world. *Aggressive Behavior, 17,* 121–134.

Mintz, A. (1951). Nonadaptive group behavior. *Journal of Abnormal and Social Psychology, 46,* 150–159.

Mischel, W. (1998). Metacognition at the hyphen of social-cognitive psychology. *Personality and Social Psychology Review, 2*(2), 84–86.

Monteith, M. J., Devine, P. G., & Zuwernik, J. R. (1993). Self-directed versus other-directed affect as a consequence of prejudice-related discrepancies. *Journal of Personality and Social Psychology, 64,* 198–210.

Montgomery, B. M. (1988). Quality communication in personal relationships. In S. Duck (Ed.), *Handbook of personal relationships.* New York: Wiley.

Moreland, R. L. (1987). The formation of small groups. *Review of Personality and Social Psychology, 8,* 80–110.

Moreland, R. L., & Levine, J. M. (1982). Group socialization: Temporal changes in individual-group relations. In L. Berkowitz (Ed.), *Advances in experimental social psychology* (Vol. 15, pp. 137–192). New York: Academic Press.

Moreland, R. L., & Levine, J. M. (1989). Newcomers and old-timers in small groups. In P. Paulus (Ed.), *The psychology of group influence* (2nd ed., pp. 143–186). Hillsdale, NJ: Erlbaum.

Moriarty, T. (1975). Crime, commitment, and the unresponsive bystander: Two field experiments. *Journal of Personality and Social Psychology, 31,* 370–376.

Morrison, B. (1994, February 14). Letter from Liverpool: Children of circumstance. *The New Yorker,* 48–60.

Morrison, S. E. (1965). *The Oxford history of the American people.* New York: Oxford University Press.

Morrow-Howell, N., Lott, L., & Ozawa, M. (1990). The impact of race on volunteer helping relationships among the elderly. *Social Work, 35,* 395–403.

Morton, T. L. (1978). Intimacy and reciprocity of exchange: A comparison of spouses and strangers. *Journal of Personality and Social Psychology, 36,* 72–81.

Moscovici, S. (1980). Toward a theory of conversion behavior. In L. Berkowitz (Ed.), *Advances in experimental social psychology* (Vol. 13, pp. 209–239). New York: Academic Press.

Moscovici, S. (1985). Social influence and conformity. In G. Lindzey & E. Aronson (Eds.), *Handbook of social psychology* (3rd ed., pp. 347–412). Hillsdale, NJ: Erlbaum.

Moscovici, S., & Lage, E. (1976). Studies in social influence III: Majority versus minority influence in a group. *European Journal of Social Psychology, 6,* 149–174.

Moscovici, S., Lage, E., & Naffrechoux, M. (1969). Influence of a consistent minority on the responses of a majority in a color perception task. *Sociometry, 32,* 365–369.

Moscovici, S., & Zavalloni, M. (1969). The group as a polarizer of attitudes. *Journal of Personality and Social Psychology, 12,* 124–135.

Moskos, C. (1990). *A call to civic service.* New York, Free Press.

Moskos, C. (1991, August 5). How do they do it? *The New Republic,* 16–21.

Moyer, K. E. (1987). *Violence and aggression.* New York: Paragon House.

Mugny, G. (1975). Negotiations, image of the other and the process of minority influence. *European Journal of Social Psychology, 5,* 209–228.

Muir, G., Lonsway, K. A., & Payne, D. L. (1996). Rape myth acceptance among Scottish and American students. *Journal of Social Psychology, 136,* 261–262.

Mullen, B. (1986). Atrocity as a function of lynch mob composition: A self-attention perspective. *Personality and Social Psychology Bulletin, 12,* 187–197.

Mullen, B. (1991). Group composition, salience, and cognitive representations: The phenomenology of being in a group. *Journal of Experimental Social Psychology, 27,* 262–284.

Mullen, B., & Baumeister, R. F. (1987). Group effects of social self-attention and performance: Social loafing, social facilitation, and social impairment. In C. Hendrick (Ed.), *Review of personality and social psychology* (Vol. 9, pp. 125–206). Beverly Hills, CA: Sage.

Mullen, B., Futrell, D., Stairs, D., Tice, D. M., Baumeister, R. F., Dawson., K. E., Riordan, C. A., Radloff, C. E., Goethals, G. R., Kennedy, J. G., & Rosenfeld, P. (1986). Newscasters' facial expressions and the voting behavior of viewers: Can a smile elect a president? *Journal of Personality and Social Psychology, 51,* 291–295.

Mullen, B., & Riordan, C. A. (1988). Self-serving attributions for performance in naturalistic settings: A meta-analytic review. *Journal of Applied Social Psychology, 18,* 3–22.

Mullen, E., & Skitka, L. J. (2000, May 4–9). Who deserves help? A cross cultural comparison. Paper presented at the annual meeting of the Midwestern Psychological Association, Chicago, IL.

Mummendey, A., Kessler, T., Klink, A., & Mielke, R. (1999). Strategies to cope with negative social identity: Predictions by social identity theory and relative deprivation theory. *Journal of Personality and Social Psychology, 76,* 229–245.

Mummendey, A., & Wenzel, M. (1999). Social discrimination and tolerance in intergroup relations: Reactions to intergroup differences. *Personality and Social Psychology Review, 3,* 158–174.

Muraven, M., Tice, D. M., & Baumeister, R. F. (1998). Self-control as limited resource: Regulatory depletion patterns. *Journal of Personality and Social Psychology, 74,* 774–789.

Murdoch, D. D., & Pihl, R. O. (1988). The influence of beverage type on aggression in males in the natural setting. *Aggressive Behavior, 14,* 325–335.

Myer, C. B., & Taylor, S. E. (1986). Adjustment to rape. *Journal of Personality and Social Psychology, 50*, 1226–1234.

Myers, D. G., & Lamm, H. (1975). The polarizing effect of group discussion. *American Scientist, 63*, 297–303.

Myer D. G., & Lamm, H. (1976). The group polarization phenomenon. *Psychological Bulletin, 83*, 602–303.

Myrdal, G. (1962). *An American dilemma: The Negro problem in American democracy.* New York: Harper & Row.

Nadler, A., Altman, A., & Fisher, J. D. (1979). Helping is not enough: Recipient's reactions to aid as a function of positive and negative information about the self. *Journal of Personality, 47*, 615–628.

Nadler, A., Fisher, J. D., & Ben Itchak, S. (1983). With a little help from my friend: Effect of single or multiple act aid as a function of donor and task characteristics. *Journal of Personality and Social Psychology, 44*, 310–321.

Nadler, A, Fisher, J. D., & Streufert, S. (1976). When helping hurts: Effects of donor-recipient similarity and recipient self-esteem on reactions to aid. *Journal of Personality, 44*, 392–409.

Nasco, S. A., & Marsh, K. (1999). Gaining control through counterfactual thinking. *Personality and Social Psychology Bulletin, 25*, 556–568.

Neimeyer, G. J., & Rareshide, M. B. (1991). Personal memories and personal identity: The impact of ego identity development on autobiographical memory recall. *The Journal of Personality and Social Psychology, 60*(4), 562–569.

Nemeth, C. (1986). Differential contributions of majority and minority influence. *Psychological Review, 93*, 23–32.

Nemeth, C. (1992). Minority dissent as a stimulant to group performance. In S. Worchel, W. Wood, J. A. Simpson (Eds.), *Group process and productivity.* Newbury Park, CA: Sage.

Nemeth, C., Swedlund, M., & Kanki, B. (1974). Patterning of the minority's responses and their influence on the majority. *European Journal of Social Psychology, 4*, 428–450.

Neuberg, S. L. (1989). The goal of forming accurate impressions during social interactions: Attenuating the impact of negative experiences. *Journal of Personality and Social Psychology, 56*, 374–386.

Neuberg, S. L., Cialdini, R. B., Brown, S. L., Luce, C., & Sagarin, B. J. (1997). Does empathy lead to anything more than superficial helping? Comment on Batson et al., 1997. *Journal of Personality and Social Psychology, 73*, 510–516.

Neuberg, S. L., & Fiske, S. T. (1987). Motivational influences on impression formation: outcome dependency, accuracy-driven attention, and individuating processes. *Journal of Personality and Social Psychology, 53*, 431–444.

Newcomb, T. M. (1961). *The acquaintance process.* New York: Holt, Rinehart & Winston.

Newton, L. (1990). *Overconfidence in the communication of intent: Heard and unheard melodies.* Unpublished doctoral dissertation, Stanford University, California.

Nichols, K. A. (1974). Severe social anxiety. *British Journal of Medical Psychology, 74*, 301–306.

Niedenthal, P. M., Setterlund, M., & Wherry, M. B. (1992). Possible self-complexity and affective reactions to goal-relevant evaluation. *Journal of Personality and Social Psychology, 63*, 5–16.

Niedermeier, K. E., Horowitz, I. A., & Kerr, N. L. (1999). Informing jurors of their nullification power: A route to a just verdict or judicial chaos? *Law and Human Behavior, 23*(3), 331–352.

Niedermeier, K. E., Kerr, N. L., & Messe, L. A. (1999). Jurors' use of naked statistical evidence: Exploring bases and implications of the Wells effect. *Journal of Personality and Social Psychology, 76*, 533–542.

Nisbett, R. E. (1968). Determinants of food intake in human obesity. *Science, 159*, 1254–1255.

Nisbett, R. E. (1993). Violence and U.S. regional culture. *American Psychologist, 48*, 441–449.

Nisbett, R. E., Polly, G., & Lang, S. (1995). Homicide and U.S. regional culture. In R. B. Ruback & N. A. Weiner (Eds.), *Interpersonal violent behaviors* (pp. 133–151). New York: Springer-Verlag.

Nisbett, R., & Ross, L. (1980). *Human inference: Strategies and shortcomings of social judgment.* Englewood Cliffs, NJ: Prentice-Hall.

Nisbett, R. E., & Wilson, T. D. (1977). The halo effect: Evidence for the unconscious alteration of judgments. *Journal of Personality and Social Psychology, 35*, 250–256.

Noel, J. G., Forsyth, D. R., & Kelley, K. N. (1987). Improving the performance of failing students by overcoming their self-serving attributional biases. *Basic and Applied Social Psychology, 8*, 151–162.

Noller, P. (1985). Negative communication in marriage. *Journal of Social and Personal Relationships, 2*, 289–301.

Noller, P., & Ruzzene, G. (1991). Cognition in close relationships. In G. J. O. Fletcher & F. D. Fincham (Eds.), Hillsdale, NJ: Erlbaum.

Noller, P., & Ruzzene, G. (1991). Communication in marriage: The influence of affect and cognition. In G. J. O. Fletcher & F. D. Fincham (Eds.), *Cognition in close relationships.* Hillsdale, NJ: Erlbaum.

Notarius, C., & Markman, H. (1993). *We can work it out: Making sense out of marital conflict.* New York: Putnam.

Nowak, A., Szamrej, J., & Latane, B. (1990). From private attitude to public opinion: A dynamic theory of social impact. *Psychological Review, 97*, 362–376.

Oakes, P. J., Haslam, S. A., & Turner, J. C. (1994). *Social stereotyping and social reality.* Oxford, England: Blackwell.

O'Connell, R. L. (1989). *Of arms and men: A history of war, weapons and aggression.* New York: Oxford University Press.

Ohbuchi, K. (1981). A study of attack patterns: Equity or recency? *Japanese Psychological Research, 23*, 191–195.

Ohbuchi, K., & Kambara, T. (1985). Attackers intent and awareness of outcome, impression management, and retaliation. *Journal of Experimental Social Psychology, 21*, 321–330.

Oliker, S. J. (1989). *Best friends and marriage: Exchange among women.* Berkeley, CA: University of California Press.

Oliner, S. P., & Oliner, P. M. (1988). *The altruistic personality: Rescuers of Jews in Nazi Europe.* New York: Free Press.

Olweus, D. (1984). Development of stable reaction patterns. In R. J. Blanchard and D. C. Blanchard (Eds.), *Advances in the study of aggression* (Vol. 1, pp. 103–138). New York: Academic Press.

Opdyke, I. G., & Elliot, J. M. (1992). *Into the flames: The life story of a righteous Gentile.* San Bernardino, CA: Borgo Press.

O'Rourke, D. F., Houston, B. K., Harris, J. K., & Snyder, C. R. (1988). In B. K. Houston & C. R. Snyder (Eds.), *Type A behavior pattern.* New York: Plenum.

Osborn, M., & Osborn, S. (1994). *Public speaking.* Boston: Houghton Mifflin.

Osgood, C. E., Suci, G. J., & Tannenbaum, P. H. (1957). *The measurement of meaning*. Urbana, IL: University of Illinois Press.

Osherow, N. (1988). Making sense of the nonsensical: An analysis of Jonestown. In E. Aronson (Ed.), *Readings about the social animal* (5th ed., pp. 68–86). New York: Freeman.

Oskamp, S. (1991). *Attitudes and opinions* (2nd ed.). New York, Prentice-Hall.

Paicheler, G. (1979). Polarization of attitudes in homogeneous and heterogeneous groups. *European Journal of Social Psychology, 9,* 85–96.

Paludi, M. (Ed.). (1991). *Ivory power: Sexual harassment on campus*. Albany, NY: SUNY Press.

Patterson, G. R., DeBaryshe, B. D., & Ramsey, E. (1989). A developmental perspective on antisocial behavior. *American Psychologist, 44,* 329–335.

Paulhus, D. L., & Reid, D. B. (1991). Enhancement and denial in socially desirable responding. *Journal of Personality and Social Psychology, 60,* 307–317.

Paulus, P. B., Dzindolet, M. T., Poletes, G., & Camacho, L. M. (1993). Perception of performance in group brainstorming: The illusion of group productivity. *Personality and Social Psychology Bulletin, 19*(1), 78–89.

Pavelchak, M. A., Moreland, R. L., & Levine, J. M. (1986). Effects of prior group memberships on subsequent reconnaissance activities. *Journal of Personality and Social Psychology, 50,* 56–66.

Peele, S. (1988). Fools for love: The romantic ideal, psychological theory, and addictive love. In R. J. Sternberg & M. L. Barnes (Eds.), *The psychology of love*. New Haven, CT: Yale University Press.

Pelham, B. (1991). On confidence and consequence: The certainty and importance of self knowledge. *Journal of Personality and Social Psychology, 60*(4), 518–520.

Pelham, B., & Swann, W. B., Jr. (1989). From self-conceptions to self-worth: On sources and structure of global self-esteem. *Journal of Personal and Social Psychology, 57,* 672–680.

Pennebaker, J. W. (1989). Confession, inhibition, and disease. In L. Berkowitz (Ed.), *Advances in experimental social psychology* (Vol. 22). San Diego, CA: Academic Press.

Pennebaker, J. W., & Beall, K. S. (1986). Confronting a traumatic event: Toward understanding of inhibition and disease. *Journal of Abnormal Psychology, 95,* 274–281.

Pennebaker, J. W., Colder, M. L., & Sharp, L. K. (1988). Accelerating the coping process. Unpublished manuscript, Southern Methodist University, Dallas, Texas.

Pennington, N., & Hastie, R. (1986). Evidence evaluation in complex decision making. *Journal of Personality and Social Psychology, 51,* 242–258.

Pennington, N., & Hastie, R. (1988). Explanation-based decision making: Effects of memory structure on judgment. *Journal of Experimental Psychology: Learning, Memory, and Cognition, 14,* 521–533.

Pennington, N., & Hastie, R. (1992). Explaining evidence: Tests of the story model for juror decision making. *Journal of Personality and Social Psychology, 62,* 189–206.

Peplau, L. A., & Perlman, D. (1982). Perspectives on loneliness. In L. A. Peplau & D. Perlman (Eds.), *Loneliness: A sourcebook of current theory, research, and therapy* (pp. 1–18). New York: Wiley.

Pepler, D. J., King, G., & Byrd, W. (1991). A social-cognitively based social skills training program for aggressive children.

In D. J. Pepler & K. H. Rubin (Eds.), *The development and treatment of childhood aggression* (pp. 361–379). Hillsdale, NJ: Erlbaum.

Perdue, C. W., Dovidio, J. F., Gurtman, M. B., & Tyler, R. B. (1990). Us and them: Social categorization and the process of intergroup bias. *Journal of Personality and Social Psychology, 59*(3), 475–486.

Perlman, D., & Oscamp, S. (1971). The effects of picture content and exposure frequency on evaluations of Negroes and whites. *Journal of Experimental Social Psychology, 7,* 503–514.

Perloff, L. S. (1987). Social comparison and the illusion of unique invulnerability to negative life events. In C. R. Snyder & C. E. Ford (Eds.), *Coping with negative life events: Clinical and social psychological perspectives* (pp. 217–242). New York: Plenum.

Perrett, D. L., & Penton-Voak, I. (1999, February 25). Reply. *Nature, 397,* 6721, 661.

Perrin, S., & Spencer, C. (1981). The Asch effect—A child of its time?. *Bulletin of the British Psychological Society, 33,* 405–406.

Peterson, C. (1988). Explanatory style as a risk factor for illness. *Cognitive Therapy and Research, 12,* 117–130.

Peterson, L. (1984). The influence of donor competence to aid on bystander intervention. *British Journal of Social Psychology, 23,* 85–86.

Pettigrew, T. F. (1979). The ultimate attribution error: Extending Allport's cognitive analysis of prejudice. *Personality and Social Psychology Bulletin, 5,* 461–476.

Pettigrew, T. F. (1986). *Racially separate or together?* New York: McGraw-Hill.

Pettigrew, T. E. (1991, July 16). *The New York Times*, p. 31.

Pettit, G. S., Bakshi, A., Dodge, K. A., & Coie, J. D. (1986). The emergence of social dominance in young boys' play groups: Developmental differences and behavioral correlates. *Developmental Psychology, 26,* 1017–1025.

Petty, R. E., & Cacioppo, J. T. (1979). Effect of forewarning of persuasive intent and involvement on cognitive responses on persuasion. *Personality and Social Psychology Bulletin, 5,* 173–176.

Petty, R. E., & Cacioppo, J. T. (1986). *Communication and persuasion*. New York: Springer-Verlag.

Petty, R. E., Cacioppo, J. T., & Goldman, R. (1981). Personal involvement as a determinant of argument-based persuasion. *Journal of Social Behavior and Personality, 41,* 847–855.

Petty, R. E., Schumann, D. W., Richman, S. A., & Strathman, A. J. (1993). Positive mood and persuasion: Different roles for affect under high and low elaboration conditions. *Journal of Personality and Social Psychology, 64*(1), 5–20.

Petty, R. E., & Wegener, D. T. (1993). Flexible correction processes in social judgment: Correcting for context induced contrast. *Journal of Experimental Social Psychology, 29,* 137–165.

Petty, R. E., Wegener, D. T., & White, P. H. (1998). Flexible correction in social judgment: Implications for persuasion. *Social Cognition, 16,* 93–113.

Peukert, D. (1987). *Inside Nazi Germany: Conformity, opposition, and racism in everyday life*. New Haven, CT: Yale University Press.

Phillips, D. P. (1983). The impact of mass media violence on U.S. homicides. *American Sociological Review, 48,* 560–568.

Phillips, D. P. (1986). Natural experiments on the effects of mass media violence on fatal aggression: Strengths and weaknesses of a new approach. In L. Berkowitz (Ed.), *Advances in experimental social psychology* (Vol. 19). New York: Academic Press.

Pihl, R. O., & Lemarquand, D. (1998). Serotonin and aggression and the alcohol-aggression relationship. *Alcohol and Alcoholism, 33,* 55–65.

Pihl, R. O., & Peterson, J. B. (1993). Alcohol, serotonin and aggression. *Alcohol Health and Research World, 17,* 113–116.

Pihl, R. O., Peterson, J. B., & Lau, M. A. (1993). A biosocial model of the alcohol-aggression relationship. *Journal of Studies on Alcohol, 11,* 128–139.

Pihl, R. O., Smith, M., & Farrell, B. (1984). Alcohol and aggression in men: A comparison of brewed and distilled beverages. *Journal of Studies on Alcohol, 45,* 278–282.

Pihl, R. O., & Zaccia, C. (1986). Alcohol and aggression: A test of the affect–arousal hypothesis. *Aggressive Behavior, 12,* 367–375.

Piliavin, J. A., & Piliavin, I. M. (1972). Effects of blood on reactions to a victim. *Journal of Personality and Social Psychology, 8,* 353–361.

Piliavin, I. M., Piliavin, J. A., & Rodin, J. (1975). Costs, diffusion, and the stigmatized victim. *Journal of Personality and Social Psychology, 32,* 429–438.

Piliavin, I. M., Rodin, J., & Piliavin, J. A. (1969). Good samaritanism: An underground phenomenon? *Journal of Personality and Social Psychology, 13,* 284–299.

Pittman, T. S., & Pittman, N. L. (1980). Deprivation of control and the attribution process. *Journal of Personality and Social Psychology, 39,* 377–389.

Pliner, P., & Pelchat, M. L. (1986). Similarities in food preferences between children and siblings and parents. *Appetite, 7,* 333–342.

Plomin, R. (1989). *Nature and nurture: An introduction to human behavioral genetics.* Pacific Grove, CA: Brooks/Cole.

Plomin, R., Corley, R., DeFries, J. C., & Fulker, D. W. (1990). Individual differences in television viewing in early childhood: Nature as well as nurture. *Psychological Science, 1,* 371–377.

Polivy, J., & Herman, C. P. (1983). *Breaking the diet habit.* New York: Basic Books.

Polivy, J., & Herman, C. P. (1985). Dieting and binging. *American Psychologist, 40*(2), 193–201.

Prager, K., Fuller, D. O., & Gonzalez, A. S. (1989). The function of self-disclosure in social interaction. *Journal of Social and Personal Relationships, 4,* 563–588.

Pratkanis, A. R., & Aronson, E. (1992). *The age of propaganda.* New York: Freeman.

Pratkanis, A. R., & Greenwald, A. G. (1989). The cognitive representation of attitudes. In A. R. Pratkanis, S. J. Breckler, & A. G. Greenwald (Eds.), *Attitudes structure and function* (pp. 71–98). Hillsdale, NJ: Erlbaum.

Pratkanis, A. R., Greenwald, A. G., Leippe, M. R., & Baumgardner, M. H. (1988). In search of reliable persuasion effects. III. The sleeper effect is dead. Long live the sleeper effect. *Journal of Personality and Social Psychology, 54,* 203–218.

Pratto, F., & Bargh, J. H. (1991). Stereotyping based on apparently individuating information: Trait and global components of sex stereotypes under attention overload. *Journal of Experimental Social Psychology, 27,* 26–47.

Pratto, F., & John, O. (1991). Automatic vigilance: The attention-grabbing power of negative social information. *Journal of Personality and Social Psychology, 51,* 380–391.

Prentice-Dunn, S., & Rogers, R. W. (1989). Deindividuation and the self-regulation of behavior. In P. B. Paulus (Ed.), *Psychology of group influence* (2nd ed., pp. 87–110). Hillsdale, NJ: Erlbaum.

Pritchard, R. D., & Watson, M. D. (1992). Understanding and measuring group productivity. In S. Worchel, W. Wood, & J. A. Simpson (Eds.), *Group process and productivity.* Newbury Park, CA: Sage.

Pruitt, D. G. (1968). Reciprocity and credit building in a laboratory dyad. *Journal of Personality and Social Psychology, 8,* 143–147.

Pryor, J. B., Reeder, G. D., & McManus, J. A. (1991). Fear and loathing in the workplace: Reactions to AIDS-infected co-workers. *Personality and Social Psychology Bulletin, 17*(2), 133–139.

Pulkkinen, L., & Pikanen, T. (1993). Continuities in aggressive behavior from childhood to adulthood. *Aggressive Behavior, 19,* 249–263.

Punam, A. K., & Block, L. G. (1997). Vividness effects: A resource-matching perspective. *Journal of Consumer Research, 24,* 295–304.

Quattrone, G. A. (1982). Behavioral consequences of attributional bias. *Social Cognition, 1,* 358–378.

Quattrone, G. A., & Jones, E. E. (1980). The perception of variability within in-groups and out-groups. *Journal of Personality and Social Psychology, 38,* 141–152.

Quigley, B. M., & Leonard, K. E. (1999). Husband alcohol expectancies, drinking and marital-conflict styles as predictors of severe marital violence among newlywed couples. *Psychology of Addictive Behaviors, 13,* 49–59.

Rajecki, D. W. (1990). *Attitudes* (2nd ed.). Sunderland, MA: Sinauer.

Raven, B. H., & Kruglanski, A. W. (1970). Conflict and power. In P. Swingle (Ed.), *The structure of conflict.* New York: Academic Press.

Raven, B. H., & Rubin, J. Z. (1983). *Social psychology* (2nd ed.). New York: Wiley.

Rawlins, W. K. (1982). Cross-sex friendship and the communicative management of sex-role expectations. *Communication Quarterly, 30,* 343–352.

Rawlins, W. K. (1992). *Friendship matters: Communication, dialectics, and life course.* New York: Aldine De Gruyter.

Regan, D. T. (1971). Effects of a favor and liking on compliance. *Journal of Experimental Social Psychology 7,* 627–639.

Regan, P. (1998). What if you can't get what you want? Willingness to compromise ideal mate selection standards as a function of sex, mate value, and relationship context. *Personality and Social Psychology, 24,* 1294–1303.

Register, L. M., & Henley, T. B. (1992). The phenomenology of intimacy. *Journal of Social and Personal Relations, 9*(4), 467–482.

Reinisch, & Sanders (1986). A test of sex differences in aggressive response to hypothetical conflict situations. *Journal of Personality and Social Psychology, 50,* 1045–1049.

Reisman, J. M. (1981). Adult friendships. In S. W. Duck & R. Gilmour (Eds.), *Personal relationships 2: Developing personal relationships.* New York: Academic Press.

Reiss, M. J. (1984). Human sociobiology. *Zygon, 19,* 117–140.

Reynolds, V., Falger, V., & Vine, I. (1987). *The sociobiology of eth-nocentrism.* Athens, GA: University of Georgia Press.

Rhodewalt, F. T. (1986). Self-presentation and the phenomenal self: On the stability and malleability of self conceptions. In R. F. Baumeister (Ed.), *Public self and private self.* New York: Springer-Verlag.

Rhodewalt, F. T., Morf, C., Hazlett, S., & Fairfield, M. (1991). Self-handicapping: The role of discounting and augmentation in the preservation of self-esteem. *Journal of Personality and Social Psychology, 61,* 122–131.

Rice, M. E., & Grusec, J. E. (1975). Saying and doing: Effects on observer performance. *Journal of Personality and Social Psychology, 32,* 584–593.

Richards, J. M., & Gross, J. J. (1999). Composure at any cost? The cognitive consequences of emotion suppression. *Personality and Social Psychology Bulletin, 25,* 1033–1044.

Richardson, D. R., Vandenberg, R. J., & Humphries, S. A. (1986). Effect of power to harm on retaliative aggression among males and females. *Journal of Research in Personality, 20,* 402–419.

Ringelmann, M. (1913). Research on animate sources of power: The work of man. *Annales de l'Institut National Agronomique,* 2e serie—tome XII, 1–40.

Rochat, F., Maggioni, O., & Modgiliani, A. (2000). The dynamics of obeying and opposing authority: A mathematical model. In T. Blass (Ed.), *Obedience to authority: Current perspectives on the Milgram paradigm* (pp. 161–192). Mahwah, NJ: Lawrence Erlbaum Publishers.

Rodin, J. (1974). Effects of distraction on the performance of obese and normal subjects. In S. Schachter & J. Rodin (Eds.), *Obese humans and rats* (pp. 97–109). Potomoc, MD: Erlbaum.

Rodin, J. (1981). Current status of the internal–external hypothesis for obesity: What went wrong? *American Psychologist, 36,* 361–372.

Rodin, J., & Langer, E. (1976). Long term effect of a control relevant intervention. *Journal of Personality and Social Psychology, 35,* 897–902.

Rodin, S., & Salovey, P. (1989). Health psychology. *Annual Review of Psychology, 40,* 533–579.

Roese, N. J., & Olson, J. M. (1997). Counterfactual thinking: The intersection of affect and function. In M. P. Zanna (Ed.), *Advances in experimental social psychology* (Vol. 29, pp. 1–59). San Diego, CA: Academic Press.

Rogers, R.W. (1983). Cognitive and physiological processes in fear appeals and attitude change: A revised theory of protection motivation. In J. T. Cacioppo & R. E. Petty (Eds.), *Social psychophysiology.* New York: Guilford.

Rohsenow, D. J., & Bachorowski, J. (1984). Effects of alcohol and expectancies on verbal aggression in men and women. *Journal of Abnormal Psychology, 93,* 418–432.

Rokeach, M. (1968). *Beliefs, attitudes, and values: A theory of organization and change.* San Francisco: Jossey-Bass.

Rokeach, M. (1973). *The nature of human values.* New York: Free Press.

Rokeach, M. (1979). *Understanding human values: Individual and social.* New York: Free Press.

Roles, W. S., Simpson, J. A.,Orina, M. M. (1999). Attachment and anger in anxiety-provoking situations. *Journal of Personality and Social Psychology, 76,* 940–957.

Romer, D., Gruder, C. L., & Lizzadro, T. (1986). A person–situation approach to altruistic behavior. *Journal of Personality and Social Psychology, 51,* 1001–1012.

Ronis, D. L., & Kaiser, M. K. (1989). Correlates of breast cancer self-examinations in a sample of college women: Analysis of linear structural variations. *Journal of Applied Social Psychology, 19,* 1068–1085.

Rosenbaum, M. E. (1986). The repulsion hypothesis: On the nondevelopment of relationships. *Journal of Personality and Social Psychology, 51,* 1156–1166.

Rosenberg, M. L., & Fenley, M. A. (1992). The federal role in injury control. *American Psychologist, 47,* 1031–1035.

Rosenman, R. H., Swan, G. E., & Carmelli, D. (1988). Definition, assessment, and evolution of the type A behavior pattern. In B. K. Houston & C. R. Snyder (Eds.), *Type A behavior pattern.* New York: Wiley.

Rosenthal, R., & Jacobson, L. (1968). *Pygmalion in the classroom: Teacher expectation and pupil's intellectual development.* New York: Holt.

Roskos-Ewoldsen, D., & Fazio, R. H. (1992). On the orienting value of Attitudes: attitude accessibility as a determinant of an object's attraction of visual attention. *Journal of Personality and Social Psychology, 63,* 198–211.

Ross, L., Amabile, T., & Steinmetz, J. L. (1977). Social roles, social control, and biases in social perception process. *Journal of Personality and Social Psychology, 35,* 484–494.

Ross, L., Greene, D., & House, P. (1977). The "false consensus effect": An egocentric bias in social perception and attribution processes. *Journal of Experimental Social Psychology, 13,* 279–301.

Ross, L., & Nisbett, R. E. (1991). *The person and the situation.* New York: McGraw-Hill.

Ross, M., & Holmberg, D. (1992). Are wives' memories for events in relationships more vivid than their husbands'? *Journal of Social and Personal Relations, 9*(4), 585–606.

Ross, S. L., & Jackson, J. M. (1991). Teachers' expectations for black males' and black females' academic achievement. *Personality and Social Psychology Bulletin, 17,* 78–82.

Rowlinson, R. T., & Felner, R. D. (1988). Major life events, hassles, and adaptation in adolescence: Confounding in the conceptualization and measurement of life stress and adjustment revisited. *Journal of Personality and Social Psychology, 55*(3), 432–444.

Rubin, M., & Hewstone, M. (1998). Social identity theory's self-esteem hypothesis: A review and some suggestions for clarification. *Personality and Social Psychology Review, 2,* 40–62.

Rubin, Z. (1970). Measurement and romantic love. *Journal of Personality and Social Psychology, 16,* 265–273.

Rubin, Z. (1973). *Liking and loving: An invitation to social psychology.* New York: Holt, Rinehart & Winston.

Rubin, Z., Hill, C. T., Peplau, L. A., & Dunkel-Schetter, C. (1980). Self-disclosure in dating couples: Sex roles and the ethics of openness. *Journal of Marriage and the Family, 42,* 305–317.

Rule, B. G., & Ferguson, T. J. (1986). The effects of media violence on attitudes, emotions, and cognitions. *Journal of Social Issues, 42,* 29–50.

Rusbult, C. E. (1987). Responses to dissatisfaction in close relationships: The exit-voice-loyalty-neglect model. In D. Perlman & S. Duck (Eds.), *Intimate relationships: Development, dynamics, and deterioration* (pp. 209–237). Beverly Hills, CA: Sage.

Rusbult, C. E., Verette, J., Whitney, G. A. Slovik, L. F., & Lipkus, I. (1991). Accommodation processes in close relationships: Theory and preliminary empirical evidence. *Journal of Personality and Social Psychology, 61,* 641–647.

Ruvolo, A. P., & Rotondo, J. L. (1998). Diamonds in the rough: Implicit personality theories and views of partner and self. *Personality and Social Psychology Bulletin, 24,* 750–758.

Ryan, K. M., & Kanjorski, J. (1998). The enjoyment of sexist humor, rape attitudes, and relationship aggression in college students. *Sex Roles, 38,* 743–756.

Ryckman, R. M., Robbins, M. A., Thornton, B., Kaaczor, L. M., Gayton, S. L., & Anderson, C. V. (1991). Public self consciousness and physique stereotyping. *Personality and Social Psychology Bulletin, 18,* 400–405.

Sabato, L. J. (1983). *The rise of political consultants.* New York: Basic Books.

Saks, M., & Hastie, R. (1978). *Social psychology in court.* New York: Van Nostrand Reinhold.

Sales, S. M. (1972). Economic threat as a determinant of conversion rates in authoritarian and nonauthoritarian churches. *Journal of Personality and Social Psychology, 23,* 420–428.

Sampson, R. J. (1987). Urban black violence: The effect of male joblessness and family disruption. *American Journal of Sociology, 93,* 348–382.

Sanbonmatsu, D. M., Akimoto, S. A., & Biggs, E. (1993). Overestimating causality: Attributional effects of confirmatory processing. *Journal of Personality and Social Psychology, 65,* 892–903.

Sanna, L. J., & Shotland, R. L. (1990). Valence of anticipated evaluation and social facilitation. *Journal of Experimental Social Psychology, 22,* 242–248.

Sanna, L. J., Turley-Ames, K. J., & Meier, S. (1999). Mood, self-esteem, and simulated alternatives: Thought-provoking affective influences on counterfactual direction. *Journal of Personality and Social Psychology, 76,* 543–558.

Sayers, S. L., & Baucom, D. H. (1991). Role of femininity and masculinity in distressed couple's communication. *Journal of Personality and Social Psychology, 61,* 641–647.

Schachter, S. (1951). Deviation, rejection and communication. *Journal of Abnormal and Social Psychology, 46,* 189–207.

Schachter, S. (1973). Some extraordinary facts about obese humans and rats. In N. Keill (Ed.), *The psychology of obesity: Dynamics and treatment* (pp. 15–38). Springfield, IL: Thomas.

Schachter, S., & Rodin, J. (1974). *Obese humans and rats.* Washington, DC: Erlbaum/Halstead.

Schachter, S., & Singer, J. E. (1962). Cognitive, social, and physiological determinants of emotional state. *Psychological Review, 69,* 379–399.

Schaller, M. (1991). Social categorization and the formation of group stereotypes: Further evidence for biased processing in the perception of group-behavior correlations. *European Journal of Social Psychology, 21,* 25–35.

Scheir, M. F., & Carver, C. S. (1987). Dispositional optimism and physical well being: The influence of generalized outcome expectancies on health. *Journal of Personality, 55*(2), 172–210.

Scheir, M. F., & Carver, C. S. (1988). A model of behavioral self-regulation: Translating intention into action. In L. Berkowitz (Ed.), *Advances in experimental social psychology* (Vol. 21, pp. 303–346). New York: Academic Press.

Scheir, M. F., Matthews, K. A., Owens, J., Abbott, A., Lebfevre, C., & Carver, C. S. (1986). Optimism and bypass surgery. Unpublished manuscript, Carnegie-Mellon University, Pittsburg, PA.

Scherwitz, L. & Canick, J. D. (1988). Self reference and coronary heart disease. In B. K. Houston & C. R. Snyder (Eds.), *Type A behavior pattern.* New York: Plenum.

Schiffenbauer, A., & Schavio, S. R. (1976). Physical distance and attraction: An intensification effect. *Journal of Experimental Social Psychology, 12,* 274–282.

Schleiter S. J., Keller, S. E., Bond, R. N., Cohen, J., & Stein, M. (1989). Major depressive disorder and immunity. *Archives of General Psychiatry, 46,* 81–87.

Schlenker, B. R. (1986). Self-identification: Toward an integration of the private and public self. In R. F. Baumeister (Ed.), *Public self and private self* (pp. 21–62). New York: Springer-Verlag.

Schlenker, B. R. (1987). Threats to identity: Self-identification and social stress. In C. R. Snyder & C. Ford (Eds.), *Coping with negative life events: Clinical and social psychological perspectives* (pp. 273–321). New York: Academic Press.

Schlenker, B. R., & Leary, M. R. (1982). Social anxiety and self-presentation: A conceptualization and model. *Psychological Bulletin, 92,* 641–669.

Schlenker, B. R., Soraci, S., Jr., & McCarthy, B. (1976). Self-esteem and group performance as determinants of egocentric perceptions in cooperative groups. *Human Relations, 29,* 1163–1176.

Schlenker, B. R., & Trudeau, J. V. (1990). Impact of self-presentations on private self-beliefs: Effects of prior self-beliefs and misattribution. *Journal of Personality and Social Psychology, 58,* 22–32.

Schlenker, B. R., Weigold, M. F., & Hallam, J. R. (1990). Self serving attributions in social context: Effects of self-esteem and social pressure. *Journal of Personality and Social Psychology, 58,* 855–863.

Schmidt, G., & Weiner, B. (1988). An attribution–affect–action theory of behavior: Replications of judgments of help giving. *Personality and Social Psychology Bulletin, 14,* 610–621.

Schneider, D. J. (1991). Social cognition. *Annual Review of Psychology, 42,* 535–557.

Schoen, R., & Wooldredge, J. (1989). Marriage choices in North Carolina and Virginia, 1969–71 and 1979–81. *Journal of Marriage and the Family, 51,* 465–481.

Schopler, J., & Matthews, M. (1965). The influence of perceived causal locus of partner's dependence on the use of interpersonal power. *Journal of Personality and Social Psychology, 2,* 609–612.

Schutz, W. (1983). A theory of small groups. In H. H. Blumberg, A. P. Hare, V. Kent, & M. F. Davis (Eds.), *Small groups and social interaction* (Vol. 2, pp. 479–486). New York: Wiley.

Schwartz, S. H. (1975). The justice of need and the activation of humanitarian norms. *Journal of Social Issues, 31,* 111–136.

Schwarz, N. (1999). Self-reports: How the questions shape the answers. *American Psychologist, 54,* 93–105.

Schwarz, N., Bless, H., & Bohner, G. (1992). Mood and persuasion: Affective states influence the processing of persuasive communications. In M. P. Zanna (Ed.), *Advances in experimental social psychology* (Vol. 24, pp. 161–201). San Diego, CA: Academic Press.

Schweder, R. A., Much, N. C., Mahapatra, M., & Park, L. (1997). The "big three" of morality and the "big three" explanations for suffering. In A. Brandt & P. Rozin (Eds.), *Moralization* (pp. 119–169). New York: Rutledge.

Scott, W. A. (1957). Attitude change through reward of verbal behavior. *Journal of Abnormal and Social Psychology, 55,* 72–75.

Sedikides, C., Campbell, W. K., Reeder, G. D., & Eliot, A. D. (1998). The self-serving bias in relational context. *Journal of Personality and Social Psychology, 74,* 378–386.

Segal, M. W. (1974). Alphabet and attraction: An unobtrusive measure of the effect of propinquity in a field setting. *Journal of Personality and Social Psychology, 30,* 654–657.

Senchak, M., & Leonard, K. (1992). Attachment styles and marital adjustment among newlywed couples. *Journal of Social and Personal Relationships, 9,* 221–238.

Sereny, G. (1974). *Into that darkness: An examination of conscience.* New York: Vintage.

Shaffer, D. R., & Sadowski, C. (1979). Effects of withheld evidence on juridic decisions II: Locus of withholding strategy. *Personality and Social Psychology Bulletin, 5,* 40–43.

Shanab, M. E., & Isonio, S. A. (1982). The effects of contrast upon compliance with socially undesirable requests in the foot-in-the-door paradigm. *Bulletin of the Psychonomic Society, 20,* 180–182.

Shanab, M. E., & O'Neill, P. (1979). The effect of contrast upon compliance with socially undesirable requests in the door-in-the-face paradigm. *Canadian Journal of Behavioural Science, 11,* 236–244.

Shanab, M. E., & Yahya, K. A. (1977). A behavioral study of obedience in children. *Journal of Personality and Social Psychology, 35,* 530–536.

Shanab, M. E., & Yahya, K. A. (1978). A cross-cultural study of obedience. *Bulletin of the Psychonomic Society, 11,* 267–269.

Shapiro, E. G. (1980). Is seeking help from a friend like seeking help from a stranger? *Social Psychology Quarterly, 43,* 259–263.

Shaver, P., & Hazan, C. (1985). Incompatibility, loneliness, and limerence. In W. Ickes (Ed.), *Compatible and incompatible relationships* (pp. 163–184). New York: Springer-Verlag.

Shaver, P., Hazan, C., & Bradshaw, D. (1988). Love as attachment: The integration of three behavioral systems. In R. Sternberg & M. Barnes (Eds.), *The anatomy of love.* New Haven, CT: Yale University Press.

Shaw, J. I., Borough, H. W., & Fink, M. I. (1994). Perceived sexual orientation and helping behavior by males and females: The wrong number technique. *Journal of Psychology and Human Sexuality, 6,* 73–81.

Shaw, J. M., & Scott, W. A. (1991). Influence of parent discipline style on delinquent behavior: The mediating role of control orientation. *Australian Journal of Psychology, 43,* 61–67.

Shepperd, J. A. (1993). Productivity loss in performance groups: A motivation analysis. *Psychological Bulletin, 113*(1), 67–81.

Shepperd, J. A., & Taylor, K. M. (1999). Social loafing and value-expectancy theory. *Personality and Social Psychology Bulletin, 25,* 1147–1158.

Sherif, C. W., Sherif, M., & Nebergall, R. E. (1965). *Attitude and attitude change: The social judgment-involvement approach.* Philadelphia: Saunders.

Sherif, M. (1936). *The psychology of social norms.* New York: Harper & Row.

Sherif, M. (1972). Experiments on norm formation. In E. P. Hollander & R. G. Hunt (Eds.), *Classic contributions to social psychology.* New York: Oxford University Press.

Sherif, M., Harvey, O. J., White, B. J., Hood, W. E., & Sherif, C. (1961). *Intergroup conflict and cooperation: The robber's cave experiment.* Norman: University of Oklahoma Book Exchange.

Sherif, M., & Hovland, C. I. (1961). *Social judgment.* New Haven: Yale University Press.

Sherman, S. L., Hamilton, D. K., & Roskos-Ewoldsen, D. R. (1989). Attenuation of illusory correlation. *Personality and Social Psychology Bulletin, 15,* 559–571.

Shotland, R. L., & Heinhold, W. D. (1985). Bystander response to arterial bleeding: Helping skills, the decision making process, and differentiating the helping response. *Journal of Personality and Social Psychology, 49,* 347–356.

Showers, C. (1992). Evaluatively integrative thinking about characteristics of the self. *Personality and Social Psychology Bulletin, 18*(6), 719–729.

Showers, C. J., & Kling, K. C. (1996). Organization of self-knowledge: Implications for recovery from sad mood. *Journal of Personality and Social Psychology, 70,* 578–590.

Shultz, T. R., & Lepper, M. R. (1996). Cognitive dissonance reduction as constraint satisfaction. *Psychological Bulletin, 103,* 219–240.

Shultz, T. R., & Lepper, M. R. (1999). Computer simulation of cognitive dissonance reduction. In E. Harmon-Jones & J. Mills (Eds.), *Cognitive dissonance: Progress on a pivotal theory in social psychology.* Washington, DC: American Psychological Association.

Shultz, T. R., Leveille, E., & Lepper, M. R. (1999). Free choice and cognitive dissonance revisited: Choosing "lesser evils" versus "greater goods." *Personality and Social Psychology Bulletin, 25,* 40–48.

Shuntich, R. J., & Taylor, S. P. (1972). The effects of alcohol on human physical aggression. *Journal of Experimental Research in Personality, 6,* 34–38.

Sia, T. L., Lord, C. G., Blessum, K. A. Thomas, J. C., & Lepper, M. R. (1999). Activation of exemplars in the process of assessing social category attitudes. *Journal of Personality and Social Psychology, 76,* 517–532.

Sibicky, M., & Dovidio, J. F. (1986). Stigma of psychological therapy: Stereotypes, interpersonal reactions, and the self-fulfilling prophecy. *Journal of Counseling Psychology, 33*(2), 148–154.

Silverstein, B., Perdue, L., Peterson, B., & Kelly, E. (1986). The role of the mass media in promoting a thin standard of bodily attractiveness for women. *Sex Roles, 14,* 519–532.

Simon, L. (1977). *The biography of Alice B. Toklas.* Garden City, NY: Doubleday.

Simonton, D. K. (1985). Intelligence and personal influence in groups: Four nonlinear models. *Psychological Review, 92,* 532–547.

Simonton, D. K. (1988). Presidential style: Personality, biography, and performance. *Journal of Personality and Social Psychology, 55,* 928–936.

Simpson, J. A. (1990). Influence of attachment styles on romantic relationships. *Journal of Personality and Social Psychology, 59,* 971–980.

Simpson, J. A., Gangestad, S. W., Christensen, P. N., & Leck, K. (1999). Fluctuating symmetry, sociosexuality, and intrasexual competition. *Journal of Personality and Social Psychology, 76,* 159–172.

Simpson, J. A., Ickes, W., & Grich, J. (1999). When acuracy hurts: Reactions of anxious–ambivalent dating partners to a relationship-threatening situation. *Journal of Personality and Social Psychology, 76,* 754–769.

Simpson, J. A., & Kenrick, D. T. (Eds.). (1997). *Evolutionary social psychology.* Mahwah, NJ: Erlbaum.

Sistrunk, F., & Clement, D. (1970). Cross-cultural comparisons of the conformity behavior of college students. *Journal of Social Psychology, 82,* 273–274.

Skowronski, J. J., Betz, A. L., Thompson, C. P., & Shannon, L. (1991). Social memory in everyday life: Recall of self-events and other-events. *Journal of Personality and Social Psychology, 60,* 831–843.

Skowronski, J. J., Carlston, D. E., Mae, L., & Crawford, M. T. (1998). Spontaneous trait transference: Communicators take on the qualities they describe in others. *Journal of Personality and Social Psychology, 74,* 837–848.

Sleet, D. A. (1987). Motor vehicle trauma and safety belt use in the context of public health priorities. *Journal of Trauma, 27,* 695–702.

Slovic, P., & Fischoff, B. (1977). On the psychology of experimental surprise. *Journal of Experimental Psychology: Human Perception and Performance, 3,* 544–551.

Smeaton, G., Byrne, D., & Murnen, S. K. (1989). The repulsion hypothesis revisited: Similarity irrelevance or dissimilarity bias. *Journal of Personality and Social Psychology, 56,* 54–59.

Smith, E. R. (1988). Category accessibility effects in simulated exemplar-based memory. *Journal of Experimental Social Psychology, 24,* 448–463.

Smith, E. R. (1990). Content and process specificity in the effects of prior experiences. In T. K. Srull & R. S. Wyer, Jr. (Eds.), *Advances in social cognition, 3.* Hillsdale, NJ: Erlbaum.

Smith, E. R. (1998). Mental representations and memory. In D. T. Gilbert, S. T. Fiske, & G. Lindsey (Eds.), *Handbook of social psychology* (4th ed., Vol. 1, pp. 391–445). New York: McGraw-Hill.

Smith, R. E., Keating, J. P., Hester, R. K., & Mitchell, H. E. (1976). Role and justice considerations in attribution of responsibility to a rape victim. *Journal of Research in Personality, 10,* 346–357.

Smith, K. D., Keating, J. P., & Stotland, E. (1989). Altruism reconsidered: The effect of denying feedback on a victim's status to empathetic witnesses. *Journal of Personality and Social Psychology, 57,* 641–650.

Smith, T. W., Allred, K. D., Morrison, C. A., & Carlson, S. D. (1989). Cardiovascular reactivity and interpersonal influence: Active coping in a social context. *Journal of Personality and Social Psychology, 56*(2), 209–218.

Smith, T. W., & Frohm, K. D. (1985). What's so unhealthy about hostility? Construct validity and psychosocial correlates of the Cook and Medley Ho Scale. *Health Psychology, 4*(6), 503–520.

Sniderman, P. M., & Piazza, T. (1994). *The scar of race.* Cambridge, MA: Harvard University Press.

Snodgrass, M. A. (1987). The relationships of differential loneliness, intimacy and characterological attributional style to duration of loneliness. *Journal of Social Behavior and Personality, 2,* 173–186.

Snowden, F. M., Jr. (1983). *Before color prejudice: The ancient view of blacks.* Cambridge, MA: Harvard University Press.

Snyder, C. R., Ford, C. E., & Harris, R. N. (1987). The effects of theoretical perspective on the analysis of coping with negative life events. In C. R. Snyder & C. E. Ford (Eds.), *Coping with negative life events.* New York: Plenum Press.

Snyder, M. (1987). *Public appearances as private realities: The psychology of self monitoring.* New York: Freeman.

Snyder, M. (1993). Motivational foundations of behavioral confirmation. In M. P. Zanna (Ed.), *Advances in experimental social psychology* (Vol. 25). San Diego, CA: Academic Press.

Snyder, M., Bersheid, E., & Glick, P. (1985). Focusing on the interior and exterior. Two investigations of the initiation of personal relationships. *Journal of Personality and Social Psychology, 48,* 147–1439.

Snyder, M., & Cunningham, M. (1975). To comply or not to comply: Testing the self-perception explanation of the foot-in-the-door phenomenon. *Journal of Personality and Social Psychology, 31,* 64–67.

Snyder, M., & Swann, W. B., Jr. (1978). Hypothesis-testing processes in social interaction. *Journal of Personality and Social Psychology, 36,* 1201–1212.

Snyder, M., Tanke, E. D., & Berscheid, E. (1977). Social perception and interpersonal behavior: On the self-fulfilling nature of social stereotypes. *Journal of Personality and Social Psychology, 35,* 656–666.

Solano, C. H., & Koester, N. H. (1989). Loneliness and communication problems: Subjective anxiety or objective skills? *Personality and Social Psychology Bulletin, 15,* 126–133.

Solomon, S., Greenberg, J., & Pyszczynski, T. (1992). A terror management theory of self-esteem and its role in social behavior. In M. Leary (Ed.), *Advances in experimental social psychology* (Vol. 25). New York: Academic Press.

Sommer, K. L., Williams, K. D., Ciarocco, N. J., & Baumeister, R. F. (1998). *When silence speaks louder than words: Explorations into interpersonal and intrapsychic consequences of social ostracism.* Unpublished manuscript. Case Western University, Cleveland, Ohio.

Sommer, R. (1969). *Personal space.* Englewood Cliffs, NJ: Prentice-Hall.

Spacapan, S. (1988). Psychosocial mediators of health status. In S. Spacapan & S. Oskamp (Eds.), *The social psychology of health.* Beverly Hills, CA: Sage.

Spivey, C. B., & Prentice-Dunn, S. (1990). Assessing the directionality of deindividuated behavior: Effects of deindividuation, modeling, and private self-consciousness on aggressive and prosocial responses. *Basic and Applied Social Psychology, 11,* 387–403.

Sprafkin, J. N., Liebert, R. M., & Poulos, R. W. (1975). Effects of a prosocial televised example on children's helping. *Journal of Experimental Child Psychology, 20,* 119–126.

Sprecher, S. (1999). "I love you more today than yesterday": Romantic partners perceptions of changes in love and related affect over time. *Journal of Personality and Social Psychology, 76,* 46–53.

Stalder, D. R., & Baron, R. S. (1998). Attributional complexity as a moderator of dissonance-produced attitude change. *Journal of Personality and Social Psychology, 75,* 449–455.

Stangor, C., Carr, C., & Kiang, L. (1998). Activating stereotypes undermines task performance expectations. *Journal of Personality and Social Psychology, 74,* 1191–1197.

Stangor, C., & Lange, J. E. (1994). Mental representations of social groups: Advances in understanding stereotypes and stereotyping. In M. P. Zanna (Ed.), *Advances in experimental social psychology* (Vol. 26). San Diego, CA: Academic Press.

Stasser, G. (1992). Pooling of shared and unshared information during group discussions. In S. Worchel, W. Wood, & J. A. Simpson (Eds.), *Group process and productivity*. Newbury Park, CA: Sage.

Stasser, G., Kerr, N. L., & Davis, J. H. (1989). Influence processes and consensus models in decision making groups. In P. Paulus (Ed.), *Psychology of group influence* (2nd ed., pp. 279–326). Hillsdale, NJ: Erlbaum.

Stasser, G., & Stewart, G. (1992). Discovery of hidden profiles by decision-making groups: Solving a problem versus making a judgment. *Journal of Personality and Social Psychology, 63,* 426–434.

Stasser, G., Taylor, L. A., & Hanna, C. (1989). Information sampling and unstructured discussions of three- and six-person groups. *Journal of Personality and Social Psychology, 57,* 67–78.

Stasser, G., & Titus, W. (1987). Effects of information load and percentage of shared information on dissemination of unshared information during group discussion. *Journal of Personality and Social Psychology, 53,* 81–93.

Stattin, H., & Magnusson, D. (1989). The role of early aggressive behavior in the frequency, seriousness, and types of later crime. *Journal of Consulting and Clinical Psychology, 57,* 710–718.

Staub, E. (1985). *The roots of evil: The origins of genocide and other group violence*. Cambridge, England: Cambridge University Press.

Steele, C. M. (1988). The psychology of self-affirmation: Sustaining the integrity of the self. In L. Berkowitz (Ed.), *Advances in experimental social psychology* (Vol. 21, pp. 261–302). New York: Academic Press.

Steele, C. M., & Aronson, J. (1995). Stereotype threat and the intellectual test performance of African Americans. *Journal of Personality and Social Psychology, 69,* 797–811.

Steele, C. M., & Josephs, R. A. (1990). Alcohol myopia. *American Psychologist, 45,* 921–933.

Steil, J. M., & Weltman, K. (1991). Marital inequality: The importance of resources, personal attributes, and social norms on career valuing and the allocation of domestic responsibilities. *Sex Roles, 24,* 161–179.

Steil, J. M., & Weltman, K. (1992). Influence strategies at home and at work: A study of sixty dual career couples. *Journal of Social and Personal Relationships, 9,* 65–88.

Steiner, I. D. (1972). *Group process and productivity*. New York: Academic Press.

Stellman, J. M., & Bertin, J. E. (1990, June 4). Science's anti-female bias. *The New York Times*, p. 34.

Sternberg, R. J. (1986). A triangular theory of love. *Psychological Review, 93,* 119–135.

Sternberg, R. J. (1988). Triangulating love. In R. J. Sternberg & M. L. Barnes (Eds.), *The psychology of love*. New Haven, CT: Yale University Press.

Sternberg, R. J., & Gracek, S. (1984). The nature of love. *Journal of Personality and Social Psychology, 47,* 312–329.

Still, W. (1968). *The underground railroad*. New York: Arno Press. (Originally published 1872.)

Stipek, D., Weiner, B., & Kexing, L. (1989). Testing some attribution-emotion relations in the People's Republic of China. *Journal of Personality and Social Psychology, 56*(1), 109–116.

Stone, G. S. (1979). Patient compliance and the role of the expert. *Journal of Social Issues, 35,* 34–59.

Stone, J., Aronson, E., Crain, A. L., Winslow, M. P., & Fried, C. B. (1994). Inducing hypocrisy as a means of encouraging young adults to use condoms. *Personality and Social Psychology Bulletin, 20,* 116–128.

Stoner, J. A. F. (1961). *A comparison of individual and group decisions involving risk*. Unpublished masters thesis, Massachusetts Institute of Technology, Cambridge.

Storms, M. D. (1973). Videotape and the attribution process: Reversing actors' and observers' points of view. *Journal of Personality and Social Psychology, 27,* 165–175.

Straus, M. A. (1991). Discipline and deviance: Physical punishment of children and violence and other crime in adulthood. *Social Problems, 38,* 133–152.

Suls, J., & Sanders, G. S. (1989). Why do some behavioral styles place people at coronary risk? In A. R. Siegman & T. M. Dembroski (Eds.), *In search of coronary prone behavior: Beyond type A*. Hillsdale, NJ: Erlbaum.

Sulthana, P. (1987). The effect of frustration and inequity on the displacement of aggression. *Asian Journal of Psychology and Education, 19,* 26–33.

Swann, W. B., Jr. (1984). Quest for accuracy in person perception: A matter of pragmatics. *Psychological Review, 91,* 457–477.

Swann, W. B., Jr. (1992, February). Seeking "truth," finding despair: some unhappy consequences of a negative self-concept. *Current Directions in Psychological Science 1,* 15–18.

Swann, W. B., Jr. (1996). *Self-traps: The elusive quest for higher self-esteem*. New York: Freeman.

Swann, W. B., Jr., & Gill, M. J. (1997). Confidence and accuracy in person perception: Do we know what we think we know about relationship partners. *Journal of Personality and Social Psychology, 73,* 747–757.

Swann, W. B., Jr., Hixon, J. G., & De La Ronde, C. (1992). Embracing the bitter truth: Negative self-concepts and marital commitment. *Psychological Science, 3*(2), 118–121.

Swann, W. B., Jr., Pelham, B. W., & Krull, D. S. (1989). Agreeable fancy or disagreeable truth? Reconciling self-enhancement and self-verification. *Journal of Personality and Social Psychology, 57,* 782–791.

Swann, W. B., Jr., Stein-Seroussi, A., & McNulty, S. (1992). Outcasts in a white-lie society: The enigmatic worlds of people with negative self-conceptions. *Journal of Personality and Social Psychology, 62*(4), 618–624.

Swann, W. B., Jr., Stein-Seroussi, A., & Giesler, R. B. (1992). Why people self-verify. *Journal of Personality and Social Psychology, 62,* 392–410.

Swann, W. B., Jr., Wenzlaff, R. M., Krull, D. S., & Pelham, B. W. (1992). The allure of negative feedback: Self-verification strivings among depressed persons. *Journal of Abnormal Psychology, 101,* 293–306.

Swim, J. (1994). Perceived versus meta-analytic effect sizes: An assessment of the accuracy of gender stereotypes. *Journal of Personality and Social Psychology, 66,* 21–36.

Swim, J. K., Cohen, L. L., & Hyers, L. L. (1998). Experiencing everyday prejudice and discrimination. In J. K. Swim & C. Stangor (Eds.), *Prejudice: The target's perspective* (pp. 37–60). San Diego, CA: Academic Press.

Switzer, R., & Taylor, R. B. (1983). Sociability versus privacy of residential choice: Impacts of personality and local social ties. *Basic and Applied Social Psychology, 4,* 123–136.

Sykes, C. J. (1992). *A nation of victims*. New York: St. Martins Press.

Tajfel, H. (1981). *Human groups and social categories.* Cambridge, England: Cambridge University Press.

Tajfel, H. (1982). *Social identity and group relations.* Cambridge, England: Cambridge University Press.

Tajfel, H., Billig, M., Bundy, R., & Flament, C. (1971). Social categorization and intergroup behavior. *European Journal of Social Psychology, 1,* 149–178.

Tanford, S., & Penrod. S. (1984a). Social inference processes in juror judgments of multiple-offense trials. *Journal of Applied Social Psychology, 47,* 749–765.

Tanford, S., & Penrod, S. (1984b). Social influence model: A formal integration of research on majority and minority influence processes. *Psychological Bulletin, 95,* 189–225.

Tarnow, E. (2000). Self-destructive obedience in the airplane cockpit and the concept of obedience optimization. In T. Blass (Ed.), *Obedience to authority: Current perspectives on the Milgram paradigm* (pp. 111–123). Mahwah, NJ: Lawrence Erlbaum Publishers.

Tarvis, C. (1982). *Anger: The misunderstood emotion.* New York: Simon & Schuster.

Tarvis, C. (1990, August). *Mismeasure of woman: Paradoxes and perspectives in the study of gender.* Master lecture presented at annual meeting of the American Psychological Association, Boston.

Taylor, S. E. (1979). Hospital patient behavior: Reactance, helplessness, or control? *Journal of Social Issues, 35,* 156–184.

Taylor, S. E. (1981). The interface of cognitive and social psychology. In J. H. Harvey (Ed.), *Cognition, social behavior, and the environment.* Hillsdale, NJ: Erlbaum.

Taylor, S. E. (1983). Adjustment to threatening events: A theory of cognitive adaptation. *American Psychologist, 38,* 1161–1173.

Taylor, S. E. (1986). *Health psychology.* New York: Random House.

Taylor, S. E. (1989). *Positive illusions: Creative self-deception and the healthy mind.* New York: Basic Books.

Taylor, S. E. (1990). Health psychology: The science and the field. *American Psychologist, 45,* 40–50.

Taylor, S. E., & Brown, J. D. (1988). Illusion and well-being: A social psychological perspective on mental health. *Psychological Bulletin, 103,* 193–210.

Taylor, S. E., & Fiske, S. T. (1978). Salience, attention, and attribution: Top of the head phenomena. In L. Berkowitz (Ed.), *Advances in experimental social psychology* (Vol. 11, pp. 249–288). New York: Academic Press.

Taylor, S. E., & Gollwitzer, P. M. (1995). Effects of mindset on positive illusions. *Journal of Personality and Social Psychology, 69,* 213–226.

Taylor, S. E., Kemeny, M. E., Aspinwall, L. G., & Schneider, S. G. (1992). Optimism, coping, psychological distress, and high risk sexual behavior among men at risk for acquired immunodeficiency syndrome (AIDS). *Journal of Personality and Social Psychology, 63,* 460–473.

Taylor, S. E., & Thompson, S. (1982). Stalking the elusive vividness effect. *Psychological Review, 89,* 166–181.

Tec, N. (1986). *When light pierced the darkness: Christian rescue of Jews in Nazi-occupied Poland.* New York: Oxford University Press.

Tennen, H., & Affleck, G. (1987). The costs and benefits of optimistic explanations and dispositional optimism. *Journal of Personality, 55*(2), 377–393.

Tennov, D. (1979). *Love and limerence: The experience of being in love.* New York: Stein & Day.

Tesser, A. (1988) Toward a self-evaluation maintenance model of social behavior. In L. Berkowitz (Ed.), *Advances in experimental social psychology* (Vol. 21, pp. 181–228). New York: Academic Press.

Tesser, A. (1993). The importance of heritability in psychological research: The case of attitudes. *Psychological Review, 100,* 129–142.

Tesser, A., Campbell, J., & Mickler, S. (1983). The role of social pressure, attention to the stimulus, and self-doubt in conformity. *European Journal of Social Psychology, 13,* 217–233.

Tesser, A., & Collins, J. E. (1988). Emotion in social reflection and comparison situations: Intuitive, systematic, and exploratory approaches. *Journal of Personality and Social Psychology, 55,* 695–709.

Tesser, A., & Shaffer, D. (1990). Attitudes and attitude change. *Annual Review of Psychology* (Vol. 41, pp. 479–523). Palo Alto, CA: Annual Reviews.

Tetlock, P. E. (1985). Accountability: A social check on the fundamental attribution error. *Social Psychology Quarterly, 48,* 227–236.

Tetlock, P. E. (1986). Is categorization theory the solution to the level-of-analysis problem? *British Journal of Social Psychology, 25,* 255–256.

Tetlock, P. E., & Levi, A. (1982). Attribution bias: On the inconsistencies of the cognition-motivation debate. *Journal of Experimental Social Psychology, 18,* 68–88.

Tetlock, P. E., Peterson, R. S., McGuire, C., Shi-jie Chang, & Feld, P. (1992). Assessing political group dynamic: A test of the groupthink model. *Journal of Personality and Social Psychology, 63,* 403–425.

Thibaut, J. W., & Kelley, H. H. (1959). *The social psychology of groups.* New York: Wiley.

Thompson, B., & Borrello, G. M. (1992). Different views of love: Deductive and inductive lines of inquiry. *Psychological Science, 1*(5), 154–155.

Thornhill, R., & Gangestad, S. W. (1994). Human fluctuating asymmetry and sexual behavior. *Psychological Science, 5,* 297–302.

Tindale, R. S., Smith, C. M., Thomas, L. S., Filkins, J., & Sheffey, S. (1996). Shared representations and asymmetric social influence processes in small groups. In E. Witte & J. Davis (Eds.), *Understanding group behavior* (Vol. 1, pp. 81–104). Mahwah, NJ: Erlbaum.

Toklas, A. B. (1963). *What is remembered.* New York: Holt, Rinehart & Winston.

Tonnesmann, W. (1987). Group identification and political socialisation. In V. Reynolds, V. Falger, & I. Vine (Eds.), *The sociobiology of ethnocentrism.* Athens, GA: University of Georgia Press.

Tornstam, L. (1992). Loneliness in marriage. *Journal of Social and Personal Relationships, 9,* 197–217.

Treisman, A., & Souther, J. (1985). Search symmetry: A diagnostic for preattentive processing of separable features. *Journal of Experimental Psychology: General, 114,* 285–310.

Trenholm, S. (1989). *Persuasion and social influence.* Englewood Cliffs, NJ: Prentice-Hall.

Trepanier, M. L., & Romatowski, J. A. (1985). Attributes and roles assigned to characters in children's writing: Sex differences and sex-role perceptions. *Sex Roles, 13,* 263–272.

Triandis, H. C. (1989). The self and social behavior in differing cultural contexts. *Psychological Review, 96*(3), 506–520.

Triandis, H. C. (1994). *Culture and social behavior.* New York: McGraw-Hill.

Triplett, N. (1898). Dynamogenic factors in pacemaking and competition. *American Psychologist, 9*, 507–533.

Trivers, R. (1972). *Social evolution.* Meno Park, CA: Benjamin/Cummings.

Trope, Y. (1983). Self-enhancement and self-assessment in achievement behavior. In J. M. Suls & A. G. Greenwald (Eds.), *Psychological perspectives on the self* (Vol. 2, pp. 93–121). Hillsdale, NJ: Erlbaum.

Trope, Y. (1986). Identification and inference processes in disposition attribution. *Psychological Review, 93*, 239–257.

Trope, Y., & Alfieri, T. (1997). Effortfulness and flexibility of dispositional judgment processes. *Journal of Personality and Social Psychology, 73*, 703–718.

Trope, Y., Cohen, O., & Alfieri, T. (1991). Behavior identification as the mediator of dispositional inference. *Journal of Personality and Social Psychology, 61*, 873–883.

Tuchman, B. (1978). *A distant mirror.* New York: Ballantine.

Turner, J. C. (1987). *Rediscovering the social group: A self-categorization theory.* Oxford, UK: Basil Blackwell.

Turner, J. C., Wetherell, M. S., & Hogg, M. A. (1989). Referent informational influence and group polarization. *British Journal of Social Psychology, 28*, 135–147.

Tversky, A., & Kahneman, D. (1973). Availability: A heuristic for judgment frequency and probability. *Cognitive Psychology, 5*, 207–232.

Tversky, A., & Kahneman, D. (1974). Judgment under uncertainty: Heuristics and biases. *Science, 185*, 1124–1131.

Tybout, A. M., Sternthal, B., & Calder, B. (1983). Information availability as a determinant of multiple request effectiveness. *Journal of Marketing Research, 20*, 280–290.

Tyler, T., & Schuller, R. A. (1991). Aging and attitude change. *Journal of Personality and Social Psychology, 61*, 689–697.

Tyler, T. R. (1994). Governing amid diversity: Can fair decision-making procedures bridge competing public interests and values? *Law and Society Review, 28*, 701–722.

Tyler, T. R. (1997). The psychology of legitimacy: A relational perspective on voluntary deference to authorities. *Personality and Social Psychology Review, 1*, 323–345.

Tziner, A., & Eden, D. (1985). Effects of crew composition on crew performance: Does the whole equal the sum of its parts?. *Journal of Applied Psychology, 70*, 85–93.

Vallone, R. P., Griffin, D. W., Lin, S., & Ross, L. (1990). Overconfident prediction of future actions and outcomes by self and others. *Journal of Personality and Social Psychology, 58*, 582–592.

Vallortigara, G. (1992). Affiliation and aggression as related to gender in domestic chicks. *Journal of Comparative Psychology, 106*, 53–58.

Vandello, J. A., & Cohen, D. (1999). Patterns of individualism and collectivism across the United States. *Journal of Personality and Social Psychology, 77*, 279–292.

Van den Bos, K., Wilke, H. A. M., & Lind, E. A. (1998). When do we need procedural fairness? The role of trust in authority. *Journal of Personality and Social Psychology, 75*, 1449–1458.

Van Kippenberg, D., de Vries, N., & Van Kippenberg, A. (1990). Group status, group size and attitude polarization. *European Journal of Social Psychology, 29*, 121–134.

Van Velsor, P. (1990). *Eating behavior: Externality and social influence.* Unpublished manuscript, University of Toledo, Ohio.

Vaughn, D. (1986). *Uncoupling: Turning points in intimate relationships.* New York: Oxford University Press.

Vinokur, A., & Burnstein, E. (1974). Effects of partially shared persuasive arguments on group-induced shifts. *Journal of Personality and Social Psychology, 29*, 305–315.

Vinokur, A., & Burnstein, E. (1978). Depolarization of attitudes. *Journal of Personality and Social Psychology, 36*, 872–885.

Vissing, Y. M., Straus, M. A., Gelles, R. J., & Harrop, J. W. (1991). Verbal aggression by parents and psychosocial problems of children. *Child Abuse and Neglect, 15*, 223–238.

Vlaander, G. P. J., & van Rooijen, L. (1985). Independence and conformity in Holland: Asch's experiment three decades later. *Tijdschrift Voor Psychologie, 13*, 49–55.

Vonk, R. (1999). Effects of outcome dependency on correspondence bias. *Personality and Social Psychology Bulletin, 25*, 382–389.

Von Lang, J., & Sibyll, C. (1983). *Eichmann interrogated.* New York: Farrar, Straus, & Giroux.

Waaland, P., & Keeley, S. (1985). Police decision making in wife abuse: The impact of legal and extralegal factors. *Law and Human Behavior, 9*, 355–366.

Walford, R. (1986). *The 120 year diet.* Los Angeles, CA: UCLA Press.

Wallach, M. A., & Kogan, N. (1965). The roles of information, discussion and consensus in group risk taking. *Journal of Experimental Social Psychology, 1*, 1–19.

Wallach, M. A., Kogan, N., & Bem, D. J. (1962). Group influence on individual risk-taking. *Journal of Abnormal and Social Psychology, 65*, 75–86.

Walster (Hatfield), E., & Festinger, L. (1962). The effectiveness of "overheard" conversations. *Journal of Abnormal and Social Psychology, 65*, 395–402.

Walster, E., Walster, G. W., & Berscheid, E. (1978). *Equity theory and research.* Boston: Allyn & Bacon.

Walton, M. D, Sachs, D., Ellington, R., Hazlewood, A., Griffin, S., & Bass, D. (1988). Physical stigma and the pregnancy role: Receiving help from strangers. *Sex Roles, 18*, 323–331.

Ward, C. H., & Eisler, R. M. (1987). Type A behavior, achievement striving, and a dysfunctional self-evaluation system. *Journal of Personality and Social Psychology, 53*(2), 318–326.

Watson, P. W., & Thornhill, R. (1994). Fluctuating asymmetry and sexual selection. *Trends in Ecology and Evolution, 9*, 21–25.

Weary, G., & Edwards, J. A. (1994). Social cognition and clinical psychology: Anxiety, depression, and the processing of information about others. In R. S. Wyer & T. K. Srull (Eds.), *Handbook of social cognition* (2nd ed., Vol. 2, pp. 289–338.). Hillsdale, NJ: Erlbaum.

Webb, E. J., Campbell, D. T., Schwartz, R. D., Sechrist, L., & Grove, J. (1981). *Nonreactive measures in the social sciences* (2nd ed.). Boston: Houghton Mifflin.

Webster, T. M., King, H. N., & Kassin, S. M. (1991). Voices from the empty chair: The missing witness inference and the jury. *Law and Human Behavior, 15*, 31–42.

Wegner, D. (1986). Transactive memory: A contemporary analysis of the group mind. In B. Mullen & G. Goethals (Eds.), *Theories of group Behavior* (pp. 185–208). New York: Springer-Verlag.

Wegner, D. (1988). Stress and mental control. In S. Fisher & J. Reason (Eds.), *Handbook of life stress, cognition, and health*. Chichester, England: Wiley.

Wegner, D. M. (1989). *White bears and unwanted thoughts*. New York: Viking/Penguin.

Wegner, D. M. (1993). Thought suppression. In M. Zanna (Ed.), *Advances in experimental social psychology* (Vol. 25, pp. 193–225). Academic Press: New York.

Wegner, D. M. (1996). A computer network model of human transactive memory. *Social Cognition, 13,* 319–339.

Wegner, D. M., Ansfield, M. E., & Pilloff, D. (1998). The pun and the pendulum: Ironic effects of mental control of action. *Psychological Science, 9,* 196–199.

Wegner, D. M., & Bargh, J. (1998). Control and automaticity in social life. In D. Gilbert, S. Fiske, & G. Lindsey (Eds.), *Handbook of social psychology* (4th ed., pp. 446–496). Boston: McGraw-Hill.

Wegner, D. M., & Erber, R. (1992). The hyperaccessibility of suppressed thoughts. *Journal of Personality and Social Psychology, 63*(6), 903–912.

Wegner, D. M, Lane, J. D, Dimitri, S. (1994). The allure of secret relationships. *Journal of Personality & Social Psychology, 66*(2), 287–300.

Wegner, D. M., & Pennebaker, J. W. (Eds.). (1993). *Handbook of mental control*. Englewood Cliffs, NJ: Prentice-Hall.

Wegner, D. M., & Wheatley, T. (1999). What cognitive mechanism makes us feel as if we are acting consciously and willfully? *American Psychologist, 54,* 462–479.

Weinberg, A. (1957). *Attorney for the damned*. New York: Simon & Schuster.

Weinberg, A., & Weinberg, L. (Eds.). (1961). *The muckrackers*. New York: Capricorn Books.

Weiner, B. (1986). *An attributional theory of motivation and emotion*. New York: Springer-Verlag.

Weiner, B. (1991). Metaphors on motivation and attribution. *American Psychologist, 46,* 921–930.

Weiner, B. (1993). On sin versus sickness: A theory of perceived responsibility and social motivation. *American Psychologist, 48,* 957–965.

Weiner, B., Figueroa-Munoz, & Kakihara, C. (1991). The goals of excuses and communication strategies related to causal perceptions. *Journal of Personality and Social Psychology, 17,* 4–13.

Weiner, B., Perry, R. P., & Magnusson, J. (1988). An attributional analysis of reactions to stigmas. *Journal of Personality and Social Psychology, 55,* 738–748.

Weisman, A. D. (1991). Bereavement and companion animals. *Omega: Journal of Death and Dying, 22,* 241–248.

Weisse, J., Neselhof-Kendall, B., Fleck-Kandath, B., & Baum, A. (1990). Psychosocial aspects of AIDS prevention among heterosexuals. In J. Edwards, R. S. Tindale, L. Heath, & E. Posavek (Eds.), *Social influence processes and prevention* (Vol. 1). New York: Plenum.

Weisz, C., & Jones, E. E. Some consequences of expectancies for person perception: Target-based versus category-based expectancies. Unpublished manuscript, Princeton University.

Wells, G. L. (1995). Scientific study of witness memory: Implications for public and legal policy. *Psychology, Law, and Public Policy, 1*(4), 726–731.

Wells, G. L., & Gavanski, I. (1989). Mental simulation of causality. *Journal of Personality and Social Psychology, 56*(2), 161–169.

West, S. G., Whitney, G., & Schnedler, R. (1975). Helping a motorist in distress: The effects of sex, race, and neighborhood. *Journal of Personality and Social Psychology, 31,* 691–698.

Wheeler, L., Reis, H., & Nezlek, J. (1983). Loneliness, social interaction, and sex roles. *Journal of Personality and Social Psychology, 45,* 943–953.

Whitney, J. C., & Smith, R. A. (1983). Effect of group cohesiveness on attitude polarization and the acquisition of knowledge in a strategic planning context. *Journal of Marketing Research, 20,* 167–176.

Whyte, G. (1989). Groupthink reconsidered. *Academy of Management Review, 14,* 40–56.

Wicker, A. W. (1969). Attitudes versus actions: The relationship of verbal and overt behavioral responses to attitude objects. *Journal of Social Issues, 25*(4), 41–78.

Wicklund, R. A. (1975). Objective self-awareness. in L. Berkowitz (Ed.), *Advances in experimental social psychology,* (Vol. 8, (pp. 319–342). New York: Academic Press.

Widom, C. S. (1992, October). The cycle of violence. *National Institute of Justice Research in Brief,* 1–6.

Wiebe, D. J. (1991). Hardiness and stress moderation: A test of proposed mechanisms. *Journal of Personality and Social Psychology, 60,* 89–99.

Wiegman, O., Kuttschreuter, M., & Baarda, B. (1992). A longitudinal study of the effects of television viewing on aggressive and prosocial behaviors. *British Journal of Social Psychology, 31,* 147–164.

Wilder, D. A. (1977). Perception of groups, size of opposition, and social influence. *Journal of Experimental Social Psychology, 13,* 253–268.

Wilder, D. A. (1986). Social categorization: Implications for creation and reduction of intergroup bias. In L. Berkowitz (Ed.), *Advances in experimental psychology* (Vol. 19, pp. 293–355). New York: Academic Press.

Wilder, D. A., & Shapiro, P. (1984). The role of outgroup salience in determining social identity. *Journal of Personality and Social Psychology, 47,* 177–194.

Wilder, D. A., & Shapiro, P. (1991). Facilitation of outgroup stereotypes by enhanced ingroup identity. *Journal of Experimental Social Psychology, 27,* 431–452.

Wilford, J. N. (1992, February 11). Nubian treasures reflect black influence on Egypt. *The New York Times,* P.C.I.

Williams, A. W., & Lund, A. K. (1992). Injury control. *American Psychologist, 47,* 1036–1039.

Williams, K. D. (1994). *The relations between intentions to vote and actual voting behavior*. Unpublished manuscript, University of Toledo.

Williams, K. D. (1997). Social ostracism: The causes and consequences of "the silent treatment." In R. Kowalski (Ed.), *Aversive interpersonal relations*. New York: Plenum.

Williams, K. D., Harkins, S. G., & Latane, B. (1981). Identifiability as a deterrent to social loafing: Two cheering experiments. *Journal of Personality and Social Psychology, 40,* 303–311.

Williams, K. D., & Karau, S. J. (1991). Social loafing and social compensation: The effects of expectations of co-worker performance. *Journal of Personality and Social Psychology, 61,* 570–581.

Williams, K. D., & Sommer, K. L. (1997). Social ostracism by one's coworkers: Does rejection lead to loafing or compensation? *Personality and Social Psychology Bulletin, 23*(7), 693–706.

Williams, K. D., & Williams, K. B. (1989). Impact of source strength on two compliance techniques. *Basic and Applied Social Psychology, 10,* 149–160.

Williams, K. D., & Zadro, L. (In press). Ostracism: On being ignored, excluded and rejected. In M. Leary (Ed.), *Rejection* New York: Oxford University Press.

Williams, R. (1989) The trusting heart. *Psychology Today, 23,* 36–42.

Williams, R. B., Jr., & Barefoot, J. C. (1988). Coronary-prone behavior: The emerging role of the hostility complex. In B. K. Houston & C. R. Snyder (Eds.), *Type A behavior pattern,* New York: Plenum.

Williams, S. S., Kimble, D. L., Covell, N. H., Weiss, L. H., Newton, K., Fisher, J. D., & Fisher, W. A. (1992). College students use implicit personality theory instead of safer sex. *Journal of Applied Social Psychology, 22,* 921–933.

Williams, W. M., & Sternberg, R. J. (1988). Group intelligence: Why some groups are better than others. *Intelligence, 12,* 351–357.

Williamson, G. M., & Clark, M. S. (1989). Providing help and desired relationship type as determinants of changes in mood and self-evaluation. *Journal of Personality and Social Psychology, 56,* 722–734.

Williams v. Florida (1970). 399 U.S.

Wills, T. A. (1987) Help seeking as a coping mechanism. In C. R. Snyder & C. E. Ford (Eds.), *Coping with negative life events.* New York: Plenum.

Wilson, E. O. (1975). *Sociobiology: The new synthesis.* Cambridge, MA: Harvard University Press.

Wilson, E. O. (1978). *On human nature.* Cambridge, MA: Harvard University Press.

Wilson, G. (1981). *The Coolidge effect: An evolutionary account of human sexuality.* New York: Morrow.

Wilson, J. P. (1976). Motivation, modeling, and altruism: A person x situation analysis. *Journal of Personality and Social Psychology, 34,* 1078–1086.

Wilson, M. G., Northcraft, G. B., & Neale M. A. (1989). Information competition and vividness effects in on-line judgments. *Organizational Behavior and Human Decision Processes, 44,* 132–139.

Wilson, T. D., Dunn, D. S., Kraft. D., & Lisle, D. J. (1989). Introspection, attitude change, and attitude behavior consistency: The disruptive effects of explaining why we feel the way we do. In L. Berkowitz (Ed.), *Advances in experimental social psychology* (Vol. 22, pp. 287–344). New York: Academic Press.

Wilson, T. D., & Kraft, D. (1988). [The effects of analyzing reasons on affectively-versus cognitively-based attitudes.] Unpublished raw data. Cited in Wilson, T. D., Dunn, D. S., Kraft., D., & Lisle, D. J. (1989), Introspection, attitude change, and attitude behavior consistency: The disruptive effects of explaining why we feel the way we do. In L. Berkowitz (Ed.), *Advances in experimental social psychology* (Vol. 22, pp. 287–344). New York: Academic Press.

Wilson, T. D., Lindsey, S., & Schooler, T. Y. (2000). A model of dual attitudes. *Psychological Review, 107,* 101–126.

Winch, R. G. (1958). *Mate Selection: A theory of complementary needs.* New York: Harper & Row.

Winquist, J. R., & Larson, J. R., Jr. (1998). Information pooling: When it impacts group decision-making. *Journal of Personality and Social Psychology, 74,* 371–377.

Woike, B., Gershkovich, I., Piorkowski, R., & Polo, M. (1999). The role of motives in the content and structure of autobiographical memory. *Journal of Personality and Social Psychology, 76,* 600–612.

Wolf, S. (1979). Behavioral style and group cohesiveness as sources of minority influence. *European Journal of Social Psychology, 9,* 381–395.

Wollenstonecraft, M. (1792). *A vindication of the rights of women.* Garden Grove, CT: World Library.

Wong, M. Mei-ha, & Csikzentmihalyi, M. (1991). Affiliation motivation and daily experience. *Journal of Personality and Social Psychology, 60,* 154–164.

Wood, C. (1978). The I-knew-it-all-along effect. *Journal of Experimental Psychology: Human Perception and Performance, 4,* 345–353.

Wood, W. (1982). Retrieval of attitude relevant information from memory: Effects on susceptibility to persuasion and on intrinsic motivation. *Journal of Personality and Social Psychology, 42,* 798–810.

Wood, W. (1987). Meta-analytic review of sex differences in competence. *Psychological Bulletin, 102,* 53–71.

Wood, W., Wong, F. Y., & Chachere, J. G. (1990). Effects of media violence on viewers' aggression in unconstrained soocial intereaction. *Psychological Bulletin 108,* 137–147.

Woodall, K. L., & Mathews, K. (1993). Changes in and stability of hostile characteristics: Results from a 4-year longitudinal study of children. *Journal of Personality and Social Psychology, 64*(3), 491–499.

Worchel, S., Coutant-Sassic, & Grossman, M. (1992). In S. Worchel, W. Wood, & J. A. Simpson (Eds.), *Group process and productivity.* Newbury Park, CA: Sage.

Worchel, S., & Shackelford, S. L. (1991). Groups under stress: The influence of group structure and environment on process and performance. *Personality and Social Psychology Bulletin, 17,* 640–647.

Wright, E. F., Luus, C. A. E., & Christie, S. D. (1990). Does group discussion facilitate the use of consensus information in making causal attributions? *Journal of Personality and Social Psychology, 59,* 261–269.

Wright, P. H. (1982). Men's friendships, women's friendships and the alleged inferiority of the latter. *Sex Roles, 8,* 1–20.

Wrightsman, L. S. (1969). Wallace supporters and adherence to "law and order." *Journal of Personality and Social Psychology, 13,* 17–22.

Wyer, R. S., Jr., & Srull, T. K. (1986). Human cognition in its social context. *Psychological Review, 93,* 322–359.

Yakimovich, D., & Salz, E. (1971). Helping behavior: The cry for help. *Psychonomic Science, 23,* 427–428.

Ybarra, O. (1999). Misanthropic person memory when the need to self-enhance is absent. *Personality and Social Psychology Bulletin, 25,* 261–269.

Ybarra, O., & Stephan, W. G. (1999). Attributional orientations and the prediction of behavior: The attribution-prediction bias. *Journal of Personality and Social Psychology, 76,* 718–727.

Youngstrom, N. (1991, November). Campus life polluted for many by hate acts. *APA monitor,* pp. 22–24.

Zaccaro, S. J. (1984). Social loafing: The role of task attractiveness. *Personality and Social Psychology Bulletin, 10,* 99–106.

Zaccaro, S. J., & Lowe, C. A. (1988). Cohesiveness and performance on an additive task: Evidence for multidimensionality. *Journal of Social Psychology, 128,* 547–558.

Zacarro, S. J., & McCoy, M. C. (1988). The effects of task and inter-personal cohesiveness on performance of a disjunctive group task. *Journal of Applied Social Psychology, 18,* 837–851.

Zajonc, R. B. (1960). The process of cognitive tuning in commu-nication. *Journal of Abnormal and Social Psychology, 61,* 159–167.

Zajonc, R. B. (1965). Social facilitation. *Science, 149,* 269–274.

Zajonc, R. B. (1968). Attitudinal effects of mere exposure. *Jour-nal of Personality and Social Psychology, 9,* 1–27.

Zajonc, R. B. (1985). Emotion and facial efference: A theory re-claimed. *Science, 228,* 15–21.

Zajonc, R. B., Heingartner, A., & Herman, E. M. (1969). Social en-hancement and impairment of performance in the cock-roach. *Journal of Personality and Social Psychology, 13,* 83–92.

Zajonc, R. B., & Rajecki, D. W. (1969). Exposure and affect: A field experiment. *Psychonomic Science, 17,* 216–217.

Zanna, M. P., & Rempel, J. K. (1988). Attitudes: A new look at an old concept. In D. Bar-Tal & A. Kruglanski (Eds.), *The so-cial psychology of knowledge* (pp. 315–334). New York: Cambridge University Press.

Zebrowitz, L. A., Collins, M. A., & Dutta, R. (1998). The relation-ship between appearance and personality across life-span. *Personality and Social Psychology Bulletin, 24,* 736–749.

Zebrowitz, L. A., & Lee, S. Y. (1999). Appearance, stereotype-in-congruent behavior, and social relationships. *Personality and Social Psychology, 25,* 569–584.

Zebrowitz, L. A., Olson, K., & Hoffman, K. (1993). Stability of babyfaceness and attractiveness across the lifespan. *Journal of Personality and Social Psychology, 64,* 453–466.

Ziemer, G. A. (1972). *Education for death: The making of the Nazi.* New York: Octagon Books.

Zillman, D. (1971). Excitation transfer in communication-medi-ated aggressive behavior. *Journal of Experimental Social Psychology, 7,* 419–434.

Zillman, D. (1984). *Connections between sex and aggression.* Hillsdale, NJ: Erlbaum.

Zimbardo, P. G. (1969). The human choice. In W. J. Arnold and G. Levine (Eds.), *Nebraska symposium on motivation* (Vol. 17). Lincoln: University of Nebraska.

Zimbardo, P. G., & Leippe, M. R. (1992). *The psychology of atti-tude change and social influence.* New York: McGraw-Hill.

Zucker, G. S., & Weiner, B. (1993). Conservatism and perseptions of poverty: An attributional analysis. *Journal of Applied So-cial Psychology, 23,* 925–943.

Zuckerman, M. (1990). The psychophysiology of sensation-seek-ing. *Journal of Personality, 58,* 313–345.

Zuckerman, M., Keiffer, S. C., & Knee, C. R. (1998). Conse-quences of self-handicapping: Effects on coping, academic performance, and adjustment. *Journal of Personality and Social Psychology, 74,* 1619–1628.

Zuckerman, M., Mann, R. W., & Bernieri, F. J. (1982). Determi-nants of consensus estimates: Attribution, salience, and representativeness. *Journal of Personality and Social Psy-chology, 42,* 839–852.

Zuckerman, M., Miyake, K., & Hodgins, (1991). Cross-channel effects of vocal and physical attractiveness and their impli-cations for interpersonal perception. *Journal of Personality and Social Psychology, 60,* 545–554.

NAME INDEX

Abbot, A.S., 307
Abbott, B. B., 11, 12
Abelson, R. P., 163, 178
Abrahams, D., 336
Abrams, D., 299
Acker, M., 329
Adesso, V. J., 375
Adorno, T. W., 116
Agocha, V. B., 345
Aikwa, A., 443
Ainsworth, M. D. S., 331
Ajzen, I., 160, 176–177, 179
Akimoto, S. A., 91
Albert, D. J., 373, 374
Albright, L., 57
Aldrich, A., 316
Alfieri, T., 80, 81
Allen, J., 172, 330, 331, 443
Allen, J. L., 411
Allison, S. T., 144
Allport, G., 126, 138, 143, 144, 145, 158–159
Altermatt, T. W., 306
Altman, A., 444
Altman, I., 346
Alwin, D. F., 227
Amabile, T., 83
American Psychological Association, 23, 25, 112, 113
Andersen, B. L., 41, 42
Anderson, D. E., 75
Ansell, E., 327–328
Ansfield, M. E., 67, 75
Arbuthnot, J., 253
Archer, J., 367, 368
Arendt, H., 262
Arnabile, T., 132
Aron, A., 274, 330, 331, 333–334
Aron, E. N., 274, 330, 331, 333–334
Aronson, E., 5, 145, 223, 228
Aronson, J., 139–140
Aronson, V., 336
Arrington, L. J., 106
Ascani, K., 256, 257, 260
Asch, S., 241–243, 246, 248, 249, 251
Ashmore, R. D., 336
Aspinwall, L. G., 95–96
Atkin, R. S., 310

Baarda, B., 392
Bachorowski, J., 375
Back, K .W., 334
Badaway, A., 375
Bailey,, 344
Bailey, J., 123
Baker, J., 117–118
Baker, R. L., 386, 387
Bakshi, A., 370
Ball-Rokeach, S., 161
Balls, P., 444
Banaji, M. R., 35, 110, 111, 161
Bandura, A., 170, 381–382
Bargh, J. A., 52, 67–69, 69, 90, 146
Barkow, J. H., 128
Barnett, R., 422
Baron, R., 221
Baron, R. A., 392
Baron, R. S., 247, 294, 431
Barrett, L. F., 325
Bartell, P. A., 422
Bartholomew, K., 334
Bassett, R., 259
Batson, C. D., 408–409, 412, 413, 423, 436

Baum, A., 225
Baum, L., 180
Baumeister, R. F., 51, 52, 53, 67, 128, 221, 301, 325, 327, 328, 329, 330, 331, 356, 421
Baumgardner, A. H., 52, 55
Baumgardner, M. H., 196
Baumrind, D., 274
Baxter, K., 171
Bee, H., 397
Bell, M. L., 368
Bem, D. J., 33–34, 224, 255
Ben Hamida, S., 344
Benson, J. E., 81
Benson, P. L., 424, 426
Berglas, S., 55, 56
Berkowitz, L., 47, 246–247, 377, 424, 439, 443
Berndt, T. J., 357
Bernieri, F. J., 68–69, 69, 73, 87
Berreby, D., 341
Berry, D., 337
Berscheid, E., 54, 89, 330, 337, 346, 348, 355
Bettencourt, B. A., 368
Betz, A. L., 36, 168
Bickman, L., 246–247, 268, 423
Biernat, M., 348
Biggs, E., 91
Billig, M., 126, 298
Bissonette, V., 337
Bitton, D., 106
Bjorkqvist, K., 368
Blaine, B., 84
Blaine, B. E., 37
Blanchard, D. C., 377
Blanchard, F. A., 146
Blanchard, R. J., 377
Blank, A., 182
Blascovich, J., 312
Blass, T., 272
Block, A., 214
Block, L., 214
Blumberg, S. J., 98–99
Bodenhausen, G. V., 68, 110, 111, 125, 146
Boggs, L. W., 106
Bonner, B. L., 306
Bordens, K. S., 11, 12, 21
Borello, G. M., 328
Bornstein, R. F., 168, 335
Bourgeois, M., 91, 208
Bourough, H. W., 428
Bowdel, B. F., 388, 389
Bradshaw, D., 332
Brannon, J., 291
Bratslavsky, E., 52, 325, 328, 329, 356
Bray, R. M., 310
Breakefield, X. O., 8
Breckler, S. J., 159
Brehm, J. W., 218, 219, 225, 243, 244
Brehm, S. S., 225, 244, 330, 356
Brewer, M. B., 125, 144, 299
Brickman, P., 433
Bridstock, R., 341, 342
Briggs, S. R., 337
Broadnax, S., 84
Brody, S., 180–181
Brolly, I., 309
Bromley, S., 427
Brown, D. L., 415
Brown, J. D., 291
Brown, R., 126, 262
Brown, R. P., 140
Brown, S. L., 413
Brownstein, R. J., 260

Brunner, H. H., 8
Bryan, J. H., 433
Bryant, F. B., 379
Bryne, D., 336
Buehler, R., 36, 37
Bundy, R., 298
Burger, J. M., 260
Burgoon, M., 256
Burnett, A., 324
Burnstein, E., 240, 313
Burt, M., 394
Bush, M., 259
Bushman, B. J., 374, 375
Buss, D., 339, 342
Buss, D. M., 337
Buunk, B., 297, 342, 344
Byrd, C., 113
Byrd, J., 125
Byrd, W., 398

Cacioppo, J. T., 167, 200, 206, 207, 211, 215, 227, 259
Calder, B., 255
Caldwell, N. D., 37
Callero, P. L., 435
Calley, W., 261
Campbell, D. T., 166
Campbell, J., 244
Campbell, J. T., 239, 247
Campbell, W. K., 49
Cantrill, J. G., 255
Caporael, L. R., 291, 299
Carducci, B. J., 256
Carli, L. L., 248–249, 336
Carlo, G., 368
Carlsmith, J. M., 217
Carlson, D., 63
Carlson, N. R., 372
Carnegie Commission on Higher Education, 211–212
Carothers, L. E., 386, 387
Carr, C., 141
Carrere, S., 350
Carroll, J., 31–32, 33, 58
Cartwright, 317
Carver, C. S., 41, 50
Casey, R. J., 338
Castro, M. A. C., 443
Caverly, R., 191–193, 206, 228
Center for Disease Control and Prevention (CDC), 226, 227
Chaiken, S., 80, 195, 215
Champan, J., 131
Chang, S.-J., 317
Chanowitz, B., 182
Chapman, L. L., 131
Charlton, K., 74
Chartrand, T. L., 52, 67–69
Check, J., 394
Chen, H., 78
Cheong, J., 375–376
Chermack, S., 385
Chesner, S. P., 421
Christenfeld, N., 342
Christensen, C., 307
Christensen, P. N., 327, 341–342
Christiansen, K., 372
Chrvala, C., 249
Cialdini, R. B., 127, 256, 257, 258, 259, 260, 412, 413
Ciarocco, N. J., 301
Clark, M. S., 349–350, 441, 442
Clark, N. T., 259

Empathy
  definition of, 408
  egoism versus, 409–411
  emotional, becoming rescuer and, 432
Empathy-altruism hypothesis, 408–409
  challenging, 411–413
Empathy-punishment hypothesis, 412
Endomorphs, 339
Enlightenment effect, 272
Entity theories, of implicit stereotypes, 111
Equity theory, 347–348, *349*
Ethics, social psychological research and,
  23–25
Ethological theory, of aggression, 369–370
Evaluation apprehension, social
  facilitation/inhibition and, 293, *295*
Evil
  banality of, 261–263
  responsibility for, 262–263
Evolutionary psychology, beauty and, 340–345
Exchange theories, 347–348
Experience, direct personal, in attitude
  formation, 168–169
Experiment(s)
  evaluating, 15–16
  factorial, 14
  field, 19–20
Experimental group, definition of, 13
Experimental research, 12–16
  definition of, 12
  equivalence of groups in, 13–14
  manipulating variables in, 13
Expertise, of communicator, 195
Explicit attitudes, 160–161
Exposure, mere, in attitude formation,
  167–168
Extermination, prejudice and, 139
Extraneous variable(s)
  controlling, 14–15
  definition of, 14

Facilitation, social, 293
Factorial experiment, 14
False consensus attribution bias, 87
Family
  disruption of, aggression and, 386–387
  reducing aggression in, 396–397
Fear
  effectiveness of message and, 197–200
  protection/motivation explanation of, 200
Field experiment, 19–20
Field research, 19–20
Field study, 19
Field survey, 19
Fixation time, attractiveness and, 338
Flexible correction model (FCM), 210
Foot-in-the-door technique, of compliance,
  253–256
  definition of, 253
  hypotheses explaining, 255–256
  limits of, 256
Four horsemen of the apocalypse, relationship
  dissolution and, 354–355
Free choice, in dissonance theory, 217–218
Free riders, in group, 297–298
Friendships, 355–357
  gender differences in, 356–357
  over life cycle, 357
Frustration-aggression link, 376–380
  components of, 377
  factors mediating, 377–380
Fundamental attribution error, 82–83
  discriminatory stereotypes and, 132–134
  reasons for/correction of, 85

Gender
  aggression and, 367–369
  authoritarianism and, 115–118

conformity and, 248–249
friendships and, 356–357
obedience and, 269–270
prejudice and, 117–118
Gender roles, in children's books, attitude
  formation and, 171–172
Genetic explanation, of altruism, 413–415
Genocide, 116
Genovese, Kitty, death of, 415–416
Group(s), 287–322
  affiliative, 289
  characteristics of, 289–290
  cohesiveness of, 290
    group decision-making ability and,
      310–311
  composition of, group decision-making
    ability and, 309
  control, definition of, 13
  decision making by, 304–318. *See also*
    Decision making, group
  definition of, 289
  deviates in, 292
  equivalence of, 13–14
  experimental, definition of, 13
  formation of, 290–292
  functional quality of, problem difficulty and,
    305–306
  influence on behavior, 292–298
  instrumental, 289
  in meeting basic needs, 291
  members of, obeying leaders, 308
  newcomers in, 292
  obedience and, 269
  participation in, performance and, 294–298
    enhanced, 295–296
    free rides and, 297–298
    social loafing and, 296–297
  polarization of, 312–313
  punishment by, 301–302
  roles in, 291–292
  self-identity and, 298–303
  size of, group decision-making ability and,
    310
  social, identification with, 300
  transactive memory systems of, 304–305
  use of information by, 306–307
  violence by, 302–303
Group norms, 289–290
Groupthink, 313–318
  conditions favoring, 314
  definition of, 313
  preventing, 316–317
  symptoms of, 314–316

Happiness
  cognitive optimism and, 96–97
  future, effects of distressing and joyful
    events on, 98–99
  incompetence and, 97–98
Hate crimes, 112–113
Heider, Fritz, on attribution, 76
Heinrich, Ingo, 262–263
Help
  increasing the chance of receiving, 428
  receiving, reaction to, 443–445
  seeking, 440
    decision model for, 440–442
    decision on, factors influencing, 442–443
Helping behavior
  altruistic, 405–445. *See also* Altruism
  biological explanation of, 413–415
  egoism and, 409–411
  in emergencies, 415–428
    empathy-altruism hypothesis of, 408–409
    five-stage decision model of, 415–428
      applied to long-term helping, 437–440
  long-term, 437–440
  mood and, 423–424

in nonemergencies, 429–437
race and, 426–428
recipient of, 428
rewards and costs of, 423
sexual orientation and, 428
Heritability factor, in attitude formation,
  173–174
Heterosexism, 146–147
Heuristic and systematic information-
  processing model, 215–216
Heuristics
  availability, 92–93
  judgmental, stereotypes as, 111
  representativeness, 93–94
Hindsight bias, 22
Historical differences, in conformity, 249–250
History, social psychology and, 10–11
Homophobia, gender and, 117–118
Hormonal influences, on aggression, 372–374
Hostile aggression, 366
Hypothalamus, in aggression, 371
Hypothesis, definition of, 11–12

Ideal self, 45
Ideology, in attitude-behavior relationship,
  180–181
Ignorance, pluralistic, bystander effect and, 420
Illusion(s)
  of efficacy, in small groups, 310
  of invulnerability
    groupthink and, 314
    unique, AIDS and, 226
  positive, 95–96
  of unanimity, groupthink and, 316
Illusory correlations, stereotypes and, 131–132
Imagine-other perspective, on empathy, 408
Imagine-self perspective, on empathy,
  408–409
Implicit attitudes, 161
Implicit personality theory, 88
Impression(s)
  on others, awareness of, 56–5
  of others on us, 71–75
    accuracy of, 71–72
    constructing, 87–94
      first impressions in, 87–88
      heuristics in, 92–94
      schemas in, 88–90
      stories in, 90–91
    formation of, confidence and, 72–73
Impression management, 53–56
  self-esteem and, 54
  self-monitoring and, 54–55
Incompetence, happiness and, 97–98
Incremental theories, of implicit stereotypes,
  111–112
Independence, paths to, 243–244
Independent variable, 13
Individual characteristics, in social behavior,
  5–6
Individual self, 37
Inequity, perceived, aggression and, 379–380
Information, group use of, 306–307
Informational social influence, 238–240
Information-processing strategies for self-
  serving bias, 49
Informed consent, 25
In-group bias, 126–127
  biological perspective on, 128–129
  language in maintaining, 129–131
Inhibition, social, 293
Injustice, perceived, aggression and, 379–380
Inoculation theory, 202
Instrumental aggression, 366
Instrumental groups, 289
Instrumental values, 162
Intellective issue, social influence on, 245
Interactionist view, of altruism, 435–437

Personal experience, direct, in attitude formation, 168–169
Personality
    altruistic, 429
    authoritarian, 116–117
    becoming rescuer and, 432
    prejudice and, 115–118
Personality psychology, aggressiveness and, 9–10
Person attribution, 77
Persuasion, 193
    cognitive approach to, 205–216. See also Cognitive approach, to persuasion
    cognitive dissonance theory of, 216–223
    elaboration likelihood model of, 206–208
    group polarization from, 312–313
    heuristic model of, 215–216
    limits of, 228
    of masses, 225–228
    of multiple audiences, 204–205
    vividness of message and, 213–215
    Yale model of, 193–205. See also Yale communication model
Phrasing, attitude survey bias and, 165
Physical attack, prejudice as, 139
Physical attractiveness
    dimensions of, 337–339
    in interpersonal attraction, 336–337
Physical proximity effect, 334–335
Physiological responses, in attitude assessment, 167
Physiology, of aggression, 371–374
Physique, attractiveness bias and, 339–340
Planned behavior, theory of, 176–178
Pluralistic ignorance, bystander effect and, 420
Polarization, group, 312–313
Positive correlation, 17
Positive illusions, 95–96
Postdecision dissonance, 218–219
Prejudice, 105–153
    against African Americans, 118–120
    authoritarianism and, 115–118
    cognitive roots of, 125–137
    color, historical view of, 115
    coping with, 142–144
    definition of, 108
    dynamics of, 108–113
    everyday, 139
    gender and, 117–118
    against Jews, 132–134
    jokes based on, 139
    against Mormons, 105–106
    persistence and recurrence of, 113–115
    personality and, 115–118
    reducing, 144–148
        contact between groups in, 144–145
        personalizing out-group members in, 145–146
    reducing expression of, through social norms, 146–147
    social roots of, 118–125
    stereotypes and, 108–109
    target of, consequences of being, 137–144
    ways to express, 138
    See also Discrimination; Racism; Sexism; Stereotype(s)
Primacy effect
    in impression-formation process, 87
    of message, 200, 201
Process loss, group size and, 310
Prosocial behavior, in reducing aggression, 397
Protection/motivation explanation of fear, 200
Psychological field, in Lewin's model of social behavior, 4–5
Psychological reactance, 225
    independence and, 243–244

Psychology
    evolutionary, beauty and, 340–345
    of legitimacy, 308
    social. See Social psychology
    social psychology and, 9–10
Psychophysiological measurements, of attitudes, 167
Public health campaigns, 225–228
Punishment, by group, 301–302
Punitive ostracism, 301

Question format, attitude survey bias and, 166

Race, helping behavior and, 426–428
Racism
    aversive, 121
    changing social norms and, 124–125
    definition of, 108
    modern, 120–123
    symbolic, 121
    in U.S. Army, disarming, 147–148
    See also Discrimination; Prejudice; Stereotype(s)
Random assignment, 14
Rape, myths about, 393–394
Rating scale, 165
Rationalization
    groupthink and, 314–315
    self-affirmation theory and, 224–225
Reactance, psychological, 225
    independence and, 243–244
Reagan, Ronald, trustworthiness and, 195
Reasoned action, theory of, 176
Rebound effect, 70
Recency effect, of message, 200, 201
Reciprocal altruism, 414–415
Reciprocity, norm of, 257–259
Reflected appraisal, in self-knowledge, 333
Reinforcement, vicarious, observational learning and, 382
Rejection, latitude of, in social judgment theory, 204
Relational devaluation, 327
Relational model, of legitimacy, 308
Relationships
    close, 323–362
        attachment styles and, 333–334
        communal, 349–350
        development of, 345–346
        dissolution of, predicting, 354–355
        dynamics of, 345–357
        evaluating, 346–350
        formation of, 331–345
        friendships as, 355–357
        kinds of, 354
        love and, 328–331
        over time, 350
        responses of, to conflict, 352–354
        roots of, 325–328
        sculpting, 350–352
        working model of, 332–333
    inequity in, 443–444
Relative deprivation theory, 143
Relevance, personal, message processing and, 211–212
Reno, Janet, credibility and, 195
Representativeness heuristic, 93–94
Representative sample, 14
    for attitude survey, 165
Rescuer
    becoming
        personality factors in, 432
        situational factors in, 431–432
    righteous, 429–430
        five-stage decision model applied to, 437–440

Research, social psychological, 11–20
    correlational, 16–18
    ethics and, 23–25
    exceptions and, 22–23
    experimental, 12–16. See also Experimental research
    field, 19–20
    hindsight bias in, 22
    laboratory, 19
    lessons from, 21–23
    settings for, 19–20
    theory in, 20–21
Responsibility, diffusion of, bystander effect and, 420
Reverse incentive effect, in dissonance theory, 217
Righteous rescuers, 429–430
    five-stage decision model applied to, 437–440
Role strain, disobedience and, 275–277

Sanctioned aggression, 367
Scapegoating, 116–117
Schema(s)
    aggressive, 382–383
    assimilating new information into, 90
    behavior and, 88–90
    definition of, 41, 88
    origins of, 88
Schindler's List, film, 146
Scientific method, definition of, 11
Secret love, 331
Self
    actual, 45
    collective, 37–38
    cultural influences on, 37–43
    enhancing, 47–48
    group influences on, 37–43
    ideal, 45
    individual, 37
    ought, 45
    social, 31–61. See also Social self
Self-affirmation theory, rationalization and, 224–225
Self-awareness, 50–53
    self-knowledge and, 52
Self-categorization theory, 300–301
    discrimination and, 127–128
Self-censorship, groupthink and, 316
Self-concept, 33–43
    definition of, 33
    influence of culture on, 39–40
    memories and, 35–36
    personal attributes and, 34–35
Self-consistency, maintaining, 49–50
Self-control, cost and ironic effects of, 52–53
Self-defense, as sanctioned aggression, 367
Self-disclosure, in relationship development, 346
Self-esteem, 44–50
    definition of, 44
    impression management and, 54
    internal influences on, 44–50
    maintaining, in interactions with others, 47
    receiving help and, 444–445
    self-regulation and, 45–47
    stigma and, 44–45
Self-evaluation maintenance (SEM) theory, 47–48
Self-focus, 50–51
Self-fulfilling prophecy, 88–89
Self-handicapping, 55–56
Self-identity
    groups and, 298–303
    identification with social group and, 300

PHOTO CREDITS